INTRODUCTION TO GLOBALIZATION AND BUSINESS

INTRODUCTION TO GLOBALIZATION AND BUSINESS

Relationships and Responsibilities

Barbara Parker

SAGE Publications
London • Thousand Oaks • New Delhi

SAGE Publications
1 Oliver's Yard
55 City Road
London EC1Y 1SP

SAGE Publications Inc
2455 Teller Road
Thousand Oaks, California 91320

SAGE Publications India Pvt Ltd
B-42, Panchsheel Enclave
Post Box 4109
New Delhi 110 017

Library of Congress Control Number: 2004116095

A catalogue record for this book is available from the British
Library

ISBN 0 7619 4495 8
ISBN 0 7619 4496 6 (pbk)

Typeset by Pantek Arts Ltd, Maidstone, Kent
Printed on paper from sustainable resources
Printed in Great Britain by Alden Press, Oxford

Contents

Visit the SAGE Companion Website at **www.sagepub.co.uk/parker** to find valuable resources including:

- Suggested videos
- Assignments
- Exercises
- Supplemental questions
- PowerPoint slides.

The website also contains a suggested "Global Enterprise Project" with assignments for each chapter. This approach encourages students to apply concepts to the same organization over an entire course term.

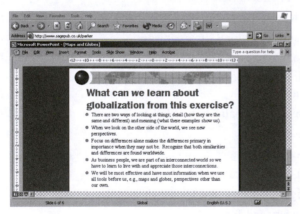

Lecture slides to facilitate group discussion

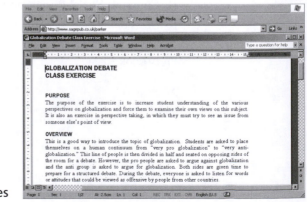

Class exercises

List of Figures and Tables

FIGURES

TABLES

to William Nichols

with thanks to Michelle Eldridge

Preface

Virtually all fields of human endeavor are affected by growing worldwide interconnections. This book outlines challenges and opportunities associated with these interconnections, and it considers important questions about globalization. An operating premise is that organizational leaders and employees can better manage chaotic global interconnections by recognizing, analyzing, and addressing shifts occurring in six major global environments: industries and businesses, the natural environment, culture, economics, politics, and technology. This book also argues that successful global managers cope with global externalities by integrating internal resources of people, processes, and structures (PPS).

ORGANIZATION AND USE OF THE TEXT

The book is appropriate for several audiences. First, it is an excellent resource for university students who wish to learn more about the globalization process and its effects on organizations. The multidisciplinary nature of globalization requires that the topic be examined through many lenses, resulting in a book that incorporates theories from many disciplines. Principles introduced are applicable to any organization, but the main focus is on business management. The book provides many organizational examples drawn from organizations of every size, found in every country, and guided by managerial motivations and practices that emerge from different cultural roots. The book's emphasis on global relationships and responsibilities also makes it useful to those interested in business/government/society interfaces. Finally, timely and thorough coverage of global shifts in culture, politics, economics, technology, industries, and the natural environment make the book an excellent resource for libraries and researchers.

Any course should begin with the introductory material found in Chapters 1–3. Chapter 1 defines globalization, distinguishes it from international activities, and presents competing worldwide perspectives on both causes and consequences of globalization. Chapter 2 outlines a systems-based model to analyze global shifts and organizational activities. The model shows that mediating organizations such as other businesses, suppliers, buyers, governmental, and nongovernmental organizations also shape an organization's responses to global shifts. Relationships with these mediating organizations further interconnect global organizations to their world. Chapter 3 outlines characteristics of the global enterprise applicable to organizations in any sector. This chapter argues that global organizations of every type face the same general challenges as do businesses.

Chapter 4 outlines the global landscape of business, demonstrating that small to medium-sized organizations as well as global giants participate in this world. Chapters 5–11 separately focus on each of the six global environments that create the context for global management. These are global industries and businesses (Chapter 5); globalization of the natural environment (Chapter 6); global culture (Chapter 7); global economics (Chapter 8 covers issues of trade, FDI, capital and financial institutions; Chapter 9's topic is global labor); Chapter 10 addresses progress and concerns of global politics; and Chapter 11 examines the impact of global technologies, especially information technologies.

In addition to laying out evidence of globalization in each global sphere, Chapters 5–11 also examine challenges of globalization. For example, Chapter 7 weighs alternative arguments of increased diversity or increased worldwide homogeneity from cultural globalization; Chapter 8 examines competing theoretical perspectives on economic development to identify a middle ground; and Chapter 9 weighs evidence for and against the benefits of labor migration. Each chapter from 5–11 presents alternative views on chapter topics to generate debate and encourage readers to develop and defend their own perspectives on globalization.

Chapters 12–16 look more specifically at how managers adapt internal structures, people, and processes to enhance global performance. Chapter 12 examines challenges for structuring global organizations. Chapter 13 and 14 concentrate on managing people. For example, Chapter 13 reviews literature on global leadership to identify common characteristics. Chapter 13 also examines managerial traits among those who are not leaders, presents career options, and outlines challenges for global human resource management systems. Chapter 14 examines the role of diversity in global organizations and weighs options for on-site and virtual teams. Chapter 15 examines two increasingly important organizational processes: corporate social responsibility and global ethics. Chapter 16 reviews processes important to global organizations such as decision-making, innovation, conflict and risk management. Chapter 17 briefly reviews text findings, further to consider managerial challenges for a global world. References are conveniently integrated and found just before a comprehensive index of course topics, organizations featured, and principles and theories presented.

Each chapter:

1 begins with a short case study to introduce chapter topics—companies from around the world are represented, including small ones;

2 provides an overview of chapter objectives;

3 contains "boxed" examples from many sources that illustrate chapter concepts; these examples come from organizations of every size and type around the world;

4 concludes with a brief chapter summary;

5 and provides a series of review and discussion questions

Chapter 1
AN INTRODUCTION TO GLOBALIZATION

FRENCH FRIES GO GLOBAL

Both large and small businesses in the fast-food industry serve growing numbers of people worldwide who are too busy to cook. Combined revenues for large global competitors like McDonald's, Burger King, Pizza Hut, and KFC top $40 billion per year. McDonald's alone is the world's number one fast-food company by sales, serving burgers and fries in 100 countries in more than 30,000 restaurants. When fast-food companies such as McDonald's open stores or sell franchises in new locations, they often add or subtract items to appeal to local taste and culture. The beef-free Maharaja Mac serves India, Japan samples the Teriyaki McBurger, and there is the McSpaghetti in the Philippines and the Beetroot Burger in New Zealand.

But one thing on the menu almost never changes: the French fry. Consumers love them, and so do restaurant owners because they are the second-biggest profit maker in fast-foods. In 1989 wholesale fries sales were $1.7 billion, but they'd grown to more than $3 billion by 2003. The Netherlands is the world's largest exporter of frozen fries. Below we follow a single batch of French fries to illustrate how globalization forges interconnections worldwide.

Our fries were grown in the US Pacific Northwest by a small colony of Hutterites, a Pacifist group that fled Russia in 1873 to avoid military service. They settled first in the US, then in Canada during World War I to avoid conscription. Today they have colonies throughout North America. Members of the group sometimes speak a Tyrolean dialect of German, sometimes English. They are isolated culturally and geographically, but their fortunes rest on world trends and in part on fast-food sales a half a world away.

The Hutterites grow potatoes in circles of land that contain 5,000 tons of potatoes, or enough to make 14 million servings of fries. Seen from the air, the circles look like aliens carved them, but they are centered around pivot irrigation systems that revolutionized agriculture regions like Oregon where rainfall is sparse. The otherwise simple lives of the Hutterites are complicated by sophisticated tractors and other farm equipment that meet demands for farm specialization, efficiency, and flexibility. Although they don't have television, the Hutterites use personal computers for work and education to keep up with global trends that affect the agricultural industry.

After harvest, the potatoes are trucked to a J.R. Simplot plant. Simplot is credited with inventing the frozen French fry, but it was Ray Kroc of McDonald's who popularized it on a worldwide basis. Mass production of the fries for McDonald's drove down costs, and increased profits on the French fry.

Simplot buys raw potatoes for about five cents per pound, processing adds 25 cents per pound, and when cooked they are sold at US outlets for about $3.65 per pound. Simplot's company produces more French fries for McDonald's than any other producer, and sends about 4 million pounds of frozen fries to Asia each week. Exporting to Muslim nations such as Indonesia requires Halal certification to assure Islamic customers that the food is prepared according to strict Muslim standards. This required Simplot to hire Mohamad Joban, an Egyptian-trained Muslim cleric to conduct the inspection. When approved, the fries can be readied for Indonesia's market.

After arrival at the Simplot plant, the Hutterite potatoes are dumped on a conveyor belt made by Spudnik Equipment Company—a small Idaho company. Water pressure of ▶

35 mph shoots the potatoes to laser-guided brass blades that yield perfect quarter inch slices. The fries are then partially cooked, dried, flash frozen, and packaged. The entire process from conveyor belt to frozen fries takes 45 minutes.

Ninety-five percent of all foreign trade travels by ship, and our fries are no exception. In the process, the transaction will pass through many hands, including freight forwarders, truckers, longshoremen, shippers, agents, importers and franchisers before arriving at Indonesian tables. One hundred and thirteen thousand servings of the Hutterite fries are loaded onto refrigerated trucks bound for the Port of Tacoma. There they meet the *Dagmar Maersk*, which sails under the Danish flag. The ship was built in South Korea; a German captains it; its crew comes in part from the Pacific islands, and it is bound for Asia. Above the fries, the longshoremen load a box of apples heading for Kuwait.

The *Dagmar Maersk* heads to Asia. Port cranes are so speedy that the crew has little off ship time in Yokohama, Shimizu, and Kobe, Japan stops. The *Dagmar Maersk* sails on to Indonesia. Rough weather in Taiwan, and a failed emergency beacon halt progress. Part of a global system for shipping,[1] the beacon must be fixed. An Australian engineer climbs on board, makes the adjustments, and the fries are back on their way.

Meanwhile, there is trouble in Asia. In 1997 currency traders observed that Thailand had a growing trade deficit. To hedge their risk in the Thai bhat, traders converted their holdings to dollars. These sales depressed the value of the bhat, leading to further sell offs that eventually took the bhat to half of its former dollar value.

The economic crisis spread as currencies in other Southeast Asian nations also began to drop. The Indonesian rupiah began to fall in December, and eventually would lose more than 80 percent of its dollar value. Meanwhile, about $50 million dollars per day were transferred out of Indonesia to the relative safety of Singapore's banks.

The French fry is but one indicator of economic prosperity. The more a country develops economically, the more French fries people consume. The reverse is also true; when economies falter, French fries and fast-foods become a luxury that fewer can afford.

In Indonesia, the currency crisis saw the price of a Big Mac triple. Because restaurants paid for imported wholesale fries in dollars, their costs soared. Customers could not meet price increases, and began to consume rice and egg dishes that McDonald's added to their Indonesia menus. But McDonald's sales plunged. Theirs and other US stores became targets for critics of globalization. One third of the restaurants that purchased French fries from Simplot were burned, including about 10 McDonald's. Anti-foreign and anti-Chinese riots to follow took 500 lives.

In view of the Indonesian crisis, the Hutterites' potatoes were diverted to Singapore's more stable economy. On an early evening there Ernest Enver—a descendant of Russian Jews—met his wife Becky and three children in one of Singapore's McDonald's. Becky is of Chinese heritage, and the family is Roman Catholic. They ordered up servings of fries that took only seven minutes to reach crispy brown perfection.

▶

The Aftermath

Mercy Corps, an international nongovernmental organization (INGO) that provides food and medical relief, distributed donated US wheat to Indonesians. Farmers in Canada and Australia who usually sell wheat to Indonesia were not happy to be edged out of wheat sales. And fast-food restaurants witnessed a drop in sales of fries.

Thanks to International Monetary Fund (IMF) pressures, several nations cut tariffs on French fries. One of the forces behind that pressure was the American Potato Trade Alliance, a nongovernmental organization of growers, processors, marketers, and fast-food managers.

Due to the Asian economic downturn, a planned factory to convert rejected French fries into ethanol was shelved. South Korean distillers wanted to ship the ethanol to South Korea for soju production, but they had to back out as lead investors when the cost of debt increased due to the currency crisis

In China, Liu Zai Jiang plows four acres planted with potatoes for J.R. Simplot. These potatoes will go to a small Beijing plant that produces about the same amount of French fries in a year as can be made in a week in US plants. But Simplot is always looking for new sources of potatoes, and through small ventures with farmers like Liu, his company now produces 70 percent of the fries for McDonald's China stores.

McDonald's managed to increase its market share in Japan, even as it lost sales in Indonesia. McDonald's has more than 2,500 Japanese outlets. In Singapore where the economy remained stable, sales of fries and other fast-food remained stable. During the currency crisis, McDonald's announced plans to invest over a billion in Asia for the coming years. The strong dollar would reduce ordinary costs of land and equipment for expansion. McDonald's also expanded in Russia and Brazil. All over the world it is installing McInternet—McDonald's digital inclusion project. New products such as the McCafe have been introduced, and cultural demands for healthier food motivate McDonald's to offer salads and other low-calorie fare.

Parent Diageo sold Burger King Restaurants to a private investor group; they vow to compete to win against McDonald's for world fast-food sales. Fast-food giant Jollibee has expanded from its base in the Philippines into US markets, and Hong Kong based Café de Coral means to make Chinese fast-food the next global food source.

In June of 1998 the financial panic spread from Asia to Russia and Latin America. In 2000 a technology-led boom in the US turned to bust, plunging the US and much of the world into economic slowdowns. In Africa, trade fell from small numbers to even smaller numbers, further plunging sub-Saharan Africa into dire economic conditions.

By 2005, French-fry consumption had slowed due to nutritional concerns, and worldwide evidence of "globesity" traced to consumption of fat-laden foods. McDonald's responded to these concerns with new offerings that included salads and smaller portions.

Examples above cover many topics we will study in this book. Global economics, politics, businesses and industries, as well as culture, technology, and the natural environment all interconnect. Their effects on business practices and the lives and livelihoods of the planet's six billion people vary. As the example above shows, there are critics of globalization as well as champions for it.

Source material: Richard Read (1998, Oct. 18–21) The French fry connection. *The Oregonian*, multiple pages.

CHAPTER OVERVIEW

This chapter defines globalization, showing how studies of globalization differ from studies of internationalization. The chapter also describes critical managerial abilities and skills for a more global world. Three competing perspectives on globalization are presented to show how each informs management practice. The chapter concludes with a look at the challenges globalization creates for managing organizations and careers.

DEFINITIONS FOR GLOBALIZATION

The word "globalization" is in daily use throughout the world. Variously referred to as *mondialisation* in French, *globalisierung* in German, or *Quan qui hua* in China (Scholte, 1996), news articles, television, and even textbooks often use the word "globalization" to mean many different things. Author Jan Pieterse (1995) asserts there are almost as many conceptualizations of globalization as there are disciplines in the social sciences. Teachers and scholars in disciplines such as management, marketing, finance, accounting, and economics also use the word "globalization" to mean different things.

For example, some believe globalization is the absence of borders and barriers to trade between nations (Ohmae, 1995), but also it has been described as a shift in traditional patterns of international production, investment, and trade (Dicken, 1992). Another popular conception of globalization is that it is a business strategy that means doing everything the same everywhere (Kanter and Dretler, 1998). Others believe globalization is interconnections between overlapping interests of business and society (Brown, 1992; Renesch, 1992). As you can see, these definitions differ in significant ways. Because definitions, descriptions, and visions of globalization vary widely, it is difficult to know what it means for businesses to go "global." We therefore begin to explore globalization by defining the term.

Globalization Defined
Globalization is a process whereby worldwide interconnections in virtually every sphere of activity are growing. Some of these interconnections lead to integration/unity worldwide; others do not. Together global interconnections and the relationships they forge represent a historically unprecedented process that is rapidly reshaping the context for many activities (Held et al., 1999). The result is blurred boundaries within and between organizations, nations, and global interests. This book is about how globalization affects organizations, and it concentrates on six spheres of activity where global interconnections are occurring. These are: global business and industry activities; the natural environment; global culture; global politics; global economics; and global technologies.

Worldwide interconnections occur within single spheres of activity such as economics to create tighter links within the global economy. These links are reflected in relationships between foreign direct investments, capital, and labor. But globalization is more than direct and discrete linkages. Multiple relationships interconnect different environments when global activities occurring in one sphere interact with activities in other spheres. An example is the middle-class phenomenon of global teens who share interests, fashions, and musical tastes worldwide. Emergence of a global teen is a cultural phenomenon, but the worldwide spread of common interests occurs because there is a global telecommunications infrastructure, and businesses and industries able to produce global brands for the global teen. A global political environment facilitates trade, and a global economy and natural environment support it.

Thus, what might seem like an isolated activity in a single global sphere creates first-order effects, then spills over into second-, third-, and subsequent-order effects as they relate to one another. A great example of the spillover effect begins with satellite technology.

Order Effects of a Simple Change

1 One first-order effect of satellite technology is to make television broadcasts available almost everywhere in the world.
2 A second-order effect is that people watch more television and then interact less with members of their own local communities. Ideas that television fosters may help people align more with national or global communities of interests.
3 These new interrelations create cultural sharing or borrowing.
4 Television also exposes people to new products and services to create needs and wants that differ from existing habits. The effects of these shifts are multiple: more global opportunities arise for businesses and other organizations; governments may face new challenges to create rules and regulations for businesses that cross traditional borders; growing trade stimulates the local economy and the world economy; and so on.

There are many other ways that a seemingly simple service like satellite television interconnects the world. What this example demonstrates best is that first-order effects of globalization in each sphere forge interconnections and stimulate subsequent-order effects in other spheres of global activity. Many of these effects are unpredictable and, as shown later in this chapter, some argue that unpredictability alone is a reason to comdemn globalization.

FOUR MAIN CHARACTERISTICS OF GLOBALIZATION

Globalization is characterized by: growing worldwide interconnections; rapid, discontinuous change; growing numbers and diversity of participants; and greater managerial complexity. Each of these is explored below.

Growing Worldwide Interconnections

Growing worldwide interconnections is one characteristic of globalization. Examples above from satellite television and the global teen show us that distinct events stimulate global interconnections, but the path for these interconnections is not always clear or steady. Some interconnections can be predicted, others cannot. Moreover, factors other than globalization also shape events. For example, proximity to vibrant markets, a transportation infrastructure, and abundant natural resources draw a people, nation, or region into global trade and other activities. Poor infrastructure and "poor geography" are some reasons countries like Chad and Mali are not well integrated in the global economy (Dollar and Kraay, 2002). These and many different reasons including, political corruption, opportunity, educational constraints, natural disasters, limited resources, and interest in being global explain why a nation and its people are more or less globally connected.

Rapid, Discontinuous Change

A second characteristic of globalization is that this process has occurred rapidly but not at a steady pace. In other words, a chart of global interconnections would follow an upward slope, but the regression line would not be a smooth one. Instead, growing interconnections are discontinuous, following a jagged upward slope. For example, global interconnections tended to slow after the 1997 Asian economic crisis, then they surged, slowed again, and repeated that pattern. According to a study produced by the US Institute of International Finance, nations affected by the Asian economic crisis also experienced different effects. Japan's estimated loss was 1.4 percent of its 1997 GDP compared to a 0.7 percent loss in the US and 0.6 percent in the EU. In turn, China and Mexico witnessed estimated losses of $21 billion and $6 billion due to reduced export opportunities to the US and Canada (Lachica, 1998). Discontinuities in the pace of change make it difficult for organizations and individuals to anticipate, interpret, or plan for the future.

Another source of discontinuity is that events that have global importance travel the world at different speeds and with differential effects. Accordingly, interconnections can affect nations, industries, businesses, and individuals at different times and in different ways. In other words, the effect of the same global event can differ. The example of the 1997 Asian economic crisis also shows how this happens. The world economy took a dip, but major effects were felt first and later most affected the economies of Thailand, Indonesia, and South Korea. This suggests that when we look at global events and interconnections, we must remember that nations and businesses can experience these connections in different ways. In other words, the process of globalization is disorganized and incoherent (Veseth, 1998).

Increased Number and Diversity of Participants

A third characteristic of globalization is growth in the numbers and diversity of actors involved in global activities. For example, participants in global business activities now include many small-to-medium-sized enterprises (SMEs) as well as large ones. Companies from developing and small economies also participate, as do firms that are owned privately and publicly. The boundaries that once constrained business activities now are more permeable to many more people and organizations worldwide. This increases diversity among participants. To the extent that global markets are characterized by multiple competitors that vary in size, shape, motives, and behaviors, global management may be said to be both less certain and therefore more complex than when market competitors, buyers, and other organizations are of equal size, share motives, or come from similar national cultures.

The Global Spice Trade

Spices have moved globally for thousands of years. For example, Egyptian records indicate that laborers were strengthened with imported spices as early as 2600 BC. Wars were fought, dominion established, and businesses founded to move spices around the world. Today the spice trade is populated by large and small businesses. The world's biggest spice-trading firm Man Producten is located in the Netherlands, spice suppliers operate in India, China, Indonesia, Brazil, the Seychelles, and many other countries, and the livelihood of individual dealers such as Thomas Thomas in Kerala, India depends on understanding this global market. Accordingly, when buying spices Mr. Thomas knows the latest prices in New York and Rotterdam. But he too is affected by global information expansion because individual farmers now find it possible to ship their produce directly to trading centers.

Source material: A taste of adventure. (1998, Dec. 19) *The Economist*, pp. 51–55.

Growing Complexity

Finally, the "one world" characterization of globalization exposes most of us to many more people and ideas whose perspectives on globalization differ. Domestic questions that once seemed to have simple answers become more complex when we realize that others worldwide have different "simple" answers to the same questions. Complexity increases again when there are different answers to the same question, and it gives rise to new questions about values and preferences. Later chapters explore the challenges of complexity in much greater depth. Here it is sufficient to note that although the world's people are increasingly interconnected, they have different perspectives on interconnections. Put another way, the strength, experience, and evaluations of global interconnections differ around the world. The same global event may be perceived to create opportunities for some and create threats for others. Neither does the world think as one with respect to business activities: some believe global business benefits the world and others believe it degrades it.

These four characteristics of globalization generate complex management challenges. In the following section we see that these challenges can differ in important ways from challenges that arise when managing in a strictly international world.

DISTINCTIONS BETWEEN INTERNATIONAL AND GLOBAL MANAGEMENT

The many differing definitions of globalization can be confusing. One source of confusion is that some use the term "globalization" to mean the same thing as "internationalization." This book distinguishes between the terms in two ways: the relative emphasis of each on nations, and managerial abilities and skills required.

Emphasis on Nations vs. the World

As the definition implies, international business focusses on relationships *between* nations. In global business the focus is on activities that transcend nations. Author Koh Sera clarifies this distinction in the following paragraph:

> ... *internationalization connotes expanding interfaces between nations sometimes implying political invasion or domination. Internationalization of business, therefore, is a concept of an action in which nationality is strongly in people's consciousness. It means the flow of business, goods or capital from one country into another. Globalization, by contrast, looks at the whole world as being nationless and borderless. Goods, capital, and people have to be moving freely ... (1992: 89)*

For businesses, the internationalization process often involves extension of existing economic activities into new nations. Dicken describes this as "essentially, a *quantitative* process that leads to a more extensive geographical pattern of economic activity" (1998: 5).

International studies typically examine similarities and differences between nations that facilitate the extension process. For example, international business courses look at theories of business internationalization. A guiding principle for international business is that national differences influence organizational behavior. In international management courses, the extension process would emphasize learning about other nations and cultural awareness. Content emphasis is likely to include background knowledge about various nations such as geographic location, languages in use, religion, government, and how to apply existing theories in international settings. Additionally, an international management course examines cross-cultural theories for conducting business between nations. This means examining the values, assumptions, and behaviors that guide business practices in each nation. For example, US students learn that Japanese business people bow in greeting. By contrast, Japanese business students learn that US business people shake hands as a greeting. Often the adaptive process means learning the "best way" for a manager to navigate in another culture. Thus, a US business person might bow to a Japanese business person and the reverse.

International vs. Global Management Skills and Abilities

Skills emphasized in international management include self- and cultural-awareness, as well as appropriate interpersonal and communication skills for managing between national cultures. Cross-cultural negotiation, decision-making, or motivating and leading in another country also are skill-based topics for international management.

Global management is defined by interconnections and interdependencies among people and organizations rather than simply between nations. Accordingly, global managers need to learn more about these interconnections and what it means to do business in "one world" as well as in an international world. As noted above, this interconnected world is more complex and affects how we manage organizations and ourselves. Dicken (1998) notes that with globalization, businesses do more than extend existing practices because they must alter existing practices to be integrated worldwide. This represents a *qualitative* difference from internationalization processes. At the managerial level, we see the challenge of integration when a US manager meets one Japanese business manager who shakes hands, another who bows, and a third who does neither. Each has been exposed to the world and adopted different practices from it. The point is that in a global world we need to reconsider appropriate behavior, and examine skills and abilities that a manager needs for an interconnected world.

A Global Mindset

Many argue that global managers need to develop a global mindset (Moran and Riesenberger (1994), but there are different definitions of it. For example, Harveston et al. describe a global mindset as "the propensity of managers to engage in proactive and visionary behaviors in order to achieve strategic objectives" (2000: 92). Begley and Boyd (2003) describe it as "the ability to develop and interpret criteria for business performance that are not dependent on the assumptions of a single country, culture or context and to implement those criteria appropriately in different countries, cultures and contexts" (2003: 25). In general, most agree that a global mindset is a way of thinking that shapes action. Both thought and action require simultaneity, for example to see the "big picture" and the details; to acknowledge and reconcile norms that may differ worldwide; to balance among conflicting objectives, and so on. Finally, a global mindset calls for disciplined managerial effort to weave together diverse strands of knowledge about others into a cohesive and integrated framework (Gupta and Govindarajan, 2002). Stephen Rhinesmith (2000) argues that the global mindset differs profoundly from mindsets more typical for a domestic Western environment. Some of these differences are listed in Table 1.1 to show that Western firms encourage a domestic mindset in several ways: by hiring people trained in a particular specialist function, for example, marketing, accounting, finance, and management, by encouraging decision-making that follows a rational, step-by-step process, by using hierarchical organizational structures, and by rewarding individual initiative.

A Comparison of International and Global Mindsets

Table 1.1   *A comparison of international and global mindsets*

Domestic Mindset	Global Mindset
1 Expertise in a functional area, e.g., marketing, accounting, finance	1 Expertise in many areas supported by a broad view of the organization
2 Prioritizing in a step-by-step linear fashion	2 Need to balance contradictions and paradoxes that are non-linear
3 Emphasis on hierarchical structure	3 Emphasis on processes
4 Individual responsibility is encouraged	4 Teamwork and diversity are encouraged
5 Eliminate surprises because they are threats	5 View change as an opportunity

Source material: Stephen H. Rhinesmith (1993) *A Manager's Guide to Globalization*. Homewood, IL: Business One Irwin.

By contrast, a more global mindset calls for generalized and broad expertise rather than a narrow specialty, a less definitive set of decision rules, and an emphasis on processes. Global mindsets also call for teamwork and diversity. This comparison of a Western domestic mindset and a more global one shows where problems might arise. That is, teamwork produces a challenge for individuals who best know how to "go it alone."

The global mindset also calls for managers to balance among conflicting priorities and contradictions. This also creates a challenge for Westerners when custom includes using straightforward and rational decision-making techniques. These examples show why people trained in a Western culture may find it difficult to adapt to a global mindset.

Domestic Mindsets Outside the Western Tradition

Looking outside the Western tradition shows different challenges for developing a global mindset. Throughout much of Asia and Latin America, for example, a traditional domestic mindset emphasizes a form of collectivism that puts group needs ahead of individual ones (Hofstede, 1980). For example, Japanese people traditionally are socialized to work in groups. In the workplace, the group's importance is reinforced by mechanisms that include:

1 At the level of persons, permanent employees are hired once a year in a group; assigned to a work group rather than a job; function in and are evaluated on the basis of their team's work.
2 At the organizational level, Japanese firms operate as horizontally integrated industrial groups to join forces with companies in different industries or vertically integrated keiretsus to join forces with buyers and suppliers within the same industry (Sai, 1995).

High homogeneity in Japan also causes some managers there to view cultural diversity as a threat (Dufour, 1994). Thus we see that domestic mindsets in Japan will facilitate team-work required by a global mindset, but may at the same time discourage the diversity that also is part of a global world.

In the Vedantic tradition that emerged from Hinduism, appropriate domestic mindsets include putting aside individualism to strive for human unity. This requires ultimate reliance on people and human processes rather than on organizations or systems (Chakraborty, 1995). This example suggests that a person with a Vedantic mindset may emphasize the processes important to a global mindset, but may not want to develop them within organizations. The examples Rhinesmith provides and those from Japan and India illustrate that people come from different traditions. Each person is challenged to develop a more global mindset, but the nature of this challenge varies according to the values instilled by distinctive domestic traditions. Thus, developing a global mindset may begin with examining one's own domestic mindset and its applicability to a global world. This begins with an understanding of how a domestic mindset develops.

Framing Information

One's mindset is shaped by how we frame information. Goffman (1974) describes framing as the process whereby a decision-maker organizes a set of occurrences into a coherent framework. Most of us develop mental frameworks to identify priorities and shape action. Although the framework may not be a conscious one, it nevertheless shapes action. To paraphrase Albert Einstein—our theories determine what we measure and where we put our attention. The frames managers use to interpret domestic business must expand for global business. A universal challenge is to expand one's global mindset to solve problems and make decisions when change is rapid and uncertainties many.

The Global Mindset in Business

According to a review by Morgan McCall, Jr. and George Hollenbeck (2002), the term "global mindset" was introduced by Christopher Bartlett and Sumantra Ghoshal in 1992. Researchers agree that a global mindset is important to global managers. Research conducted by Harveston et al. (2000) showed that managers of "born global" firms have a more global mindset than do managers of firms that globalize gradually. Kobrin (1994) found that larger firms with a more world-oriented mindset were more likely to enter international markets quickly, and Cavusgil and Knight (1997) similarly found that managers of born global firms create their own opportunities when they think in terms of the world as their market. These findings suggest that a global mindset may be an important predictor of both how the leader views the business world and the business activities that follow. The boxed example shows how Eastman Kodak's CEO views mindsets.

Mindsets at Eastman Kodak

Wiley Bourne, CEO of Eastman Kodak, argues that being global also means changing mindsets at every organizational level. In the case of Eastman Kodak, this meant doing more than talking about being global. It meant educating others about how a global stance differed from Kodak's traditional stance as an "opportunistic exploiter," and it required training, rewards, resources, and alterations in existing processes, structures, and hiring patterns. For example, Kodak began to send women abroad as expatriate managers, and they began to hire and develop foreign nationals for leadership positions.

Source material: Wiley Bourne (1996, June/July) Old lessons, new perspectives: Moving toward a global mindset. *Executive Speeches*, pp. 1–4.

Changes in organizational mindsets require more than cosmetic changes. For example, Prahalad and Lieberthal (1998) argue that corporate success in emerging markets such as China, India, Brazil, or Indonesia depends on developing new mindsets that lead to new business models.

Developing the Global Mindset

Ways to develop a more global mindset are outlined by Gupta and Govindarajan (2002) who indicate that the speed with which an individual develops a global mindset is driven by four forces:

1 Curiosity about the world and a desire to become smarter about how the world works
2 Self-conscious awareness of one's current mindset
3 Exposure to different experiences and to diversity
4 A disciplined effort to weave together diverse strands of knowledge about others into a cohesive and integrated framework.

In summary, a global world requires a global mindset. Managers develop this mindset by incorporating complexity in their thinking. This helps managers develop a broader perspective on events, it helps them organize these events into broader frameworks, and it helps them make decisions that incorporate more data and more contradictions in decision-making. It follows that a global mindset is particularly useful when responding to problems and challenges that represent global dilemmas.

Global Management Skills

Many studies of global managers have been conducted in the past decade. Those studies—reviewed in greater depth in Chapter 13—show that the global manager calls upon many different skills and abilities, including six upon which most scholars agree. That is, important skills and abilities recommended for all global managers are:

1 A global mindset
2 Know the business and its environment
3 Create and convey a clear vision with integrity
4 Develop self-awareness and self-understanding
5 Be able to manage diversity
6 Continuously learn.

Because the globalization process is discontinuous and events that interconnect us vary around the world, managers may best prepare for a global world by developing expertise with varied managerial tools and techniques. Global techniques and theories may be needed to address one set of challenges, but international techniques may be more useful in another setting. This blending of techniques and constant re-examination of activities and options creates challenges for global organizations and managers. Put another way, the either/or approach to managing between nations becomes a "both/and" and even a "many/and" approach to managing in one world. The leadership task becomes more complex and uncertainties are many when managing the tensions among local, international, and global demands.

MANAGEMENT THEORY AND GLOBALIZATION

Henry Luce characterized the twentieth century as "the American century," a characterization that seemed to be borne out by post-1945 events. Organizational research also was characterized by "American researchers focussed on American firms, American perspectives, and those questions most salient to American managers" (Boyacigiller and Adler, 1991: 264). Although most would agree that US organizations are important players in global business, theories based solely on their experiences or on the experiences of only large, or only Western, or only Japanese firms necessarily impose limits on our understanding of managing globally.

In a more complex and global business world, there may be few management universals (Hu, 1992; McCall and Hollenbeck, 2002). According to Scott Cowan in his 1996 address as outgoing President of what was then the American Assembly of Collegiate Schools of Business (AACSB), for the first time management theory lagged behind management practice because practitioners more than academics were at the leading edge of management. For those schooled in competition, the fact that practitioners lead theorists might appear to be a threat. But for those engaged in the more cooperative world of global business and global-business theory, the important thing may be how academics and practitioners jointly learn more about survival and success in global business.

It is also important to look at activities and theories that reflect diverse organizational efforts in a global world. In the business world, we learn most by examining activities of global business giants and also at the roles SMEs play in business globalization. Additionally, given growing interconnections and other characteristics of globalization, it is important to look at the roles that governmental and nongovernmental organizations play in shaping global business. That is, the interconnections that shape one world have implications for managing everywhere and in all kinds of organizations. Moreover, as demonstrated in chapters to follow, a trend among global organizations is to position themselves as world citizens as well as residents of more localized communities. The many managerial implications of these and other global business shifts are explored throughout this book. In the next section we see that the process of globalization is not a smooth one, nor do people see it in the same way.

PERSPECTIVES ON GLOBALIZATION

There are many differing perspectives on globalization. These have been organized around three broad schools of thought which Held and others (1999) define as skeptical, hyperglobalist, and transformationalist. A review of these three perspectives shows how the same category can encompass ideas whose underpinnings differ significantly. Additionally, we look at the managerial implications of each.

The Skeptical Thesis of Globalization

Some assert that globalization is, in a word, "globaloney." This "skeptical" thesis is based on two main arguments: history has seen other periods of growing interconnections, and the future will be much like the past.

History Repeats Itself

Historical support for the skeptic's argument focusses on different time periods, but the general point is the same: globalization is nothing new. In a UN address delivered in 2001, Ugandan President Museveni (2001) argued that African slaves have been globalized since the 1440s. Flynn and Giraldez (2002) argue that the world economy began in the 1570s with trade links that emerged between Asia, Africa, Europe, and the Americas. Silver mined in the Spanish colony of Manila was shipped to China, providing direct connections among all the world's populated continents.

According to Anthony Sampson, author of *Company Man* (1995), the forerunners of today's corporations were collaborative arrangements among European merchants during the Crusades. The charters of these business organizations were to return profits to owners. The less successful fell prey to pirates, to each other, to resistance to colonization, to weather, or to other forces, but the successful ones returned from abroad with new wealth for owners. According to John Keay, author of *The Honourable Company: A History of the English East India Company* (1991), at the height of its influence in the early nineteenth century, the English East India Company controlled nearly half of the world's trade in a business empire that stretched from England to India and throughout Asia. In the same time period, the Dutch East India Company established itself as a rival firm by supplying spices and other valuables to a willing European market. Wealth creation stimulated significant export activity throughout the 1800s and 1900s. Like today, this wealth was based on all types of industries.

For example, Worcestershire sauce was developed and introduced to the world in 1834. Its basis is an Indian recipe that contains vinegar, molasses, sugar, Spanish anchovies, black Calcutta tamarinds, Dutch shallots, Chinese chiles, Madagascar cloves, French garlic, and secret ingredients. In the 1990s, autos, motorcycles, food, and even insurance were sold outside their home countries. The profit generated by global sauces, autos, and services was an important factor in the 1800s, and it remains an important business objective in a more global world.

Other authors believe globalization began in about 1840. In comparing the post-1945 process of globalization to the years between 1840 and 1914, economists Kevin O'Rourke and Jeffrey Williamson (2000) note that in the earlier period transportation costs fell faster, cross-national trade barriers were fewer, more capital flowed across national boundaries with more volatility, and cross-border migration was far greater than it is today. Contemporary increases in economic inequalities in rich countries and decreased economic inequalities in poor countries also occurred in the nineteenth century (Williamson, 1996).

What's Important Remains the Same

The second thread of the skeptic argument is that nations remain central to business activities. That is, the historical events and geographic concerns that shaped today's nation-states will also be important in the future (Veseth, 1998). This thread of the skeptic's argument is bolstered by evidence showing that many global firms are as firmly rooted within national cultures and practices as in the past. For example, membership on boards of directors in all corporations is drawn almost exclusively from a company's headquarters (Hu, 1992), and stock ownership is concentrated largely in country of origin, often in the hands of just a few. Others argue there are no or few truly global organizations. For example, Lipsey et al. (2000) note that large corporations account for about the same amount of the world's output in 1990 (22 percent) as they did in 1980. Using a definition that requires a business to both produce and sell in global pools, Veseth (1998) also claims there are few global businesses. Rugman (2001) believes that businesses are national or at best regional.

The Skeptical Thesis and Business Activities

Since, as was argued earlier, business activities result from a manager's frame of reference, it follows that how one defines the organization's place in the world shapes strategy and other business activities. The skeptic's point of view on globalization is that business is and remains international. If globalization is nothing new, then globalization of business is simply business as usual. Having defined itself as nation-based, the leader who perceives globalization to be internationalization is likely to scan external boundaries from a domestic base, fixing attention on flows of business, goods or capital from one country into another. Assessing these flows involves boundary scanning that begins at a national level and expands to encompass international opportunities. Rather than scan the latter directly, the firm defined as international might rely on its national government to identify emerging business opportunities abroad. This firm also might draw guidance from existing theories of internationalization, perhaps adopting an evolutionary approach such as internationalization processes, product life cycles (Vernon, 1966), or portfolio theories when operating abroad.

In summary, nation-based firms that view globalization as "nothing new" will respond with activities consistent with the more international or country-to-country approach developed over the last fifty years. In a practical sense, this means that businesses can best expand into international markets by following principles built around a world largely defined by commerce between nations.

The Limits of Skepticism

Van Bergeijk and Mensink (1997) refute the skeptical argument. They argue that when recalculated in current dollars the trade figures cited by Krugman (1996) and others show that real growth of trade is extremely strong and persistent and that the export ratio of GDP has also increased very rapidly since the mid-1980s. Similarly, Govindarajan and Gupta (2000) calculate that world trade in services and goods is about 25 percent of world GDP as compared to 10 percent about thirty years ago. Points made by the latter authors suggest that globalization represents something other than a repeat of past occurrences.

The skeptical argument takes a limited view of the world by comparing today's activities to those of an earlier era. According to Keohane and Nye, the issue is not how old globalization is, but rather "how 'thin' or 'thick' it is at any given time" (2000: 7). These authors illustrate their point as follows:

> *An example of "thin globalization," the Silk Road provided an economic and cultural link between ancient Europe and Asia, but the route was plied by a small group of hardy traders, and the goods that were traded back and forth had a direct impact primarily on a small (and relatively elite) stratum of consumers along the road. In contrast, "thick" relations of globalization involve many relationships that are intensive as well as extensive: long-distance flows that are large and continuous, affecting the lives of many people.*

Keohane and Nye conclude that globalization today represents "thick" relationships that involve many people and relationships in interconnected networks.

The Hyperglobalist Thesis of Globalization

A different perspective on globalization called "hyperglobalism" asserts that globalization is a new stage of human history through which the power of nation-states is supplanted by business activities (Ohmae, 1995). This means that businesses more than nation-states will become the "primary economic and political units of world society" (Held et al., 1999: 3). Hyperglobalists usually agree that globalization is an economic phenomenon, but they disagree on why and how businesses participate in the process. Two different perspectives are reviewed below.

Businesses as Self-interested Actors

The self-interested nature of business motivates managers to pursue profit in an interdependent world. The self-interest perspective views organizations as dispassionate actors on a global scale working pragmatically in pursuit of their own ends, e.g. profits and survival. Luttwak (1999) believes businesses are victims of a turbo-charged capitalism. They are forced to rapid action because competitors otherwise will do it first. Under these conditions, businesses are little more than isolated actors in a global market where rules of profitability and survival are governed by supercharged market forces. According to Scholte (1996), this more liberal perspective on globalization can view organizational actors and market forces as part of a benign and even beneficial process.

In a global world, self-interest could mean linking with suppliers and buyers or even with competitors to satisfy self-interest. It almost certainly means relocating jobs to low-wage economies because to do otherwise is to lose out to competitors. It can then be argued that linked worldwide production chains simply help businesses operate efficiently and survive in a competitive world. Although some believe that markets will correct themselves to assure that abuses do not occur, a concern is that governments may be motivated to comply with lower labor standards or compromise environmental protections to attract business investments. In this way the interests of global business may overpower national interests.

Businesses Conspire to Supplant National Power

The hyperglobalism theme explored above looks primarily at how indifferent markets displace or reshape the authority of national governments. A different perspective asserts that business self-interest has a malevolent character. This perspective is explored below.

The Anti-globalization Protest Movement

Anti-globalization protesters share three general concerns about globalization. They believe that capitalism as a system cannot reasonably address social-justice issues; they believe that multinational corporations are at the heart of the globalization problem; and they believe that even if globalization increases overall wealth worldwide, it will have malignant effects on poverty, literacy, diversity, gender equality, and cultures. The main charge leveled against businesses is that they create monopolies that exploit workers abroad. They cannot be stopped because there are no globally shared regulations coming from the political sphere.

Source material: Jagdish Bhagwati (2002) Coping with anti-globalization. *Foreign Affairs*, 81 (1): 2–8.

A New World Order perspective on hyperglobalism argues that global-business primacy is coming about by design and it is not indifferent. First given voice by Mikael Gorbachev in a 1988 speech, the concept of a New World Order was popularized by then-US President George Bush during the 1989 Gulf War. Since then, the meaning of a New

World Order has been appropriated most often by those who view it as consolidation of power among already-powerful business and governmental interests.

Some believe that businesses collude with other powerful entities to further consolidate and enhance their own positions (Barnett and Cavanagh, 1994; Klein, 2000; Korten, 1995). An example they might highlight is the role that global advertising agencies played in India's 2004 elections. This example shows interconnections, but some will wonder if these are helpful interconnections.

Advertising/India

Politics dominated India's television advertising in the 2004 elections. Ads prepared by global powerhouses Grey Global Group (GGG) and Publicis' Leo Burnett helped articulate opposing views of India, and for the first time political parties used ad campaigns to "brand" their activities. For example, GGG was commissioned by ruling party Bharatiya Janta to create an "India Shining" campaign that highlighted the government's role in recent economic advances. Leo Burnett worked for opposition party Indian National Congress to reach the millions of poor and rural Indians who had not benefitted from India's economic boom. These ad campaigns mark a sharp departure from Indian political campaigns of the past which were more grass roots in nature and they demonstrate how ideas from one nation move rapidly to others in an age of globalization.

Steingard and Fitzgibbons (1995) believe that management literature may be partly to blame for the New World Order backlash to globalization. They argue that academic publications promote myths like "Globalization leads to one healthy world culture," "Globalization brings prosperity to person and planet," or "Global markets spread naturally." They argue that globalization ideals represent primarily Westernized perspectives. They further assert that management educators have given little thought to the fact that not everyone wants to be a member of a global village. These authors argue that it is important for scholars and citizens to balance unbridled enthusiasm for capitalism with evidence of its results. They call for an open and egalitarian dialogue among those who promote globalization and those who believe it has negative consequences.

Hyperglobalism and Business Activities

Managers who adopt a hyperglobalist view recognize that globalization is not business as usual. If globalization is perceived to be "survival of the fittest" on a global scale, managers are likely to scan the world for pragmatic opportunities that satisfy their interests. This might lead to dispassionate decisions when relocating jobs or shifting investments. Although managers may recognize that their actions create unpleasant consequences for others, they may believe that relentless competitive markets allow few alternatives.

The Limits of Hyperglobalism

The rubric for globalization as a "New World Order" is very scary indeed. But it does not tell all we need to know about globalization or the role businesses can or should play in this process. Defining globalization as a New World Order may over generalize and cause people to overlook options for a more global world. For example, although large firms have the potential to abuse their economic power, not all do and some work to enhance world-wide opportunities. Ironically, the more extreme anti-globalization protestors share a belief with defenders of business that the relationship between business and society is a zero-sum game where one can gain only when the other loses. Ellis (2001) notes that this is a false dichotomy, arguing that the same forces that drive business globalization also can facilitate social progress. This suggests that businesses can play a role in creating a win/win world. Business roles in creating win/win options may not be explored or developed when businesses are viewed as a source of evil. Finally, when the global dialogue concentrates only on winners and losers, it reinforces win/lose approaches to resolving challenges.

Three Faces of Global Culture

Peter Berger (1997) outlines three perspectives on the creation of a global culture:

The Davos culture: Until 2002 when they met in New York, a group of business and political leaders from advanced economies annually met in Davos, Switzerland at the World Economic Summit. Samuel Huntington coined the phrase "Davos culture" to suggest that global culture is a culture of the elite. Berger further describes this culture as a Western business elite and those who want to be like them. This cultural group aligns with the New World Order perspective on hyperglobalism because it focusses on those whose main interests are in globalizing economic development and business activities.

The McWorld culture: Benjamin Barber (1992) characterized cultural polarization as "Jihad vs. McWorld." In particular, he argued that Western culture and particularly US culture transmitted through various media are a form of cultural imperialism that has begun to dominant the world. The McWorld culture is populated by the Davos elite and companies that produce global brands representing Western culture. This perspective is analogous to the benign self-interest perspective on hyperglobalism.

Faculty club international culture: In contrast to the Davos culture that organizes to sell products abroad and the McWorld culture that supports it, the faculty club international culture promotes Western ideals such as feminism or environmentalism. According to Berger, this group is an elite of the intelligentsia that spreads Western ideals through existing systems such as education, think tanks, and mass media. Berger suggests that the tensions between the Davos culture and the faculty club international culture revolve around how progress can be achieved. That is, the Davos culture assumes economic development leads progress, but the faculty club culture assumes it follows human development such as human rights initiatives.

The Transformational Thesis of Globalization

In contrast to the hyperglobalist thesis, a transformational thesis of globalization argues that the end-point of the globalization process is not yet decided, although most agree that global interconnections and interdependence will forge new links and dissolve some existing ones. Relationships among nations and people will be reconfigured and power relationships restructured (Held et al., 1999). The Unocal example below shows how transnational voluntary organizations work to hold businesses accountable for worldwide activities.

Unocal

In the late 1990s, the US prohibited investments in Burma, putting Unocal in a difficult spot as the biggest US investor there. The public accused Unocal of human rights violations there because they collaborate with the State Law and Order Restoration Council in Burma—the military junta that seized power in 1988. Public pressure mounted against this and other businesses to withdraw from Burma, but Unocal divorced itself from the nation to become more "stateless."

In 2002 a US court ruled that companies could be held liable in US courts for aiding and abetting human-rights violations committed outside the US. This opened the way for a lower court to hear a case against Unocal. The suit claimed that Myanmar government soldiers forced Burmese villagers to labor on a $1.2 billion natural-gas pipeline in which Unocal was an investor. Plaintiffs claim that Unocal knew about the abuses, but did nothing to stop them because the project benefitted from them. At least ten similar lawsuits are pending against US corporations. These and similar lawsuits demonstrate growing interest in the activities of companies everywhere. They also show that new mechanisms emerge to hold companies accountable for worldwide activities.

Source material: Sherri Prasso (1997, May 5) A company without a country? *Business Week*, p. 40.

According to Richard Falk, transnational voluntary organizations are "animated by environmental concerns, human rights, hostility to patriarchy, and a vision of human community based on the unity of diverse cultures ..." (1993: 39). Working toward a vision of human community driven less by consumption than by caring, these organizations aim to enhance worldwide justice. The anti-personnel mines treaty, the Jubilee debt forgiveness movement, and alliances for sustainability and against poverty, illiteracy, terror, and HIV/AIDs are all examples of recent and global progress.

Although many proponents of transformation come from the voluntary sector, some businesses also reflect a transformationist view that works toward a better world. Ellis (2001) believes that the same forces that drive business globalization can also aid social progress. For example, global businesses often pay their workers more than the national average, spend more on R&D in countries where they invest than their domestic counterparts, and export more than domestic firms do (Foreign friends, 2000); the effects of business activities like these are greater in poorer economies than rich ones. Over

68 percent of large companies in Western Europe and 41 percent in the US report on "triple bottom line" objectives (profits, people, and the planet), showing that they integrate social and profit goals (Management barometer, 2003).

Global Business as a Force for Good

Vernon Ellis believes that the global advance of business is inexorable, but that the consequences are not. Businesses have choices to make, and Ellis believes that businesses will make choices that benefit the global society as well as themselves. He argues that the interests of society and business are not played out in a "zero-sum" game where one can gain only at the expense of the other. Although Ellis acknowledges that businesses often resist social change, they have "always had a long-term commonality of interest with wider society ... business has constantly evolved to meet society's goals and fuses them into its own interests" (2001: 16).

Source material: Ellis Vernon (2001) Can global business be a force for good? *Business Strategy Review*, 12 (2): 15–20.

Some businesses promote social justice as part of ordinary activities. For example, Benetton's advertisements highlight social issues like peace, caring, and hunger prevention. The Body Shop endorses Amnesty International and other social causes. DuPont is a champion for sustainable development. Businesses also contribute to justice via direct action in activities less traditional to the business sector. Some participate in cause-based business/nonprofit partnerships and others contribute to philanthropic ventures to satisfy social objectives. Numerous foundations operate to help businesses contribute to social goals. Other businesses engage in corporate philanthropy. An example of the latter is the Global Alliance for Vaccines and Immunization, a $1.01 billion aid project launched in the late 1990s with major funding from Microsoft Corporation and the Bill and Melinda Gates Foundation. The project immunizes for childhood diseases, concentrating on nations where many children do not live to the age of five.

Merck's Charter

In 1950 chairman of Merck George W. Merck said "medicine is for the people. It is not for the profits. The profits follow." In 1987, this vision of business motivated Merck to donate a drug to treat river blindness to millions in sub-Saharan Africa. By 2002, Merck had donated $100 million in vaccines, worked to build better healthcare systems to treat AIDs in Africa, and was selling AIDs-treatment drugs at an 85 percent discount in Africa.

Activities of Transformationalist Enterprises

The business that views globalization through a transformational filter also finds it important to generate wealth. It may do this (as the hyperglobalist does) by forging links with suppliers and customers. Unlike the hyperglobalist, the manager who adopts this perspective would consider the longer-run ramifications of these linkages. For example, a central concern for the board of British Petroleum is the economic and social health of places where BP does business. Wealth may be broadly defined to embrace both financial and social goals, for example to enhance quality of life and financial wealth. Further, this firm may alter its activities to ensure that human and other species survive. Some may operate from a double or triple bottom-line perspective to balance interests of people, profit, and the planet. Others may engage in single issues that improve local communities.

Reconfiguration of existing links sometimes comes about through interconnections among businesses, governments, and members of civil society. Voluntary and governmental organizations may take on business roles just as businesses may play social as well as profit-generating roles. In these ways they transform their own organizations. Thus the transformationist view of globalization suggests that businesses and voluntary organizations do not divide neatly into opposing camps for good and evil, but that they cross boundaries and borders to interconnect their activities and initiatives. This point is further explored in Chapter 2.

Limitations of the Transformationist Perspective

Held et al. (1999) assert that transformation is a process that will yield different power hierarchies and shift authority systems, but no one can say what the results will be. Changes thus far are both positive and negative. Interconnections between businesses and other organizations and interconnections among people around the world are making it easier to identify and address social injustice. But this process is not pretty. Some of what we see is disturbing, and some events that occur are destructive. However, seeing world realities helps all of us to recognize that common concerns cannot be addressed unless we operate as part of one world. The better world envisioned is one based on partnerships that realize gains made when civil society, businesses, and governments worldwide collaborate.

PERSPECTIVES ON GLOBALIZATION INFORM ACTION

Having suggested that business leaders operationalize different views of globalization, it is important to note advantages as well as disadvantages associated with each. For example, if globalization is not internationalization, then firms relying exclusively on traditions of practice and theory may not be well served by them. At worst, this approach can fragment rather than strengthen boundary-spanning activities. If globalization is something new, then both transformations and hyperglobalists must find new ways to operate. There are no rulebooks to guide them through the globalization process. This means that many will experiment, and it probably means that mistakes will be made. For example, donations of second-hand clothing to Zambia have all but destroyed textile production there. This suggests that all organizations should consider the second- and third-order global consequences of their activities.

There is no definitive answer to the question: what is globalization? But we do see that many organizations in addition to businesses shape the global agenda. Although many businesses are shaped by globalization, others play an active role in shaping the agenda for defining globalization and its consequences. Accordingly, it is important for business leaders to make explicit and clear choices when interpreting what growing worldwide interconnections mean for their organizations.

Finally, in this more global world of interrelatedness and interdependence, it is important to recognize that organizational activities result from human decisions. It is people who generate positive or negative outcomes. As individuals, as organizational participants, and as citizens of nations and of an interconnected world, we need not become victims of globalization. At the same time, developing the potential and avoiding the threats of globalization demands attention and action. A compelling reason to learn about and involve ourselves in globalization is that global decisions made without participation may lead to outcomes that serve few interests—outcomes that could realize the worst qualities of the feared New World Order.

THE GLOBAL CHALLENGE FOR MANAGING CAREERS AND ORGANIZATIONS

In summary, growing interconnections brought about by the globalization process require that both managers and organizations expand on traditional repertoires of roles. Subsequent chapters examine how this can occur, and so the examples below are limited in scope.

As national economies, political systems, cultures, technologies, resources, and industries increasingly converge—perhaps to meld, perhaps to take shape in new forms—global management skills and abilities become more important to all organizations. These skills will be diverse. Traditional knowledge and skills remain important. For example, some managerial competencies such as leading, planning, organizing, and controlling will persist. Yet global managers can better respond to global demands by learning continuously, managing diversity, and developing a global mindset. This encourages managers to think "outside the box" of tradition. For the individual manager, the task is to prepare for projects, jobs, and careers in a future where direction is unclear. This requires that many learn to live with ambiguity.

For organizational leaders as well, the challenge is to manage tradition and change. Global firms may mix and match traditional principles with newly developed ones that borrow best practices worldwide. Many Western firms once articulated their strategy as profit-seeking alone, and established stand-alone hierarchical structures. Few in the global sphere are able to pursue profits alone, and many now experiment with flatter organizational structures. Most link with others to accomplish their goals. Western traditions of scientific management, Japanese traditions of lifetime employment, Chinese traditions of family ownership, and many other traditions are under review. Under similar review are high wage rates and quality of life issues in German firms, ethics of work in Eastern Europe and other former Communist countries, and the relationship between global business and global society. Proliferation of global options creates new challenges for balancing organizational structures, people, and processes. Ways that global managers achieve balance are explored in Chapter 2.

CHAPTER SUMMARY

Globalization is a process that is increasing worldwide interconnections in virtually every sphere of activity.

The four characteristics of globalization are increasing worldwide interconnections, rapid, discontinuous change, an increased number and diversity of participants in business and other activities, and growing complexity.

Distinctions between international and global business can be made based on the relative emphasis on nations, and management skills and abilities needed for each.

A global world requires a more global mindset. Developing this mindset requires changes from everyone, but the specific changes depend on one's existing mindset.

Three perspectives on globalization are offered: the skeptical view, the hyperglobalist view, and the transformationist view. Each provides a different explanation of globalization, and suggests different activities for managers subscribing to the view.

Organizational activities result from human decisions. As individuals, as organizational participants, and as citizens of nations and of an interconnected world, we need not create nor ourselves become victims of globalization. But this takes knowledge, thought, and action. It also requires that we look beyond first-order effects to understand how our actions affect others worldwide.

REVIEW AND DISCUSSION QUESTIONS

1 Evaluate yourself on the six managerial skills required of a global manager. Rate your progress on each and set goals for how you can improve on each.

2 Three perspectives on globalization were presented: it's nothing new (the skeptical thesis), it's hyperglobalism, it's transformational. Select the perspective that is closest to your own beliefs and provide arguments to support your point of view.

3 What does your answer to #1 suggest about how you should prepare yourself for global business? What classes should you take? What academic interests should be your specialty? What skills will be most important to you?

4 Find a recent headline from a newspaper or magazine that reports on an event that occurred somewhere in the world. A war? An economic recession? Discovery of a new drug? A natural disaster? Examples: North Korea's withdrawal from the Treaty on the Nonproliferation of Nuclear Weapons; the Iraqi war; inter-tribal warfare in African nations; terrorist bombings; organized crime in the illicit drug trade. Trace how this event or activity can go global. How might this event affect your daily life? How might it affect your job opportunities?

NOTE

1 In the event that a ship sinks, its emergency beacon floats free. The beacon sends a signal to a Russian satellite that is beamed down to a Moscow technician who records and sends the location and the ship's identification number to rescue ships.

Chapter 2
A SYSTEMS VIEW OF GLOBAL MANAGEMENT

NAPSTER FORGES GLOBAL INTERCONNECTIONS

Organizations and individuals face global shifts in six external environments: 1) businesses and industries; 2) the natural environment; 3) economic; 4) political; 5) technology, particularly information technologies; and 6) culture. Although each of these six external environments is distinctive, they also interact with one another, and are additionally shaped by mediating organizations and even individual activities. This point is illustrated by a simple change in music *technology* that began with Shawn Fanning's Napster.

Having provided consumers with a way to share files and download music from the Internet, Napster altered *cultural* habits for music acquisition worldwide. At the same time, another *cultural shift* occurred when the teen-pop fad faded but no new music fad replaced it. *Businesses* in the music *industry* witnessed an almost immediate downturn in sales of tapes and CDs: billions of dollars reported for the global *economy* were no longer counted because consumers had no costs. This downturn together with illegal copying of CDs caused many music companies to drop recording contracts for local artists, finding it cheaper to promote established international artists than to develop local ones. Hardest hit were recording artists in nations where CD piracy is particularly high. At the time 30 percent of music CDs in Spain and 60 percent of music CDs in Thailand were pirated. Thus, absence of *political/legal* sanctions against both CD piracy and file sharing over the Internet affected music companies.

Between 1999 and 2003 the record industry witnessed a 14 percent drop in revenue. This impacted not only on record producers but also on performing artists. Industry businesses created different strategies in response to file sharing services. For example, Bertelsmann loaned Napster more than $100 million to develop it as a legitimate business model complementary to its own recording unit BMG Entertainment. New organizations such as KaZaA—incorporated in Vanuatu—and Morpheus entered the industry. These and other activities further altered recording-industry dynamics. Mediating organizations such as the Recording Industry Association of America filed lawsuits against Napster, putting a *political/legal* spin on music downloading. Both Universal Music Group and EMI Group—competitors to BMG—filed direct suits against Bertelsmann. Others with mediating interests include recording artists themselves as well as buyers and suppliers to the industry.

This brief example illustrates how a global change in an information technology was followed by global shifts in the industry, in politics, in culture, and in economics. Although it might seem that the natural environment plays no role in this event, consider the packaging, plastic, and other materials that are ordinarily required to sell a CD or tape. The point is, each external environment is affected by a global change in any other but the felt effect may not be immediately obvious.

But this story continues. Napster liquidated assets after losing a battle over copyrights in 2001. Roxio bought Napter's name and remaining assets in 2002, then relaunched it as a subscription and pay-per-song service. Meanwhile Apple Computer introduced its iTunes store, charging just about $1 dollar per downloaded song. Musicmatch Inc., RealNetworks Inc's Rhapsody, and bigger competitors such as Amazon.com, Sony, and Wal-Mart followed this lead. Sony and Bertelsmann announced merger plans for their music division, ▶

and peer-to-peer computing developed as a viable option. These new competitive configurations and technologies further altered the global landscape for music and other industries. But the beat continued: RIAA filed suits against individuals backed by angry claims that music downloaders are thieves (Gomes, 2003). Pepsi featured these individuals in a promotional campaign for free (and legal) downloads, and smaller businesses emerged to handle legal issues and burn CDs for customers. The Dutch supreme court ruled that KaZaA's makers cannot be held liable for copyright infringement due to file sharing, but record-industry investigators raided firm offices. What's next? Stay tuned.

Source material: Peter Burrows (2003, Oct. 20) Napster lives again—Sort of. *Business Week*, pp. 66, 68; Charles Goldsmith and Keith Johnson (2002, June 4) Music piracy forces industry to reduce signing new artists. *The Wall Street Journal*, p. B10; Lee Gomes (2003, Sept. 15). RIAA takes off gloves in mounting its fight against music thieves. *The Wall Street Journal* (Eastern Edition), p. B1; Ethan Smith (2003, Oct. 16) Universal Music to cut work force as industry sags. *The Wall Street Journal*, pp. A3, A8.

CHAPTER OVERVIEW

A review of contemporary business history provides the context for understanding how organizations interconnect with global environments. Systems and chaos theories are introduced to provide a framework for examining organizations in global environments. Six sources of globalization are described and their interactions in a global system are outlined. Attention then turns to the organization to show how managers adapt people, processes and structures for a more global world. Finally, the chapter examines organizational interconnections through which global businesses manage external adaptation and internal integration.

WITH HISTORY AS THE GUIDE: SETTING THE CONTEXT

Writing in 1981, Richard Robinson classified post-World War II business into four distinct periods of international business expansion. During each time period, business leaders focused their attention in different ways, and different theories emerged to set the stage for global management.

The Postwar Decade (1945–1955): Reasons for Efficiency in the Postwar Decade

The end of World War II brought an urgent worldwide need for materials and services. Firms best able to respond were located principally in the US and a few other industrialized economies, such as Switzerland. Nestlé is an example; it had relocated to the US during the war years from which it developed a significant Latin American presence. Many of these businesses relied on principles of scientific management to meet growing worldwide demand.

Scientific Management

Frederick Taylor's principles of "scientific management" argued for "one best way" to accomplish work. Writing at the same time as Taylor, Henri Fayol also sought to uncover universal business truths based on a "science" of management. Fayol is credited with introducing the five managerial universals of planning, organizing, coordinating, controlling, and commanding, and he outlined how each could best be used. For example, command is facilitated by a clear chain of command through which employees answer to a single superior.

Max Weber's ideal for a bureaucratic organization complemented and expanded on the developing "science" of work management by showing how jobs could be organized into a cohesive organizational whole. This bureaucratic ideal is the pyramid-shaped hierarchy many use today. The pyramid shape is supported by clear divisions of labor, delegated authority and control, and sustained by written rules and regulations.

Features of Bureaucracy and Scientific Management as "One Best Way"

1 Division of labor or specialization occurs—people are trained as experts in narrow areas
2 Tasks are standardized to perform the same job in exactly the same way
3 Hierarchy of authority is established
4 Unity of command is established so no employee answers to more than one boss
5 Span of control is limited to no more than seven for any one supervisor
6 Line and staff responsibilities are divided—line makes decisions, staff advises
7 Decentralization locates authority at the lowest level possible without losing control over critical issues
8 Structure is established according to purpose, function, geography, or by customer served to organize work in logical groupings
9 Activities of the manager include planning, organizing, leading, coordinating, controlling

---

Economic success and both public and academic reinforcement doubtless confirmed an impression that bureaucratic management practices in US firms were superior. As Dunning puts it: "The argument in the 1950s and early 1960s seemed to run something like this. US industry in the US is efficient; its technology, management and marketing skills are the best in the world. Therefore when US industry goes abroad, US products, skills and production methods should follow it" (1993: 9–10).

Cross-border business activities in this time period relied primarily on trade in tangible goods, and managers were encouraged to concentrate on efficient transfers of resources from home to host countries. Senior managers abroad usually were expatriates from the home country. Many businesses were described as ethnocentric (Heenan and Perlmutter, 1979) because they put home-country interests above those of host countries. Finally, with respect to the external environment, businesses in the postwar decade tended to see boundaries between the organization and its environment (Wright and Ricks, 1994), and nations were viewed primarily as closed systems defined by clear borders.

The Growth Years (1955–1970)

World manufacturing and trade increased after the mid-1950s. Businesses with a presence in multiple countries came to be called multinational enterprises (MNEs) or multinational corporations (MNCs). For some, expansion produced revenues larger than the entire gross domestic product (GDP) of smaller nations. The growing economic clout of businesses often was equated with real or perceived political clout. When foreign businesses used this power, they were viewed as extensions of national governments. Although international business activities in the growth years still came from industrialized nations, growing consumer demand attracted firms from many more nations.

International Expansion as a Rational Economic Decision

Early theories of international business growth helped shift emphasis from nations (how businesses help nations develop) to organizations (how businesses achieve competitive advantage to grow for their own benefit). Writing in the 1960s, Raymond Vernon (1966) argued that limits on domestic growth led to four expansion stages for US firms. The theory linked foreign direct investment decisions to economic rationality over a life cycle:

1   At the product's introductory stage when sales growth is uncertain and production runs limited, the firm uses excess productive capacity domestically to produce and export to similar industrialized economies
2   At the product's growth stage, firms will increase exports to developing economies to further expand their markets and ease growing competition in the domestic market
3   As the product matures and competition increases, costs become more important and the firm may then use improved process technologies to produce more abroad and export less; manufacturing abroad often occurs first in other industrialized countries for export to developing economies
4   At the decline phase of the product life cycle, almost all production moves to lesser developed economies for worldwide distribution

Expansion in many firms conformed to a life-cycle process, but others did not. This led to an eclectic theory for foreign direct investment (Dunning, 1988). Dunning argued that location-specific advantages combine with the business's own special abilities to shape FDI decisions. An example is Coors Brewery which is unlikely to expand to locations where there is no clean mountain water.

Time of Trouble (1970s)

Many European and Japanese firms expanded internationally in the 1960s and beyond. Business-to-business competition increased, showing that national governments could not always protect businesses from competition or external pressures such as nationalization or oil shocks. Robinson (1981) described the 1970s as watershed years when developing economies began to reject the dominant role that large multinational businesses had played. Some developing economies expelled businesses; others nationalized them under government control.

The interface between an organization and its environment (Emery and Trist, 1965) took on a special urgency in this "time of trouble." The developing and direct link between organizations and their international environments led to new complexity. Organizations viewed international expansion in rational economic terms, but also began to view it as a learning process for future expansion (Beamish et al., 1991).

The greatest practical concern for firms operating in the increasingly complex 1970s was integration of strategy, structure, and systems (Bartlett and Ghoshal, 1995). Since organizations differ, integration also could come about in different ways. Thus, there was no longer a single "best way" for conducting business. Researchers began to explore growing complexities worldwide. For example, increased political emphasis and a more competitive environment for international business encouraged studies of political risk and competitive advantages for firms and industries.

Internationalization Theory

Working at the University of Uppsala, researchers Jan Johanson, Jan-Erik Vahlne, and Finn Wiedersheim-Paul (1975, 1977) developed a theory of internationalization that expanded on economic rationality. Specifically, the Uppsala model argues that firms internationalize as they gain experience and knowledge of foreign markets. Because direct, hands-on learning is usually acquired slowly, internationalization can be viewed as an incremental process that occurs in four distinct stages. Each stage of this internationalization process is based on knowledge gained in a previous stage:

- In the first stage where firms are not engaged in export activities there is little learning about international markets.
- In the second stage, independent representatives are hired to facilitate exporting. Interactions with this representative help the exporting firm learn about the foreign market.
- An overseas sales subsidiary is established when the firm has sufficient learning.
- Following additional learning, the company can establish a foreign production facility.

The Uppsala model, Vernon's model, and Dunning's theory all suggest that internationalization follows a series of defined steps. But these theories differ in important ways. Whereas economic models explain FDI in economic terms, the eclectic model suggested and the Uppsala model showed that managerial behaviors and learning are different yet important inputs for internationalization. Thus we see that as business diversity increased, theorists began to examine new variables to better explain behaviors.

The New International Order (1980 and Beyond)

Research in the 1980s pointed out that some firms did not follow expected internationalization stages. For example, some skipped the exporting phase to enter markets with foreign licensing or manufacturing (Carstairs and Welch, 1982/1983; Reid, 1984; Root, 1987). Other research showed that firms from different countries could follow different paths to internationalization (see Knight and Cavusgil, 1996 for a review of these studies). Reid (1983) noted that stage models of internationalization also paid insufficient attention to factors like the industry, the company, or people involved in the company. These findings called for broader-based theories better able to explain variations in how businesses expand internationally.

Expanding complexity also focused attention on culture and national interests. This was followed by studies of cultural traits (Hofstede, 1980, 1983). Other theories combined ideas from different fields to create interdisciplinary research. An example of the latter is network theory.

Network Theory

Earlier we saw that FDI and product life-cycle theories view economic rationality as a key determinant for international expansion. By contrast, internationalization according to the Uppsala theory focuses on learning as a key determinant. Network theory attempts to wed these two theories, arguing that both economic rationality and learning influence firm decisions (Johanson and Mattsson, 1988, 1992; Sharma, 1992). The resulting decision network for organizations involves relationships such as interactions with customers, suppliers, and competitors; networks can involve family and friends. This theory therefore suggests that one can better understand decisions to go international by considering how economic variables and social relationships jointly influence firm activities.

Internationalization of Small and Medium-sized Enterprises (SMEs)

How do theories of international expansion apply to small and medium-sized firms? Nicole Coviello and Andrew McAuley (1999) explored this question by looking at sixteen empirical studies of small international businesses. They concluded that using more than one theoretical framework better captures the internationalization concept. They also suggest that internationalization and life-cycle theories might not apply to small firms.

SMEs Defined

Small and medium-sized enterprises are variously defined. The OECD defines them as independent firms that are not subsidiaries of other companies. The upward limit on size often is 250 employees, but in the US SMEs can employ as many as 500 employees. Small firms are categorized as those that employ fewer than 50 people. Financial assets also are used to define SMEs. For example, in the European Union, SMEs must have annual revenues of €40 million or less and balance-sheet valuations of less than €27 million.

Source material: Small and medium-sized enterprises: Local strength, global reach. (2000, June) OECD Policy Brief. http://www1.oecd.org/publications/pol_brief/2000/2000_02.pdf.

Small firms may rely more on networks to go international (Coviello and Munro, 1995; Holmlund and Kock, 1998). Specifically, managing business and social network relationships can increase rates of international development among smaller firms. This view is supported by much of the SME research. Zafarullah and others (1998) concluded that the network perspective is perhaps most useful in understanding SME internationalization. More recently, Jones (2001) studied small, high-technology firms to note that for many of them international involvement was importing not exporting. She further noted that first steps towards internationalization among her sample of SMEs included activities other than trade. This evidence shows why tradition alone may be insufficient to analyze the internationalization process.

Pencils Go Global

Dixon Ticonderoga Co. is a relatively small company that makes pencils—not the fancy retractable ones but the plain wood-encased graphite grasped by many primary-school students. Dixon buys erasers from Korea, some of its wood from Indonesia and wooden parts from near Beijing, and it is shifting more operations to Mexico. Once protected by US tariffs, Dixon faces stiff world competition especially from Chinese pencil makers who can make cheaper and better pencils. This example illustrates how smaller firms are affected by and engage in global activities.

Growing Emphasis on Processes and People

By the 1990s, the international era had reached a more global stage that demanded integration, particularly with suppliers worldwide. This shift in behavior led to shifts in managerial emphasis, and more attention to integrative processes and people to manage them. Bartlett and Ghoshal (1989) indicate that the strategy/structure/systems concerns of the 1970s and 1980s gave way to *how* links within and between firms and their constituents are managed. Some of these processes were borrowed from other nations. For example, because Japanese firms had gained a manufacturing advantage in the 1970s with "lean" production techniques, other firms began to adopt techniques like "just in time" inventory management. Other techniques ensured high-quality consistency or low inventories of finished goods (Schonberger, 1996). In borrowing these techniques from the Japanese, businesses worldwide began to learn from each other.

Ways to manage the global firm today vary widely, but a common theme is that they take their strength not only from structures but from concentrating also on people and processes. Thus, there is a need to integrate among these. Second, business success depends on managing trade-offs that are difficult to balance in a world that does not think or act as one. Additionally, organizational adjustments intended to achieve flexible efficiencies for the dynamic and competitive global business world add to rather than displace other concerns like efficiency.

According to Jeffrey Garten (2003), businesses face a new geopolitical reality and a new managerial era due to economic slowdowns, increased terrorism, and corporate governance scrutiny. Companies that wish to create lasting value will need to:

■ Focus anew on the fundamentals, but put less emphasis on speed and untested theories and more emphasis on people and systems.

■ Rethink their role in society because society will value companies that have a broader focus on more shareholders.

■ Embrace the new ethos for good corporate governance but sustain the courage to take educated investment risks.

■ Redefine the character of leadership.

Peter Drucker (1999) notes that when business conditions change, business assumptions also should change. Table 2.1 outlines underlying business assumptions in the past and those that may be more relevant today.

Table 2.1 *Postwar and new assumptions for management practice*

Assumptions Underlying Postwar Management Practices	Assumptions Underlying Management Practice Today
1 Technologies, markets and end-users are given and abundant	1 There are limitations to technologies, markets, and end-users; organizations are driven by customer values
2 Management's scope is legally defined	2 Managers need to focus on the entire management process at every phase of the economic chain
3 Management is internally focused	3 Management exists to produce results; managers answer to others outside the organization
4 The economy is defined by national boundaries	4 National boundaries largely function as restraints on a firm

SOURCES OF GLOBALIZATION: SIX INTERCONNECTING SPHERES

As already noted, there are many definitions of globalization. Differing definitions of globalization give rise to different hypotheses about causes. Some believe globalization can be traced to a single or finite set of sources. For example, some think technology is the driving force behind globalization (The case for globalisation, 2000; Friedman, 1999; Naisbitt, 1994; Ostry and Nelson, 1995). Others believe globalization is powered by economics (Govindarajan and Gupta, 2000; Ohmae, 1995; van Bergeijk and Mensink, 1997), business (Bannock et al., 1998; O'Neill, 1997; Reich, 1991b), cultural factors (Barber, 1992; Huntington, 1993), or communications and transportation innovations (Can there be, 2000; Mandel and Ferleger, 2000).

This "primary driver" approach to thinking about globalization first emerged from the popular press, but scholars use it too. It is a flawed approach because it encourages people to think about globalization as "prefiguring a singular condition or end-state" (Held et al., 1999: 11). Viewing globalization as static or as caused by a single force is not consistent with definitions and characteristics of globalization presented in Chapter 1 and reinforced throughout this book.

Recent scholarship demonstrates a growing tendency to examine interconnections. Some combine two or more global "drivers" when analyzing change, particularly technological shifts and business shifts (Mandel and Ferleger, 2000). Others note there are many more than two or three drivers for globalization and it is important also to look at their interrelationships (Clough, 1996; Dicken, 1998; Lodge, 1995). For example, Manuel Castells (1998) notes that three independent processes occurred to stimulate globalization: the information technology revolution, the economic crisis that brought capitalism and nation-states into conflict, and worldwide social and cultural movements such as human rights, feminism, and environmentalism. He argues that interactions among these processes create a network society.

Global Environments Examined

Businesses and other organizations operate in an increasingly interconnected world. These interconnections occur at three levels shown in Figure 2.1. At the center of this figure is the organization whose leaders integrate people, processes, and structures (PPS) to shape outcomes in a global world.

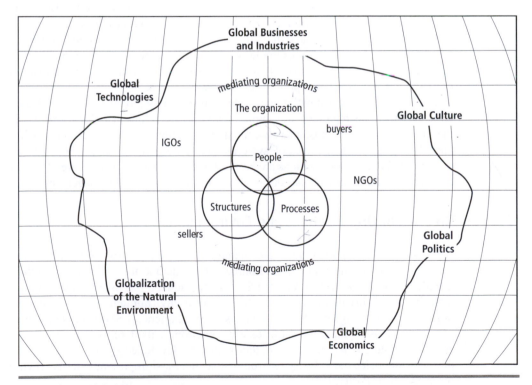

Figure 2.1   *Global interconnections*

Outcomes also depend on activities that occur outside the firm. As shown in Figure 2.1, these activities are organized around six major global environments: 1) businesses and industries; 2) the natural environment; 3) the economy; 4) political/legal activities; 5) technology, particularly information technologies; and 6) culture.

The third level of interconnection occurs because others, such as suppliers, nongovernmental organizations, competitors and unions, mediate the interface between one, some, or all of the six external environments and the focal firm. Figure 2.1 examines characteristics of each of these three levels of interconnections, beginning with the six external environments.

Interconnections of Global Environments

For the sake of simplicity, Figure 2.1 shows the six external environments as discrete and separate entities. However, an event occurring in any one of the six usually interacts with events in the other five external environments. Hence a change in one environment is often followed by, causes, or is concurrent with, changes in others. These shifts in global environments as well as interactions among them affect organizations, but each organization can be affected in a different way. This occurs for two reasons: 1) mediating organizations stand between an organization and its external environment and they shape available organizational options; and 2) organizational leaders pursue different approaches to manage global shifts. The case example introducing this chapter illustrates the latter point: the technological shift that opened a market for Internet music exchange led Bertelsmann to collaborate with Napster even as Apple introduced its own iTunes service.

Mediating organizations and individuals also can reshape the meaning of global events for a particular business. For example, when customers began to download music rather than purchase CDs, this motivated record companies to alter their activities. An example of mediation occurred when police raided KaZaA offices.

Locating organizations within the circle represented by global environments and mediating organizations represents a systems view of organizations in a global world. "Systems theories" describe relationships between an organization and the system in which it operates. Many different theories of systems have emerged, but at the core of each is a common belief that organizations are part of larger systems. A look at several systems theories below shows that each has different implications for global management.

Systems Theories of Organizations and Environments

Almost all contemporary strategic management theorists examine the relationship between an organization and its environment. One method for analyzing this relationship is called a *SWOT analysis*. Using the SWOT technique, a manager analyzes the opportunities (O) and threats (T) posed by the external environment and compares them to organizational strengths (S) and weaknesses (W). A general SWOT model usually provides variations on the same set of external environments described above, for example economy, politics, and culture. Another approach developed by industrial organization theorists identifies the industry environment as the most important external environment for every firm (Porter, 1980).

Biological systems theories look at relationships between groups of organizations, applying concepts like Darwin's survival of the fittest. When biological concepts are applied to organizations, explanations for organizational growth and demise are explained in terms of natural selection in markets. That is, one organization survives when the market values its attributes. Another expires because its attributes fail to meet market needs.

Although the systems theories above differ from one another, they share several underlying assumptions for how organizations and external environments interact. First, the external environment is believed to exert considerable influence on the organization. Second, these theories assume that it is possible for managers to assess external environments and respond with internal adaptations. Third, managers are believed to be rational decision-makers. For example, if an industry analysis reveals few opportunities for a particular business, then managers would be expected to exit the industry. This occurred at ICI when top managers sold low-margin commodity businesses.

These underlying assumptions support a fairly deterministic view of how organizations operate within systems. They argue for a cause–effect relationship between environmental assessment and organizational activities. Application of these deterministic theories to global environments motivates managers to monitor global activities as well as international ones to conduct a SWOT or industry analysis. For example, an industry analysis would look at worldwide industry competitors in addition to domestic and international ones.

Unlike more deterministic rational systems theory and biological systems theories, *chaos theories* posit that some phenomena involve so many factors that they are inherently unpredictable. Although some external shifts could be orderly, others are chaotic or random. Further, the patterns that emerge from one series of events are not necessarily repeated. Thus, a chaotic system creates complex and unpredictable managerial challenges.

Domino Effects and Butterfly Effects

Another way to compare rational and chaotic systems is to think of them as having domino or butterfly effects. In rational systems, dominoes are lined up one next to another. The first domino to fall leans into the next and the next until all have fallen one by one. The dependency and relationships among the dominoes is clear. The butterfly effect is the propensity of a system to be sensitive to initial conditions in an iterative pattern. Such systems over time become unpredictable. This approach is called the butterfly effect because in a chaotic system a butterfly flapping its wings in one area of the world can cause a tornado or similar weather event to occur elsewhere in the world.

When chaos is part of a system, managers cannot rely on logic alone to assess the boundaries of the system or outcomes from particular global shifts because both are quite difficult to assess or predict. Managers operating in chaos might be expected to use rationality some of the time, but also would be encouraged to plan for and manage unpredictability and paradox. For example, they might be encouraged to develop intuitive reasoning skills. Additionally, managers in chaotic systems need to be flexible because systems tend to alter in fairly unpredictable ways.

The systems perspective adopted for this text combines elements of determinism, chaos, and biology. What is determinable is that globalization is occurring in each of the six global environments. The source of chaos in this system is three-fold: some events are not predictable, others are reshaped by interactions with each other, and mediating organizations shape the meaning and importance of activities that do occur. Thus mediating organizations also contribute to activities that cause businesses to thrive, survive, languish, or die.

The following sections introduce the six global environments of greatest concern to global managers. Examples that follow show how interconnections among these spheres affect business practices. This systematic view helps managers see the "big picture" needed to adopt a global mindset and anticipate some outcomes. The chapter later looks at internal features of organizations and the expanding roles of mediating organizations.

KEY ASPECTS OF THE SIX EXTERNAL ENVIRONMENTS

Globalization of the Natural Environment

Few need to be convinced that sustaining the natural environment is important to everyone's future. Examinations of this environment include a look at the "global commons" of air, water, and space. Most of these resources are beyond the jurisdiction of nations and intergovernmental agreements. Yet individual and organizational consumption affects everyone worldwide. Raw materials of every type also are important parts of what can be thought of as the earth's "natural" environment. Nations may have greater and lesser deposits of raw materials such as wood, rubber, minerals, ores, or oil, but as one world there is a finite amount of these resources available. Demand for natural resources varies. For example, 20 percent of costs for the commercial airline industry come from fuel. Thus oil price fluctuations have a significant impact on this industry.

Three other aspects of the natural environment demonstrate the global significance of the natural environment. First, it is increasingly evident that species biodiversity so important to all life is diminishing. Second, globalization of diseases such as AIDs, malaria, and hepatitis challenge existing resources and opportunities. Finally, natural and human disasters can also have a global impact and demonstrate global interconnections.

Each of these five elements of the natural environment connects to every other; those interconnections are explored in much greater depth in Chapter 6. Additionally, each and all of these elements of the global natural environment interconnect with business, with the economy, and with other global environments. The following example illustrates these interconnections.

Natural Disasters and Business
Tsunamis swept the Indian Ocean in December of 2004, hitting eleven nations and carrying hundreds of thousands out to sea. The aftermath of this tragic event demonstrates all too clearly how shifts in the natural environment interconnect the world. Satellite transmissions of surging water transfixed the world. Nongovernmental organizations, such as Mercy Corps and Doctors Without Borders, quickly dispatched help; IGOs, such as the UN, sent fact-finders to devise responses; and businesses sent supplies of food, medicine, and water. National governments in water-swept nations quickly mobilized; nations and individuals donated funds; and many embassies had the sad task of searching for lost tourists. A lingering image is of an Indonesian tribesman, arrow aimed at a helicopter to prevent a landing that would connect him to the world.

Globalization of Political/Legal Environments

The world today is organized principally around nation-states that operate within different political infrastructures. At the heart of virtually every political system is the need to balance between individual (self) and collective (national) interests. The shift from command to market principles in many nations and the propensity of nations to privatize state-owned enterprises indicates that many governments believe free markets can help them achieve the individual/collective balance. But this is difficult to do on a worldwide scale because every government has created different rules, standards, and regulations to address issues like taxes, tariffs, and business activities.

On a worldwide scale, creating a common and global "good" society involves many more than governmental actors in the political/legal environment. Intergovernmental organizations, nongovernmental organizations, businesses, and members of global gangs, pirates, and terrorist organizations also shape global political/legal environments. At the periphery are rebel groups vying for control within nations and they too affect the global political/legal environment. These points are examined in greater detail in Chapter 10.

Globalization of Culture

A principal challenge of globalization today focuses on the tension between the cultures of nation-states and an emerging global culture. Because culture is known to shape meaning and create values as well as lead to common habits, many worry that cultural globalization will result in a homogeneous world culture that drives out individual variation. Products ranging from cola beverages to denim blue jeans, autos, and televisions are consumed throughout the world. English increasingly is a global language for business; some food habits are converging; travel is global; artifacts of popular culture from television and film are viewed worldwide; and business activities increasingly are viewed as modes of distributing information and other resources around the world. For example, the Doha-based news agency Al-Jazeera has increased informational access for the world to the entire Middle East.

The activities of businesses and other global enterprises transcend barriers of every type. These activities shape and reshape cultural beliefs not only within organizations but also among individuals, groups, and nations that interact with them. Many cultural clashes between conflicting value sets also are taking place. Religious habits, language standards, operating assumptions concerning bribery, learning styles, sex roles, cultural diversity, and even the purpose of work are only a few issues being played out within global enterprises. These and other cultural concerns are further examined in Chapter 7.

Global Technologies

International business expansion emphasizes a product or process life-cycle that extends the life of a technological change. Technological breakthroughs in medicine, in television broadcasting, and in most other fields of endeavor combine to make the world a smaller place where in-person or electronic access to people and other resources around the world is almost as great as to next-door neighbors. This access to information, opportunity, products, and markets is an argument for a global technological revolution.

The global technological environment often focuses on those processes and products with greatest global impact, but there is a propensity to examine products more than processes. Frozen yogurt, squeeze-bottle condiments containers, microwave cooking, and virtual-reality video games are all examples of product developments due to technological breakthroughs. Certainly one of the most profound technological changes has been the introduction of telecommunications to link the whole world, and computers that facilitate those links.

In addition to very visible products and services, it is important to recognize that less evident work *processes* are also part of the global technological environment. Examples of breakthrough process technologies include just-in-time inventory management, total quality management, and organizational learning.

Telecommunications and similar technologies provide opportunities for far-flung business interactions, and people from Bulgaria to Buenos Aires seize, rethink, and retool them to create more business opportunities. With little more than a computer, a modem, a telephone, and fax capability, it is possible to establish, maintain, and expand a business reaching outside traditional boundaries, borders, and barriers, including barriers of economies of scale and scope that previously restricted worldwide business to larger firms. For many small businesses, technological access has extended their reach worldwide.

Breakthroughs also generate new questions about justice, for example the digital divide, privacy, and the organization's ability to stimulate creativity at arm's length. William Knoke (1996) argues that in the face of technological change, particularly the "fourth dimension" of computerization, nation-states will lose sovereignty, and physical place will become almost irrelevant. According to Knoke, the impact on business is to create companies that use these linking technologies to quickly assemble and disassemble project teams throughout the world. Others similarly argue that technological breakthroughs of every kind are changing traditional assumptions as organizations become virtual (Davidow and Malone, 1992), as the gap between the "haves" and "have nots" becomes evident (Green and Ruhleder, 1996), as relationships between large and small organizations in a global sphere alter and make it possible for small firms to compete globally (Naisbitt, 1994), as jobs and work roles adapt to an information-driven world.

Global Economics

Many trace the roots of globalization to the many events that together shape an increasingly interconnected global economy. Interconnections between elements of the global economy such as trade, FDI, labor, and currency have implications for world development as well as for organizations operating in a global economy. Governments and not-for-profit organizations contribute to GDP, but businesses generate significant amounts of world GDP.

In 1994, world trade in tangible goods or products rose 12 percent to total $5.2 trillion. Trade in commercial services or intangibles such as banking, transportation, and travel also rose to represent some 26 percent of all world exports by 1994 (*WTO Annual Report*, 1996). By 2002 world trade was $6.2 trillion in tangible goods and $1.4 trillion in commercial services like banking. This growth occurred at discontinuous rates: 4 percent in 1999, 12.5 percent in 2000, and less than 4 percent in 2001 (WTO News, 2002).

FDI are also part of the global economy. FDI occurs when a company purchases buildings, equipment, or other resources in a foreign location, when it merges with or acquires other firms, or when it invests in another company's stock. All three forms of FDI are more global than in the past. For example, whereas once the direction of FDI went primarily from one industrialized country to another, recent activity shows industrialized countries now invest in each other *and* in the developing world. And developing economies are more than recipients of investment; they are major FDI participants as well.

The global economy also is characterized by worldwide capital markets that previously were closely aligned with nations. Globalization of the economy has not only disrupted some traditional economic roles, for example the role of central banking, but also brought more participants into the global economy. Both small and large enterprises from all parts of the world find it attractive and possible to participate in global economics because global capital can move easily across borders. Chapter 8 further explores trade, FDI, capital, and other forms of global economic integration.

Labor also contributes to wealth creation and other effects of economic development. A look at the economic consequences of labor globalization focusses attention on compensation, job and human migration, safety and other work conditions. The interconnections between global labor and global business create new demands on organizations to facilitate job and human equities. Global staffing, leveraging and accounting for knowledge, and managing intellectual capital are a few among many other organizational challenges associated with managing a global workforce. Nations also confront important issues because of labor globalization. For example, nations are better able to develop economically when they offer an educated workforce attractive to foreign direct investments. Additionally, the relative attractiveness of any economy—be it local or national—can make it more or less vulnerable to brain drain or to legal and illegal forms of migration. Labor concerns such as these are discussed in Chapter 9.

Global economic interconnections are increasingly evident in shifting patterns for trade, FDI, capital, and labor. Many of these interconnections are forged or brokered by intergovernmental financial institutions, for example the International Monetary Fund, or the profit-oriented, Citigroup. This demonstrates the link between economics, politics,

political

and business. Additionally many ponder the meaning of wealth, wondering if it is reflected only in financial assets or also in human development or attainment of social goals such as justice.

Political shifts also link economies. Among main reasons that China and India are increasingly a part of the global economy is that national governments in both have liberalized trade and investment rules. These and other nations operating in newly opened national economic systems are more permeable. World Trade Organization rules also facilitate economic interconnections by establishing standards for trade and investment.

Global Business Activities and Industries

Industrial development that took more than a hundred years in North America and Western Europe occurred in as little as ten years in newly industrialized nations such as China and South Korea (A game of international leapfrog, 1994). This growth pace has been powered by a wide array of organizations, including businesses that are small and large, publicly held, family owned or sponsored by "overseas" or "nonresident" groups. The latter are those who retain or develop business ties with their nations of origin, for example the overseas Chinese or overseas Indians. With them also come new reasons to study smaller, less well-known, and privately owned firms as they too operate globally. Finally, although many organizations are not global, virtually all are affected by globalization. This provides a reason to look at many types of businesses and also at organizations that do not perform a business function.

Many examine global business by looking at the tens of thousands of transnational corporations whose activities are reported in annual *World Investment Reports*. These firms directly control hundreds of thousands of subsidiaries worldwide and the trillions their combined assets represent make them important to worldwide growth and development. Greatest interest often revolves around the relatively narrow group of global businesses that produce highly visible branded goods or services like Sony, Sanrio (Hello Kitty), Nestlé, Coca-Cola, PepsiCo, or Benetton. But focusing only on firms in consumer products and services tends to obscure the fact that many other businesses operate around the world. Any list of the largest among these organizations—*Fortune*'s Global 500, *Business Week*'s Global 1000, or the *Financial Times* 100—provides names that are not well known outside founding nations but that are nevertheless global. This list includes both publicly and privately held companies such as ABB, Hanson, Saint Gobain, Sony, Itochu, Amoco, Michelin, Samsung, and Pemex to name a few.

Late-mover businesses from developing economies also have carved out global business space (Bartlett and Ghoshal, 2000). Also operating on the global business scene are many thousands of SMEs (Simon, 1996), some of which are launched as global startups (Hordes et al. 1995) or born globals (Madsen and Servais, 1997). According to Adrian Slywotzky (1996), smaller companies are enjoying success worldwide because they are playing by new rules that are redefining their industries. Many smaller firms are family owned, but larger ones are also owned by families, for example Pirelli, Ferrero, and Henkel. This brief look at the many different types and motives of global businesses suggests they are diverse. Other organizations also populate the global landscape for business including nongovernmental organizations, IGOs, and even crime and terrorist groups. These diverse global participants are discussed in Chapter 4.

As business activities cross or recross established borders, the boundaries shift, reshape, and even dissolve to assume new shapes. In turn, these shifts create challenges for businesses. When industry borders blend, opportunities and threats also change. One example is the "cosmeceuticals" industry that blends cosmetics with pharmaceuticals. This industry developed rapidly, stimulated by growing cultural emphasis on youth and an increasing number of financially solvent older women in developed economies. Overall cosmeceutical sales grew by 41 percent from 1995–99, but sales per person were highest in Germany where the population is aging faster than in other countries (Cosmeceuticals, 2000). When industry borders shift as they have done to create this new industry, business assumptions also may be reshaped. Chapter 5 further examines global industry challenges.

Organizations are not simply affected by globalization: the combined activities of organizations pursuing profit, social, political, personal, family or other goals stimulate, facilitate, sustain, and extend globalization. In the search for new products and markets, business enterprises spread not only consumer goods but ideas concerning wealth creation; ideals concerning how people should live and work; ideologies concerning political and business governance. Nor are the parameters of business in the global world easily controlled: a telephone link to the Internet yields tips on guerilla tactics or access to kiddie porn almost as readily as it provides the latest Dow Jones Index; mafia organizations and drug cartels operate in a worldwide arena with as much expertise as Shell, Imperial Chemical Industries, or Sony. Global business is not, then, just about business: it has cultural, legal, political, and social effects as much as economic ones. The combined experience and learning of firms of every size and type operating in diverse industries is shaping global business and global industries.

A look at each of the six global environments above illustrates only some of its features. It also demonstrates some of the ways these environments interconnect with one another. In view of the dynamic relationships among these global spheres, it is important to look not only at individual sources of globalization but also to view global events as part of an integrated system. Standing at the center of this system is individual organizations whose people, processes, and structures are internally integrated to respond to a more global world.

MANAGING ORGANIZATIONAL INTEGRATION

Each organization can be located within the shifting boundaries of the six global environments reviewed above. Organizations differ because each uses different people, processes, and structures. This difference in configuration means that each will respond in a distinctive way to shifts it might experience. Multiple internal changes generate managerial complexity and uncertainty. This complexity increases exponentially as the firm goes global because global change is more difficult to recognize and to monitor than is domestic change. Further, because globalization is a new phenomenon, managers often do not have abundant experiences from which to draw. Finally, research is limited on global change and what it means for managers.

Managing Organizational Structure

Structures provide a framework for action by showing relationships between people and their jobs. Organizational structures are similar in some ways to the skeletal frame of mammals that make it possible for the organism to move. Organizational structures differ from one another just as the skeletons of mammals differ. Sometimes an organization's formal structure is made visible in an organizational chart that shows reporting relationships, but these charts rarely capture informal relationships that also shape structure. A classic example is the secretary to a CEO or managing director who often has considerable power even though secretarial jobs rarely appear on the organizational chart. Organizational charts also are difficult to draw as relationships become more complex. In this text we will examine both simple and complex structures in use today.

Table 2.2 *Words that reflect managerial attention to structure*

Bureaucracy	Chain of command
Reporting relationships	Flat or horizontal structures
Board of supervisors	Pyramid or hierarchical structures
Communication flows	Control mechanisms
Organizational form	Product divisions; geographic divisions
Keiretsu; chaebol	Managing directors
Formalization	Networks; spiderwebs
Centralization	Shamrock organizations
Division of labor	Alliances; joint ventures
Line of authority	Autonomy vs. collaboration

Because structures, people, and processes relate to one another as shown in Figure 2.1, a change in one is bound to bring about a change in the others. Sometimes these changes are anticipated; other times not. For example, when battery supplier Exide discovered that country managers were undercutting one another's European prices, they replaced their geographic divisional structure with a product division structure. This change altered the selling process, and it profoundly affected people; half their European managers resigned. Ford Motor Company also made a change from a geographic to a product-line structure. The result was a savings of $5 billion in three years, but sales processes were affected, and new managers were needed to oversee European operations. Efforts to fix these problems led Ford to relocate some of its employees and restore some of the regional managers' lost authority (Lublin, 2000). Interconnections among people, processes, and structure show that managers need to monitor not only external change, but also the likely effects of internal changes.

Managing Organizational Processes

Processes are systematic or continuous activities to accomplish organizational purposes. Unlike programs that can be added or deleted to meet temporary needs, processes tend to be long term and embedded within the organization. In most firms, for example, strategic management is part of a continuous process. Creating a strategy, sustaining a vision, and managing a culture are three processes all organizations develop, but how they develop, what they are called, and why they are introduced can vary from one firm to the next. This partially explains why statements of company objectives often use different words such as vision, mission, values, or commitments.

Processes like internal supply chain management help to coordinate organizational activities. For example, textile manufacturer and retailer Inditex—parent to the Zara brand—links all its stores to company headquarters so that individual store sales are immediately available to production managers. This process helps Inditex introduce over 20,000 new garments per year because it cuts the time between design and delivery to an average 10–15 days (Crawford, 2001).

The success and retention of processes depends on how well they fit with each other and with structure and people in the organization. According to James Champy (1995) many process re-engineering attempts failed when people viewed them as a prelude to job losses. In other words, a perception that re-engineering would cost them their jobs caused people to resist them. Table 2.3 lists only some of the processes in which businesses engage.

Managing People

Organizations exist because people create and sustain them. Perhaps more than processes and structures, people are the factors that make or break organizations. Critical people are not just top managers, but all the employees in an organization. Much of the emphasis in the field of human resources has been on how to select, develop, train, compensate, and otherwise manage human resources efficiently. These are the definable dimensions of managing people. Another dimension looks at the intangibles that people bring to organizations like diversity, intellect, skills, abilities, or attitudes toward work. In the global sphere, differences in culture make it difficult to unite human resources to achieve common purpose. Differences in how people think, the time they are willing to devote to organizations, the skills and abilities they have or can acquire, or the compensation they expect vary widely.

Table 2.3 *Words that reflect managerial attention to processes*

Strategy, vision, mission, objectives	Organizational learning processes
Organizational culture	Life-cycle stages of birth, growth, decline
Change management	Ethics and social responsibility
Innovation management	Stakeholder management
Information systems	Managing functions, e.g., accounting
Operations management	Financial auditing
Just in time inventory management	Environmental auditing
Supply chain management	Entrepreneurship; intrapreneurship
Value chain management	Intranet management
Organizational renewal	Core competencies; competitive advantage
Re-engineering	Empowerment
Loyalty	Trust management
Codes of conduct	Decision-making

Managing people globally creates many managerial challenges. The global manager balances among them to create an effective organization. With respect to people, questions to ask are: what people do we need and where do they need to be located to achieve current and future goals? While the two parts of this question might once have been answered by hiring males from the dominant domestic culture, today the answers are less clear-cut. When managerial attention is on people, the words that might be used are like those found in Table 2.4.

Achieving fit among, within, and between these three categories of internal environment is an important and demanding task for managers who more than most must achieve integration among the people, processes, and structures shown at the center of Figure 2.1.

Table 2.4 *Words that reflect managerial attention to people*

Human resource planning	Conflict, violence; resistance at work
Hiring, firing	Substance-abuse program
Selection	Organized labor; co-determination
Deployment	Attitudes, values, behaviors
Workforce diversity	Religion at work
Employee rights and responsibilities	Age and seniority
Compensation; benefits; incentives	Leaders; coaching; following
Staffing; the mix of full- to part-time	Teamwork
Outsourced labor	Virtual teams
Work/personal life balance	Motivation; satisfaction
Jobs, careers, professions	Portfolio of skills
Job security	

WORKING WITH MEDIATING ORGANIZATIONS

According to Jeffrey Garten (1998), making globalization work humanely is becoming a dominant issue. He describes the efforts of John Browne, CEO of British Petroleum, who believes that for BP to thrive so must the communities in which it does business. Although community involvement is mandated, operating units may choose their mode of involvement. Computer-based technology to control recurrent flooding has been introduced in Vietnam, and in Zambia the company installed 200 solar-powered refrigerators to store anti-malaria vaccine. According to Browne, "These efforts have nothing to do with charity, and everything to do with our long-term self-interest." He maintains the four steps to follow are: think long term; invest heavily in the communities where the business operates; be obsessive about achieving profits; and fully integrate social responsibility into policies on governance and compensation.

Businesses play important roles in the societies where they operate. Few organizations are autonomous and most increasingly operate in relationship with other organizations, including governmental actors, members of civil society, business suppliers and competitors, and global gangs and terrorists.

> **Mediating Across Sectors**
>
> Many international non-governmental organizations (INGOs) provide seed money to establish tiny businesses in developing economies such as Bangladesh, India, Central and Latin America, and the Philippines. With this practice INGOs play roles such as stimulating economic development that are more traditional to governments. INGOs also play private-sector roles traditional to banks by lending. Possible effects may be changed assumptions about work and business practices that merge business and social norms.
>
> The Xavante Indian tribe still uses bows and arrows in their Brazilian homes, but outside influences have changed their lives in many ways. Diets, for example, now include tobacco, refined and processed food, and rice. The latter was introduced by the Brazilian government to encourage farming. The net result is tooth decay, a problem that Colgate Palmolive has addressed in partnership with Brazilian dentist Rui Arantes. Dr. Arantes visits each Xavante village about every four months, bringing along Colgate toothpaste and toothbrushes as well as dental instruments and education on tooth care. Colgate's managers acknowledge that their activities could not be called "a classic business-building process" (Jordan, 2003: B1), but note that the Xavante project is a socially responsible investment. This example demonstrates the role businesses can play to address social challenges.
>
> Source material: Miriam Jordan (2003, July 23) Brushing in the bush. *The Wall Street Journal*, pp. B1, B5.

Mediating organizations stand between the focal organization and global shifts. The mediating organizations shape global business in two principal ways: they shape the meaning of global shifts, and they shape the options available to businesses. As shown in Figure 2.1, some events are filtered through many intermediaries. We may be better able to understand differences between sectors with the comparison shown in Table 2.5.

Integrating Activities with NGOs and Civil Society Organizations (CSOs)

NGOs typically represent the interests of civil society (as compared to the interests of business or governmental sectors). NGOs distribute more aid than the World Bank, their annual spending exceeds $1 trillion, and they are the most important constituents of governmental agencies to distribute aid (Sins of the secular missionaries, 2000; Salamon and Anheier, 1998).

NGOs share five common features: 1) they are formally constituted; 2) they are separate from the government; 3) they do not distribute profits; 4) they are self-governing; and 5) their labor is to a significant extent voluntary (Salamon, Sokolowski, and List, 2004). Nonprofit organizations can be grouped into 12 categories, each of which has many subcategories such as culture and recreation, social services, environment, law, religion, unions, international activities, and business and professional associations. For example, a professional group such as a potato growers association qualifies as an NGO, although it chiefly supports business activities.

Table 2.5 *Traditional sectoral differences*

	Government Sector	Market Sector	Civil Society Sector
Primary Interest	Political/legal	Economic	Social needs
Dominant organizational form	Government	Profit-generating businesses	Not-for-profit organizations
Primary controls on the sector	Voters/leaders	Owners	Communities
Goods/services produced	Public goods	Private goods	Group goods
Core competencies	Enforcement	Production of goods and services	Community mobilization
Temporal framework	Election cycles	Business and reporting cycles	Sustainability and regeneration cycles
Primary resources	Legal system and police/military	Capital and other resources	Volunteers, vision, and shared values
Primary weaknesses	Rigidity; conflict between voter and global interests	Markets often do not factor in social or environment concerns	Can fragment interests

Source material: Steve Waddell (2001/2002) Societal learning: Creating big-systems change. *The Systems Thinker*, 12 (10): 1–5.

Frequent use of the term NGO, to describe large, formal organizations such as Oxfam or Greenpeace, causes some to use another term—civil society organizations (CSO)—to refer more generally to all the small and large organizations whose work distinguishes them from government and business sectors (Glasius and Kaldor, 2002). CSOs can be religious, labor, nongovernmental or community-based groups (Waddell, 2001). They range in size, source, intent, and attitudes toward globalization.

The Global Stakeholder 2020 Panel Survey

The 2020 Fund at the King Baudouin Foundation and supporting organizations conducted a series of surveys that led to their first report titled "Towards the Future We Want for our Children." More than 300 responses were received from 63 countries; the survey was conducted in five languages. Results included:

■ Three in four of the mainly NGO stakeholders agree that increasing globalization is inevitable.

■ Four in ten view trade as making a positive contribution to the world they want to live in for 2020; three in ten see international trade as negative.

■ Nine in ten believe that globalization focuses too much on increasing trade and investment and not enough on human rights and environmental protections.

Source material: http://www.2020fund.org

CSOs can be grassroots groups that coalesce around the interests of a few people, or they can be membership groups that serve interests of many thousands. CSOs can be consumer groups like Global Trade Watch, environmental groups like Friends of the Earth, think tanks like the Heritage Foundation or the International Forum on Globalization, protest groups like Direct Action Network, and coalitions within and among religious bodies. An example of the latter is the World's Council of Churches. CSOs also can emerge from professional groups. The Center for International Environmental Law is a CSO that emerged from the legal profession; Doctors Without Borders emerged from the medical profession.

CSOs mediate between global environments and business in two principal ways: opposition and proposition. Opposition occurs when CSOs engage media support or initiate e-mail campaigns to influence business activities. For example, Global Exchange threatened a global "roast Starbucks" campaign unless the latter promised to sell fair-trade coffee. On a global scale, environmental groups like Greenpeace lead boycotts, demonstrate, and disrupt business activities. CSOs also use protests, marches, sit-ins, negotiations, and other mechanisms to oppose businesses and thereby influence subsequent activities.

Many CSO leaders increasingly use a propositional approach when working with global businesses. This marks a shift among many CSOs whose traditional stance toward business has been more oppositional. Propositional approaches vary to include community dialogue with businesses, cross-sector partnerships, and interlinked board memberships. Topics for mutual interest include human and labor rights initiatives, fair trade, child-labor standards, and environment protection to name a few. Business activities include development of fair labor standards, compliance with externally determined standards, codes of ethics, and the like. For example, insurance companies and organizations like Human Rights Watch pursue mutual interests in tracking weather patterns and consumption of global commons like air and water. Although CSO activities can take these two different forms, both link businesses and CSOs to one another and to global communities.

Integrating Activities with Governmental Organizations

The fall of the Berlin Wall in 1989 touched off a worldwide rush to capitalism. The resulting emphasis on consumerism, entrepreneurism, and their conceptual cousins focusses world attention on businesses. Deregulation and privatization transfers some part of governmental authority to the business sector. According to Peter Drucker (1987), business ownership of these important services increases the power of business when the public depends upon them to get to work, manage their money, heat their homes, and communicate with one another. By creating business/government partnerships, governments further involve businesses in decisions formerly made by politicians alone.

National governments partner formally and indirectly with businesses to attract FDI and jobs. Firms operating on a global scale are major employers, and job growth among the largest of them has occurred principally in developing economies. The foreign affiliates of UNCTAD transnational corporations employed about 40.5 million people in 1999, up from 23.6 million in 1990 (*World Investment Report*, 2000). Governments mediate access to employees, but CSOs also become involved to ensure fair labor standards. In this way job growth creates tighter links between governmental organizations, businesses, and CSOs. Although relationships between CSOs and business can generate innovations, often governments play a key role by "establishing the appropriate 'enabling environment'" (Waddell, 2001: 59).

The link between government, business, and civil society is also evident in education. Many governments develop or increase enrollments in schools of business. At the same time, businesses educate to develop the global work force they need. Anticipating an employee shortfall by 2005, Cisco Systems initiated Indian academies to train 100,000 network professionals. The company's plans were to invest about $8.6 million in this arm of a Networking Academy through which Cisco could teach people to design, build, and maintain computer networks.

The government/business interface occurs in many different ways. Coca-Cola experimented with a vitamin-fortified drink for Botswana's children to improve child health. CARE, GlaxoSmithKline, and the Bangladeshi government collaborated on a joint effort to educate parents and medically treat parasites in children. Many intergovernmental organizations like the United Nations also play intermediary roles related to trade and economic and human development. Following the September 11, 2001 attack, the US government invited Disney to help ease travel delays, Nike provided brand advice to the Secret Service, and Marriott International and FedEx suggested ways to measure security screeners' performance (Power, 2002). In 2004 elections, companies like Cebu Pacific Air, Globe Telecom, Jollibee Foods, San Miguel, McDonald's, and Pure Foods sponsored an effort to count ballots in the Philippines' presidential election (Hookway, 2004). Integrative activities like these between national governments and businesses create the potential to change the essential nature of each.

Integrating Activities with Suppliers and Competitors

Global production and distribution systems depend on cooperative activities between organizations (Borrus and Zysman, 1998), including supply chain linkages with SMEs worldwide. Some SMEs are captives of these production networks, but others use them to establish autonomy. For example, SMEs use communication technologies to network with each other, through which they establish cooperative ventures that enhance collective bargaining power or create niche markets (Castells, 1996). Global businesses also link with suppliers to achieve price advantages and facilitate rapid knowledge transfer. These activities increasingly link the focal organization with diverse supplier groups that mediate between the organization and other factors in its extended environment.

Businesses create alliances not only with competitors in their own businesses but also with businesses in other industries. For example, American Express, Visa International, Banksky SA of Belgium and ERG Ltd of Australia formed Proton World International that allows consumers worldwide to use a single smart card for functions ranging from cash withdrawals, mobile-phone networks, and Internet transactions. Competitor

MasterCard was pushing the Mondex system that relies on different technologies and standards. This example indicates that competitors like MasterCard and American Express compete with one another by cooperating with others in the Mondex and Proton ventures. Procter & Gamble creates external connections to enhance innovation and business growth. Alliance networks that link industries help organizations cooperate and develop opportunities much faster than if each remained isolated in its own industry (Gomes-Casseres, 1994).

Integrating Activities with Customers

Companies today also incorporate customers in their value networks. Some of these customers are business customers, while others are end-users. Companies who use this type of value network with end-users have to shift their emphasis from internal interests also to external ones. For example, the consumer has to be integrated in the company's system for value creation, and influence how value is generated (Prahalad and Ramaswamy, 2002). Saturn developed a co-creation approach, working with customers to develop a design, manufacturing, and sales process responsive to customer interests. Saturn continually solicits new ideas from customers, and its advertisements represent it as a company that partners with its customers. According to Prahalad and Ramaswamy (2002), the building blocks for integration with customers are:

- Engaged dialogue with customers
- Providing access to a broad array of products that anyone could use
- Be more forthcoming about product risk so that consumers can make informed choices
- Increase transparency so that customers can "see for themselves" what the company is doing and how it is doing it.

Integrating Activities with Other Organizational Entities

An entirely different type of organization also mediates global business activities. Global gangs based in Russia, China, Hong Kong, Japan, Colombia, Italy, and the US, for example, transport heroin, cocaine, and other illicit drugs throughout the world, traffic in human cargo, and use the global-banking system and computer technology to launder billions in revenues. The United Nations estimates that annual illegal drug sales are US$400 billion, half of which is financed by crime (Revenue from illicit drugs, 1997).

Reduced national barriers make it easier for gangs and terrorists to extend their reach. For example, many of the hijackers who destroyed the World Trade Center entered the US via student visas and learned how to fly at US schools. The operating practices of Al Qaeda and other organizations challenge not only tenets of civil society, but they also affect business practices by putting new emphasis on issues of bribery, corruption, and safety for global managers and employees alike.

Many other organizations and individuals also mediate between businesses and global events. The spread of capitalism has created many more sophisticated consumers and the Internet makes organizations much more accessible to them. For example, people create Internet "hate sites" to oppose a targeted company; others create sites that applaud organizational actions. These and other activities interconnect businesses with a wider society. Although the approach a mediating organization takes to interact with a business can differ, the common denominator is that mediators link businesses to a vast array of stakeholders.

Businesses worldwide increasingly are held accountable for real and perceived transgressions even at a time when the potential for error has grown. As Chapter 11's discussion on global technology demonstrates, public scrutiny of business becomes possible because of improved modes of global communication. Expectations for businesses are greater and they are more closely scrutinized for decisions made, even as those decisions occur against a backdrop that is complex, dynamic, and uncertain. Expanding relationships between businesses and a larger global society alter managerial habits, and lead to new management theories for a global world. They pose new questions as well, such as: how should businesses function in global society and to whom should they answer?

This chapter's review of recent business history illustrates that business practices emerge from a particular context. In a more global context, businesses are most concerned about internal and external forms of integration that help them respond appropriately to global opportunities and threats. External global shifts affect businesses, and they are also affected by mediating organizations whose activities alter the impact of global shifts. Finally, the experience of each organization with respect to global shifts and the influence of mediating organizations depends in large part on internal integration mechanisms that include people, processes, and structures. Chapter 3 looks more specifically at how global organizations manage within systems that contain elements of both dynamism and determinism.

CHAPTER SUMMARY

Historical reviews of business reveal that management principles usually emerge to deal with challenges at a particular point in time.

Many argue that globalization emanates primarily from one source. This book asserts that a distinctive feature of globalization is that it emanates from multiple sources. The interrelationships and interdependencies among these disparate sources converge to create global shifts.

Three different theories of organizational systems are the basis for analyzing a global world: rational systems, biological systems, and chaotic systems.

Every global organization is affected by global shifts occurring in six distinct environments: 1) businesses and industries; 2) the natural environment; 3) economic; 4) the political/legal sphere; 5) technology, particularly information technologies; and 6) culture.

Events in global environments often interconnect to reshape their impact. Sometimes this impact directly affects an organization, but more often it is mediated by other organizations, including governmental groups, members of civil society, business suppliers and competitors, and global gangs and terrorists.

In the context of global environments, internal firm issues are of three general types that concern: 1) people; 2) processes; and 3) structures. The people, processes, and structures that absorb much of a manager's time require internal integration.

Decisions and activities consistent for building a just world depend on the ability to analyze complex and rapidly changing global conditions, to see interrelationships, and to visualize a dynamic future.

REVIEW AND DISCUSSION QUESTIONS

1 Consider each of the three systems theories presented in the text: rational, biological, chaotic. Which is most attractive to you as a way to see the world? Why?

2 Many theories of management emerged from the study and experiences of US firms. In what ways has this influence shaped business expectations in a global world? Identify three concepts presented in this chapter and describe the ways they reflect US influence.

3 Select a recent global event, and classify it according to the single external environment into which you think it belongs. Then, working alone or in a group, decide how the event relates to other global environments. Finally, if time permits, conduct library or Internet research to see how different firms responded to that event. For example, in the wake of terrorist attacks, FedEx Corporation started its own ten-person police force.

4 The Napster case provided a snapshot of the industry in 2004. But global shifts occur rapidly for this industry. Illustrate this point with an update on Napster and/or Internet music downloading.

Chapter 3
CHARACTERISTICS AND CHALLENGES FOR GLOBAL ENTERPRISES

ROYAL DUTCH/SHELL ENTERS A NEW PHASE

In both 1994 and 1995, Anglo-Dutch giant Royal Dutch/Shell Group led the *Fortune* Global 500 list as the world's biggest firm. But by the end of 1996, Shell announced a drop in profits, layoffs, a restructuring plan to eliminate 30,000 people in management positions, and a new determination to focus on refining operations. Although Shell predicted that world energy demand could grow by 70 percent for the next 30 years, they had also become aware that global survival depended on acquiring new skills, implementing new processes, and restructuring. Two factors no doubt contributed to this realization.

First, like other firms in oil-production and refining industries, Shell leaders recognized that growth depends on a global workforce and on a capacity to meet global demands, particularly in developing economies where energy growth is greatest.

But competitive pressures on costs and profits were only one of Shell's global challenges. It also faced increased global public scrutiny that began in 1995 when Royal Dutch/Shell quietly announced a government-approved plan to sink the Brent Spar oil platform in the North Sea. Shell proposed to sink the platform with 100 tons of oil sludge that could not be removed; their studies indicated that the sludge would be so far below the water surface that it would not affect sea life. Alerted to the plan, Greenpeace commissioned their own study, then argued that more than the estimated amount of marine life would be damaged. Greenpeace activists later boarded the Brent Spar, and were pictured being forcefully ejected; water cannons kept the Greenpeace helicopter from landing on the rig. Shell leaders adamantly refused to meet with environmentalists, but that attracted ever-wider television audiences. An informal boycott spread from Germany to the Netherlands and Denmark causing a 20 percent drop in European retail sales. Internal dissent at Shell increased, but eventually Shell managers gave up their plans for the Brent Spar.

Then in October, Shell Nigeria was implicated in the hanging of eight pro-democracy political prisoners in Nigeria. The best known of the executed was Ken Saro-Wiwa, a popular writer who had become an activist. World opinion again turned against Shell. Greenpeace activists argued that Shell's importance to the Nigerian economy could have been used to save Saro-Wiwa. Again, Shell was taken by surprise. They had a formal operating principle that demanded they stay out of the political affairs of host countries.

The results of Shell's actions were financial as well as social. Toronto rejected a contract with Shell Canada, the International Finance Corporation canceled its planned participation with Shell to open a $4 billion liquefied natural gas project in Nigeria, and Saro-Wiwa's heirs filed a lawsuit against Shell charging it with complicity in the hanging deaths.

According to an editorial that later appeared in the *Oil and Gas Journal*, accusations against Shell and their aftermath made it evident that international oil companies were increasingly being held accountable for misdeeds committed by host-country governments. Evidence provided in this chapter suggests that the Shell experience is indicative of growing public expectations that global businesses have a different role to play than "business as usual."

According to representative Gerry Matthews (2001), events like Brent Spar and the hangings in Nigeria forced Shell to rethink their roles. They recognized that social expectations of multinational corporations were changing, and Shell needed to develop a value proposition ▶

that would give them a license to operate in the long run. Shell made internal and external changes. Externally, they began to collaborate with CSOs, and pursued dialogue with organizations like Greenpeace to better understand society's expectations. They developed a Tell Shell website (www.shell.com/tellshell) to solicit comments. Results of these and other interactions were included in the introduction of 10 Shell principles in 1997 followed by an ethics report in 1998 and annual reports such as the 2001 Shell Report titled "People, planet and profits." In 2003, Royal Dutch/Shell promised to avoid exploration or drilling in places designated as United Nations' World Heritage sites in 170 nations.

Internal changes also were many. In 1995 the matrix structure formerly used at Shell headquarters was judged to be too bureaucratic and slow for a global market, and it was replaced with a centralized structure that assigns executives oversight for worldwide divisions. Shell did away with national businesses and organized its structure around five global businesses, including refining and renewable energy.

As Shell changed its structure, it also needed to change the decision-making process and reorganize jobs. Shell Chemical introduced a five-member business management team to coordinate strategy with leaders of worldwide businesses. Low-profit divisions like chemicals were sold, high-end businesses like refining attracted more attention from headquarters, and plans included developing new operations in developing economies. Employees experienced job changes and transfers to fulfill company principles. Management development also changed. For example, in the past promising young executives typically completed jobs in "tough" spots like Nigeria before they could expect to be promoted at headquarters. That practice changed to one that allowed employees to apply for openings, but it meant that many talented people did not gain experience in locations where Shell faced its greatest challenges. To make sure that the ten Shell principles were borne out in performance, Shell introduced an implementation mechanism to measure performance against the principles. Creating value for the future became a key business value for Shell. Some believe that changes at Shell diverted attention from fiscal responsibilities. By 2001 internal auditors had begun to warn that bonuses might be encouraging managers to inflate booked oil reserves, but change did not come until early 2004 when Shell began to recategorize filings to reduce total reserves by about 23 percent. Fines, firings, and public outcry followed. These in turn led to a corporate overhaul to combine the two parent companies into a single one named Royal Dutch Shell PLC. Changes in people and other processes followed.

Shell's example illustrates growing public demand for social, political, and environmental accountability on the part of business organizations. This demand cannot be met without changes in how the company interacts with external stakeholders, and with changes in internal structures, people, and organizational processes. A lingering question, however, is whether Shell's involvement with stakeholders caused them to forget the interests of shareholders. For many firms, it illustrates how challenging it can be to balance needs of multiple and sometimes competing objectives.

Source material: A new political risk. (1996, Feb. 5) *The Oil and Gas Journal*, 94 (6): 25; Giant outsmarted. (1995, July 7) *The Wall Street Journal*, pp. Al, A4; Patricia L. Layman (1996, July 29). Gerry P. Matthews (2001, Aug. 10) Address to the social issues in management division, Academy of Management, Washington, DC; *People, Planet and Profits: The Shell Report 2001* (2001) The Hague, Netherlands: Shell International B.V.

CHAPTER OVERVIEW

This chapter differentiates between domestic, international, multinational, and global businesses. It outlines and describes five characteristics of global enterprises applicable to organizations in any sector. Attention then turns to four common challenges that these global enterprises face: they confront problems that cannot be "solved" but must be managed; their success increasingly is derived from intangibles that the organization cannot own; leaders increasingly manage many forms of diversity; and business managers and organizations assume new roles for which the past has not fully prepared them.

A CONTINUUM FOR BUSINESS ACTIVITIES

Chapter 1 distinguished between activities that are international and activities that are global. Below we differentiate among domestic, international, multinational, partially global, and fully global enterprises. All are affected by globalization but each responds in different ways.

Domestic Businesses

Domestic businesses are defined as profit-generating entities operating principally within a single nation. Many such as shoe shining or childcare operate on a small scale, and often their activities take place only in a local community. Every major city and many minor ones are populated with thousands upon thousands of enterprises that serve local needs. The result is millions of domestic firms throughout the world. Some operate in a "shadow" or hidden economy and their activities are not counted in official government measures. Others are small entrepreneurial businesses whose activities are the subject of Global Entrepreneurship Monitor (GEM) studies. The 2000 GEM study looked at entrepreneurship in 29 developed and developing economies to estimate that 147 million people were involved in entrepreneurial activities (Reynolds et al., 2001). By 2003 the GEM studies included 40 nations whose combined population represent almost 4 billion of the world's 6 billion plus population. As many as 300 million people tried to start new companies in 2002, demonstrating that worldwide entrepreneurial activities are quite high. Although some entrepreneurial companies operate on a global scale, the vast majority operate within national borders and often within a single city or region. In summary, the activities of domestic businesses take place primarily within local, regional, and national settings.

Although located within a domestic economy, the domestic firm is affected by globalization. For example, local restaurants are affected when food prices for sugar, coffee, and other commodities change due to global supply and demand. However, managers for small or localized firms can and should become more globally savvy by monitoring global shifts.

Distinguishing among Firms Outside Domestic Markets

A wide variety of firms operate outside the nations where they were founded. But it can be difficult to distinguish between international, multinational, transnational, and global enterprises. Confusion ensues when some use the same terms to mean different things, and others use different terms to mean the same thing. For example, Daniels and Radebaugh (1992) argued that a transnational corporation was synonymous with a multinational enterprise, but the United Nations Conference on Trade and Development (UNCTAD) uses the term 'transnational' as an umbrella term for any business that controls or owns value-added activities in two or more countries. Thus, gathered under the UNCTAD umbrella are firms that operate in one country other than their own, those that operate in several countries, and those that this book would classify as global. UNCTAD estimates there were about 60,000 "transnational" businesses operating worldwide in 2000 with a total of about 800,000 affiliates (*World Investment Report*, 2001). This represents an increase from 40,000 firms and 206,000 affiliates in 1994 (*World Investment Report*, 1995).

Inconsistent use of terms has led to misconceptions and confusion about all the different types of businesses operating outside domestic spheres. Another source of confusion is that while some describe international, multinational, or global businesses according to where subsidiaries are located, others focus on how they are organized or for what purpose. For example, Bartlett and Ghoshal (1989) used organizational design to distinguish among firms as follows:

1 The international organization is a coordinated federation in which the parent company transfers knowledge and expertise to foreign markets.
2 The multinational organization is a "decentralized federation of assets and responsibilities" (p. 49) that allows foreign operations to respond to local differences.
3 The global organization is a centralized hub where most assets and decisions are centralized.
4 The transnational organization is characterized by an integrated network where efficiency can be balanced against local responsiveness to obtain both global competitiveness and flexibility in an organization dedicated to learning and innovation.

The resources reviewed above show varied descriptions for the many enterprises that function outside their own national borders. The following sections distinguish among them.

The International Business

The international business actively participates in at least one national market outside its own. According to Hordes et al. (1995), the international firm is rooted within its own nation, and its headquarters are almost always based in the single country it calls home. This makes the home country the frame of reference for the international firm. The international company adopts standardized technologies and business processes throughout its operations, regardless of where they are located, and it uses similar policies to manage human resources wherever it operates. The parent company also transfers knowledge and expertise to foreign markets (Bartlett and Ghoshal, 1989). Managers of international organizations typically view their activities as an extension or addition to domestic activities. This being the case, managers often apply domestic skills to international settings.

Active international participation can take different forms. For example, a restaurant could be international because it actively obtains supplies from another country via importing. It could also open restaurants in another nation. Either activity requires knowledge of business activities in other nations. This factor requires that international managers become more actively involved in cross-national business activities than would occur for most domestic firms.

Managers of international businesses usually will learn about the politics, cultures, and economies of nations in which they operate, and they may adapt home practices abroad. However, the extent of learning acquired may depend on how important that knowledge is to them. For example, the company that acquires international resources through an intermediary might need less knowledge than the company that directly acquires its own supplies.

The Multinational Corporation

A multinational corporation (MNC) sometimes is referred to as a multinational enterprise (MNE). Whichever term is used, the multinational company is distinguished from the international one because the former usually operates in several nations beyond its "home." However, like the international firm, it is typically headquartered in a single nation that it thinks of as home. Like the domestic and the international firm, the MNC is affected by global business activities, but it plays a more active role in managing non-domestic activities than does the international firm. This occurs because operating in more than two nations means the focal company must coordinate and control across nations and among cultures rather than just between them as the international firm does. In the case of a multinational restaurant owner, supplies are obtained from multiple locations and/or new stores must be managed in several nations. The multinational manager often must balance competing interests of these nations.

Characteristics of the Global Enterprise

As compared to the international and the multinational enterprise, the global one differs by virtue of the worldwide interconnections it forges. But it too has been defined in many ways. Hordes et al. (1995) describe the global firm as one that creates links around processes; it is organized around a few core values; it is most often managed by a team operating in diverse locations; and it adopts an organizational culture that values diversity. Except for a few standardized policies, its processes, policies, and technologies are diverse. Others suggest that this interconnected firm combines mission, vision, education, and training with an emphasis on processes of global corporate culture (Evans et al.,

1990) or that knowledge (D'Aveni, 1995; Senge, 1990) and diversity among people, processes, or structures (Hoecklin, 1995; Rhinesmith, 1993; Trompenaars, 1994) are essential to sustain flexibility and adapt quickly to opportunities and threats in a rapidly globalizing world. As may be evident from the examples above, although the global firm has been described in many ways, there are two common themes: global interconnections and reliance on internal integration techniques.

Globality is a multidimensional phenomenon (Govindarajan and Gupta, 2000), meaning that global firms can be arranged along a continuum anchored by low to high engagement in global activities. Accordingly, organizational globalization is measured with multiple criteria, for example where a firm operates, how it operates, and the degrees to which it operates globally on each criteria.

In practice, few firms are altogether global (Bartlett and Ghoshal, 1989). However, one can assess firm globalization by examining how closely an organization conforms to five characteristics of a global enterprise: 1) acquires resources from a global pool; 2) views the world as its home; 3) establishes a worldwide presence in one or more businesses; 4) develops a global *business* strategy for its businesses that operate worldwide; 5) and transcends internal and external boundaries. Such an assessment reveals that organizations fulfill the characteristics of a global enterprise in different ways. For example, global restaurants include worldwide franchisers like McDonald's and companies like Burger King that operate only with wholly owned subsidiaries. The following look at the five characteristics of a global enterprise further demonstrates diverse action among organizations.

Acquires Capital, Labor, and Materials from Global Sources

Whereas an international business acquires its resources from one or a few countries, the global enterprise scans the world to identify best sources for capital, labor, and materials. In this context, "best" sources are viewed as those offering greatest benefits at the low cost important to competition on a global scale. Although low-cost efforts might mean relocating jobs abroad, the cost/benefit tradeoff also could motivate a global enterprise to pay higher labor prices for productive workers.

Global Capital

Most businesses finance growth with borrowed or equity capital, but the cost of capital depends on two factors: return the lender can earn elsewhere, and the borrower's ability to generate revenues sufficient to cover the loan. Worldwide integration among financial institutions has led to an increasingly integrated world market for capital in which capital costs have begun to converge (Fukao, 1993, 1995). The inconsistencies and imperfections of this system are many (Held et al., 1999). For example, rapid capital movement sometimes creates "hot money" that disrupts stable economies such as occurred after Mexico's 1994 crisis when investors rapidly withdrew resources from stable Latin American economies as well as from Mexico, and when Russia's 1998 bond default affected other emerging economies.

In practice a global capital market means that almost any firm (global, international or domestic) competes in a global market for capital. Thus, this measure cannot be used alone to identify a global enterprise. Global materials and labor are more variable and less accessible than the global cost of capital, and this may make them more accurate indicators of this global characteristic.

Global Materials and Labor

Parent company location often requires organizations to acquire materials from a global pool. For example, limited natural resources in Japan force Nippon Steel to draw its 60 million plus tons of ore per year from companies located in Australia, North and South America, Africa, Asia, and Europe. Using supply chain management techniques that link buyers and sellers, the global enterprise attempts to gain access to resources around the world via integrative systems. These integrated systems can help a company find the lowest prices worldwide.

Global enterprises also tap into a global labor force. Labor is the least portable resource for global firms, and global firms gain access to labor worldwide in different ways. One way is to build manufacturing facilities in nations where labor is cheap, but this advantage is difficult to sustain when competitors follow this approach. As an alternative, some companies subcontract labor through local companies. If labor costs rise, then the contract can be moved elsewhere. A third approach is to tap into a global labor pool with telecommunications interconnections. For example, Microsoft contracts with software engineers in Bangalore and ATT contracts with India for back-office functions such as bookkeeping and customer service. Businesses also foster global labor mobility when they send expatriate managers from headquarters to postings throughout the world.

The global search for labor pulls many firms into public debates about labor rights, child labor, and the like. For example, when organizations realize lower-cost advantages by switching suppliers, this creates challenges for existing suppliers and their workforce. Accordingly, some perceive global sourcing to result in social costs that businesses also should confront. Dialogue around these issues links businesses with social and national development issues as well as business costs. In addition, the public increasingly demands that global firms monitor subcontractors and their labor practices. As a result, many global companies have developed codes of conduct that extend to subcontractors. For example, apparel retailer H&M requires that all contractors and subcontractors conform to a code of conduct that (among other things) forbids child labor and supports workers' rights and safety. Posting expatriate workers around the world often illustrates pay or benefit differentials that also can lead to heated discussion about what is "fair" company compensation worldwide.

In summary, organizations have access to three types of global resources. Accordingly, we can assess firm globalization by measuring the extent to which capital, resources, and labor are obtained from a global pool. The most global firm on this dimension would be the one that sources capital, labor, and materials globally. As we have seen, global businesses that utilize these global resources often increase their interconnections with organizations such as NGOs or governments whose interests are broader than those of wealth creation alone.

Views the World as Its Home

Earlier in this chapter, we noted that international and multinational companies operate from domestic bases that they consider home. This approach to managing abroad is often ethnocentric, meaning that managers use their own culture as the standard for activities abroad. Global firms view the world as a single market (Ohmae, 1995), making it less likely that they would call only one place home. However, as illustrated below there are many ways to view the world as one's home.

Reduce Existing Links

First, a global enterprise can relocate its headquarters altogether. This occurred when Caltex Petroleum Corporation moved its California headquarters to Singapore in 1998. Pharmacia similarly transferred its entire headquarters from London to New Jersey two years after its 1995 merger with Upjohn. Alcatel pursues a second approach by dispersing headquarters to several different locations. Oil and natural-gas giant Unocal remains headquartered in California, but Unocal no longer considers itself a US company. It describes itself as a global energy company; and in April, 1997 opened "twin" headquarters in Malaysia to serve as the base for several senior executives.

Yet a third way to reduce national links is to relocate headquarters for single businesses or functions outside the nation of origin. Over 829 global firms pursued this option from January 2002 to March 2003 (UNCTAD, 2003), but in three different ways:

1 Set up regional headquarters outside the home country. For example, UK GSK established a regional headquarters in the US.
2 Relocate headquarters' functions. Examples: Novartis relocated its global research hub from Basel to Boston; Imperial Chemical manages worldwide explosives from Toronto; and DuPont's Lycra business is headquartered in Germany.
3 Relocate global headquarters. For example, Viatron moved its world headquarters to the Netherlands.

The examples above show how structural changes—relocating divisions or functions— expand links beyond a single geographic place. These types of activities make a company less national than it once was, and perhaps even "stateless." Questions one might answer to assess the "stateless" organization are outlined below:

1 Where are the bulk of assets and people found?
2 In which nation is firm ownership located and who owns and controls foreign subsidiaries?
3 What are the nationalities of senior executives at headquarters and decision-makers in subsidiaries abroad?
4 What is the legal nationality of the firm and to what nation does it turn for political or diplomatic protection?
5 Can tax authorities in a nation choose to tax corporate earnings worldwide? (Hu, 1992: 121)

Another way to be at home in the world is to reduce *perceived* connections with a single place. For example, Exxon used a single advertising campaign to promote its portfolio of brands in the 100 markets where it operates. In 2004 Nokia similarly adopted a global advertising campaign. Thus, instead of localizing image, these companies try to globalize it. Finally, the global enterprise can view the world as home by being a virtual organization that operates from no fixed geographic place.

Activities that Reflect World Citizenship

Above we saw that labor issues often engage global businesses in global social challenges. Some businesses actively embrace social issues to establish themselves as world citizens more than local or national ones. So-called "civil corporations," such as Stora Enso, are willing and able to take greater responsibility for their activities (Zadek, 2001).

Stora Enso's Expanding Community

Lumber mills traditionally developed within limited geographic areas. Around them communities developed, and this usually made social responsibility of business a local concept. However, according to Jukka Harmala, CEO of integrated forest products giant Stora Enso, "today one must also consider responsibility at the global level … Updating quality, management systems, and socio-economic areas are examples of actions to be taken." By enlarging its sense of global community, Stora Enso demonstrates its desire to transcend individual communities and take global responsibility for communities that interact with forest product companies.

Source material: Stora Enso endorses principles for corporate social responsibility. (2002, Dec. 12) (electronic version] *PR Newswire*.

In summary, a company that views the world as its home can be assessed according to geographic location, for example where headquarters and operations are located, by perceptual positioning, or by operating as a global citizen.

The Global Enterprise Establishes a Worldwide Presence

Establishing a worldwide presence in one or more businesses can come about by chance or by design. R. Griggs, maker of Doc Martens' boots and shoes, established a global presence almost by accident when trend-setting teens worldwide adopted their shoes and boots. Conversely, Eastman Kodak went global by design to open a Kodak Express shop in Antarctica because it was the only continent the company had not yet reached. Its stated purpose was "to demonstrate our commitment to serve customers literally everywhere" (Klein, 1999). Thus, the defining characteristic for establishing a global presence in a business is not its initial intent but subsequent efforts to sustain a worldwide presence in one or more businesses.

Nestlé and Unilever purposefully seek to establish a worldwide presence in many product lines. For example, Unilever promotes Lipton tea around the world. Similarly, firms like Pepsi Cola, CNN ("the global news network"), Al-Jazeera (which reaches 35 million viewers in the Arab world alone), and Benetton are identifiable on this characteristic because they purposefully establish and maintain a global presence in virtually all their businesses. Firms like DaimlerChrysler, Hanson, GlaxoSmithKline, McDonald's, Siemens, Saint Gobain, Sony, Itochu, Amoco, Michelin, and Diageo also have brands that are recognized worldwide. Large companies can be global in one, some, or all their businesses. Firms like Chupa Chups and R. Griggs show that smaller firms also can establish a global presence, although usually in a single business or with a narrow product line.

These examples show that organizations of any size can establish a global presence. They also demonstrate that it is possible to establish a global presence in one, many, or all product or service businesses. This suggests that the global enterprise might be more or less global depending on the number of its businesses that maintain a worldwide presence.

Develops a Global Business Strategy

Much like the term "globalization," the word "strategy" conjures up many different images. In 1998, Rosabeth Kanter and Thomas Dretler argued that definitional differences have created several myths and misunderstandings about global strategy. One of these myths is that global strategy means doing everything the same everywhere. This misconception may arise because many businesses initiated global activities in the 1990s with a worldwide product standardization strategy. This means that they produced virtually the same product worldwide, an approach that leads some to argue that global strategies realize economies of scale from worldwide integration and standardization (Hout et al., 1982; Levitt, 1983).

However, George Yip (1995) notes that worldwide standardization is not necessarily synonymous with a global firm since the latter can sustain an integrated standard for one business line and be locally responsive in other business lines. The latter approach to strategy is to balance worldwide standards with demands for the localization of products and services, and it also has been called a global strategy (Hamel and Prahalad, 1985). Yip called this approach *multilocal* (1995: 8), and Phatak (1992) and Ashkenas et al. (1995) call it *glocal*. These examples show why there is confusion about what constitutes a global strategy.

Kanter and Dretler (1998) believe that the key variable for a global business strategy is not a specific activity. Instead, they argue that the shared feature among global firms is that they integrate activities on a worldwide scale. This means that while worldwide standardization business strategy would integrate its supply chains, local adaptation strategy might mean integrating business operations with local environments where the firm operates. In other words, the form of integration depends in part on the desired end.

In summary, different uses of the word "global" may be diluting any specific meaning it has in describing a strategy (Yip, 1995: 8). Such definitional differences are perhaps one unavoidable result of the rapid pace of global change. They are a compelling reason to look more closely at how strategy is defined.

Strategy is the limited set of important, nonroutine, nonprogrammable decisions that guide organizational direction. It is a comprehensive construct that encompasses all levels of organizational activity and thought. Five levels are discussed below—enterprise, corporate, business, operational, and individual strategy.

Enterprise Strategy

Enterprise strategy answers "big picture" organizational questions such as: why do we exist as an organization and what is our purpose in society? In a global world where it is not possible to be all things to all people, it is important for any organization to clarify its overall purpose.

Top managers usually set enterprise strategy, but they may use different words to describe it, for example mission, vision, or shared values. Research shows that approaches to setting strategy vary by country. For example, a comparison of company missions for British and French firms showed processes of mission development vary, reflecting major differences in how the mission is developed, its content, and even its impact (Brabet and Klemm, 1994). When studying organizations, the researcher should be aware that some organizations espouse one thing but actually pursue another. Accordingly, one can best understand enterprise purpose by examining behaviors as well as explicit statements from top leaders.

By definition, businesses exist to generate wealth, but in a global world definitions of wealth as well as the relative importance of wealth can vary. In some nations wealth is financial alone, but other nations define wealth as one measure in the total quality of life. The boxed examples that follow show that overall purpose or enterprise strategies vary considerably from one global organization to the next.

Enterprise Strategy Varies Between Firms

Evergreen Marine transports containerized cargo around the world. Their purpose is reflected in three mottoes: create profits, look after employees, and reciprocating society.

(Taiwan Business Information, 2002)

In working the Carlsberg Breweries it should be a constant purpose, regardless of immediate profit, to develop the art of making beer to the greatest possible degree of perfection in order that these breweries as well as their products may ever stand out as a model and so, through their example, assist in keeping beer brewing on a high and honourable level.

(J.C. Jacobsen, who founded this Danish Brewery in 1847, established this enterprise purpose as "The Golden Words": http://www.carlsberg.com.cy/)

It is our mission to improve the lives of customers and communities where we all live, work and play ... Our established directions for the 21st century provide a balance of fun for the customer and responsibility for society and the environment.

(Honda Motor Company website, 2002)

At the heart of the corporate purpose, which guides us in our approach to doing business, is the drive to serve consumers in a unique and effective way.

(Unilever: http://www.unilever.com/company/ourpurpose/)

Our goal is to provide superior returns to our shareholders. Profitability is critical to achieving superior returns, building our capital, and attracting and keeping our best people.

(Goldman Sachs: http://www.gs.com/about/principles.html)

In the case of Carlsberg, the enterprise strategy far outlived the person who developed it. Other enterprise strategies change with top leaders. Organizational purpose also can change when the organization's relationship with external or internal environments alter. For example, Sony's 1950 enterprise strategy was to become the company most known for changing the low-quality image of Japanese products, but Japanese products have long since met Sony's original purpose. Accordingly, Sony's overall purpose also changed.

In summary, some enterprise strategies emphasize profits alone, and others balance profitability with social objectives. Global participation may encourage firms to specifically address balance or global citizenship in their enterprise strategy statements. Whether articulated explicitly or reflected primarily by behaviors, enterprise strategy typically flows into four other levels of organizational strategy.

Corporate Strategy

Corporate strategy follows enterprise strategy, and it answers portfolio questions such as: what businesses shall we be in now, and in the future? One way to observe corporate strategy is to look at businesses in the corporate portfolio. For example, although Asahi Breweries was established initially as a brewery, by 2002 its portfolio contained businesses ranging from beer to pharmaceuticals, food, and soft drinks. A growing challenge for global managers is deciding which businesses provide current and future global opportunities.

Portfolio Expansion

The merger or acquisition activities in which Asahi engaged showed a shift in corporate strategy that expanded its portfolio. The corporate portfolio also can expand when organizations use their own resources to extend a product line or to develop new products and businesses. For example, confectioner Ferrero Company—maker of Kinder Surprises and Tic Tacs—has never acquired any other business, choosing instead to develop its own new products. PepsiCo established its bottled water business by using existing water treatment facilities at soft-drink bottling plants to purify tap water.

Portfolio Changes

Hong Kong-based Hutchison Whampoa Ltd. made plans to acquire Kdruidvat Group of the Netherlands for $1.27 billion to expand its beauty and health retail operations in Europe. Costs also would be decreased because Hutchison intended to combine Kdruidvat's operations under the A.S. Watson drugstore franchise that Hutchison already owns. This would increase its drugstores in Europe from 250 to over 2,000. Additionally, the deal was expected to assist Hutchison's riskier venture into 3G handsets and subscriptions; the new stores would sell both, giving Hutchison an instant European distribution channel.

Source material: Hutchison Whampoa sets sights on 3G network with purchase. (2002, Aug. 23) *The Wall Street Journal*, p. A3.

Portfolio Contraction or Exchange

The examples above illustrate ways organizations expand their portfolios. Companies also can narrow their portfolio by divesting themselves of existing businesses. For example, in 2002 steel manufacturer Corus Group PLC consolidated its portfolio by selling ancillary businesses such as aluminum and stainless steel. By 1999 Turkish conglomerate Haci Omer Sabaci Holding AS began to divest many of the 69 businesses it had collected to concentrate on energy, the Internet, and telecommunications. Other companies spin off businesses rather than retain them as subsidiaries in the corporate portfolio. An example is Sara Lee's spin-off of the Coach line. Still others may exchange the portfolio, replacing one business with another.

When evaluating businesses for the corporate portfolio, leaders may choose to divest businesses even when they are profitable in favor of businesses that generate profits less weighted by social costs. DuPont did the latter by withdrawing from CFC production. Tobacco giant Phillip Morris retained its portfolio, but changed its name to Altria so that known brands in the portfolio such as Kraft, Nabisco, and General Foods could be better differentiated from tobacco and cigarettes.

In summary, answers to the questions posed by corporate strategy are found by looking at what businesses the organization has assembled and retains in its portfolio of businesses. The corporate portfolio can expand by means of internal organic growth, via mergers, acquisitions, or investments, or some combination of these. Corporate portfolios also can contract, and exchanges can be made. Thus, corporate strategy can be observed by looking at decisions to "make or buy" new businesses or to sell, close, divest, or otherwise dispose of existing businesses.

Business Strategy

Business-level strategy questions include: what is the basis of our advantage, and how shall we compete and/or collaborate in this business? But opportunities and hence business strategies depend not just on the organization and its preferences but also on the industry in which each business is located. For example, Deloitte Touche's long-term business strategy is to offer one-stop global services for accounting, tax, risk management, consulting, and (outside the US) legal work. The viability of this business strategy is uncertain in the wake of the Andersen/Enron debacle (Kahn, 2002). This is one example of how industry activities shape business strategy choices.

A look at Asahi Breweries shows how business strategy develops for a company that owns both pharmaceutical businesses and breweries. On a global scale, the success of beer sales depends on marketing, but in pharmaceuticals success is more dependent on research and development. Additionally, companies in the pharmaceutical businesses tend to collaborate, particularly when responding to global regulations but breweries collaborate infrequently. As a result of these industry differences, we observe different business strategies for Asahi Beer and pharmaceuticals. At the same time, both are expected to meet Asahi's enterprise purpose for "creating a fun and affluent lifestyle culture for a new era" (Asahi homepage, 2002: http://www.asahibeer.co.jp/english/).

Creating a Business Advantage

There are many different ways to create a distinctive business advantage. Jay Barney (1991) suggests advantages can be based on physical, human or capital advantages. Hunt and Morgan (1995) classify advantages as financial, physical, legal, human, organizational, information, or relational. Examples of different advantages include: a price advantage, a product advantage, innovation in the product or service, quality, ease of access to it, worldwide integration, or local responsiveness. The latter two approaches are outlined in the box below, but any advantage can be explored to examine how a firm develops its business advantages.

Business Strategy: Worldwide Standardization or Local Responsiveness?

A worldwide product standardization strategy means producing virtually the same product worldwide. The main benefit of this strategy is cost reductions due to economies of scale that occur when the same process is used over and over. This business-level strategy is similar to Porter's (1980) cost-leadership strategy of reduced costs across an entire product line. It is supported by supply-chain management processes that identify low-cost inputs worldwide. The advantages of worldwide standardization may be offset by higher coordination costs, additional reporting requirements, reduced morale among managers whose autonomy is limited, or a product that does not fully satisfy customers anywhere (Yip, 1995). Ford's Contour/Mondeo product pursued a worldwide standardization strategy, but it has not proved successful.

Businesses that pursue a local responsiveness strategy tailor products to the specific preferences or tastes of buyers worldwide. Production costs usually are higher for firms that are locally responsive. Nestlé and Unilever both pursue local responsiveness strategies by tailoring products to the varied countries where they operate. This "tailoring" can occur in different ways. For example, Hindustan Unilever sells the same soap in India as elsewhere, but it packages it in the smaller sizes that Indian buyers prefer. Products also can be reformulated for different markets.

Most organizations base their business advantage on combined rather than single attributes. For example, a hospital might provide many services, but create its distinct advantage by combining smooth patient flow with innovative medical care. Rapid information retrieval combined with accuracy and honesty might be core advantages for a data retrieval firm. Chocolatier Lindt and Sprungli AG competes by ensuring quality, providing competitive pricing, and employing highly qualified people. Often the combination of advantages that constitute a business strategy is described as core competencies—those three to five major strengths or advantages that differentiate one organization from another.

How Shall We Position in the Industry? Competition, Collaboration, or Coopetition?

Another critical business strategy decision is how to position the business against industry competitors. A business can pursue competition, collaboration, coopetition or all of these options. The choice depends on industry characteristics as well as organizational choice. For example, neither Coca-Cola nor Pepsi is altogether likely to abandon the head-to-head competitive tactics that characterize the soft-drinks industry.

Writing in *The Winner-take-all Society*, authors Robert Frank and Philip Cook (1995) observe that some societies define competition as a win/lose option. In the US the star system makes it difficult for firms to embrace anything other than a sole survivor, competitive stance within industries. At the business level, efforts to "win" usually involve besting all other competitors. According to James Moore's *The Death of Competition* (1996), product superiority and industry dominance are no longer the driving force behind organizational success. Instead, what matters is a form of systematic leadership that integrates technologies and develops new markets. Growth can come about through cooperation.

Some industries are more cooperative than others, creating an industry environment in which firms are expected to collaborate. In 2001 music-industry competitors Bertelsmann, AOL Time Warner and EMI jointly purchased MUSicNet to provide subscriptions to music downloads through America Online. In other industries, collaboration came about because of bad experiences with competition. For example, following a costly competitive war over worldwide VCR standards, Sony and RCA collaborated to develop the digital camera.

Some global organizations can accommodate both competition and cooperation at the same time. For example, having collaborated to develop a common digital camera technology, Sony and RCA then became competitors for sales. In effect, the camera technology is the same, but each shapes the product and its features, and their packaging and advertising also differ.

Firms that compete and cooperate simultaneously face challenges of two types. The first challenge is externally when partners act on different expectations for what it means to combine cooperation and competition. The second occurs internally when managers cannot adopt behaviors appropriate for both competitive and cooperative interactions. Despite evidence of successful cooperative arrangements, leaders at many firms feel collaborating with competitors compromises their own position in an industry.

Coopetition can include both competitive and cooperative elements. It is based on game-theory arguments for new mindsets and new games capable of changing industry and organizational strategy from win/lose to win/win (Brandenburger and Nalebuff, 1996). Dowling et al. call these relationships "multifaceted" when a supplier, buyer, and/or partner is also a major competitor (1996: 155). Examples include: a) vertical cooperation between buyers and suppliers in direct competition, such as occurs between IBM and Intel when the latter supplies IBM with microprocessor chips and also competes in a variety of markets; b) buyers or suppliers who are in indirect competition as in Apple/Microsoft connections because the former buys software from Microsoft, and also is involved in a lawsuit against the Windows platform; and c) partners in competition via a joint venture, research consortium, or licensing agreement as a way to pool resources against other competitors. For example, the 1986 alliance between Canon and Hewlett-Packard captured 70 percent of the US market in laser printers and provided a barrier to other entrants. Partners in the latter arrangement remain intense rivals in ink-jet technology.

Operational Strategy

Operational strategy looks at what gets done in the organization. Typically it is consistent with and satisfies enterprise, corporate, and business strategy objectives. A main operational challenge is to assemble the people, processes, and structures needed to achieve higher-level strategies. For example, athletic-shoe company K-Swiss adopted a Softshoe software system to automate their global product development and sourcing operations. This integrated system represents a process that facilitates global efficiencies by linking geographically dispersed users to one another.

Systematic and continuous processes to accomplish a firm's specific tasks are many, ranging from knowledge transfer to creation of information systems, change management, or development of internal cultural attributes and work processes. Strategic planning itself also is a process. People hired and their ability to accomplish organizational objectives also reflect operational strategy decisions.

Individual-level Strategy

Organizational leaders often fail to push strategies through to the individual level, but strategy should be embedded in the work each person does. For example, in Levi's pay-based Partners in Performance program, each employee forms a partnership with the company to align their objectives with the company's global business plan. Vivendi Universal signaled their intention to be a technological leader by providing each employee with a computer and unlimited Internet access. This demonstrated what employees were to do (use the Internet freely) and why (to help Vivendi be a technological leader).

Every organization should convey its purpose and reinforce it at every organizational level, although as noted earlier in the chapter, purpose can be conveyed either explicitly or implicitly. The example that follows shows how Reinhard Mohn developed an enterprise strategy that fed into each of the four lower levels of strategy reviewed above.

Five Levels of Strategy at Bertelsmann AG

Carl Bertelsmann founded Bertelsmann AG in 1835. His great-grandson, Reinhard Mohn served in World War II, returning home in 1947 to find family factories reduced to rubble. Fifty years later, the rebuilt firm had become the world's third largest media giant, including publishers like Bantam Doubleday Dell, record label RCA, and Europe's biggest broadcasting company RTL group. By 2002, Bertelsmann operated in 56 countries, and generated revenues/turnover of $17.8 billion.

Reinhard Mohn rebuilt Bertelsmann around an *enterprise strategy* or purpose that puts contribution to society ahead of profit maximization. The Bertelsmann Foundation contributes millions to philanthropic interests, and it shares profits with employees in the form of an annual dividend. *Corporate strategies* preserve the firm and protect employees by reducing risk: there is a mandatory 15 percent rate of return on any project to reduce costly mistakes that might lead to layoffs, and one result is that Bertelsmann has not acquired businesses it could well afford financially. Within the TV

▶

industry, Bertelsmann businesses such as for-pay television have grown through cooperation rather than head-to-head competition, showing a preference for a *business-level strategy* characterized more by collaboration than competition. This might explain Bertelsmann's purchase of Napster and a music industry merger to create Sony/BMG that showed willingness to collaborate and compete. *Operational strategies* to coordinate among processes, people, and structures include a structure that is decentralized and includes employees on the company's supervisory board, and decision-making processes that involve partnerships between managers and employees. According to some sources, the early 2000 go-go acquisition strategy of CEO Thomas Middelhoff disrupted these processes because operations had become centralized and collaboration had declined. This conflict between enterprise strategy and operational activities created a challenge that was resolved in 2002 when Reinhard Mohn fired Mr. Middelhoff. At the *individual level*, executives are well aware they are expected to be servants to society and to their employees, and employees follow Mohn dictates to be modest and share credit for work rather than focus on individual ambitions.

Source material: Matthew Karnitschnig and Neal E. Boudette (2002, July 30) Battle for the soul of Bertelsmann led to CEO ouster. *The Wall Street Journal*, pp. A1, A6; Bertelsmann homepage: www.Bertelsmann.com; Cacilie Rohwedder (1997, Jan. 15) Reinhard Mohn: The quiet media mogul. *The Wall Street Journal*, p. A10.

The hierarchy of strategy described above can be used to analyze any type of organization. Ideally, enterprise strategy is reflected in all that organizational participants do. In practice, this does not always occur.

Sometimes strategy mismatches occur when organizational leaders fail to convey a clear vision or sense of organizational purpose. In other cases, the vision may be clear but the goals unattainable. For example, Allianz's vision of an integrated banking and insurance empire caused it to add Dresdner Bank to its corporate portfolio, but a culture clash between the two companies impeded integration. Problems also occur when people at lower organizational levels misinterpret or subvert enterprise strategy; when top leaders are weak; or when employees will not follow them.

Since mismatches can occur, organizational analysts should pay attention not only to what organizations say they do, but also to what they actually do. This is one lesson to be learned from business debacles that began with Enron. Enron's managers, for example, said that they were expanding and realizing profit growth. In fact, the company was pressuring employees to take unsustainable risks. At the end of the day, organizational behaviors illustrate what organizations really value at each level of strategy. This is why it is important to observe business activities as well as review statements of strategic intent.

Transcends Boundaries

In addition to the four characteristics described above, the global enterprise also must be able to transcend both external and internal boundaries (Ashkenas, et al., 1995). Boundary transcendence means that a global organization must redefine its boundaries for itself and others better to integrate its activities across them. According to Ashkenas and his colleagues, boundaryless behavior is necessarily fluid. The process of reducing boundaries between the organization and other actors can occur in many ways.

Transcending External Boundaries

Obvious external boundaries that the global organization transcends are geographic or national (Ohmae, 1995) or those of time or space. Our earlier look at systems examined relationships businesses manage with other organizations, including suppliers, buyers, governments, nongovernmental organizations, and stakeholders. Managing these relationships requires integrative activities that transcend external boundaries between one organization and another. These external integrative activities can be horizontal (between competitors in the same industry) or vertical (between buyer and supplier). Vertical relationships are exemplified by supply-chain linkages with SMEs located throughout the world.

Transcending Internal Boundaries

Global organizations also transcend two types of internal boundaries: vertical boundaries between levels and ranks of people and horizontal boundaries between functions and disciplines (Ashkenas et al., 1995). Both are achieved via integration activities. Often vertical boundaries are created by job descriptions of tasks or ranks (Ghoshal and Bartlett, 1995); others can be the result of an organizational structure. For example, a steep hierarchical structure clearly denotes that some people are higher than others, and this creates a vertical barrier. Typically there are access barriers between the top person in an organization and the vast majority of workers. However, vertical barriers also can be embedded in organizational culture. For example, veneration for age in Japan makes it difficult for experienced engineers to value talented young computer engineers. In Toshiba older engineers have found it difficult to acknowledge innovative ideas coming from young computer wizards.

Boundaries created by professional training also can create a vertical boundary, particularly when one group perceives itself to be more important to the organization than another. For example, Whirlpool acquired Philips' European appliance divisions but found they had to transcend thinking established by the latter's engineering-driven history. Shared belief in the importance of engineering to the firm was well ingrained in people's sense of who they were and how work was to be accomplished. Managers felt this boundary had to be transcended to help people understand the horizontal relationship of each function to every other.

Many internal boundaries are intangible. For example, belief systems like how creativity can be stimulated, or how conflict operates, or even how one should spend work time are intangibles. Their intangibility makes them difficult to describe and difficult to measure. Even when acknowledged, belief systems may be difficult to alter if people cannot view themselves objectively relative to others. These reasons suggest that belief systems and the intangibles of organizational life that are most difficult to measure will be the most difficult to change in organizations.

> **Managing Intangibles at Nissan Design International**
>
> Traditional practice in many organizations is to hire new employees who will work well and "fit" in with existing employees. This has been particularly true among Japanese firms where collective values are held in high regard and individualism often is avoided. So when Nissan Design International began to hire people in contrasting pairs the company was not only violating principles of Japanese business harmony, they were violating principles of national culture and collectivity. Motivating this change was a desire for "creative abrasion" among employees sufficient to stimulate new ways of thinking and new ways to design Nissan products. Employees were asked to cross boundaries of behavior and boundaries of thought. The creativity the company sought is an intangible believed to be stimulated by difference and even conflict. For existing employees long-schooled in conflict avoidance, crossing boundaries of behavior must have been difficult. Moreover, since creativity is not easily assessed, positive results were not measurable. How then can organizational leaders convince employees that these changes are worthwhile? In some cases, they can't and organizational changes lead to voluntary departures. Leaders then must weigh and perhaps defend the benefits of intangibles like hoped-for creativity against measurable losses experienced when seasoned employees leave.

In summary, the global enterprise transcends external and internal boundaries by means of integration techniques, perhaps breaking through national borders and nationalistic thinking to reconceptualize its activities or bridging internal barriers that impede its ability to gain or sustain a global position. Every firm is likely to have distinct priorities for reshaping these internal and external boundaries because each varies in size, industry, strategy, leadership, and so on. For example, a start-up in an Internet-dependent industry might place highest priority on leveraging internal and external knowledge technology; whereas an established firm might see a greater need to break down internal barriers to diversity to leverage knowledge throughout the organization.

Applying Global Enterprise Characteristics to Other Organizations

The principal emphasis in this book is on global business activities. However, it is important to note that many of the characteristics of a global business can be applied to other types of global enterprises. Although international NGOs most often pursue social rather than profit goals, global characteristics presented here can be used to assess them. For example, one might assess the extent to which an NGO obtains paid and volunteer labor from a global pool, if their revenue base depends on global sources, and the extent to which it views the world rather than a single place as home. The increasingly global nature of NGO activities makes many of them world rather than national advocates alone, and many achieve their objectives via internal integrative activities and external ones with other organizations, including businesses and governmental organizations.

COMMON CHALLENGES FOR THE GLOBAL ENTERPRISE

Global enterprises face many challenges. Some of those challenges are identical with those found in domestic or international arenas. For example, a common challenge for all businesses is to earn a profit; for a voluntary organization the common challenge is to meet social objectives. In an international country-to-country era, businesses face currency conversion challenges that also persist in a global world. Finally, competition is a reality for all businesses wherever they operate. In addition, global businesses face challenges that emerge from a more global world. It is important to recognize that while every organization faces these challenges, the exact nature of the challenge and organizational responses to them will vary, and this is something that is demonstrated in the following sections.

Challenge 1: Problems that Cannot be Solved but Must be Managed

A paradox is a statement or proposition that seems contradictory. Writing in *The Age of Paradox*, Charles Handy (1994) identified nine paradoxical challenges or situations that cannot be resolved so much as managed. At the global level, one paradox is how all nations can benefit economically from competitive business activities since competition usually implies that there will be winners and losers. At the level of national governments, paradox includes balancing between global interests and domestic interests. At the organizational level, paradoxes might include cooperating to compete, and managers might see profitability as a trade-off between self-interest and the interests of a larger society. At the individual level, the statement expresses an apparent paradox: "the more I do, the less I get done." Students often face this paradox: "the more I learn, the more questions I have." Individuals also face a paradox when they are encouraged to think in linear and process-oriented fashions; to be autonomous and yet to be team members; to have a full life and yet to devote all free time to the organization.

A Center for Creative Leadership Conference created a list of these and similar organizational paradoxes or trade-offs such as balancing individual achievement against team achievement, focussing on people or on the bottom line, emphasis on processes or on results, and viewing organizations as engines for economic development or for human development (Tornow, 1994).

In personal lives and professional worlds, many are taught to look at paradoxes and other challenges as problems that need solving. However, according to Charles Handy, a major managerial challenge of paradox is to learn to live with it. In effect, managing paradox is the first global challenge all organizations face: *there are problems that cannot be solved so much as managed.*

Few certainties characterize globalization, but one among them is the increased number of multiple and competing objectives every person and organization faces. In view of cultural, political, economic, and other differences throughout the world, it is currently impossible to reconcile many of these objectives. Thus, one of the primary challenges associated with globalization is balancing conflicting and/or competing objectives such as the apparent trade-off between profits and social responsibility, individual and collective interests, autonomy and collaboration, innovation and order, heterogeneity and homogeneity. Many of the chapters which follow explore how firms manage these and other uncertainties. The following examples illustrate the range of paradoxical challenges organizations face.

Sample Problems that Cannot be Solved so much as Managed

Global pharmaceutical firms invest in research and development that cannot be recaptured in many developing economies. Yet, growing networks for medical information make it impossible to withhold knowledge about useful remedies; often the formulas are copied with no reimbursement to the originator, and few worldwide legal conventions provide universal protection.

Merck's product Crixivan has been shown effective against the AIDs disease, but neither Merck nor its subcontractors can produce sufficient supplies worldwide to keep up with the spread of this disease.

Many companies face challenges that cannot be solved when markets and economies take a turn for the worse. Grupo Televisa suffered financial difficulties with the breakdown of the peso and losses due to foreign investment. Although these were problems that Televisa could not solve themselves NAFTA helped by eliminating trade barriers.

Companies are encouraged to grow, but face risks when doing so. This causes a decline in the profitability that investors seek. For example, when the market was growing rapidly Matsushita Electric intended to grow via US expansion with a new semiconductor plant. But Matsushita encountered delays, the market slowed, and the semiconductor plan was abandoned. The company is believed to have lost around $90 million instead of fostering growth. Balancing the risks of growth is a problem that cannot be solved so much as managed.

Mercy Corps faces risks when it decides how to use limited resources. It must choose the right project to provide the greatest long-term social benefits. Choosing the wrong project reduces their ability to leverage resources worldwide.

As Sony expands throughout the world and becomes an ever-larger company, its organizational structure becomes very large and complicated. Sony has recognized this and formulated new corporate strategies to deal with the problem, but still must manage the trade-off between being small enough to be innovative and large enough to manage all their operations worldwide.

During times of economic slowdown companies face challenges in trying to maintain a balance between lay-offs and social responsibility. After eliminating jobs in Germany, Siemens drew criticism from the union. They were accused of being short sighted as well as adhering to a hire-and-fire policy. The union argues that Siemens cannot just fire employees during an economic slump, then rehire when times are better. At the same time, investors expect Siemens to be profitable, and this may be hard to achieve if they have too many workers on their payrolls.

The World Health Organization is faced with the challenge of reduced funding by the member states. This has led them to partner with large pharmaceutical companies that in turn could influence their decisions on important health issues. For example, the WHO launched a campaign against smoking, but this could benefit drug-company partners that produce nicotine replacement drugs. Balancing how to reinvent themselves as an organization concerned about lung cancer in addition to clean water or disfiguring diseases is a major challenge for WHO.

In response to consumer activists who target companies regarding wages and working conditions, Mattel generated Global Manufacturing Principles. The principles govern Mattel factories and vendors worldwide and provide a way to manage regulations that are both beneficial to the workers and the company. But this forces Mattel to be involved not only in their own activities but also those of suppliers.

Because of the large, global nature of the World Wildlife Fund, as well as the large amount of money flowing through it, the organization has had to find ways to manage corruption risk. The WWF has attempted to form alliances to assist in problem solving and to assist in avoiding corruption problems by basically implementing a check-and-balance system among countries and governments that they align with.

Challenge 2: Organizational Success Increasingly is Derived from Intangibles that Organizations Cannot Own

Rapid growth in knowledge-based industries has drawn attention to the roles intellect and knowledge play in organizations. Knowledge is critical to organizational achievement, and the ability to link and leverage knowledge is increasingly a factor for differentiating among organizations that survive (Bartlett and Ghoshal, 1989). Unlike other productive factors like land, capital, and equipment, intelligence does not belong to the organization. Further, information is not a scarce resource (Henderson, 1996), and it cannot be taken, redistributed, owned, accurately measured, or monopolized (Handy, 1994). Finally, although organizations depend heavily on knowledge as a critical resource, many do not know how to value it. Thus, many organizational resources may not be reflected in public valuations of the enterprise. The "bricks and mortar" upon which traditional valuations are built often do not capture the value of "clicks" established through Internet knowledge and information transfer.

Knowledge frequently is leveraged via means of intangible processes such as relationship building, or trust enhancement. Intangibles based on qualities like these are difficult to measure, assess, or implement. Rosabeth Kanter (1995: 152) believes these knowledge-based intangible assets are of three kinds:

1 Concepts are leading-edge ideas, designs or formulations for products or services that create value for customers.
2 Competence is the ability to translate ideas into applications for customers.
3 Connections are alliances among businesses to leverage core capabilities, create more value for customers, or simply open doors and widen horizons.

The intangible quality of knowledge is reflected in relationships and also in employee skills and abilities. A change in the employee base, particularly among top management, often results in a knowledge deficit or increase, and many analysts examine these changes to anticipate the likely effect on an organization. In addition to looking at employee shifts, analysts also can better understand organizational reliance on intangibles by looking at some of the factors described in the following box.

Examples of Increased Reliance on Intangibles

Philips lost market share when compact-disc technology was used by other companies and in other countries even though a patent was in place.

The Boeing Company is committed to developing the human capital of their employees. The Boeing Company annually commits a minimum of $4.5 million towards education, training, and career-development training.

For Sony it is very important to hire, retain, and foster knowledge workers. Furthermore, Sony offers a pleasant working environment where people can make the most of their abilities.

Panasonic's founder was famous for promoting the concept of coexistence and co-prosperity in countries in which Panasonic conducts business.

The core values of IKEA were codified in Ingvar Kamprad's 1976 "Furniture Dealer's Testament" which are taught to all IKEA employees.

Shiseido depends on connections with prominent and talented artists, designers, and places to support its business activity. For example, Shiseido appointed a French artist, Serge Lutens, as its international image creator.

Because of the increasing importance and complex nature of environmental problems, the World Wildlife Federation increasingly relies on its employees and volunteers to use current technology and practices to solve environmental problems.

Mercy Corps subscribes to the idea that "few firms could achieve industry leadership or be competitive globally without some global strategic partners." One of Mercy Corps' strengths is its ability to partner with a multitude of corporations, government agencies, foundations, faith organizations, the United Nations, and the World Bank. However, the resulting synergies are often intangible.

Challenge 3: Organizations Increasingly Manage Many Forms of Diversity

Diversity of people—their color, their nationality, their gender—emerged as an issue almost simultaneously around the globe, fostered by global economics and immigration, government regulations, and transnational human-rights mandates. Whatever the motivation, many in organizations initially viewed increased diversity as a problem. Initial business responses to the "problem" of diversity often followed national legislation based on differences of color, gender, or nationality. Many firms assumed that assimilation was the most desirable response to diversity. In other words, early business efforts involved training women, ethnic minorities, and/or immigrants to behave more like existing employees. Organizational managers soon discovered the impracticalities of assimilation, recognizing that diversity of experience is exactly what is required in a more diverse and global world.

The boundaries of diversity also have expanded. Studies of diversity show that sometimes similarities are found where differences had been assumed. Organizations also house not only diverse people, but diverse systems, diverse structures, diverse ways of thinking and acting, and diverse processes. All are aspects of managing diversity. The challenges associated with managing these many forms of diversity will be explored in Chapter 14, but some examples of how organizations manage diversity appear below.

Examples of Managing Diversity

Mattel increased diversity in its product range to stabilize sales. This was done by implementing a mixture of year-round toys with seasonal toys.

As a result of re-engineering efforts to improve market share, Philips Components initiated a joint venture with LG Electronics of South Korea. Philips expects further growth through alliances and acquisitions. One reason for these alliances is that it has become necessary to locate facilities in many places to attract talent. Thus, this example shows that diversity in structure and with people often are managed simultaneously.

IKEA moves into markets slowly, and looks at how they can complement existing trends in a market. This "fusion" helps to minimize culture clash with employees and customers. IKEA job applications in all countries have the following statement at the top, setting the tone for celebrating diversity from an employee's first interaction with the company: "In our IKEA family we want to keep the human being in the center and to support each other' —Ingvar Kamprad."

Honda Motor Company believes that cultural differences can be a source of extraordinary performance results when integration of different perspectives results in a unique competitive advantage. The paradox is that diversity can mean difficulties, but diversity is also the cornerstone for creativity. The philosophy of Honda is that diversity begins with respect for the individual. Based on this philosophy, thousands of diverse individuals work together as a team toward a common goal. Honda implements dozens of internal training programs to help those working in diverse groups.

Unilever acknowledges the potential problems that result from cultural diversity, but the company believes it gains an advantage by honoring differences between people as well as similarities. Unilever has implemented many corporate diversity initiatives dealing with communication and training that enhances the advantages of diversity.

To address diversity issues the Boeing Company's human resources department has created an internal company website devoted to diversity. The website includes information related to diversity issues such as: how employees can respect each other's differences, working with people from different cultural backgrounds, and information on diversity classes for employees and managers.

▶

An example of how Nokia manages employee diversity is that most of the daily work is carried out by cross-functional teams within the Finnish corporate office. By drawing teams comprised from different groups, Nokia is better able to foster efficiency and productivity. For example, an accountant may be able to offer a unique perspective when confronted with a marketing problem. This cross-functionality allows employees to understand and visualize problems that Nokia faces on a company-wide scale, instead of just how it relates to them within their own department or function.

Today, a company's growth and development are intrinsically linked to how that company can attract people to its organization and motivate them to create value. In April 1998, Toyota established a Corporate Diversity Department to guide the company in making diversity an integral part of every aspect of their business. Specifically, it provides strategic guidance, support for diversity initiatives, and helps develop and promote education and diversity awareness throughout the organization.

Diversity at the World Wildlife Fund goes beyond the traditional anti-discrimination, equal employment paradigm. The WWF has created an organizational structure that allows the national branches to be in control of their employment practices. This allows each national organization to hire individuals from their own country.

Eastman Kodak is firmly committed to building and managing a truly diverse work force, both from a worldwide perspective and in all of its local operations. Grounded in the five Kodak values (respect, integrity, trust, credibility, and continuous improvement of personal renewal), Kodak's efforts are guided by its Global Performance Expectation on Diversity, one of six corporate business imperatives articulated by CEO George Fisher.

Challenge 4: Business Managers and Organizations Assume New Roles for which the Past has Not Prepared Them

Business research necessarily looks at the past and the present more than at the future. However, global firms face a future that could be quite different from the past. For example, most worldwide business research studies manufacturing firms, but today services such as banking, telecommunications, tourism, and education are important contributors to globalization. Service globalization may require different strategic capabilities than those used in manufacturing (Campbell and Verbeke, 1994).

In practice, many assumptions about how businesses can or should operate are being re-evaluated. For example, having instituted "open book" management by making financial details available to all employees, Sara Lee managers realized a first step was to teach employees how to interpret financial data. Thereafter, managers observed employees were just as adept as they in recognizing gains and losses, and perhaps more adept in finding ways to balance them (Lee, 1994). This sudden empowerment among employees meant that managers had to share roles that previously were theirs alone. The examples below illustrate other events for which managers were ill prepared.

Examples of Challenges for which Managers are Not Prepared

The failed merger between Mattel and the Learning Company demonstrates an example of managers assuming roles for which the past has not prepared them. The deal closed in May 1999, and from the start the two companies struggled to integrate. Management on both sides was not prepared to deal with the differences in company culture.

Sony Group shifted from manufacturing output to a network global enterprise. Under the leadership of the Sony Group headquarters, strategic alliances among the five pillars and integrated group-wide strategies bolster and maximize the company's corporate value.

Grupo Televisa faced new challenges due to industry changes. At its inception it faced little competition; however, Televisa later faced competition from high-powered multimedia corporations around the world as well as at home with TV Azteca. Grupo Televisa has found it necessary to become more aggressive and to search out markets rather than have the market come to them.

The greatest strength Mercy Corps has is their people. Employees encounter situations and environments that reflect dire desperation. Few past experiences can prepare them for the work ahead. On the ground, relief workers often confront atrocities and risk severe illness for which they can scarcely prepare.

Mitsubishi's management ran into situations that they were not prepared for when they began doing business internationally. Comfortable with Japanese cultural norms, management was faced with a sexual-harassment lawsuit due to improper behaviors at work. Mitsubishi's managers seemed to be unaware that such activity was unacceptable elsewhere and were ill prepared for the consequences.

Privatization at Deutsche Telekom and in many other telecommunications companies forces employees to transition from providing a government benefit to running a profit-generating business. Employee roles change when organizational purpose changes.

Japanese employers less frequently endorse lifetime employment, and this means Japanese students at Tokyo University are no longer guaranteed jobs. The result is that young people in Japan increasingly look for work among smaller firms, but they were unprepared for this change.

Worldwide, many larger firms are finding their newer competitors to be the women, minorities, or immigrants they themselves wouldn't hire or didn't promote. Fastest growth among small businesses in the US, Western Europe, and Japan are those established by women. Managers in many firms must learn how to work with people "not like us."

This look at characteristics of and challenges for global enterprises shows that achieving global "fit" depends on more than good intentions. Managers must juggle among multiple and sometimes competing interests put forward by forces both internal and external to the firm. The integration that connects an organization to its external environment clearly involves complex tasks. Further, it should also be clear that managers and other employees increasingly make decisions and engage in global activities that carry risks and often have a high cost of failure. The chapters to follow outline some of those risks and provide a context for understanding the true challenge of managing on a global scale.

CHAPTER SUMMARY

Inconsistent use of terms has led to misconceptions and confusion about all the different types of businesses operating outside domestic spheres. This occurs in part because while some define businesses according to where they operate, others define them in terms of how they are organized.

The international business actively participates in at least one national market outside its own. The multinational company can be distinguished from the international one because the former operates in more than one and usually several national markets beyond its "home" nation. The global enterprise differs from international and multinational firms by virtue of its interconnections worldwide.

There are five characteristics of a global enterprise: the enterprise acquires resources from a global pool, establishes a worldwide presence in one or more businesses, views the world as its home, develops a global *business* strategy for those of its businesses that operate worldwide, and achieves integration by transcending internal and external boundaries. With these five characteristics in mind, one can measure the extent to which any particular firm can be thought of as global.

Strategy is the limited set of important, nonroutine, nonprogrammable decisions that guide organizational direction. It is a comprehensive construct that encompasses all levels of organizational activity and thought. This text examines strategy as it unfolds at five organizational levels: enterprise strategy outlines the firm's purpose; corporate strategy determines which businesses will be held in the company's portfolio; business strategy defines sources of advantages and ways to compete or collaborate in the business; operational strategy determines how internal people, processes, and structures will be configured; and individual strategy outlines how each person's job satisfies higher level strategies.

Global organizations face four common challenges: they handle problems that cannot be "solved" but must be managed; their success increasingly is derived from intangibles that the organization cannot own; leaders increasingly manage many forms of diversity; and business managers and organizations assume new roles for which the past has not fully prepared them.

Globalization has meant more opportunities for businesses to operate on a worldwide basis, and the experience of operating globally has caused many business managers to rethink the basic assumptions of how their firms are organized and operated. Global management may require mixing and matching among tools and techniques derived from a variety of cultures perhaps to meld Western-style financial techniques with Eastern-style team-oriented work techniques. While it is relatively easy to think about altering systems and ways of thinking, it is much more difficult to alter the practices of a lifetime or of organizational generations.

REVIEW AND DISCUSSION QUESTIONS

1 Think for a moment about the factors that fueled fast-food restaurant growth in the industrialized world. What are some of these factors? Are they the same factors fueling growth for fast foods in the developing world? Do you think certain groups of people, for example younger people, will adopt fast-food habits earlier than other groups? Why?

2 As a group, brainstorm all the services and products you consume. Then organize the businesses that supply these needs into categories that are local, domestic, international, or global.

3 The 2001 GEM study (Reynolds et al., 2001) showed that about 147 million people were involved in entrepreneurial activity in the 29 developed and developing economies that participated in the study. These nations represent only about one third of the world's 6+ billion people. What is everyone else doing?

4 Will globalization make it more or less possible for small firms to participate in business? In what ways does globalization create similar challenges for any size firm? What are the key differences between large and smaller firms that make each more and less adaptive to globalization?

Chapter 4
THE LANDSCAPE OF GLOBAL BUSINESS

DR MARTENS AND FICKLE FASHION

Over 500 million global teens share tastes and habits. To prove this point, ad agency BSB Worldwide videotaped teenagers' rooms in 25 countries from the Pacific Rim, Europe, and Latin and North America to reveal similarities that made it difficult to know just where each tape was made. Closets contained baggy Levi's or Diesel jeans, Nikes or shoes from Timberland and Doc Martens, and similar sports jackets. Tabletops held similar PCs in identical colors; televisions played MTV; the same video games whirred; recordings from hip-hop and world bands dominated; Coke and Pepsi were the beverages of choice.

So just how does a firm tap into this global teen market? There are many pathways, one of which goes by Dr Martens shoe store—those ubiquitous boots showing up on teens and young adults all over the world, first as steel-toed black boots and later in a rainbow of colors. Global teens might be surprised to learn that this once-standard issue for their generation was fashioned originally from auto tires and other products to cushion the foot. The patented model created by Bavarian doctor Claus Maertens was a postwar invention to alleviate Maertens' foot pain.

Bill Griggs, chairman of Northamptonshire footwear manufacturer R. Griggs and Co., spotted ads for the comfortable shoes, then acquired global rights for the invention. After Anglicizing the name to Dr Martens, small, privately held R. Griggs began to manufacture and sell the shoes in England in 1960. Although the shoes were expected to appeal to postal carriers, police, and others who work on their feet, they were an immediate hit among Britain's early skinheads. The Griggs group adapted quickly to this counter-cultural shift, and by watching how buyers customized the shoes, they kept pace with fashion demands of skins, mods, punk, ska, psychobilly, Goths, grunge, and other buyers. In the process, the company expanded its reach from the UK to the Caribbean, North America, and finally to world consciousness. By 2002 there were 65,000 variations on the DM brand, including a "vegan" version manufactured from leather-like material.

In 1990, readers of *New Musical Express* named Dr Martens as the fashion item of the year. The company's market research also was limited to observing how buyers customized the shoes they purchased. And until 2000, R. Griggs had never advertised globally for the boot, finding that their best business came from word of mouth and celebrity endorsements. Calvin Klein sent model Kate Moss down the fashion runway wearing nothing but underwear and her Docs, and rock star Madonna also posed in her Docs.

By 1999, youth fashion interests had shifted to sports wear. Dr Martens followed by introducing a new footwear brand called AirWave in the US, Western Europe, Japan, Hong Kong, and the Philippines. The main reason for creating a new brand name was to expand beyond the Dr Martens name and brand without undercutting street credibility for the boot. And as they'd done with the original boot, the company sought feedback via direct customer communication. This time they used the Internet. In 2000, Dr Martens launched a new and global print campaign to pursue a fresh, fashion-forward look intended to showcase its vast array of product offerings in addition to the basic boot.

At that point, Dr Martens began to experience problems. The sports range did not meet with enthusiastic welcome, and other manufacturers began to introduce boots that cut into Dr Marten's existing lines. For example, John Fluevog Shoes began to turn up on ▶

many of the same celebrity feet that popularized Doc Martens. "Angel" soles were particularly popular in 1998 in both the Buicks line and Derby Swirl boots. The latter boots are not only comfortable—they offer an environmental advantage because they are made from biodegradable rubber of the Amazonia Hevea tree.

In 2002 Dr Martens reported losses of almost $38 million—a significant loss for a company whose annual revenues were estimated to be $600 million. In 2003 R. Griggs announced intentions to shift manufacturing from Northampton to China, and a decision to go back to its utility-boot roots to control declining sales. In particular, the company expected to target the boot to original customers by introducing sub-brands such as the Industrial, the Uniform, the Office, and the Terrain boot for workers who are on their feet most of every day. According to its managing director, "We were losing so much money that if we didn't do something we wouldn't have a future" (Jardine, 2003: 1).

This example illustrates that small firms can compete globally and they too can sponsor global brands. It also shows that not all firms consciously plan to go global. In the case of Dr Martens, teen consumers made them global. Then it was up to the firm to retain that status. R. Griggs made many efforts to retain their global brand position: the company rolled out a global advertising campaign, introduced new products in response to consumers' interests in sports wear, and shifted production to China. In the fickle world of teen fashion, Dr Martens faces the same challenge as that of larger firms: to stay ahead of their global competitors by anticipating the next big trend among global teens.

Source material: Mercedes M.Cardona (2000, March 6) Dr Martens moves beyond punk roots. *Advertising Age*, 71 (10): 26; Dr Martens: Great British brands. (2002, Aug. 1) *Marketing*, p. 19; http://www.drmartens.com; Alexandra Jardine (2003, May 29) Dr Martens plans "utility" return to fight sales slump. *Marketing*, p. 1; Richard C. Morais (1995, Jan. 16) What's up, doc? *Forbes*, pp. 42–43; Ali Qassim (1999, Sept. 13) Cult brand Dr Martens steps into new market. *Advertising Age International*, p. 9; Al Stewart (2000, Oct. 16) Dr. Martens retools. *Adweek* (Western edition) 50 (42);12; Shawn Tully (1994, May 16) Teens, the most global market of all. *Fortune*, pp. 90–96.

CHAPTER OVERVIEW

This chapter introduces global businesses that range in size from global giants to small "global startups." Ownership arrangements for these global businesses also vary. Diversity among these businesses creates opportunities and threats for competitors, and these are reviewed. The chapter concludes by looking at how growing diversity and interconnections among businesses, shareholders, and stakeholders affect management traditions.

THE GLOBAL POPULATION OF BUSINESS

Organizations of every size and shape populate the global business landscape. Businesses operating globally range in size from giants to medium-sized, small and even minuscule organizations. Some are private or family owned; others are publicly owned in the form of stocks or equities. Most global businesses operate from one or more geographic bases, but some are "virtual." Each in its own way contributes to growing diversity in worldwide business.

Business activities also are shaped by organizations that operate outside the business sector. Nongovernmental organizations pressure and partner with businesses, sometimes adopting business tools and techniques to achieve their objectives. Some organizations in the voluntary sector also generate revenues, sometimes by setting up quasi-businesses. These varied activities among nongovernmental organizations also shape global business practices. Still other profit-generating organizations are fully or partially government owned. Additionally, organizations such as global gangs, pirates, drug cartels, and the like interact with and challenge businesses on a global scale. These various organizations are looked at below. Global organizations range in size, form of ownership, and place of origin.

GLOBAL GIANTS

Many could quickly name businesses whose products or services they know or use. The resulting list might include global brand powerhouses like Coca-Cola, Sony, Nokia, Mercedes, Louis Vuitton, Benetton, Guinness, or Nestlé. This occurs because global brands enhance public awareness and because most of us are most alert to what occurs in our own communities and nations. Information access is another way for global giants to become well known. Names like ICI, Unilever, Sony, Danone, and Hanson are known throughout the world because these and other publicly owned organizations are major players in manufacturing, exporting and/or investing throughout the world. Public owner-ship also requires public reports, making the activities of these organizations more accessible to everyone. These firms also are frequently cited in newspaper and magazine articles because reporters can easily obtain information about them.

Hidden Giants

Sometimes there is limited public awareness of global giants. Three reasons for this are: information on them is not available; the industry or business does not generate public interest; or their activities are purposefully obscured.

Rarely is as much information available or sought from firms whose products are not in the public eye or whose products or services are of limited consumer interest. An example is Cemex, a global giant headquartered in Mexico. This company was the number three supplier of cement worldwide in 2003 with sales exceeding $7 billion, but relatively few know it by name. The name of 17-year-old Haier Group is little known out-side China, but it is the number two refrigerator manufacturer in the world and threatens US markets of Maytag, Electrolux, and General Electric on goods like wine chillers, air conditioners, and mini-freezers. Chinese companies such as computer brand Lenovo Group Ltd. and Beijing Li-Ning Sports Goods are working to establish global brand con-sciousness. Recent advertisements from Saint-Gobain demonstrate this company's efforts to be more recognizable on a global scale (see Table 4.1).

Table 4.1 *Saint-Gobain, Global Giant*

Product	Output
Frames and panels	For the Louvre pyramid, the Shanghai Opera House, and the Rodin Museum in Seoul, Korea
Insulation	For ½ the homes in Europe; 1/4 in the US
Pipes	For the 80 world capitals that use Saint-Gobain water systems
Bottles	Produces 30 billion per year, enough to stretch to the moon 15 times
Building supplies	Distributed via 2,500 outlets
Quartz filaments	For NASA's space shuttle
Insect screening	To screen out mosquitoes
Roofing shingles	Manufacture 300 square miles per year; enough to cover 160,000 US football fields

Source material: Saint-Gobain advertisement. (2002, April 1) *Business Week*, pp. 7–8. www.saint-gobain.com

Other business giants—such as food producers—tend to operate quietly in global markets. Thus, although Barilla is the world's largest pasta producer, the firm itself is little known outside Europe. According to Hermann Simon (1996), other global firms are "hidden" even though they have worldwide market shares of 50, 60, and even 90 percent. Examples include Mabuchi of Japan (50 percent of the small motor market worldwide), or Hauni from Germany (90 percent of the market for high-speed cigarette makers). Table 4.2 on hidden "champions" shows many hidden giants have become global "giants" within their own niches.

Table 4.2 *Hidden champions*

Company	Primary Product	Sales in millions USD	Employees	World Rank in Niche
Brahler	Rental of conference, translation systems	45	390	1–2
Carl Jager	Incense cones, sticks	3	10	1
Soring	Ultrasonic dissectors	3	20	1
Grenzebach	Computer-controlled management of float-glass production	67	450	1
Carl Walther	Sports guns	17	200	1

Source material: Hermann Simon (1996) *Hidden Champions*. Boston, MA: Harvard University Press, pp. 20–21.

Global firms sometimes obscure their identity if public knowledge could alter public perception. Accordingly, many large food producers retain an original name when they acquire smaller firms. For example, Ben and Jerry's Homemade Inc. trades on its premium ice-cream image, but global giant Unilever owns it. Similarly Coca-Cola owns Odwalla Juice, Adolph Coors owns Belgian White beer, and General Mills purchased Small Planet Foods Co.

Privately held firms become the subject of public interest and inquiry when their products or activities attract global attention. Mars Candy, Levi Strauss, Sainsbury, Guess?, Domino's Pizza, Deloitte & Touche, Thomson, Heineken, Hallmark Cards, Henkel, Benetton, Salim Group, and Toyota are only a few among many privately owned global giants. Some like Mars or Ferrero remain secretive; others like Levi Strauss regularly report their activities. The public is most likely to know the names of these and other privately held firms when they consume the product or live near the company headquarters.

Privately Owned Firms

Often there is limited information available on privately owned firms. This too can occur for many reasons, but private ownership usually means the company is not required to report its activities to the public. The example below describes two global giants that are privately owned.

Ever Heard of Koch? Or JCB?

Koch Industries (pronounced "coke") is the second-largest private US company (after Cargill), with extensive holdings in petroleum, agriculture, and chemicals. Its two refineries process about 600,000 barrels of crude oil a day. Koch also processes natural-gas liquids and operates gas-gathering systems and a 35,000-mile pipeline system between Texas and Canada. KoSa, its venture with Mexico's Saba family, is a leading polyester producer. Other operations include minerals trading and transport, asphalt marketing, manufacturing equipment for processing industries, and ranching. Brothers Charles and David Koch control the company. In 2002 they employed about 11,000 people, and earned an estimated $40 billion in revenue. This puts their revenues way ahead of two US companies that are much better known globally. That would put them about 87th on *Fortune*'s Global 500 list for 2002, ahead of Microsoft whose revenues were $28 billion and McDonald's $15 billion. So why isn't Koch listed on the *Fortune* 500 or the *Business Week* 1000 or the *Financial Times* 500? Because Koch is a privately held firm and does not provide information to the public.

JC Bamford Excavators is such a popular brand in the UK that people often use the initials "JCB" interchangeably with a backhoe. English dictionaries often define JCB as a "type of mechanical excavator." The company produces various equipment for construction and farming, including crawler excavators, backhoe loaders, front-end loaders, material handlers, and speed tractors. Despite being Europe's largest maker of construction equipment, the company is less well known worldwide than competitors like Caterpillar and Komatsu. But JCB is the fourth largest construction machinery manufacturer in the world. One reason we may know less about it is that JCB is family owned. The family of founder Joseph Cyril Bamford owns JCB.

Family-owned Companies

Family-owned firms—be they domestic or global—account for the vast majority of world GDP, but often there is limited information available on them. Some exceptions appear in Table 4.3. Yet family-owned firms are important actors in the global business landscape. For example, families control as much as a third of the largest 20 companies in most advanced economies and more than one third in developing economies (La Porta and Lopez-de-Silanes, 1999).

Table 4.3 *Family-owned global giants and 2003 revenues*

Country	Company	Revenue ($ billion)
Hong Kong	Hutchison Whampoa	18.66
Australia	News Corp	22
Canada	Thomson Corporation	7.608
Japan	Toyota	128.965
India	Tata Group	12.8
US	Anheuser-Busch	12.6
Germany	BMW	52.122

Source material: Annual reports from each company.

Between Firm Rankings

Global giants are ranked against one another on lists such as the *Fortune* Global 500, the *Financial Times* Global 500, and the *Business Week* Global 1000, although the basis of these relative rankings vary. Measurement differences and rapid worldwide changes can mean they vary on the same attributes even within the same year. For example, the *Financial Times* 500 looks at market capitalization on a single day, reporting the number of shares the company has issued multiplied by market share prices. But absolute valuation depends on events other than those directly related to firm activities, and so market capitalization can vary depending on when it was measured. For example, stock-market volatility in 2000 resulted in significant rankings changes in the *FT* 500 list for the following year.

The *Fortune* Global 500 compares firms on profits. However, this approach fails to account for differences that arise because of one-time expenses such as write-offs. Many firms have different fiscal years. For example, the end of Microsoft's fiscal year is July 31, but other companies follow the calendar year. Additionally, annual revenue rankings tend to improve ranks for trading companies that have very high sales. In other words, results are not always comparable. The *Fortune* 500 guide also reports the number of employees worldwide, a figure that makes it possible to calculate sales per employee, profit per employee or similar ratios.

Every list of global giants has advantages and disadvantages, but none perfectly tracks the rapid pace of change found in global firms. For example, firms can be added and subtracted from any list of global giants via mergers and acquisitions, such was the case with Ciba-Geigy and Sandoz who merged to become Novartis. Additionally, global giants fall off the list of giants because they falter or fail, such as Enron. Finally, there is a tendency to look only at firms at the top of the global giants list. A look at the middle and the bottom of these lists shows they are populated by corporations about which the world knows less. Thus, the disadvantages of these lists and the differences between them are reasons to consult more than one source when assessing global giants.

Nation of Origin

Firms from advanced economies often dominate lists of the Global 500 or 1000. For example, only one global giant from a developing economy was listed among UNCTAD's largest corporations. This was Petroleos de Venezuela that holds $8 billion in foreign assets, including a US subsidiary and partnerships in Germany and Finland (*World Investment Report*, 2000). *Business Week's* list of the "Top 100 Companies" shows these firms come from large and small countries, for example Switzerland and Singapore are home to firms representing many industries including automotives, pharmaceuticals software, consumer products, commodities, banking and investment, and healthcare.

Whereas firms in developing economies once concentrated their energies on domestic activities, increasingly they seek opportunities beyond national borders. Late-mover businesses from developing economies have carved out global business space (Bartlett and Ghoshal, 2000). While most UNCTAD businesses are headquartered in advanced economies, the role of large firms from developing and transitional economies has increased. For example, the share of outward foreign direct investment originating in developing economies rose from about 3 percent in the early 1980s to 9 percent by 2000 (*World Investment Report*, 2001). According to the UN's 1995 *World Investment Report*, heightened business competition can be expected as companies from the fastest-growing developing economies, such as China, India, and South Korea, operate in many more nations. For example, Indian companies such as Ranbaxy, Infosys Technologies, and Wipro are quickly becoming global actors.

In summary, this review of global giants shows there are many of them, but rankings among them depend on who is doing the ranking and measures used. Privately held giants also exist, but often information on them is difficult to acquire. Another way to explore these companies is to examine Forbes.com and its annual lists of global billionaires; then explore how these billionaires sustain their wealth. The same information paucity also occurs for many smaller firms examined in the following section.

GLOBAL BRANDS

Global brands enhance awareness of global businesses of any size. Branding reflects the product, but often global brands convey a message about the company that produces it. Researchers show consumer purchases are influenced when they perceive a brand to offer quality and reflect prestige (Steenkamp, Batra, and Alden, 2003). This may be particularly important in developing economies when consumers cannot be sure of product quality among non-branded goods. Steenkamp et al. (2003) also found that certain consumers, for example individualists, avoid globally branded products.

Some global brands and companies are very well known, while others seek to establish global brands, for example the Chinese companies Kejian in cellular telephones, and Haier in appliances. Haier's main focus has been on innovative products such as wine-cooling cabinets and dormitory refrigerators that are advertised widely in airports and appliance outlets.

Global Branding for Smaller Businesses

The concept of branding has appeal for small as well as large enterprises. One successful brand has become the "Copper River" salmon from Alaska. More recently, Canada's diamond industry—the $8 billion global diamond trade—has begun to brand their diamonds to distinguish them from "blood diamonds" mined in war-torn countries or to finance armed conflict. Canada's Beny Sofer & Sons LLC markets their wholesale diamonds under the brand name Canadia, borrowing from Canada's reputation as a peaceful and socially responsive nation. Sirius Diamonds in Vancouver, BC etches a tiny polar bear on their stones to demonstrate Canadian authenticity. And in another effort to brand, the government of Canada's Northwest Territories provides a certificate to demonstrate that diamonds sold are mined, cut, and polished there.

Source material: Joel Baglole (2003. Apr. 17) Political correctness by the carat. *The Wall Street Journal*, pp. B1, B3.

An interesting challenge for measuring global brand impact is that standards are emerging rather than well established. This leads to competing lists of global brands generated by Interbrand and AC Nielson.

Interbrand Rankings

Interbrand was the first organization to assess global brands, beginning in 1990 with an initial list of 1,200 brands named by Interbrand staff. The list was reduced to 500 brands evaluated on four criteria:

- the brand's weight measured by market share within its category (35 percent)
- the brand's breadth measured by brand appeal to age, character, and nationality (30 percent)

- the brand's depth measured by customer loyalty (20 percent)
- the brand's length measured by stretch of the brand beyond its original product type (15 percent).

The Interbrand calculations for 2003 started with global brands valued greater than $1 billion. Each had to derive more than a third of its sales from outside their home country (up from 20 percent in 2001), and have significant distribution in the Americas, Europe, and Asia. However, because the Interbrand index relies on publicly available information, brands owned by privately held firms are not included in the Interbrand analysis. This eliminates Snickers candy because family-owned Mars manufactures it, and the British Broadcasting Corporation (BBC) because it is state owned. This suggests that brand consideration sometimes must go beyond available measures.

Table 4.4 *World's top 10 branded goods, 2003 (global brand position in 1996)*

1	Coca-Cola (#2 in 1996)	6	Nokia
2	Microsoft (#9 in 1996)	7	Disney (#3 in 1996)
3	IBM	8	McDonald's
4	GE	9	Marlboro
5	Intel	10	Mercedes

Source material: Brands in an age of anti-Americanism. (2003, Aug. 4) *Business Week*, pp. 69–78.

Interbrand research to date reflects that global brand rankings fluctuate over time. This occurs because of changing global tastes, new products that edge out an existing brand's franchise, and brand management activities. For example, Chupa Chups created a global candy presence by giving away lollipops to globally known celebrities at fashion shows, nightclubs, and MTV events.

AC Nielsen Rankings

AC Nielsen first rated global brands in 2001, but they maintain that branding activities began in the sixteenth century when tavern owners used branding irons to burn their names on barrels of alcohol (Perrin and Nishikawa, 2003). Although the 2001 Nielsen ratings used $1 billion in worldwide sales as the baseline, they developed an interest in global mega brands by 2003, using the following criteria:

- they looked only at consumer packaged goods;
- products must be marketed under the same brand name in at least three different categories; and
- products must meet the brand-franchise criteria above in at least three of five geographic regions.

A Nielsen restriction not imposed by Interbrand is that consumers had to be able to find the same product with the same name in multiple markets. This could eliminate from consideration the many Unilever products that sell identical products but with different names worldwide. Only nine of the 62 global mega brands identified were found to be available in each of the 50 countries studied: this included Nivea, L'Oreal, Revlon, Nestlé, Dove, Lipton, Pond's, Gillette, and Oral B. Over 50 percent of Nielsen's global mega brands were in personal care and cosmetics categories.

Less well-known global giants often appear on developing economy lists of companies. For example, the *Financial Times* website lists top Middle Eastern and Latin American firms whose capitalization exceeds $1 billion. Although these firms may not be well known beyond their nation of origin, their names could soon be global.

SMALL AND MEDIUM-SIZED GLOBAL ENTERPRISES (SMEs)

Although SMEs usually concentrate on domestic markets, many expand internationally to one or more other nations. In 1999, smaller firms accounted for over 90 percent of companies in the EU and many were export-oriented (Demick and O'Reilly, 2000). About 25 percent of manufacturing SMEs operate across national boundaries (Small and medium-sized enterprises, 2000).

Some SMEs—family owned and publicly owned—operate as global enterprises. Communication and transportation infrastructures allow SMEs to participate in global production processes. SMEs, especially those in Japan, are increasingly investing in developing countries (Fujita, 1995), suggesting they may be more attracted to opportunities large firms reject. And there are many opportunities worldwide that have been absorbed by small firms. For example, Jinwoong is based in South Korea but controls 35 percent of the world market for tents, Hongjin Crown makes motorcycle helmets that command a 40 percent share of the US market alone, and Hong Kong-based Boto International is the world's largest manufacturer of artificial Christmas trees.

The German *Mittelstand*: From Local to Global

Once operating as one of the many medium-sized companies in Germany known as the *Mittelstand*, Knorr-Bremse now manufactures about 40 percent of the world's braking systems for trains and buses. Company owner Heinz Hermann Thiele notes that when he purchased the company in 1985, he refocussed strategy to concentrate on braking systems for customers who were themselves increasingly global. In addition to global sales of over $1 billion, some 70 percent of Knorr-Bremse's 11,000-member staff is employed outside Germany. According to Thiele, Knorr-Bremse is "now a global company" (p. 62).

Source material: Rising above the sludge. (2003, Apr. 5) *The Economist*, pp. 61–63.

Information technology allows many SMEs to participate in a global business world on their own terms. For example, information technology allows native Indians in the Amazon basin to decide which goods they will sell, when, where, and to whom instead of being economically "captured" by firms with capital and other resources. In India, many small firms have developed to satisfy growing worldwide demand for business-support services such as billing, information management, data mining, and call answering (Back office to the world, 2001). While some SMEs are suppliers captured by bigger firms' production networks, others use communication technologies to network with each other, through which they establish cooperative ventures that enhance collective-bargaining power or create niche markets (Castells, 1996).

Tortellini Takes Rana Global

Gianluca Rana intends to make his family-run business a global enterprise as the new CEO of Pastificio Rana SpA. The firm was founded by father Giovanni Rana, who, recognizing that women working in factories didn't have time to cook, filled a demand for ready-made tortellini. Now the younger Rana intends to address that same need on a global scale, starting with an intense advertising campaign in France and Spain. Although the company is little known, its tortellini are consumed in many European countries under private labels sold by Sainsbury in the UK and Auchan in France. Similar plans are afoot in other nations, including a venture in the US and a factory in Argentina to produce and distribute Rana products in Latin America. Success depends not only on innovation and marketing, but also on the company's ability to go head-to-head with Italian firm Barilla SpA and Nestlé's Buitoni, Italy's second largest fresh-pasta company.

Source material: Maria Sturani (1998, June 19) For Italy's Rana, recipe for tortellini begins with innovation and marketing. *The Wall Street Journal*, p. B7A.

The fluid structure of many smaller firms allows them to act quickly, and technological changes facilitate access to information and capital once available only to larger firms with significant research capabilities. An example is Spectramind, an Indian start-up that used telecommunications technologies to transcend traditional barriers of time and place with business services.

Global Start-ups/Born Globals

According to Gary Knight and S. Tamer Cavusgil (1996), born globals—firms that are global at inception—rely on cutting-edge technology to develop relatively unique products or processes. They are typically small in size, view the world as a single marketplace at birth, and begin exporting about a quarter of their production soon after their founding. Madsen and Servais (1997) note there are different names for what they also call born globals, including global start-ups (Oviatt and McDougall, 1995), high-technology start-ups (Jolly et al., 1992), and international new ventures (McDougall et al., 1994). More recently, Jim Bell et al. described "born again" globals as well-established firms that suddenly embrace "rapid and dedicated internationalization" (2001: 174) despite having previously focussed on their domestic markets. Born again activity can occur in either large or small organizations, and this characteristic differentiates them from smaller born globals and global start-ups.

Start-ups to the Rescue

According to a study conducted by IP Strategies and commissioned by the nonprofit group Europe 500 association (linked to the European Foundation of Entrepreneurship Research), entrepreneurial start-up companies in Europe are making gains in creating jobs and profits. Whereas Europe's biggest companies slashed payrolls by 4 percent or by more than 500,000 jobs during 1991–1996, the 500 small companies studied increased their employment by 183,000 jobs or 16 percent annually over the same time period. These companies are primarily privately owned, and most succeed by identifying niches created by cultural, political, and economic shifts. For example, Telepizza of Spain capitalized on growing demand for fast food because more women were working, while regional airlines such as Britain's Cityflyer Express Ltd are able to compete because air travel across the European continent is less regulated. Many firms are succeeding simply because they are responsive to consumers' demands for better service than that provided by many larger firms. Although most of these start-ups created hundreds rather than thousands of jobs, collectively they generated millions in sales in industries such as computers, wine production, advertising, medical services, and manufacturing.

Source material: Start-ups to the rescue. (1998, Mar. 23) *Business Week*, pp. 50–2.

According to Benjamin Oviatt and Patricia Phillips McDougall (1995), a prototypical global start-up is Logitech, Inc., which went global to manufacture computer mice. Founded by a Swiss and two Italians, the firm was established in 1982 with headquarters in both California and Switzerland. Research and development as well as manufacturing were conducted in both places, but soon expanded to include Taiwan and Ireland. By 1989, Logitech had revenues of US $140 million and held 30 percent of the world market for computer mice. By 2004 the company posted $1.2 million in revenues of about $944 million, employed just under 5,000 employees, and had expanded their product portfolio to include Internet video cameras, keyboards, personal computer, audio and telephony products, and interactive gaming controllers.

Oviatt and McDougall (1995) believe global start-ups share these characteristics:

1 a global vision exists from inception
2 managers are internationally experienced
3 their entrepreneurs have strong international business networks
4 they exploit pre-emptive technology or marketing

5 they have a unique intangible asset, e.g., tacit knowledge
6 product or service extensions are closely linked
7 the organization is closely coordinated worldwide.

Many small to mid-size firms have become leaders in business globalization by following leaders, but others succeed with new business approaches.

EMERGING GLOBAL BUSINESS PARTICIPANTS

Organizations of many sizes, types, and ownership forms populate the global business landscape, and they increase its diversity. Emerging participation from all parts of the world and segments of society will increase this diversity further.

Latin America

Many business practices in South American countries migrated there via colonists and settlers from throughout the world, whereas other values emerged from practices of indigenous peoples. The melding and merging of many cultures has created country-specific habits in Latin America, but some commonalities are identifiable. For example, many business practices are part of a system of interlocking extended family and social community. Among the values applicable to work are that destiny or fate guides life. Social and organizational hierarchies reinforce veneration for tradition. Results depend on networks of relationships, and family and friendship connections are central to obtaining jobs and promotions. Finally, families more than work define human existence, and often one owes greater loyalty to the latter than to the former (Harris and Moran, 1996).

Several characteristics found among Latin American business people particularly help to explain Latin American business traditions. Simpatia or warmth in personal relationships places great value in good relationships in business. Criticism or insults resulting in loss of face are viewed as affronts to personal dignity. Personalism creates loyalty via relationships, and also creates a strong desire for personal attention. Face-to-face contact is more highly valued than bureaucratic procedures (Osland et al., 1999).

Yet, the globalization process may alter Latin American traditions. Many Latin American countries are more actively promoting corporate governance standards. Brazil, Argentina, Chile, and Colombia all have instituted new rules to promote business transparency and improve corporate governance standards. For example, Brazil launched a stock market that requires companies to adopt international accounting practices. The following example illustrates a particular change within a family-owned Venezuelan firm.

> ### Cisneros Family Values
>
> Venezuela's Cisneros family conglomerate is privately held, but generated over $4 billion in sales for 2002. The family has targeted their efforts toward international growth and this has meant changes in long-standing relationships. For example, in August of 1996, bottler Hit de Venezuela abandoned its 50-year relationship with PepsiCo to align long-term growth interests with Coca-Cola. Overnight Pepsi products disappeared from Venezuelan store shelves, and thousands of Hit trucks were repainted as the 18 bottling plants switched to Coke products. The subsequent lawsuit filed by Pepsi was settled with fines against Coke and Cisneros, but allowed the Coke–Cisneros venture to continue. Pepsi struck a new venture with Empresas Polar, the country's major distributor of beer and hopes to regain their national reputation and distribution capability. Six months later, the Cisneros family sold most of their newly acquired bottling interests to Panamco, part of a long-term strategy to move out of retail and consumer goods and into global telecommunications. Cisneros family decisions showed that traditions of business in Latin America such as developing and maintaining long-standing relationships might be undergoing change in a more global world.

Entrepreneurship

Entrepreneurship—the propensity to start new businesses—has increased in many nations worldwide and among a diverse range of people. For example, downturns in big business were followed by new business starts in South Korea. In 2002 the Global Entrepreneurship Monitor noted that firms less than four years old employed 9 percent of Korean adults (Entrepreneurial fresh air, 2001). Some of these firms prove responsive to their investors. For example, the chief executive of Humax holds monthly meetings with institutional investors to review company finances and management activities. Conversely, in Japan entrepreneurial behavior is decreasing as the nation loses more companies than are added. Japanese entrepreneur Tsutomu Shida shows one reason why this is happening.

> ### Barriers to Entrepreneurial Behavior
>
> Entrepreneurs in any nation face barriers that are both financial and psychological. In Japan both are institutionalized. For example, an entrepreneur must have considerable capital to establish a venture; these ventures do not receive favorable tax treatment; and they are not allowed to raise capital with stock or junk bond offers. Further, Japanese cultural emphasis on saving face discourages many from starting a venture that could fail, and entrepreneurs are held in low regard in Japan.
>
> None of these barriers were impediments to Tsutomu Shida who made his fortune in food ventures in ice-cream, restaurants, karaoke bars, and catering. Unlike most Japanese entrepreneurs who keep quiet about their ventures, Mr. Shida frequently appears before government committees to promote entrepreneurism, courts Japanese media, and has written two books about his entrepreneurial adventures. Mr. Shida

feels strongly that Japan should encourage entrepreneurial behavior, and he is helping to do that with an institute that offers courses on every phase of the business start-up process. Although Mr. Shida does not charge for institute classes, he is first in line to provide venture funds for promising start-ups. Isn't that just like an entrepreneur?

Source material: Show them the money. (1999, Feb. 13) *The Economist*, p. 67.

Larger firms also encourage entrepreneurial behaviors among their employees. Ghoshal and Bartlett (1995) assert that entrepreneurial behavior in global giants requires:

■ An organizational culture that emphasizes people's abilities.
■ A structure that reduces reliance on formal controls and rules; this does not mean that there would not be rules, but rather that people would agree to abide by the ones that do develop.
■ People who are stimulated by creativity.

Entrepreneurial Women

Management researchers often examine if and how women's management styles, interests, and business approaches differ from those of men (Gibson, 1995; Rosener, 1990). A tendency toward entrepreneurial behavior is one indicator of difference, but others include a longer-run profit horizon, participative management styles, and efforts to create structures and processes designed to meet human needs. Data about women business owners is somewhat sparse, but they are estimated to own between a quarter and a third of businesses worldwide. Additionally, the number of women-owned businesses is growing faster than overall economic growth in many nations (Women entrepreneurs are a growing international trend, 1997).

In the US, about 10.1 million firms are at least 50 percent owned by women, and women entrepreneurs generated about $2.3 trillion in revenues for the US economy in 2002 (Top 10 facts about women business owners, 2003). In Japan five out of six new businesses in 1993 were created by women (Fisher, 1993), and entrepreneurship is credited with advances for even the world's poorest women (*Human Development Report*, 1995).

Female Entrepreneurship in Saudi Arabia

Hundreds of women gathered in Riyadh, Saudi Arabia in 1998 to learn how to start their own businesses. Although many wealthy Saudi women traditionally have worked, women from other economic classes now are taking jobs outside the home or starting their own businesses. More than 6,000 commercial licenses have been issued to businesswomen in Riyadh and Jeddah and an estimated 250,000 women are at work in Saudi Arabia. Despite restrictions on women, for example they are not allowed to drive or have contact with male workers, women are circumventing these traditions via technology, using the telephone, fax, and e-mail to engage in business.

Source material: Putting Saudi women to work. (1998, Sept. 26) *The Economist*, p. 48.

The Family-owned Business

Earlier we saw that some global giants are family owned. But most family-owned businesses are small ones, and only some operate on a global scale. Small, family-owned businesses are quite common in Africa, Europe, throughout Central and Latin America, and in Asia. For example, about 90–95 percent of Mexican companies are family owned or run (A firm focus on family affairs, 2003). Although there may be a perception that North America is dominated by global giants, family and private ownership is quite strong there; family-owned firms are about 95 percent of incorporated US businesses (Dunne, 2003). For firms listed on the US Standard and Poor ratings, over a third include managers from a founding family (Family Inc., 2003). Almost half of US GDP is generated by family-owned or closely held businesses.

There are about 50,000 private family-owned German companies with sales of $13–250 million; these are the Mittelstand—small or owner-run companies—that account for most of Germany's GDP. According to the French Association of Medium-Sized Family-Owned Companies, family-owned businesses there account for 80 percent of companies with sales from $7 million to $290 million (Raghavan and Steinmetz, 2000). Three-quarters of UK companies are family-held enterprises (Blackhurst, 2002).

Family ownership allows broad latitude for management practices, and this increases diversity of business objectives in the global sphere. Family-owned businesses take a longer planning horizon than firms under pressure to produce periodic profits. According to Imanol Belausteguigoitia (A firm focus on family affairs, 2003), advantages of family businesses in Mexico can be greater loyalty, stronger commitment, easier understanding, low staff turnover, longer-term vision, and long time frames to train employees and family members.

A Change in Business Strategy Leads to Internal Personnel Changes for a Would-Be Global Firm

Chupa Chups is a candy maker based in Spain that is becoming increasingly well known for its lollipops. Growing a global brand did not occur by chance; company managers planned it that way. But when the founding Bernat family decided to position themselves against global competitors like Hershey, Tootsie Rolls, and Ferrero, they realized they'd also have to change their staffing habits. Accordingly, the family gave up all their active management positions and transferred responsibility for them to a supervisory board. They reshuffled their board of directors and from 2001 chose their managing director from outside company ranks to promote worldwide expansion. In 2003 the Bernat family transferred ownership of the Chupa Chups brand from the family to the company itself.

Source material: … while Bernat family transfers brand ownership. (2003) *Candy Industry*, 168 (2): 12–18.

Family-owned businesses also can face problems. Family dynamics and succession decisions can divide them; family membership does not guarantee managerial ability; and differences of opinion about the company's direction or financial decisions can confuse enterprise strategy. For these and other reasons, many businesses do not make it beyond the third generation of family ownership.

Koc Holdings

Koc Holding's business interests range widely to cover autos, supermarkets, energy, appliances, financials, and foods. The company employs over 50,000 people, and generates annual revenues in excess of $10 billion. Established by Vehbi Koc in 1985, the company is based in Turkey. In 2003, the company moved to its third generation of family direction when Rahmi Koc appointed eldest son Mustafa to lead the company. Mustafa Koc earned a management degree from a US university, but has developed his managerial experience through a variety of jobs in the Koc conglomerate. What remains to be seen is if Koc can make the transition beyond a third generation of family leadership.

The family clearly recognizes that links beyond Turkey are important for its global survival and to Turkey. The company is growing globally and now exports a third of its production. Koc also is attempting to bring the world of business to Turkey. For example, the family established Koc University in Istanbul, and is staffing it principally with Turkish nationals educated in top US business schools.

Source material: Face value: The retiring Mr. Koc. (2003, Apr. 19) *The Economist*, p. 58.

Koc's promotion of US-style business education in Turkey is one example of how a family business introduces diverse business practices. Another example of diverse business practices is found in Italy's relationship-based system. For example, when Fiat automotive needed a cash infusion in 1993, family and friends of Chairman Gianni Agnelli provided capital and agreed that Mr. Agnelli could decide how much of a dividend to pay on these investments (Che non ci sera, 1995).

The Extended Family in Global Business

"Overseas" or "nonresident" groups, for example Chinese, Indians, Hungarians, or Burmese, often build businesses in their home nations that also develop or renew cultural links, make a difference for people in the country of origin, or fulfill perceived obligations for home-country development. Some, like Raj Bagri, chairman of the London Metal Exchange, invest in India because of cultural attachments there; others feel that family connections or patience facilitate business opportunities (Passage back to India, 1995). Whatever their investment reasons, overseas groups fuel many economies. An example is the Salim Group.

Salim Group

The history of Liem Sioe Liong's business interests and the Salim Group tracks the post-World War II history of Indonesia. Liem is a resident of Indonesia, but he is an ethnic Chinese—one of many Chinese who helped to develop Indonesia's business interests. Working in collaboration with the Indonesian government, Liem founded Salim Group, which by 1997 was a global conglomerate involved in businesses ranging from soap and shampoo in Indonesia to car sales in the Philippines, and from mortgage loans in San Francisco to portable phone delivery in Malaysia.

Salim Group's growth was halted in 1997 by an Asian economic crisis. Many in Indonesia blamed this crisis on ethnic Chinese and concessions that had been made long ago to develop businesses like the Salim Group. For example, Liem invested in steel and cement industries during the 1970s and 1980s when the government called for infrastructure projects. In return, the government offered Liem a wide range of trading privileges, cheap financing, and exclusive licenses. In the 1980s Salim Group firm Indomobil was granted sole assembly and distribution rights for Suzuki, Volvo, Nissan, and Mazda cars in Indonesia.

After the fall of President Suharto in 1998, Indonesian Chinese experienced business losses and violence against them. Although many left the country, the Salim Group stayed. It and many other ethnic Chinese businesses were blamed for many of Indonesia's economic ills, and held liable for debts to the government. This resulted in sales of over 100 Salim companies. Today the Salim Group operates fewer companies, but it is not out of the running. In 2002, its flagship company Indofoods—the world's largest manufacturer of noodles by volume—was voted the top Indonesian firm for overall leadership according to a *Far Eastern Economic Review* annual company survey.

Source material: Michael Shari (2000, Oct. 9) Wages of hatred. *Business Week*, pp. 71–74; Adam Schwarz and Jonathan Friedland (1991, Mar. 14) Indonesia: Empire of the sun. *Far Eastern Economic Review*, pp. 46–53.

Two important overseas networks are overseas Chinese and Indians who create "social networks composed of family members, friends and trusted colleagues that influence business operations and environments" (Haley and Haley, 1998: 301). Overseas Chinese probably number about 50 million (Kapur and Ramamurti, 2001). Firms often succeed via unrelated diversification. Haley and Tan (1996) and Haley and Haley (1997) propose that in terms of strategic management practices, these overseas networks share common characteristics different from those found in Western firms. In particular, managers of these networks tend to make decisions quickly based on qualitative data, and they use intuition when making decisions (Haley and Haley, 1998).

The overseas Chinese generate billions in economic output. In 2001, overseas Chinese owned an estimated 73 percent of market capitalization in Indonesia, 69 percent in Malaysia, 50–60 percent in the Philippines, and 81 percent in both Thailand and Singapore. Except for Singapore where 78 percent of the population is Chinese, this represents asset control well in excess of population representation. For example, Chinese comprise only 3–4 percent of the Indonesian population, 2 percent of the Filipino population, and 14 percent of Thailand's population (Asian business survey, 2001).

Although overseas Chinese receive the lion's share of attention for global expansion, subcontinent Indians also have established global networks. Further, like the Chinese, overseas Indians have migrated for generations to establish merchant businesses in nations as diverse as Africa, Mauritania, Fiji, the US, and Europe as well as Asia. Many overseas Indians have established successful dot.com, Internet, and software businesses, and overseas Indians operate in mainstream industries such as hotel and restaurant management. Many overseas Indians view financial success as a family duty (Gidoomal and Porter, 1997), especially for an oldest son. As becomes evident in the following focus on Planar Systems, sometimes family practices of overseas Indians alter traditional practices in the nations where they settle.

Planar Systems' Inverted Bonus Plan

Planar Systems' CEO is Dr. Balaji Krishnamurthy, who formerly worked as a Tektronix Inc. executive and in General Electric research. As at most US companies, the CEO is paid the most, followed by middle managers, and then the rank and file. But the bonus system at Planar turns this around. First in line for profits are shareholders. Then if targets are met, rank and file workers get quarterly or annual bonuses. Next in line are middle managers who get no bonus until junior managers get theirs, or who miss their own targets. Last in line is the CEO who becomes the ultimate shock absorber during downturns. Krishnamurthy explains that the reasoning behind this system is that "the higher the degree of influence, the greater the stewardship responsibility you have for ensuring others have been taken care of."

Source material: Joanne Lublin (2003, Apr. 14) Bottom up. *The Wall Street Journal*, p. R4.

Many Indians practice Vedantic principles that are reflected in business values and behaviors such as the following (Chakraborty, 1995):

1 Striving for a pure mind is more important than sharpening the intellect because feelings more than intellect lead to decisions and behaviors.
2 Primary organizational reliance should be on humans rather than on systems or structures.
3 "Work must be done without personal claims to egocentric results (i.e. rewards) as the primary driving force" (p. 10).
4 Ego-led decisions return unfavorable results; this is the notion of karma.
5 Striving for unity and "oneness" is true development.

Many Indian families prefer to operate "behind the scenes" more than do Chinese families, but the two groups share several characteristics (Haley and Haley, 1998):

■ There is little differentiation between the company and its controlling family.
■ The companies have very strong and informal networks organized around family norms.
■ The companies have good relationships with the public sectors in India and China.
■ The companies usually are diversified in unrelated businesses.

DIVERSE BUSINESS PARTICIPATION AND MANAGEMENT PRACTICE

Firms of every size and from every part of the world now cross boundaries of size, economies, and nations to participate in business. This process is occurring quickly because of rapid changes in other external environments. For example, almost anyone can gain access to global technology, capital, components, and even labor. Differences among these firms generate diverse business practices that often transform industries and organizations.

The Effects of Increased Business Participation on Global Giants

Many global giants grew in size due to capital access used to merge, acquire, and expand globally. They also had advantages of economic scale and scope. These advantages may not persist. Liberalization of commercial rules in the developed and developing countries ease market entry for enterprises of any size. Deregulation and standardization of commercial rules means that larger firms may lose advantages they once had as experts on regulatory standards in most of the world. Traditional large-firm dominance of global production and distribution systems also may be eroding (Held et al., 1999: 237) because entrepreneurs are newly able to enter markets with little more than a personal computer and a link to world markets. For example, born-global firms increasingly participate in business around the world (Knight and Cavusgil, 2004).

Cyrus Friedheim (1998) notes that global giants find it difficult to grow because consumer tastes change quickly, governments are more hostile to them, and the cost of projects have grown beyond the ability of even these firms. Globalization also has reduced the following "natural advantages" for larger firms (Who wants to be a giant, 1995):

1 Deregulation and lower trade barriers have reduced the value of relationships large firms cultivate with government leaders.
2 The spread of modern management techniques has reduced the monopoly position of large firms on management wisdom.
3 Large, bureaucratic organizations find it difficult to adapt rapidly to change.

The Effects of Increased Business Participation on Family-owned Businesses

When family-owned firms raise capital on global markets, their management practices become subject to external review. In Italy, many managers did not stand up to scrutiny, leading to the ousting of Giovanni Agnelli from Fiat, Carlos De Benedetti from Olivetti, and the Ferruzzi family from top jobs at agrochemical Ferruzi SpA. These changes signal a change in some family-ownership systems. Still another challenge for family-owned firms arises from the original means for acquiring family wealth. For example, in the Philippines and in Indonesia, many businesses that collaborated with replaced governments fell into disfavor.

A challenge for family-owned business under any circumstances is to acquire appropriate managerial skills. Hiring relatives reduces the selection pool. Moreover, even when there is managerial talent in the family, aging leaders may not acknowledge it. The world is changing quickly, and a leader guided more by family interests than by externalities may not be as quick to gauge and respond to environmental changes. Growing uncertainties of globalization may increase family strife and disrupt the firm.

The Effects of Increased Business Participation on the Extended Family

Growing desire to expand into high value-added industries like automotives has altered traditional family-ownership patterns. For example, Indonesia's Raja Garuda Mas Group financed expansion in the pulp and paper products industry by consolidating factories under Asia Pacific Resources International Holdings. Following the consolidation, billionaire founder Sukanto Tanoto took the company public and subsequently raised $150 million on equity while maintaining 60 percent family ownership (Asia's competing capitalisms, 1995). Public ownership exposes business practices to people outside the family.

Peter Drucker (1994b) believes challenges for the overseas Chinese multinational will include: a) the founders are aging, and successors have grown up in a different world; b) in order to grow, the multinational will have to engage in joint ventures with all manner of foreigners; and c) growth is impeded by relying on clan membership alone—multinationals will grow by hiring and maintaining talented people, regardless of their family connections. Overt conflict is unusual among ethnic Chinese, but it may increase as younger family members become educated outside their own countries.

The Effects of Increased Business Participation on SMEs

The presence of global SMEs increases the diversity of organizations in the global market-place. Most assume that smaller firms operate in different ways than larger firms, but this has only recently been explored in studies of SME internationalization (Coviello and McAuley, 1999; Knight and Cavusgil, 2004). Like their larger counterparts, leaders of small firms also find that the constantly shifting parameters of industry competition create opportunities for boundary transcendence. Many countries have reduced restrictions and stimulated business start-ups. Additionally, improvements in information technology facilitate worldwide matches between investors and people with business ideas. These technological improvements decrease some of the uncertainties associated with start-ups by providing more information to entrepreneur and investor alike.

Small firms traditionally challenge conventional management practices with their creativity. While some of these managerial challenges can reshape how or where work is organized—recall that Logitech set up headquarters in more than one country—others alter external conditions. For example, small global firms increasingly raise equity capital with direct sales of shares while others tap into venture capital networks. These practices expand and stretch options for raising capital.

THE GLOBAL COMMUNITY FOR BUSINESS

Shareholders own stock or equities in the firm. Together with employees and managers, shareholders have a very direct stake in the firm's performance. The demands these "owners" make on any given company depends in part on traditions in the company's nation of origin. Globalization is altering those traditions in two ways. First, around the world, shareholders have begun to demand a greater voice in business governance. Second, stakeholder demands worldwide also have escalated. Both of these trends affect global businesses.

Shareholder Activism

Shareholder activism has escalated worldwide. In Europe and in Asia, more individuals are shareholders because of privatization. In Europe, shareholders who previously remained silent increasingly question executive pay packages and poor economic or managerial performance (Viotzthum, 1995). Shareholders monitor company decisions, and react negatively when surprised by company decisions or performance. Individual shareholders disrupt annual meetings or initiate anti-corporate media campaigns to influence organizational activities. Poor corporate performance from 2000–2002 and corporate scandals and upsets at Worldcom, Andersen, Merrill Lynch, Alcatel, Vivendi, ABB, Deutsche Telekom, Ahold, and Martha Stewart (to name only a few) motivate individual shareholders to voice their concerns.

Siemens and its Shareholders

In 1997, SGZ-Bank in Frankfurt ranked companies according to how friendly they are toward shareholders. Siemens finished 26th among 27 German companies. In response, Siemens AG began to sharpen its focus on shareholders and erase its reputation for inefficiencies. To do so, it set up a system to measure different business segments in terms of value creation, introduced performance-based pay, spun off businesses in which it could not be a world leader, downsized, and became more aggressive in marketing its products and services.

Source material: Greg Steinmetz (1998, Feb. 19). Siemens AG remembers its shareholders. *The Wall Street Journal*, p. A17.

In some cases individual shareholders organize others to increase their influence on company decisions.

> ### Shareholder Activism
>
> Sophie L'Helias organizes alliances of individual shareholders to nudge French firms toward shareholder value. If management is not responsive to shareholders Ms. L'Helias might solicit proxy votes from small shareholders. In the case of the Eurotunnel, Ms. L'Helias's magazine advertisement won replies from 25,000 shareholders. She used their clout to threaten a veto for any Eurotunnel initiative that did not treat shareholders fairly. Ms. L'Helias trained in law in Paris, but earned an MBA and a second law degree in the US. This education provides a grounding in governance much broader than found in a single nation.
>
> Source material: Fair shares. (1997, Feb. 15) *The Economist*, p. 65.

Individual shareholder activism is on the rise, but the main pressure on corporate governance worldwide is from institutional shareholders, for example pension and mutual funds, and from INGOs. These usually are well-capitalized and well-organized groups, such as TIAA/CREF, Hermes, the Association of British Insurers, Deutsche Boerse, and Association Française de la Gestion Financière, all of which hold equities in companies worldwide. NGOs also monitor corporate activities and encourage transparency. For example, the Foundation for the Investigation of Corporate Information (SOBI) filed a suit against Reed Elsevier PLC, claiming that it had wrongfully adjusted the amount of goodwill in its 2001 report and thereby had artificially boosted its earnings. Since 1993 INGO Transparency International has reported annually on the extent of corporate transparency found within nations; this information can be found on their web site www.transparency.org.

In the UK and the US, over 50 percent of the equity of the largest 25 companies is held by financial institutions, such as pension funds and investors' groups. In Japan, France, and Germany, a much greater percentage of equity is cross-held by banks and corporations. However, the trend in the latter three nations and around the world is greater ownership by and accountability to institutional investors (The global investor and corporate governance, 2001).

Institutional shareholders increasingly intervene in company decisions. The International Corporate Governance Network lists five activities their members pursue (ICGN, 2000):

- They annually send corporate governance guidelines to every company in which they invest.
- They regularly meet with companies in which they invest.
- They use media management to let the press know institutional investor opinions on company activities.
- They take direct action such as publishing annual lists of companies to be targeted for corporate governance practices.
- They create alliances with local investors and try to learn from them about key issues in local markets.

Increased shareholder activism has forced some CEOs to resign; mergers that favor one group over another have been blocked; and most companies have become increasingly aware that shareholders monitor their activities. Two divergent views on the role of shareholders are the Rhine view and the Anglo-Saxon view; each is described below.

The Rhine Model versus the Anglo-Saxon Model

Shareholder activism as described above tends to focus primarily on wealth creation and stockholder benefits according to what some call the "Anglo-Saxon" model (Albert et al., 1993). This model asks organizations to emphasize financial returns to shareholders. In contrast, the Rhine perspective calls on corporations to govern themselves by balancing the interests of profits with social benefits. The "Rhine" model places short-term shareholder interests behind longer-term interests of the company, its employees, and society. For example, Philips Electronics NV cited shareholder value as a reason to restructure the company, and paper and packaging firm KNP BT cited shareholder interests when it withdrew financial support from its money-losing KNP Leykam division (Schiffrin, 1996).

The Anglo-Saxon model appears to be dominant among individual and institutional shareholders. The Rhine model is more often adopted by CSOs and NGOs whose members believe that companies have social as well as profit obligations. One example of the latter occurred in 2001 when Friends of the Earth introduced a shareholder resolution requiring the company to adopt clean energy rather than fossil fuels. Shareholder resolutions worldwide are increasingly sponsored by individual or institutional shareholders and by NGOs. These activities reflect increased stakeholder activism.

Stakeholder Activism

Direct stakeholders are employees, unions, managers, and owners who are affected directly by firm activities. Less direct stakeholders might include governments in the immediate geographic community where an organization operates or the community where the company's products are sold. Also counted among indirect stakeholders are groups like Friends of the Earth that attempt to influence business activities. Indirect stakeholder groups believe they have a stake in the organization because they or issues they represent are affected by corporate decisions and activities. An environmental group like Friends of the Earth believes that fossil fuels pollute the earth, and thus it believes itself to be a stakeholder for fuel companies.

The important trend with respect to stakeholder activism is that many more individuals and groups perceive themselves to have a stake in company decisions. This increases worldwide scrutiny of corporations. In Japan, for example, where outside influences have had limited historical impact on firms, businesses are the subjects of greater stakeholder pressure (Steadman et al., 1995) coming from outside forces. For example, foreigners held 18.3 percent of Japanese stocks by value in March 2002, up from about 4 percent a decade ago (Scandals reduce US sparkle as icon of marketplace ideas, 2002). Outside investors are knowledgeable about corporate governance practices worldwide, and they pressure Japanese firms to adopt best practices.

The two trends reviewed above influence business activities. Table 4.5 shows how these concerns are reflected in national legislative activities of business activities. As a group, these legislative changes reflect a trend for greater corporate transparency and adoption of global more than local practices, for example adoption of International Accounting Standards. The next section looks at how influences such as investor activism and legal changes reshape management traditions.

Table 4.5 *Laws governing corporate governance*

Nation	Effects on Corporate Governance
France	The Viernot Report led French companies to appoint independent directors and separate the duties of Chairman of the Board and CEO.
Germany	Proposals of the 2001 Cromme Commission urges listed German companies to set up independent audit committees. Large companies are switching to International Accounting Standards.
Hong Kong	The government adopted stringent measures in 2002 to promote corporate transparency. Behaviors that once were accepted, e.g., insider trading, now are criminal offenses.
Italy	Government rules attack the tradition of corporate control via "shell" companies. This is forcing secretive companies to be more transparent.
Japan	The Japanese commercial code was amended in 2001, giving businesses the choice of adopting US-style corporate practices such as independent auditing and compensation committees.
US	The 2002 Sarbanes-Oxley Act introduced an array of new rules requiring more accountability for top executives and board members; tougher criminal penalties for violations; and more disclosure of off-balance sheet transactions

Source material: John Rossan, Jack Ewing and Brian Bremner (2002, May 6) The corporate cleanup goes global. *Business Week*, pp. 80–81.

MANAGEMENT TRADITION AND CHANGE

The priorities, preferences, interests, and practices among firms in leading industrialized nations differ. Some of the major differences are summarized in Table 4.6:

Table 4.6 *National models of businesses*

US Model	Japanese Model	Western European Model
Emphasis on economic returns to shareholders	Emphasis on long-term growth; little or no influence by shareholders	Emphasis on cultural and humanistic values; stakeholders like government have more clout than shareholders
Product versus customer orientation	Quality orientation to customers' needs and continuous improvement	Customers to be satisfied include stakeholders
Compete universally for short-run economic returns	Compete externally and cooperate internally to achieve market share	Compete and cooperate globally and locally to balance short- and long-run objectives
Individualism expressed in organizational autonomy and individual actions	Collectivism and groupism creates primary loyalty to the firm and the work group over self	Obligation to sacrifice some economic gains for the community quality of life
Cultural diversity viewed as a legal challenge	Cultural diversity viewed as a threat	Cultural diversity viewed as business as usual
Personal and professional life interrelate	Personal and professional life are the same	Personal and professional life are distinct

Source material: Bruno Dufour (1994, Winter) Dealing in diversity: Management education in Europe. *Selections*, pp. 7–15.

Table 4.5 shows that corporate governance activities differ based on nation of origin. These differences will make it difficult for companies to converge toward common practices. However, Ira Millstein (2000) suggests four fundamentals of corporate governance that can transcend national boundaries. These are:

■ Fairness that protects shareholder rights and contract enforceability with providers.
■ Transparency that requires timely disclosure of information concerning corporate financial performance, for example international accounting standards and comparable disclosure requirements.
■ Accountability to clarify governance roles and responsibilities and that support voluntary efforts to align shareholder and managerial interests.
■ Responsibility to ensure that corporations comply with the laws and regulations that reflect a society's values.

Global Demands and Limits of Tradition

Many firms respond to external pressures by borrowing managerial traditions from other nations. An ideal governance system could be one that safeguards against abuses in the Anglo-Saxon model by combining longer-term and more cooperative relationships found in Japan, Latin America, and Western Europe with market incentives and safeguards (Kester, 1996). Global challenges outlined above create more rather than fewer pressures to wrestle efficiencies from organizations; more rather than less need to value diversity; compelling reasons to develop skills useful to managing tangibles and intangibles; and less room for error.

Growing Demands for Global Community

Shareholder and stakeholder activism draws businesses into relationships with representatives of both government and civil society organizations. Juanita Brown (1992) suggests that growing emphasis on global community will lead organizations to adopt new corporate models with features such as the following:

- The corporation as a dynamic community
- linked by networks of interdependent teams composed of
- self-managing people with diverse characteristics and talents
- guided by a shared purpose, and
- leaders committed to continuous learning and improvement
- in service of maximum long-term customer satisfaction, employee and shareholder enrichment, and the health of the larger society.

Many firms combine elements from different traditions to create hybrids. Because they are experiments, some will succeed and others will fail. For example, combining the advantages of both hierarchies and horizontal organization may make it possible for employees to be both generalists and specialists, for organizations to take on characteristics of being both big and small, for strategies to be both global and local. At the same time, coordination can become more difficult since much depends on shared understandings that may not be in place. These hybrids are inherently "messy" because they tolerate uncertainties. Additionally hybrids could replicate the worst qualities of multiple systems rather than the best of each. For example, when hierarchies and horizontal structures are combined, the worst case is distributed decision-making where everyone is accountable but no one has authority. Some businesses will cling to tradition, others will abandon them, and still others will create hybrids that draw on best practices around the world. In this way, global interconnections will multiply.

CHAPTER SUMMARY

Organizations of every size and shape populate the global landscape for business. Global giants are best known worldwide because many offer branded products. SMEs increasingly compete in global businesses and industries. Some of these are global start-ups, but others may be born-again global businesses.

Emerging global players in the business world include Latin American businesses, entrepreneurs, women, family-owned businesses, and overseas Chinese and overseas Indians. Each of these types of organizations introduces different values, perspectives, and traditions to global management.

As diverse businesses enter the global marketplace, the "natural advantages" of size and scope may erode for global giants. At the same time, new entrants to global business also face their own challenges.

The Anglo-Saxon governance model emphasizes shareholder or owner interests above all others. The Rhine model emphasizes collaboration between businesses and stakeholders such that the business serves social as well as wealth-creation needs. These perspectives are in direct conflict, and further confuse the management task for global leaders.

Shareholders are increasingly active, placing growing demands on businesses to be profitable. At the same time, stakeholders in all sectors and especially members of CSOs demand that companies be more socially responsive.

REVIEW AND DISCUSSION QUESTIONS

1 Does globalization make it more or less likely that SMEs will complete worldwide? Why or why not?

2 Many global brands have very short and easy to recall names such as Sony, Exxon, Acura, Coca-Cola, Prada, BMW, GAP, Canon, Avon, and Adidas. What are other common characteristics of global brands?

3 Many theories of management emerged from the study and experiences of US firms. In what ways has this influence shaped business expectations in a global world? Identify three concepts presented in this chapter and describe the ways they reflect US influence.

4 Compare the corporate model to the community model of business. Consider how the differences between the two are likely to affect people, processes, and organizational structures in a global firm.

Chapter 5
GLOBAL INDUSTRIES

STARBUCKS EXPANDS

In 2003 Starbucks announced plans to acquire Seattle Coffee—parent firm for Seattle's Best Coffee and Torrefazione Italia. The market response was both joy and consternation (though not necessarily in that order). SBC and Terrafazione aficionados mourned perceived losses, industry competitors saw new forces looming, and anti-consolidationists cried "foul." Starbucks shareholders and many business analysts were delighted. This event represents a global industry shift of consolidation and responses show there are varying perspectives on the same industry activity.

The Consolidation Argument

Starbucks is coming late to the acquisitions party. Most of the $3+ trillion in worldwide foreign direct investment since 1998 comes from mergers and acquisitions in a wide range of industries: advertising, aerospace, paper and pulp, pharmaceuticals, energy, telecommunications, and steel are a few. By comparison Starbucks' $72 million domestic purchase of Seattle Coffee is small. But as a symbol, it highlights growing and global concerns about industry consolidation.

Among other things, critics perceive that industry consolidation concentrates the power of global corporations. Some believe corporations leverage power to enforce wage inequalities that further enhance their wealth. This argument is usually followed by concerns that weak governments, civil society, the already marginalized, and so on, lose economic ground. Others believe global firms hasten cultural homogeneity which they see as problematic. On the other hand is evidence from Ghemawat and Ghadar (2000) whose study of globalizing industries shows industry consolidation has *decreased* since 1945. The "I hate Starbucks" website notwithstanding, the fact is that Starbucks purchases only 1 percent of the world's coffee beans.

Among benefits from global M&A activities are: foreign direct investors pay their workers more than the national average and spend more on R&D in countries where they invest. As a foreign direct investor, Starbucks employs 62,000 people in 30 countries. These 'partners' (Starbucks' term for employees) receive benefits that include stock ownership and training. Starbucks expands internationally by partnering with local businesses. Both jobs and partnerships stimulate economic development at home and abroad.

Companies like Starbucks demonstrate another trend among global firms. They increasingly enhance the quality of life with community-building activities. An example is the Starbucks/Conservation International partnership to encourage shade-grown coffee development. Starbucks' trademarked Commitment to Origins program offers Fair Trade-certified coffee and purchases single-origin coffee directly from the farmer. These and other activities deserve mention when weighing the pros and cons of global business expansion.

The Competition Argument

Starbucks purchased Seattle Coffee to establish a beachhead in the wholesale segment of the coffee industry. Thus, existing firms in the wholesale coffee industry face new competition with Starbucks' acquisition. At the same time, Starbucks' entry could stimulate ▶

growth in the wholesale segment of the specialty coffee industry. At best it could follow the explosive growth pattern that satisfied CEO Howard Schulz's vision for retail coffee. Twenty years ago coffee was a declining industry—a dog—but Starbucks is largely responsible for industry growth that now generates billions in annual revenues. Starbucks is only one beneficiary of an expanded industry that includes firms like Gloria Jean, Aroma Therapy, Coffee Republic, World Coffee, Caffè Nero, and "mom and pop" coffee stores around the world.

With lamentable exceptions, good retail coffee is available almost everywhere. But good coffee is rarely found in outlets that buy wholesale beans, such as universities, places of worship, supermarkets, or parks. As occurs whenever competition shifts, some existing competitors in wholesale coffee will disappear. Companies that seek to avoid that alternative will be motivated to streamline and improve operations. New opportunities are likely to emerge for the entrepreneurs who are the backbone of every economy. In this sense, competition is good for business development, and it is good for Starbucks whose value will rest on a broader base.

CHAPTER OVERVIEW

This chapter explores industry globalization to illustrate world changes. It starts by presenting alternative ways to describe an industry, and then looks at reasons for industry globalization. Measures of industry globalization are reviewed. The chapter also examines ways that global industries change. The chapter examines five different ways leaders monitor their industry to analyze coming change and identify distinctive advantages for their firms. Finally, the chapter examines perspectives on national versus business competitiveness.

DEFINING AN INDUSTRY

An industry is composed of all the organizations operating within it. Its essential shape results from activities of many actors, including those of competitors, buyers, suppliers, lenders, governments, terrorists, and others. There are many different types of industries, and there are many ways to classify them. For example, industries can be categorized as product or service industries. They can be cyclical like heating oil which is purchased mostly during cold weather or noncyclical due to year-round demand. Durability is another way to classify an industry. Durables are products like automobiles that last many years, whereas shampoo or soap are nondurable because their value is depleted relatively quickly. Industries can be basic ones found in most nations such as textiles or agriculture or high value-added ones concentrated in advanced economies.

> **Value-added Industries**
>
> The value a business adds to a product is determined by subtracting the total cost of production such as labor, materials, administrative overhead, or sales expenses from price. A high value-added product results when a product's price far exceeds its actual costs such as occurs in industries like aircraft, heavy equipment, electronics, automobiles, or fashion clothing. When firms from developing economies initiate trade relationships, traditionally they have done so with low value-added goods such as textiles or agricultural products. For low value-added products there is usually little gap between price and production costs.

There can be significant differences between industries, such as cost, that help define the industry. For example, high initial costs of nuclear-power production make it difficult for new firms to enter this industry. As a result, nuclear-power plants are often fully or partially government owned, sales are to industrial users, planning is long range, and there are few competitors. By contrast, the pet-food industry is organized by the private sector, and product sales are to consumers' owners whose fickle tastes demand constant innovation in relatively short product-planning cycles. The costs of producing pet food are relatively low, competitors can be many, and there are many substitutes. These examples show there are many ways to differentiate one industry from another.

Despite differences among them, a commonality among industries is that almost all are increasingly affected by global activities. Whether located in basic industries like chemicals, food, and textiles, extractive industries such as oil, aluminum, coal, and water, or value-added industries, industry opportunities increasingly are defined by myriad global activities. Industry globalization is a complex process whose outcome is shaped by many diverse actors.

Industries are Shaped by Many Activities

Opportunities within any given industry are usually limited, and managers compete for them by developing or promoting unique organizational competencies. The combined activities of these managers help shape the character of an industry and as a result industries can differ significantly from one another, especially in terms of rivalry. For example, fierce competitive rivalry between Coca-Cola and PepsiCo in the soft-drink beverage industry continued abroad with head-to-head combat over bottling in Latin America, skirmishes in Eastern Europe, and warfare in the bottled-water beverage segment. Cost-cutting and pre-emptive strikes by these rivals make the industry more volatile. Competitive activities make it difficult for other soft-drink beverage firms to predict or plan for the industry, and they demonstrate that would-be entrants also must be fierce competitors. Virgin Cola demonstrated competitive ferocity in their failed 1990s attempt to penetrate Coke/Pepsi hegemony in the soft-drink industry. Industries such as athletic footwear and most global team sports also are characterized by fierce interorganizational rivalry.

Little Kola Real Delivers a Competitive Punch

In the late 1980s Eduardo and Mirtha Añaños recognized a business opportunity in Peru's cola markets. Rebel forces, leaving the rural populace cola-less, routinely hijacked Coca-Cola trucks. The Añaños mortgaged their home and started a small business making cola for local markets. By 2003 their Kola Real product had become a genuine threat to both Coca-Cola and Pepsi in not only Peru but also Ecuador, Venezuela, and Mexico. Interestingly, Kola Real's low-cost product has gained market share because global giants like Wal-Mart increased price sensitivity throughout Latin America. The Añaños family used this approach to create a competitive cost advantage. Only time will tell if they are able to sustain their advantage. But what is clear is that rivalry in the industry persists. Further, this example shows that sometimes industry change comes from outside the industry, in this case political activities.

Source material: David Luhnow and Chad Terhune (2003, Oct. 27) A low-budget cola shakes up markets south of the border. *The Wall Street Journal*, pp. A1, A18.

Competitors in many other industries are far less rivalrous than those involved in the "cola wars." For example, Samsung and Sony collaborated to develop flat-screen televisions. Global pharmaceutical firms also collaborate with one another, although usually not on product development. Significant examples of the latter's collaborative activities include HIV/AIDs drug programs for many African nations and unified resistance to Internet sales. In recent years, global air carriers joined alliances such as OneWorld or Star Alliance that permit member code sharing. These and other activities by industry competitors shape the nature of the industry as surely as rivalry shapes the beverage industry.

Industries also are shaped by activities on the part of buyers, suppliers, lenders, governments, and other actors like nongovernmental organizations. For example, growing pressures on companies to be good global citizens motivated Coca-Cola to extend its product line with a vitamin-fortified drink for Botswana; when other competitors followed the same strategy, the industry expanded to accommodate healthy products. Similarly, opportunities in the global coffee industry have been reshaped by environmental concerns and consumer demands for free-trade and shade-grown coffee. These pressures may help explain collaborative activities described in the Starbucks case.

Monitoring Industry Conditions

Even within domestic markets, many organizations find it difficult to monitor the economic, political, cultural, and other factors that reshape industries. It is often difficult to obtain good information about an industry's future because competitors tend to be secretive and buyers rarely announce their intentions. Gathering external information is costly in terms of employee time or consultant costs. These and similar monitoring challenges compound globally because competitors are distant and cannot be observed daily. Additionally, customers, lenders, and inputs can be located a world away, creating challenges for managers to keep up with the events that affect them. The result can be industry shifts that sometimes seem to occur almost overnight.

Managers who realize that they are affected by factors outside their control usually concentrate greatest attention on external environments that they believe affect them. Often they monitor externalities that have historically affected them. For example, a global corn processor like Archer Daniels Midland whose success has historically depended on weather patterns is likely to look first to the natural environment to anticipate future opportunities. Businesses in the machine-tool industry might look first to economic indicators, because a good economy usually is followed by capital expenditures. However, because the boundaries and barriers of industries have the capacity to shift due to global events, managers also must recognize where future dependencies lie. Thus, it is not enough to remain fixed on industry history or present industry condition. It also is critical to monitor the entire global horizon to identify trends in other industries that are likely to impact on the firm. Relevant trends emerge not just from within a given industry but also from other industries and from other global environments.

REASONS FOR INDUSTRY GLOBALIZATION

Throughout the 1980s, globalization of capital, knowledge, and technology made it easier for businesses worldwide to participate in industries previously closed to them. National industrial policies also encouraged large and small organizations worldwide to enter industries previously dominated by Western or Japanese firms. Together, the collective activities of these myriad firms have reshaped the nature of many industries, making many more global in scope. Development and production of the Mazda Miata provides an example of the global nature of the automotive industry, but many other industries similarly finance, design, produce, and sell worldwide.

The Miata MX-5
Financing for the Miata came from Tokyo and New York; it was designed in California but the first prototype was created in Worthing, England. The automobile is assembled in Michigan and Mexico using advanced electronic components invented in New Jersey and fabricated in Japan. Technological, economic, and cultural tastes on a global scale have combined to produce global demand for this sporty little car.

Increased global participation on the part of companies from developing economies is only one reason for growth among industry competitors. Slowing growth in developed economies motivates domestic firms to look beyond their borders for business opportunities. Increased participation of firms in a wide variety of industries worldwide led theorists to argue that industry-specific events occurring in one country were likely to be replicated in other countries. Thus firms faced an industry environment where economic forces were dominated not by single nations but rather by worldwide collective economic forces (Bartlett and Ghoshal, 1992a). Efforts followed to examine the characteristics of a global industry.

MEASURES OF INDUSTRY GLOBALIZATION

Michael Porter defined a global industry as one "in which a firm's competitive position in one country is significantly affected by its position in other countries or vice versa" (1990: 18). Porter recommended that firms create an advantage in these global industries by integrating activities on a worldwide basis. According to Porter, globalization of industry competition had become more the rule than the exception as early as 1986, brought about by increased interconnections among domestic industries. He suggested that those with a high industry trade ratio (Porter, 1980) are more global, and can be assessed according to the amount of industry influence that comes from outside domestic markets.

Another measure of industry globalization is intrafirm flows of resources (Kobrin, 1991) or resources that move between subsidiaries of the same company. Using product measures from 1982 data, Kobrin discovered that intrafirm flows accounted for 25 percent of international sales for ten industries studied. Motor vehicles were the most global industry followed by communications equipment, electronics including semiconductors, computers and office machinery, and farm machinery. Comparisons between Kobrin's 1982 and 1986 data showed dramatic increases in global integration for many industries. Kobrin's work provides a useful way of thinking about global industries because it indicates that global integration within and across boundaries is shaped not within single sectors but through relationships between global technology, global industries, global culture, and other environments. Integration of the type measured in Kobrin's study continued through the last decade.

According to Govindarajan and Gupta (2000), other key indicators of industry globalization are: cross-border investment as a ratio of total industry capital invested; proportion of industry revenues generated by players competing in all the major regions of the world; and cross-border trade within the industry as a ratio of total worldwide production. Using 1996 OECD data, these authors note that the manufacturing index was higher for the computer industry than for automotives or pharmaceuticals on cross-border trade. Accordingly, they argue that the computer industry was more global than either the automotive or pharmaceuticals industries.

A 1999 UNCTAD measure used the magnitude of cross-border mergers and acquisitions to identify ten industries where national border transcendence was particularly apparent. These included life insurance, radio telephone and telephone communications, pharmaceuticals, commercial banks, electric services, cigarettes, and man-made organic fibers (*World Investment Report*, 2000).

Makhija et al. (1997) argue that industry globalization is a complex process that can be better conceptualized as a continuum that ranges from low to high industry globalization. On the left hand side of the continuum would be the multi-domestic industry wherein virtually all company value-added activities are located in a single country. Until recently, a perfect example of this was the funeral industry which operated within nations. The country-based approach for this industry means that each company has few opportunities to develop activities linking them with industries in other countries.

Second on the continuum would be a simple global industry that has some or limited external linkages, but where the focus remains on the domestic market. The third position would reflect higher industry globalization or integrated global activities; this occurs when value-added activities of firms are significantly driven by the need for global scale. For example, the furniture industry is increasingly global, driven by low labor costs in

China and improved information technology. Finally, industries that are highest on globalization are ones where companies integrate most or all value-added activities with similar industries in other countries; these are fully global industries. According to these authors, a systematic analysis of industry globalization should have three attributes:

1 It should explain the combined effects of all firms within the industry.
2 It should be able to distinguish industries with significant international linkages in other countries.
3 It should measure functional integration within the firm of value-added activities the firm conducts across national boundaries.

These authors measured globalization in chemical and manufacturing sectors, examining published data on a total of 27 industries represented by four-digit International Standard Industrial Classification Codes (ISIC). The time frame was 17 years (1970–1986) and cross-national comparisons were for the five largest OECD countries: the US, Japan, Germany, France, and the UK. The results shown in Table 5.1 reveal that only three worldwide industries were fully global at that point: industrial chemicals, fertilizers and pesticides, and resins and plastics. The authors explain their findings by noting that some industries that seem global, such as aircraft, are more or less global depending on the nation of origin. For example, Boeing manufacturing for commercial aircraft is far more global than its defense manufacturing. Thus, the student of industry globalization needs to clearly distinguish between industry segments when studying company activities.

Table 5.1 *Examples of multidomestic to fully global industries*

Multidomestic	Simple Global	Integrated Global	Fully Global
Cutlery and hand tools	Automobiles	Engines and turbines	Industrial chemicals
Structural metal products	Motorcycles	Specialized industrial machinery	Fertilizers and pesticides
Furniture	Watches	Office and computing machinery	Resins and plastics
Agricultural machinery		Radio and telecommunications equipment	
Metal and woodworking machinery		Shipbuilding	
Electrical industrial machinery		Railroad	
		Aircraft	
		Photographic and optical goods	

Source material: Mona V. Makhija, Kwangsoo Kim and Sandra D. Williamson (1997, 4th quarter) Measuring globalization of industries using a national industry approach: Empircal evidence across five countries and over time. *Journal of International Business Studies*, pp. 679–710.

Using multiple measures, the Makhija et al. study illustrates several important points about industry globalization. That is, when compared, some industries are more global than others. Second, some global industries such as resins and plastics attract little public attention. Third, it shows industry globalization to be a process in which the degree of industry globalization differs. Finally, this study illustrates that industry globalization is a growing trend. Accordingly, we can reasonably expect that many more industries will become measurable on a continuum of industry globalization.

Industry Globalization

Many think that industry globalization is a relatively new phenomenon. But nineteenth-century entrepreneur Frederic Tudor proves us wrong. Tudor faced considerable ridicule when he decided to combine technological innovation and marketing skills to globalize a simple process: ice making. Tudor harvested ice in Massachusetts, then sold it to nations as geographically distant as India and Cuba. Tudor also encouraged bartenders to use ice in drinks, and thereby created a following for iced drinks. In this instance, Tudor created a demand and then he satisfied it with a product that was relatively easy to replicate. In the process, he created an industry with a following that demands iced drinks.

Source material: Gavin Weightman (2003) *The Frozen-Water Trade*. New York: Hyperion.

WAYS GLOBAL INDUSTRIES CHANGE

Measures above show global industries can be assessed in many different ways. Moreover, this is not a static process. Subsequent to Kobrin's study, services as well as manufacturing industries went global. Advertising, consulting, engineering, leisure and tourism, forest products, chemicals, and steel are by virtue of sales more global than domestic, and smaller industries such as watches, copiers, pet foods, cereals, eyeglasses, and athletic shoes also have gone global.

As is true for global firms, some industries are well known and others attract little interest. For example, the insurance industry generates some $3 trillion worldwide in revenues, but few insurance companies are well known. The worldwide pet-food market amounted to about $30 billion in 2001, and ice-cream was a $20 billion industry. According to the International Trade Center, a monitoring group linked to the United Nations, the global organic-farming industry grows by as much as 20 percent per year, particularly in advanced economies and where recent effects of animal diseases such as mad-cow and hoof-and-mouth have been most severe, for example England and Europe (Boston, 2002). The porcelain toilet industry is global, as is the $9.2 million industry in human-hair swatches. Other industries are global because they encompass companies whose products are globally branded.

Just as boundaries of nation-states, economies, and cultures are increasingly permeable, industry boundaries also are subject to rapid change. Industries converge, disintermediate, integrate, contract or relocate, and dissolve. These industry changes are brought about in many ways, including competitor activities, technological changes such as computers, changes in cultural norms and habits, politics, and economic conditions, to name a few. Each industry alteration creates new challenges for existing firms and opportunities for those able to define, develop, or grow firms and industries.

Industry Convergence

Industry convergence occurs when autonomous industries overlap. This is a lateral form of industry convergence shown by the "edutainment" industry that combines software with books and "infotainment" made possible by fiber optic telephones and television coaxial cables. Pharmaceutical and cosmetics industries overlap to produce "cosmeceuticals," and natural foods and pharmaceuticals blend to create "neutriceuticals."

Industry Disintermediation

A second way that industries change is disintermediation in which processes or traditional industry structures are reshaped (Hamel and Prahalad, 1994) to reduce or sometimes eliminate the role of intermediaries. In the airline industry, disintermediation occurs when buyers use the Internet to purchase tickets; it occurs in equity markets when investors circumvent traders; it occurs in retailing when consumers make purchases on line instead of visiting a retail store. Some of these changes create opportunities for "infomediaries" that specialize in on-line information management (Evans and Wurster, 2000), showing that sometimes disintermediation reduces industry entry barriers.

Disintermediation affects many within industries. They reshape jobs when intermediaries such as travel agents, stockbrokers, and retailers lose jobs or when Internet service agents gain them. They affect organizational processes when work is shifted from in-person to telephone sales. They affect organizational structures when the jobs themselves are outsourced to new locations around the world. New infrastructures are needed to manage employees in new places, and existing structures may be downsized.

Industry Integration

Unlike industry convergence that usually involves blending of two different industries, integration often comes about when competitors link themselves to one another or to suppliers in the same industry. Below we examine three integration modes important to globalization: consolidation via mergers and acquisitions; alliances; and production-chain management.

Consolidation

Whether motivated by costs, efforts to establish technological leadership, fear of industry shakeout, or other factors, consolidation tends to reduce the number of competitors in an industry.

Mergers and acquisitions usually result in industry consolidation. The $1.2 trillion posted in worldwide 1997 mergers and acquisitions reached $2.489 trillion in 1998 and $3.4 trillion in 1999 before declining in 2000 and dropping to $560 billion by 2003. At least initially, integration on the scale of Daimler-Benz/Chrysler and Volkswagen/BMW in the auto industry, Ciba-Geigy/Sandoz in the pharmaceuticals industry, and WorldCom/MCI in the telecommunications service industry generated a sense that we live in a "winner take all" society (Frank and Cook, 1995). This belief itself may have motivated more mergers and acquisitions, especially among firms that feared they would be left behind. However, other firms like Luxottica had a specific plan in mind.

Luxottica's Growth

Luxottica Group S.p.A is a leading maker and seller of eyeglass frames, but 30 years ago it was a small Italian start-up supplying products to other companies. Chairman Leonardo Del Vecchio grew his company by taking some big risks that paid off. In 1970 he took a daring step by competing directly against companies he'd been supplying. Then, instead of outsourcing research and development, payroll, or distribution, Del Vecchio vertically integrated so that he owned every phase of the research to sales process. An example is that Del Vecchio himself designed the machines he first used to automate frame manufacture. More recently, Del Vecchio has grown through acquisitions that enhance further integration. For example, his purchase of LensCrafters gave him a retail base for optical stores. Later purchase of Sunglass Hut International provided a new product line and also a new outlet. Luxottica manufactures and sells its frames in more than 120 nations, generating more than $3 billion in annual revenues. But the company is still 70 percent owned by founder Leonardo Del Vecchio.

Source material: Sharen Kindel (1995, Aug.) *Hemispheres*, pp. 31–34; Luxottica Group S.p.A. (2003) http://www.hoover.com/luxottica (accessed Nov 19, 2003).

Alliances

A second approach to industry integration involves long-term or temporary alliances with competitors. As compared to mergers that require structural changes and often impede flexibility, Peter Drucker (1999) believes that alliances provide a more flexible approach to managing in a global world. For example, Sony and Samsung collaborate on flat-screen television technology. In these and other cases, firms are enjoined to collaborate to compete (Perlmutter and Heenan, 1986). Others engage in temporary alliances. An example is United Airlines which ended its code-sharing arrangement with British Airways when the former was granted its own London route.

Strategic alliances also can include collaborative arrangements between businesses from multiple countries, governments and not-for-profits partnering with businesses, and cooperation among firms that collaborate in one line of business and compete in another. On a national level European and US firms compete in the computer industry but collaborate to produce a new computer chip, and IBM and Apple compete in the personal computer market but collaborated in the lab to develop a non-DOS platform for personal computers. Some believe activities like these represent the death of competition as we know it (Moore, 1996), arguing for coopetition involving win/win solutions (Brandenburger and Nalebuff, 1996).

Links with Buyers and Suppliers

An important way to achieve worldwide integration is with links between the company and its buyers and suppliers. Some call this supply chain management, but Dicken defines this as production chain management, "a transactionally linked sequence of functions in which each stage adds value to the process of production of goods or services" (1998: 7). Dicken further notes there are two ways that production chains can develop: external production chains occur when a firm buys supplies from a second firm in a transactional exchange conducted in an open market; internal chains develop when a company uses a vertically integrated supply system where buying and selling is within the company's subsidiaries. As Dicken notes, company decisions about whether to use market or internal transactions continually shift, creating many different challenges for production chain coordination.

Value Chain Management

Another approach to integration with suppliers and buyers is value-chain management (Porter, 1986). Using the value chain, one looks at different firm activities to separate the primary ones such as operations, logistics, marketing and sales, and services, from those that are support activities, such as human resource management, structure, or R&D. Ideally, an analysis of each shows where value is added and where it is subtracted. The example below shows how grocer Tesco used value-chain analysis to enhance their operations.

Value-chain Analysis at Tesco
A value-chain analysis for global grocer Tesco tracked activities that provide a single can of carbonated cola for store shelves (Jones and Womack, 1996). Manufactured from Australian bauxite, the various stages of smelting, rolling, label application, cola addition, and sales took a total of 319 days. Only three hours of this time was spent in activities that added value to the firm's profits. The balance of time was expended in storage and transportation. This analysis then helps Tesco managers decide whether these activities are appropriate for the competitive market they face.

Value chains include all businesses that are part of the manufacture and production of a good or service. Following this chain helps managers recognize and repair weak links in the value chain. However, as knowledge is outsourced, it may be more appropriate to think of this more as a value network than a value chain. In other words, relationships with mediating organizations that provide value create richer, more complex relationships than a linear value chain. This network is doubtless more difficult to manage than a more linear one.

The Effects of Industry Integration

Chapter 1 reviewed evident concerns about industry consolidation and integration, suggesting that evidence for and results of industry integration are decidedly mixed. Based on their study of 20 industries over 40 years, Ghemawat and Ghadar (2000) concluded that industry consolidation does not result from global mergers, and that concentration in globalizing industries has decreased since 1945. A KPMG report indicates half of recent mergers destroyed company value while others had no measurable effect on parent's success (How mergers go wrong, 2000). A look at US global giants from 1984 to 1997 showed that equity value of them relative to assets was 9–17 percent lower than similar domestic companies, suggesting that globalization is far from a sure shot at profits (Click and Harrison, 2000). As a group data like these challenge assertions that industry consolidation is occurring or that it leads to company wealth and dominance.

It is likely that global M&A activity will continue, but at a more measured pace perhaps in cycles that track the pace of globalization. In other words, when globalization moves at a rapid pace, so will M&A activity, and both will slow at the same time. Finally, as has occurred in the past, M&A activity worldwide will usually be led by specific industries. For example, telecommunications sales led M&A lists in the late 1990s, but pharmaceuticals defined these activities in 2003. Both alliances and production chain activities seem to be on the rise, which also suggests that these forms of integration will remain important to global firms and industries.

Industry Contraction and Relocation

Diverse industry participation leads to contraction for some global industries. For example, despite growing worldwide demand for steel, the introduction of steel mini-mills reduced the number of manufacturers and an industry shake-out followed. Consumer acceptance of screw tops and plastic reduced cork demand that shrinks the cork industry. Contraction also can occur because of global shifts from outside the industry. For example, a 2001 advertising industry slowdown was due to the combined effects of economic contraction and loss of consumer confidence. The industry experienced its worst performance for the last 50 years.

Industries also relocate or are reshaped because of globalization. An example of reshaping occurred when Russia entered the global diamond industry to alter the dominant position De Beers had long held. Additionally, once it became evident that rebel groups were selling "blood" diamonds to fuel African civil wars, sales of Canadian diamonds increased. These shifts reshape the industry's public image, and bring new entrants to the industry. Growing worldwide demand for fresh fish is met less frequently by open sea fishing, and more by farmed fish. This creates industry substitution.

Low-cost labor has shifted much textile industry production to developing economies. At the same time, technological breakthroughs produce textiles with fewer people. Thus while textile sales increase, the number of companies needed to produce them decreases, shrinking the number of industry competitors. Some industries shrink because high-quality products do not need to be replaced so frequently. Patagonia aims to benefit the planet by producing long-lasting textiles. Thus we see that there are a number of ways that industry size can contract.

Industry Dissolution

Industries also can disappear altogether, usually because they are phased out by a new industry. Buggy whips are the classic example, but a more recent example is vacuum tube televisions and computers. These virtually disappeared with the advent of transistor technologies. Another is oven-cleaning products—the industry for these products is gradually disappearing with the advent of self-cleaning ovens. Hazel Henderson (1996) believes that whole industries and sectors could disappear with globalization. She argues that industries based on fossil fuels or those that pollute or create disposable products will be less desirable than sustainable ones. Examples of the latter include pollution control, natural foods, and waste recycling and reuse.

COMPANY LONGEVITY

Within any industry, the life of most firms is relatively short. For large US firms, life expectancy is 40–50 years, but most small firms in the US fail within one year of founding. According to Stratix Consulting Group, both Japanese and European firms have an average life expectancy of less than 13 years (How to live long and prosper, 1997). There are relatively few studies of long-lived firms, but among those reviewed below, success characteristics appear to be threefold: a clear strategy, investments in people, and luck. Industry may also be a factor. For example, one notes that among firms known as "Les Henokiens" (shown in Table 5.2), surviving firms often operate in industries like confections, alcoholic beverages, textiles, and construction supplies that have been important in every period of human history. Candidates for Les Henokiens must meet four conditions of membership: 1) the companies they own are in business for at least 200 years; 2) they are run by the founders' descendants; 3) the company enjoys sound financial health; and 4) the majority of capital is still held by the original family.

Table 5.2 *Les Henokiens*

Date of Foundation	Name	Headquarters	Businesses
718	Hoshi	Japan	Hotels
1460	Barovier & Toso	Italy	Glass products
1526	Beretta Corporation	Italy	Firearms
1551	Codorníu	Spain	Sparkling wines
1568	Poschinger Glashutte	Germany	Glass products
1613	Mellerio dits Meller	France	Jewelry
1637	Gekkeikan Sake Company Ltd.	Japan	Liquors
1639	Hugel & Fils	France	Vineyards
1664	Friedr. Schwarze	Germany	Liquors
1679	Viellard-Migeon & Cie.	France	Metal products
1680	Tissages Denantes	France	Textiles
1685	Maison Gradis	France	Wine
1690	Delamare Sovra	France	Wood products
1733	Fratelli Piacenza	Italy	Textiles
1745	Daciano Colbachini & Figli	Italy	Bells
1755	Marie Brizard & Roger International	France	Liquors
1757	Lanificio G.B. Conte	Italy	Textiles
1760	Griset	France	Metal products
1762	F.V. Möller	Germany	Metal products
1770	Silca	Italy	Keys and key-making equipment
1779	Ditta Bortolo Nardini	Italy	Distilleries
1783	Confetti Mario Pelino	Italy	Candies

Source material: The Henokiens Society: An association of bicentennial family-owned companies. http://www.Henokiens.com

Although not on the Les Henokiens list, Tiger Balm is another example of an old firm that is now global. Its success stimulates an emerging global industry for balms and ointments.

Tiger Balm Goes Global

Tiger Balm ointment is recognized today as a sports balm, but it got its start more than 130 years ago as an Asian cure-all for bodily aches and pains. Tiger Balm was first developed by a herbalist in Rangoon, Burma, who on his deathbed asked his sons to perfect the product. True to their promise, sons Aw Boon Haw and Aw Boon Par experimented to create the perfect product. They marketed from Burma to Singapore, drawing attention to the product with a car decorated with a tiger head and stripes, and building a customer base with free samples. This word-of-mouth approach to marketing created a huge customer base that eventually led to headquarters in Singapore and untold wealth for the brothers. Today Haw Par Healthcare Ltd. distributes the Tiger Balm product worldwide to over 100 countries on five continents. This is a small company that has stood the test of time.

Source material: http://www.tigerbalm.com

According to Arie de Geus, author of *The Living Company* (1997), long-lived firms are those that meet four conditions:

- their financial affairs are managed conservatively
- they are sensitive to their external environment and adapt appropriately
- they have a strong sense of cohesion around a common goal-set and are able to convey common values to succeeding generations of employees
- and they show internal tolerance that fosters creativity and camaraderie.

Unlike "economic" companies that expend their energy in achieving high economic returns over short time periods, the returns for de Geus's "living companies" are not correlated with maximized financial returns or with country or industry. But they survive. Thus, these studies suggest that survival over the long term is not a matter just of fiscal performance but of other, perhaps more qualitative criteria, including a clear vision of both internal and external capabilities and needs.

A globalizing industry environment creates demands for balancing among multiple and sometimes competing objectives and disparate findings. The process for discovering industry futures may begin with managers who ask why and "what if" type questions as they monitor conditions in their own and other industries.

SOURCES OF INDUSTRY CHANGE

Growing interdependence in global spheres makes it nearly impossible for firms to survive without interacting on a global level. In the aerospace industry, for example, access to capital, labor, and sales depend on global rather than domestic economies, global rather than domestic politics. Stephen Kobrin (1991) recognized that industries like automotives, microelectronics, and telecommunications were being forced toward globalization, but he also observed that globalization is imperative for businesses operating in industries too small to survive or thrive except on a worldwide basis. For example, costly research and development investments at Merck pharmaceuticals is justified only by worldwide sales.

Industry change due to globalization generates threats and also creates opportunities, often for smaller firms. For example, a US-based entrepreneur uses the Internet to sell industrial music CDs worldwide. The domestic market is simply too small for him to thrive, but by taking a global approach, he is able to establish a retail CD-sales channel for the relatively small industrial music industry. Even neighborhood restaurants that give every sign of being local interact at a global level to purchase food made globally available through advances in food production and distribution. These restaurants can turn industry globalization to opportunity by introducing new foods to clients who recognize that they too need exposure to a wider world.

For these local businesses and for the purposefully global corporation, a critical and strategic challenge is to develop internal systems responsive to a global industry. At the same time they must remain alert and responsive to the shifting customs, preferences, and needs of individual nations, regions, and mediating organizations. For example, anti-smoking initiatives headed by the World Health Organization and other political and private organizations constitute a serious threat to the tobacco industry. Integration of local and global concerns suggests that organizational leaders must pay attention to what is happening locally and globally both within and outside one's own industry.

Often trends that change industries begin outside them. For example, airline "hubbing" migrated from airlines to wholesale and food retailing industries that ship to large, regional warehouses for dispatch to smaller markets. This technique reduces the costs of inventory for each store, saves on shipping costs, and requires computer programs to queue and dispatch merchandise expeditiously. Interestingly, by 2002 hubbing was less frequently used in the airlines industry. In the global personal computer industry, Acer's Stan Shih adopted the "fast food" concept of McDonald's to create a distinctive competency for his firm.

Industry shifts also begin within industries when participants discover new ways to accomplish objectives. For example, IKEA learned that they could sell more furniture by packaging it in boxes for home assembly. Carrefour changed its own industry when it introduced superstores, but then Sam Walton altered it yet again by focussing almost exclusively on low price. The Mattel example below demonstrates how this company monitored external events to produce internal changes that redefined industry assumptions.

The Barbie Doll Goes Global

Industries change, and companies that monitor them can benefit from those changes. This is what Mattel Inc. discovered with consumer research. In the past, Mattel had tailored their popular Barbie doll to local cultures. So the Japanese Barbie doll had Asian facial features and black hair, while the US Barbie was blond and blue-eyed. Traditional assumptions were that children in different countries wanted toys most like themselves, but Mattel learned that children were global in their preferences. In particular, certain Barbies could be global. An example is the Rapunzel Barbie whose long hair and ball gown appeals to children throughout the world. These changes occur because children worldwide now are exposed to the same media that create popular culture on a global scale. In addition, mass retailers like Wal-Mart or Carrefour are able to roll out media campaigns on a worldwide scale. For example, the Rapunzel Barbie was promoted by ad campaigns in 35 languages, and combined with Barbie website stories and games in eight languages. The Rapunzel Barbie launch was complemented by promotional ventures that included a video, parties, and other special activities. In the end Mattel learned that toys are not always local.

Source material: Lisa Bannon and Carita Vitzthum (2003, Apr. 29) One-toy-fits-all: How industry learned to love the global kid. *The Wall Street Journal*, pp. A1, A8.

Monitoring global industry shifts requires that managers know their own industries and also study activities in other industries. Mattel did both of these using gathered information to alter their own practices and those of the industry.

Businesses encounter shifting boundaries for global industries that require constant review of industry parameters and redefinition of business activities. Demands to be many things simultaneously creates a paradox for organizational leaders who compete as autonomous actors more than as representatives of nations but also are expected to cooperate with former and current competitors. This creates organizational challenges addressed at the business level (within an industry) by organizations trying to create a sustainable advantage within its industry. They must be future oriented, but neither should they ignore the past.

CREATING INDUSTRY ADVANTAGE

Evidence presented above shows that industry change comes from many sources. Organizations monitor these sources to identify distinctive advantages to exploit. The sections below examine five different ways that organizations try to create a distinctive global advantage: industry analysis, diagnosing industry globalization, anticipating the future, revolutionizing the industry, and reshaping the organization.

Industry Analysis

When assessing industry history or current conditions, many managers use a technique popularized by Michael Porter (1980). In his successful book *Competitive Strategy*, Porter described how industry analysis could be used to identify the potential for earning above-average profits from an industry. Five industry characteristics important to this analysis are shown in Figure 5.1. The five forces affecting an industry are: buyers, suppliers, substitute products, barriers to new entrants, and competitive rivalry. Once the industry is analyzed and competitor moves analyzed in the same way, then the focal firm can identify the competencies it has for the industry and develop appropriate competitive moves consistent with its own competencies. At the heart of all this is the industry analysis itself.

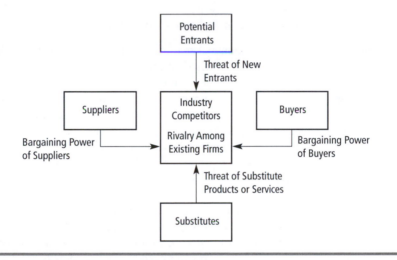

Figure 5.1 *Five forces of industry competition*

Rivalry

The degree of rivalry in an industry establishes parameters for action. Competition in domestic and international business has been placid in some industries and fierce in others. Fierce competition may well be a deterrent to new entrants.

Barriers to Industry Entry

High initial costs, existing brand loyalty, economies of scale, government actions that limit entry, or access to distribution channels all create opportunities for existing firms that make it difficult for new firms to enter the industry.

Availability of Substitutes

The availability of substitute products or services makes it more difficult for firms within an industry to earn above-average profits. If they raise prices, sales may go to substitute products, making the industry less attractive than one with few or no substitutes.

Buyer or Supplier Power

The relative strength or bargaining power of buyer or supplier groups shapes the firm's ability to set prices autonomously. For example, if buyer groups purchase large volumes of a firm's or industry's output, they can command better prices than when buyers are dispersed or uninformed.

Weighing the Porter Approach to Industry Analysis

The volatility of globalization makes it more difficult to conduct an industry analysis than when businesses operate in domestic or international markets. First, industry participants span the globe creating many more activities to monitor. Although managers have access to abundant information sources, important ones may be unavailable or difficult to interpret. Information over-abundance may motivate managers to pay attention only to their own industries. This could keep them from recognizing synergies generated by other industries.

Additionally, the set of competitive activities firms conduct with an industry analysis views the world from the perspective of the firm rather than from the perspective of the customer (Keen and Knapp, 1996). Finally, industry analysis is based usually on historical or present activities.

Jeffrey Pfeffer (1994) believes that these and similar weaknesses with industry analysis suggest that we need new tools to assess changing industry conditions. In summary, industry analysis provides a framework for organizations to assess historical and current industry factors, but there is a growing need to analyze industry globalization and assess organizational competencies with an eye toward future industry globalization.

Diagnosing Industry Globalization

In his book *Total Global Strategy*, George Yip (1995) outlines four factors that drive industry globalization: market, cost, government, and competitive globalization. An examination of these four factors helps managers assess the degree of industry globalization for their worldwide businesses.

Market Globalization

This form of industry globalization can be assessed by examining a) common needs of end use customers worldwide; b) national and multinational global customers who search the world for suppliers but use the purchased product or service either in one country or in many; c) ease with which marketing can be transferred worldwide; and d) lead countries where the most important industry product or process innovations are located. By assessing these four elements of market globalization, managers are able to see when consumer tastes converge; when buyers consolidate their buying; when marketing can be used globally; and where they need to invest.

Cost Globalization

Cost globalization drivers depend on the economies of the business. These can vary by industry. For example, global economies of scale are a cost globalization driver only when they can be realized with sales in many rather than one country. Other cost globalization drivers include global economies of scope; experience curves; sourcing efficiencies; favorable logistics; fast-changing technology; high product development costs; and differences in country costs. For example, in Chapter 9 on global labor, we note that differences in the cost of labor are a major factor for job migration.

Government Globalization

Drivers for government globalization are those emanating from the global political/legal environment. These include: favorable trade policies that make it desirable to expand into new nations; compatible technical standards; common marketing regulations; host government concerns; and government-owned competitors and customers. For example, the potential for industry globalization can increase when a government-owned entity is a competitor because government actors can marshal resources and may subsidize industries to take them global. For example, the aerospace industry began to globalize due to subsidies from the multiple nations that established Airbus.

Competitive Globalization

Central themes include economic integration via increased exports and imports; the existence of competitors from many nations; increased economic interdependence among countries; and increased rivalry on a global scale. These reflections of globalization are occurring across industries of every kind and in every sector. As developing countries seek out "value-added" industries, manufacturers in the industrialized world simultaneously surrender some of their profits or offer additional product value in order to retain buyers. Thus, prices for value-added products are likely to decline as more business participants enter the market and as additional technological efforts lower costs and improve quality and access simultaneously. Moreover, as value-added industries globalize, businesses offer better prices to consumers, but profits may be more difficult to attain.

Yip, Johansson, and Roos (1997) studied 63 worldwide businesses to examine the effects of industry globalization drivers and management processes on them. Both factors influenced global strategy, but the authors also observed significant nationality effects. In particular, European and Japanese businesses made more use of global strategy than did US firms.

Anticipating the Future

Gary Hamel and C.K. Prahalad (1994) believe that a historical look at industries using an industry analysis is insufficient. Technological, demographic, regulatory and other changes occurring worldwide have the potential to transform industry boundaries and create new space for firms. These authors argue that managers must create a vision of the future when diagnosing the past and present. Jorma Ollila, CEO of Nokia, believes questions that address industry futures will not be asked unless the CEO understands each business in the company portfolio—otherwise the CEO will end up reading reports based on financial criteria rather than developing an understanding of where the future lies.

Metanational and Triad Strategies

Diversity of academic opinion also characterizes globalization. The two books referenced below envision very different futures for global strategists.

Doz et al. (2001) argue that the future will favor the metanational corporation. These companies will not draw their advantages from home countries, or even from a defined set of national subsidiaries. Instead, they will view the world as a broad canvas of untapped knowledge. Successful metanationals will be those that can mobilize globally dispersed knowledge to innovate better than competitors. They will also be able to effectively manage operations to maximize sales and profit growth.

Alan Rugman (2001) believes that firms do not operate globally. At best, they operate in Triad-based regions defined by NAFTA, the European Union and Asia. Accordingly, Rugman argues that firms need to develop regional rather than global strategies.

Source material: Yves Doz, Jose Santos and Peter J. Williamson (2002) *From Global to Metanational: How Companies Win in the Knowledge Economy.* Boston: Harvard Business School Press; Alan M Rugman (2001) *The End of Globalization.* New York: AMACOM/McGraw-Hill.

Envisioning the future begins with hands-on knowledge of the organization and its businesses. Ticketmaster Corporation sells seats to sporting and entertainment events, but a change in the airline industry caused Fredrick Rosen of Ticketmaster to ask: why does it have to be the same way? If airlines can disintermediate, Rosen reasoned that Ticketmaster could use its interconnectivity to sell airline tickets, sea and ski travel packages, or coordinate parking, restaurant, and show tickets. The importance of this kind of "what if?" thinking at Intel is described in the example that follows.

Intel's Paranoid Thinking Alters Strategy

Until the mid-1980s, Intel's core business was designing and manufacturing memory chips for computers, but the industry changed in 1984 when Japanese firms entered with high-quality, low-price competitive products. Memory chips were abundant and Intel was losing money. According to Intel chief Andy Grove, he asked then-CEO Gordon Moore what he thought a new CEO and president would do. The answer was to get out of the computer-memory business, and that is exactly what Intel did, even though Grove himself felt the idea was far-fetched and even paranoid. However, the shift from memory into microprocessor production led to development of the 386 chips that became an industry mainstay and made Intel an industry giant in microprocessors. According to Andy Grove, Intel made this decision at what he called a "strategy inflection point" where the whole life of the business was about to change because fundamental forces acting upon it were undergoing fundamental change. In this case, history now shows those fundamental changes in the chip industry included: global industry change as competitors from other nations entered markets previously dominated by one or a few nations; global technological change hinging on microprocessor breakthroughs; global economic change creating a computer-buying middle class; and global political change leading to commercialization of the Internet and growing demand for computers to access its offerings.

Source material: Andrew S. Grove (1997) *Only the Paranoid Survive*. New York: Currency Doubleday.

Revolutionizing the Industry

Whatever their size or strategy, global firms often take unconventional approaches to their industries, developing strategic innovations that change the rules of the competitive game in a particular industry (Hout et al., 1982) or that reinvent their businesses to create new profit zones (Slywotzky et al., 1998). Deutsche Morgan Grenfell changed the rules of global banking by raiding employees from other firms, and Suisse Bank similarly broke away from conservative Swiss banking traditions to invest in riskier opportunities in Eastern Europe. Nike reshaped the trainer/sneaker market by creating shoes for athletes, and Reebok followed with athletic shoes for women. Dell Computer revolutionized computer purchasing by introducing a direct-sales model responsive to each individual's needs. Richard Branson did the almost unthinkable by introducing Virgin Soda to the highly rivalrous global soft-drink beverage market. The boxed example explains how McDonald's Corporation hoped to revolutionize its industry. This and other industry revolutions result from someone, somewhere questioning the industry status quo.

McDonald's Intentions

Jack M. Greenberg took over as president and CEO of McDonald's Corporation in August of 1998, intending to "reinvent the category in which we compete" and to "grow and change at the same time." According to Hellinker and Gibson (1998), this approach was different from the three CEOs before Greenberg whose missions were to expand the chain and protect the McDonald's formula for growth. Greenberg expected hamburgers to play a diminished role on the menu with the addition of more fish, white meat, salads, and other items. Greenberg's prior efforts at McDonald's included decentralizing US operations and shifting responsibilities to promote newcomers, especially women. His style often was described as "inclusive," with ideas coming from the stores rather than from headquarters. One example is the McFlurry ice-cream treat invented in Canada. Despite these efforts, McDonald's profits stalled and Greenberg was subsequently replaced with Jim Cantalupo who instituted additional changes until his death in 2003. But his successors will doubtless continue to make changes to sustain the company's industry leadership.

Source material: Kevin Helliker and Richard Gibson (1998, Aug. 24) The new chief is ordering up changes at McDonald's. *The Wall Street Journal*, pp. B1, B6.

According to Gary Hamel (1996), except for industry leaders with an unassailable position, most businesses have a larger stake in revolution than in the status quo. He proposes nine ways firms can revolutionize their industries. These are listed below.

Reconceive a Product or Service

- Radically improve the value ratio by 500 percent or more like Hewlett-Packard did in the printer industry and IKEA did for furniture.
- Separate function and form as the security industry did by using the credit-card industry's magnetic stripe idea to authorize entry to rooms, buildings, copiers.
- Achieve joy of use as Trader Joe's did by making grocery shopping surprising and fun.

Redefine the Market

- Push the boundaries of universality to identify new opportunities; the single-use camera is accessible to children who were not users of other types of cameras; Domino's Pizza is popular in Japan with squid and other offerings.
- Strive for individuality to respond to needs people have to feel special; Levi Strauss now uses computer measurements to manufacture personalized jeans.
- Increase accessibility via telephone, expanding hours, locating fast foods in buildings where people work.

Redraw Industry Boundaries

- Rescale industries, making local services national or national ones global or the reverse to create micromarkets for standardized goods like bakery products or microbrew beers.
- Compress the supply chain by removing steps from processes, for example cutting out the cost of shipping paper worldwide by using electronic media.
- Drive convergence between industries, a process grocery stores have fostered by offering prepared meals equivalent to restaurants.

According to Hamel, true industry revolutionaries do not care what industries they are in because existing boundaries are not meaningful. What is more meaningful are emerging industries that create tomorrow's advantages.

Reshaping the Organization

Chapter 2 described how managers adapt people, processes, and structures to create advantage in a global world. As other chapters show, organizations do this in many ways. For example, some create a structural advantage via an important alliance; others create a process-oriented advantage such as a proprietary information system. Below we look at how Jeffrey Pfeffer (1994) believes competitive advantage can be created with people.

Pfeffer (1994) argues that traditional sources of success such as product and process technologies, protected or regulated national markets, access to financial resources, and economies of scale provide fewer advantages than they once did. This elevates the importance of organizational culture and capabilities created from managing people well. Organizations find many ways to derive sustainable advantage from people, and so none will use exactly the same criteria. Yet, Pfeffer identified 16 interrelated practices that often help companies achieve sustainable advantage through people. Among practices listed are some that contrast with current practice, for example provide employment security or pay high wages, and others like cross-utilization and cross-training that reinforce current practice. Examples from Pfeffer's list include:

- High wages—you get what you pay for.
- Incentive pay—shared gains.
- Information sharing.
- Cross-utilization and cross-training.
- Long-term perspective.
- An overarching philosophy.

Pfeffer believes that achieving sustainable advantage though people and human resource practices is more enduring than sustainable advantage created by a new piece of equipment. But as compared to new equipment, it may take longer to create a sustainable advantage through people. This longer-time horizon is more easily achieved in family-owned or privately-owned firms less answerable to stockholder demands for short-term profits. Global organizations also need to take this longer-run view to develop the knowledge or customer-oriented workers they need, but face difficult trade-offs with stockholder demands for short-term profitability.

Pfeffer also believes that external barriers to achieving sustainable advantage through people include national and even world veneration for the wrong heroes and economic theories, and models that emphasize neoclassical principles like agency theory and transaction costs. The latter's emphasis on opportunism, for example, fosters distrust within and between organizations. Making heroes of people who have made money or claimed fame based on lay-offs and "lean and mean" behavior suggests people are an expendable resource. Internal barriers include using language that undermines rather than develops employee confidence or loyalty, for example thinking of others as foreigners. Finally, Pfeffer suggests heroes, theories and language used within a firm should be integrated and consistent with a desire to build advantages through people. Managing these intangibles may be more important to sustaining advantage than a short-lived economic advantage, but is difficult for analytical managers who prefer to manage concrete and tangible assets.

THE GLOBAL FIELD FOR COMPETITION: DO NATIONS OR FIRMS COMPETE?

Business activities as well as customer preferences, suppliers, and other stakeholders shape industries. National governments also shape industries through industrial policy, subsidies, regulations, patents, trademarks, and similar mechanisms. Theories of absolute and comparative advantage help to explain the historical link between companies and nations.

Absolute and Comparative Advantage

Adam Smith's (1776) theory of absolute advantage asserts that nations differ in their ability to produce goods efficiently. This being the case, a country can improve its economy by producing goods or services in which it has an absolute advantage over other nations. David Ricardo (1817) provided an alternative explanation for trade called comparative advantage. This theory argues that even when a country has absolute advantage, it might make sense to specialize in efficient industries and buy goods it produces least efficiently. This argument acknowledges that there is likely to be a continuum of advantage with any nation having most and least productive industries.

Nations take different routes to achieve absolute and comparative national advantages. For example, many Western nations provide subsidies such as tax breaks that stimulate selected industries whereas Japan and Korea formalized industrial development by establishing keiretsu and chaebols whose interlinked activities in targeted industries were intended to create national comparative advantage. In these and other ways, each nation tries to link national economic development to business activities. Many governments play an active role in shaping business and industry environments. Their activities raise an important question for global businesses and for industry globalization: is it nations or industries and firms that compete in global markets? This is an important question because its answer determines the extent to which businesses are unfettered actors on the world stage.

Joseph Clougherty (2001) indicates that researchers have two points of view on this question. "Globalists" believe that global business mobility compromises national autonomy, arguing that nations must be involved with businesses to keep important ones within their own nations. "Institutionalists" believe national autonomy is not compromised by global business, arguing that businesses compete more than nations. These perspectives shape national activities which in turn shape industry and business opportunities. Nations adopt different perspectives on the globalist/institutionalist debate and resulting activities also affect industry and firm development on a worldwide scale.

Nations Compete

In the bordered world of international expansion, business development and national development are viewed as complementary activities. Trade across national borders created systems that reinforced the notion of competition between nations reflected in an annual *World Competitiveness Report* ranking of nations according to eight criteria: domestic economic strength; international activity; government policy; financial markets; infrastructure; management; science and technology; and people. In 1996, the World Economic Forum and IMD produced separate reports using different criteria, but both ranked nations according to their competitiveness. Union Bank of Switzerland produces annual assessments of nations' future competitiveness, and on occasion *The Economist* has done the same. Selected rankings to 2004 are shown in Table 5.3:

Table 5.3 *National competitive rankings 1995, 1998, 2002, 2004*

Nation	1995	1998	2002	2004
United States	1	1	1	2
Singapore	2	2	5	7
Hong Kong	3	3	9	21
Finland	18	5	2	1
Netherlands	8	4	4	12
Norway	10	6	17	6
Denmark	7	8	6	5
Switzerland	5	7	7	8
Canada	13	10	8	15
New Zealand	9	13	19	18
Japan	4	18	30	9
Britain/UK	15	12	16	11

Source material: International Institute for Management Development (IMD), World Competitiveness Scorecard 2002: http://www01.imd.ch/wcy/ranking (accessed 2002, June 20).

Business researchers compare business activities by nation more than by industry to produce categories like those shown above. The relative ease of access to national data encourages this practice, and clear national differences in politics, economics, and national sentiment make this approach logical. At the same time, national comparisons tend to obscure differences between firms from the same country, and changes in ranking are reason enough to exercise caution when examining data at a single point in time. Further, data like these reinforce notions of national competition that may be irrelevant to borderless competition.

Determinants of National Competitiveness

Michael Porter (1990) argued that nations became more important as a result of global competition. He proposed that national competitiveness stems from four industry determinants: the availability of productive factors; demand; proximity of related or support industries; and firm strategy, structure, and rivalry consistent with national norms. Porter's argument is that nations play a role in shaping their own economic destiny by providing support for education and other productive factors that enhance national productivity, by creating a national work ethic, encouraging rivalry, and passing regulations that make it possible for firms to cluster geographically and gain support from related industries. Concentration on software, biotech, genetic research, and telecommunications industries in Iceland has created an active and thriving economy. Liechtenstein benefits by concentrating on false-teeth production. The Irish government has invested in education to attract foreign investment. The four national competitiveness factors described below explain how a national competitive advantage is created through business.

Factor Conditions

Factors of production such as skilled labor or infrastructure of roads or telephone communications are necessary to compete in a selected industry. Therefore nations succeed in industries where they are particularly good at factor creation. For example, a contributory factor for the successful Netherlands flower industry is that the nation invests in research into cultivation, packaging, and shipping of flowers.

Demand Conditions

Demanding and exacting consumers in domestic markets force companies to develop a clear or early picture of consumer demands.

Related and Supporting Industries

Supporting industries, for example myriad software houses that surround industry hardware and software firms, provide a competitive advantage because they innovate, make constant industry upgrades, and provide cost-efficient inputs.

Firm Strategy, Structure, and Rivalry

Porter argues that fierce rivalry improves firms as they compete for technical excellence and public recognition of the "best" firm, and this toughens them as they move beyond domestic markets.

Domestic rivalry and geographic concentration of firms within the same geographic area are especially powerful in transforming the four factors into a system because domestic rivalry "promotes improvement in all the other determinants and geographic concentration because it elevates and magnifies the interaction of the four separate influences" (Porter, 1990: 83).

National Branding

Simon Anholt (2000) argues that nations compete with national branding. Although several nations have successfully branded themselves, for example the US, many more could attract buyers with national branding. For example, Anholt notes that Brazil has a strong brand personality that includes attributes like samba, football, and carnival that could be successfully translated into product brands. He further argues that many developing economies have a branding advantage not available to former European powers with a legacy of colonialism and military dominance. Finally, he argues that if a company from a poor economy can sell brands to consumers in a rich economy, then the overall balance of trade can be addressed in ways not addressed when rich economies sell branded goods to people in poor economies.

Only Firms Should Compete

Economist Paul Krugman (1994) argues that a national focus on industrial policy creates trade wars that harm everyone in their single-minded pursuit of "winning" when world trade is not and need not be played as a "zero-sum" game in which trade opportunity is limited. He further argues that thinking in terms of national competitiveness leads to bad economic policies that hinder national development. For example, using government money to protect failing industries is a waste and protectionism hurts competition. Krugman believes that the real pain of job losses or downsizing could blur issues of competitiveness, and perhaps divert government attention from policies that have important long-term implications for nations. In summary, Krugman believes the role of government is to govern rather than set the terms of competition.

Turner (2001) supports Krugman's argument that companies more than nations should compete for business. He argues that the contrary assumption (nations compete for business) is counterproductive because it implies that there is only so much prosperity available in the world. However, Turner argues that one nation's prosperity does not have to come from another's.

The debate surrounding national competitiveness is a crucial one for businesses. It is one among many factors that businesses monitor on a global scale. A nation that subscribes to the idea that nations compete will create mechanisms to assist companies within its boundaries. In addition, national leaders can erect barriers such as tariffs to protect current producers. An example is US introduction of steel tariffs in 2002; these were intended to protect domestic producers. Conversely, national competitiveness policies may be used to attract foreign producers to a country to create jobs or other national development benefits.

Having looked at globalization of industries, we can reach several conclusions. The trend to date has been toward industry globalization. This has meant increased integration activities among firms—whether they choose to be global or remain domestic in their approach. This suggests that businesses will increasingly be affected by global industry shifts. The extent to which governmental actors mediate these shifts may depend on domestic policy within nations. Chapter 10 on global politics further examines how national/business relationships operate on a global scale.

CHAPTER SUMMARY

Industries are described and classified in myriad ways such as industry type, product or service, value-added, durability, and the like. An industry commonality is that all are increasingly global and each can be classified as multidomestic, simple global, integrated global or fully global.

Suggested measures of industry globalization include: the amount of an industry's trade ratio, intrafirm flows of resources, and cross-border industry activities.

Industry reshaping occurs in one or more of five ways: convergence, integration, disinter-mediation, contraction, and dissolution.

Businesses encounter shifting boundaries for global industries that require constant review of industry parameters and redefinition of business activities.

Organizational leaders hope to create sustainable advantages in a global world. They analyze their environments better to recognize sources of distinctive advantages that they can exploit. Five ways that organizations use to identify a distinctive advantage are: industry analysis, diagnosing industry globalization, anticipating the future, revolutionizing the industry, and reshaping the organization.

Competition on a global level raises the question of whether it is nations or firms that should compete on a global scale. The answer to this question shapes allocation of government resources and government–business relationships within and between nations.

REVIEW AND DISCUSSION QUESTIONS

1 What is meant by blurring boundaries of industry? What are the long-term effects of blurred industry boundaries for managers?

2 Select a firm like Nike, Dell Computer, or Virgin, known for its propensity to revolutionize the industry (others are listed in the chapter section titled "Revolutionizing Industries" on pp. 139–41). Then examine recent firm activities to demonstrate a continuation of this practice.

3 Select a global industry to study, for example premium ice-cream, advertising, cosmetics. To what extent is the industry affected by factors such as convergence, integration, disin-termediation, contraction or dissolution? In the long run, will this industry survive?

4 Competition on a global sphere raises the question of whether it is nations, firms or both that compete globally. Develop a four-cell box to present arguments for and against competition and collaboration for either nations or businesses.

Chapter 6
GLOBALIZATION AND THE NATURAL ENVIRONMENT

BAMBOO HARDWOODS: A VISION FOR SUSTAINABILITY

Bamboo Hardwoods is a young firm with a global mission: save the earth one tree at a time. As company founder Doug Lewis tells the story, his initial business inspiration came from his mother's observation that bamboo is a sustainable source of wood fiber. To himself he said "this is what I have to do with my life"—develop this sustainable resource. He recalls huddling around coffee-shop tables with like-minded investors to create a business plan that could "make a difference." On its cover were Margaret Mead's much-quoted words: "Never doubt that a small group of thoughtful, committed citizens can change the world. Indeed, it is the only thing that ever has." Mr. Lewis's vision to make that difference has not wavered in the ten-plus years since he founded Bamboo Hardwoods, but as the following paragraphs show, he has traveled at high speed on global roads that are neither smooth nor direct. The Bamboo Hardwoods experience demonstrates the rapid pace and discontinuous nature of globalization; it shows how small firms participate globally; and it illustrates how sustainable development concepts lead to business opportunities.

The story begins with bamboo, most of which grows in Asia. This reedy grass emerges from rapidly grown clumps or culms that reach full height in 2–3 months by growing as much as a meter per day. Bamboo is evergreen, photosynthesizes year around, and takes very few nutrients from the ground. Harvested properly, bamboo is a sustainable food crop and can also be used to make paper or building materials such as flooring for Bamboo Hardwoods. There are over 1,000 species of bamboo, but only a few are thick, hard, and durable enough for flooring. Its strength-to-weight ratio is the best of any natural product, and it has a tensile strength stronger than steel. The lasting value of bamboo flooring is that the product can be replenished in a matter of years instead of the decades hardwoods take.

Mr. Lewis had previous business experience as a founder of Bamboo Gardens. In 1990 he traveled to Guangzhou, China to explore bamboo business possibilities there. Although China has plots of bamboo that stretch as far as the eye can see the plants were not harvested for sustainability. For example, collective ownership often motivated farmers to harvest bamboo too early, killing culms or producing bamboo too soft for flooring. Discouraged by this use of a natural resource, Lewis returned to Seattle without a contract. Discussions with a Vietnamese refugee there resulted in a joint venture to develop bamboo flooring and panels in Vietnam. Although the two had different reasons to partner, bamboo flooring provided a way to achieve their separate goals.

Vietnam business development proved challenging in the early 1990s. For example, the US embargo on Vietnam trade discouraged US FDI there. As a communist country, Vietnam's infrastructure provided few business incentives and many restrictions on foreign asset ownership. For example, the Vietnamese government would not issue a manufacturing license without land ownership, but a non-citizen could not purchase land. Thus although Mr. Lewis purchased land to build a factory, it had to be registered in the names of Vietnamese citizens. Additionally, once purchased, the land was turned over to the government and leased back on a 50-year contract. Lewis further found that a poor communications infrastructure and weak rules of law made it impossible for him to enforce a contract. To minimize dealings with the Vietnamese government, Lewis tried to control his own supply sources of tamvong bamboo.

▶

The first factory employed about 200 workers who in 1992 earned an average $3 per day—more than state companies were paying. Upon receipt of mature poles of 60 to 80 feet, workers rip the bamboo into strips and run them through planers before gluing and laminating it into flooring. In the early days of manufacturing, workers and Lewis could work into the night to prepare an order—sometimes sleeping on the floor. Today materials and labor sourcing to engineer bamboo flooring reflect one characteristic of a global business. Machinery comes from Germany, good table saws come from Italy, glue comes from Scandinavia, and finish resins might come from Germany but they are mixed in Singapore. The flooring itself is manufactured and sourced from China, Vietnam, and Indonesia, and it is installed or "floats" on recycled tires from Canada. But true to the dream, materials used can be replenished and thereby reduce demands on the natural environment.

Bamboo flooring products are available worldwide, but the greatest interest in them is in Europe, the US, and Asia. Growing demand is powered by both cultural and natural environment concerns. Interest in bamboo products is growing in Europe because of high commitments to sustainable products. This causes scientists in the United Kingdom and the Netherlands to study bamboo and encourages business people to found companies that market bamboo.

There is also growing worldwide interest in all things Asian, showing how this sustainable product transfers cultural influences worldwide. According to Stanley Murashige (Sherrod, 2003), the qualities of bamboo make it a metaphor for desirable characteristics such as strength, resilience, longevity, and good luck. For example, bamboo is resilient because it can bend with the wind but not be broken by it. In many Asian nations, bamboo resilience also makes it a metaphor for individuals to hold steady when confronting external pressures. The evergreen nature of bamboo also associates it with longevity, and its hollow interior is a metaphor for a person whose unbiased and unprejudiced attitudes improve insight into all possibilities.

Bamboo Hardwoods' competitors are found around the globe. They include US and Canadian companies, Dutch ones, and many companies from Asian nations that include the Philippines, Indonesia, and China. In addition, consumers now have other options for sustainable flooring such as cork. According to rumors in the bamboo flooring industry, small bamboo producers may face competition from IKEA, but Doug Lewis thinks it is a good thing for his vision when giant firms like IKEA begin to spread the word about bamboo's qualities as a durable and sustainable natural fiber.

Like many small firms, Bamboo Hardwoods operates with relatively few employees; the Seattle office employs 20 and a new Vietnam factory employs about 200 people. Mr. Lewis himself has a partial interest in the Vietnam factory, and owns part of Bamboo Technologies which manufactures bamboo homes. The latter sent its first shipment of 12 houses from Vietnam to the Cook Islands in 2004. Most internal communication is face-to-face, and to save resources Mr. Lewis keeps globally linked through frequent e-mails. Although the company's small size requires relatively few management systems, it also exposes the firm to risk. For example, fraud eviscerated Mr. Lewis's investment in the original Vietnam plant, and a spate of Internet check-fraud schemes also caught the company by surprise. Introduction of a new information management system to track costs, inventory, and other information also consumed time. Despite these challenges, the company ▶

continues to grow, still powered by a vision for sustainability. This case shows that preservation of the natural environment depends on global shifts in other environments such as the economy, industries, culture, technology, and politics.

Source material: Bruce Ramsey (1996, Apr. 1) Grass-roots effort. *Seattle Post-Intelligencer*, p. B3; Pamela Sherrod (2003, Feb. 16) Et tu, bamboo? The reedy grass is newest trend in home décor. *Northwest Life Sunday*, *The Seattle Times* (electronic version).

CHAPTER OVERVIEW

Many individuals and organizational leaders are well aware that their activities affect the natural environment. This awareness grows out of growing evidence of the effects of environmental use and some thirty years of environmental activism. This chapter begins with a look at worldwide interconnections in the natural environment that result from use of the global commons and other resources, globalization of disease, and natural disasters that are rarely controllable. The emphasis then shifts to examine the combined effects of population growth and industrialization as pressures on the natural environment. Principles of sustainable development are introduced and applied to business activities. Finally, the chapter examines how businesses and other organizations address challenges for a shared earth.

BOUNDARIES FOR THE EARTH

In crossing boundaries of time and space and nations, one recognizes that earth is a complex eco-system where activities in one part of the world increasingly affect some or all of the world. For example, disease, pollution, and environmental degradation move across geographic boundaries affecting people and places indiscriminately. The following look at the global commons, disease, and natural disasters illustrates how boundary transcendence globalizes the natural environment and globalizes the dialogue on use of the natural environment worldwide.

GLOBAL DEMAND FOR NATURAL RESOURCES

There are many types of natural resources. Among globally shared resources are "global commons" such as the air and water, which are essential to everyone. The global commons also are described in broader terms to include the atmosphere, space, and the Internet (Buck, 1998; Henderson, 1999). It follows that use or abuse of the global commons shapes everyone's future.

Natural resources provided by the earth include land, energy, trees, metal, other raw materials, and living species. Some are the source of food or shelter; others such as oil, gold, and other minerals foster economic and cultural development. There is a growing concern that those in the richer economies benefit more than most others from use of natural resources such as these, and that all lose with species decline; and further that national governments alone cannot readily address global environmental challenges that are global in nature (French, Hilary 2003).

The Global Commons: Water

Both fresh and ocean water are important components of the global commons. Water absorbs and stores heat for the earth, provides energy and food resources, and transports much in the world. Almost 70 percent of the earth is water, and 90 percent of all planetary fresh water is found in Antarctica (which is owned by no country). Aquifers and lakes beneath nations supply many, and almost all rivers cross more than one nation. Yet, many nations operate independently in their use of the ocean and fresh water—often in the name of business and individual self-interest—and this has led to shared concerns and problems.

Nine out of ten people on the planet had enough water in 1995 (1,700 cubic meters per person), but by 2003 almost one billion people had little access to safe, clean drinking water. For some, poor access to clean water is due to geographic conditions; for example, desert conditions in Kuwait, Qatar, Gaza, and Saudi Arabia make water scarce. Others face human-induced water challenges; for example, industrial pollution and poor waste treatment reduce the quality of water (*World Water Development*, 2003) contributing to 80 percent of disease in the developing world and killing ten million people annually.

Water scarcity occurs with growing population, urbanization, and environmental degradation. By 2050 some two billion people could face scarce water supplies, becoming a trigger for global and international conflict (see Shiva, 2002 and Ward, 2002 for additional insight on this issue). The criticality of water resources generated a water–poverty index that grades nations according to their water resources, access, use, and environmental impact. On average, and with some exceptions such as Guyana and Suriname, developing economies scored lower on the index than advanced ones. The following examples show how most water is consumed.

Water Use and Abuse

Only about 10 percent of water consumed on a worldwide basis is for household and personal use. Organizations consume about 20 percent of the world's water, using it to produce goods and services. But a staggering 70 percent goes to agriculture. In the developing economies agricultural use of water is high because of dependence on crops. In developed economies, agricultural use often remains high because governments subsidize water use, providing little incentive for farmers to conserve water. For example, drip irrigations systems use 30–70 percent less water than conventional irrigation systems, but these systems are used on less than 1 percent of irrigated land. Organizations working together through the World Water Council argue that changes in agricultural use can come about only through transnational water use standards and regulations.

Source material: Fen Montaigne (2002, Sept.) Water pressure. *National Geographic*, pp. 2–32; World Water Council: http://www.worldwatercouncil.org

National interests can impede development of global water use or standards. For example, in the US Midwest, the government subsidizes water to help farmers, but golf courses and swimming pools benefit too and thereby deplete resources (de Villiers, 2000). In a world bounded by national politics, autonomous governments may be poorly equipped to manage global water access or development. Few economies have the resources to build an infrastructure for worldwide water systems, and developing ones often cannot maintain or develop even national systems.

Almost by default, global businesses such as private companies like Suez Lyonnaise des Eaux have become water systems builders. The latter has invested in deteriorating pipes and built modern facilities in many nations further to develop the $400 billion global water industry. But many worry that when businesses manage global commons like water, the result will be reduced access for the poor. This fear has resulted in failed water privatization efforts in Latin America, Indonesia, Pakistan, India, South Africa, Poland, and Hungary. Perhaps the most spectacular failure occurred in Cochabamba, Bolivia, where "water warriors" disrupted a planned water consortium between Bechtel Corporation and Bolivia's government (Finnegan, 2002).

To prevent negative effects of water privatization, local governments increasingly create regulations to mediate relationships between water providers and suppliers. For example, the 1993 Suez contract to provide water to Buenos Aires called for a 27 percent price drop, an investment pledge of $3 billion over thirty years to bring water to new and mainly poor customers, and replacement of 15,000 miles of rusting pipes (Tully, 2000).

The Global Commons: Air

Some also view air as a "free" global common. Although no one disagrees that air quality depends on human activities, they do conflict when trying to disentangle the human impact on air from other natural ones. An example is climate change. Scientists agree this is occurring, but few agree about why. Some believe the principal cause is human use; others argue that climate change is due to natural variations, alterations in the universe, or unexplained roles of the ocean in a global ecology. However, it is evident that some businesses play a role in shaping air quality and others are affected by climatic change.

Business Activities and Air

Trees convert carbon dioxide to oxygen. But many forests—especially in developing economies—are falling victim to growing demand for timber for construction, paper, fuel, and other industries. Over one-fifth of all harvested wood ends up as paper; paper and pulp is the fifth largest industrial consumer of world energy (Abramovitz and Mattoon, 1999); and despite electronic communication modes, global paper use has increased sixfold since 1950. Worldwide, as many as 80,000 square miles of tropical forests are cleared each year. By one estimate, Indonesian forests the size of New Jersey or New Caledonia are harvested each year (Mapes and Madani, 2001). This is but one example of how business activities on the part of global giants and individuals influence air quality. Other examples include "slash and burn" agricultural practices.

The Effects of Climate Changes

Global warming causes ecosystems to disappear, deserts to expand, and storms to become more violent and frequent. These and other climate changes affect people and business formation and development in myriad ways. In shipping, for example, a result of global warming is higher costs to remove barnacles. Insurance companies face huge claims due to climate changes.

Natural Resources: Species

Estimates of total species range from 1.4 to 1.7 million, of which about 50,000 disappear each year. This rate far exceeds the United Nations' estimate of 1,000 as the "natural" rate of extinction. According to the World Resources Institute (1996/1997), in each decade between 1995 and 2015 somewhere between 1 percent to 11 percent of the world's species will move toward eventual extinction. Globalization of travel and trade is partly to blame because they introduce new species that account for a third of species reduction. Examples below illustrate how global transplant of plants and animals disrupt existing eco-systems or cause species demise.

Species Migration
Guam had no snakes until they hitchhiked in via incoming aircraft 30 years ago. Now brown tree snakes are so prevalent on the island that they have killed off virtually all species of birds and many animals. Increased air travel increases the potential for similar impacts elsewhere. Zebra mussels traveling on Russian ships now clog intake pipes in the US Great Lakes, costing $500 million per year. European green crabs introduced to San Francisco Bay have wiped out indigenous East Asian clams. Rainbow jellyfish that entered Black Sea waters in the water of ship ballasts are wiping out plankton, fish eggs, and the larvae of existing mussels and oysters there.

Biodiversity Hotspots

About two-thirds of all species are found in humid lowland tropical forests. These and other species-rich locations are known as biodiversity "hotspots" because a disproportionate number of species found in them are rapidly losing habitat (Environmental Literacy Council, 2003). Most of the world's 25 biodiversity hotspots (see Figure 6.1) are in developing economies that face pressure to increase income from sales of timber and other natural resources. For example, about 85 percent of plants and animals in Madagascar are only found there, but they are being consumed by Madagascans whose existence depends on slash and burn agriculture. Many biodiversity hotspots have been reduced to less than 10 percent of their original vegetation.

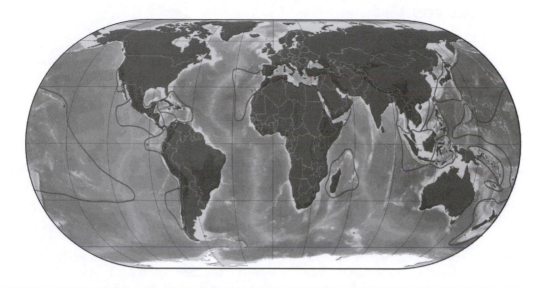

Figure 6.1 *Locations for biodiversity hotspots*
Source material: Conservation International. Reproduced with permission.

Business and Biodiversity Prospecting

Shaman Pharmaceuticals is a California-based company that uses indigenous knowledge of plants to create drugs and diet supplements, and their approach is one that
develops other people and nations. The company has "bioprospected" since 1991 in
countries around the world, first getting permission from communities, then allotting
15–20 percent of its research expense budget to local projects. Local scientists share
in the lab work to improve their training. The company also set up a nonprofit association called the Herb Forest Conservancy to distribute a share of its eventual profits to
host countries and community groups in the countries where it works.

Source material: Anthony Faiola (1999, July 18) Is it 'biopiracy'—or just business? *The Seattle Times*, p. A2.

Threats to Human Species

Among threats to the human species are those that reduce or corrupt the global commons.
But others believe the species is further threatened by air- and food-borne chemicals that
interfere with reproductive hormones (Colborn et al., 1996). For example, hundreds of
synthetic chemicals mimic human hormones like estrogen and testosterone. When introduced to humans through food ingestion or air-borne particles, they can alter reproduction.

Loss of other species also has a negative impact on human well-being. For example, half
of all medicines are derived from natural resources (Cetron and Davies, 2001). No one
knows what the long-range implications of those losses will be. In summary, boundarylessness may reduce the gene pool of animals, plants, and people, making survivors more
vulnerable to future disease. This reduction in variety increases extinction threats for all.

Natural Resources: Land

Among resources that all people need is food and the land upon which it is grown. According to detailed satellite photos of the earth, nearly 40 percent of worldwide farmland is seriously degraded (Pilot analysis of global agrosystems, 2001) due to erosion, loss of organic matter, nutrient depletion, and increased salinity. Some degradation is due to industrialization; other to overpopulation, poverty, overgrazing, and many other factors related to human use. Together, these factors raise concerns about the world's ability to feed itself, particularly in developing economies where food growth is most needed.

Tragedy of the Commons

In an article titled "The tragedy of the commons," author Garrett Hardin (1968) explained why it is difficult—if not impossible—to manage use of an unfenced global common like land. He used the example of herdsmen to argue that self-interest encourages each to add to herds until the total number of animals grazing on the global common moves beyond saturation. Thus, freedom to use a common resource brings ruin to all. Hardin proposed several alternatives for resolving conflicts that arise from use of the global commons, concluding that mutual agreements among the majority of those affected is needed to avert ruin.

Source material: Garrett Hardin (1968) The tragedy of the commons. *Science*, 162: 1243–1248.

GLOBALIZATION OF DISEASE

Diseases that afflict people, plants, and animals also are going global—often with devastating effects. For example, increased agricultural trade stimulated by multilateral alliances such as NAFTA, the EU, MERCOSUR, or the World Trade Organization help spread potato fungus or mad cow disease. Business travel and tourism increases the reach of many human diseases such as HIV/AIDS. In *The Coming Plague: Newly Emerging Diseases in a World Out of Balance* (1994), author Laurie Garrett argues that disease interconnects individuals, societies, and governments. Two recent tomes pursue the same theme: global interdependence between human and ecological health is both causing and spreading global disease (French, Hilary, 2003; Walters, 2003). It also is clear that the spread of disease in many nations occurs when governments cannot afford to treat or will not acknowledge a disease. Top US scientists (Microbial threats to health, 2003) believe that over the last 30 or so years worldwide spread of infectious diseases such as AIDS, West Nile, hantavirus, Ebola, Hendra, and Nipah are due to 13 specific world changes. Some of these changes are alterations in human activities such as economic development or land use, international travel and commerce, war, famine, and bioterrorism.

> **Global Disease**
>
> Tuberculosis: About a third of the world's population is infected with tuberculosis. Over 8 million people contract TB each year; the disease kills about 2 million people annually. Almost 98 percent of those affected by TB live in developing economies. However, the growth of new infections is slowing, and more than 60 percent of the world's population now has access to standard diagnosis and treatments. (World Health Organization, 2002, http://www.who.int/gtb)
>
> SARS: Severe Acute Respiratory Syndrome (SARS) emerged as one new member of the family of germs called coronaviruses. This disease appeared in Hong Kong, China, and Vietnam in early 2003. Although the initial number of people affected by SARS was relatively small, global travel and information access led to worldwide concerns. The economic implications of SARS were greatest for Asian nations where the virus began with immediate effects on travel, tourism, and education when each nation closed borders to stem spread of the disease.
>
> Malaria: Malaria causes or contributes to three million deaths per year; most are children in Southeast Asia, India, and South America. Tourism and travel, increased immigration, migration from rural to urban areas, and growing drug resistance are four reasons that this disease now kills more people than it did three decades ago. Malaria Foundation International. (2003, Apr. 13). http://www.malaria.org/
>
> Childhood Diseases: Annual deaths from preventable diseases include almost a million each lost to hepatitis B and measles. Almost half a million die from contracting tetanus, influenza B and pertussis (whooping cough). These and other diseases such as yellow fewer and diphtheria can be nearly eliminated with childhood vaccinations.

AIDS has had a significant worldwide effect, infecting more than 80 million people. By the end of 2003, an estimated 40 million adults and children globally were living with HIV/AIDS (AIDS epidemic, 2003). Of this number about 28.5 million were in sub-Saharan Africa where AIDS is a leading cause of death and made orphans of about 16 percent of children. AIDS and other global diseases have social as well as economic costs. Economic costs are weakened national economies due to resource shifts from production and education to healthcare and early loss of productive workers. The greatest effect may be on the poor because AIDS deprives them of the main resource they bring to the economy: their labor (International Food Policy Research Institute, 2003). Global diseases also have business costs. For example, the estimated economic cost of SARS in the first three months after its emergence was expected to be almost $10.6 billion of GDP decline in affected Asian economies (SARS deals blow to Asian economies, 2003).

Efforts to combat diseases are globalizing. For example, the Global Alliance for Vaccines and Immunizations (GAVI) was formed in 1999 by UNICEF, the World Health Organization, and the World Bank with a five-year $750 million grant from the Gates Foundation. GAVI's purpose is to immunize children in lesser-developed economies. (Global Alliance for Vaccines and Immunizations, 2003). As the example of HIV and SARS indicates in the box below, a global response to disease identification led to very good results.

HIV and SARS: A New Approach to Global Disease

Scientists were baffled by the HIV virus when it first appeared in the early 1980s. Competitive battles emerged to identify and name the virus, resulting in a two-year lag to isolate the germ. In contrast scientists worldwide isolated the SARS coronavirus in only two months of 2003, using Internet links and new scientific techniques to share their findings worldwide. Central players were the World Health Organization and Dr. Klaus Stohr who in mid-March organized 12 labs around the world to search for the cause of SARS. Information shared led to an April 16 announcement from WHO that SARS was a new coronavirus.

Source material: Marc Pottinger, Elean Cherney, Gautam Naik and Michael Waldhoz (2003, April 16) Cellular sleuths: How global effort found SARS virus in matter of weeks. *The Wall Street Journal*, pp. A1–A8.

NATURAL DISASTERS HAVE GLOBAL IMPACT

Weather also affects people and business activities. Sometimes these effects are not well publicized worldwide. For example, in the same year that 3,000 died in a terrorist attack on New York's World Trade Center, more than 15,000 died in an earthquake in Gujarat, India and over 41,000 died in a 2003 earthquake in Iran. Weather-related disasters such as floods, drought, and hurricanes increased from 200 per year in 1993–97 to 331 a year from 1998–2002. In 2003, natural disasters killed three times the number of people they had killed in 2002 (*World Disasters Report 2004*). Natural and industrial disasters more than tripled from 2001–2, requiring resources of food, shelter, and medical aid for those affected (*World Disasters Report 2003*). Tsunamis in 2004 killed over 200,000.

Floods and Economics

2002 was a bad year for floods that swept China, Thailand, and Europe. In Europe alone, reinsurer Swiss Re estimated about $15 billion in damage, some of which would be paid by privatization revenues or budget cuts. Thus less was available to invest in more productive activities. Cultural treasures also were lost. In Prague, museums and libraries were flooded, and many books badly damaged. Also affected were the infrastructures on which business activity depends: bridges, roads, and waterways.

Source material: After the deluge, moi? (2002, Aug. 24) *The Economist*, pp. 39–40.

GROWING PRESSURES ON THE NATURAL SYSTEM

Together population growth and economic development hasten natural resource consumption, putting pressure on the global commons, spreading disease, threatening species, and extending the impact of global natural disasters. The interrelated nature of these pressures is shown in Figure 6.2.

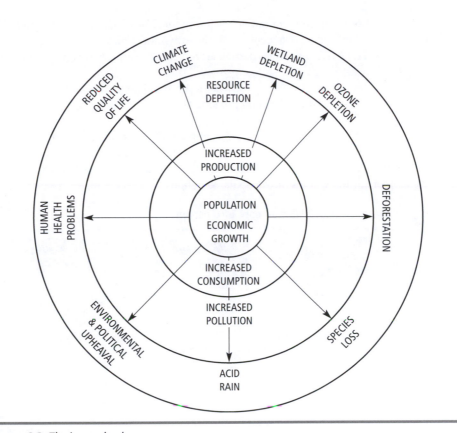

Figure 6.2 *The issue wheel*
Source material: W. Edward Stead and Jean Garner Stead (1996) *Management for a Small Planet.* Thousand Oaks, CA: Sage, p. 22.

World Population

According to Zero Population Growth (2003) it took four million years for human population to reach its 1927 total of two billion. World population had reached six billion by October 12, 1999 (The United Nations Population Fund, 1999) leading to fears that by 2050 population growth would exceed the upper end of earth's 4–16-billion carrying capacity. However, a dramatic and worldwide decline in fertility by 2000 resulted in World Bank and UN population division forecasts of 9–10 billion people by 2100 or about 20–30 percent below 1970s projections. Among reasons for declining fertility rates are:

■ Women are becoming more educated, leading to more employment opportunities and more financial independence for women who then choose to have fewer children.
■ Contraceptives are more readily available worldwide.

- Some government initiatives limit family size, particularly in India and China, and others create disincentives for bearing more children.
- The AIDS epidemic, particularly in Sub-Saharan Africa, is killing women of child-bearing age.
- Television creates aspirations for the small yet happy and healthy families shown on worldwide television broadcasts.

About 81 percent of the world's population lives in developing economies, but China and India alone account for one-third of births worldwide. It follows that global growth could reach new peaks if birth rates rise in either. Table 6.1 provides data on these and others of the world's most populated nations.

Table 6.1 *The world's most populated nations*

Rank	Nation	Population (millions)	Estimated Population (millions) 2025
1	China	1,281	1,394
2	India	1,050	1,628
3	United States	287	413
4	Indonesia	217	316
5	Brazil	174	247
6	Russia	144	102
7	Pakistan	144	322
8	Bangladesh	134	204
9	Nigeria	130	304

Source material: 2002 World Population Data Sheet. (2003, Apr. 13) World Population Bureau. http://www.prb.org

Effects of World Population on Natural Resources

In most advanced and industrialized economies, population growth began to equal or drop below zero population growth (ZPG) in the 1970s, while growth soared in the developing economies. Europe experienced nearly 50 consecutive years of fertility decline, from 2.66 children per woman in 1955–1960 to 1.34 by 2000–2005. By 1976 fertility rates were 1.3 in Italy (Politics of population, 1994). In the same time period, Japan's fertility declined from 2.75 to 1.33 (The future of fertility in intermediate-fertility countries, 2002). Except for the US, which has high birth rates among immigrants and other subgroups, the fertility rate in most developed economies was 1.7 by 2000. The challenges of population decline include reductions in the labor supply, lower potential GDP, and more illnesses associated with aging.

Until recently, low birthrates in developed economies were more than offset by high rates in developing ones, which were 5.6 per couple as recently as 1997 (Population Reference Bureau, 1998). Population challenges of growth differ from those of decline: nations cannot easily feed, educate, or shelter growing populations, and economic development often must take a back seat to basic needs. In recent years, fertility in developing economies plummeted from 6.2 in 1960 to about 3.4 by 2000. One UN scenario is that less developed economies are heading toward a fertility rate of 1.85 (The future of fertility in intermediate-fertility countries, 2002). But these declines are uneven. Population growth is fastest in some Islamic nations (*Arab Human Development Report*, 2003) but not others. In Bangladesh, Grameen Bank and the Bangladesh Rural Advancement Committee's efforts to help women start businesses and gain access to contraceptives are associated with an average Bangladeshi birthrate of 3.3 compared to 4.9 as recently as 1990 (Zwingle, 1998).

Population Challenges Differ for Developed and Developing Economies

Although world population growth may be converging to ZPG or below, developed and developing economies still face different population challenges. These include age structure, gender imbalance, immigration, and consumption habits. Each has different implications for business activities. For example, aging creates opportunities to develop new products and services, but it creates a challenge for retaining and making best use of older workers.

The relatively small populations in advanced economies consume most of the world's resources. For example, richer nations consume 86 percent of all goods and services while the poorest fifth consumes only 1.3 percent. This imbalance leads to growing concern on two related issues: justice and resource depletion. Economic development and prosperity usually lead to higher consumption patterns. This pattern in the advanced economies is one that many in developing economies wish to emulate. Thus, a logical consequence of population growth and worldwide economic development is likely to be a growing demand for limited natural resources, and depletion of natural resources. This is why products such as those Bamboo Hardwoods produces are needed.

The justice issue is one of future distribution. Few in developing economies want to give up acquired goods, and many in developing economies also want to own autos, televisions, refrigerators, and DVD players. The latter may be willing to sacrifice natural resources like trees or air quality to obtain goods or achieve economic development. Both types of consumption strain the natural environment.

Urbanization is another result of population growth linked to production and consumption. About 2.9 billion people of the world's population now live in cities, an increase of roughly a third since 1960 (Zwingle, 2002). The world counts 41 cities with five million or more people and expects another 23 to reach that number by 2014. All but 11 of the total will be in developing economies where most urbanization is occurring (Urbanization, 2000). Rapid growth in these cities puts a further strain on scarce natural resources, particularly global commons of air and water, and needed resources such as shelter and food.

Additionally, the waste that consumption creates is globalized. For example, US waste in appliances, paper, plastic, metal, and other materials is exported to China, India, and other nations as raw materials. US exports of waste to China alone were $1.2 billion in 2002 (Hilsenrath, 2003). Many nations that receive these exports have low environmental, health, or safety standards, and this further strains the natural environment.

Finally, over-consumption is also responsible for diseases of affluence such as obesity (now described as "globesity"), heart failure, circulatory disease, and lung cancer. These are the leading causes of death in the industrialized world. Development worldwide has increased diseases of affluence. For example, lung disease is the leading cause of death in China. Diseases of affluence have resource implications as well as business ones when organizations such as tobacco manufacturers defend against mounting lung-cancer lawsuits.

Industrialization

The industrial model of economic growth has been one driver for worldwide economic integration and for global interconnections of culture, politics, industries, technologies, and the natural environment. Factories that spew pollutants also create jobs and a standard of living that individuals as well as nations seek. Factories also draw people to densely populated areas where urban problems of garbage and water treatment as well as noise, air, and water pollution may occur.

Industrialization may improve world prosperity according to measures of wealth such as GDP, but it also increases potential for ecological disruption and may lead to a declining quality of life. For example, Western observers estimate that a 1994 oil leak in Russia's Komineft pipeline network in arctic western Siberia poured millions of gallons of crude oil into Arctic water. Because the pipeline was important to their livelihood, Russians did not want to abandon it but they found it too costly to fix. However, as the following example shows, the global reach of television technology has stimulated citizen awareness of environmental threats. This has led many to demand more social and environmental responsibility from businesses.

Citizens Meet Capitalism

Globalization of capitalism together with traditional Russian skepticism of almost everything has made many wary of business motives. This has created unusual citizen-initiated demands for Amoco Oil in Novy Port, Russia. The following example illustrates one challenge business enterprises face when citizens are well informed by television, historically cautious about promises, and motivated to avoid environmental mistakes of the past.

Novy Port is a town of 1,000 residents located on top of one of the largest oil fields in the world. While the citizens of Novy Port recognize advantages of oil field development, they also are aware of environmental costs. The legacy of environmental damage to air and water that occurred under Soviet management is visible, underscored by a high cancer rate believed to result from environmental damage. Now that

▶

television has exposed Novy Port citizens to the world "people are beginning to under-stand the concepts of a market, rights and potential profit" (Specter, 1994). Having invested tens of millions of US dollars in the area, Amoco representatives remained tied up in local meetings answering questions like "How much money are you going to earn from all this?" Novy Port citizens, like citizens in many parts of the world, acted to assure themselves that private enterprises would not exploit them in future. Oil companies British Petroleum and Arco gain permission to drill oil wells in places like Siberia and Alaska by guaranteeing that they will build schools and airports or act as stewards of the environment.

Source material: Michael Specter (1994, Aug. 14) A Russian outpost now happily embraces Asia. *New York Times*, p. A1.

As in Novy Port, many people worldwide view business organizations with varying degrees of suspicion or skepticism. Although suspicions may be more perceptual than real they nevertheless shape actions. How, then, is an organization involved in global business expected to operate in a world that both encourages and rejects its activities? This is a challenge facing most if not all business enterprises today. Diverse responses to the same business activities has led many business leaders to re-evaluate and explicitly consider their global roles in preserving the natural environment.

BOOM AND DOOM

Many recognize needs to protect the natural environment, but few agree on how. Some envision a future "boom" leading to unprecedented prosperity that will foster environ-mental preservation; others predict "doom." Champions of each perspective acknowledge that population growth and industrialization affect the natural environment, but suggested next steps have different implications. According to Edward Wilson (2002), where boom and doom differ is:

- forecasting the state of the world
- how far proponents look into the future
- how much proponents value non-human life.

The "Boom" Perspective

Those taking the boom perspective argue that rapid economic growth will generate tech-nologies needed to address environmental problems. Examples might include on-line systems that require less paper, reduced industrial waste due to recycling breakthroughs, or improved resource use due to solar power or biotechnology. Their forecast is positive for the near future, and mostly silent on non-human life.

Until his death in 1998, Julian Simon (1981, 1998) was a champion for the "boom" point of view. Central to his argument is that the key factor in natural and world economic growth is the capacity for new idea creation. Gregg Easterbrook (1995) also sees a boom in development. He argues that the natural world is far more resilient than many think, and that economic development itself leads to improvements in environmental usage. For example, emission controls on gas-powered vehicles have reduced pollution. Other perspectives that support the boom mentality—that economic growth and technology will resolve environment concerns—appear in the following box.

Evidence to Support the "Boom" Mentality

Despite concern that industrialization would lead to pollution for the developing economies (as it had when advanced economies developed), a six-year study by the World Bank (*Greening Industry*, 1999) showed that total emissions are declining in some areas where industry is growing rapidly. In China where economic development is rapid and pollution rife, air quality has remained stable or improved in the last decade.

Bjorn Lomborg argues that the litany of an ever-deteriorating environment promulgated by press, political statements, and individuals is overstated. In his book *The Skeptical Environmentalist*, he argues that the lot of humans has vastly improved. He further suggests that those who warn that the earth is worse off are scaring people and causing them to spend resources on "phantom problems while ignoring real and pressing (possibly non-environmental) issues" (2001: 5).

Von Weizsacker et al. (1998) argue that technological innovations improve people's relationships with the natural environment even as they reduce consumption. For example, drip irrigation is efficient and more effective than other irrigation systems, and battery-powered cars use less rather than more resources. These and other examples show why technology is a key factor for environmental preservation.

To one degree or another, proponents of the "boom" perspective believe that checks and balances in economic systems can be trusted to develop new technologies if old ones fail. For example, if fossil fuels reach depletion, businesses will develop alternative energies. The following example shows how one innovation resolved a particular environment challenge.

New Product, New Approach to Saving the Earth

Mike Pelly's television viewing led him to the world of biodiesel, a fuel generated from "yellow grease" or leftover kitchen oil from restaurants. After seeing a documentary about the product, Pelly enrolled in college to study chemistry and renewable energy, then started working on his own conversion machine. Once a week Pelly picks up yellow grease, and puts it through a machine that screens, adds chemicals, and converts the fuel to biodiesel. Biodiesel will run any diesel motor without modification, and it costs sixty cents per gallon. Although Pelly believes the product is far from commercial use, he formed a cooperative to distribute the fuel, and hopes to make his machine available to cooperatives everywhere.

Source material: John Wolfson (2002, Sept. 30) Cooking oil can fuel the car after it helps feed the driver. *The Seattle Times*, pp. A1, A11.

The "Doom" Perspective

Paul Erlich (1969) is a consistent champion for the "doom" view of the earth's future (Erlich and Erlich, 2004). According to Erlich, environmental impact (I) is equal to population (P) multiplied by consumption or evidence of affluence (A), then multiplied again by technology (T) or I = PAT. This equation expresses a contrast with the "boom" view by showing that technology is part of the environmental problem rather than its solution. Lester Brown, lead author since 1992 of *Vital Signs*, and president of Worldwatch Institute, believes that industrial production is on a collision course with the earth's natural limits. Observable acceleration of economic, cultural, and political globalization described in Chapters 7, 8 and 10 are believed to strain the natural environment, leading to concerns about food, air and water quality, or fuel and other natural resources. Paul Hawken (1993) also argues that technological breakthroughs—such as ability to extract natural resources of water more rapidly—have hastened environmental decline. These examples show that those in the "doom" camp tend to look at the long-run implications of environmental use, and they fear an environmentally impoverished future.

Although economists often view economic growth as providing the answer to most problems, more are weighing the trade-offs between rapid growth and the natural environment to rethink this position. Some join Erlich in expressing concerns about the carrying capacity of the earth. For example, economist Herman Daly (1996) argues that economic growth cannot be sustained at present levels, asserting that economic growth has increased environmental costs faster than the benefits of production.

There is support for both the boom and the doom perspectives. This is one result of technological globalization; information abundance provides empirical support for almost any argument. But deciding where you believe the truth lies is important because action follows analysis. Those associated with the "boom" school deride predictions of "doom," claiming that environmentalists are alarmists whose most dire predictions did not materialize. The bottom line on this debate may be that the cost of being wrong about "the coming boom" is extremely high. Error could mean irreversible planet degradation.

Win/Win Outcomes

Those who argue that the "growth versus environment" debate leads to win/lose thinking (Porter and van der Linde, 1995) call for new perspectives in which "economic success and ecosystem survival are both worthy and necessary goals for individuals, organizations, society and Nature" (Stead and Stead, 1996: 131). According to Edward Wilson, the short- and long-run visions of boom and doom can be combined in a universal environmental ethic (2002). Futurist Hazel Henderson (1996) believes win/win solutions are not only possible but imperative to human and business survival. Often a win/win approach moves the debate to the common ground of "sustainable development," or development that ensures a viable world for future generations.

SUSTAINABLE DEVELOPMENT

Sustainable development, like many other global constructs, can be considered from multiple perspectives. Some definitions emphasize biological minimums (sustaining life), others call for improvements in quality of life, and still others describe trade-offs among competing goals of biological and economic systems.

Regardless of perspective, all definitions of sustainable development force us to think about obligations to the future. A common feature is that most proposals for sustainable development call for fundamental changes in how life is organized. For example, market-based economics accepts there are likely to be rich and poor, but sustainable development calls for increased economic equity. Creating this equity is likely to require a change in economic systems, in organizations, and in individual behaviors.

Principles of Sustainable Development

The following points demonstrate the relevance of sustainable development principles to businesses, governmental actors, and members of civil society:

1 Tensions between economic growth and environmental protection and regeneration have to be resolved.
2 Poor nations cannot nor should they imitate the production and consumption patterns of rich nations.
3 Lifestyles in the rich nations must change.
4 Maximization of income must be replaced with the expansion of opportunities.

Each principle of sustainable development presents a challenge to many traditional business and individual practices. People in rich economies are asked to alter established consumption patterns, and people in developing economies are urged to defer consumption that the rich nations enjoy. Individuals in poor nations may sense that the principles provide yet another way for the rich world to withhold resources from the poor.

Business demands for environmental accountability now come from domestic and global regulations and voluntary codes, consumer demands, ethical investors, employees, environmental interest groups, lenders and insurers (Stead and Stead, 1996), and the business community itself. They create conflicts among governmental and nongovernmental actors, and they provide direction for nongovernmental organizations committed to environmental preservation. The balance of this chapter shows how organizations and individuals address these challenges.

ENVIRONMENTAL ROLES OF GOVERNMENTAL AND INTERGOVERNMENTAL ACTORS

Almost all governments manage business activities via laws, rules, and regulations. Early phases of environmental regulation relied on local and domestic communities to regulate industries and govern behaviors. Hawken (1993) recounts the example of Curitiba, Brazil, where inaccessible streets in slums made garbage collection impossible. Local mayor Jaime Lerner managed the problem with an exchange system that provided bus tokens for recycling garbage and food chits for organic waste. The city's gains from selling wastes not only offset costs but also showed how a win/win approach can succeed.

Local and National Action

Many communities, regions, or nations industrialize by exploiting natural resources such as fossil fuels or trees. Only some have developed rules, regulations, and laws to preserve or protect these resources. National laws in advanced economies govern many business activities, covering specific environmental problems like air and water pollution or species protection, specific industries like paper pulp or agriculture, and geographic regions requiring special protection such as wetlands, forests, or coastal areas (Stead and Stead, 1996). These regulations usually are strictly enforced in the US and throughout Western Europe. In France, for example, manufacturers must document waste creation, where it goes, and how it is disposed of or used. Manufacturers must further receive local approval for waste generated, prove there is no cleaner way to produce their product, and bear costs to take waste to special landfills (The environment is good business in France, 1992). Germany makes it mandatory for manufacturers to take back and recycle materials used in every phase of production. National laws like these extend to local communities to standardize environment practices at least within nations.

Many developing economies have both fewer environmental laws and weaker enforcement mechanisms. In some the government is unable to enforce rules or they overlook damaging environment activities to promote economic growth. For others the costs of anti-pollution or other measures are deemed too high.

Trade-off in the Forests

The trade-off between development and environmental costs is illustrated with a look at logging activities in Pacific Islands. There tropical rain forests are being destroyed by logging and farming practices. Logging companies benefit as do landowners. But their profit-maximizing behaviors accelerate deforestation. Environmentalists argue that forests produce breathable air. Once the tree stock is depleted, Pacific Islanders may have little choice but to become migrants in a world employment market for which they are ill prepared.

Other developing economies find ways to develop and preserve the natural environment. For example, in 1996 Kathmandu, Nepal, introduced battery-run buses to improve air quality. Example of changes in national environmental law appear in the following box.

National Culture Shapes Environmental Practices and Laws

In 2003 Taiwan passed a law banning free distribution of plastic bags and disposable tableware such as chopsticks, cups, or plates from restaurants, supermarkets, fast-food outlets, and other enterprises. According to officials there, Taiwan's citizens use 20 billion plastic bags per year. Because the population is not strong on recycling, these bags are incinerated with other waste, releasing pollutants into the air. About 75,000 businesses in Taiwan will be affected. These laws make Taiwan one of many countries (including Ireland, South Africa, Australia, Britain, Singapore, and Thailand) that has implemented or considered restrictions on plastic use. Like Taiwan, some of these nations restrict use through bans; others tax use.

Source material: John Boudreau (2003, Mar. 7) Taiwan faces plastics ban. *The Seattle Times*, p. A7.

Nations also develop industries to preserve or protect the natural environment. For example, Costa Rica sponsors tours to rain forests and South Africa advertises safaris that showcase a wide range of animals. The principles of sustainable tourism described below often are a guide. Tibet is one among several nations that takes a sustainable approach to natural resource use. In addition to developing nature-based and cultural tourism, Tibet also has introduced a few environmentally friendly industries. These and similar projects stimulate economic development without compromising natural resources, but it is not a model that all nations can adopt.

Sustainable Tourism

Sustainable tourism development meets the needs of present tourists and host regions while protecting and enhancing opportunities for the future. It is envisaged as leading to management of all resources in such a way that economic, social, and aesthetic needs can be fulfilled while maintaining cultural integrity, essential ecological processes, biological diversity and life support systems.

Source material: World Tourism Organization. (2002) http://www.world-tourism.org

---

Most environmental laws punish violations, but often they do little to encourage innovative approaches. The academic field called "ecological economics" calls for re-evaluating economic principles and shifting taxation away from income and toward resource use. This and other practices provide incentives for businesses and other resource users to reduce use and waste of resources like air that are "free" to most industrial producers.

Intergovernmental Activities

A compelling reason for regional and global preservation initiatives is to broaden the scope of enforcement of environmental mandates such that unprotected resources become less vulnerable to exploitation. This is being accomplished through regional as well as global intergovernmental activities.

Regional Associations

Environmental norms and laws to enforce them often emerge from national alliances such as the EU which is a leader on many environmental laws. For example, a clean-air mandate was part of the European Community's 1987 Single European Act. Specific legislation followed to preserve and protect many other natural resources such that EU environmental laws have become the prototype for other multilateral agreements. For example, NAFTA environmental agreements are patterned after EU models. Operating in the EU or selling products there also requires that companies from around the world must comply with "green" dictates. When global companies adopt EU standards on a worldwide basis, environmental practices are improved worldwide.

Multilateral Agreements

Most nations are signatories to more than 150 environmental treaties—over half of which were introduced since 1970. In the 1950s these agreements were of limited scope but by the 1980s there was growing focus on trans-boundary issues such as pollution and ozone depletion. Growing numbers of multilateral agreements address global concerns such as climate change, discharges at sea, endangered species, biodiversity, and nuclear safety (Clark, 2000). These varied treaties are reviewed by Susan Buck (1998) in her book *The Global Commons: An Introduction*.

The Earth Summit

An important intergovernmental environmental activity occurred in 1992. Organized by the UN Conference on the Environment and Development, the so-called Earth Summit brought together 170 nations that agreed to develop regulations and programs to address environmental threats. Because the group met in Rio de Janeiro, Brazil, it is sometimes referred to as the Rio Summit.

Earth Summit delegates specifically considered trade-offs between economic development and environmental preservation, looking at contributing factors such as population, poverty, pollution, and consumption. Delegates reached five main agreements:

1 The *Rio Declaration* articulated principles tying economic growth to environmental issues.
2 The *Biodiversity Treaty* aimed to protect endangered species and better share profits from use of global genetic resources.

3 The *Climate Change Treaty* called for voluntary reductions of carbon dioxide and other gas emissions leading to the threatened "greenhouse effect" of global warming.

4 The *Statement of Forest Principles* recommended protecting forests against development-related damage.

5 *Agenda 21* provided an 800-page non-binding recommendation for how to carry out the Rio principles.

The 1995 follow-up to the Earth Summit demonstrated limited progress on global warming and delegates reconvened in 1997 for the Third Conference of Parties to the UN Framework Convention on Climate Change (commonly known as the Kyoto Conference). Findings included:

■ Despite declining fertility rates in many nations, poverty had grown.

■ One-third of the world's population lived in countries with moderate to severe access problems for fresh water.

■ 34 million acres of forest were lost each year to cutting and burning.

■ Worldwide annual carbon emissions rose from 5.9 billion tons in 1990 to 6.2 billion in 1996.

Efforts to correct these failings resulted in the Kyoto Accord to establish clearer and legally binding emissions targets for carbon dioxide and other greenhouse gases. A Clean Development Mechanism also was introduced to globalize greenhouse gas emissions limits.

ENVIRONMENTAL ROLES OF NONGOVERNMENTAL ORGANIZATIONS

Many nongovernmental groups preserve and protect the natural environment. They operate at local, regional, national, and global levels. Often they play roles that governments do not or will not play. For example, where birth control is banned, groups like Planned Parenthood may be the sole source for family planning assistance.

Transnational environmental groups include those like Greenpeace, Survival International, Friends of the Earth, Worldwatch Institute, Zero Population Growth, Oxfam, and many others whose names may be less well known. Businesses activities increasingly intersect with those of environmental transnational nongovernmental organizations. For example, Greenpeace leads boycotts and demonstrations against businesses that are perceived to use environmentally unsound practices. Protests, marches, sit-ins, and other mechanisms also are used to influence business behaviors.

In recent years, global environmental groups have influenced business activities with propositional as well as oppositional tactics. For example, Human Rights Watch works with insurance companies to track and report the effects of changes in weather patterns or consumption of global commons like air and water. Some INGOs collaborate with one another to influence government and intergovernmental policies affecting business. For example, alliances of NGOs helped generate Earth Summit 1992 agreements to control greenhouse gas.

Other global nongovernmental organizations adopt practices from businesses. For example, the box below shows the mission statement for the Worldwatch Institute is very similar to a business mission statement. The World Wildlife Fund (WWF) increasingly supports their activities with income generation, and others assist with business development or shape business efforts to preserve the environment. For example, the WWF fosters global partnerships to accomplish priorities like species conservation.

Research on environmental groups notes they differ on four dimensions (Clair et al., 1995):

1 Their philosophies range on a continuum from affective, process-oriented approaches to technological, data gathering, linear approaches.
2 Their approaches to advocacy range from low key to confrontational.
3 They differ on desired end states.
4 They differ according to the degree of professionalism, size, and complexity found in the group. For example, an advocacy group like Greenpeace operates as a large, technically sophisticated global organization, but another advocacy group can be four concerned individuals gathered around a card table in someone's basement.

Differences among environmental groups make it difficult for many to coalesce around common concerns. When environmental groups take different approaches, businesses may find it difficult to identify or respond to them. Finally, while few question the motivation of these groups or their desire to bring about what they regard as worthwhile solutions to potentially serious problems, their global scope has been questioned. For example, some local and regional NGOs at the 2002 Johannesburg Earth Summit felt their concerns were overshadowed by international NGOs that had different agendas. Others invite global INGOs to meet the same accountability standards as other organizations (Adair, 1999).

Mission Statement for the Worldwatch Institute

2003: The Worldwatch Institute is an independent research organization that works for an environmentally sustainable and socially just society, in which the needs of all people are met without threatening the health of the natural environment or the well-being of future generations.

1997: The Worldwatch Institute is dedicated to fostering the evolution of an environmentally sustainable society—one in which human needs are met in ways that do not threaten the health of the natural environment or the prospects of future generations.

Source material: Worldwatch Institute. (1997, June 19 and 2003, Nov. 14) http://www.worldwatch.org

ENVIRONMENTAL ROLES OF BUSINESSES

The first Earth Day was celebrated April 22, 1970. Some dismissed these public concerns for pollution, respect for the earth, and ecologically sound activities. At that time few businesses embraced environmental principles without struggles that sometimes included ignoring or fighting environmental regulations. Major concerns were three: that environmental activities were not the responsibility of businesses; that environmental efforts would make businesses less competitive worldwide; and that stricter environmental standards from developed to developing economies would bring charges of business extraterritoriality (imposition of one nation's standards on another). These and other concerns persist, but many businesses now play active roles in environmental development and preservation. Earth Day is observed in over 140 nations, and for some, environmental initiatives are key business strategies. For example, a 1990 United Nations survey showed that a growing number of global firms published policy statements on environmentalism (United Nations Conference, 1993), and others are members of the World Business Council for Sustainable Development or the Global Compact.

Five common practices found among environmentally responsible firms are:

1 Corporate values that promote environmental advocacy such as a clear mission statement.
2 A framework to manage environmental initiatives and activities.
3 Introduction of process and product designs that are environmentally sensitive.
4 Stakeholder partnerships that focus on the environment.
5 Educational initiatives with internal and external stakeholders to inform on environmental concerns.

According to Rondinelli and Berry (2000), businesses tend to organize these practices around internal activities and external ones of three types: incentives for employees to collaborate with external stakeholders on environmental improvement projects; philanthropic activities that support efforts to improve the environment; and strategic alliances between businesses and environmental or public interest groups to solve environmental challenges. The sections below examine some of the ways businesses organize internally to improve environmental activities.

Environmental Leadership

In 1990, August A. Busch III, CEO of brewing giant Anheuser-Busch, expressed a sentiment widely shared among leaders for environmental sustainability. He said: "The world we all share is given to us in trust. Every choice we make regarding the earth, air, and water around us is made with the objective of preserving it for all generations to come." Organizational leaders who take responsibility for the trust passed on by past generations often become champions or leaders for environmental initiatives. Carlsberg A/S signals its leadership commitment by noting that their environmental intent is to go beyond statutory demands and regulations (Graham and Havlich, 1999). Sony leads in another way shown in the following box.

> ### Sony's Green Management 2005
>
> Sony's environment action program titled "Green Management 2005" pursues multiple objectives including: decreasing the impact of business activities on the natural environment, environmental risk management, and protecting the health and safety of Sony employees. Thirty-five Sony manufacturing plants had reached "zero landfill" status by 2001, meaning that they had reduced or recycled waste by 95 percent. Their 2005 goal is to earn this status for all Sony manufacturing plants. All Sony manufacturing plants are ISO 14001 certified, and 19 non-manufacturing plants were awarded Occupational Health and Safety Management System status—another international standard that reflects good management of employee health and safety standards.
>
> Source material: Sony environmental vision. (2002) http://www.sony.co.jp/en/SonyInfo/IR/financial/ar/2001/Enviromental.html (accessed 2002, Apr. 21).

Costs of Environmental Leadership

Firms whose leaders put environmental principles before or equal to profits can encounter opposition and criticism. Body Shop products are not tested on animals, they are available in recyclable containers, and customers are offered an economic incentive to reuse cosmetic containers. But many criticize the Body Shop to say they should do more. This shows that environmental leaders in business may be more closely monitored or held to higher standards than others. In other cases, business approaches to environmental issues may conflict with public preferences. For example, Monsanto CEO Robert Shapiro invested in biotechnology to address population growth problems. But many believe their needs are not served by genetically altered seeds or food additives.

> ### Businesses and Environmental Preservation Activities
>
> McDonald's will not purchase beef raised on rain forest (or recently deforested rain forest) land.
>
> Canon played a leadership role in developing the Caux Principles for a Global Business Ethic.
>
> Forestry giant Weyerhaeuser introduced a program called "Weyerhaeuser Freeways" that gives employees free, unlimited bus or car-pool passes, promotes telecommuting, and offers compressed work weeks, guaranteed rides home, expanded transportation between Weyerhaeuser buildings, and even $1 a day to any employee who car pools, rides a bicycle, or walks to work.

The public also finds it difficult to decide who to trust on environmental issues. For example, although McDonald's developed a biodegradable plastic burger wrapper, the product was withdrawn due to public fears (Halal, 1996). A similar furor in the US weighed the environmental costs of paper versus cloth diapers for babies. The latter consume water and leave detergent and chlorine residue in water supplies; the former are not biodegradable like cloth. Which product is environmentally superior remains a mystery. One result of these debates is that the public is more aware of concerns, but has insufficient data to reach easy conclusions. Consumer uncertainty may be a deterrent to environmental leadership.

Accounting for Environmental Use

The relationship between environmentalism and business is an issue of increasing importance worldwide. Dutch computer consulting firm BOS/Beheer BV was one of the first companies to develop an ecological accounting system to calculate costs of ozone depletion due to BOS's use of styrofoam cups, pollution caused by an employee's plane trip, and even how much sewage employees contribute per year. Environmental accounting as a process requires accountants trained in new skills. The role organizations must play in training and educating their own employees as well as issues of sustainable development are business challenges to consider when studying the globalization of environmental issues.

Cost-reduction and Profit Objectives

Others embrace environmental objectives because they help them achieve business goals. According to the Dow Jones and Sustainable Asset Management Index (Green is good, 1999; Dow Jones Sustainability Indexes 2004), companies with an eye on the triple bottom line of economic, environmental, and social sustainability outperform their peers, particularly in technology and energy. Below we see there are many ways to reduce costs or improve profits and also preserve the environment.

Reduction Programs

Many businesses reduce the amount of resources consumed. In offices, this might mean sending e-mail rather than paper. In marketing it might mean reducing the amount of packaging. For example Lever Brothers, manufacturers of Wisk detergent, used recycled plastic and reduced container size. In manufacturing, it might mean using materials in new ways or reducing emissions as has occurred at Royal/Dutch Shell, Monsanto, British Petroleum, and many other global firms. Sometimes these changes can improve profits. For example, a new Dow Chemical plant in Canada used 40 percent less energy and required less maintenance to release 10 gallons of waste water per minute as compared to 360 gallons/minute for older plants. This also reduced longer-term environmental costs.

Recycling and Reuse

Many firms combine environmental programs. For example, McDonald's Earth Effort program is an integrative recycling program based on three waste reduction principles: reduce, reuse, recycle. McRecycle USA is a commitment to buy a minimum of recycled products every year. Carry-out bags are made from recycled corrugated boxes and newsprint, and take-out trays from recycled newspapers. Insulated concrete blocks made from recycled photographic film are used for building construction, roofing tiles are from used computer casings, and recycled automobile tires are used in play areas. In the photographic imaging industry, Kodak recycles 70 percent of disposable cameras and reuses 86 percent of materials at their Guadalajara plant. Canon, a global firm headquartered in Japan, established the "E" Project ("E" for environment, ecology, energy). The Clean Earth Campaign, a cartridge-collection program, is an outgrowth of this concern for the environment that keeps the environment clean by paying postage for consumers to return used toner cartridges. Portions of the returned cartridges are reused and Canon USA also makes a contribution to The National Wildlife Federation and The Nature Conservancy.

Remanufacturing

Remanufacturing processes include efforts to engineer products designed for disassembly (DFD). A primarily goal of DFD is to design and build a product whose components can be rebuilt, reused, or disposed of safely at the end of the product's life. This approach becomes essential for products like computers that can quickly become obsolete. For example, as early as 1995, two computers were made obsolete with every three purchased. In personal computers, IBM takes back machines from large customers, and helps consumers dispose of unwanted personal computers. For a relatively low fee, useful computers are shipped to Gifts in Kind International for distribution to not-for-profit firms worldwide. Obsolete machines are recycled to prevent hazardous materials from going into landfills.

Reasons for adopting DFD include regulations that make the original manufacturer responsible for product waste, buyer pressure for environmentally sustainable products, and manufacturer incentives to reduce the cost of assembly and disassembly. The results of DFD adoption are that BMW and other German automakers disassembled about 20 million autos for reuse in 2000.

Loss Prevention

Firms in some industries face losses due to environmental degradation. Insurance firms are especially vulnerable to the effects of global warming. For example, a five-degree (Fahrenheit) average heat increase in the US Midwest could turn Kansas into a dust bowl, or a 15 percent increase in hurricane wind speeds would double insurance losses. Similarly, banks face risks from natural disasters caused by atmospheric change. It serves their own long-term self-interest for these businesses to monitor and alleviate environmental challenges.

In summary, businesses commit to environmental objectives for reasons that include personal commitment among leaders, cost reduction, loss prevention, and business survival. The examples above illustrate only a few activities reflective of each. Other approaches include development of appropriate technology, use of renewable resources, participation in writing regulatory legislation, development of social goals, and so on. For example, an appropriate technology usually is one that connects the technology used to the place, culture, and impact of its use. Thus, wind or solar energy might be considered appropriate technologies where both are abundant. Usually renewable resources are those that can be replaced. For example, bamboo and cork have become substitutes for hardwood flooring because both are abundant and regrow naturally.

Sustainable Development Principles for Businesses

Paul Hawken (1993)—one of the founders of Smith and Hawken—writes that sustainable development can be achieved when businesses are organized around three goals:

1 Entirely eliminate waste from industrial production—this would shift emphasis from the current one of efficient disposal and waste recovery to a system design that produces little or no waste.
2 Change from an economy based on carbon to one based on hydrogen and sunshine.
3 Reverse the pattern of production and consumption to create systems of feedback and accountability that support and encourage resource restoration.

The first of Hawken's three goals is consistent with cost-reduction activities described above. However, reversing the pattern of consumption and production highlights important challenges of equity and access. Thus, one of the challenges of sustainable development is to manage the paradox of economic growth against protection and regeneration of the natural environment. Hawken's second two points suggest that business leaders need to transform assumptions about how life and business are organized. This transformation may occur independently, but also occurs when leaders collaborate with others on environmental challenges. Some examples of cross-sector activities are described below.

ENVIRONMENTAL ACTIVITIES THAT CROSS SECTORS

Marstrander (1994) and Bendell (2000a) note that businesses, governments, and civil society organizations increasingly collaborate across sectors on a global level. Some efforts are limited in scope. For example, insurance companies collaborate with Human Rights Watch to predict the effects of weather patterns and consumption of global commons like air and water. British Petroleum's trading emissions plan was developed jointly with the Environmental Defense advocacy group. BP also partners with the World Wildlife Fund in Bolivia and China to preserve biodiversity, and with Oxfam in Angola and Save the

Children in Vietnam. They believe these cross-sector partnerships represent a proactive approach to environmental preservation. These multi-sector projects can take many forms, include many partners, and produce different results as the examples below indicate.

ISO 14000 Standards

Members of resource-dependent industries increasingly partner to develop standards that meet industry and environmental objectives. For example, timber-reliant companies increasingly collaborate with the Forest Stewardship Council to certify that products meet environmental standards. ISO 14000 and 14001 established worldwide standards for environmental management systems. Interest in developing these standards emerged from the Uruguay round of the GATT negotiations and the 1992 Rio Summit on the Environment. Both created commitments for protecting the earth's environment that the ISO 14000 series helped realize. For example, according to the International Chamber of Commerce, some 5000 companies worldwide certify their environmental management systems using the ISO 14001 guidelines. People who developed the ISO 14000 standards worked in committees and sub-committees that included representatives from businesses, standards organizations, government, and nongovernmental environmental organizations. They came from many nations to show that large-scale collaborative activities can be successful.

ISO 14001 requires that organizations develop an environmental policy. Supported by senior management, ISO outlines company environmental policies, integrates them into employee practice, and publicly reports them. Examples of ISO 14001 certification activities include:

- environmental management systems
- environmental auditing
- environmental performance evaluation
- environmental labeling
- life-cycle assessment
- environmental aspects in product standards.

These standards draw worldwide attention to the environment and encourage a cleaner, safer, healthier world for all. Further, standards provide a way for businesses to benchmark their environmental efforts against internationally accepted criteria. Just as occurred in Europe when ISO 9000 quality registration became almost necessary to do business in many sectors, ISO 14000 management system registration may become the primary requirement for doing business in many regions or industries.

The Natural Step

Before founding the Natural Step in 1989, Swede Karl-Henrik Robert observed that unlike himself, many environmental groups perceived business people to be "enemies." Today the Natural Step is a federation of free-standing and autonomous associations committed to the concept of sustainability. For example, one group is Doctors for the

Environment. These associations collaborate with businesses and other organizations and professions to improve environmental use. Managers there believe that good environmental practices and good business economics are not mutually exclusive.

The Natural Step is based on four principles for sustainability. Bradbury and Clair (1999) describe these as:

1 Substances that are extracted from the earth's crust such as fossil fuels or minerals must not systematically increase in the ecosphere.
2 Substances produced by society such as plastic must not systematically increase.
3 The physical basis for the productivity and diversity of nature must not be systematically diminished.
4 Global sustainability requires fair and efficient use of resources to meet human needs. What this means is that we cannot destroy forests to meet survival needs.

A business that adopts Natural Step principles might first measure their own approach to the four principles such as the amount of fossil fuel used and the estimated effect of continued use. This information helps leaders weigh alternatives for use reduction. The success of the Natural Step in Sweden and elsewhere in Europe led to its worldwide introduction. This organization provides a model for successful collaborative activities in which members of different sectors meet to achieve sustainable development.

The Global Compact

Initiated by UN Secretary-General Kofi Annan in 1999, the Global Compact is a voluntary agreement between the UN and businesses. This Compact is a value-based platform to promote institutional learning; it is neither a regulatory instrument nor a code of conduct. Businesses that sign on to the Global Compact agree to enact nine core principles built around human rights, labor, and environmental concerns. Environmental principles spelled out in the Global Compact (http://www.unglobalcompact.com) are:

■ Principle 7: support a precautionary approach to environmental challenges.
■ Principle 8: undertake initiatives to promote greater environmental responsibility.
■ Principle 9: encourage the development and diffusion of environmentally friendly technologies.

Companies that have signed on to this voluntary Global Compact include textile and apparel manufacturers Inditex and Hennes & Mauritz and publisher Pearson Publications.

Table 6.2 *Cross-sector environmental partnerships*

Lead Partner	Main Partners	Purpose
International Petroleum Industry Environmental Conservation Organization	World Bank, UN, US Environmental Protection Agency	Phase out leaded gasoline in sub-Saharan Africa by 2005
UN AIDS Program	Merck, GlaxoSmithKline, UNICEF, World Bank	Improve access to AIDS care in regions hardest hit by the disease
Conservation International	Starbucks, Songbird Foundation	Stimulate growth of shade-grown coffee

The Earth Charter

The cross-sector partnerships described above were initiated and largely developed through organizational action. In contrast, the Earth Charter emerged from citizen action over many years to include representatives in over 70 nations. Defined as a work in progress, the Earth Charter's environmental focus notes that caring for the Earth and caring for people are two parts of the same task. The Earth Charter asserts that humanity must together choose a future with but two options: form a global partnership to care for Earth and one another or risk the destruction of ourselves and the diversity of life (Preamble, 2003).

ENVIRONMENTAL ACTIVITIES AND CONSUMERS

Activist Jane Goodall may speak for many when she admits to feeling overwhelmed by the too-many environmental problems of the world. She concludes that:

We love to point fingers when we try to deal with difficult problems such as the environment, to lay the blame on industry or science or politicians. But who buys the products? We do, you and I, the vast, amorphous general public. Each of our actions has a global impact. (Goodall, 1995: 102)

Three ways individuals can engage in and influence business impacts on the natural environment are "green" consumption, recycling and reuse, and socially responsible investing. "Green" products are "of high quality, durable, made with nontoxic materials, produced and delivered using energy efficient processes, packaged in small amounts of recyclable material, not tested on animals, and/or not derived from threatened species" (Stead and Stead, 1996: 161). Green consumers range widely to include those who buy only when a product meets all of the above characteristics, those who buy when one or more important attributes are met, and those who will substitute green products for lower-price products some or all of the time. Whatever their own practices, most green consumers expect and even demand that businesses be environmentally responsible.

Gaps between what consumers say and do may discourage businesses. For example, Philips Electronics found few buyers for their eco-friendly, energy-saving fluorescent bulbs. Following repackaging and a promotion campaign that emphasized the seven-year life of the bulbs, Philips saw a 12 percent annual growth in sales (Fowler, 2002). In developing economies, green campaigns may be attracting more adherents than in advanced ones. For example, in a 1999 study, Environics International found that more than half of buyers polled in Venezuela, China, India, and Egypt were willing to pay a 10 percent premium for a greener cleaning product as compared to only one-fifth of consumers in Britain, Japan, and France. "Affinity" cards that generate charitable donations for environmental organizations such as the Rainforest Action Network provide another way for consumers to be "green."

Investors can purchase mutual funds that hold socially responsible equities. Usually these funds do not purchase shares of so-called "sin" products such as liquor or tobacco but focus on environmentally active companies. Growing demand for socially responsible funds makes investment counselors and businesses more aware of consumer concerns. Investors who purchase equities only from firms that are members of groups like CERES, the Global Compact, or the Natural Step signal activity approval. Finally, investors propose or participate in shareholder resolutions to influence environmental policy. For example, shareholder resolutions urged American Electric Power Company to reduce greenhouse gas emissions, and similar resolutions related to global warming have been raised at global companies like Exxon Mobil, Eastman Chemical, and General Electric. These and other activities help companies recognize that shareholders want environmentally responsible business leadership.

Whether we interact with the environment as consumers, business people or as members of governmental and nongovernmental organizations, what should be clear from this chapter is that we all have a vested interest in preserving the Earth. This suggests that each of us must more actively engage in resolution of the continuing debate between economic development and environmental preservation

CHAPTER SUMMARY

Globalization of disease, pressures on the global commons, and the growing global importance of natural disasters are three factors that create global pressures on the Earth's natural environment. These pressures are exacerbated by demands for economic growth and by the needs of a growing world population.

Many argue that technological breakthroughs make the "boom" of economic and population growth infinitely possible. Others assert that economic and population growth are consuming and degrading resources faster than they can be replaced by any technology and will lead to "doom."

Principles of sustainable development are that tensions between economic growth and environmental protection and regeneration have to be resolved; poor nations cannot nor should they imitate the production and consumption patterns of rich nations; lifestyles in the rich nations must change; and maximization of income must be replaced with the expansion of opportunities for people.

Growing demands for environmental accountability now come from domestic and global regulations and voluntary codes, from consumer demands, from ethical investors, from employees, environmental interest groups, from lenders and insurers, and from the business community itself.

Common practices found among environmentally responsible firms are: 1) a mission statement and corporate values that promote environmental advocacy; 2) a framework for managing environmental initiatives; 3) green process and product-design systems; 4) environmentally-focussed stakeholder partnerships; and 5) internal and external education initiatives.

Being "green" consumers, investing in socially responsible investment funds, and changing consumption habits are three ways individuals can reduce their use of natural resources and motivate businesses to become environmentally responsive.

REVIEW AND DISCUSSION QUESTIONS

1 Environmentalist/population ecologist Garrett Hardin (1968) asserted that unlimited population growth is likely to have dire results as more people are needed to produce and they in turn consume and ultimately degrade commonly held, life-sustaining resources. A contemporary example of this phenomenon occurs in sub-Saharan Africa. Tribal groups and nomadic families earn income by reducing trees to charcoal they can sell; more family members equal more earnings, but as more produce charcoal, air is polluted and there are fewer trees to offset the effects. The eventual loss of all trees in an area forces relocation and may stimulate greater population growth because families need still more productive members. Consider the next steps in this process in terms of immigration and use of the global commons. In other words, how might these local concerns go global?

2 Find an article that appeared in a trade journal or newspaper in the last six months that describes how an organization is responding to environmentalism. Describe at least three ways the organization is showing environmental responsibility; describe the costs of taking on environmentalism when competitors do not. Use your own words and examples from the article to explain why environmental challenges are global in their impact on businesses.

3 Industrialized nations may be those whose cultures are most aligned with concepts of consumerism and economic development. Less developed economies may not have cultural mechanisms supportive of capitalism. For example, many in Africa are members of tribes and similar social groups whose history is nomadic and agrarian. How can nomadic people stay in control of their own development when the very concept of development is contrary to their culture? If people are unable to anticipate political, cultural, economic, and technological change, how can they plan for or cope with sustainability?

Chapter 7
GLOBALIZATION OF CULTURE

I WANT MY ... MTV

Founded with about $15 million, Music Television (MTV) became a part of television music history at 12:01 am on August 1, 1981. Its initial promotional image was global: a suited astronaut planted MTV's flag on the moon. Today's MTV images are similarly irreverent, reflective perhaps of a tendency among MTV's 18–24-year-old demographic group to question the status quo. Music Television is an organization with a strong internal culture whose icons are likely to be recognizable to music devotees throughout the world. Viewers learn not only about the culture MTV reflects but become part of an emerging global culture that melds words, music, and symbols worldwide.

MTV's original station and later additions such as DD2 Metro in India, VH-1 in England, Nickelodeon, and MTV Asia reach one billion people worldwide. The MTV family of cable channels covers 164 countries using 18 languages, and with present rates of growth MTV could have 2.8 billion viewers by 2010. MTV leaders are particularly interested in the biggest population markets—India and China—and they were the first to launch a 24-hour channel in China. Interbrand identified MTV as the number-one media brand in the world.

MTV reaches more households in both Europe and the Asia Pacific region than in the US where it was founded. And there is plenty of room for world growth because the penetration of cable and satellite outside the US is only 38 percent or about where the US market was in 1983.

MTV worldwide caters to local as well as global tastes. This means hiring local video hosts and decentralizing decision-making to local managers. This means that some shows are the same worldwide while others are specific to a single market. For example, MTV Russia introduced "12 Angry Viewers" during which intellectuals debate the merits of music videos. It may not play in Helsinki.

Vee-jays speak in local dialects and languages, but they also make liberal use of a developing music language fostered by consumers of world music. According to Tower Records' head of retail operations, even in the US "foreign music is where all the hipsters are."

MTV's stated mission is to be "television's most powerful source of freedom, liberation, personal creativity, unbridled fun and hope for a radically better future." The reception desk in MTV's head office reflects some of the fun; it is a huge plastic rock symbolic of rock and roll. At the studios for the head office the monitors are always tuned to MTV, and among the staff it is considered uncool to ask someone to turn down their music.

College interns and production assistants populate MTV studios, and most are in MTV's demographic target group. Except for a very few—including the CEO—aging is synonymous with leaving MTV. Development of MTV programs or new formats for showing video-music tapes often is in the hands of 24-year-old associate producers who can create an idea on Monday, "sell" it to a producer on Tuesday, write it on Wednesday, shoot the video on Thursday, cut and edit on Friday, and air the show on Saturday. The organization has adopted a horizontal structure that enhances the speedy decision-making necessary to track fads and constantly evolving interests among young people. In summary, the mission, the language, the tangible symbols, and the behaviors of MTV employees underscore the solutions MTV has created to remain viable in a society where its audience is increasingly global. ▶

An exemplar employee is Li Yifei—head of MTV's China operation. Like many MTV employees, she didn't follow a traditional career route. Instead she was a national tai chi champion at 13, then attended Beijing's most elite foreign-language university, followed by political science studies in Texas, an internship at the United Nations, and employment by MTV's rival News Corp.

Among reasons for MTV's success are globalization of culture, industries, technologies, economies, and politics. First, the number of television sets and satellite transmissions has increased all over the world. Second, global businesses are heavy advertisers on MTV because it gives them access to young people. Finally, there is the demographic: the world is home to 2.7 billion people between the ages of 10–34. Due to political changes, these and others find it easier to study abroad and work for foreign companies.

Despite its successes, MTV faces challenges typical to any global enterprise. It is costly to develop different programs for each international market, and decentralized decision-making can lead to the occasional misstep. For example, Indian vee-jays refused to play the Hindi film music they viewed as old-fashioned. Their audience abandoned them, but soared by some 700 percent when Hindi film music returned. MTV leaders would like to go global or at least multinational with some programs, but this means finding programs that have near universal appeal. To reach this goal, MTV International created a centralized pool of money for national channels to use in developing joint programs. Meanwhile, MTV continues to meld the local and global, providing new opportunities for local stars to go global.

Source material: Kerry Capell (2002, Feb. 18 MTV's world. *Business Week*, pp. 81–84; Charles Goldsmith (2003, July 21) MTV seeks global appeal. *The Wall Street Journal*, pp. B1, B3; Robert La Franco and Michael Schuman (1995, July 17) How do you say rock 'n' roll in Wolof? *Forbes*, pp. 102–103; John Seabrook (1994, Oct. 10) Rocking in Shangri-La. *The New Yorker*, 64–78.

CHAPTER OVERVIEW

The chapter defines culture, showing how the construct can be applied to both nations and organizations. Many dimensions of culture are shaped within nations, but as businesses transcend boundaries, these cultural dimensions are reshaped to generate cultural interconnections. The chapter concludes with debates that characterize thinking about the relationships between national and global cultures.

AN INTRODUCTION TO CULTURE

There are many competing explanations for why nations and groups perform better economically than others (Harrison and Huntington, 2000). Among these arguments are:

1 External influences such as colonialism, discrimination or differential access to resources such as education account for economic differences.
2 Geography or access to valuable natural resources explains economic performance differences.
3 Cultural differences in beliefs and values affect economic performance.

This chapter explores the relationship between culture and factors such as economic performance. Although culture alone is not the only determinant of outcomes, it does exert a powerful influence on people, organizations, and nations (Landes, 1998).

The border crossings of time and space, of nation-states and economies, and of organizations and industries focus increased attention on how culture facilitates global interconnections. For example, emerging information technologies expose us to cultural norms, values, and behaviors of many nations; telecommunications provide access to much of the world, and movies, music, and the Internet reflect behaviors that may differ from our own. Travel also exposes us to new experiences and different behaviors.

At the same time, one observes similarities among nations such as worldwide enthusiasm for profit-generating activities or global brand popularity. These similarities and differences in culture affect and are affected by national cultural habits. How and in what ways these activities lead to a global culture is a subject this chapter explores.

DEFINITIONS OF CULTURE

Growing international commerce in the 1970s and 1980s made it evident that national cultures shape expectations. In the same time period, it also became evident that businesses have cultures. The book *In Search of Excellence* (Peters and Waterman, 1982) identified strong organizational culture as an important contributor to performance success. "Strong" organizational cultures were expected to help organizations develop and implement common goals, while "weak" organizational cultures were viewed as a drag on organizational purpose (Schein, 1992). Thus culture became an important concept for businesses.

Culture has been analyzed at many different levels including group or subgroup, organization, industry, region, and nation. Hofstede (2001) provides a useful metaphor for distinguishing among levels of cultural analysis, suggesting that nations are cultural gardens, organizations are cultural bouquets gathered from the garden, and individuals are cultural flowers assembled for the bouquet. Culture is also defined in different ways: farmers culture the soil, biologists culture microbes, and in many societies "cultured" people attend the opera. Anthropologists alone have over 200 definitions for the word "culture."

Management scholars also define culture in different ways. For example, Geert Hofstede (1980) describes culture as collective mental programming that shapes individuals' responses to their environment. Vern Terpstra and Kenneth David (1991) describe culture as a learned, shared, compelling, interrelated set of symbols whose meanings provide a set of orientations for members of a society. Edgar Schein (1992) describes culture as the pattern of basic assumptions that are invented, discovered or developed by a given group. These patterns emerge to help the group cope with problems of external adaptation and internal integration. A definition of culture broad enough to apply to the global, national, industry, and organizational cultures examined in this chapter is: culture is the learned, shared, interrelated set of symbols and patterned assumptions that help a group cope with the challenges it faces.

Cultural groups serve similar purposes: to protect against common enemies, manage resources, distribute power, handle deviations from cultural norms, and help people find meaning in life. All require both external adaptation and internal integration. Assembling an army is an example of national external adaptation; systems that feed, clothe, and shelter people reflect internal integration. Although the type of challenges culture addresses are similar, changing contexts require new forms of adaptation. For example, urbanization due to industrialization required internal integration for food transportation systems. Global terrorism as an external threat and Internet privacy as an internal one also require cultural adaptation. For businesses, cultural challenges include external adaptation to global environments as well as internal integration among an organization's people, processes, and structures.

TRANSITIONS IN CULTURAL GROUPINGS

People historically satisfy common needs by forming cultural groupings or societies. According to John Bennett and Kenneth Dahlberg (1993), five transitions occurred in cultural groupings as people developed:

> Transition 1: People living in family units as part of hunting and gathering societies *joined other families in larger groups* whose undertakings were directed and organized by group members.
> Transition 2: Nomadic group hunting became localized and *people settled in geographic territories* where they established one or more encampments.
> Transition 3: People began to raise plant foods and breed animals in *emerging village communities*.
> Transition 4: The rise of trade and craft manufacturing led to an urban revolution where people in groups began to *concentrate geographically in cities or towns*.
> Transition 5: Discovery of means to extract and concentrate energy and other resources in great quantities led to *the modern state* which balances between business interests and community interests.

A global world may represent a sixth transitional stage as people transcend geographic and national barriers to meet common needs. This sixth stage could produce a more global form of culture.

A Global Culture Generates Smaller Cultures

The Internet and other communication media may make it possible for smaller cultural groups to form worldwide. For example, Joel Kotkin (1993) believes that transnational ethnic groups or tribes like the overseas Indians or Chinese have the capacity to transcend national borders, arguing that via common and shared values spanning the globe, these tribes have been instrumental in fostering global business and will remain a force for stability. According to Kotkin, tribes poised to span the globe in future include Filipinos, Lebanese, Palestinians, Mormons, and people from Eastern Europe. People from most of these groups come from nations least involved in global business, and global entry of these groups to business also may reshape business practices globally.

Most of today's cultural challenges are mediated by nations whose citizens learn, share, and appreciate an interrelated set of values, beliefs, and behaviors. Virtually every aspect of a particular national culture develops to support it. Economic and political systems reflect national beliefs about how to manage resources, and national cultures traditionally are a powerful influence on people and organizations. They help define who you are, and they define what is expected of you.

NATIONAL CULTURES SHAPE BEHAVIORS

Having answered the questions of *why* culture emerges, we are better prepared to look at *how* national cultures operate. A shared national sense of values leads to behavioral expectations. This explains why people in most nations derive the same general meaning from the signs they read, words they hear, behaviors observed, and other artifacts of culture.

Many cultural tasks within nations are delegated to groups and organizations. For example, businesses are cultural mechanisms to manage work and transfer resources; charitable organizations ensure that people obtain needed resources; religious organizations help people derive meaning from life; governments mediate between interests that maintain a society and those that disrupt. Nations persist when people adopt a shared culture; they dissolve or explode when they do not.

Cash and Culture

Money is inanimate, but the pictures on it, the language used, even the choice of name for a nation's money animate and reinforce national culture. Take a look at your own currency to illustrate this point; what images are found on money? What do they mean to you? These symbols reinforce a shared sense of national identity that is often protected. For example, one reason that Britain decided not to adopt the euro in 2002 is because the pound sterling remains an important symbol for national sovereignty; at about the same time Sweden also opted out of using the euro.

ANALYZING CULTURE

Like an iceberg, cultural attributes are both above and below the surface of awareness. As shown in Figure 7.1, aspects of culture such as language, behaviors, customs, and norms are accessible or observable.

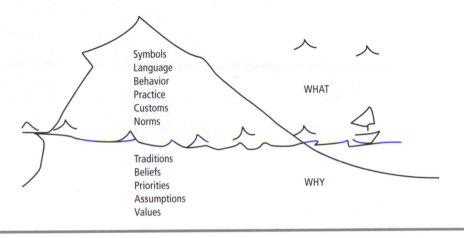

Symbols
Language
Behavior
Practice
Customs
Norms

WHAT

Traditions
Beliefs
Priorities
Assumptions
Values

WHY

Figure 7.1 *The cultural iceberg*

Language and Symbols

Language transmits information and cultural messages in verbal and nonverbal form. For example, parents teach children about culture via language liberally dosed with "no," but the same message is conveyed nonverbally with a sharp glare or hands on hips.

One of the language differences between national cultures is the extent to which information is conveyed via verbal versus nonverbal forms of communication. A *high context* culture is one in which a great deal of information is conveyed by nonverbal behaviors. These nonverbals are embedded in the context of the communication such as who is speaking, the tone of voice used, where they are located in a room, or body language. Many Asian cultures are high context ones. This makes people from them very attentive to symbols and meanings. For those who practice a *low context* form of communication, more of a communication's meaning is conveyed by words alone. The latter communication style is most evident in Western nations where people are most attentive to verbal and written forms of communication. This may explain why many Western cultures rely on written business contracts more than on the handshake or verbal commitment more typical in Asian cultures.

Stories, Rites, and Cultural Myths

Cultural groups use stories and develop rites and myths that reinforce beliefs and values. For example, a family story about Uncle's triumph against adversity encourages others. National stories also function to reinforce desired values and behaviors. The example below shows that learning about culture starts early.

The Smart Brothers and the Stupid Little Brother

A group of immigrant parents from East India initiated a program to teach their children about Hindu religion and culture. They used Panchatantra tales—similar to Aessop's fables—because they contain important moral messages. One such story describes a pilgrimage for three smart brothers and their "stupid" sibling. When the four happen upon a lion skeleton, the smart brothers try to demonstrate their magical powers by bringing it to life. The little brother cautions against using magic, worrying that the lion will eat all of them. The smart brothers persist, so the stupid brother climbs a tree, and he alone is saved when the lion does indeed eat the three "smart" brothers.

When asked to describe the moral of the story, the children answered in different ways. Several thought the message was to get away from wild animals; another thought the story cautioned against bringing dead things back to life; still another said it showed that the stupid brother was right. But the real moral of the Hindu story was more complicated than that: always listen to other people; treat others with respect; have common sense even when you have great knowledge and powers. This example shows how culture is "taught" and it shows that the moral of stories can be more complex than what appears on the surface.

Source material: Rasmi Simhan (2002, Sept. 18) Learning culture through child's play. *The Seattle Times*, pp. F5.

Rites are patterned ways to transition through stages of life. In higher education, for example, the graduation ceremony celebrates a passage from carefree childhood to adult labors. The black robes, distinctive colors for each discipline, and the pomp and circumstance of the ceremony all are symbols for this important rite of passage. Often repeated stories about national leaders become myths that symbolize treasured national values. For example, stories about Ataturk reinforce belief that Turkey can be a bridge between Europe and Asia. In summary, communication, advertisements, symbols, stories, rites, and myths reinforce cultural beliefs about how life is or ought to be organized.

Norms, Customs, and Practices

Culture defines what is "normal" or expected, outlining appropriate behaviors for a particular situation. In the business world, national norms usually dictate when meetings start, who convenes them, who speaks during a meeting, and when it adjourns. A member of the culture knows these norms, and while outsiders can observe them, they often do not know why particular norms arise.

Customary expectations often are broadly defined. It is customary to dress a particular way at work, but some workplaces endorse a very relaxed style of dressing while others do not. One typically dresses differently for a university or sporting event than for work. Practices such as what people ordinarily do also reinforce cultural standards, such as beach nudity. Religious holidays are practices that reinforce the role of religion in life. Other holidays such as Bastille Day celebrate the nation's founding. This is an example of an observable norm, but it need not be a celebration to be a norm. For example, Parisians normally leave the city during August.

Underlying Cultural Values

The cultural iceberg shows there is more to a culture than what is observable. What lies below the surface are the traditions, assumptions, and values that shape the "why" of culture. These values shape behaviors, and help people evaluate themselves, other people, and events (Schwartz, 1992). Values are important because they shape language, behaviors, economic systems, political systems, uses of technology, relationships with the natural environment, and other ways of being. Perhaps even more than behaviors, values are complex and often difficult to describe or explain. Even people within a culture sometimes find it difficult to explain the "why" of their culture. Values tend to vary between nations. The unseen and underlying values of culture can sink a cross-cultural business transaction just as the unseen iceberg can sink a ship.

Culture Frames Our Sense of What's "Right"

Chapter 2 introduced the concept of "framing" to show that people pay attention to what they think is important. Framing also applies culturally because most people interpret behaviors based on their own cultural frames. In other words, we perceive people from other cultures according to what is considered valued and therefore normal in our culture. This can lead to cultural misunderstandings. For example, many in the Arab world believe eyes are a window to one's human qualities. Thus, a Saudi Arabian will stare deeply into another's eyes to observe those qualities. In Nigeria, however, averting the eyes is a sign of respect. Thus, a Saudi and Nigerian who interpret behavior only according to their own cultural frames may misinterpret one another's behavior. This means that cultural learning requires analysis of how behaviors, norms, assumptions, and values embedded in culture shape persons and organizations, including one's own assumptions about work, personal life, business, government, and even globalization.

National Orientations to Values

Many compare one culture to another by looking first at value dimensions to discover that nations differ on values.

Kluckhohn and Strodtbeck Values Orientations

Kluckhohn and Strodtbeck (1961) identified six value orientations that one can use to compare cross-cultural behaviors. These dimensions and the questions one could ask to discover them are:

1 Beliefs about human nature: are humans inherently good, bad or some combination of the two?
2 Relationship to nature: should people dominate, submit or live in harmony with nature?
3 Human activity: are people in the culture oriented toward being, toward doing, or toward thinking?
4 Relationships with others: is greatest concern for oneself and immediate family, to teamwork, or to hierarchical orderings?
5 Space: is physical space public, private, or a mixture of the two?
6 Time: are people oriented to the past, to the present, or to the future?

Cultural Contrasts

Value differences can be polar opposites as shown in Table 7.1. Some of these contrasts relate to metaphysical questions, for example the purpose of life; others are behavioral. The last example looks at learning modes grounded by one pole that is "listen and memorize" and another that is "actively participate." In the US, active learning is encouraged, but traditional learning in Asia or Germany has been to listen and memorize. A US student in a German or Asian school might have few practical skills for succeeding in these systems and vice versa. Follow the line of values down the middle of the table to see how underlying values shape assumptions, priorities, beliefs, and traditions as well as behaviors.

Fatalism and Control

In a society where fatalism is prevalent, negative events at work or in personal life are attributed to the will of a supernatural force, to fate, or to luck. Since these events are perceived to be outside individual control, people rarely fight against them. Conversely, a cultural belief that people control their own destiny almost certainly will motivate individual efforts to alter negative outcomes.

Although national values can be polar opposites, in practice most operate along a continuum from most to least of a characteristic. The sections below look at three important studies that categorize national values used to explain organizational behaviors.

National Values

The Hofstede Studies

Dutch researcher Geert Hofstede (1980) collected questionnaire responses from 117,000 people in more than 50 countries to identify values useful to cross-cultural management. Hofstede originally described four dimensions of national cultural values to which a fifth was later added.

Table 7.1 *Cultural contrasts*

Outcomes are influenced by a higher authority or by fate.	*Fatalism vs. control*	Individuals control their own destiny.
Humans should accommodate themselves to nature.	*Harmony vs. domination*	Nature is a resource for people to use.
Tradition is revered and reveals today's lessons.	*Tradition vs. change*	Change is in most cases desirable.
Live for today.	*Present vs. future*	Plan for the future.
Nurture the human spirit.	*Purpose of life*	Create material wealth.
Life is part of an interdependent whole.	*Ways to know*	Life is rational.
Quality of life determines life success.	*Definitions of success*	Wealth and status reflect success.
Use time to build relationships.	*How to use time*	Use time to acquire resources.
Friendships are lifelong.	*The role of friends*	Friendships are quickly made and dissolved.
Age is venerated.	*Age vs. youth*	Youth is valued; the old discarded.
Identity is derived from group membership.	*Source of identity*	Individual acts define the person.
Depend on the group.	*Self vs. group*	Personal independence is paramount.
Action results from compulsion and force.	*Cause for action*	Persuasion and reason direct action.
Boasting disrupts harmony.	*Modesty vs. boasting*	Self-aggrandizement is the only way to attract attention.

Table 7.1 *Continued*

Mistakes result in a loss of face.	*Risks that fail*	Mistakes show one is trying.
Find ways to maintain harmony and save face for all parties.	*Responding to others*	Tell it like it is, even if information criticizes.
Cooperation leads to desired outcomes.	*Cooperate or compete*	Winning is the important outcome.
Be indirect to avoid rudeness.	*How to ask questions*	Be direct; ask for what you want.
Avoid conflict.	*How to manage conflict*	Confront conflict directly.
Information is in the context and in the words.	*How messages are conveyed*	Words embody meaning.
Listen and memorize.	*Way to learn*	Actively participate to learn.

Source material: Sandra Thiedemann (1991) *Bridging Cultural Barriers for Corporate Success.* Lexington, MA: Lexington Books.

Individualism/Collectivism

This dimension reflects relationships an individual develops. High individualism is a preference to act independently and it is reflected in a greater desire to work independently rather than in groups. High collectivism reflects a greater preference to work in relationship with others. In family life, individualism might create nuclear families whereas collectivism would be associated more with extended families.

Uncertainty Avoidance

This dimension measures the extent to which people prefer certainty in their lives. Individuals high on uncertainty avoidance prefer formal rules and absolute truths. Individuals low on uncertainty avoidance enjoy lax rules and relative truths. Those low on uncertainty avoidance enjoy working with few rules. In contrast, uncertainty avoiders tend to prefer clear rules.

Power Distance

This dimension reflects the extent to which a society accepts that power is distributed unequally in society, its institutions, and organizations. Inherent to a monarchy or caste system, for example, is a belief that some are born to power and others are not. This inequality is expected and accepted in a society high on power distance. In contrast, members of a low power distance society believe that status differences between individuals are not inherent although they may be associated with work roles, for example one is the boss. A preference for high power distance translates into behaviors that suggest one's position in life is determined, into a clear family hierarchy, and at work into a clear definition of who is to lead and who to follow. In a low-power distance society, social inequities are minimized, there is substantial belief in individual equality, and belief that hierarchies are convenient but not unalterable.

Masculinity/Femininity

This dimension of Hofstede's work is perhaps the least well understood. Part of the challenge is that words like masculine and feminine carry different sex-role expectations in various nations. As Hofstede defined them, these scales have little to do with sex roles *per se*, but rather reflect a society's preference for things versus people. In a masculine society, the emphasis is on valuing money and things; assertive acquisition of these things is reflective of a masculine society. Conversely, a feminine society is more likely to emphasize quality of life values, relationships, and nurturing behavior toward people in society.

Time

Hofstede also suggests that time orientation is a fifth dimension of culture which organizes national preferences on a continuum anchored by long-term versus short-term orientations (Hofstede, 1994).

Hofstede's cultural dimensions appear often in organizational studies using scores shown in Table 7.2. However, critics remind us that this and other cultural frameworks should be viewed only as partial explanations for complex cultural phenomenon. Critics of Hofstede's work caution:

- Nationality in the various samples was limited to countries in which IBM had a subsidiary.
- Results may have been influenced by IBM's corporate culture.
- Data were gathered from 1967–1973; major cultural changes are and have occurred since then.
- The dimensions are based on country rather than individual averages; individual differences may be lost with country score averaging.
- Specific items measuring culture may not have the same meaning in each culture.
- Surveys may not be a suitable measure of cultural differences.
- The value dimensions are not exhaustive; the four dimensions described in the 1967–73 studies may not be enough to describe cultural differences. (Bangert and Pirzada, 1992; Harzing and Hofstede, 1996; Lane, 1989).

Trompenaars' Dimensions of Culture

In a ten-year study, Alfons Trompenaars (1994) collected cultural data from 15,000 managers from 23 nations to propose the following dimensions for comparing national cultures.

Universalism/Particularism

Universalism is the belief that the same ideas and concepts can be applied everywhere; particularism argues that circumstances differ and so managerial tools and techniques need to be adapted to particular situations and nations.

Individualism/Collectivism

Like Hofstede's scale, this continuum represents individual orientation. In an individualistic culture, the person puts their own interests before group interests; the reverse is the case in a collectivist culture.

Neutral/Affective

Members of a neutral culture are expected to mask feelings whereas in an affective culture it is considered normal to show emotions. In the latter culture, emotions are assumed to be a natural part of the communication process.

Specific/Diffuse

A specific culture calls for large amounts of public space and small amounts of private space. A diffuse culture would support equal amounts of space for both public and private space, although public space may be more guarded because it provides entry into private space.

Achievement/Ascription

An achievement orientation represents belief that successes and failures depend on personal effort. An ascriptive orientation assumes that success and failure is due to accidents of birth such as gender, ethnicity, nationality, birth order or other factors. This dimension is similar to Hofstede's power distance dimension.

Changing a Culture

Because national behaviors and values are closely interconnected, it is often difficult to change cultural habits within a nation. The following examples demonstrate that pressures to adapt to a more global culture come from both outside and within nations.

Language: Those who communicate globally often adapt English words to create hybrid languages such as Janglish (Japanese/English), Spanglish (Spanish/English) and Chinglish (Chinese/English). Examples from Japan include 'biru' for beer, 'defuro' for deflation, and 'safety drive' to connote defensive driving. 'To mackuru' is to eat at McDonalds and 'haageru' is to consume Häagen-Dazs. Repeated often enough, these words become local standards that can thwart or lead to a more global language. For example, in Russia the definitions for short-term government bills and longer-term bonds somehow were transposed, creating both language and investment challenges.

Education: Japanese public schools revamped their curriculum to focus less on rote memorization and more on developing the individuality the government believes important to a high-tech society. Similar thinking in Singapore led to the development of the Singapore Management University which was to foster creativity and risk-taking among future leaders.

Legal change: Social programs in Western Europe face global workforce pressures to which nations have responded with legal change. For example, in 2005 France moved to alter its controversial 35-hour cap on the working week.

Table 7.2 *Hofstede's cultural dimensions for 53 nations*

Country	Power Distance Index (PDI)	Rank	Individualism/ Collectivism Index (IDV)	Rank	Masculinity/ Femininity Index (MAS)	Rank	Uncertainty Avoidance Index (UAI)	Rank
Argentina	49	18–19	46	31–32	56	33–34	86	39–44
Australia	36	13	90	53	61	38	86	17
Austria	11	1	55	36	79	52	51	29–30
Belgium	65	35	75	46	51	32	70	48–49
Brazil	69	40	38	27–28	49	27	94	32–33
Canada	39	15	80	49–50	52	30	76	12–13
Chile	63	29–30	2	16	28	8	48	39–44
Columbia	67	37	13	5	64	42–43	86	3
Costa Rica	35	10–12	15	8	21	5–6	86	26
Denmark	18	3	74	45	16	4	23	22–23
Ecuador	78	45–46	8	2	63	40–41	37	49–44
Finland	33	8	63	37	26	7	59	25
France	68	38–39	71	43–44	43	18–19	86	39–44
Germany, FR	35	10–12	67	39	66	44–45	65	53
Great Britain	35	10–12	89	51	66	44–45	35	51
Greece	60	26–27	35	24	57	35–36	112	53
Guatemala	95	51–52	6	1	37	11	101	9

Table 7.2 *Continued*

Country	Power Distance Index (PDI)	Rank	Individualism/ Collectivism Index (IDV)	Rank	Masculinity/ Femininity Index (MAS)	Rank	Uncertainty Avoidance Index (UAI)	Rank
Hong Kong	68	38–39	25	17	57	35–36	29	4–5
India	77	43–44	48	33	56	33–34	40	22–23
Indonesia	78	45–46	14	6–7	46	23–24	48	12–13
Iran	58	24–25	41	30	43	18–19	59	35
Ireland	28	5	70	42	68	46–47	35	31
Israel	13	2	54	35	47	25	81	2
Italy	50	20	76	47	70	19–50	75	35
Jamaica	45	17	39	38	68	46–47	13	31
Japan	54	21	46	31–32	95	53	92	47
South Korea	60	26–27	18	11	39	13	85	37–38
Malaysia	104	53	26	18	50	28–29	36	8
Mexico	81	48–49	30	22	69	48	82	36
Netherlands	38	14	80	49–50	14	3	53	19
New Zealand	22	4	79	48	58	37	49	14–15
Norway	31	6–7	69	41	8	2	50	16
Pakistan	55	22	14	6–7	50	28–29	70	29–30
Panama	95	51–52	11	3	44	20	86	39–44

Table 7.2 *Continued*

Peru	64	31–33	16	9	42	16–17	87	45
Philippines	94	50	32	23	64	43–43	44	10
Portugal	63	29–30	27	19–21	31	9	104	52
Salvador	66	35–36	19	12	40	14	94	48–49
Singapore	74	41	20	13–15	48	26	8	1
South Africa	49	18–19	65	38	63	40–41	49	14–15
Spain	57	23	51	34	42	16–17	86	39–44
Sweden	31	6–7	71	43–44	5	1	29	4–5
Switzerland	34	9	68	40	70	49–50	58	21
Taiwan	58	24–25	17	10	45	21–22	69	28
Thailand	64	31–33	20	13–15	34	10	64	24
Turkey	66	35–36	37	26	45	21–22	85	37–38
Uruguay	61	28	36	25	38	12	100	50
USA	40	16	91	53	62	39	46	11
Venezuela	81	48–49	12	4	73	51	76	23–33
Yugoslavia	76	42	27	19–21	21	5–6	88	46
Region								
East Africa	64	31–33	27	19–21	41	15	52	18
West Africa	77	43–44	20	13–15	46	23–24	54	20
Arab nations	80	47	38	27–28	53	31	68	27

Source material: David C. Bangert and Kahkashan Pirzadas (1992) Culture and negotiation. *The International Executive*, 34 (1): 43–64.

Orientation to Time

Trompenaars concludes that cultures have different concepts of time that lead to sequential or synchronous preferences in time use. A sequential preference focussed on the present or the future usually occurs in cultures that value schedules and keep appointments. In a more synchronous time-oriented culture that values relationships of the past or the present, time is viewed as more flexible and less definite.

Orientation to the Environment

Cultural orientations to the environment generate different approaches to control. Defined as locus of control in much of the management literature, this cultural dimension has two poles. An external locus of control is found in those who believe events are outside their control. An internal locus of control is found among those who believe their own activities affect outcomes. According to Trompenaars' data, locus of control is viewed as external in many nations where collectivism is also encouraged, for example China, Singapore, and Japan. External locus of control also would be strong among most Muslims.

Entrepreneurship, Collectivism, and Individualism

A study of business owners explored the relationship between entrepreneurial behavior generated by individualism and collectivism to suggest that the "best" mix may come from balancing these two conflicting values. Similar results were found with a South African sample; with high levels of individualism or collectivism labeled as dysfunctional to entrepreneurial behavior (Morris et al., 1994).

Dimensions of national values can be used to examine cross-national as well as organizational behaviors. For example, there are fewer management education programs in "ascription" cultures than in "achieving" cultures because people in the former usually believe that leaders are born and not made. "Achieving" cultures believe that leaders can be developed. These cultures sponsor educational programs to facilitate leadership development.

Dominant Cultures and Subcultures

Most studies of national cultures focus on the "dominant" culture or the one that most people know. However, it would be wrong to say that nations are unified in terms of their cultural orientations—many if not most nations are home to subordinate as well as dominant cultures. Subordinate cultures arise due to membership in a particular group, for example Pashtuns in Afghanistan, or religious membership, or due to attributes such as gender, age, and national origin. Subcultures also are geographic, such as urban/rural or the region from which one comes. The preferences and tastes of these groups also can be important to organizations. Singapore's population, for example, is composed of Malays, Indians, and Chinese with different habits, and the business practices appropriate to dealing with each may vary even though all are Singapore citizens.

Subcultures among Kiosk Owners in Southern Brazil

Tomasz Lenartowicz and Kendall Roth (2001) identified four subcultures among kiosk owners in southern Brazil. Their values varied on four cultural value dimensions: achievement, self-direction, security, and conformity. The researchers were able to show a relationship between business performance and membership in each of the four cultural groups.

TRADITIONAL SOURCES OF ORGANIZATIONAL CULTURE

Like the larger societies from which they spring, businesses are a collection of people who come together to resolve common problems such as earning a living or providing a response to a social need. Just as national cultures provide solutions to the problems societies face, organizational cultures address organizational challenges. Principal among business challenges are wealth creation and organizational survival.

Organizational cultures are like an organization's personality. They too develop symbols, behaviors, practices, customs, norms, values, assumptions, and even specialized language to achieve their objectives. Organizations also accommodate dominant and subordinate cultures such as professional groups, teams, or gender and ethnic groups that work in the same organization. For example, MTV has a well-developed cultural personality reflected in norms, behaviors and widely shared values. As people who work for MTV get older, they are expected to retire. This reinforces norms for MTV to be by and for young people. An organization with easily recognized symbols and habits like those of MTV is considered one with a strong culture. The following example shows how the British Broadcasting Corporation changed its culture to adapt to listeners' demands and growing competition.

Evolving Mission at the BBC

The BBC was founded in 1922 to counter the growing influence of US mass culture. Sometimes it is referred to in Britain as "Auntie Beeb;" suggesting the BBC is part of the family there. The BBC's original business strategy was to focus on cultural improvement by offering symphony, opera, and chamber music programs. Thus, like family members sometimes can do, the BBC gave the public what it "ought to have." Under growing pressure to give people what they want and in the face of growing competition worldwide, BBC expanded its mission by September 1996 "to remain the touchstone of quality in the new global multimedia environment."

The BBC's position further altered in 2002 when Britain changed laws to allow foreign media giants into their market. Then it altered once again during the 2003 Iraqi war, winning viewers from all over the world who were looking for more objective coverage than found on Fox and CNN.

By 2003 BBC radio broadcasts were translated into more than 43 languages for 150 million listeners worldwide, BBC online also was available, and BBC World's international TV news channel was in 254 million households in virtually every country.

Source material: Kerry Capell (2003, Apr. 28) Suddenly, the BBC is a world-beater. *Business Week*, p. 98; C. Dignam (1995, Mar. 2) Media industry reels over BBC. *Marketing*, p. 9; LeMahieur, D.L. (1995) British Broadcasting Corporation. *Twenty-first Century Britain: An Encylopaedia*, pp. 101–104. London: Garland.

Like the BBC at its founding, organizations traditionally borrow cultural habits from the nations in which they were established. In this way national culture shapes many organizational cultures as illustrated by Figure 7.2.

Figure 7.2 *Traditional influences of culture on business activities*

Deviations from National Cultural Norms
Values in some organizations deviate from national norms. Those that adopt higher standards often survive, but those that deviate with a lower standard usually face challenges. An example of a firm that adopted a higher standard is Ben and Jerry's ice-cream. This Vermont-based business was founded to achieve the profitability important to US culture, but it also pursued environmental and social standards well in excess of those expected from US firms. In contrast, Enron pursued lower ethical and legal standards than those demanded in the US, landing its executives in court and leading to organizational dissolution.

When organizations operate across national boundaries, it may be impossible or undesirable for them to operate according to national values. IBM, for example, found that the strong culture and standards critical to their early success required adaptation and more flexibility in a global world. Similarly, the corporate Disney culture was resisted by French employees who were unwilling to conform to corporate norms for personal appearance, for example no facial hair on men. The Disney experience suggests that the unifying strength of a strong organizational culture can prove a weakness when companies cross cultures. Accordingly, businesses adapt their cultures or confront unpleasant consequences.

Analyzing Organizational Cultures

Attributes of national culture also can be used to analyze organizational culture. As in nations, observable attributes of organizational culture are "above the waterline" on the cultural iceberg. Organizations also convey messages in verbal and nonverbal forms. For example, logo colors and pictures convey a particular image of the organization.

Accessible information in the form of symbols or written information provide insight and direction for organizational members. Nonaka and Takeuchi (1995) call this type of information explicit knowledge because it is usually formalized and widely distributed in printed statements of values, beliefs, or mission. Other organizational knowledge is implicit, passed along in more subtle stories, rites, and myths. Implicit as well as explicit forms of knowledge permeate organizations to shape culture.

Organizational Symbols

Organizations convey information via symbols such as website or annual report pictures of the top management team. Organizations sometimes develop their own unique language to convey a particular cultural value. For example, Nike's "Just do it" campaign reflects a preference for action.

Organizational Stories and Myths

Organizational stories outline expectations such as what one is supposed to do when in doubt, when a high-status person breaks the rules, or how the little person advances (Martin et al., 1983). The World Bank story below illustrates how employees overcome difficult challenges. Although every story has a message, the listener must analyze it for insight. In other words, the storyteller is unlikely to say: listen up for an important lesson. Myths about leaders or outstanding employees outline desirable employee characteristics. An example is a story about Wal-Mart founder Sam Walton, who brought sweets and coffee to loading docks when it was cold. This story exemplifies equity values, showing that one is never too "big" to relate to all employees.

Storytelling at the World Bank

As the story goes, a World Bank health worker was frustrated by the inability to treat malaria in a remote and isolated Zambian town. After repeated efforts in every direction, the worker found an Internet link to the Centers for Disease Control that aided treatment. With this story, Stephen Denning, head of knowledge management, hoped to inspire World Bank employees to reorganize internal expertise. The story tells us several things about how the World Bank can and should function. First, it tells us that the Bank did not have a mechanism for sharing its own information. Thus, one moral of the story is that employees should find ways to improve access to their information and research findings. Second, the story tells us that even when isolated, people are encouraged to maintain links with the world. Third, the story suggests that success among World Bank workers depends on individual persistence. Thus, it tells us that to succeed at the World Bank, employees may have to work hard and against the odds on important tasks such as malaria reduction.

Source material: Stephen Denning (2000) *The Springboard: How Storytelling Ignites Action in Knowledge-era Organizations*. Oxford: Butterworth-Heinemann.

Organizational Rites

Organizational rites also reinforce culture. For example, organizational rites of passage such as a promotion party honor transition from one role to another. Rites of renewal such as year-end parties help to lubricate social relations, and rites of integration such as team-building exercises or executive retreats may revive or develop a shared sense of organizational purpose. Table 7.3 describes some organizational rites of passage and their functions. People who observe these rites are better able to understand the organization and its values.

Table 7.3 *Rites of passage and their purposes*

Rites of degradation	dissolve a person's organizational identify
Rites of enhancement	recognize accomplishments or enhances power
Rites of renewal	lubricate social relations
Rites of conflict reduction	reduce conflict by partitioning it
Rites of integration	revive common feeling

Source material: Harrison M. Trice and Janice M. Beyer (1984) Studying organizational culture through rites and ceremonials. *Academy of Management Review.* 9: 657.

Cross-cultural Differences in Organizational Values and Behaviors

National culture differences can produce culture clash when businesses from different nations interact, when companies from different cultures merge, or when companies create strategic alliances. At the individual level, culture clash often results when people from different cultures first begin to work together.

Culture clash may occur even among nations that others consider similar. For example, Table 7.4 illustrates that value differences lead to different behaviors. For example, higher collectivism in Germany results in group projects and decisions by committee whereas in the more individualistic Netherlands consensus is valued but individual decisions also are possible.

EMERGING SOURCES OF ORGANIZATIONAL CULTURE

Increasing worldwide heterogeneity has brought about changes in organizational culture. For example, IBM abandoned its "blue suit" mentality in favor of casual clothes days to relax formal relationships. The Mercedes Benz "Made in Germany" label was replaced with "Made by Mercedes Benz." The French company Tabacalera and Spanish Seita merged to become Altadis SA whose company language was English (Altadis SA annual report, 2000: 42). Also English is the common language among senior managers at Deutsche Bank. Thus, going global may mean that organizations reflect national cultures less than they once did.

Table 7.4 *Country comparisons on six dimensions*

Country	Universalism vs Particularism	Individualism vs Collectivism	Neutral vs Affective	Specific vs Diffuse	Achievement vs Ascription	Time Concept
Germany	Universalistic: Focus on rules more than relationships 'A deal is a deal'	Collectivist: Decision by committee Group projects	Middle of the road May appear stuffy but warm under surface Devoted to order	Somewhat diffuse Formality is maintained at all times	Achievement: High status given achievement	Sequential: Future-oriented Honor appointments/ schedules
UK	Universalistic: Inner pride History of colonialism (universal rules) Common law	Individualistic: Quaint Eccentric Individual achievement emphasis Inventive	Neutral: Stoic and reserved Polite Gentlemanly Unflappable	Specific: Use of titles in formal settings Slow to form strong bonds	Achievement: Strong emphasis on business hierarchy Task orientation Goal-oriented	Sequential: Future-oriented Honor appointments/ schedules
Netherlands	Universalistic: History of colonialism Highly structured Proceduralized	Individualistic: Balance between knowledge and social factors Consensus also valued	Balanced, tending towards affective: Sociable once they know you Neighborhood orientation Enthusiastic with known entities	Specific: Long-term employment creates work/ home-life bonds Loyal	Achievement: Often use aptitude testing to recruit Less careerist than some Tend to recruit from top echelon of schools	Sequential: Present- and future-oriented One activity at a time undertaken
Switzerland	Universalistic: Follow rules carefully Systematic	Balanced: Social contract is important	Affective: Outgoing Social	Specific: Tight inner circle of friends	Achievement: Personal achievement is important	Sequential: Present orientation Punctual and precise
Denmark	Universalistic: Monarchy Highly structured Idealistic	Individualism: Individual responsibility for own actions Initiative rewarded Broad social support system	Neutral: Emotions controlled, but direct critique accepted	Diffuse: Long-term employment (work and private lives often closely related)	Achievement: Highly focussed on education Small size but high quality, aggressive	Sequential: Keep appointments Act in present but look to future

Table 7.4 *Continued*

Country	Universalism vs Particularism	Individualism vs Collectivism	Neutral vs Affective	Specific vs Diffuse	Achievement vs Ascription	Time Concept
Spain	Particularistic: Focus on relationships Personal systems Trust Duty to friends, family, etc.	Individualistic: Focus on individual achievement Personal responsibility Standing out is desirable	Affective: Physical contact more open and free Expressive, vocal Strong body language	Diffuse: Indirect Avoid direct confrontation More closed, introverted Link private and work lives	Ascription: Status based on position, age, schooling, or other criteria More homogeneous workforce	Synchronous: Relationships most important, time not concern Flexible Present-oriented
Greece	Particularistic: Pride in own history, and ideas Not subject to others	Collectivist: Family and groups highly valued Church plays significant role in sense of community	Affective: Open and confident Expressive	Specific: Open/extroverted Private and tight inner circle	Balanced: Belief in experts and expertise Traditional family ties important	Synchronous: Long, distinguished history, time not definite

Global organizations take shape by borrowing best practices and new ideas from among multiple cultures, but they must at the same time create an internal culture that instills unity and provides direction. Common worldwide processes and structures often are introduced for this purpose, but human decisions to aid or subvert a new process or structure make or break the global organization as it struggles to learn and grow a culture responsive to the dynamics of global change. Lisa Hoecklin (1995) lists three ways ways organizations create global unity out of local differences:

1 Permit local interpretations of values statements.
2 Incorporate local views when creating values statements.
3 Implement a formal process to discuss how the values should be interpreted locally.

Business cultures also overlap with traditions in other organizations. Nongovernmental organizations loan funds to the disenfranchised who use it to start businesses, public universities are encouraged to provide customer service, and government entities are under pressure to provide objective evidence of successful service delivery. These examples illustrate growing pressures for non-business organizations to adopt myriad practices formerly associated primarily with businesses. Thus, there is increased pressure to adopt business practices to settings that were not established to generate wealth. These adaptations can affect how businesses themselves operate.

Converging business activities and values such as these alter cultural roles for businesses that take their cues from the world. This being the case, the relationship of organizational culture to national culture is reconceptualized to reflect that global businesses are both recipients of and conduits for cultural globalization. The example below shows how McDonald's has become a cultural conduit in Asia.

McDonald's Changes "Tastes"

McDonald's has helped change Asia, not only by altering how people behave and consume but also by adapting itself to countries in which it operates. For example, children's birthdays in Asia are often not celebrated, but "Uncle" and "Aunt" McDonald now honor birthdays, including mainland Chinese children whose names and birthdays are recorded in "The Book of Little Honorary Guests" to whom McDonald's sends cards just before their birthdays. Other children throughout Asia now celebrate birthdays by dining at McDonald's where it is almost impossible to lose face because limited menu choices do not allow upstaging from other diners. Watson believes that McDonald's experiences are not so much manipulation of cultural habits as adaptation to them, but other authors note cultural changes that are both helpful and problematic. For example, Japanese were accustomed to dining while seated but now will stand to eat at a McDonalds; Hong Kong Chinese rarely submitted to standing in queues but are more accustomed to it because of habits learned at McDonald's.

Source material: James Watson (Ed.) (1998) *Golden Arches East: McDonald's in East Asia*. Cambridge: Cambridge University Press/Palo Alto: Stanford University Press.

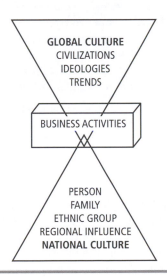

Figure 7.3 *Global businesses as cultural conduits*

In summary, globalization of business changes more than organizational culture; it also affects national cultures and leads to cultural globalization. The following sections illustrate these relationships with a quick look at business/culture interactions related to global entertainment and electronic media, travel, language, demographic groups, and values.

GLOBAL ENTERTAINMENT AND ELECTRONIC MEDIA

A major source of cultural globalization is entertainment media such as films, television, athletic events, live and recorded performances, theme parks, and the Internet.

Film

Films are idealized or incomplete representations of a nation or its culture. Although people within a nation may know their culture well enough to see distortions in film, outsiders may believe that films represent reality in another culture.

Film Shapes Aspirations

In the 1960s, former Indonesian president Sukarno summarized cultural concerns about film to show how access to outside images can alter a national culture:

The motion picture industry has provided a window on the world, and the colonized nations have looked through that window and have seen the things of which they have been deprived. It is perhaps not generally realized that a refrigerator can be a revolutionary symbol—to a people who have no refrigerators. A motor car owned by a worker in one country can be a symbol of revolt to a people deprived of even the necessities of life ... [Hollywood] helped to build up the sense of deprivation of man's birthright, and that sense of deprivation has played a large part in the national revolutions of postwar Asia.

Source material: Marshall McLuhan and Quentin Fiore (1964) *The Medium is the Massage*. New York: Bantam.

Television

Five hundred and thirty-eight million people watched the first moon walk, and television viewership continues to increase. People wringing out a scarce living on a falucca in Egypt, a shakara in Kashmir, or on a plot of land in Peru share priorities for television ownership. Those who cannot purchase their own television often pool village or family resources to get one. Access is stimulated by organizational development. Television news CNN established its global news network during the Gulf War. Doha-based Al Jazeera made a similar splash in 2002 by satisfying growing interest in the Middle East;

it now broadcasts to over 35 million worldwide. Because of television, World Cup soccer and other sports have extended their global reach. By one estimate, 1 in 5 people on the earth or a total of about 1.2 billion people watched the 2002 World Cup soccer finals.

Globo Network

Rede Globo or Globo Network is the largest television network outside the US. Like many other Latin American broadcasters, Globo has experienced success with telenovelas that appeal to rich and poor viewers alike in over 130 nations. These television novels tackle controversial issues of every sort. In October 2001 Globo introduced O Clone, featuring a young woman caught between the traditions of Muslim culture and those of her adopted Brazil. The writer and director believed it important to increase exposure to Islamic life, and producers were responding to growing curiosity in Brazil to learn about Islam.

Source material: Miriam Jordan (2002, Jan. 8) Soap opera exploring interfaith relations captivates Brazilians, will come to US. *The Wall Street Journal*.

Music and Television

Music also has gone global. Globalization has altered popularity patterns and changed modes of music access. This point was illustrated by the Napster case outlined at the beginning of Chapter 2. Many enjoy "world music," providing an audience for recording artists with whom they share no language. Access to this form of entertainment exposes more of the world's people to one another.

Perhaps more than any other form of popular culture, music television is most reflective of globalizing culture. Where once trendy behavior was a spontaneous local occurrence, people can learn and copy trends from everywhere, immediately. Thus music television may convey values associated with wealth creation and consumption. Music television also blurs the line between real life and fantasy life. For example, MTV broadcasts a program called "Real Life" which chronicles experiences of groups of young people. Is what we see life, or is it ... MTV? Is there a difference?

Electronic Media

Part entertainment, part form of mind travel, the Internet is a hybrid mode of information exchange. The falling costs of computers and Internet use improve access to electronic images, ideas, and information across traditional boundaries of time, convention, and national borders. It would be difficult to overestimate the potential effects this form of information exchange has on culture. Other technological breakthroughs with a great impact on culture include improved telephone communication which has enhanced information exchange.

Electronic images and telecommunications are very democratic. Those who are educated know that pop culture represented in film or video is often a poor source of cultural information. However, for many poorly educated people, visual media may be a major information source and from it they may take behavioral and ideological cues. In this way, these media and business activities may shape a more global culture.

GLOBAL TRAVEL

Business, tourism, and educational travel are particularly relevant to globalization of culture. Many if not most of these activities are motivated by or responses to global business activities.

Business Travel

Globalization of business sends business travelers worldwide. Some professionals are sent abroad to work for their own firms, others search for opportunity on their own. For example, many Filipinos work abroad as ship crew members, as maids, nurses, teachers, cooks, and housekeepers, sending millions of dollars to the Philippines each year (Frank, 2001). Earnings repatriation in many nations further links national opportunities to the world.

Tourism

Tourism figures reported in Table 7.5 show travel growth, which is important to economies when it generates jobs and revenues. The boxed example illustrates how Spain has grown due to tourism. This remarkably resilient and growing industry rests primarily on global businesses involved in air, cruise, and travel industries. Growing interest in sustainable tourism brings tourists to many regions of the world that especially need jobs and revenue, particularly Africa where many nations sponsor eco-tourism trips that expose visitors to Africa's animals and other natural resources.

Table 7.5 *Tourism numbers grow*

Year	Number of International Travelers (million)
2002	715
2001	639
1996	593
1995	540
1994	321

Source material: World Tourism Organization (2003, Jan. 27) http://www.world-tourism.org

Spain's Travel and Tourism Industry

In 2003, Spain surpassed the US as the number two tourist travel destination. (France remains number one). Spain's travel and tourism is critical to its economic growth, contributing more than 12 percent of its gross domestic product. Travelers visit Spain in part due to its lower expense as compared with other European nations. Spain has an attractive combination of cultural sites including castles and museums, as well as beaches. But more importantly, Spain's current position may be due to worldwide shifts. For example, global terrorism and conflict in the Middle East has kept some away from Turkey and Tunisia where prices are cheaper. Additionally, Spain's increased number of visitors is at least partially due to a global downturn in the airline industry that has produced cheaper air fares. Thus Spain's future in travel and tourism remains vulnerable to shifts in global environments.

Source material: Keith Johnson (2003, Oct. 23) How Spain lures 53 million tourists—At a price. *The Wall Street Journal*, p. A19.

Business activities resulting from growing travel and tourism stimulate economies, and move new products and new ideas around the world. With worldwide integration, and particularly increased human mobility, these activities also globalize problems like prostitution and child pornography that demand global solutions.

Education

The relatively low cost and ease of air travel also facilitates student sojourns abroad, but other factors operate simultaneously. For example, limited access to higher education in many nations and a growing belief that education enhances economic development encourage nations and families to invest in study abroad. Upon return, students bring cultural practices and ideals from host nations. For example, they encourage businesses to carry foreign products, they start businesses based on experiences gained abroad, or they question national norms. Nations may be more responsive to cultural shifts when they are linked to economic gains that students represent. *New York Times* author Michael Specter (1994) describes how this looks in one part of Russia.

Dateline ... Khabarovsk, Russia

A popular Korean takeout place has opened at the corner of Leo Tolstoy and Kin Yu Chen Streets. Women are wearing cotton sundresses bought from Chinese salesmen who live across the border, 20 miles away. A visitor from Seattle has set up an espresso bar. And at the top of the city's Intourist Hotel, part of a chain that in most Russian cities still seems about as innovative as an old Communist Party boss, Japanese businessmen perform karaoke and eat Tokyo-quality sushi.

Global Food

Forty years ago pizza was a new item in the heartland of the US, and Ricky's Russian restaurant was the closest Hong Kong came to Western food. Today pizza is a global food, and Hong Kong offers food from Thailand, Japan, France, the US, and everywhere else. In Japan, Kentucky Fried Chicken is more popular than it is in US and in Britain home-delivered pizza is the fastest growth segment of the fast-food market. In the US, many eat more like the rest of the world; cilantro, shiitake mushrooms, dulce de leche, and sun-dried tomatoes are only a few *de rigueur* flavors scarcely known in the US a decade ago.

Introduction and adoption of similar eating habits throughout the world is stimulated by fads, travel, business, and a globalizing work place. Younger people like to try new tastes, and many want to be like others their age worldwide. Throughout the world, more women work outside the home, and in many countries there are growing numbers of single-parent households. This leaves little time for daily shopping or cooking, and stimulates the number of households relying on fast foods, quick takeout, and frozen meals.

Convergence in food preferences also has created business opportunities, but as the example of Domino's Pizza shows, those opportunities often require business people to create food hybrids to bridge cultures.

Domino's Pizza in Japan

Ernest M. Higa is a Hawaii native who took the Domino's Pizza concept to Japan in 1984. Domino's corporate leaders were skeptical, and Higa's family members feared that pizza would fail in Japan because Japanese were unaccustomed to eating with their hands, did not universally enjoy cheese, and tended to avoid foods that were not Japanese. As it turned out, Higa had read his market correctly. Young Japanese ready for changes were willing to give pizza a try. Moreover, there were other cultural reasons driving this change. Globalization draws more women and men into the workplace, increasing demand for easy meals such as pizza. Ten years after opening their first store in central Tokyo in 1985, Domino's had expanded to include 106 stores in Japan with $140 million in annual sales and over 4,200 Japanese employees. While the pizza product remains essentially the same, cultural adaptations include tuna and squid toppings, and food presentation that reflects Japanese belief that "one eats with one's eyes" first.

Honoring 20 years of international activities, in 2003 Domino's Pizza created a news release called "Twenty lessons in twenty years of global growth." Included among these lessons was one learned in Japan which is that unlike other places, Japanese buildings are not numbered according to where they are located but when they were constructed; this made it hard to deliver pizzas!

Source material: Carol Steinberg (1995, March) Millionaire franchisees. *Success*, p. 65; Twenty lessons in twenty years of global growth. (2003, Nov. 18) Accessed Nov. 2004. http://www.dominos.com/C1256B420054FF48/vwContentByKey/W25TLJLG823DOMBEN

In addition to changed food habits, commercial holidays once contained within nations spread to include celebrations of Valentine's Day and Halloween in many nations. Indofood now offers both Chinese New Year and Valentine's noodles in Indonesia. Style of dress and other consumption habits, for example use of cellular telephones and beepers, also are more global. US-style football is gaining in popularity in Europe, and soccer is gaining adherents in the US. However, as the boxed example below shows, companies must be careful to introduce new products in ways that are culturally acceptable.

Candy and Politics

Mars Inc. introduced Snickers candy to Russia in 1991 through a grass-roots network of small distributors supported by an aggressive advertising campaign. Initially this successful strategy catapulted Snickers into the top of a Russian confectionery market valued at $2.5–3.2 billion. By 1998, Snickers had become an icon for a perceived pop culture invasion of Russia from the US. According to *US News and World Report*, this shift occurred because Mars' ad campaign was aggressive, used US images and slogans, and its style was similar to that in the former Soviet Union when political messages were repeated endlessly. Further, the cultural environment in Russia changed rapidly from an embrace of Western culture in the early 1990s to later "Russianization." In the chocolate market, foreigners' share dropped from 80 percent in 1992 to about 33 percent by 1998.

Source material: Christian Caryl (1998, Jan. 26) We will bury you … with a Snickers bar. *US News and World Report*, pp. 50–52.

GLOBAL LANGUAGE

Michael Krauss of the University of Alaska at Fairbanks believes there may have been as many as 20,000 languages spoken 10,000 years ago (Miller, 2002) by a total human population of perhaps 10 million. Today more than 6 billion people speak more than 6,000 languages.

National Languages

- According to Dalby et al. (1999), Papua New Guinea has 750 languages and Nigeria has 400 languages.
- There are 150 different Aboriginal languages in Australia, more than all the total languages in Europe.
- There are 11 official languages in South Africa.
- Arabic is the third most used language in Canada.
- The US has no official language.

Language Loss and Global Environments

Technology—unwritten languages are not transmitted electronically, but technology could be used to save some minor languages by creating data bases and allowing linguists to confer on line about language loss and techniques to preserve them.

Culture—as languages fade so do the cultures that support them, leading to less cultural diversity; at the same time, education levels may rise if people can speak a common language.

Economics—the promise of economic benefits will attract young people to dominant languages and businesses feed this interest because they don't hire people who don't speak dominant languages.

Natural environment—native speakers have knowledge of native plants that is likely to be lost.

Political/legal—pressures will induce governments to protect indigenous languages even as simultaneous pressures will be for single languages that reduce costs.

Source material: Rosemarie Ostler (1999, Aug.–Sept.) Disappearing languages. *The Futurist*, pp. 16–21.

The United Nations Educational, Scientific and Cultural Organization (UNESCO) warns that 3,000 languages are endangered, seriously endangered, or dying. By contrast, a healthy language is one that is acquiring new speakers and being passed along to future generations: English fits this definition. English is the language for much entertainment media, and more than half of Internet sites are in English. About 380 million people speak English as a first language, but many more speak it as a second language (Worldwatch Institute, 2001). English is the main language of commerce and of the Internet. The pervasive reach of English is demonstrated by the following examples.

English and Other Global Languages

About 80 percent of worldwide websites are in English (down from 90 percent in 1997), and over 80 percent of information stored in all the world's computers is in English.

English is the dominant or official language in over 60 countries, and it is routinely used in 75 other countries.

Over forty years ago, Voice of America began using Special English to transmit to non-native English speakers.

Caterpillar developed a system of printed communication called Caterpillar Fundamental English (CFE)—a condensed, simplified, and specialized form of English providing non-English speakers with a reading vocabulary of less than 1,000 words sufficient to service Caterpillar machinery.

Edward Johnson at Cambridge University created an operational language for communications at sea, and is in the process of developing about 5,500 words for global "police speak."

McDonald's Corporation employees worldwide ring up sales by punching symbols of Big Macs, french fries, or colas instead of words or numerals. Software does the rest.

Many worry that business English will corrupt other cultures. For example, the "sexually active unmarried individuals" described in the English "Program of Action" of the 1994 United Nations population conference would be criminals under Islamic law. The document also included words like empowerment, reproductive rights, and birth control that are difficult to translate because they are neither practiced nor approved in many nations.

Academie Française

France established the Academie Française in 1635 to legislate French-language use. This body often bars use of words from outside the culture, for example "le weekend," "le parking", and "le cheeseburger" to protect the language and its culture from outside influences. By state decree France advised the French to say "le site" instead of "le site web" to describe a web-based site.

GLOBAL DEMOGRAPHIC GROUPS

Global Elites

Global elites are people from high income groups. Often they are from the highest social class, they tend to be well traveled, and many are well educated. Members of the global elite share family names that are known worldwide, for example Rothschild, DuPont, Agnelli, Kennedy, Rockefeller, Porsche, Michelin. Others are best known within nations or regions, such as Salim or Ly. Nakshatra Reddy is an Indian biochemist married to a prominent businessman; her daughter Meghana is a former VJ on MTV and model. Another daughter also models and a third works for Swatch. All are part of India's contingent of global elite (Swerdlow, 1999). These elites demand high quality, and they consume global products. Although the global elite are not a new phenomenon, growing world wealth may mean there are more global elites than there once were. Characteristics of the global elite are listed in table 7.6.

Table 7.6 *Characteristics of the global elite*

Shared values	Wealth, success, status
Demographics	Very high income, social status and class, well traveled, well educated
Mode of access to them	Up-scale publications, direct marketing, global telemarketing
Distribution channels they use	Up-scale retailing
Price range	Premium
Related segments and clusters	Affluent women, top executives, highly educated professionals, professional athletes
Factors influencing emergence	Increased wealth, global travel and communication

Source material: Salah S. Hassan and Lea Prevel Katsanis (1994) Global market segment strategies and trends. In Salah S. Hassan and Erdener Kaynak (Eds). *Globalization of Consumer Markets: Structures and Strategies*, p. 58. Binghamton, NY: International Business Press/Haworth.

Global Teens

Global teens represent a new phenomenon. Using a broad definition global teens are some 500 million 12–19-year-olds worldwide who share behaviors, interests, and values. They are usually from the middle class and reachable through similar services businesses provide: television, film, the Internet, music. According to a study of more than 27,000 teenagers in 44 countries, global teens can be classified into six distinct groups (see Table 7.7).

Table 7.7 *Six segments of the global teen population*

Teen Segment	Key Definers	What They Enjoy	Their Attitudes
Thrills & Chills (18%)	Friends, family, irreverence and sensation	Fun, friends, going out, experiencing life	Easily bored; seeking good times
Upholders (16%)	Family, custom, tradition and respect for individuals	Conforming to social and family traditions	Dutiful and adhere to family and social beliefs
Quiet achievers (15%)	Success, anonymity, anti-individualism, social optimism	Conform to social norms; strong family ties	Determined and hard-working
Resigned (14%)	Friends, family, fun and low expectations	Negative and destructive images	Low expectation for the future
Bootstrappers (14%)	Achievement, individualism, optimism, determination and power	Achieving	Eager for achievement and power but want to improve the world
World savers (12%)	Natural environment, humanism, fun and friends	Helping others; making a difference	altruism

Source material: Elissa Moses (2000) *The $100 Billion Allowance: Accessing the Global Teen Market*. New York: John Wiley & Sons.

The cultural phenomenon of the global teen provides opportunities to sell products and shape ideals. MTV may sell music, but Benetton ads shape concerns that teens share such as world conflict, responses to AIDS, and hunger relief.

GLOBAL VALUES

The World Values Survey

Introduced in 1981 the World Values Survey examines the values of 65 societies (Ingelhart and Baker, 2000) or about 80 percent of the world's population. Results show that economic development has a powerful relationship with cultural values. That is, people from low-income societies differ significantly from those in high-income countries on two dimensions: traditional vs. secular-rational values and survival vs. self-expression values.

Traditional vs. Secular-rational Values

Low income societies tend to emphasize *traditional* orientations toward authority that include a strong emphasis on religion, a belief in authoritarianism, male dominance in economic and political life, respect for authority, a strong sense of national pride, and relatively low tolerance levels for abortion or divorce. *Secular-rational* societies are found in advanced economies whose citizens place less emphasis on religion, and are less likely to encourage male dominance or accept authority without questioning it. Results from these studies show that the shift from an agrarian to an industrial society seems to bring about shifts from traditional to more secular-rational orientations.

Survival vs. Self-expression Values

In contrast to higher-income societies where are found self-expression values and greater personal happiness, survival values are found mostly in low-income economies. People in survival societies tend to describe themselves as not very happy, and most believe one has to be very careful about trusting people.

During its 25 years' administration, the World Values Survey has shown increased emphasis on environmental protection, women's rights, and participation in decision-making in economic and political life in advanced economies and a worldwide move toward secular-rational values. Based on these data, Ronald Ingelhart and Wayne Baker (2000) conclude that changes in gross national product and occupational structure have important influences on values. At the same time, they caution that traditional cultural influences persist, nations remain a key influence on the values of most people from that nation, and national cultures are not easily categorized. In other words, although economic development does push societies in the same general direction, they tend to move along paths shaped by national culture. However, these findings suggest that links between culture and economic performance go both ways. A shift in economic performance can affect a culture, and a cultural change can affect economic performance.

CHALLENGES OF CULTURAL GLOBALIZATION

Chapter 1 notes that some believe globalization is a negative while others think it can lead to positive outcomes. These same arguments are part of discussions of cultural globalization. Some believe that cultural merging is a form of neo-imperialism that will eliminate cultural variety (Tomlinson, 1991). Others believe cultures will clash (Barber, 1996) or lead to destructive conflict (Huntington, 1993). Given the potential of these negative outcomes, an important question is: What does globalization of culture mean? Is it convergence and compression into a single culture such as a Western or a US culture? Or is it expansion in cultural options? These perspectives are further explored below.

Many take a bleak view of cultural globalization, focussing on rising evidence of cultural violence, armed reactions to cultural imperialism, and growth of a consumer- and self-oriented society capable of displacing spiritual and community-oriented values worldwide. Terrorism, vigilantism, and extremism are three examples of violent responses to culture clash.

Samuel Huntington (1993) believes that culture is a dominant source of potential conflict among the seven or eight major civilizations: Western, Confucian, Japanese, Islamic, Hindu, Slavic-Orthodox, Latin American, and possibly African civilizations. According to Huntington, the highest level of cultural groups can be organized within single nations, for example Japan, or as multiple nations, for example Western civilization. Culture clash between civilizations could arise from unresolvable differences based on important social issues such as equality, individuality, and human rights. Said (1998) criticizes this view of the contemporary world, arguing that thinking in terms of civilizations is a simplistic approach to thinking about groups of people who are complex, diverse, and contradictory.

National culture clash could be encouraged by increased access to and knowledge of each other combined with a growing need for a sense of common identify, and trends toward economic regionalization that make it appear that cultural similarity is important to economic prosperity. These points of view also suggest that global culture is a convergent culture that will have winners and losers. Losers could emerge if globalization of culture is only transformation to a culture of consumption (Bannerjee and Linstead, 2001).

Others worry that cultural globalization constitutes threats to nation-states. Particular worries are that globalization of culture will reduce variation or that national, regional, and affinity cultures such as religion will be subsumed by global culture. Few are willing to give up their own values, and many fear traditional values will be corrupted. As television, Internet, and other media influences skirt legal and value-based sanctions against them, they stimulate growing fear that global media rather than families and nations will shape the values of the next generation. Much of this programming comes from the US, and it is often targeted at the lowest common denominator (Feigenbaum, 2001). This leads to fears that US values of mass consumption will displace world variation in values and behaviors. Thus, the world will become not only homogeneous but Westernized.

The material presented in this chapter shows that globalization of culture has increased most options. One argument is that cultural borrowing such as with "creolization," "mestizaje," or "orientalization" enhances, but does not redefine culture (Pieterse, 1995). "Glocalization" or loose connections between what is local and what is global may instead be forged (Robertson, 1995), leading to multiplication of cultural differences (Kahn, 1995). Robertson (1995) further argues that new awareness of the boundaries that define people and the planet serve not to homogenize but instead to help us understand that cultural differences expose us to greater diversity.

This is the paradox and the challenge of global culturalization. There are growing pressures for homogeneity within cultures, but increased heterogeneity worldwide. As time and space compression bring us to a realization of one world, they also expose us to the infinite variety and diversity of the world. These tensions create opportunities and they exact costs for nations, and for businesses.

Businesses must balance between cultural tensions of homogeneity and heterogeneity. The need for a common culture to direct firm activities is offset by external demands for responding to many needs. Traditionally, organizations have been structured to program out or control diversity. Hierarchical systems, for example, regularize, standardize, and reinforce sameness. Differences in perspective stimulate organizational creativity at the same time they challenge order, structure, and "the way we do things." These tensions exact costs and provide opportunities for organizations to which they respond by adapting internal mechanisms of people, processes, and structures.

Most importantly, this chapter argues that people have options with respect to the cultural norms they adopt. Just as it is now possible for individuals to live within cultures of home, family, religion, subgroup, region or nation, it is also technically possible to operate well within organizational, national, and global cultures. However, since global culture is emerging rapidly, many may feel that they do not have the knowledge they need, and for others the transition to yet another new culture may be painful.

CHAPTER SUMMARY

There are many competing explanations for why some nations and groups perform better economically than others. Cultural differences are one explanation.

Culture is defined as the learned, shared, interrelated set of symbols and patterned assumptions that help a group cope with the challenges it faces. Chief cultural challenges for nations and organizations are external adaptation and internal integration.

Most societies are organized as nation-states. The culture of each nation is reflected not only in how individuals act and react, but also in how political and economic systems are structured, how natural resources are allocated, how technology is used, and how industries and businesses are organized.

Studies of culture show that organizations also have their own cultures. Organizational cultures can be thought of as an organization's personality.

Organizations traditionally adapt their culture to that of their home country, but global business activities cause businesses to adopt new cultures that they then transmit worldwide.

The advantages people and nations derive from globalizing culture include the ability to confront and amend stereotypes, identify with new affinity groups, improve knowledge and understanding, and become aware of new options. Disadvantages include potential conflict, culture clash, and cultural homogeneity.

Just as people find it possible to live within the same nation and subscribe to different cultural rules of family, religion, ethnic group, and nation, so too it is technically possible for people to live comfortably with a global business culture and a differing national culture.

REVIEW AND DISCUSSION QUESTIONS

1 Think of your "work ethic" or how you orient to work. Trace this work ethic to your own cultural experiences with family, friends, and organizations. Use this example to support the assertion that culture is learned, shared, and interrelated.

2 Identify a cultural "story" with which you are familiar and explain what it means. For example, most of us are familiar with stories of the boy who cried wolf, or the boy who put his finger in the dyke. We are less familiar with cultural stories that exist within a single culture. Tell a story from your own nation that you believe imparts an important cultural message.

3 Is cultural globalization convergence and compression into a single culture such as a Western or a US culture? Or is it expansion in cultural options? Weigh the pros and cons of each argument.

Chapter 8
GLOBAL ECONOMY 1— TRADE, FDI, CURRENCY, WEALTH MEASURES, AND FINANCIAL INSTITUTIONS

SO MUCH DATA, SO LITTLE INFORMATION: BARINGS BANK

Barings Bank's first foray into derivatives was part of a 1993 joint venture. At the time Peter Baring, chair of conservative bank Baring Brothers, said 'Derivatives need to be well controlled and understood, but we believe we do that here.' By spring 1995, Barings PLC was bankrupt. This is a story of 'unauthorized' trading in derivatives on the part of one man that led to the demise of the organization he represented. According to differing perspectives on the Barings bankruptcy, it is also a story of dangers with derivatives, of rapid industry change that outpaced current capabilities, or how financial markets went global. In sum, it is the story of opportunities and challenges in worldwide financial markets.

Until spring 1995, 28-year-old Nick Leeson was a Singapore-based trader in the Barings Futures (Singapore) Pte. Ltd. division of Britain's Barings PLC. According to published reports, Leeson had been a successful futures trader in 1992 when Barings sent him to their Singapore office as head of the settlements department. In 1995, he was supposed to be arbitraging between Japanese- and Singapore-based derivatives, which in this case involved simultaneously buying Nikkei-225 futures contracts in Japan and selling them on the Singapore Monetary Exchange. In reality, he was engaged in different activities. Between 1992 and 1995 Leeson was betting on a healthy Japanese stock market by trading in futures contracts and options contracts on the Nikkei Exchange. For Neeson's bet to pay off, the Japanese stock exchange had to stay in the 18,500–19,500 range. On January 17, a disastrous earthquake in Kobe rocked Japan and a few days later the Tokyo stock market plummeted. Mindful of the £450,000 bonus he stood to gain in February, Leeson tried to recoup his losses with further investments in Nikkei futures. He failed, and Barings' losses eventually totaled about £900 million (US $1.3 billion), leading to bankruptcy after 223 years of operations.

This failure illustrates how global banking changes affected Barings. First, Barings' reputation was built on cautious and conservative banking practices such as corporate finance and asset management. But when global competition caused Barings to lose some traditional sources of income, the company took on riskier businesses such as securities and derivatives—a financial contract whose value is linked to or derived from some underlying asset. Options, swaps, and futures contracts are derivatives on which huge bets can be made with small amounts of capital.

As compared to traditional bankers, derivatives managers often are more risk-tolerant. Additionally, they tend to be youthful like Leeson. These differences in style and age made it difficult for traditional bankers to understand or manage derivatives or their managers. Barings had also increased its worldwide staff by 30 percent between 1993 and 1995, spreading people too thin worldwide. Additionally, there were problems with Barings' internal controls. Contrary to prudent practices, Leeson was head of both trading and settlements. In other words, only he monitored his trades, letting him hide evidence of derivatives purchases. Second, according to the Bank of England report on the collapse, Barings officials regularly remitted significant amounts to Barings Singapore without any clear understanding about how the money would be used. For example, at the time of the collapse, funds sent to Singapore were approximately equal to the bank's entire share capital and reserves. Barings' officials could not have missed knowing how much they had sent to Singapore, yet they kept sending money.

▶

The Barings case shows how challenging it is to keep pace with rapid change. In a global-izing economy, rules that once seemed reasonably robust in explaining economic events now seem less well able to explain global occurrences. Blurring boundaries of every type contribute to greater complexity and fewer certainties for every aspect of the global econ-omy. In this emerging global economy, many markets have become global, and most organizations and individuals are ill prepared to manage within them. According to author Frank Partnoy, financial problems like those Barings faced are due to the steady growth of increasingly complex financial instruments.

Leeson's staggering losses of $1.3 billion now seem relatively small in the wake of Sumitomo Corporation's $2.6 billion losses in unauthorized copper trading, Yamaichi Securities' $24 billion bankruptcy, or Enron and WorldCom losses. But each of these terri-ble events shows that data does not necessarily yield information.

Source material: Bank of England report on Barings. (1995, July 18) London: Bank of England; Nicholas Bray (1996, July 22) Ex-boss of Barings' Leeson fights back. *The Wall Street Journal*, p. A8; The collapse of Barings. (1995, Mar. 4) *The Economist*, pp. 19–21; Frank Partnoy (2003) *Infectious Greed*. New York: Times Books; Nick Leeson, with Edward Whitley (1996) *Rogue Trader*. New York: Little, Brown; Charles M. Seeger (1995, Aug. 8) How to prevent future Nick Leesons. *The Wall Street Journal*, p. A15; Who lost Barings? (1995, July 22) *The Economist*, p. 16.

CHAPTER OVERVIEW

This chapter introduces global economics by looking at three principal contributors to a global economy: trade, foreign direct investment, and currency. (The fourth element of the global economy is labor, which is the topic of Chapter 9.) Components of trade, FDI, and currency worldwide are examined and followed by global measures that calculate wealth and development. The chapter reviews challenges national economies face in a more global economy. The chapter concludes with a look at the roles financial institu-tions such as intergovernmental organizations and private entities play in managing the global economy.

THE PURPOSE OF ECONOMIC SYSTEMS

Economic systems provide the means for generating and distributing resources within a society. Economies are supported by production systems that create goods; distribution systems; currency that provides a medium for exchange; and a wide variety of financial institutions that facilitate resource generation, distribution, and investments. Until the twentieth century, most national economies were more closed than open, and within these economies people used the same currency, the same distribution systems, and the same institutions. Further, these closed national economies principally relied on domestic busi-nesses to generate and distribute economic resources. In a closed system, the economic indicators to watch became those associated with the health of the domestic economy. For example, personal income or business investments in capital equipment reflect individual decisions. Macroeconomic activities that reflect the economy as a whole include fiscal policies that extract assets from the system in the form of taxes or add assets in the form of transfer payments and subsidies or monetary policies relating to money supply.

As a result of industrialization, many domestic economies became more open to economic interactions with other nations. This marked the beginning of an active international trading era that required international solutions to the problems of payment, resource acquisition, and distribution. For example, payment for traded goods is more difficult when there is no commonly recognized currency. Thus, new—more international—systems developed to manage exports and imports, to calculate the balance of trade between trading countries, to determine currency exchange rates, and to foster direct investments abroad. These systems evolved to manage international commerce, and as this chapter shows, many are not well suited for managing commerce in a more global world.

How Market Economies Work

By definition, market-based economies are a forum for people to come together to exchange goods and services. Some basic assumptions of free markets are: economic decisions are made by markets rather than by governments; buyers and sellers can freely enter markets; and all have full access to knowledge of prices, quantities, and the activities of others. Market capitalism further assumes that market participants make rational decisions based on their own economic self-interests. The theory is that rational and independent economic actors create a supply and demand market responsive to collective wants and needs. If independent decisions lead individuals to stop purchasing a good, then producers respond by lowering prices or they can halt production. Conversely, if all want the same goods, this creates a scarcity that permits producers to raise prices. As prices go up, ardor for the desired product decreases and alternatives are sought. This up-and-down movement in availability and price is the law of supply and demand, but it is difficult to predict with any certainty. Markets are governed largely by costs, prices, and profits, but the underlying factors for those markets are rarely visible and therefore difficult to predict. This is why market activities are often said to be managed by an "invisible hand."

Creation of economic wealth via free-market economics is a driving force for economic globalization. This system is one driver for globalization, and ways to manage it are evolving. Global interconnections link elements of the global economy to one another, and they link economic issues to cultural and political issues. These interrelationships create dependencies that make it more difficult for individual nations to manage their own economies. They raise the same question for each nation: what happens as the world globalizes and outstrips the ability of any individual country to control the economic events affecting its own prosperity? This chapter explores the question of economic interconnections, beginning with three principal elements of a global economy: trade, FDI, and currency.

TRADE

Both goods and services are part of trade figures. Cross-national trade in visible merchandise is a major source of revenue and expenditures for many countries. Trade also includes services such as accounting, travel, consulting, investments management, and personal services.

Overall growth in world trade increased dramatically from 1982 until 1998 when it fell. The World Trade Organization also reported a decrease in both the volume and the value of world trade beginning in 2001 (WTO Annual Report, 2002) which has since rebounded. The effects of declines and increases are worldwide, but they have had a greater relative effect on the developing economies. This raises questions about how equitable the global economy is or should be, a topic explored later in this chapter. Nevertheless, world trade in goods and services is about 25 percent of world GDP as compared to 10 percent about thirty years ago (Govindarajan and Gupta, 2000).

Trade in Goods

Virtually every nation is involved in export and import activity. Trade in visible goods or merchandise is a major source of international revenue and expenditures for many countries, and about 70 percent of world trade is in goods. Many national leaders pay most attention to trade statistics on visible goods. Their tangibility makes this aspect of trade relatively easy to count. Traded merchandise includes jeans, cola beverages, and other highly visible consumer products. Trade also includes durable goods such as aircraft, automobiles, machine tools, and furniture. Less visible tangible commodities like silver, gold, sugar, and many agricultural products are also part of global trade. The latter "low value" products are the basis of trade in many developing economies.

Developing Economies and Trade

According to the World Bank, the share of world exports accounted for by developing economies expanded from 5 percent to 22 percent between 1970 and 1993. Developing economies accounted for 217 percent of real growth in exports from 1985 to 1996 as compared to 69.6 percent from industrialized nations (Emerging nations win major exporting roles, 1997). Manufactured goods rose from 25 percent of developing economy exports in 1980 to more than 80 percent by 1998 (Globalization, growth, and poverty, 2001). Developing economies were expected to contribute 38 percent of growth in world output in 1995–2010, compared to 22 percent in the 1980s (Reverse linkages—Everybody wins, 1995).

Traders and Investors in Developing Economies

According to Dollar and Kraay (2002), there may be two categories of traders and investors in the developing economies: a globalizing group of countries and a non-globalizing group. The annual per capita growth rate for the globalizing group, for example, India, China, South Korea, Thailand, and Eastern Europe, went from 1 percent in the 1960s to 5 percent in the 1990s. This compares favorably to the 2 percent growth rate experienced in developing economies. In contrast, nonglobalizing nations, many of which are located in Africa, grew at only 1 percent.

Source material: David Dollar and Aart Kraay (2002, Jan. Feb.) Spreading the wealth. *Foreign Affairs*, pp. 120–133.

Firms from developing economies compete in many industries, sometimes by leapfrogging intermediate stages of national development and industrial production to compete in aircraft, heavy equipment, electronics, automobiles, and computer indutries. Exports almost doubled Samsung's electronics sales between 1989 and 1993; Taiwan's Mitac and Acer have become major world producers of inexpensive but reliable personal computers sold throughout the world (Kraar, 1994). The example to follow describes Mexican participation in global industries.

Mexico's Companies Trade Globally

In 1993 Mexico ranked 26th on the list of world exporters. By 2000, it was eighth on the list, shipping more than $120 billion abroad in the form of glass, steel, cement, and automobiles. Although half of this total is generated by US firms, the balance comes from both small and large businesses created in Mexico. Together they employ more than 700,000 people in more than two dozen nations and they generate about $8 billion in annual revenue. For example, Grupo Industrial Bimbo employs tens of thousands worldwide and generated 2003 sales of $4.1 billion. Part of that revenue came from its Czech production of gummy bears. The head of the Czech plant reflects some of the reality of going global: he is an Indonesia Cantonese with a German passport. Although McDonald's rejected Bimbo's initial bread product for buns, today Bimbo supplies buns not only in Mexico but to McDonald's in many markets. Smaller companies such as auto-parts manufacturer Corp. Industrias San Luis SA has become the world's biggest producer of light-vehicle suspension springs. Imsa SA is Latin America's top producer of auto batteries. KoSa—a US/Mexican joint venture—is the world's leading polyester maker. These examples show how firms from one developing economy use trade to grow on a global scale.

Source material: Grupo Industrial Bimbo SA website. http://www.grupobimbo.com (accessed 2004, Nov. 30); Joel Millman (2000, May 9) The world's new tiger on the export scene isn't Asia: It's Mexico. *The Wall Street Journal*, pp. A1, A10.

Changing Import Patterns

From 1981 to 1990, North America, the European Union, and Japan increased the amount of manufacturing imports from the developing world. For example, North American manufactured goods imported from developing economies rose to total 42 percent of consumption in 1991 as compared to 22 percent in 1981.

Developing economies increased import activity as well. Between 1990 and 1993 developing economies' imports grew by 37 percent (The missing link, 1994). These goods came from the industrialized world and from other developing economies. For example, Thailand's exports to six other ASEAN members increased by 34 percent in 1995.

Trade in Services

Trade in services such as transportation, entertainment, financial services, computer and data processing, and telecommunications is growing. Service-trade growth also occurs due to consultants, janitorial services, engineering, tax and accountancies, royalties and licensing fees, and education. The intangible component of these activities makes them more difficult to calculate than visible merchandise trade.

Trade in services is about 20 percent of world exports, but about 60–70 percent of economic productivity in advanced economies is based on services. Principal service traders are the US, France, Italy, Britain, and Japan (World exports of commercial services by region and economy, 2002); 80 percent of the US economy is based on services.

The same rapid development in visible trade in Asia has also occurred with less visible global services. Taiwan-based EVA Airways, Malaysia Air, and Singapore Airlines are growing contenders in commercial air travel, and Singapore's Y.Y. Wong is only one among many Asian entrepreneurs selling telecommunications and family entertainment services globally. Growing desire for branded products is also increasing service-trade activities associated with franchising, licensing, fees, and royalties paid for selling tangible goods such as Prada handbags or Gucci luggage.

The examples above show that growth and volume of trade varies over time to illustrate the rapid yet discontinuous nature of globalization. There has been an overall trend toward greater export growth in every region of the world except sub-Saharan Africa. While the greatest growth comes from developing economies, the advanced economies seek to maintain their lead in value-added activities.

FOREIGN DIRECT INVESTMENT

Foreign direct investment (FDI) takes many forms, but all interconnect economic assets globally. Reasons for business FDI abroad are many including market expansion, acquisition of needed resources, enhanced global position, or even efforts to gain political influence in a host country. Some companies make "greenfield" investments to build a new facility abroad. In this case, FDI is in real-estate purchase or lease, new plant and equipment, and new jobs. Mergers and acquisitions of existing companies are another FDI form, but some of these do not create new jobs or require new facilities. FDI also is reflected in equity investments such as partial purchases of company stock or equity. All types of FDI have increased on a global scale. Between 1976 and 1990 alone, FDI tripled worldwide from under $50 billion to more than $150 billion (*World Investment Report 1993*). Growth in the years to follow was erratic, reaching a high of $1.4 trillion in 2001, then down to $560 billion by 2003. According to UNCTAD (*World Investment Report 2001*), FDI inflows reflect the degree to which nations integrate with the world economy. Outflows reflect which countries control global distribution of FDI investments. Both are reviewed below.

FDI Inflows

Developed Economies

The majority of FDI inflows—about $1 trillion in 2001—go to advanced economies (*World Investment Report 2001*). Economic Triad nations—the US, the EU, and Japan—attracted about 70 percent of these inflows. More recently, China has been the major recipient of FDI inflows.

Why FDI Investments in the US?
Reasons to manufacture in the US are many. One is to circumvent tariffs or import quotas. Another is to reduce currency-exchange risk. More recent reasons to manufacture in the US include moving closer to customers and competitors, or to take part in development of new technology development. For example, Samsung Electronics Corporation built a semiconductor plant in Texas to improve proximity and responsiveness to the US market. Similarly, Infosys Consulting created US jobs better to link India/US outsourcers.   Both industrialized and developing economies have contributed to FDI growth in the US. Asian, Latin American, and Eastern European firms also initiate FDI to spread their risks, reduce costs, and otherwise benefit from a world economy.

Developing Economies

One hundred years ago the inflow of foreign capital to developing economies typically went to infrastructure projects like canal building or natural resource extraction. Today the majority of FDI inflows to developing economies are in manufacturing and services (Dollar and Kraay, 2002). In practice, these types of FDI inflows help nations create competitive global businesses; earlier in this chapter we saw how Mexican businesses achieve this. Developing countries received about 40 percent of global FDI inflows between 1992 and 1994, compared with 23 percent in the early 1980s (Reverse linkages—Everybody wins, 1995). The *World Investment Report 2001* notes that FDI to developing economies also increased in 2000 to $240 billion, but the percentage share of FDI declined.

Where FDI Inflows Go in the Developing Economies

Among the developing economies, South, East, and Southeast Asia have attracted most FDI followed by Latin American and the Caribbean. Asian economies attracting most FDI are headed by China. Latin American countries attracting most FDI are Chile, Brazil, and Venezuela. Eastern European nations such as Poland and Hungary also have attracted FDI. Despite trade liberalization, Africa does not attract significant FDI. For example, Africa receives less that 1 percent of the world's FDI, and much of that is concentrated in diamond and oil mining (*World Investment Report 2001*).

Merger and Acquisitions Activities

FDI also occurs via mergers and acquisitions. Many companies extend their global reach by acquiring equity in the same or complementary businesses. For example, global advertising giant WPP Group acquired all of US ad agencies Ogilvie and Mather and J. Walter Thompson. This was in response to globalization of the advertising industry.

Major industries subject to mergers and acquisitions in recent years include automobiles, aerospace, airlines, pharmaceuticals, energy, and telecommunications. These activities are motivated by many factors such as costs, efforts to establish technological leadership, fear of industry shakeout, or executive hubris. The global value of merger and acquisition activities was $1 trillion in 1996; $1.2 trillion in 1997; $2.489 trillion in 1998; and $3.4 trillion in 1999. This was followed by a decline in 2001, a 12 percent increase in 2002, then another decline, which altogether illustrates the uneven pace of global economic activities.

Pharmaceuticals Pursue Mergers and Acquisitions

M&A results in any given year often reflect industry-specific activities. This occurs because industries globalize at different paces. For example, in the late 1990s many M&A activities were due to privatization of utilities and airlines. Banking was a subject for much 2000 M&A activity. Telecommunications experienced most M&A activity in 2001. In 2002, the focus shifted to pharmaceutical companies. Under pressure to boost earnings, many pharmaceutical companies merged with one another and with smaller biotechnology firms to gain access to new products.

Source material: Geoff Dyer (2003, Feb. 10) Pharma deals lift M&A activity. *Financial Times*, p. 19.

Merger and acquisition activities often raise concerns for host countries. These include the following:

1 Productive capacity does not increase, it is just transferred.
2 Large, acquiring firms may dominate local markets.
3 Efficient implementation from the company's point of view may not be favorable to the host country.

4 Some purchases do not go well and assets are then devalued.
5 Purchases transcend economic boundaries to affect social and cultural norms.
   (What concerns do cross-border M&As raise for host countries?, 2000)

FDI Outflows

FDI outflows come principally from developed economies, including the United Kingdom, the US, France, Germany, and other Western European nations. These outflows usually go to larger developing economies such as China, Singapore, Hong Kong, and Malaysia. However, as with trade, developing economies increasingly invest in one another. This suggests that economic integration is occurring among developing economies as well as between them and developed economies.

Equity Investments

Business Equity Investors

A firm can also foreign direct invest by purchasing shares in a foreign firm. This type of FDI can be full or partial and involve cash payments or stock swaps. When stock is swapped, FDI may involve *control* or influence over a company in another country via voting shares. This occurred when Denmark-based Novo Nordisk—manufacturer of insulin for diabetes—purchased 49 percent of stock in Seattle-based ZymoGenetics. Shared management can create challenges, particularly when assumptions about appropriate managerial behaviors differ.

As compared to FDI in plant and equipment, which tends to be relatively stable, equity FDI investments can be more volatile because shares are more liquid. This creates special vulnerabilities for nations whose economic prospects depend on few rather than many thousands of companies. Most vulnerable are the poorest economies with least companies.

Growth of the Equity Culture

Individuals and institutional investors make a different sort of foreign direct investment when they purchase stocks. A look at their activities illustrates another dimension of global economic integration.

More People Own Equity Shares

More people worldwide now own equity shares of businesses due to many factors. For example, privatization puts public companies in private hands, returns on stock often are more attractive than other forms of investment, and the demise of company pensions encourages people to invest in stock markets. These and other factors generate a global "equity culture" (A survey of global equity markets, 2001) wherein many more worldwide invest in foreign companies. Following poor corporate performance in the early 2000s, market losses between 2000 and 2003 (shown in the box below), and economic downturns, the equity culture is no longer as vibrant as it once was.

Calculating Losses on Global Stock Markets

- Downturns in equity markets destroyed some $13 trillion in wealth between 2000 and 2003. According to a *Financial Times* report, $13 trillion is the equivalent of a $2,000 loss for every man, woman, and child on the planet (Dimson et al., 2003).
- Wealth depletion was uneven, because only about 2 percent of the world's population even owns equities.
- According to the *Wall Street Journal* (Webb, 2002), the world's wealthiest households—those with net investment assets of more than $250,000—had 5.6 percent or $2.6 trillion of their wealth wiped out in 2001 alone. In the Asia Pacific region, net investment assets fell 16.4 percent, showing they were most affected (on a percentage basis) by stock-market declines.
- What did these declines mean for businesses? Equity sales by nervous investors and lowered stock prices further reduced investor confidence, which in turn provided less investment income. Many businesses responded to these conditions with cost-cutting measures that included lay-offs and other reorganizing activities.

Source material: Alex Skorecki (2003, Feb. 12) Shares are safe enough—if you have 50 years to spare. *Financial Times*, p. 28; Sara Webb (2002, July 9) *The Wall Street Journal*, p. C14.

Shares are Listed on Multiple Exchanges and Traded Worldwide

The equity culture to buy and sell stocks translates into annual turnover in the hundreds of *trillions* for thousands of publicly listed companies. For example, the New York Stock Exchange traded 107 million shares in 1985; this increased to 1.2 billion shares daily in 2001 (Exchange places, 2001).

Global Changes in Share Trading

In the 1970s cross-border transactions of all stock and bond trades as a ratio of overall GDP for Japan, the US, and Germany were less than 5 percent. By 1996 this ratio had increased to 100 percent in Japan, 150 percent in the US, 200 percent in Germany (Govindarajan and Gupta, 2000).

In 1970, 66 percent of the world's equity capitalization was in US stocks; by 1995 the US share was 38 percent.

Source material: Vijay Govindarajan and Anil K. Gupta (2000) Analysis of the emerging global Arena. *European Management Journal*, 18 (3): 274–84.

A global equity culture is facilitated by availability, and global share offerings shift a company's dependency from a single nation to the world. As early as 1985, Volvo's Pehr

Gyllenhammer campaigned to get more individuals outside Sweden to hold Volvo stock; 48 percent of Olivetti shares are owned abroad. Over 600 foreign stocks are traded on the New York stock exchange and electronic trading has made it even easier for individual investors and companies to purchase an equity position in publicly traded firms located anywhere in the world. This opportunity is offset by challenges such as the one Bridgestone faced due to global equity ownership.

Bridgestone's Dilemma

In August 2000, Bridgestone's Firestone tires were recalled due to safety problems. According to some, heavy selling of Bridgestone shares by foreign holders was a major factor contributing to a 50 percent drop in the company's stock price. Equities of the tire maker—like most other companies in corporate Japan—are held not only by Japanese, but also increasingly by foreign investors. Selling on the part of the latter is a major factor behind the drop in Bridgestone shares.

Interconnections between Japanese firms and world investors began when Japanese markets were opened to foreign brokerage firms. Overseas investors became active traders in Japanese stocks. For example, in the week of May 14, 2001 foreign securities firms accounted for about 50 percent of trading volume in Japanese shares; this is compared with only 27 percent in 1995. Overseas investors also own 18.6 percent of Japanese shares by value, up from 4 percent a decade earlier.

Overseas investors create another threat to companies like Bridgestone. Unlike the many Japanese banks that tend to hold investments over decades, overseas investors sell when they are not happy with financial returns. Increased turnover in Bridgestone stock produces downward pressure on share prices. This could motivate institutional and portfolio managers to agitate for more change in corporate Japanese practices.

Source material: Jason Singer (2001, May 30) Bridgestone is test case in new market climate. *The Wall Street Journal*, p. A19.

In the US, foreign stocks are available via ADRs (American Depository Receipts). These are dollar-denominated certificates held by US banks. Stocks from more than 80 countries total 2,200 non-US issues traded in US equity markets (The ADR Reference Guide, 2002/2003), up from 1,300 in 1996. Bank of New York—the leading manager of ADR programs—reported that in the first half of 1996, 62 non-US companies and 11 governments raised about $6.7 billion through ADR programs, an increase of 75 percent over the previous year.

ADR shares are not altogether liquid, but they offer access to a broader range of investments for companies worldwide. For example, the ADR trading volume for many Latin American companies exceeds that of corresponding shares in their domestic markets. This can be an advantage for high-performance firms whose market values may be artificially depressed by poor local economies.

Global Shares

In 1998, DaimlerChrysler began trading as a global share in the US, Germany, Japan, and five other countries. What this means is that the same shares are traded in multiple currencies around the world. Global share trading is not yet popular, and is available only for a few companies such as financial services giant UBS, Celanese, DaimlerChrysler, and Deutsche Bank.

Worldwide Equity Ownership Synchronizes Market Effects

Almost everyone has better access to information, and overlapping time zones for stock markets combined with electronic communications facilitate transactions. This provides equal exposure to both profits and losses from global interconnections. The record $1 trillion loss of New York Exchange equity on April 14, 2000 was followed by losses on exchanges in Tokyo, Singapore, Australia, South Korea, and Europe.

Stock ownership also causes people to factor in stock prices when estimating their confidence in an economy. When stock prices fall, shareholders perceive they have less money. They curtail spending. In this way equity markets worldwide affect consumption patterns within economies.

Stock Market Exchanges

Many stock exchanges operate worldwide. In August 2001, their total capitalization—the market value of all listed companies—was about $30 trillion. This was only slightly less than 2001 world product. Markets extend the trading day from Tokyo through London to New York and back again. There are almost 100 stock markets worldwide; 30 are in Europe alone. The cultural and political bases of stock markets make it difficult to coordinate among them. In Europe, for example, stock exchanges located in different nations celebrate 57 different national holidays as compared to nine holidays for the New York Stock Exchange (Ascarelli, 1999). The following example illustrates yet another problem with 24/7 trading.

24-hour Trading

The New York Stock Exchange operates only during weekdays, but the "after hours" market increasingly provides trading opportunities. According to the *Wall Street Journal*, millions of shares are routinely traded after the markets close, even seven days a week. For example, a Florida jury verdict against a tobacco company drove Philip Morris to a $102 close on Friday's market, but after hours trading resulted in a Monday morning opening price of $95. Because after hours trading results are not reported widely, only some buyers and sellers were aware of the weekend price drop. Those relying on published results from Friday's market close must have been dismayed to learn Philip Morris shares had lost $7 in market value over the weekend.

Source material: Dave Kansas (1996, Aug. 12) Nicked at night: Even after the market closes, stock prices can take wild swings. *The Wall Street Journal*, pp. A1, A8.

Other Financial Instruments

The same factors that stimulate equity purchases also attract investors to debt instruments like bonds and newer financial instruments such as derivatives, swaps, and options. These too are going global. For example, Malaysia issued the first Islamic global bond, aiming to raise $350–500 million. These bonds are structured according to Islamic religious principles forbidding interest payments. Instead, the bonds carry a zero coupon or pay a profit rate, returns that are permissible under Islam law (Malaysia plans Islamic global bond, 2002). Although demand for global debt issues may be going global, markets to manage them are as yet regional or national.

In summary, rapid, discontinuous economic integration has occurred because of world-wide economic activities. This integration in turn makes it more difficult for nations to make independent fiscal and monetary decisions. The following look at global currency shows that this third indicator of a global economy has also become more complex, has reduced national autonomy, and, because of rapid changes, has increased uncertainties.

CURRENCY

Exchange of goods and services between nations requires a payment system. Barter is used in some cases, but currency is more often the basic of that system. Except for goods that universally trade in the same currency (oil is purchased with US dollars), most settlements require conversion from the buyer's currency into that of the seller's. Motivations for current currency exchange systems are outlined below. Although global trades would be facilitated by a global medium for exchange, such a system is not yet in place. National and regional currencies are the best substitute, but another suggested approach is electronic currency. The evidence favoring each approach also is reviewed below.

Currency Exchange

As we saw when examining global stock markets, investors worldwide seek return on capital. Capital in the form of currency is especially easy to move globally. Capital can migrate 24 hours a day in search of higher returns, and many make their living while trading from the comfort of home via computer links to stock and capital markets.

Exchange rates are the number of units of one currency required for a unit of another currency. Variations in currency exchange rates have price implications for firms and for individuals when goods are purchased from other nations. Global price comparisons prepared by Runzheimer International illustrate this point. For example, the 2002 price of 100 aspirin tablets range from a high of $35.93 in Tokyo to a low of $1.16 in Mexico City. Travelers have little choice but to pay the current price for aspirin when in Tokyo, but doing so reduces the amount available to purchase other goods and services.

Cost variations resulting from exchange rate variations have similar implications for the firm. These fluctuations make it difficult to plan for costs and they necessarily affect profits. The box below provides some examples.

An Example of Currency Fluctuations

In 1985 the yen to dollar ratio was 258 yen to $1; by April 1996, it was 79 yen to $1. In effect, the dollar could be bought for fewer yen in 1996 as compared to 1985 and so each yen bought more goods in the US than in earlier years. This stimulated investment decisions. For example, when the Japanese yen was at a peak relative to the US dollar in April of 1996, Japanese automakers initiated construction of auto manufacturing plants in the US because each yen then bought more real estate, more plant and equipment, and more labor than in the past. But the reverse also occurs with respect to currency exchanges. As the dollar strengthened against the yen through late 1996 and 1997, commitments to build plants in the US then had to be paid in more yen per dollar. This roller-coaster ride of yen/dollar exchange rates illustrates one problem of the currency exchange system—they alter. This same problem occurs every day on currency exchange markets worldwide.

Exchange Rate Systems Emerge: The Bretton Woods Agreements

In the 150 years prior to the Bretton Woods agreements, the world's exchange rate system operated on a gold standard managed by the Bank of England. This world system was disrupted by two devastating world wars that left much of the world in shambles. Representatives of the 44 nations gathered at Bretton Woods in 1944 believed that economic instabilities had caused two wars and could soon cause another. They intended to avert future wars by stabilizing exchange rates worldwide. These delegates "fixed" currencies to a standard that valued gold at $35 per ounce.

Seventy percent of the world's gold reserves in 1947 were held in the US as a currency guarantee for countries represented at Bretton Woods. Accordingly, member currencies were denominated in gold and in US dollars. Because it was far easier to trade in dollars than in gold, governments as well as businesses bought and sold dollars rather than gold. This fixed-rate system was altered in 1971. Nevertheless, the US dollar remains in use worldwide. Its suitability for the role of a global currency is explored later in the chapter.

The three approaches used most when setting currency exchange rates are:

1 To "peg" currency rates against one or several other currencies—this approach usually compares a market basket of the same goods in two or more countries.
2 To allow currency rates to fluctuate around some relatively stable currency standard.
3 To allow currency exchange rates to float freely in response to the market.

Globalization has witnessed a move away from the relative safety of pegged exchange rates that were the norm (63.5 percent) as recently as 1984. By 2002 only a few major currencies still fixed their exchange rates; this included Hong Kong, Malaysia, and China. The safety mechanism of pegged rates is that they are established by central bankers whose managers can factor in the effects of currency rate exchanges.

Conversely, free-floating currency exchanges are determined by market factors, and the market can be fickle, wrong, and opportunistic. According to Gregory Millman (1995), free-floating currencies let self-interested currency speculators play a key role in determining currency values. Their role in futures and options markets can sometimes outstrip the role of central banks and cause currency panics that have little to do with the underlying strength of the affected currency. This creates a phenomenon known as "hot money," the implications of which appear in the box below.

"Hot" Money

Chapter 3 introduced the concept of "hot" money or rapid capital movement sufficient in speed and volume to disrupt economies—even stable ones. For example, 1994 economic challenges in Mexico caused many investors quickly to move their money out of all of Latin America, despite the fact that only Mexico faced severe economic challenges. This left too little capital within many nations, putting a damper on business lending and borrowing. In 1997, during the Asian economic crisis, as much as $50 million per day was being wired from Jakarta, Indonesia to Singapore. This capital movement stimulated Singapore's economy, but left Indonesia with few assets to rebuild. These kinds of "hot" money activities lead to financial panic that creates problems even for stable economies. For example, when confidence is low, the price of capital increases. Hot money can cause even more problems for nations with poor economic policies.

Global Currency

There is a growing need for a global currency to manage global financial transactions. Accounting for paper or actual gains and losses due to exchange rates would all but disappear; organizations could more readily gain access to payments; and tourists could throw away calculators and conversion charts. This same advantage would benefit businesses vulnerable to exchange-rate variations. In lieu of a global currency, much trade is exchanged in the US dollar, the euro, and the yen. Virtual currency is a suggested response to the need for a global payment system.

US Dollar

In the absence of a true global currency, the US dollar is in frequent use around the world. For example, in 2003 many Iraqi transactions were conducted in US dollars. As a partial substitute for the discredited Iraqi dinar, Iraqi civil servants and dock and maintenance workers were paid in USD. According to a 1999 estimate, $425 billion in US currency circulated worldwide, but only 35 percent was within the country (The life cycle of money, 1999). By 2003, $562 billion dollars were in circulation. The US dollar is the official currency in Panama, Peru, Ecuador, and El Salvador, providing opportunities and threats described in the box to follow. Many other nations allow dollarized bank accounts.

Still others use the dollar as a *de facto* currency. For example, dollar-based transactions occur daily in many nations of Africa, Asia, Latin America, and Eastern Europe. Dollar-based transactions are particularly heavy in countries where the local currency is unstable and where there is limited confidence in the government.

Dollarization in El Salvador

In 1994 El Salvador pegged its currency to the dollar, and began to phase out the *colon* in 2001. By 2002, almost 85 percent of transactions were in USD. Some two million US-based Salvadorians send over $2 billion per year to El Salvador; none of these funds are reduced due to currency conversion. Businesses and the government have been aided by cheaper international financing, and they too have enjoyed a reduction in transaction costs. On the negative side, El Salvador competes with other Latin American nations whose currencies are cheap relative to the USD. This makes their goods less expensive than dollar-denominated Salvadorian ones.

Source material: El Salvador learns to love the greenback. (2002, Sept. 28) *The Economist*, pp. 34–35.

Worldwide use of the US dollar links the US economy with the world economy. The dollar's use as a world currency causes the world's economists to track the strength of the dollar very closely. The latter attention may make it more difficult for US policy-makers to pursue longer-run monetary or fiscal policies. When sales are invoiced in dollars, those involved are directly or indirectly affected by dollar strength or weakness. These effects grow in a dynamic global marketplace when the number and size of worldwide transactions can be completed at near lightning speed. Widespread dollar use also makes the currency more vulnerable to counterfeiting; $44 million in counterfeit currency was detected in 2002 alone. US businesses lost about $5.5 billion to counterfeiting in 1985; that figure was $200 billion annually by 2001.

Centrality of the US dollar may be a vestige of history, and its volatility in global markets demonstrates that this currency plays a role it was not designed to play. As global events occur, problems associated with the dollar's role as a global currency become more evident.

The Euro

The Economic Monetary Union issued the euro to 12 member nations in January 2002. There are many evident advantages of the euro, for example ease of trade, elimination of exchange rate fees, economic stimulation within the EU. For example, investors can avoid currency exchange fees when they purchase equity shares of member nations with euros.

Many believed that cultural and political differences among member nations would impede conversion to the euro. But they were wrong. By March of 2002, most member nations had replaced national currencies with the euro. The expanded area for a single currency may provide the economies of scale needed to establish the euro as a global currency. The example below shows that firms responded to euro introduction in different ways.

Organizational Adaptations to Introduction of the Euro

For consumers, one benefit of the euro is that prices can be easily compared throughout Europe. But many consumers were confused about the currency change. Businesses also face opportunities and threats because of the euro's introduction, and each responded with different forms of adaptation. Because a single currency made it possible to establish shared and centralized accounting and administrative systems, organizations such as DaimlerChrysler contemplated a more centralized structure. But Sara Lee stayed with their decentralized structure, and focussed their efforts on adapting the company's culture. In particular, local managers at Sara Lee needed to operate less as autonomous actors in each country and more as part of a federation of businesses that share common responsibilities. Because the glue of this cultural change is information, it means altering the communication process so that information flows freely between managers throughout Europe. Battery supplier Exide restructured by eliminating country managers, then developed a hybrid that permitted some country autonomy. Imperial Chemical did not focus on structure as their main form of adaptation. Instead, they refocussed their strategic processes in response to the euro by shifting their portfolio away from commodity businesses that compete on price alone and more toward specialized goods that can be differentiated.

Source material: Nicholas G. Carr (1999) Managing in the euro zone. *Harvard Business Review*, 77 (1): 47–48.

The Yen

Despite financial problems that began in the early 1990s, Japan is the second largest economy in the world. Some suggest that if used as a global or regional currency, the yen could reduce exposure to dollar volatility. According to C.H. Kwan (1996), a yen bloc is needed because traditional reasons to use the dollar no longer apply. For example, Asian countries are less dependent on the US and more dependent on each other for economic growth. Impediments to introduction of a yen bloc or a euro currency are impediments to every other suggested form of global currency: the players cannot agree on the rules by which they will play.

Virtual Currencies

Virtual currency is a response to demand for a global payment system. The latter include beenz, flooz, idollars, e-gold, and others used mostly for Internet transactions.

The sections above examined three major elements of the global economy—trade, FDI, and currency—to show there are more interconnections among these three than ever before. This is demonstrated by linkages among them, and by recent evidence that economic upturns and downturns move in synchronicity in much of the world. Examples follow in the box.

Synchronicity in the Global Economy

For most of the last half century, economies tended to grow and ebb based on local factors. However, the evidence below shows that global interdependence stimulates economic synchronicity:

■ World trade dropped in 2001; few countries were unaffected. World FDI drops in 2001 also were experienced worldwide, although the biggest hit was to the US.

■ Stock markets increasingly move together; a downturn in one has ripple effects in all others; an upturn also affects all.

■ Big companies have worldwide supply chains so that a downturn in one part of their world affects their hiring and inventory decisions everywhere.

Source material: Christopher Rhoads and Jon E. Hilsenrath (2001, Mar. 18) Following a synchronized stumble, economies hint at a joint rebound. *The Wall Street Journal*, pp. A1, A8.

MEASURES OF WORLD WEALTH

Comparisons of trade, FDI, and capital flows above provide one view of the global economy. Below we look at how measures like these reflect national and world wealth.

According to almost every World Bank and United Nations measure, the world is better off than it was a generation ago: fewer people live below the poverty line; food production is rising faster than population growth; educational levels are rising; life spans are longer; and infant mortality has decreased substantially (*Human Development Report 2000*; *World Development Report 2000/2001*). These improvements are not uniform; in particular many in African countries are worse off than they were a generation ago. Those who attribute evident gains to economic activities tend to calculate world wealth according to measures such as those reviewed below.

Examples of Worldwide Development Improvements

■ According to UN reports, the average life expectancy at birth in emerging economies is 70 years—up 16 years from 1955.

■ The World Bank reports that 80 percent of adults in the developing economies are literate compared to 58 percent in 1960.

■ On a per capita basis, nutritional intake in developing economies has climbed 17 percent in the past three decades.

Source material: John Marks Templeton (1999, Jan.) A worldwide rise in living standards. *The Futurist*, pp. 17–22.

World Product

GDP and GNP

World domestic product measures are compiled by adding gross domestic product (GDP) or gross national product (GNP) numbers of nations. As an indicator of a society's well-being, GDP counts all finished goods and services produced within a nation, even if they were produced by foreign companies. Gross National Product (also known as GNI or Gross National Income) tells a slightly different story because it totals goods produced only by domestic companies. Both measures are based on final goods and services. For example, a loaf of bread is counted at purchase with price reflecting value added by everyone who contributed to the final product, for example the wheat farmer, the miller, the manufacturer, the distributor.

World GNP stood at $26 trillion in 1994 (A dynamic new world economy, 1994), climbing to somewhere between $36–50 billion in 2003. The $14 billion gap in estimates is a measurement artifact because some use market exchange rates to calculate GNP ($36b) and others use Purchasing Power Parity (PPP of $50b). The box below explains why some prefer to use PPP calculations. At over $10 trillion, the US is the world's largest economy, followed by Japan and Germany. These Triad nations total 50 percent of world GNP (World Bank figures for 2000, 2002).

Comparing Apples to Apples with PPP

GDP comparisons often are adjusted to compare different currencies and nations using *purchasing power parity* (PPP). The guiding assumption is that the underlying value of goods is the same, even when costs of living vary. A great illustration of PPP is *The Economist's* annual "hamburger index." If the Big Mac is $2.71 in the US, and the ingredients are exactly the same in Japan, then the Biggu Macku should cost $2.71 in yen. But this is rarely the case. For example, in 2003 the Biggu Macku went for the equivalent of $2.18 in yen. PPP is calculated by dividing the local price by the US price. Using the $2.71 example shows the yen was undervalued by 19 percent. Thus, PPP makes it possible to see where costs are higher or lower than values. The advantages of PPP are offset by some limitations. For example, some argue that PPP theory works only in an ideal or abstract world without trade barriers and without real differences, and that labor, rents, and inflation can and do change all the time. What this means is that PPP figures can over- or under-state GDP. Nevertheless, many argue that PPP remains a better comparative measure of economic performance than figures based on market exchange rates. In 2004 *The Economist* also calculated a Starbucks tall-latte index.

The overall increasing rate of GDP differs by nation. The highest growth rates are in developing economies and especially large nations such as India and China, as shown in Table 8.1. As the box below indicates, they and others will witness GDP growth in the future as well. This globalizing group of developing economies is open to FDI and foreign trade and their faster growth rates generally translate into higher incomes for the poor (Dollar and Kraay, 2002). However, the same cannot be said for nonglobalizing nations in sub-Saharan Africa, some of whose GDPs are lower per capita than 20 years ago.

GDP Rankings for the Future

According to a Goldman Sachs study of the fast-growing BRIC (Brazil, Russia, India, and China) economies, their combined output in GDP will be greater than those of today's largest economic entities. China's economy alone is expected to be bigger than that of the entire G7 (the US, Japan, Germany, France, Britain, Italy, and Canada) by mid-century, overtaking Germany by 2007, Japan by 2015, and the US by 2041.

Source material: Follow the yellow BRIC road. (2003, Oct. 11) *The Economist*, p. 74.

Table 8.1 *Percentages of GDP growth in selected economies*

Nation	1970–1979	1980–1989	1990–1996	1997	2000–2001
Hong Kong	9.2	7.5	5.0	5.4	0.1
Singapore	9.4	7.2	8.3	7.4	−2.0
Taiwan	10.2	8.1	6.3	6.6	−2.2
South Korea	9.3	8.0	7.7	5.8	3.0
Malaysia	8.0	5.7	8.8	7.4	0.4
Thailand	7.3	7.2	8.6	0.9	1.8
Indonesia	7.8	5.7	7.2	6.3	3.3
China	7.5	9.3	10.1	9.3	7.3
The Philippines	6.1	1.8	2.8	4.9	3.4
Industrial economies	3.4	2.6	2.0	2.9	0.7

Source material: Is it over? (1997, Mar. 1) *The Economist*, p.23; www.asiarisk.com; 1998 estimates from multiple forecasters; 2001 figures from World Development Indicators. (2003) New York: World Bank: http://www.worldbank.org/data/wdi2003/tables/table1-1.pdf

Mature industrial economies now contribute less in relative terms to world growth than they once did. For example, in 1994, most of the mature industrial economies listed above experienced GDP growth of less than 5 percent. That pattern continued through the 1990s; economic downturns beginning in 2000 most affected growth in advanced economies and the poorest developing ones.

Measures like GNP, GDP or growth comparisons of economic wealth tell one part of the development story. However, that story has limited scope because many measures of economic activity are incomparable, incomplete, and even false. The following example illustrates how this can affect business decisions.

Data Inaccuracy and Business Planning

China is one of the fastest-growing consumer markets, but many businesses find it difficult to plan because of variance in reported data. For example, state estimates of the television advertising market in China is $2.8 billion annually, but Nielsen Media Research estimates the same market at $7.5 billion per year. That's quite a difference, especially for would-be investors. Data variance makes it hard to plan for business expansion. According to one set of data Bacardi was encouraged to compete directly against hard liquor markets in China; another data set argued for market entry with premixed bottles with appeal to beer drinkers. Thus different market reports made it difficult for Bacardi to select an appropriate strategy.

Source material: Gabriel Kahn (2003, Oct. 15) Chinese puzzle: Spotty consumer data. *The Wall Street Journal*, pp. B1, B10.

The preceding review of GDP and GNP measures described how these figures are calculated to estimate economic wealth. They demonstrate why businesses should exercise caution when using GDP alone to assess absolute or relative national prosperity.

ECONOMIC DATA TELL ONLY PART OF THE PROSPERITY STORY

Some argue that prosperity should not be measured by economic statistics alone. For example, economists William Nordhaus and James Tobin (1972) believe that a more focussed measure of economic welfare would include the value of leisure and unpaid at-home work. The following sections examine measures that provide a broader look at national and world prosperity. Businesses that use these approaches together with GDP measures may have a more accurate notion of which nations offer the best investment climate.

The Human Development Index

In 1990 the United Nations Development Program developed an alternative scale of national wealth called the Human Development Index (HDI). The HDI measures five factors: life expectancy, adult literacy, average years of schooling, educational attainment, and adjusted income. The HDI is based on the following philosophy:

> … *human choices extend far beyond economic well being. Human beings may want to enjoy long and healthy lives, drink deep at the fountain of knowledge, participate freely in the life of their community, breathe fresh air and enjoy the simple pleasures of life in a clean physical environment. (Human Development Report, 1994: 15)*

Human development is higher than GDP in many economies. For example, Iceland, Norway, and Sweden were highest ranked in the 2003 HDI, but the GDP per person for each is lower than many other nations (see the annual report for the United Nations Development Program; HDI calculations usually are released from July to August each year). Malaysia, Turkey, South Africa, and Indonesia also earn higher HDI scores than per capita GDP.

The gap between GDP and HDI is least in wealthy industrial economies and greatest in developing economies. Interestingly, the industrial nations have a human development index only 1.6 times more than developing economies even though GDP gaps can be more than five times as high. These examples demonstrate why GDP is a limited measure of national wealth. Futurist Hazel Henderson provides a different perspective in the box below.

GDP as a Development Stage?

Futurist Hazel Henderson (1996) takes another perspective on market-based measures of development like GDP. Henderson believes that market economics represent a very early "stage" in human development that emerged because it reinforces boundary-based identification of people living in groups and nations. She argues that long-held beliefs about money, wealth, productivity, and efficiency of market economics are "rooted in immature, often infantile states of mind—easily manipulated by politicians and advertisers" (1996: 153). Further, she suggests that as people expand the calculus of human interest to include social objectives, the species will evolve to transcend divisive, boundary-based loyalties and reach fully integrated planetary identity. Although it is almost impossible to imagine how a planetary identity will transcend markets, equity and survival issues challenge business leaders and politicians to rethink "traditional" assumptions.

Human and economic development do not always move together. Thus while we can say that worldwide people eat better, get cleaner water, and survive to live longer lives, in sub-Saharan Africa economies are smaller than twenty years ago. Many live in the crushing poverty defined and described below. These prosperity gaps focus world attention on how worsened conditions can be improved.

Defining Poverty

Poverty is defined not only as material deprivation but also low achievements in education and health. This multidimensional measurement of poverty makes it more difficult to compare achievements in the overall assessment of poverty. For example, health could improve even as real income worsens.

Between 1987 and 1999, population in developing and transitional economies living on $1 a day fell from 28 percent to 24 percent. But this figure does not reflect the uneven nature of declines even within regions. For example, East Asia dramatically reduced the number of people living on $1 a day, but South Asia experienced an increase among this group of poor.

Source material: *World Development Report 2000/2001*. (2001) Attacking poverty. World Bank: Oxford University Press.

DEVELOPMENT ALTERNATIVES

Dominant thinking after World War II was that economic growth leads to fiscal wealth, national security, and human development. Capitalist systems such as those described in the box below developed in different ways because nations tended to adopt different points of view about the mix of roles private (business) and public (government) sectors play to stimulate economic growth.

What is Capitalism?

Capitalist approaches vary. In their book *The Seven Cultures of Capitalism*, Charles Hampden-Turner and Alfons Trompenaars (1993) outline how the unique cultural values of the US, Japan, Germany, France, Sweden, the Netherlands, and the United Kingdom have resulted in different approaches to wealth creation.

The "frontier capitalism" of Russia and mainland China is characterized by a three-stage evolutionary process (Farrell, 1994). First, following alteration or collapse of a state-run economy, black marketeers or gangsters gain enormous profits, and government corruption spreads. In the second phase of frontier capitalism, independent business people and entrepreneurs with limited capital begin to flourish. Because commercial laws have not yet developed, these entrepreneurs develop operating standards that can become commercial rules. Finally, in the third stage of frontier capitalism, economic growth is brisk, particularly as financial markets begin to evolve. This attracts foreign investors who demand higher returns to offset their risks

Two forms of capitalism operate in Asia. The Southeast model is practiced by Singapore, Thailand, Malaysia, and Indonesia, countries that export goods and ideas. They are open to foreign direct investment, they are much less likely than South Korea and Japan to establish government-directed industrial policies, and they have allowed financial markets to develop (Asia's competing capitalisms, 1995).

US businesses stress competitive and individualistic forms of capitalism, but Margaret Sharp (1992) believes the world needs more cooperative forms of capitalism stressing group harmony and consensus like in Japan, Germany, and Sweden. According to Sharp, cooperative capitalism embraces new forms of collaboration, particularly vertical collaboration between makers and users, customers and contractors, 'just in time' relationships, and quality control. It calls for a new approach to accounting standards that recognizes the long-term value of company investments in R&D, education, and training.

Government Intervention

Followers of John Maynard Keynes believe that frequent government intervention stimulates private spending and can compensate for private-sector inactivity. Governments that adopt this line of thinking might adapt fiscal policy to stimulate internal activities, for example provide incentives for businesses to develop. On the international scene, governments could increase foreign aid to stimulate economic development elsewhere. This approach was adopted by most developed economies post-World War II, and it has been credited with significant development within them. Conversely, foreign aid has had limited permanent affect on the poorest of the developing economies. Failure of this approach to stimulate developing economies led to support for a more *laissez-faire* approach wherein markets were relatively unfettered.

Unfettered Markets

Friedrich von Hayek, Milton Friedman, and other Chicago School economists best represent this perspective. Their point of view is that only free economies can organize efficient resource distribution. Contrary to Keynesians who view fiscal and monetary policies as mechanisms for managing problems like inflation and unemployment, these economists believe that problems like unemployment occur because of government interventions. Thus they argue that the best government policy is to let the market operate with minimal government inference. This position is consistent with those of hyperglobalists whose positions were reviewed in Chapter 1. It is reflected in and supported by reports such as the Index of Economic Freedom described below.

Index of Economic Freedom

The Index of Economic Freedom was initiated in 1997 to assess annual links between living standards and economic freedom in 150 countries. The report examines trade policy, taxation, government intervention, monetary policy, capital flows and foreign investments, banking policy, wage and price controls, property rights, regulations, and black-market activities. Findings over the years lead to the same general conclusion: countries with the most economic freedom also have higher rates of long-term economic growth. The 2002 study noted that economically free countries also show greater civility and tolerance for variation than do economically repressed nations, leading authors to conclude that economic repression fosters hopelessness and isolation that leads to fanaticism and terrorism (O'Driscoll and Holmes, 2002). By 2004, ratings had improved in 75 countries, declined in 65, and remained the same in 11. Rankings appear in Table 8.2.

Although the Economic Freedom Index associates economic development with more open economic markets, it does not reflect some results of unfettered markets. In many of the poorer developing economies, unfettered markets have increased misery. In Zambia for example, open markets were flooded by second-hand textiles that ruined the local industry. Privatization of Zambian copper led to that industry's abandonment as well. Without jobs, people were worse off than they had been with government controls. Thus, the unfettered market approach to economic development also proves faulty. Combined with conditions such as corruption, repeated natural disasters, and weak infrastructure, inhabitants of some developing nations find it difficult to succeed in open markets. Further, few among them participate in markets that meet free market assumptions such as information abundance, economic rationality, or ease of entry. The following example illustrates that economic rationality does not operate in the same way worldwide, showing why free-market assumptions have not been a panacea for economic development.

Table 8.2 *Index of economic freedom, selected 2004 rankings*

Free	Mostly Free	Mostly Unfree	Repressed
1 Hong Kong	17 Iceland	72 Senegal	144 Cuba
2 Singapore	18 Germany	73 Macedonia	145 Belarus
3 New Zealand	19 Netherlands	79 Moldova	146 Tajikistan
4 Luxembourg	20 Austria and Bahrain	88 Guatemala and Malaysia	147 Venezuela
5 Ireland	22 Belgium and Lithuania	95 Burkina Faso, Egypt, Mozambique	148 Iran
6 Estonia	29 Israel and Latvia	97 Cameroon, Gabon, Macedonia, Zambia	149 Uzbekistan
7 UK	32 Czech Republic	101 Ethiopia	150 Turkmenistan
8 Denmark	36 Trinidad and Tobago	114 Malawi and Russia	151 Burma and Laos
9 Switzerland	39 Botswana and Uruguay	117 Ukraine	153 Zimbabwe
10 USA	50 Costa Rica	120 Dominican Republic	154 Libya
14 Cyprus and Finland	71 Mauritius	121 Honduras, India, Nepal	155 North Korea

Source material: Marc Miles, Edwin Jr. Feulner, and Mary Anastasia O'Grady (2004) *The 2004 Index of Economic Freedom.* Washington, DC: Heritage Foundation.

People Are More than Economically Rational Actors

A group of anthropologists studied economic rationality in 15 small-scale societies. The premise was a game in which the first player had $100 to split with the second player. The only catches were that the second player knew how much the first player had and could refuse the offer. In the latter case no one got anything. Because the societies varied, so did the actual amount of money offered.

In a strictly rational economic system, people would be expected to act as follows: the first player should offer as little as possible to keep more, and the second should take any offer so long as he or she got something. But that is not how it worked out.

The researchers found that the self-interest model failed in all of the societies studied. They concluded that in addition to self-interest, people also care about fairness and reciprocity, even when that involves personal economic costs.

Source material: Joseph Heinrich, Robert Boyd, Samuel Bowles, Herbert Gintis, Ernst Fehr, and Colin Camerer (Eds) (2004) *Foundations of Human Sociality: Ethnography and Experiments in 15 Small-scale Societies.* London: Oxford University Press.

A Middle Ground?

In view of failures associated both with the Keynesian view and the unfettered markets approach, development economists seek a middle ground to balance government interventions with market activities. This approach differs from earlier theories of development economics in three ways:

1 It recognizes that markets have limits, and acknowledges that government interventions can help some be better off without causing others to be worse off.
2 It recognizes a knowledge gap between developing and advanced economies that needs to be addressed.
3 It emphasizes the need to improve national government performance and activities of global financial institutions. (Emerging issues in development economics, 1997)

The latter approach to development economies assumes that few economies can remain closed to outside influences. The clean, crisp border once drawn around closed national economies blurs when factors of production, for example people, capital, and goods, flow freely into and outside national economic systems.

What Exactly *Are* Factor Flows?

Production factors include people, capital, and goods. But the practice of factor transfer expands beyond what one might assume. For example, factor flows include transfer funds from government to retirees living abroad or taxes gained from individuals and companies operating abroad. They include movement of productive factors associated with trade and direct investments, and they are reflected in currency exchange rates, international settlements, and trade balances.

The "middle ground" approach to balancing between government and market interests acknowledges a gap between what some call "have" and "have not" economies and it posits that institutions have an important role to play in achieving parity. Three types of global development entities are central banks, intergovernmental development institutions like the World Bank or the International Monetary Fund (IMF), and private financial entities. The roles each might and does play in an interconnected economy are reviewed below.

FINANCIAL INSTITUTIONS

The activities of financial institutions of every sort lag global economic changes. A look at how each operates demonstrates interconnections among them as well as changing assumptions about how the global economy functions.

Central Banks

Central banks such as the US Federal Reserve Bank, the Bank of England, the European Central Bank, the German Bundesbank, or the Bank of Japan were chartered to manage monetary policy within and between nations. Central banks determine and adjust money supply, they may intervene to buy currency on open markets to manipulate exchange rates, they often serve as a lender when others will not lend, and sometimes they supervise banks. Their ability to manage these responsibilities is challenged by globalization. For example, monetary policies that inject or withdraw currency are increasingly influenced by factors that occur outside a country. Many central banks no longer operate in the relative stability of a regulated environment. Their activities, even collaborative ones, may be insufficient to counteract forces they do not control. For example, independent traders exchange more than $1 trillion in currency daily.

This world market threatens to overwhelm the ability of central banks to manage the world money supply and exchange rates, and for some the challenge of finance in a global sphere is whether central bankers will prevail in maintaining orderly markets, or whether fickle, interest-seeking global traders will prevail in making and breaking financial markets around the world. Many fear that financial markets will be far too volatile without central banks, and they believe central banks should have increased authority for them (Solomon, 1995).

The World Bank and the International Monetary Fund

The World Bank and the International Monetary Fund (IMF) were chartered at Bretton Woods to manage global debt and wealth creation. The World Bank financed postwar reconstruction and facilitates economic development among poorer economies. The IMF managed controls on what was then a fairly rigid set of world currency exchange rates. For example, the US borrowed over $600 million from the IMF between 1963 and 1964 to stabilize its currency and restore investor confidence in the US. The IMF remains at the center of worldwide financial crises that have occurred in Mexico, Asia, Russia, and Venezuela. Usually IMF lending is exchanged for structural adjustment programs (SAPs) that force nations to privatize, improve accountability and transparency, reduce government spending and increase taxes, or remove market restraints.

The global challenge to these institutions is twofold. First, capital demand is increasingly met with funds from private rather than institutional sources, and in the developing economies private capital is displacing the need for capital from the World Bank or IMF control. Second, politicians in developing countries chafe under rules designed for other cultures and for other modes of economic development.

World Bank officials have been criticized on several fronts: for timidity in helping countries move from socialist to market economies, for applying the same economic policies everywhere, for failure to fund projects in riskier, lesser developed economies, and for limited investments in projects that educate girls, support family planning, or provide aid to small enterprises (It's time to redefine the World Bank and the IMF, 1994). The

World Bank revised its policies to respond to some of these criticisms. For example, national governments now design their own "Poverty Reduction Strategies" that are based on national dialogue among civil society organizations (CSOs) and the government. In this way CSOs play a mediating role between their governments and global institutions that assist them.

Although there seems to be general agreement that the IMF and the World Bank have outgrown their original roles, few agree on future roles. Suggested IMF roles include: watchdog and support role to prevent disasters like the 1995 economic collapse in Mexico (Why can't a country be like a firm?, 1995); a central bank for the world; a global Securities and Exchange Commission to exert pressure on governments to disclose their full financial health (Foust, 1995); or a permanent staff for advanced economies (Magnussen, 1994).

Haass and Litan (1998) suggest three different approaches to how the World Bank, the IMF or other global institutions can address problems a global economy creates:

1 Create new institutions to lend structure and direction to the marketplace. These new institutions would complement roles currently played by the IMF and others.
2 Leave the economy alone but create reforms to structure and discipline financial operations and transactions. This approach would sustain the safety net of the IMF but maintain the element of risk that is part of capitalism. The challenge would be for nations to introduce reforms, and for some organization—perhaps an NGO—to issue report cards on countries' progress. The latter report would include greater transparency and information to facilitate market transactions.
3 Embrace free markets and abandon rescue approaches like those pursued by the IMF.

Private Financial Markets

Banking

Foreign exchange and commercial and individual banking are two traditional functions for private entities such as banks. Foreign exchange brokers facilitate most currency exchanges and banks provide loans, trade in securities, and handle commercial financial needs as well as individual accounts. Banks also are intermediaries between borrowers and lenders. Advertising in 1995, the investment firm Merrill Lynch noted that the difference between crossing borders and barriers has been that while crossing borders requires limited effort, crossing cultural, economic, and political barriers to business worldwide is challenging (Merrill Lynch, 1995). Growing worldwide competition in banking and security industries also challenges financial institutions. For example, the collapse of Barings PLC described at the opening of the chapter shows how difficult it can be to keep track of rapid changes in global financial markets. The borderlessness of the industry has also fostered experiments that range from the successful to questionable, unethical, and even illegal activities. These activities occur for many reasons. The global industry for banking is not yet well defined, leading to conflict between standards and norms. For example, Credit Suisse broke with conservative national banking tradition by investing in high-risk ventures in China and Russia, and also became the first bank in Switzerland to be involved in a hostile takeover. The example below illustrates yet another challenge of global economic integration. Together these examples show how the rapid pace of global economic change creates barriers to organizational change.

Islamic Banking

Islamic and Western attitudes towards interest payments illustrate one among many challenges of global economic integration. Islamic law prohibits payment of interest, faulting Western banks that earn interest on four counts: when lending they don't take into account the social-welfare issues of a society; they legitimize and perpetuate wealth and income inequities; they allow people with money to direct their resources into production and services that can be harmful to society; and money market forces are indiscriminate and even blind to social concerns of individuals. These attitudinal differences confound relationships between Western and Islamic financial institutions.

Source material: Masoud Kavoossi (2000) *The Globalization of Business and the Middle East*. Westport, CT: Quorum Books.

Microlending

The poor have limited access to financial institutions and often must borrow from money lenders who charge very high rates. Grameen Bank is credited with microcredit innovations that changed these practices by putting small loans into the hands of the poor. Not-for-profit as well as for-profit micro lenders increasingly provide these and other banking services for the poor. They use these funds to establish very small businesses that produce food, candy, apparel, pottery, leather goods, and so on, or services such as childcare, painting, and food services including catering. In some cases micro loans go to individuals, and in others to collectives whose members contribute small amounts of money weekly. When the pool is large enough, the assets are loaned to one person whose repayments grow the pool. Microlending provides participatory access to economic development for the poor and, as the following box shows, it can change lives. Further, this innovation has reverse migrated from developing economies to advanced ones, making microenterprise lending a worldwide phenomenon.

Microenterprise Businesses

Azucena Alcantra borrowed less than $100 to change her life from scavenger to entrepreneur. Ms. Alcantra now buys promotional wrappers from Nescafé and other discarded containers, bundles them into stacks, and sells them to willing buyers (Hookway, 2001).

Delora Begum is the "phone lady" of Chandryel, Bangladesh. Using funds loaned by Grameen Bank, Ms. Begum purchased a Nokia cell phone and resells airtime to villagers. This business supports Ms. Begum and her family, and also provides telephones in a nation where 90 percent of 68,000 villages lack telephone access (Jordan, 1999).

Source material: James Hookway (2001, Nov. 5) Microfinance program helps Filipinos move from scavengers to entrepreneurs. *The Wall Street Journal*, pp. B1, B8; Miriam Jordan (1999, June 25) It takes a cell phone. *The Wall Street Journal*, pp. B1, B4.

Initial funding for many microenterprises in developing economies came from voluntary organizations like Women's World Banking and Accion International. Inspired by the success of these organizations, entities like the World Bank and the US Agency for International Development also loan small amounts of money. More recently, some microlenders seek profits. The findings to date are that women repay micro loans at better rates than men and are less likely to waste development money. Further, in many developing economies, female borrowers use their earnings to fund education, health care, or family needs.

Poor Women and Microenterprise Programs

According to the *Wall Street Journal* (Carrington, 1994), studies of loans to female entrepreneurs in developing economies showed the following:

- A World Bank study in Ivory Coast found that their project to introduce more effective farming methods was run by men and for men with few results. When women were provided with the funds, the response was positive and yielded crop increases.
- A UN program called Unifem extended credit to women in small silk-weaving businesses that gave young women an alternative to becoming sex workers.

Contrary to traditional expectations that the poor represent a bad credit risk, these experiences show that many poor—and especially poor women— are good credit risks. Their tendency to invest in health and education also plays a role in stimulating world economic growth. In the 2001 *World Development Report*, the World Bank also noted that when poor people have access to the same institutions as the rich, they will do much the same as the rich do: they will start businesses to help themselves.

Hawala

Despite innovations like microlending that bring the poor into the global economy, others remain on the margins of society with little access to financial institutions. In view of increased immigration, many require mechanisms to transfer funds between nations. Businesses like Western Union satisfy part of this need, but often they charge very high rates on a single transaction: as much as $25 for a $100 transfer. Another system is hawala, a complex exchange in use by the Mogul Empire in the sixteenth century. Interpol characterizes this system as one that involves "money transfer without money movement" (Simpson, 2001). An example begins with a hypothetical Ethiopian immigrant in France. She gives money to a hawala agent there for transfer to family in Ethiopia. The French agent contacts an Ethiopian counterpart to pay the family. Settlement then occurs through networks of agents located worldwide. This system is complex and relies heavily on trust.

The hawala system provides the poor with a less expensive method for transferring funds than banks and other financial institutions. But because it operates outside legitimate systems, it is also unregulated and subject to abuses. For example, Interpol believes that the hawala system launders drug money and finances terrorist networks. Yet this system also provides an alternative the poor can afford. The example demonstrates a growing need for financial institutions—both public and private—that can better meet myriad and global financial needs.

This look at the global economy has examined only some of the challenges associated with managing global trade, FDI, capital, economic development, and financial institutions. Companies trade, many foreign direct invest, and all must deal with currency exchange. Each bases its investment decision in part on economic criteria, but as we have seen, sometimes economic measures of growth or of prosperity are inaccurate.

The chapter also shows that relationships between economic criteria and human development are complex, creating management challenges that bring businesses into dialogue with many mediating organizations, particularly governmental groups and civil society organizations. This chapter also demonstrates a new and worldwide awareness that economic activity alone has not improved the quality of life worldwide to a desirable level. According to Kevin Watkins, these goals will best be achieved when "governments, financial institutions, and civil society" engage in "a real dialogue about how to make globalization work as a more powerful force for poverty reduction and social justice" (2002: 26). Views like these suggest that increasingly businesses will be expected to engage in global dialogue around both economic growth and economic equity.

CHAPTER SUMMARY

Economic systems generate and distribute resources within a society; these economic systems are supported by distribution systems that transfer goods, currency systems that provide a medium for exchange, and organizations such as banks and businesses that facilitate resource generation and distribution.

Trade in goods and services, foreign direct investments, and currency exchange all become more important indicators of national economic wealth with increased worldwide economic integration. The evidence shows that each of these three economic factors has expanded in the last two decades.

GDP and GNP often are used to reflect global wealth, but other measures of wealth such as human development exist. Combined wealth and development measures provide a more comprehensive picture of investment potential within and among nations.

Economic perspectives on how to stimulate world prosperity differ. The Keynesian perspective is that governmental intervention stimulates economic growth; Hayek and the Chicago school believe that government intervention retards economic growth. Others call for balance between government and free-market activities.

Competition for investment capital is keen worldwide. The efforts of financial institutions like the World Bank and the IMF, central banks, and private lending institutions show that managing this competition on a global scale creates unaccustomed opportunities and challenges.

Existing financial institutions often disenfranchise the poor. Systems such as microenterprise lending and hawala currency transfers are two mechanisms that address this gap.

REVIEW AND DISCUSSION QUESTIONS

1 How are global events in economic and other environments affecting business practices of investment bankers? What traditions of banking are changing and how do these reflect an era of global banking versus banking within nation-states?

2 Many claim that democracy and economic freedoms are linked. Yet in China we observe that economic freedoms have led to prosperity without using a democratic system. How can this be explained?

3 Based on this chapter (and possibly on other readings) what would you say are the three greatest challenges an organization faces when investing worldwide?

4 Conduct this interesting experiment: Use any Internet search engine and enter world GDP as your search term; compare the results. What can you conclude about reported measures of GDP? How can you generalize about other economic data?

Chapter 9
GLOBAL ECONOMY 2— GLOBALIZATION OF LABOR

AVON'S GLOBAL LABOR FORCE

Since 1886 Avon has been calling on people everywhere to become the world's largest direct seller of cosmetics and beauty-related items; it sells products in 143 nations. In addition to its well-known cosmetics lines, Avon also sells jewelry, apparel, and home furnishings. In recent years Avon expanded its distribution outlets to include sales from catalogs, Internet sites, and retail stores. Face-to-face direct sales in homes, schools, and workplaces is its mainstay, providing jobs for about 3.5 million independent representatives. Although Avon now calls itself "the company for women," until 1999 all CEOs were male.

Avon is one of only a few cosmetic companies that sell door-to-door. In 1996 Avon was the first direct-sales company to China, and soon had over 85,000 sales people in every region except Tibet. Avon gained a competitive advantage over other companies by bringing products to their customers. When China's government banned direct sales, Avon shifted its approach to sell in small shops and malls (Byrnes, 2001).

Aside from China, direct sales remain an important worldwide sales vehicle for Avon. In developing economies Avon recruits agents from remote and poor areas where product access is limited. Cultural factors also facilitate sales in many countries. For example, in Brazil and throughout Latin America, many people tend to buy based on relationships forged through the face-to-face contact of direct sales. Some will even spend a little bit more per purchase to buy from someone they know.

Brazil is Avon's second-biggest market by volume after the US, home to Avon's largest sales force of 800,000 people—up from 150,000 a decade ago. One thousand of Avon's Brazilian employees are subcontractors to Maria Carvalheiras—one of Brazil's top Avon representatives. On profits of $15,000 per month (based on sales for all the companies she represents), Ms. Carvalheiras makes far more than the $260 monthly average for most Brazilian workers. In addition to handling Avon sales, Ms. Carvalheiras is also a lead representative for Avon's Brazilian rival, Natura Cosmeticos, and twelve other direct-sale firms. Because catalogs help her provide products ranging from cosmetics to lingerie to saucepans, she calls her business "The King of Catalogs."

Ms. Carvalheiras recruits from among the poor, many of whom sell to the poor. When recruiting, Ms. Carvalheiras intentionally targets needy communities, recruiting women in slums by promising "extra cash." The workers themselves come from Brazil's large pool of un- or under-employed women. Unemployment in Brazil is 12 percent and the country has experienced declining real wages. Economists estimate that at least one-third of Brazil's economy is in the informal sector where many work in freelance jobs such as Avon sales.

A cultural characteristic of Brazil is that almost everyone cares about how they look. Avon's own 2003 study of women worldwide found that Brazilian women care more about their appearance than any others. Half are willing to undergo plastic surgery, and 90 percent of women polled in Brazil classify beauty products as an essential rather than a luxury. These beliefs protect Avon against economic swings in Brazil. When the economy is strong, many buy Avon products, and they continue to buy in economic downturns because Avon products are relatively inexpensive.

The King of Catalogs operates three distribution centers where workers place orders, collect, and pay for merchandise. In Brazil, Ms. Carvalheiras acts as an intermediary for ▶

sales by taking orders from agents that then go to Avon. When products arrive, workers purchase and deliver them to clients. In the case of Avon, Ms. Carvalheiras gives two-thirds of the commission to her saleswomen and keeps one-third.

Ms. Carvalheiras' business differs from traditional businesses in other ways as well. She takes on greater risk with subcontractors who could not pass a background check. She requires no deposit from agents and retains subcontractors who sell very little, even those who purchase only one or two items at a time.

Ms. Carvalheiras also trains her workforce on business skills and issues that affect them: domestic violence, drug abuse, or marital infidelity are three examples. Sometimes she must assist illiterate women in completing order forms. Ms. Carvalheiras also provides benefits uncommon to Brazil's informal economy. For example, she persuaded a local hospital to provide health insurance to about 300 women and their families at a fraction of the normal rate. For the very poor, she persuaded a bank to waive the minimum-deposit requirement for opening an account.

Despite her efforts, Ms. Carvalheiras experiences sales-force turnover as high as 30 percent per month. To improve retention, the company offers incentives such as food or small appliances for top performers. Motivation efforts include appointing team leaders to work with smaller groups.

In addition to the Sao Paulo distribution center, Ms. Carvalheiras has expanded her franchise to other cities. Her husband left his bookbinding business to be the accountant and technology officer for the King of Catalogs. In the latter capacity, he designed a King of Catalogs website through which Ms. Carvalheiras can tap into yet a different segment of Brazil's population.

Source material: Avon Products Homepage: http://avon.com; Nanette Byrnes (2001, Oct.) It took a lady to save Avon. *Fortune*, 144 (7): 202–208; Douek Timothy (2001, Feb.) China's cosmetic fever. *Global Cosmetic Industry*, 168 (2): 56; Miriam Jordan (2003, Feb. 19) An army of underemployed goes door-to-door in Brazil. *The Wall Street Journal*, pp. A1,A2.

CHAPTER OVERVIEW

Chapter 8 reviewed three of the four indicators of economic globalization. This chapter considers the fourth dimension of economic globalization: labor. It opens with a look at the global labor pool, then explores characteristics of informal and formal work sectors. Unemployment, wage and labor inequities, working children, economic migration, and other challenges of labor globalization are reviewed to provide a context for understanding labor challenges worldwide. The chapter argues that global businesses are increasingly expected to resolve some of these challenges. The chapter concludes with a look at varied initiatives undertaken by governmental entities, businesses, and civil society organizations on behalf of a growing global labor force.

LABOR IN THE GLOBAL ECONOMY

According to the International Labour Organization (*World Employment Report 2001*) the global workforce numbers about three billion men and women between ages 15–64. This represents more than a 100 percent increase over 1965 (*World Employment Report 1995*). About 380 million workers live in developed economies, but more than 1.4 billion live in economies with annual per capita incomes below $700. The global workforce toils primarily in the agricultural sector; fewer people work in service or manufacturing jobs.

Economic development within nations affects how many people are employed in wage-earning jobs. In the developing economies, only about 15 percent of workers have wage contracts, and most of them are employed by urban industrials and service providers. In the middle-income economies (those that are neither rich nor poor), 46 percent of the working population is in industrial or service employment. In the advanced economies, most people — about 70 percent or 218 million—work in service industries. While many people work in the formal sector, others toil in the "informal" sector.

THE INFORMAL WORK SECTOR

The informal sector contains jobs and exchanges that are not regulated by social institutions in "a legal and social environment where similar activities are regulated" (Castells and Portes, 1989: 12). It comprises people who are self-employed in small or unregistered enterprises or earning wages without contracts, for example occasional workers. Work and revenues generated in the informal sector are not reported in official statistics, and so informal sector work is not part of GDP or national measures of work or employment.

Work in the informal sector can be either legitimate or illegal. Legitimate work includes agricultural work and home-based work such as healthcare and childcare. Home-based workers and street vendors are two of the largest sub-groups of the informal workforce (Women and men in the informal economy, 2002), but professionals also participate in the informal sector. Examples include a computer specialist who sets up a friend's hardware for a good meal, or a teacher who agrees to tutor in exchange for other services. Almost anyone can be a member of the informal sector at some time. However, many people who work in the informal sector—including the Avon agents described in the opening case—have few other options than occasional work.

Activities such as drug dealing, prostitution, illegal gambling, and the like also are part of the informal economy. These types of activities are reflected in synonyms sometimes used to describe the informal sector, for example gray, shadow, underground, or black-market economies. *The Economist* estimates the annual size of the shadow economy at $9 trillion or almost one-quarter that of the measured economy (Black hole, 1999).

Throughout history, some work has gone unreported. However, according to a study reported by *The Economist* (Underground economy, 2001), Linz University professor Friedrich Schneider determined that the shadow economy's share of national output grew in every OECD country from 1989–1999. The shadow economy in these nations has grown three times as fast as the reported economy since 1960 (Light on the shadows, 1997) to total about 15 percent of officially reported GDP. Reasons for a rapid growth pace in the informal economy among advanced economies are several: these nations levy high tax rates that may encourage people to hide income; shifts from manufacturing to service industries provide opportunities to hide cash transactions; job losses force people to develop independent income sources; and regulations may discourage legitimate activities. For example, bans on evening or Sunday sales encourage Germans to shop at open air, cash-dependent markets.

According to Professor Schneider, underground activity is higher in developing economies than advanced ones. For example, Nigeria and Thailand each have shadow economies amounting to 70 percent of official GDP (Black hole, 1999). In Latin America, the informal labor market is estimated at 20–30 percent of the non-agricultural labor force (Gomez-Buendia, 1995), and as much as one-third of Brazil's economy is "off the books" with direct sales such as for Avon. Much legitimate work occurs on the margins of developing economies. For example, according to one estimate, up to 65 percent of legitimate labor is performed in the informal sector in developing economies (Henderson, 1999).

In developing economies, the informal sector serves two purposes. First, it provides jobs unavailable in the formal sector due to low overall economic activity. The opening case study of Avon and the following example illustrate two of many ways this occurs. Weak governance in developing economies may facilitate illegal activities that serve both local and global demand. For example, drugs like marijuana, heroin, and coca become cash crops for poor farmers, and also create wealth for drug dealers. Because drug running is illegal, jobs created by it are necessarily in the informal sector.

Life on a Dollar a Day

Rose Shanzi is one of eight in ten Zambians who live on less than $1 a day. The percentage of the world's population living on less than $1 a day may be smaller than it was 10 years ago, but in absolute numbers it has not changed much in two decades. And things have gotten worse for Rose Shanzi and her family, especially after the death of her husband.

Nearly 100,000 Zambian jobs have disappeared since 1992. Privatization of the copper industry led to eventual abandonment of that industry, and duty-free shipments of foreign clothes have shut down almost all textile production. Sub-Saharan Africa's 640 million people are 10 percent of the world's population, but they account for less than 2 percent of international trade—less than 50 years ago.

But people have to eat. So Rose Shanzi grows tomatoes for Maramba's market on Zambia's southern border. The number of vendors selling in the market was stable for almost forty years, but it has tripled in the last ten years to 4,000. Others have tomatoes to sell and they often earn too little each day to feed themselves or their children. Although Rose has a high-school diploma, there is no job for her. Nor is there government support or charity since no one has money.

There isn't much action at the Maramba market, and Rose reads a newspaper between customers. If it is a bad day, then Rose has read a lot of news, but sold very few tomatoes. On this day, Rose earns 3900 Zambian kwachas—about 97 cents or less than a euro. She remarks: "Ah today we are rich."

Source material: Jon Jeter (2002, Feb. 24) Getting by in Zambia: 75 cents makes her day *The Seattle Times*, p. A7.

Pay in the Informal Sector

Because the informal sector is neither organized nor part of official reports it is impossible to determine wages, work hours, or other conditions of work in the informal sector. However, some inferences can be made:

1 The relative size of the informal sector is greatest in developing economies.
2 The informal sector is populated primarily with women, children, and illegal immigrants.
3 The actual number of hours worked by people in developing economies is vastly under-reported when they depend on informal-sector employment. For example, the UN estimates that women's unpaid work amounted to $11 trillion in 1995.
4 Wages are lower and working hours are on average longer in the informal sector than in the formal sector (Bosch et al., 1993: 18).

Work in the informal sector is often unpaid (such as agriculture), some jobs are unsafe, and workers earn few to no benefits. These and other reasons motivate many to seek paid jobs in the formal sector.

THE FORMAL WORK SECTOR

Paid labor in the formal sector is increasing due to transitions to market economies, the perceived importance of economic wealth, and the growing number of women in the formal work sector. These and other factors elevate interest in and economic importance of organizations that create jobs. These organizations are challenged by differing worldwide parameters of work such as work hours and work conditions.

Work Hours

People in advanced economies generally have the lowest annual hours of work (1,500–1,900 hours), while developing economies in Asia have the highest (2,000–2,300 hours). According to the International Labour Organization, the estimated annual number of hours worked per worker ranges from over 2,400 hours (Republic of Korea) to less than 1,400 hours (the Netherlands and Norway). Annual hours in Latin America and the Caribbean range between 1,800 and 2,100 hours (Hours of work, 2002).

Industrialization reduces the annual average hours of work over time. In 1870, work hours per person totaled just less than 3,000 hours for most people in what are now industrialized economies. By the 1960s most of the industrialized countries adopted a standard working week of 40 or slightly more hours per week (Bosch et al., 1993). The OECD reports that between 1990 and 2002, average working hours dropped in Japan and most European countries, but were stable in the US. By 2002, the average number of hours worked in Europe was closer to 1,400 per year.

Bosch et al. (1993) observe several trends in developed economy work hours prior to 1990:

1 White-collar workers work fewer hours than blue-collar workers.
2 Male-dominated white-collar sectors like banking, finance, insurance, and real estate have shorter working hours than female-dominated sectors like retail and blue-collar sectors like manufacturing.
3 The overall pattern has been toward fewer working hours, but greater variations between countries suggest that harmonization is less.
4 In all countries reviewed there was a 20-year increase in part-time work explained mainly by women's workforce participation.
5 Lifelong working hours are highest in Japan and the US and lowest in Western Europe.

As compared with the industrialized world, normal working hours in developing economies are longer and can include long work days, weeks, and months. In the developing world, part-time employment also is high, fueled by limited numbers of jobs in the paid labor force. Some work two or more part-time jobs if they cannot find suitable full-time work.

Work Conditions

According to Gerhard Bosch et al., "agreement on international working standards were reached within the framework of the ILO [the Geneva-based International Labor Organization is part of the UN] after the First World War and in the first decades after the Second World War" (1993: 1). Although almost all nations are within the ILO framework, laws or statutory limits often are not observed.

In the industrialized countries, work hours, wages, and other conditions are governed by regulations meant to protect workers. These include limits on hours worked, or specified safeguards for handling chemicals, medical and human waste and similar materials, air and water filtration systems, monitors, and anti-pollution devices. These protections may not be available in developing countries. Even simple items such as safety goggles or earplugs that are standard safety gear in advanced economies may be unavailable or unused in developing ones. The following box shows that many work standards of developed economies were not in place in 2002 in Chinese toy factories.

Work Safety and Standards

A January 2002 report titled "Toys of Misery" examined 19 factories in Guangdong, China and observed the following work conditions in almost all:

■ Mandatory daily shifts of 15 to 16 hours.
■ Seven-day work week of 30 days per month.
■ 12 to 14 cents-an-hour wages; wages of $8.42 for a $72\frac{1}{4}$-hour work week.
■ Not a single worker interviewed received the legal minimum wage.
■ Factory temperatures of more than 100 degrees.

▶

According to report authors, managers exploit China's poor economy when they pay low wages and demand much. Typical counter-arguments are that wages and work conditions are better than what is otherwise available, and that one should not compare developed and developing economies. Company leaders often find themselves in the middle of these two sets of arguments when they hire foreign workers in developing economies.

Source material: Toys of misery: A report on the toy industry of China. (2002, Jan.) National Labor Committee: http://www.nlcnet.org

Few developing economies provide workers with the social safety net that workers enjoy in many industrialized nations. Workers in developing economies consequently face more risks from work and have fewer remedies if work affects health or well-being. For example, according to ILO estimates, only 20 percent of the world's workers have adequate social protections. Workers in developing economies are also vulnerable to abuse in the form of corporal punishment, withheld wages, verbal haranguing, or sexual harassment.

BUSINESSES AND LABOR GLOBALIZATION

Jobs are created by every sector. For example, governments often employ most people in developing economies, for example Zimbabwe. Nongovernmental jobs account for 5 percent of jobs and 23 percent of job growth in many nations (Salamon et al., 1998). The vast majority of new jobs are created within nations by small to medium-sized firms. Far fewer jobs are created by global businesses. However, because global businesses operate on a global scale, their hiring practices, labor standards, and compensation practices attract global attention. Thus globalization of labor focusses public attention on global businesses.

The Role of the Global Business

An estimated 60,000 global businesses employed about 40.5 million people in 1999, an increase from 23.6 million in 1990 (*World Investment Report*, 2000). Although global firms employ relatively few in the global labor force, they are at the center of many global labor debates for reasons such as the following:

- They are identifiable.
- They have added many jobs in the last decade, especially to developing economies where labor standards and wages can be low.
- They generate significant income in nations where they operate.
- They are viewed as much more powerful forces for change than are domestic businesses; in some cases, businesses are perceived to have more clout than national governments.

Because they create many of the jobs upon which domestic economies are based, some believe businesses are the only entity with sufficient clout to make changes (Hawken, 1993). Others think it is the government's job to improve labor forces via education or by creating sociopolitical and economic conditions that favor economic development. (Simai, 1994). Still others think change will come only when business, government, and society work together on labor concerns and rights (Annan, 2000).

High-visibility global firms take on business-level concerns about working conditions, wage rates, and worker participation in corporate governance (Applebaum and Henderson, 1995). In terms of labor conditions and standards, global businesses improve global standards when they pay their workers more than the national average, spend more on R&D in countries where they invest than do domestic counterparts, and export more than domestic firms. According to the OECD study upon which these conclusions are based, the effects of business activities like these are bigger in poorer economies than in richer ones (Foreign friends, 2000). Small global firms also raise global labor standards as the example of the fly-fishing lure industry illustrates.

Fly-Making in Thailand

Chang Mai, Thailand has become the epicenter for fishing flies. Small businesses like Targus and Brookside Flies moved their operations there over a decade ago, lured by handicrafts traditions that require the same type of dexterity and discipline as fly tying. Fierce competition for talented laborers raised wages to 3.5 times Thai minimum wages. Companies also provide benefits unusual for Thai workers. For example, Targus provides rent-free housing and free English lessons and helps workers out of extreme poverty. Brookside Flies' workers toil in a pleasant villa or in their own homes, they set their own hours, and they are eligible for retirement benefits after three years of employment. The company also hires people with handicaps and women whose husbands have left them.

Source material: Denis D. Gray (2003, Apr. 14) Thai town lures makers of fishing hooks. *The Seattle Times*, p. A13.

Some businesses actively work to raise world work standards. Sometimes this can bring charges of extraterritoriality of values, a point illustrated by the boxed example from Reebok Shoes.

Reebok's Challenge

Almost all athletic shoes are manufactured in low-wage nations. China alone manufactures 100 million pairs per year. High consumer visibility for athletic shoes has brought attention to the athletic shoe industry, and firms within the industry experience pressure to improve working conditions and standards. In 1999 US firm Reebok conducted and then published an independent report on their two main Indonesian suppliers. Among the findings were that few workers understood the Indonesian term for sexual harassment. Accordingly, Reebok encouraged suppliers to provide training in gender awareness. Charged with forcing more Western values on Indonesian suppliers, Reebok's vice-president for human rights countered that workers and managers have to learn new things. He noted that if the firm had not insisted on safe disposal, the local market would have been flooded with empty chemical containers. Additionally, although many workers hate to wear protective clothing, their best interests are served by forcing them to wear them. This example illustrates that global managers sometimes have to confront problems for which there is no perfect resolution.

Source material: Best foot forward at Reebok. (1999, Oct. 23) *The Economist*, p. 74.

CHALLENGES OF LABOR GLOBALIZATION

The expanding role of businesses in generating paid-sector jobs is one factor that draws worldwide attention to them. The public also is attuned to labor concerns that are newly global such as unemployment and underemployment, work inequalities, child labor, and both individual and job migration and immigration. These and other concerns are increasingly part of operating reality for many global businesses.

Unemployment and Underemployment

Economic slowdowns beginning in 1998 increased unemployment which grew to 180 million by the end of 2002 (*Global Employment Trends*, 2003). Additionally as many as one billion in the labor force are underemployed (*World Employment Report 2001*), meaning they work at jobs that underutilize them. Businesses often find it difficult to respond to critiques that they need to create jobs or make business decisions that factor in unemployment concerns. Table 9.1 indicates where these concerns were greatest in 2002.

Table 9.1 *Global unemployment, 2002*

Unemployment, 2002	As a percentage of the workforce
Sub-Saharan Africa	14.4
Transitional economies	13.5
Latin American and the Caribbean	10.0
European Union	7.6
Canada	7.6
Asia	6.8
United States	5.7

Source material: *Global Employment Trends* (2003) Geneva: International Labour Organization.

Work Inequalities

Businesses also face pressure to correct social inequities such as discrimination. The two examples below include women and minority groups.

Women and Work

The numbers of women who work vary. As many as 56 percent of Chinese women work compared to 50 percent of US women, 80 percent of women in sub-Saharan Africa, and 27 percent in the Middle East and North Africa. But the United Nations annually reports that no country treats its women as well as it treats its men. This gender gap is reflected in the annual editions of the United Nations' Gender-related Development Index (GDI) in the *Human Development Report*.

Differential treatment for women across and within nations includes poor access to basic safety, security, nutrition, or healthcare resources, limited access to educational opportunities, and poor access to paid jobs. Once in the paid workforce, differential treatment for women is unequal wages, possible sexual harassment, and fewer promotional opportunities than men. The example below illustrates that when improvements occur, they often elude the poor.

Women in India

According to a 1997 *World Business* article, wealthy Indian women have not experienced the same discrimination as women elsewhere in the world. Author Kathleen Cox claims that women's central role in Indian culture has exempted women from work discrimination, noting little gender equality and large numbers of women professionals operating as doctors, lawyers, engineers, scientists, and educators. Both women and men work as secretaries and in the government sector, and women have been elected to public office. In terms of religion, Cox notes that the Vedas—the Hindu holy book—describes mother as God, and sources cited say that women are to be treated with respect. Hinduism also has thousands of deities and many of the more popular ones are goddesses or *devis* who are powerful, for example Lakshmi the consort of Vishnu bestows wealth. Cox also notes that this is a matter of class status because poorer women often are abused and face gender inequalities much more serious than in the advanced nations, for example abortion of female fetuses, beating, and dowry deaths.

Source material: Kathleen Cox (1997, Jan./Feb.) *World Business*, pp. 24–32. A publication of KPGM Peat Marwick.

Women's Wages

Women are paid less for their work than men almost universally, earning about 77 percent of male wages in industrial countries and 73 percent in developing economies. Some part of wage differentials for women and men is attributable to factors that do not involve discrimination. For example, many women work part-time, take temporary absences from work to accumulate fewer years of work experience, or work in agriculture, sales, and other sectors where pay is traditionally low. However, the World Bank notes that only about a fifth of the wage gap can be explained by gender differences in education, work experience or job characteristics (Engendering development through gender equity, 2000). Instead, they argue that a large part of the reason for wage inequities is that women have unequal social, economic, and legal rights. Gender disparities like these tend to be greater among the poor than the rich.

Women and the Arab Development Report

Authors of the first *Arab Human Development Report* (AHDR) in 2002 identified three reasons that the Arab world is not more developed economically: widening gaps in freedom, too little knowledge development across the region, and very little female empowerment. Achievements on the Human Development Report were lower than the world average, in part due to women's treatment. Despite educational improvements in Arab countries (adult illiteracy dropped from 60 percent in 1980 to about 43 percent in the mid-1990s), almost two-thirds of adult illiterates in Arab countries are women. Female participation in Arab political and economic life is the lowest in the world. The report notes that Arab nations are unlikely to develop economically when half its productive potential is not allowed to contribute. The subsequent AHDR 2003 clarified that in Arab civilization, obstructions to progress are social, economic, and political. The 2003 report concludes that Arabs must remove or reform these obstructions to participate fully in a knowledge economy.

Source material: *Arab Human Development Report 2003*. (2003) New York: United Nations Development Program.

Women in Management

Women workers often have limited access to professional and managerial jobs, even when they are a significant proportion of the workforce. In Europe, for example, women are over 40 percent of the workforce, but hold only 26 percent of managerial jobs (Women in leadership, 2002). Progress is greater in the US where about 39 percent of women are in managerial or professional jobs including law, medicine, and teaching as well as business management (Families and Work Institute, 2003). Women of color hold fewer managerial jobs than do white women (Catalyst fact sheet, 1999). In Japan, most major corporations divide their workforce into two classes: those who are on the career track and those who are not. The latter are generally women whose tracks bar them from gaining experience critical to advancement in Japanese corporations. Although 40 percent of Japanese women work, fewer than 20 percent are on a management track and 9 percent are managers (French, Howard W. 2003).

The Status of Minorities at Work

Visible and invisible signs of ethnic diversity are the basis for wage and other forms of work inequalities. In the US, Brazil, and South America black people have historically had fewer educational or work opportunities than lighter-skinned people. For example, although blacks and mixed-color people are 45 percent of Brazil's population, less than 1 percent enrolls in the nation's largest public university. Over 50 percent of the unemployed in South Africa are native blacks, and among black Americans, particularly those concentrated in urban areas, as many as 30 percent are unemployed. As the box below demonstrates, color discrimination is practiced in many places. However, many nations now ban this form of discrimination and require that businesses conform by changing their hiring and promotional practices. Additionally, workers from protected classes increasingly use legal or other means to retain ethnic or cultural identities. Failure to attend to a growing sense of group dignity and identity may be costly to organizations. A US example is the growing number of EEO (equal employment opportunity) complaints.

Color Discrimination Is Global

Ethnic Chinese often own many resources but encounter discrimination throughout Southeast Asia. An example was anti-Chinese riots in Indonesia in 1998.

Indian shop owners are viewed with suspicion throughout Oceania — an example is Fiji where political rights of Indians were curtailed.

In Japan there is discrimination against people with Korean heritage who despite long heritage within Japan cannot claim Japanese citizenship.

Anti-Turkish sentiment in Germany is largely a reaction to religious differences between Christians and Muslims. Turks generally are ghettoized and until recently could not claim German citizenship.

This list can be continued as discrimination exists for Algerian immigrants to France, Pakistani immigrants to England, Mexican immigrants to the US, and so on.

Child Labor

Sixteen of every 100 children or 246 million children work. Twelve of the 16 work in hazardous conditions and too many are prostitutes, slaves, or combatants in armed conflict. In 1993, the ILO reported an increase among working children throughout the industrialized countries (An evil unbearable to the human heart, 1993), but for the most part child labor occurs in developing economies (Experts work to eradicate use of child labour, 1997). Child laborers often work to contribute to family income, sometimes in factories but more often they are self-employed or engage in street work. Thousands of street children from Nairobi to Brazil and Turkey to India have little choice but to work. Child labor is frequent among children who have been uprooted by immigration.

Children's Lives: Too Few Fun and Games

In Thailand, "child searchers" kidnap or buy children from poor families and put them up for sale to private households, restaurants, or factories. In the Dominican Republic children are sent to work in sugar plantations as virtual slaves. In Brazil, poor rural families are encouraged to send their children to the city for high wages, but the children often are charged for travel and food expenses, make low wages, and enter a form of debt bondage. In Colombia children work in coalmines. In Cairo many work in tanneries where they are exposed to strong chemicals. Between 1990 and 2000, two million children were killed in conflict. Over 100 million children do not attend primary school, and worldwide 149 million children are malnourished.

Source material: International Labour Organization. (2002, July 4) http://www.ilo.org

Most nations are signatories of International Labour Organization standards on child labor. However, when enforcement regulations against child labor are non-existent or weak or when economic pressures are high, children often have no alternative but to work. The ILO recognizes that children face limited choices but they nevertheless oppose child labor: when it is a daily necessity that deprives the child of education and other social skills; when the work is dangerous; or when the work exploits the child such as forced labor, debt bondage, or prostitution. In 1989 a United Nations convention for the rights of the child set higher standards for healthcare, education, and social services. The first World Summit on Children was held in 1990. In 2002 the group recognized progress to eradicate polio, reduce child mortality and malnutrition, and reduce the gender gap for elementary schooling, setting new goals that included a 50 percent reduction in the number of children out of school. Mandated schooling in the industrialized world decreased the numbers of children below 16 who work for pay, and there is a similar effect in the developing economies where schooling is universal and mandatory.

Child labor has implications for global business. Businesses that subcontract for labor often discover that they employ children, particularly in consumer product industries like textiles, furniture, and athletic shoes. The global community then pressures global enterprises to be change agents for children who work.

One way global businesses respond to public outcries against child labor is to terminate contracts that employ children. However, this may not yield the desired result. For example, Oxfam cautions that an unintended impact of retailers' human rights policies in Bangladeshi textile work has been that children then take dangerous jobs or prostitute themselves (Human rights, 1995). Another approach is proactive such as Levi Strauss displayed when it allowed a subcontractor to retain under-age workers but required that they also be paid to attend school until they reached the legal working age of 14 (Zachary, 1994). Because it is more traditional for families or governments to fund education, Levi's example demonstrates that businesses in a global world are taking on roles less usual for the business sector. Having found a way to indirectly pay for education, Levi's assumed a responsibility that more traditionally falls on families and/or the government sector.

Individual Migration and Immigration

The sense of boundarylessness evident in the global economy also applies to labor. In a world with fewer boundaries, people physically move to find work. Internal labor migration occurs when people move within their own countries, usually from rural to urban settings where there are more jobs. This occurs worldwide such as in Mexico where people seek paid labor in border towns like Tijuana and Juarez; among rural Nicaraguans working in Managua's free-trade zone; and in China where millions move from farms to take jobs in new urban centers. One of those millions is 19-year-old Hong Xiaohui whose story appears in the boxed example below.

A Chinese Girl Goes to the Factory

In 1996 19-year-old Hong Xiaohui joined 100 million other Chinese workers who left rural homes for factory work in urban centers. Some of the reasons for her pilgrimage are universal and almost global: she sought independence, she was bored with her life, and she sought easy money and adventure elsewhere. Other reasons are more universal for the poor: paid work for Hong eased the family's economic burden, helping to break a chain of poverty. She earned the equivalent of $24 per month to make Barbie dolls for Mattel.

Source material: Kathy Chen (1996, Oct. 29) Boom-town bound. *The Wall Street Journal*, pp. A1, A10.

After politics, economics are the second strongest driver of worldwide migration. Economic immigrants cross national boundaries in search of jobs, principally from developing to developed economies. Usually skilled workers are temporary or permanent immigrants to developed economies, but many unskilled immigrants illegally enter developed economies (Bhagwati, 2002). For example, an estimated 400,000 Nicaraguans are illegal in Costa Rica. About half of migrants settle in nations where industry is growing, and over a third are found in only seven of the world's most industrialized nations: Germany, France, the UK, the US, Italy, Japan, and Canada.

Many more women are immigrants than in the past. In 1996, about 50 percent of Asian overseas workers were women, up from less than 15 percent in 1976. By 2001, 70 percent of migrant workers were female (Frank, 2001). Women migrate when there are limited opportunities in home countries, but there are other reasons as well. For example, families may encourage wives and daughters to earn hard currency abroad or governments may facilitate female immigration to reduce national job competition.

Businesses that employ migrants or immigrants face challenges that range from cultural to economic to political. For example, most businesses must justify hiring immigrants over locals or engage attorneys to assist with work credentials. Immigrants increase workplace diversity that must be managed, and some may require training to reach potential in a new setting.

Job Migration

Labor-cost differentials among other factors stimulate global companies to move jobs to where labor is abundant. Outsourcing describes this process when jobs move from within the firm to an outside supplier, but this can occur within or across nations. For example, some countries hire prisoners to answer tourists' telephone questions. Offshore production is another term used, and it refers more specifically to cross-national job migration.

The worldwide search for labor occurs in both manufacturing and service industries, and it has occurred in three stages. First, low-skilled manufacturing jobs moved into the world, then middle-level skilled jobs such as call centers or processing credit card receipts were globally outsourced. A third stage of job migration occurs when professional knowledge labor globalizes.

Manufacturing

The lower costs of labor combined with improved distribution systems reduces barriers to hiring laborers almost anywhere in the world. Thomson Consumer Electronics employs three times as many people in Asia as in France, and most of Fila's textile output is sub-contracted in Asia with only 10 percent remaining in Italy. The following example shows why even smaller firms move manufacturing jobs to other nations.

Dr Martens' Move

Dr Martens shoes expanded production to China where over 100 million shoes are manufactured a year for global companies like Nike, Adidas, Timberland, Hush Puppy, Reebok, and Puma. Whereas the Dr Martens' factory in Northampton, England uses small groups of workers to assemble complete shoes, their Pou Chen plant uses mass-production techniques. The cost of labor in Northampton is about $490 a week; in Pou Chen it is about $100 per month. Unlike in England, Dr Martens must provide dormitories for migrants to Pou Chen who work up to 69 hours a week.

Source material: Dan Roberts and James Kynge (2003, Feb. 4) How cheap labour, foreign investment and rapid industrialization are creating a new workshop of the world. *Financial Times*, p. 13.

Despite frequent media reports to the contrary, manufacturing jobs are in decline worldwide. According to a 2003 study by Alliance Capital Management LP (reported in Hilsenrath and Buckman, 2003), manufacturing jobs worldwide declined by 11 percent between 1995–2002. These job losses include a 15 percent decline in China, a 16 percent decline in Japan, and a 20 percent decline in Brazil.

Services

On the other hand, service jobs are growing in number stimulated in part by low-wage, low-skill jobs in retailing, restaurants, and hotels. The global tourism industry is a particularly big employer of wage-workers in the developing economies. Service jobs in professions like accounting, consulting, engineering, medicine, teaching, and computing contribute most to service growth in the industrial economies. Below we look at both types of service jobs. Here are a few service industries that are increasingly global:

- Hotels and Restaurants
- Mail and Package delivery
- Advertising
- Business consulting
- Tourism and Travel
- Transportation
- Telecommunications
- Legal and Accounting
- Insurance and Reinsurance
- Cleaning and Maintenance.

Many "back office" services such as bookkeeping, call centers, credit card charges processing, loan and credit risks analyzing, or insurance claim reviews are outsourced worldwide. Jamaican service centers process data for everything from credit card applications to airline reservations; Irish laborers proofread technical manuals and process insurance claims; and by 2003, India had become "the back office to the world." In the short to medium term India was expected to be most attractive to global corporations, then become a leading provider of tradable services in the medium to long term (Kapur and Ramamurti, 2001). The boxed example shows that these back-office functions have done more than provide jobs for Indians; they also attract foreign workers to India. This example demonstrates how labor globalization can move jobs in more than one direction.

Ebookers

Ebookers is a medium-sized company, and it may be the first among online travel agencies to make an annual profit. Ebookers was founded in Britain by Dinesh Dhamija, son of an Indian diplomat. Ebookers provides around the clock service from a Dehli subsidiary called Tecnovate. On costs alone, the Dehli office may save Mr. Dhamija more than $4 million per year.

The ebookers story puts an interesting spin on labor globalization. While Tecnovate employs plenty of Indians, it also pioneered a new service. The motivation was to provide services for European travelers who don't speak English. The solution has been to recruit young people from Europe to staff the Dehli office.

Recruiting emphasizes adventure and opportunity. Although direct pay is low for this group of expatriates, so is the cost of living. Europeans enjoy company-paid

▶

housing, transportation to and from work, and after one year they earn perks like company-paid plane tickets to Europe. Although relatively few European workers are employed at Tecnovate (less than fifty), the service is growing—fueled by demand for foreign language speakers in Indian call centers and craving among young people to truly "see the world."

Source material: Kevin J. Delaney (2003) Outsourcing jobs—and workers—to India. *The Wall Street Journal*, pp. B1, B2; Face value/Click and fly. (2003, Oct. 11) *The Economist*, p. 72.

Professional Services Migrate

Global interconnections put competitive pressure on professional work as well. For example, developing economies are less willing to buy goods and services without foreign direct investments and job creation, and worldwide labor shortages in skilled jobs such as computer programming motivate companies to take jobs abroad. For example, Indian, Chinese, and Bulgarian software programmers write code for firms located anywhere in the world. India also supplies labor in many skill-intensive services such as software development, information technology (IT)-enabled services, product/project engineering and design, biotechnology, pharmaceuticals, media, entertainment, and healthcare. By 2003, India's exports of software and services had reached $9.5 billion (Delaney, 2003). India's educational system boasts several elite engineering universities that can turn out 25,000 engineering graduates and 70,000 computer software professionals annually (Greenemeier, 2002: 56). India, Ireland, China, Taiwan, Russia, and many other developing economies also provide professional services.

Business Benefits and Limitations of Outsourcing

Outsourcing provides access to skills that may not be available in local or domestic workforces. A second company benefit of outsourcing is direct labor-cost reductions. For example, IBM pays a Chinese programmer about $12.50 per hour (including salary and benefits) as compared to $56 an hour for comparable US programmers (Bulkeley, 2004). Costs are also reduced with lower tariffs, and when outsourcing improves logistical management. Outsourcing can reduce indirect costs. For example, companies that hire subcontract labor avoid recruiting costs, and may be able to cut in-house human resource managers. Finally, with outsourcing, some companies offer more services without raising prices. For example, many companies route telephone helpdesk calls worldwide around the clock.

Companies that outsource confront new and sometimes different labor challenges worldwide. For example, Irish service providers embrace a quality focus consistent with US values, and Ireland has a well-established, stable government and infrastructure consistent with Europe and the US. Their government supports the off-shoring industry directly with tax-free business zones and other tax incentives, as well as by working to maintain the necessary technological and educational infrastructure. In contrast, the Indian regulatory environment can be cumbersome, and infrastructure such as electricity requires upgrades. These national differences make it difficult for a global firm to create an integrative approach to global labor management.

Labor-cost advantages of relocation can be ephemeral or short lived. For example, direct hourly wage rates may not reflect actual costs of labor such as high benefits and bonuses, a need to train and educate a poorly developed workforce, or lower workforce productivity.

Competition for global labor also boosts labor demand, increasing both short- and long-term costs. High costs are associated with relocating outsourced jobs to still other nations. In Asia, a chronic shortage of service workers and local managers forces firms to train people in-house and then sees them leave to take better-paying jobs elsewhere. In Thailand, Japanese carmakers Toyota, Nissan, and Honda find that a quarter of their local managers quit annually for a rival job (Asia's labor pains, 1995). Finally, companies that outsource may be viewed as poor corporate citizens by nations that lose jobs to offshore hires. This is especially likely where there are strong historical links between companies and communities.

RACE TO THE BOTTOM OR SLOG TO THE TOP?

David Korten (1995) argues that global competition for jobs is a "race to the bottom" where the world is worse off at the finish line. In other words, low-wage jobs will be replaced with even lower-wage jobs. A second theme in the race to the bottom argument is that labor competition puts downward pressure on labor standards when they are adapted to attract FDI. A third concern is that hiring cheap labor worldwide may disrupt social contracts and cultural norms within domestic economies. For example, child-labor prohibitions in one country are subverted when companies from that nation substitute child labor abroad (Rodrik, 1997) and labor unions undermined if companies move to avoid them. The following example illustrates how elements of the Korean social contract were changed with partial purchase by a foreign firm.

Interbrew Buys 50 percent of Oriental Brewery

Belgium's Interbrew grows globally via acquisitions. Their partial purchase of South Korea's Oriental Brewery (OB) illustrates how business activities alter social contracts and traditions. OB was steeped in Korean business tradition: lifetime employment, hierarchical management, personal relationships and loyalty to the boss, male dominated, and meetings where everyone kept their mouths shut. Clients usually took months to pay the bills, and the sales force often financially 'sweetened' supplier deals. Enter Interbrew whose own traditions were quite different: casual relations among employees, input sought from men and women alike, and economic decisions that included prompt payments of bills and lay-offs.

Interbrew's managers had to find ways to bridge the cultural gap. One immediate problem was solved when they guaranteed no lay-offs for a three-year period. To create a more casual atmosphere, Interbrew managers brought in sodas and burgers for lunch, encouraged idea sharing, and handed control of a meeting to a female manager. They changed the pay structure to elicit prompt client payment, changed sales protocol, and were willing to listen to Korean employees.

Source material: Michael Schuman (2000, July 24) Foreign flavor: How Interbrew blended disparate ingredients in Korean beer venture. *The Wall Street Journal*, pp. A1, A6.

A counter-argument to the "race to the bottom" is that jobs anywhere aid overall economic development. For example, jobs in developing economies improve wages and other benefits as in Thailand where foreign wages are 10 percent or more above those of equivalent domestic firms. Thai firms are motivated to meet these wage hikes and offer healthcare benefits similar to those of foreign firms. There is some evidence of international wage convergence for workers in similar skill groups (Wood, 1994), and a leading Indian IT group estimates that earnings for top Indian software engineers will be equal to those of US engineers by 2020 (The new geography of the IT industry, 2003).

Job creation also has a spillover effect. For example, until the late 1960s or early 1970s manufacturing was monopolized almost entirely by Western firms, but manufacturing now stimulates growth in many developing economies (Krugman, 1998). The example of DDD shows how jobs stimulate other forms of development.

Digital Divide Data (DDD)

DDD is a small firm located in Phnom Penh, Cambodia at which workers participate in the $290 million data-entry industry. Most of these jobs have been outsourced due to low working wages. What makes DDD exceptional is that it was founded to bring digital sophistication to Cambodia. Jobs are held by people who are least likely to be employed elsewhere, including people disabled by land mines or polio, former prostitutes, and slum residents. Founded by former business colleagues for a global consulting firm, the company has nearly a dozen contracts that include entering encyclopedic data, UN surveys, and a seventeenth-century copy of Julius Caesar's *Gallic War*. The workers cannot read the data they enter, but they enjoy earnings of $16.25 a week for 36 hours of work (as compared to a Cambodian minimum wage of $11.25 per week for a 48-hour work week). Workers are encouraged to use their extra time to gain additional education for which DDD pays half the tuition.

Source material: June Shih (2003, Jan. 8) Only poor country's destitute may apply. *The Seattle Times*, p. A11.

Job globalization also stimulates business formation as demonstrated by the following examples from China and India.

Chinese and Indian Firms Alter the Global Business Landscape

Chinese company Masson Group recognized the potential for toothpaste sales by a "home-grown" Chinese company. They then launched CCP Calcium as a direct rival to Crest and Colgate toothpaste sales in China. Other Chinese companies create jobs on a global scale. For example, appliance brand giant Haier has 13 manufacturing sites outside China, including factories in Iran, Indonesia, and South Carolina. TCL, China's second biggest television maker, and its rival Konka have also invested in television manufacturing outside China. Through partnerships, these companies stimulate

▶

further job creation in the region. For example, Starlight Electronics Corporation, a major Vietnamese household appliance maker, gets technical assistance and parts supplies from Chinese firms and plans to expand its product line-up and possibly seek brand recognition beyond Vietnam.

Source material: Spreading their wings. (2003, Sept. 6) *The Economist*, p. 57.

Arvind Agarwalla's Fact Software International Pte. was established in India with a software program that enables businesses to update accounting information on a real-time basis. Mr. Agarwalla designed the software during his spare time, and then marketed to Singapore where computer use was more advanced. Fact quickly grew; its 1995 revenues were $2.6 million with offices in four nations and 130 employees. By 2003, Fact had moved its headquarters to Singapore and was doing business from 10 nations.

Source material: Fact homepage (2003, Nov. 15): http://fact.com.sg; Jeremy Mark (1995, May 9) Small Asian firm breaks into ranks of Western-dominated software firms. *The Wall Street Journal*, A16.

Changing demand shifts for more skilled labor (Blanchflower and Slaughter, 1998) could also enhance the global labor force with three principal effects:

1 Women will enter the workforce in greater numbers, particularly in the developing economies that have traditionally absorbed few paid female workers.
2 The average age of the world workforce will rise, particularly in the industrialized nations that are producing few new workers.
3 Demand for skilled labor will increase the number of people worldwide with high school and university educations. (Johnston, 1997)

The growing need for knowledge workers should cause jobs to develop where education levels also are high, providing comparative advantage to nations with an educated workforce and perhaps returning jobs to industrialized nations. The example below shows how Iceland has derived benefits from becoming a knowledge economy.

Opportunity in Iceland

The island nation of Iceland is located near the Arctic Circle and its citizens have made it a knowledge-based economy second to few worldwide. Iceland developed hydropower to produce and export aluminum and ferro-sulfates; its fishing fleet catches almost as many fish as the French with only one tenth of the labor; and they are the world leader in developing electronic tools for the fishing industry. Per capita income is among the highest in the world, pollution and crime are nil. Yet Iceland offers a good university, multiple theater companies, dozens of magazine and book publishers, television and radio stations, countless restaurants and cultural events, and up-to-date medical care.

Source material: Peter Passell (1994, June 26) A little economy that can. *New York Times*, E5.

INITIATIVES TO ASSIST GLOBAL WORKFORCE DEVELOPMENT

Governments, nations, nongovernmental organizations, and businesses all play a role in deciding if labor globalization improves or undermines work opportunities and standards. The unanswered question is: who or what entity is responsible for achieving better employment equity? Rodrik (1997) argues that unless businesses recognize links between their activities and social contracts with nations and workers, social forces will lead to political governance of business activities. Whether through voluntary or mandated action, it seems likely that businesses will be part of future initiatives for workforce development. Further, as argued elsewhere in the book, there is a growing sense that businesses must play a role in achieving social as well as economic equity. The following sections focus on global organizations that develop the global work force.

Government Initiatives in Education

Mihaly Simai (1994: 194–195) believes governments can improve the workforce by improving human resources in the following ways:

1 Optimize the quality of the labor force and human resources with educational systems, retrain labor force, promoted scientific awareness and progress.
2 Sociopolitical and economic conditions that favor developments such as improved working conditions and support for basic human rights.

The chances are this chapter is part of a university assignment. If so, you are among the privileged few who continue their studies beyond secondary school. Worldwide educational investments totaled $1.5 trillion in 2003. These expenditures are expected to double in six years to total $6 trillion in 2012. However, even within advanced economies, only about 25 percent of the population has a university degree. In contrast, more than 876 million adults are illiterate, and over 115 million children do not have access even to primary school. Most illiterates are women. More than 40 percent of children in Africa receive no education. Below we see that globalization of labor and economic development is closely associated with education.

Gregory Mankiw (1995) estimates that two-thirds of all national labor incomes result from improving workers' skills. As a percentage of GNP, world expenditures on education increased from 3.9 to 4.8 percent between 1980 and 1997. Nations with strong educational systems experienced higher economic growth and lower poverty levels than nations with poor educational standards (Up the ladder, 2000). Some examples appear in Table 9.2.

Table 9.2 *Education and GDP Growth*

Nation	Average GDP growth rate, 1990–98	Education as % males with a primary-school education	Poverty as % living on 1 $US per day
South Korea	6.1	98	Less than 2
Chile	7.9	100	4.3
Malaysia	7.4	98	5.6
India	6.1	62	44.2
Guatemala	4.2	52	39.8
Nigeria	2.6	70.2	28.9

Source material: Up the ladder. (2000, Nov. 6) *Business Week*, pp. 78–84.

Social returns from primary-education investments are higher than for secondary or tertiary education in developing economies. For example, it benefits communities by lowering fertility rates, helps families to raise healthier children, and helps farmers to improve their crop yields (Sen, 1999). When people can read and write, they have better job opportunities that may help them earn enough to break the cycle of poverty. For example, they can fund the other costs of schooling for their children such as uniforms, books, materials, and even transportation to and from school.

Many nations target education to improve the labor force. In the industrialized world where skilled and educated workers are concentrated, the average worker has completed 11 years of education compared with five in China and Mexico. Many advanced nations also encourage or subsidize post-secondary education with grants, gifts, or scholarships. South Korea used education to leapfrog neighbors that are less supportive of education. Many nations provide more educational benefits for males than for females, but others have adopted universal education. The example below shows that universal education can catapult a country to world economic growth.

Back to the Industrial Revolution

Lester Thurow argues that a technological elite catapulted Britain to world leadership in the steam age. But in the decades to follow, Britain ignored its underclass, doing little to educate them. Meanwhile, the US embarked on a bold experiment for universal education. According to Thurow, this investment in education made it possible for the US to out-produce the British using the same technologies. In other words, productivity is linked to education is linked to national development.

Source material: Lester C. Thurow (1999) *Building Wealth*. New York: HarperCollins.

Mandatory school attendance is from 5–11 years in the developing countries. At an "Education for All" conference in 1990, all but two of the world's nations pledged to provide universal basic education by 2015 (No school, 1999). But progress toward these goals has been slow. Meeting in 2002, member nations agreed to Fast Track initiatives to meet their original goals. But as is true for child-labor initiatives, the problem is not setting goals but the political will to follow through. Some nations have reshaped cultural traditions to endorse education; examples appear in the box below.

National Investments in Education

In Malawi, laws were relaxed to make primary education accessible. Indonesia's commitment to *wajib belajar* reinforces the responsibility all Indonesians have to gain as much knowledge as possible. The slogan at the University of Botswana is "Thuto Ke Thabe" translated as "education is a shield." Local government in Guadalajara, Mexico distribute pamphlets in schools that list careers and salaries at local companies. The government also subsidizes job training for new hires (Up the ladder, 2000).

When governments perceive that businesses are the linchpin in the trade-path to national prosperity, they are further motivated to improve educational levels that attract business. The Chilean example appearing below also shows that the shorter-term benefits of education affect economic development and may in turn shape the nation's commitment to education.

Chile's Social Spending

According to a 1996 IMF report, Chile's economic development has been accompanied by social spending that increased from 55 to 61 percent between 1990 and 1995; most of this spending went into health, education, and housing. Rather than producing a drag on economic development, this social spending accompanied high economic growth for Chile. Meanwhile, Chile's illiteracy rate has been reduced to less than 5 percent, and the poverty rate was cut by 30 percent in four years. Having witnessed the link between education and economic development, in 1996 Chile passed legislation calling for an increase in funding to build more schools, update curriculum, and improve teacher training.

Innovative collaborative arrangements among development agencies, governments, NGOs, and businesses also have helped to improve educational standards upon which many domestic economies rest (Waddell, 1999), and they further serve to integrate business, government, and civil society. Businesses routinely train their own employees to help them gain skills the organization needs. This is one type of educational initiative in which businesses engage. Another approach is for businesses to create free-standing educational institutions. For example, Cisco Systems founded a worldwide Networking

Academy program to meet future need for Internet networking professionals. These academies have trained over 100,000 in the US, and were expected to reach a similar number in India (Cisco aims to train 100,000 workers in India by 2006, 2001).

Intergovernmental Initiatives

The 175 member nations of the ILO have adopted 200 conventions covering labor conditions and labor rights. Most nations and businesses in them base their labor standards and practices at least in part on these and other multilateral agreements. The International Chamber of Commerce counts more than forty codes of conduct designed to govern the activities of global corporations. These include the Global Sullivan Principles, the UN Global Compact, the Global Reporting Initiative, and the Organization for Economic Cooperation and Development (OECD) guidelines on Multinational Enterprises. The global basket of human rights issues is necessarily large to encompass many and diverse concerns such as child labor, working hours and safety conditions, and ethnic and gender equity to name but a few.

Labor rights cover basic first-order rights such as rights to freedom from persecution and slavery, second-order rights such as basic healthcare, and third-order rights to peace, development, and a healthy environment (Husband, 1996). Businesses are expected to honor first- and second-order rights, and they are increasingly expected to help achieve third-order rights through hiring practices that generate job equity or production processes that preserve the natural environment.

Civil Society Initiatives

Transnational voluntary groups like the International Labor Rights Education and Resource Fund, Human Rights Watch, the Clandestine Commission on Unions, and Amnesty International are only a few among many organizations that have increased global awareness of human rights at work. Their advocacy for human rights includes pressure on national governments and direct action against corporations. More recently, the scope of these groups has expanded to combine political and economic pressures. Finally, direct consumer pressure on business organizations has caused them also to consider their labor practices.

Labor Unions

Upward convergence in labor conditions is an aim of global labor unionization, an approach that brings trade unions full circle to their early nineteenth-century roots which witnessed national and international efforts to win fair and safe work conditions. The common international voice of labor was almost extinguished by the nationalism of two world wars, causing unions to develop more within nations than among them, and giving rise to national variations in laborer/manager relationships. Examples of different union stances appear in the following box.

Union–National Relationships

In Germany, the post-World War approach of co-determination acknowledged common interest among owners and laborers to ensure a high quality of life. Union members serve on corporate boards to monitor and resolve labor/management concerns.

The fierce individualism and desire for autonomy dominant among US industrialists created an "us versus them" mentality in US labor/management relationships. US labor negotiations remain adversarial in many cases.

Postwar unionism in Japan has been one of partnership between management and labor.

National labor union membership varies as well. According to the ILO, in 1995 union members were 28.9 percent of Germany workers; 32.9 percent of British workers; and 25.6 percent of workers in the Netherlands. As a percentage of the workforce, US union membership has declined from 20 percent in 1980 to 12.4 percent by 2004.

According to Jeremy Brecher and Tim Costello, globalization creates social challenges that transcend the workplace and can be addressed only by a labor movement that promotes the interests of all workers. According to these authors "trade unions must reach out of the workplace and into the community by building coalitions with environmental, community, religious, women's human rights, farm, and other people's organizations" (1994: 160) as partners in improving job conditions rather than competitors for jobs worldwide. These authors recommend that labor movements worldwide build on past successes and forge new ones by helping corporations create worker-designed workplace solutions to emerging problems. An example of how this can occur appears below.

Motorola Finds Another Way

Motorola managers wanted to cut manufacturing costs, and they considered moving US jobs abroad. But first they asked employees for their ideas. Employees created a plan for building the product at a lower cost and a higher level quality than international competitors. Not only were they able to reduce costs, but they also developed successful new products for import. An example is a radio-paging product exported to Japan where consumers are known to be particularly demanding of quality. This example shows how collaboration reduced costs and helped workers to retain and even create jobs.

Inasmuch as many union traditions developed within nations, a major barrier to transnational labor unionism is the view that jobs "belong" to one nation or another. Like other entities, collective bargainers often find it difficult to trade short-term losses against longer-term benefits for workers worldwide. This is an impediment to transnational collective bargaining (Prahalad and Doz, 1987).

Industry and Business Initiatives

Many global firms participate in certification arrangements such as "codes of conduct, production guidelines, and monitoring standards that govern and attest to not only the corporation's behavior but also to that of their suppliers around the world" (Gereffi, et al., 2001: 56). Industries that most frequently employ certification standards are those most vulnerable to consumers, for example coffee, forest products, oil, mining, apparel, footwear, and toys. There are four levels of certification:

- First-party certification is the most common variety, whereby a single firm develops its own rules and reports on compliance.
- Second-party certification involves an industry or trade association fashioning a code of conduct and implementing reporting mechanisms.
- Third-party certification involves an external group, often an NGO, imposing its rules and compliance methods onto a particular firm or industry.
- Fourth-party certification involves government or multilateral agencies such as the Global Compact (Gereffi et al., 2001).

An example of a first-party certification appears below in the description of Mattel's audit of its own activities. It is followed by a second-party form of certification developed for the toy industry as a whole.

Mattel Audits Its Labor Practices

In the mid-1990s, Mattel and other US toy and clothing companies faced charges that they were not protecting workers' health and safety in overseas plants. In response Mattel instituted a global code of conduct and established an independent monitoring council to conduct regular audits of manufacturing plants.

Mattel's initial 1999 audit of its Asian plants noted a number of problems that the company agreed to resolve. For example, in Indonesia, the audit found that workers were exposed to chemical odors, noise, and hazardous working conditions. In China, Mattel management agreed to discontinue a hiring practice that requires a cash security deposit during employment, and to consider how they could reduce or help with recruiting and transportation fees. A 2001 follow-up in China noted that the Guan Yao Mattel plant found significant improvements in employee living and working conditions that included new dormitories for workers, an on-site medical facility, and installation of a new ventilation system. The audit also noted that the Guan Yao plant facilitated greater employee awareness of Mattel's Global Manufacturing Principles and initiated open gatherings to discuss issues of concern to employees. Programs for job-related new employee training had also been strengthened. Mattel is one of only a few companies that make its audits public; Gap is another.

Source material: Lisa Bannon (1999, Nov. 18) Mattel's Asian plants will address problems. *The Wall Street Journal*, p. B15; Mattel Company home page: http://www.mattel.com

> ### Toy Industry Code of Conduct
>
> To protect the health and safety of workers making toys, the Toy Industry Association introduced an expanded Code of Business Practices defining an appropriate standard for safe working conditions. Included in this Code are the International Labor Organization's C138 Minimum Age Convention and C182 Worst Forms of Child Labor Convention, which are obviously aimed at protecting children. Human rights always poses a challenge for global firms, and taking steps at ensuring a clean, safe working environment can only stand to benefit both sides.

The Global Compact (reviewed in greater depth in Chapter 6) is a fourth-party certification program. In terms of labor rights, the Global Compact outlines the following principles for businesses:

- Principle 1: support and respect the protection of international human rights within their sphere of influence.
- Principle 2: make sure their own corporations are not complicit in human rights abuses.
- Principle 3: uphold freedom of association and the effective recognition of the right to collective bargaining.
- Principle 4: the elimination of all forms of forced and compulsory labor.
- Principle 5: the effective abolition of child labor.
- Principle 6: the elimination of discrimination in respect of employment and occupation.

Agitation for and development of global codes and certifications has ramifications for global firms as they weigh trade-offs of autonomy and control, between patriarchy and partnership, between equality and the inequity inherent in most traditional management structures. According to chairman Robert Eckert, Mattell must consider difficult questions and trade-offs such as "Do we want to make people's lives better? Absolutely. Do we want to unilaterally do things that make us uncompetitive and therefore our products don't sell and therefore nobody gets employed? No." (Goldman, 2004).

The preceding review of some of many factors that shape the global labor force illustrates that a globalizing world of work offers almost limitless potential tempered by challenges of access and equity. Recognizing, weighing, and selecting from among these and other opportunities are only a few business challenges in a global world. Despite guidelines suggested here and elsewhere, there are as yet no hard and fast "rules" for global work. Worldwide changes in technology, organizations, culture, and other global environments generate jobs and bring challenges that confront businesses, governments, civil society, and citizens.

CHAPTER SUMMARY

About three billion people work. In the developing economies, only about 15 percent of workers have wage contracts, and most of these are employed by urban industrial firms or service providers. In the middle-income economies (those that are neither rich nor poor), 46 percent of the working population is in industrial or service employment. In the advanced economies, most people — about 70 percent — work in service industries

The informal work sector comprises both self-employment in small or unregistered enterprises, or wages earned in jobs that have no contracts. The informal work sector is not counted in GDP estimates, and conditions of informal work are unreported, but it is believed that hours of work are longer and wages are lower than in the formal work sector.

Global work challenges include high unemployment and underemployment, low status for women and members of minority groups, children at work, and human and job migration and immigration.

Global firms employ a relatively small number of the global labor force, and most paid jobs are created by small, place-bound firms. Nevertheless, because they are identifiable, have economic and political clout, and contribute to job growth, global firms are expected to take a bigger role in managing labor inequities.

REVIEW AND DISCUSSION QUESTIONS

1 What are the pros and cons for countries to send immigrants abroad to work?

2 In North America and Europe women dominate jobs that are growing and men are more frequently trapped in manufacturing jobs that are declining in number. In rapidly growing Asian nations, women's job and educational opportunities are also growing, and in many developing economies, women increasingly are taking jobs in the paid labor force. Analyze how these changes are likely to affect work organizations. What are the likely impacts of these changes on social relationships between women and men? Overall, are these changes likely to prove positive or negative; take a position and provide evidence to support it.

3 If knowledge and education are primary organizational assets, consider the following:

  a) How will traditional management techniques of your nation change?

  b) What will employee benefits packages need to stress: Wages or educational subsidies? Wage raises or healthcare? Time or money? Explain the reasons for your conclusions.

Chapter 10
GLOBAL POLITICS

NATIONAL POLITICS AND GLOBAL BUSINESS INTERESTS COLLIDE

Telefónica is Spain's largest company, and it is a telecommunications giant for Spanish- and Portuguese-speaking populations worldwide. The company operates about 43 million fixed lines, and its wireless unit Telefónica Móviles has 48 million subscribers. It is also the largest shareholder in the Terra Lycos Internet portal, and it operates call centers and directory publishing. Telefónica activities demonstrate one way that global interconnections of culture, telecommunications, business, and politics take shape.

In 1995 Telefónica de Espana was one of Europe's weakest national telephone carriers. It was accused of inefficiencies, and a top-heavy management team that deflected innovation. By 2000 it had become one of the world's most global telecoms, due in large part to the efforts of CEO Jose Villalonga.

Mr. Villalonga's experience was as a management consultant and an investment banker. He knew little about the telecom industry, but in 1996 agreed to head the company when his former schoolmate, Jose Maria Aznar, became Spain's prime minister. At the time, Telefónica de Espana was a state-controlled monopoly. Under Mr. Villalonga's leadership, the company was fully privatized by 1997, and it had begun to shed its image as a stodgy firm. He changed personnel, brought in dozens of consultants from McKinsey, overruled Telefónica managers, and even changed the company's name from Telefónica de Espana to Telefónica.

Consistent with what was happening worldwide among telecommunications companies, Villalonga pursued a bewildering blur of strategic moves that included acquisitions, spin-offs, partnerships, and expansion. For example, Telefónica leveraged its Latin American presence beyond Argentina, Peru, and Chile by quickly bidding for the newly available assets of Brazil's regional phone companies. He positioned Telefónica as a multimedia player with a $5 billion takeover of Dutch Endemol—best known for "Big Brother," a TV show in which cameras and microphones follow a group of people locked in a house. Other corporate strategy moves included a spin-off of Internet services arm Terra Networks S.A. (Madrid) and a successful bid for one of the continent's first third-generation mobile licenses. He withdrew Telefónica from Unisource, an alliance of European phone companies that sell voice and data services to multinational corporations, then began negotiations for a different alliance. Finally, he began to court larger telecoms, looking for a merger partner to catapult Telefónica into global leadership.

Some viewed Telefónica as a symbol of a renewed Spanish economy. Shareholders were especially pleased: at its peak, Telefónica stock rose 460 percent to outperform the European telecom sector average by 25 percent. But Villalonga and the new Telefónica represented a poor accommodation between Spanish politics and traditions and the new, more global politic and business practices borrowed from other traditions. The uneasy nature of this accommodation was played out in an annual Telefónica meeting when a shareholder's defense of Villalonga led to a physical attack by another. According to the *Wall Street Journal* report on the incident, it represented a culture clash between conservative European business traditions and the "sky is the limit" US-style capitalism Mr. Villalonga pursued.

▶

This clash was played out at organizational and national levels as well. Telefónica's leaders were overruled on many decisions, and Mr. Villalonga often did not consult them before making strategic moves. His sharp focus on shareholder value also included returns to Telefónica's managers in the form of generous stock options.

According to media reports, Villalonga quickly fell out of favor with Spain's power elite over issues ranging from personal to professional rumors and scandals. He did things his own way, could be personally abrasive, and drew worldwide attention to a romantic liaison. Mr. Villalonga paid less and less heed to Spanish business protocol, sometimes neglecting to return calls or acknowledge gifts.

Villalonga fell out with prime minister Aznar over a proposed business alliance to exchange shares and vice-chairmanships between Telefónica and Banco Bilbao Vizcaya Argentaria, a banking and industrial group. Political opponents used this to bolster claims that Aznar's appointees had too much power. Faced with government resistance to the deal, BBVA persuaded Mr. Villalonga to give up the role of vice-chairman at the bank. Merger talks with Dutch telecom KPN collapsed. Then the Spanish authorities announced an investigation into improper share trading. By 2000, Villalonga and Telefónica had parted ways.

But problems at Telefónica continued. Villalonga's replacement César Alierta was believed to be a much less aggressive manager, but Alierta faced global challenges. There was a downturn in Latin American markets, and currency problems that led to a 23 percent dip in Latin American revenues in the first half of 2002. Efforts to "unwind" expansion from the Villalonga era required writing off a $5 billion investment.

There were also problems with Sintel, a Spanish telecom company that had been sold to Cuban exile leader Jorge Mas Canosa. Sintel had been hollowed out, leaving nothing to pay Telefónica for its purchase. Telefónica stopped subcontracting with Sintel which then cut its staff by 1,800. In protest, some of the fired workers camped outside the finance ministry. Eventually the Aznar government succumbed to public pressure, forcing Telefónica—the fully privatized firm—to rehire employees or provide early retirement and state pensions.

Then in 2002, prosecutors charged new CEO Alierta with insider trading on shares of a tobacco group he'd earlier chaired. Alierta denied the charges and promptly sued *El Mundo*, the daily newspaper that reported on the investigation.

These examples illustrate how national politics are spotlighted by participation in global industries. Telefónica was privatized, but there was a lingering sense that the company "belonged" to Spain. Business activities across national boundaries were not well received when they opposed existing governance traditions. Individuals, in this case shareholders, enjoyed some of the changes, but those in political power recognized that global involvement reduced their autonomy to act just as they had in the past. The Spanish press picked up on corporate governance issues, the company was affected by economic downturns in Latin America, and a company that had been the pride of its nation reported its first loss in 2002.

Source material: Jennie James and Hugh Porter (2002, Aug. 12) Spanish firms run into real trouble. *Time Europe*, 160 (7):14–17; Gautam Naik, Carlta Vitzhum and Thomas Kamm (2000, May 8) Telefónica chief upsets Spain's staid customs. *The Wall Street Journal*, pp. A1, A8; Pain in Spain. (2002, Sept. 9) *Time Europe*, 160 (24): 20; Sarah Parkes (2000, Aug. 14) A new reign in Spain. *tele.com*, 5 (16): 22–24; Who's Next? (2001, Sept. 1) *The Economist*, pp. 45–47.

CHAPTER OVERVIEW

This chapter examines governmental activities that stimulate domestic prosperity. Increasingly government leaders recognize that national prosperity also depends on building worldwide interconnections. Thus world prosperity becomes an issue for national leaders who encourage more global business activities via privatization, deregulation, business stimulation, and trade agreements. The expected benefits are offset by challenges for political leaders. In a world where business is global, there is an increasing need for global rules of business conduct. The latter raise global governance issues examined in this chapter. The chapter concludes with a look at organizational activities that shape emerging global governance.

THE ROLE OF GOVERNMENTS

Governments play many roles, but their primary responsibility is to manage public policy to balance individual and collective interests of the governed. Governments play many roles such as providing goods and services that benefit the nation as a whole, for example, healthcare, education, economic development and mobilizing defense mechanisms. Governments finance their activities by collecting taxes or levies; they create laws to outline responsibilities and maintain social order; and they intervene when laws are broken. Most governments are organized as sovereign and independent nation-states defined by geographic boundaries.

Nation-State Governance Systems

Every nation's prosperity and even its survival depends in great part on smooth operation of the nation's affairs. Internal coordination among political interests needs to be balanced because these can differ at national, regional, state/province, and even local levels. When competing interests are not reconciled, civil strife may follow such as in Afghanistan when the Taliban, the Northern Alliance, and tribal groups conflicted. In some cases a government may satisfy its own citizens but clash with other nations. This too can produce conflict such as occurred when Iraq attacked Kuwait; the Gulf War that followed involved many more nations than the two.

Governmental systems and processes differ widely in the world's 193 nations, 60 dependencies, and six disputed territories. This book focusses principally on how these systems affect businesses within nations and on a global scale. Below we look at three points of difference that affect business activities within nations: who makes national decisions; how national resources are distributed and managed; and the basis for rules of law.

Decision-making

In a democracy, decisions are distributed to ensure that each individual has some say in them. Often this occurs through voting processes. Although government systems such as communism, socialism, absolute monarchies, and dictatorships differ widely from one another, they are similar because decisions are made by one or a few powerful leaders. In the former Soviet Union, the few in command were top members of the Communist Party. In Brunei, the Sultan—a monarch—makes most decisions. Absolute monarchies, dictatorships, and command economies typically seek limited citizen input.

Resource Distribution and Management

Political systems manage resource flows that vary to include *socialist control* and *market systems*. An underlying assumption of socialism is that government is best able to balance collective and individual interests, and so the state or government manages production, distribution, and exchange of goods and services. Many resources are owned by the state rather than by private businesses. Government leaders in a socialist system decide how to use productive resources like land, labor, and capital. In the former Soviet Union, for example, the Communist Party dictated not only which goods would be produced and distributed but also where, and it assigned workers to jobs. At the end of World War II about one-third of the world operated under some sort of socialist system.

An alternative approach to resource distribution is a market system that concentrates productive resources in private hands such as businesses. On balance the premise of a market system is that collective good is best served by the activities of largely self-interested actors in a free and open market. This is not to say that government does nothing. Typically, free-market governments address gaps that emerge. For example, because the market is unlikely to address social needs, such as providing for the future or protecting the natural environment, governments legislate to meet collective needs such as these. Other examples of government "corrections" to the market appear in the box below. Except for those few nations where governments almost never interfere with markets, most governments correct market imperfections and manage business and individual behavior through regulations, policies, rules, standards, and laws.

Government Corrections to a Free-market System

- To protect the future, governments are likely to build infrastructure capacity such as roads that everyone uses.
- Governments provide public goods such as police, parks, or educational facilities.
- Governments correct spillovers and externalities. For example, a government might provide a subsidy or incentive to encourage research and development that is not directly profitable but provides a public good such as "orphan drugs."
- Governments correct for business-cycle instabilities.
- Governments maintain principles of justice and equality. For example, many governments offer equal and free access to schooling.

Market Systems Develop

Two-thirds of the world was not socialist in 1945, but their market systems varied considerably. In Western Europe, for example, governments tended to own more productive resources than in the US, especially infrastructure assets such as telephones, transportation, mail, and utilities. Many of these differences persist and affect business activities today. For example, the *polder* model in the Netherlands calls for businesses, politicians, and unions to reach consensus around a common good. This reflects a general tendency in Western Europe for business and government to collaborate on public policy. In the US business interests are often perceived to conflict with those of politicians. In practice, this leads to less government/business cooperation in the US than in Europe.

The form of market system adopted also affects government spending on social programs and tax rates. Because Western European nations tend to provide a more comprehensive social safety net for citizens, government coordination costs are higher than in the US. This in part explains why tax levies on individuals and organizations are higher there than in the US.

Growing Interest in Market Systems

The fall of the Berlin Wall in November 1989 may have marked the end of a world previously divided into socialist (2nd world) and free-market capitalist (1st world) nations. This event, the later dissolution of the Soviet Union, and China's entry into the World Trade Organization all presage a worldwide shift away from government intervention and toward free-market systems. Together, these and other global political shifts profoundly affect political and legal systems within and among affected nations. In particular, these global shifts hamper autonomous activities as nations manage policies in an interconnected world. The example below illustrates that open markets are not a worldwide panacea.

Elections in Latin America Post-neoliberalism

After the fall of the Berlin Wall, many citizens of Latin American countries believed that free trade could help them. By the mid-1990s almost all Latin American countries faced growing pressure to open their markets in pursuit of free trade. This meant less government intervention in trade such as import tariffs. Nations such as Chile, Mexico, Argentina, and Peru elected US-trained free-market leaders to benefit from free markets. Part of the free-market revolution occurring in Latin America is attributed to US graduate study in economics, particularly among "Los Chicago Boys" who studied at the University of Chicago.

Sadly, free markets did not prove a panacea. For much of Latin America open-market politics have been accompanied by unrest and growing poverty rates. The poor in the region also bear the brunt of chronic shortages in healthcare, education, and other social programs. By 2002, Latin American nations witnessed elections in response to their unchanged conditions. Many nations that had embraced open markets elected left-leaning politicians; those that had been leftist began to elect conservatives. How can we explain this trend? According to Venezuela political

▶

analyst Anibal Romero, the reason for these electoral upsets is simple: political models of both left and right have failed to deliver the better life that people seek. Nevertheless, according to measures of the Latinobarometro poll (The stubborn survival, 2003) of people polled in 17 Latin American nations, 50–70% believe that a market economy is the only system that can develop their countries.

Source material: T. Christian Miller and Hector Tobar (2002, Nov. 29) Latin America is hungry for change. *The Seattle Times*, p. A19; The stubborn survival of frustrated democrats. (2003, Nov. 1) *The Economist*, pp. 33–34.

Global shifts in the late 1990s—particularly active demands for global economic and social equity—mark the beginning of renewed efforts to improve economic and social development in the Third World of developing economies. Early efforts were based largely on free-market activities, but as the prior example from Latin American nations shows, it may be impossible to create one world based on the same set of free-market principles. A particular challenge is that the beliefs, values, and behaviors that balance individual and collective interests within nations are not shared worldwide. Nor are mechanisms for taxation and public goods the same worldwide. These differences in values and behaviors make it difficult to develop worldwide market systems or global governance mechanisms to manage them. The latter point is explored in greater depth later in this chapter.

Shopping in Germany

As noted earlier, nation-states develop internal governance mechanisms to manage domestic and international cross-border activities. Underlying assumptions that shape governance, decision-making, ways to distribute resources, rules of law, property rights, and all other forms of political decisions within nations emerged from common and shared understandings among citizens about what is good, right, acceptable, or fair. For example, Germany's Free Gift Act and Discount Law protected small retailers by limiting discounts, rebates, and giveaways. These laws meant that US retailer Land's End could not advertise its unconditional guarantee in Germany, nor could American Express advertise a program that awards points for purchases (German shoppers, 2001). In a more global world these laws were repealed to open Germany to Internet retailing, but their repeal also reduced German reliance on the government's price-monitoring role. Small retailers may be affected, and German shoppers must acquire new skills. This example shows why global governance mechanisms are difficult to establish: existing national laws provide direction for people and organizations.

Rules of Law Affect Businesses

On the domestic scene, governments redistribute resources through taxation and transfers, they collaborate with businesses and other communities of interest to promote economic growth and social development, and they regulate individual and organizational activities.

Everybody Hates Them: Taxes

In the absence of income-producing activities like gambling in Monte Carlo and Las Vegas or oil production in Saudi Arabia that generate government incomes, most governments gain access to the operating income they need via taxation levied against private resources, including taxes on personal income, on sales, on property, or on corporate profits. Regardless of the sources, government revenues are typically used to support government operations, build a defense system, or redistribute them for the common good. Among projects believed to serve a common good are welfare and other social support programs, road or infrastructure projects, education, food subsidies, and even business development programs. Redistribution of resources varies widely according to nation. According to a recent *Economist* article (The tap runs dry, 1997), globalization in two spheres may make it more difficult for nations to tax corporations. First, Internet technology allows almost all organizations to cross commercial borders, and few mechanisms exist to monitor these sales. Second, multinationals as well as smaller firms increasingly earn more of their revenues abroad, and they may find it advantageous to report greatest profits in nations where tax rates are low.

National laws and regulations affecting businesses can outline small concerns such as whether a limited liability company is designated by Ltd. as in Britain, Gmbh. as in Germany, or Inc. as in the US. Other national law covers much more important concerns such as corporate governance, transparency, or employment law. For example, many developed economies require advance notice to fire or lay off workers, but the notice period ranges from 12 weeks in Belgium and Denmark to two weeks in Britain.

Rules of Law and Property Rights Enhance Business Investments

Two important legal protections for business investments are rules of law and well-defined property rights. In the absence of these systems, businesses may be unwilling to invest. If laws are in place and they are transparent—evident to all—then this lowers FDI risk for businesses. But rules of law in themselves have little value without government mechanisms such as courts to resolve disputes in a timely manner. In general, advanced economies operate with concrete and enforceable rules of law that are infrequently subject to whimsical change.

Additionally, property rights are fairly well established among advanced economies, and greatest economic growth occurs among the poorest nations when the poor have good property rights (*World Development Report 2001*). However, a common problem for the poorest economies is that property rights are often poorly defined or unenforceable (Olson, 2000). In Malawi, for example, about two-thirds of occupied land is owned by tribal chiefs. This means that individuals cannot use homes as collateral for business loans, nor can they sell land that has been in their families for generations (De Soto, 2000; No title, 2001). In Nicaragua, real-estate ownership is difficult to establish because returning citizens claim land the Sandanista government redistributed. Foreign businesses are unlikely to purchase land or develop real estate there until claims are settled.

In addition to rules of law and property rights, many other features of legal infrastructure encourage or discourage business activities. For example, high taxation and few government services tend to deter business investments. Business laws that establish standards, for example safety, professional licensing, or minimum wages also affect business investments.

Three Main Types of Legal Systems

There are three main types of legal systems used today. A *civil law* system outlines law that courts then apply; this system is used in Western Europe except the British Commonwealth and it is in limited use in East Asia. *Common law* systems also rely on written laws, but courts have much greater leeway to interpret them. The common law system originated with William the Conqueror in 1066 and it is still practiced in the British Commonwealth, in the US, and in most countries settled by Anglo-Saxons. Other nations follow *religious law.* For example, many Islamic countries follow Sharia or the laws of Islam, which defines individual behavior as well as social relations, business relations, and community life. The ideological basis of these relations is found in the Qur'an or Koran as it is often spelled in English. The Koran can be interpreted differently according to the Islamic sect in power and the nation. Elsewhere less well-codified and even unwritten religious laws direct beliefs and behaviors. For example, tribal groups such as animists believe the soul is the principle of life found in all natural objects. Magic, fate, luck, and signs also are a part of animist religious laws.

Sharia Interpreted

In 1995, Sheik Hamad bin Khalifa al Thani replaced his conservative father as leader of Qatar. Since then, Qatar has developed economically and attracted business investments. An example is Al Jazeera satellite-TV station. Qatar's leader also has lifted many prior restrictions. For example he allowed Christian migrant workers to build a church in Qatar and he lifted many restrictions on women's rights. Qatar is largely populated by Wahhabi Muslims. This same strain of Islam is also practiced in Saudi Arabia, but the two countries have interpreted it in very different ways. The dean of Qatar University's College of Sharia, Abdelhameed Alansari, comments: "I consider myself a good Wahhabi and can still be modern, understanding Islam in an open way. We take into account the changes in the world and do not have the closed-minded mentality" found elsewhere.

Source material: Yarlslav Trofimov (2002, Oct. 24) In quiet revolt, Qatar snubs Saudis with women's rights. *The Wall Street Journal*, pp. A1, A12.

A global challenge is that individuals and organizations are not easily able, nor always willing, to adopt or adapt to the laws of others. This leads to conflict within and between nations. For example, animist traditions among Aborigines often conflict with Australian law. Differences between Islamic religious law and civil or common law have become more evident as the Western world learns more about Islamic life. In other words, differences between national laws become more evident when people from these nations interact. Businesses worldwide also face challenges and incur costs to comply with different laws in each nation. This is one reason that many global businesses support global regulations and standards.

National Stability and Business Investments

The pros and cons of every form of governance are widely debated. However, most agree that whatever their ideology, stable governments tend to attract business activities and unstable ones do not. For example, many foreign businesses closed their operations in Argentina and Venezuela in 2001 following economic and military crises. Internal instability can lead to an overturn in government leadership, and this can threaten investments. But there are less radical ways that political instability affects business investments. For example, St. Croix experienced losses of $40 million per year in cruise ship revenues until local thefts were curbed.

NATIONAL GOVERNMENTS INTERCONNECT WITH BUSINESSES

For most of the twentieth century, nations viewed themselves as autonomous entities whose prosperity depended mostly on their own efforts which could include trade with other nations. In this "closed economy" scenario nations managed cross-border interactions mainly via national governance policies such as tariffs, quotas, subsidies, customs valuations, standards, licensing, reciprocal agreements, and restrictions of services.

But there is growing belief that national economic prosperity depends not only on domestic activities but also on participation in global economic activities. The interconnections that follow entry into a global economy also bring challenges. For politicians, challenges arise from managing conflicting demands of national and global interests. An example is subsidies: many countries subsidize businesses or industries, but the World Trade Organization has systematically ruled that subsidies impede world trade. Additionally, global interconnections alter the essential nature of the politician's job. For example, if a nation's ability to create wealth and prosperity depends on interconnections, then an important job for governments is to enhance these interconnections rather than preserve national interests only. Below we look at four principal ways that national governments encourage business activities that connect them to the world: privatization, deregulation, business stimulation, and trade agreements.

Privatization

Privatization is the process by which an organization is transferred from public to private ownership. General Augusto Pinochet is generally credited with kicking off the current trend toward privatization. The box below indicates where some privatization has occurred.

The Privatization Trend

As a first-mover on widescale privatization, Chile proved that economic development could follow privatization, and became the model for worldwide privatization. In 1993 alone Argentina made a public stock offering in oil and gas giant YPF; Brazil sold a major steel maker to a group of banks; Jamaica sold sugar plantations to Sugar Company of Jamaica; Mexico sold Television Azteca to the Salinas Pliego and Sabo families; and Panama sold its fruit juice company to a Colombian extractor. Since then, hundreds of similar deals have been made throughout the region, including Colombia's sale of automaker Colombiana Automotriz to Mazda and Sumitomo. Telecommunications industries also have been privatized in full or in part since 1987 from Latin and Central America to include Argentina, Chile, Peru, Mexico, Venezuela, and Caribbean countries such as Cuba and Jamaica. This was how Telefónica invested in Latin America. In 2002, Indonesia began to sell stakes in PT Indonesia Satellite Corporation (Indostat) to private investors.

Governments worldwide have divested full or partial ownership in productive factors once owned or controlled. But privatization occurs for many reasons. For example, capital-intensive businesses in industries such as airlines, railroads, and telecommunications often have high costs that governments cannot bear. Because governments want those businesses to grow they sell them, hoping that private capital will help them grow. Another reason to privatize is to preserve the original company's jobs. Privatization also can be a source of government funds. Governments also privatize activities they previously managed alone such as garbage-removal services, prison management, or even education by contracting activities to businesses or to nongovernmental organizations. When that occurs, the links between businesses, NGOs, and governments grow. In command economies such as China, Vietnam, and Cuba political changes have resulted in increased privatization in all types of industries.

Privatization also occurs in advanced economies. Among industries privatized in Europe are airlines, telecommunications, energy, banking, steel, education, and even prisons. For example, Britain divested itself of Rolls-Royce and British Airways, and Germany sold off Deutsche Telekom among others. Privatization is credited with economic growth in developed economies. For example, in the mid-1980s when the economy grew at a slow pace, government agencies in Iceland controlled everything from fish prices to interest rates. But following a government decision to create a competitive business environment, most of these industries were privatized (Baglole, 2001), and Iceland had become very prosperous by 2002.

Privatization in Hong Kong

Like most nations that undertake privatization, Hong Kong is struggling with record budget deficits. Proposed privatization of airports, mass transit systems, tunnels and bridges, and even housing could raise billions in government revenues before 2005, but they also provoke citizen concern. For example, having witnessed failures elsewhere, citizens worry that privatization will lead to more expensive services. They also fear that jobs will be lost or that services will be reduced, especially to those who need them most. Finally, others note that privatization only resolves short-run budget deficits, but does not create a capacity for future revenues. Governments favoring privatization often argue in favor of increased operating efficiencies and greater customer service orientation for privatized firms. Further, they view privatization as a lesser of other evils, such as increased taxes to support state-owned services.

Source material: Joel Baglole (2003, Oct. 17) Hong Kong plans another handover. *The Wall Street Journal*, p. A9.

Privatization in OECD countries hit a temporary peak of around $100 billion in 1998 to drop to $20 billion in 2001. This was partly due to declining stock markets and reduced availability of companies to privatize (Recent privatization trends, 2002). Nevertheless, many developed economies continue to privatize. Italy, for example, averaged over $15 billion in sales of government-owned companies between 1995 and 1999 (Privatisation, 2000), and in 2002 announced further plans to sell full or partial interests in Tabacci Italiani SPA, shipbuilders Tireenia and Fincantieri, and electricity giant Enel and airliner Alitalia.

Benefits and Costs of Privatization

Many believe that businesses more efficiently perform roles traditionally performed by government. Achieving efficiency has sometimes led to employee reductions and even factory closings such as in Eastern Europe where many buildings stand empty. These types of changes can lead to social upheaval and face-offs between businesses, governments, and civil society. When newly privatized firms are restructured, managers often run afoul of labor and citizen groups more accustomed to having a say in the organization's destiny. When too much change occurs at once, the result may be poor service or high costs that do not meet public expectations of improved quality and lower costs. This can lead to disappointment and anger toward business and government leaders. This point is illustrated in the boxed example below.

Privatization and Business Risk at F&P Holdings

In the late 1990s Romania began to privatize its factories. US firm F&P Holdings purchased can factory Amep in Tecuci, Romania as part of its efforts to produce packaging with cheaper labor. The US managers turned over day-to-day management to executives from their Polish subsidiary, who promptly fired the plant's director. But despite reports of a modest 2000 profit, F&P managers were besieged with endless

▶

requests for money to manage the Amep plant. Auditors discovered that the reported profit was bogus, but they gave plant managers more money and limited time to make a profit. Instead, the directors resigned and created their own plan to get rid of F&P owners. Workers confronted F&P representatives at the June 2001 meeting, demanding that the current managers stay. They locked F&P executives outside the plant and in one case injured an employee. Lawsuits flooded the courts even as F&P made repeated appeals to Romanian government officials. For F&P the risk of privatization did not result in the desired return.

Source material: Elizabeth Williamson (2002, June 28) In Eastern Europe, workers go sour on foreign owners. *The Wall Street Journal*, pp. A1, A8.

Examples above show that privatization represents more than a transfer of ownership from government to private hands. Shifts in ownership create managerial challenges for owners who inherit employees, processes, and structures originally organized to serve public needs more than business goals. Lay-offs, restructuring, and job redesign have been resisted, and businesses and governments face challenges in managing these and other forms of resistance to privatization.

Deregulation

Regulations outline many of the operating standards for businesses and industries. With deregulation those rules or standards are relaxed. Some industries—particularly those that serve a common, national good such as airlines or telecommunications—traditionally have been heavily regulated. In the airline industry, regulation means the government establishes routes and consumer costs or limits industry entry and exit. In other words, in a regulated industry the government rather than the market shapes business activities.

Many nations have deregulated industries such as banking, investments, telecommunications, automotives, computers, and commercial aviation. For example, airlines are deregulated in the US and most of the European Union. Banking regulations also have been relaxed worldwide to permit integration of insurance companies with investment firms or banks with investment houses. In these industries, national deregulation has led to global industry development when national firms enter global markets or foreign firms move into domestic ones.

Benefits and Costs of Deregulation

The longer-run business benefits of deregulation are that managers can base decisions on economic criteria rather than government mandates. However, as is true with privatization, there are social costs of deregulation. For example, airline deregulation increased competition and led to some bankruptcies. Lower airline ticket prices to popular destinations were offset by higher prices to less popular destinations. Given the size of global stakes and country potential to gain genuine comparative advantage via deregulation

(McRae, 1994), national leaders may feel they have little choice except to deregulate, but they are rarely applauded for benefits and often blamed for losses. Steven Vogel (1997) believes freeing markets brings new rules leading to re-regulation. This points out a paradox of deregulation: to date it has increased the number of regulations.

In the short run, deregulation is often accompanied by general concern about changing rules and their impact on markets. Those outside the industry may be pleased when entry barriers fall or subsidies cease, but current competitors view the same changes with alarm. In many nations, there is growing concern that deregulation of utilities such as power or water could deprive the poor of basic resources. The collapse of utility company Enron increases those concerns because it demonstrates that no regulatory body is monitoring the activities of global utilities. Others argue that there is simply too much at stake to deregulate utilities (World moves, 2001).

In a globalizing world there is a growing fear that reduced constraints will encourage a "free-for-all" market to edge out or eliminate domestic competitors. For example, the Japanese "Big Bang" of financial deregulation produced many economic changes in Japan such as a weaker yen and stock-market declines. When foreign investment banks and securities firms were allowed into Japan, local firms faced changes. As noted in Chapter 3, one result was that publicly traded Japanese firms faced growing shareholder demands.

Business Stimulation

National governments stimulate business development in many ways. The three principal ways are industrial policies, export development, and foreign direct investments (FDI). Each interconnects nations with businesses, with national government interest, and with the world of global politics.

Industrial Policy and Subsidies

In the postwar years, many nations encouraged private investments via industrial policies that favored particular industries. For example, under the Suharto government Indonesia targeted ten industries for growth, including steel, electronics, telecommunications, aerospace, heavy industries, transportation, and military armaments. Subsidized industries in developing economies are often capital intensive and experiencing rapid growth, but many nations also subsidize commodity industries or those deemed important to defense.

Nations with no formal industrial policies may adopt informal policies that restrict open borders. For example, George Bush's 2002 tariff protected the US steel industry, and many EU nations and the US provide billions in annual subsidies for farmers. One result is described in the box below.

> ### How Subsidies Work
>
> As of 2002, rich countries spent more than $311 billion a year in agricultural subsidies. US farmers received on average a fifth of their income from the federal government. In Europe and Japan, farmers received from 31–59 percent of their income from subsidies. Subsidized farmers are guaranteed a particular price for their products, regardless of world prices for them. This can encourage farmers to overproduce, and when overproduction occurs world prices fall. The effect on developing economy farmers is negative because they earn less on affected products. For example, businesswoman Monica Shandu in Entumeni, South Africa earned $200 after costs on her 2001 sugarcane harvest. Without subsidies on worldwide sugar, her income would have increased to about $300, providing more support for the husband, four children, two grandchildren, and several other adult relatives who rely on her earnings. In time and without government support such as tariffs to correct prices, farmers like Monica Shandu lose income or go out of business. When farmers in developing economies no longer plant crops, then the nation becomes more dependent on food production elsewhere. For these and other reasons, many people argue that agricultural subsidies in advanced nations should be reduced or eliminated.
>
> Source material: Paul Magnusson (2002, Sept. 9) Farm subsidies: A blight on the economy. *Business Week*, p. 50; Roger Thurow and Geoff Winestock (2002, Sept. 16) How an addiction to sugar subsidies hurts development. *The Wall Street Journal*, pp. A1, A10.

In a more open and global world, both overt and indirect industrial policies such as subsidies are perceived to be restraints on trade. Accordingly, national governments face increased external and internal opposition to them. For example, the World Trade Organization ruled that 2002 US steel tariffs were unfair, and they were subsequently rescinded.

Export Stimulation

Whereas national leaders once concentrated on local or domestic business development, many stimulate export opportunities with various incentives. They reduce constraints on exports, sponsor trade missions, provide subsidies for new businesses, or create centers for export assistance to stimulate trade for large and small producers alike. Many regional, state, provincial or local authorities also provide resources to stimulate export activities. Export sales earn income for domestic firms and often creates jobs, but because they rely on foreign buying power and economic cycles, many national, regional, or state politicians seek also to attract investments of fixed assets.

Attracting Foreign Direct Investments

Incentives to attract foreign direct investments include a broad array of mechanisms such as tax rebates, industrial-site development, reduced utility rates, promises for streamlined government controls, worker training, currency transaction protections, and even protection from import competition. Some governments create free-trade zones that provide a tax advantage to firms operating within it. Jobs result from FDI and free-trade zones, creating revenues and tax sources for the nation.

Another way that national governments attract FDI is to lift current restrictions on foreign ownership. France's decision to lift limits on non-EU bids for French firms is one example. From Hungary to China, the transition economies too are making it easier for foreigners to own firms or their equity. For example following a 50-year ban, foreigners to India now are allowed to own as much as 26 percent of media companies and 100 percent of tea plantations. Activities like these in India and elsewhere in the world increase interconnections among national governments and global businesses.

NATIONAL GOVERNMENTS INTERACT VIA TRADE AGREEMENTS

Government leaders also stimulate national prosperity via trade agreements with other nations that can be bilateral, regional, multinational, or global in scope. Trade agreements can include special arrangements like foreign economic zones and city-states within nations; industry alliances such as OPEC (the Organization of Petroleum Exporting Countries); regional economic agreements such as the EU, ASEAN, or the African Union of 53 nations; or global trade agreements such as the World Trade Organization.

One benefit of trade agreements is that they generate collective power. Acting as a single unit, trade group members may be able to influence world trade, defend themselves against other trading blocks, or overcome costly cross-border inefficiencies (GATT and FTAs: No longer foes, 1992). Table 10.1 offers a glimpse at a range of trade agreements.

Table 10.1 *A sample of trading groups*

AMU (Arab Maghreb Union) The AMU aims to safeguard the region's economic interests, foster and promote economic and cultural cooperation, and intensify mutual commercial exchanges as a precursor for integration and the creation of a North African Common Market (also referred to as Maghreb Economic Space). Common defense and non-interference in the domestic affairs of the partners are also key aspects of the AMU Treaty. (http://www.maghrebarabe.org)
APEC (Asia-Pacific Economic Cooperation) was established in 1989 to promote economic integration around the Pacific Rim and to sustain economic growth. In 2005, APEC has 21 members including: Australia; Brunei Darussalam; Canada; Chile; People's Republic of China; Hong Kong, China; Indonesia; Japan; Republic of Korea; Malaysia; Mexico; New Zealand; Papua New Guinea; Peru; Republic of the Philippines; Russia; Singapore; Chinese Taipei; Thailand; USA; Vietnam. (http://www.apec.org)
ASEAN (Association of Southeast Asian Nations), formed in 1967 to strengthen regional cohesion and self-reliance and emphasize economic, social, and cultural cooperation and development. Members include Brunei Darussalam, Indonesia, Malaysia, the Philippines, Singapore, Thailand, and Vietnam. (http://www.asean.or.id)

▶

Table 10.1 *Continued*

CAN (Andean Community of Nations), formerly known as the Andean Group (AG), the Andean Parliament, and most recently as the Andean Common Market (Ancom). Established May 26, 1969; present name established October 1, 1992. Their aim is to promote harmonious development through economic integration. There are five members: Bolivia, Colombia, Ecuador, Peru, and Venezuela. (http://www.comunidadandina.org/endex.htm)

CARICOM (Caribbean Community and Common Market) The Caribbean Community has three objectives: economic cooperation through the Caribbean Single Market and Economy; coordination of foreign policy among the independent Member States; and common services and cooperation in matters such as health, education and culture, communications, and industrial relations. The CARICOM member states include: Antigua and Barbuda, the Bahamas, Barbados, Belize, Dominica, Grenada, Guyana, Jamaica, Montserrat, Saint Lucia, St. Kitts and Nevis, St. Vincent and the Grenadines, Suriname, and Trinidad and Tobago. (http://www.caricom.org/)

EFTA (European Free Trade Association) is a limited free industrial trade association of Finland, Sweden, Norway, Iceland, Switzerland, and Austria.

MERCOSUR countries of Argentina, Brazil, Paraguay, and Uruguay formed a common market in 1994. They total 209 million people and a combined GNP of $655.5 millions (http://www.americasnet.com/mauritz/mercosur); the Andean Pact includes Bolivia, Colombia, Ecuador, Peru, and Venezuela with 97 million people and a combined GNP of $122.5 millions in a customs union. (http://www.iadb.org)

NAFTA (North American Free Trade Agreement) between the US, Canada, and Mexico was scheduled to eliminate all trade and investments barriers between the three countries within 5 years of its 1994 founding. Chile was invited to join NAFTA in 1994, but had not done so by mid-2003. (http://www.mac.doc.gov/nafta/)

CIS (Commonwealth of Independent States). (http://www.cis.minsk.by)

ECOWAS (Economic Community of West African States). (http://www.ecowas.int)

GCC (Gulf Cooperation Council). (http://www.gcc-sg.org/index_e.html)

SAARC (South Asian Association for Regional Cooperation). (http://www.saarc-sec.org)

SADC (Southern African Development Community). (http://www.sadc.int)

Types of Trade Agreements

Most trade agreements are regional, often conforming to one of the four types described below. A main difference is the extent of economic integration.

Free Trade Area

A free trade area eliminates trade barriers such as tariffs or quotas among member nations, but each member nation retains authority over all trade policies with non-members. The North American Free Trade Act (NAFTA) created free trade for members

Mexico, the US, and Canada. Reduction of trade barriers between Mexico and the US puts no constraints on either partner's relationships with Germany, for example.

Customs Union

A customs union also eliminates internal trade barriers among members, and members agree to common external trade policies toward non-members. For example, members of a customs union would have the same policy toward trading with Germany.

Common Market

In a common market, agreement on internal and external trade policies is complemented by reduced restrictions on productive factors such as capital, technologies, and labor. However, some restrictions may remain. For example, within the common-market framework of the European Economic Community, medical doctors and others governed by licensing standards could not practice medicine everywhere in the EEC.

Economic Integration

Economic integration incorporates all the features of a common market, and in addition integrates national economic policies to create mechanisms like common fiscal and monetary policy, a common currency, a common system of taxation, and supporting mechanisms to enhance economic union. Because decisions like fiscal policy are embedded in national politics and culture, full economic integration requires other forms of integration as well.

Whether initiated as trade unions or as mechanisms for full economic integration, regional trade agreements set common standards that shape business threats and opportunities. For example, cross-border business costs in the EU were reduced when trucks no longer filed papers at each national border. Tougher recycling rules in the Economic Union forced Carrier to bear costs to redesign its air conditioners. Carrier made these changes to offer the same product worldwide.

Development of regional standards can be a painful process that highlights differences in values and beliefs held by participating nations. An example is the proposed Free Trade Agreement for the Americas (FTAA). Proponents believe that FTAA will boost trade for Latin America and improve their access to world trade. Opponents worry that the FTAA will further burden Latin America with structural-adjustment programs and other mechanisms that disrupt existing political and economic systems. The review of European Union history below further illustrates some of the challenges and opportunities that trade agreements pose for member nations.

A Sample Regional Trade Alliance: The European Community Becomes the European Union

European nations held both political and economic sway over most of the world at the dawn of the twentieth century. But by the close of World War II, Europe found itself sandwiched between Cold War opponents. Many believed that Europe had but two options:

- reassert the balance of nation-state powers in place before the war, or
- develop some sort of common voice to generate collective economic power in Europe.

Participating nations went with the second option, establishing the 1957 Treaty of Rome common market. The terms Economic Community and European Economic Community were used interchangeably to refer to this common market arrangement, and so it may seem that the European Union (EU) is also just another term for the same entity. This is not the case as illustrated in the box below. The Maastricht Treaty officially established the EU, "marking a new stage in the process of creating an ever closer union among the peoples of Europe," defined by objectives that include:

- To promote economic and social progress which is balanced and sustainable, in particular through the creation of an area without internal frontiers, through the strengthening of economic and social cohesion and through the establishment of economic and monetary union, ultimately including a single currency.
- To assert its identify on the international scene.
- To strengthen the protection of the rights and interests of the nationals of its member states through the introduction of a citizenship of the Union.

A Chronology for the European Union

The original EC members were France, Germany, Italy, the Netherlands, Belgium and Luxembourg. The United Kingdom of Great Britain and Northern Ireland did not participate in the Treaty of Rome, and did not join the EC until 1973. Ireland and Denmark also joined the EC in 1973, followed by Greece in 1981 and by Portugal and Spain in 1985. Sweden, Finland, and Austria joined the EEC in 1995. By 2004, the EU totalled 25 member nations whose combined population is 444 million.

The European Council is the EU's political arm; the European Commission is the executive branch appointed by national governments; the Council of Ministers is the EU's top law-making body.

EMU or European Monetary Union is the EU's effort to achieve monetary and economic union. The circulating currency or euro was introduced in January 2002; the UK did not adopt the euro and both Sweden and Denmark had voted against participation by 2005.

Source material: European Union website: http://europa.eu.int

Full economic integration represents a significant step up from a common market because it permits free movement of goods, capital, and some labor. But member nations struggle with competing interests and cultures. For example, the EU classifies carrots as fruit, requiring a separate ruling for how to handle carrots in any EU fruit rule. The examples in the following box show how detailed these rules must be.

EU Rulings—When is a Strawberry just a Strawberry?

The number of perforations in a fold of toilet tissue, grams of tobacco in a cigarette, and even the size of a strawberry are subject to EU classification. In the latter case, an EU ruling specified that strawberries had to be wider than 22 mm in diameter, eliminating smaller Swedish strawberries from the retail trade. In 2002, the European Commission ruled that only Greek producers had the right to call tangy cheese "feta," giving other European producers of feta five years to find another name for their product or cease production. Other protected cheese product names in the EU include French brie de Meaux and Italy's gorgonzola. These examples illustrate the level of detail involved to create the millions of technical specifications for trade within a regional alliance; millions could become billions in the global sphere. They also show that not everyone wins from trade agreements, such as producers of the vast array of offerings known as feta cheese.

A Global Trade Alliance: From GATT to WTO

Nations also participate in global trade alliances. Examples from the GATT and WTO treaties below show that the global trade agreement process is fraught with difficulties.

An important step toward globalization of business rules occurred in 1947 when representatives of 23 nations established the General Agreement on Trades and Tariffs (GATT). GATT agreements were expected to lead to economic prosperity that many believed would ensure world security and peace. The charter was to create rules of commercial behavior to which signatory nations could agreed. The founding meeting was followed by "rounds" of talks, most of which were negotiated over many years. The national motivation to participate was that most of the world's largest traders, for example the US, nations of Western Europe, and Japan, were GATT members. Over time GATT struggled with several problems:

■ The many exceptions to GATT agreements led to constant conflict over special-status advantages for some nations and not others.
■ The mutual monitoring system established to bring complaints of violations was circumvented by many voluntary bilateral agreements.
■ GATT covered only about two-thirds of world trade, excepting important service industries such as banking and investments.

The Uruguay GATT round continued from 1987 to 1994, but concluded to cover many new industries and issues such as intellectual property, services, textiles, and direct investments abroad. It also sought to remedy a major GATT weakness with a dispute-resolution process as part of a newly constituted GATT called the World Trade Organization (WTO). Features that distinguish the WTO from GATT are:

- The WTO is an institution with a director-general and resources available to pursue trade goals; GATT was an agreement with few institutional mechanisms.
- WTO rules are binding; GATT rules were guidelines with weak enforcement mechanisms.
- Trade disputes can be brought to the WTO whose members rule on their findings; like GATT, the WTO cannot force member nations to do anything; however, part of dispute resolution allows for retaliation against members who do not comply with ruling.
- The WTO mandates equal representation of members; under GATT any powerful country could (and did) block adverse rulings with a veto.

Not without difficulty, GATT became the World Trade Organization on January 1, 1995. Many agreements followed covering financial services, information technology products, and telecommunications. But many felt that the pace of global change in these and other trade-related industries was occurring too rapidly and without sufficient deliberation. This was one reason behind protests at the 1999 WTO meetings in Seattle and beyond.

Protests Against the WTO

Protestors at the Seattle WTO meeting numbered about 100,000. They marched together against the WTO but their interests otherwise ranged from environmental sustainability to labor, human, child, and animal rights. Others had no apparent social interest. For example, one photograph shows a protestor kicking letters from the Nike Town façade wearing shoes bearing the Nike logo.

The 1999 meetings ended without agreement on a new round. In 2000, new talks began on agriculture and services and were incorporated into a broader agenda launched at the fourth WTO Ministerial Conference in Doha in November 2001. A principal topic among its 148-member nations was how to help developing countries implement agreements. As compared to the Uruguay meeting where nongovernmental organizations were excluded, the Doha meeting registered 647 NGOs. 2003 meetings in Cancun saw more protests but little progress on WTO initiatives, but new agreements were reached in 2004. The post-1999 experiences of the WTO show growing public perception that trade's effect on labor and the environment requires that all three be part of what was initially viewed as only a trade agreement. This suggests that worldwide commercial rules emerging from the political sphere effect will be affected by virtually all other spheres of interest.

> **The TRIPS Agreement**
>
> An example of the relationship between WTO agreements and business activities is found in the Trade-Related Aspects of Intellectual Property Rights (TRIPS). TRIPS is the set of rules and regulations governing the trade of intellectual property rights, including music. The impact of this agreement is that intellectual property rights are enforced on a global scale. This is intended to stem declining sales in the music publishing industry due to piracy. But there are short-term costs to achieve the longer-run benefit of protecting intellectual property rights. For example, the music industry is unwilling to sign contracts with Mexican artists because many cassettes and CDs sold in Mexico are pirated (Business Software Alliance, 2004; http://www.bsa.org). As is likely to be true for all global standards, the TRIPS agreement brought benefits to some in the form of lower prices, but hardships for others. Mexican artists, for example, find it difficult to attract publisher interest.

The same cost/benefit trade-off demonstrated by the TRIPS agreement is evident for virtually every industry and most nations covered by WTO agreements. For example, sub-Saharan Africa and other agriculture-based economies are expected to be particularly hard hit by WTO agriculture rules. Many worry that Africa has too few resources with which to develop or compete worldwide in agricultural industries. Accordingly, there are growing efforts to ensure that the WTO and other governmental entities represent the interests of the poorest economies and their citizens.

Challenges for Trade Agreements

Above we looked at examples of regional and global trade agreements. They show that trade agreements forge interconnections among nations and their political leaders. Each usually requires that member nations yield some degree of control over their own economic and political destinies. For example, trade agreements often allow entry of foreign competitors into signatory nations. Companies that enter these nations are then exposed to influences wielded by both governmental and nongovernmental actors within them, and in this way businesses become more interconnected with other organizations.

The history and development of nation-states suggests few will be eager to sacrifice national interests to global interests. Further, when the focus is on economic interests, national leaders may give priority to businesses over those of the poor or the disenfranchised. Thus the advent of global trade alliances may require new national definitions of what constitutes self-interest (Prestowitz et al., 1991).

THE RATIONALE FOR GLOBAL GOVERNANCE SYSTEMS

On-going worldwide protests over security, environmental preservation, labor rights, business activities, and other global issues demonstrate a central challenge for global forms of governance: not everyone agrees there should be global governance. Yet business activities require some form of global governance for at least three reasons. First, trade growth requires facilitation. Second, worldwide development is likely to remain uneven without global action. Third, trade and other global activities cannot easily be managed without safety and a common defense system.

The 1995 Commission on Global Governance concluded there are five basic public goods that a global governance system should provide:

- a systematic financial system to smooth worldwide volatility
- protection of the global commons and a framework to promote sustainable development
- an open system for trade, technology transfer, and investment with acceptable dispute mechanisms
- infrastructure and institutions to reach agreements on common systems like weights and measures or aviation and communication systems
- equity and social cohesion through economic cooperation that includes international development assistance and disaster relief.

Other chapters in this book look at development of the global financial system (Chapter 8) and protection of the global commons (Chapter 6). This chapter's main focus on global politics concentrates below on how global governance facilitates open systems, encourages infrastructure development, and promotes equity through economic cooperation.

Global Standards Facilitate Open Systems

Although not all agree, many believe that trade fosters economic development. However, economic progress has been uneven. Accordingly, global governance is proposed as a mechanism for "leveling the playing field" to equalize opportunities for both rich and poor economies. Our examination of the WTO above demonstrates how this is meant to occur. For example, WTO decisions are consensus based, they are enforceable, and they are transparent—meaning that everyone knows the rules.

Another suggested way to improve equal access is common standards such as those produced by governmental bodies, IGOs, NGOs, or professional organizations. The rules and regulations these groups suggest help create technical and product standards or work standards. Many cover virtually all aspects of product development, manufacturing, distribution, and even recovery. For example, worldwide compliance with "built for reuse" standards in the automotive industry requires that recyclable amounts of all products be specified.

ISO and International Accounting Standards

New regulations created by global IGOs are based on the premise that the world benefits from standardization and harmonization of commercial rules. Some of these standard-setting IGOs were chartered under the auspices of trade alliances like the EU commission, and others are associated with IGOs such as the International Telecommunications Union chartered by the UN. Still others emerge from professional associations and nongovernmental organizations. For example, the International Organization for Standardization (ISO) was formed in 1947; it published its first standard in 1951, but had created more than 12,5000 standards by 2000. ISO 9000 specifies global quality standards for manufacturing; ISO 14000 covers environmental standards.

ISO standards share three characteristics: they are voluntary, they are industry-wide, and they are developed by consensus of those involved. ISO standards are implemented via adoption. For example, ISO 9000 became an important standard because the Economic Union adopted them to facilitate economic unification and provide a universal framework for quality assurance. Thus businesses that wish to operate within the EU must adopt them; global businesses adopt them worldwide to improve internal integration of production standards. Figure 10.1 outlines the review process for meeting ISO 9000 standards.

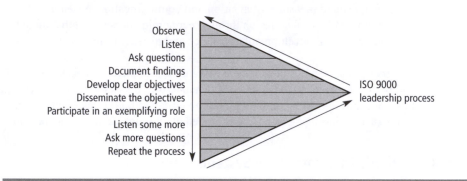

Figure 10.1 *ISO 9000 leadership process*
Source material: Adedeji Badiru (1995) *Industry's Guide to ISO 9000*. New York: John Wiley and Sons Inc, p. 10.

An international committee of accountants, financial executives, and equity analysts revised the International Accounting Standards Board (IASB) to provide a single set of accounting procedures worldwide. The implications for worldwide adoption of this system are immense because businesses find it costly to manage different accounting systems. Common accounting standards also facilitate interpretations of economic performance results worldwide and so would stimulate worldwide investments in equities. However, the London-based IASB faces opposition from the US Financial Accounting Standards Board (FASB) which claims that international standards are less comprehensive than FASB's generally accepted accounting principles. This conflict within the accounting profession shows how difficult it is to reach agreement on global standards. In the wake of the 2001–02 accounting scandals in US firms, FASB itself faces challenge.

Standards on Corruption and Transparency

Corruption occurs when people engage in activities that are dishonest or unfairly favor a limited few. Defining corruption on a global scale has proved difficult because what is perceived to be honest or dishonest is based on national cultures that differ. Thus the bribes considered dishonest in one nation could be viewed as a normal business practice in another. These differences in perspective make it difficult to develop global anti-corruption standards.

The culturally embedded nature of corruption affects business operations principally in nations that encourage or tolerate corrupt practices. These practices can include direct costs to businesses in the form of "bribes, kickbacks, 'grease,' and 'speed' money" to facilitate transactions (Doh et al., 2003: 115). Corruption also has indirect costs. For example, corruption is negatively correlated with both investment and growth (Mauro, 1995; *World Development Report 1997*). Lower growth potential stems from corrupt practices that deter investment, reduce or distort public expenditures, provide limited resources for needed infrastructures, and misdirect or waste entrepreneurial talent (Doh et al., 2003).

Acting alone or together, nations as well as businesses and civil society organizations (CSOs) fight corruption on a global scale for several reasons. First, corruption is hard to hide because of global interconnections. Second, globalization in other spheres makes it important for businesses to operate according to common and morally defensible rules. Finally, corruption is a major impediment not only to economic development but also to human development (Brademas and Heimann, 1998). The box below provides some examples of governmental actions to curb corruption.

Governments and Intergovernmental Organizations Take Aim on Corruption

The US 1977 Foreign Corrupt Practices Act covers only US companies abroad, but in 1996 the OECD similarly agreed to strengthen European rules by eliminating tax deductions for bribery. In late 1997 it adopted a proposal for OECD nations to criminalize payments made to political or business representatives to win contracts and other work. The Organization of American States also signed an anti-corruption agreement in March 1996, and the United Nations adopted a resolution against corruption in December 1996.

The World Bank declared its intention to revoke loans to government enterprises when bribes are used to allocate business opportunities. After concluding that high levels of corruption hurt a country's ability to attract capital, the International Monetary Fund (IMF) issued 1997 staff guidelines that involve the IMF in governance issues like the use of public funds. Finally, the IMF bail-out of South Korea and Indonesia in 1997 and 1998 included demands that these countries restructure and engage in more transparent business transactions.

Operational Strategies for Dealing with Corruption

Richard De George (1993: 114–121), author of *Competing with Integrity in International Business*, suggests a number of operational strategies for dealing with corruption. They include:

- Do not respond in kind by adopting the very practices you find unethical.
- Decision-makers may have to use moral imagination to respond when there are no specific rules for response.

- Be ready to act with moral courage.
- Seek joint action with others and work for ethical change.
- Be prepared to pay a price and sometimes a higher price for responding ethically to a competitor that is not ethical.

Transparency International

Transparency International is an anti-corruption INGO. According to TI, corruption undermines good government, leads to the misallocation of resources, harms the private sector and private-sector development, and particularly hurts the poor. Controlling it is only possible with the cooperation of many stakeholders in government, civil society, and the private sector. On a global scale, TI brings attention to the crippling effects of corruption, advocates and works toward reform, monitors compliance and works with others to reduce corruption. For example, TI works closely with the World Bank and the OECD. It annually publishes corruption ratings by country and a bribery index. Businesses use these indices to weigh business challenges in various countries. Information may be especially useful to SMEs whose internal intelligence is not as well funded as those of global giants.

Source material: Robin Hodess, Tania Inowlocki, and Tob Wolfe (Eds) (2003) *Global Corruption Report 2003*. London and Berlin: Profile Books and Transparency International; Transparency International (http://www.transparency.org)

Infrastructure and Institutions that Facilitate Trade

Crime, armed conflict, and terrorism have a growing influence on trade and on daily life, but as yet there are no common worldwide defense systems for them. Many existing agencies resist or are unable to make changes leading to a global police system. For example, computer limitations prevent national agencies from fighting crime globally. Growing armed conflict in Africa, rebel action in Latin America, and East Asian skirmishes in North Korea, Taiwan, Myanmar, Cambodia, East Timor, and the Spratly Islands are almost all due to economic causes, and all impede economic development (Collier, et al., 2003), yet there is no common and global defense system to manage armed conflict.

People worldwide are increasingly vulnerable to global crime and terrorism, and businesses must cope with counterfeiting, money laundering, piracy, and similar crimes. According to Interpol, crime generated about $1 trillion in 1996. But unlike legitimate business people, criminals cannot simply deposit their money in banks. Instead, they "launder" money to disguise its source or funnel it to other uses. The IMF estimates that the world financial system launders an estimated $500 billion to $1.5 trillion per year.

> **The Money Laundering Process**
>
> According to the International Financial Action Task Force on Money Laundering, "dirty" money usually is introduced into the financial system in small sums. Then a series of transactions follow—such as wiring the money to different accounts in different nations—further to disguise the source. Usually nations that receive the wired funds are those that do not have anti-money laundering rules or those with weak monitoring systems. From there, funds can be wired back to nations of origin and perhaps used to purchase real estate or legitimate businesses.

An effect of money laundering on business is that legitimate financial institutions face growing pressure to monitor cross-border financial transactions. For example, a 2001 report criticized Citigroup, J.P. Morgan Chase, Bank of America, and Bank of New York for failure to monitor activities that could include money laundering (Through the wringer, 2001). New money-laundering rules were subsequently introduced, requiring firms to implement money-laundering compliance programs, train employees to detect money laundering, and perform audits to identify suspicious activities.

Terrorism covers a wide range of violent acts meant to instill fear that will prevent action or cause people to withdraw politically. Terrorist acts once perceived to be local are increasingly acknowledged as global in impact following attacks on the New York World Trade Center, nightclub bombings in Bali, and train bombings in Spain. Freedman (2003) calls these acts "superterrorism" because of their worldwide effects. Like crimes and armed conflict, terrorism deters global business investments and depresses economic growth. For example, the net effect of attacks on September 11, 2001 was felt not only in the US but also in Asian nations that witnessed a 2.4 percent drop in GDP growth (Booth, 2001).

Examples of armed conflict, global crime, and global terrorism show that while effects are global, defense and security mechanisms are not. This occurs in part because security and defense mechanisms have deep roots in national cultures that make it difficult for internal systems to forge external relationships. At the same time, the absence of global security and defense systems facilitates opportunities for criminals. This absence also deters business investments, particularly in the poorest economies where conflict, corruption, crime, and terrorism are high.

Global Equity Efforts Require Governance

Dialogue and protests show that trade and development are not independent issues. Organizations like the WTO that incorporate labor and environmental concerns in trade negotiations acknowledge these interconnections. There is also a growing public sense that intervention is needed to alleviate human suffering and promote worldwide justice (Watson, 1995). Thus justice that goes beyond economic opportunity is increasingly sought at a global level.

MANY ORGANIZATIONS SHAPE GLOBAL GOVERNANCE

Developing public good on a global scale is a topic of great concern to most of the world, and many books are available on the subject. This text explores the issue in a more limited way by looking at principal actors shaping global public policy.

Intergovernmental Organizations

An influential political actor is the Intergovernmental Organization (IGO). *Formally* constituted IGOs like the UN or the OECD tend to operate according to a charter. Their members are official delegates from participating nations who define and observe membership conditions and pursue member-selected objectives. *Less formal* IGOs like the G-8 can accommodate fluid membership and changing objectives and be more responsive to emergent needs.

IGOs often create common policies governing member states. The Latin American Economic System headquartered in Caracas, Venezuela is a regional IGO funded by 27 member countries in Latin America and the Caribbean. Like many other IGOs it sponsors studies of economic and trade issues of common interest to its members.

The G-groups are informal IGOs whose members meet to discuss economic prospects or draft policies on worldwide economic development. The 2002 meeting of the G-8 focussed particular attention on economic development for Africa. Other informal IGOs can be task or focus groups of government representatives who meet periodically to discuss ideas and issues of multilateral concern. The decisions of many IGOs affect business activities. For example, the Spain-based World Tourism Organization is a group of 125 national leaders who explore common interests and concerns related to the tourism and travel industries.

According to Mihaly Simai (1994), the network of IGOs has expanded considerably in recent decades. There were 30 in 1900, 123 by 1950, and several hundred by the 1990s. Some nations are more inclined to be involved in IGOs than others. For example although the average nation participated in 30 IGOs in 1990, the US participated in 140 and France in 270. A criticism of IGOs is that their emergence has resulted in competing and parallel groups that are not organized according to formal designs or structures (Simai, 1994).

Two important IGOs are the United Nations and the OECD. These two were almost alone in their post-World War II roles as intergovernmental actors shaping international and global governance system. Below we look at how each came into being to examine ways in which these and similar IGOs influence global governance issues such as trade or human development.

Organization for Economic Cooperation and Development (OECD)

The Organization for European Economic Cooperation was formed after World War II to manage reconstruction aid. Despite conflicting views, the group adopted a common goal: to formulate policies promoting economic and social welfare of member nations. In 1961, the OEEC became the OECD. Members are the world's 30 most industrialized countries; an additional 70 nations have active relationships with the OECD. This IGO helps harmonize aid to developing economies and identify national governance challenges. The OECD office is also an important data source on many global issues, such as the economy, employment, and gender.

The United Nations (UN)

Also founded in the postwar era, the United Nations charter begins "We the peoples of the United Nations ..." According to the Commission on Global Governance (1995), this introduction represented hope that the world's people could unite to address common needs and goals. As the box below indicates, when common needs change, so too the focus of UN activities changes.

UN Agencies

The UN is an umbrella-type organization housing many operations under three related systems: the General Assembly; the Bretton Woods institutions such as the World Bank and the IMF; and specialized agencies such as the UN Conference on Trade and Development (UNCTAD) which houses the Division on Transnational Corporations and Investments. The Security Council responds to armed conflict, and the specialized agencies pursue human development initiatives with four agencies: the International Labour Organization (ILO) oversees work conditions; the World Health Organization (WHO); the Food and Drug Organization (FAO); and the UN Educational, Scientific and Cultural Organization (UNESCO). Programs and funds organized by the UN include many affecting business activities throughout the world. These are the Population Fund, the World Food Programme, the Environment Programme, and the High Commissioner for Refugees. Finally, the UN sponsors many more specialized and technical agencies such as the International Telecommunications Union that sets global telecommunications standards.

An example from the FAO of the UN shows how this IGO interconnects the world. FAO predictions show that agricultural production must expand by 75 percent by 2025 to match population growth, but current figures are not reassuring: the global grain harvest, for example, has increased by only 2.3 percent since 1990 but population has grown by 10 percent. Reasons for the current crisis include: agricultural collapse in Russia after 1989; government alliances like the WTO that have cut subsidies to agriculture; poor weather in the US and Russia; and dietary substitutes in China. Global weather patterns, cultural change, and governmental decisions demonstrate the interactions among global environments. These shifts create challenges that increasingly must be resolved by global organizations. Responding to growing fears of worldwide food shortages, the FAO continues to search for new approaches to helping economically poor nations to grow, buy or otherwise get more food.

During the celebration of its fiftieth year in 1996, unrealized UN ambitions drew far more attention than its successes. However, UN successes include human rights advances and bringing global attention to population and women's issues (Commission on, 1995; Simai, 1994). These successes affect global businesses when they improve educational opportunity or advance previously disadvantaged groups.

Nongovernmental and Civil Society Organizations

The "global associational revolution" (Salamon, 1994) exerts growing clout in the political arena. Organizations driving this revolution are for the most part independent from government and from businesses. As noted in Chapter 2, two terms are used to describe these organizations: nongovernmental organizations (NGOs) and civil society organizations (CSOs). These organizations act independent of the state and the market to pursue purposes important to them (Brown et al., 2002). They range in purpose, size, intent, and source (Waddell, 2001/2002).

Nongovernmental Organizations

The contemporary NGO movement originated in the 1970s in developing economies like Bangladesh, the Philippines, Zimbabwe, and Indonesia, but rapidly spread worldwide. NGOs now number in the hundreds of thousands in developing and advanced economies alike (Salamon and Anheier, 1994, 1998). Lester Salamon (1994) believes that NGOs grew rapidly because government failed to manage social problems. Improved literacy and a communication revolution make it possible to organize and mobilize groups of people worldwide, and there is a growing sense that rapid economic development has created needs that simply cannot wait. For example, environmental crises cannot be postponed for another day. Many hundreds of thousands of NGOs provide information and intervention to resolve global issues. If viewed as a single group, spending of over $1 trillion per year makes NGOs the eighth biggest economic power in the world (Salamon and Anheier, 1998).

International Nongovernmental Organizations (INGOs)

About 30,000 NGOs are global or international in scope. According to a count of the *Yearbook of International Organizations*, this number has quadrupled in the last decade (Brown et al., 2002). INGOs can be consumer groups like Global Trade Watch, environmental groups like Friends of the Earth, think tanks like the Heritage Foundation or the International Forum on Globalization, protest groups like Direct Action Network, or coalitions within and among religious bodies. An example of the latter is the World's Council of Churches.

INGOs can be grassroots groups that form around member interests, or membership groups that serve wider interests. For example, Amnesty International is a human rights group whose members number over one million. INGOs can also emerge from professional groups. For example, the Center for International Environmental Law emerged from the legal profession, and Doctors Without Borders emerged from the medical profession to provide medical care in areas of the world where there is limited or sporadic medical care. Examples in Table 10.2 provide some insight into their range.

Table 10.2 *Nongovernmental organizations, a sample*

Organizational Name	Location
African Gender Institute	Cape Town, South Africa
Amnesty International	London
Conservation International	Washington, DC
The Earth Council	San Jose, Cost Rica
Friends of the Earth	London
Greenpeace	Amsterdam
International Planned Parenthood Federation	London
International Work Group for Indigenous Affairs	Denmark
Peace Corps	Washington, DC
Physicians for Human Rights	Boston, MA
Center for Reproductive and Family Health	Hanoi, Vietnam
Revolutionary Association of the Women of Afghanistan	Pakistan
Social Watch	Uruguay
Women in Security Conflict Management and Peace	New Delhi, India
World Watch Institute	Washington, DC

Activities of INGOs

According to researchers (Brown et al., 2002), INGOs and alliances help shape and implement international decisions and policies in at least seven ways:

- They've identified problems with the consequences of globalization that otherwise might be ignored.
- They've articulated new values and norms to guide and constrain international practice.
- They've built transnational alliances that advocate for alternatives that might otherwise be ignored.
- They've motivated international institutions to respond to unmet needs.
- They've disseminated social innovations that apply internationally.
- They've negotiated resolutions to transnational conflicts and disagreements.
- They've mobilized resources and acted directly on important public problems.

Global interconnections put growing pressure on INGOs to be more accountable for their activities (Adair, 1999; Brown et al., 2002). At the 1999 WTO meetings, for example, representatives from developing economies often noted that demonstrators did not represent their interests. Second, INGOs are asked to be accountable to members, provide accurate information, manage their financial assets well, and show concern for innocent third parties, for example the person who loses a job due to an INGO boycott.

The issues that INGOs undertake often are contentious ones, making it difficult for them to speak for everyone worldwide on any single issue. Often, going global brings NGO leaders face-to-face with the same conflicting demands governments and businesses face. For example, Greenpeace seeks to save the earth but often engages in civil disobedience to accomplish their ends; the Missionaries of Charity serve many in over-populated nations but oppose birth control; and the International Red Cross is accused of political preference because they do not allow Israel to adopt a red Star of David but do use the Red Crescent in Muslim nations.

Many INGOs receive financial support from governmental entities. For example, a quarter of Oxfam's 1998 budget for $162 million was provided by the British government and the EU (Sins of the secular missionaries, 2000). Many watchdog groups in the Netherlands are funded by that government, and many African NGOs are funded either by their own or other governments. This connects global NGOs with national governments, and when they engage in global governance activities, it interconnects them to the world.

Businesses

Businesses also voluntarily forge links with governments when business coalitions pressure national governments or industries partner with them. For example, major pharmaceutical businesses partnered with national governments to improve distribution of low-cost AIDs vaccine in Africa. Indirectly, professional business groups influence rules and regulations to harmonize and standardize business practices that include manufacturing, environmental standards, and accounting rules. Businesses also influence government policy with geographic moves. For example, the merger of French and Spanish firms resulted in Altadis SA, which registered in the Netherlands to enjoy a business-friendly legal system and lower taxes (France left behind, politicians keep quiet, 2001). The example below illustrates how the US government collaborated with businesses to improve airport security.

Disney Shares Business Tips with the Government

New US air-travel precautions led to back-ups at security checkpoints in US airports. The government created a new Transportation Security Administration to manage these problems, but the agency promptly turned to businesses for advice. Several lent executives to help the agency consider its options. Disney's manager-on-loan suggested ways to reduce waiting times. A possibility is modeled on the Disney Pass system in which travelers would submit to background checks to obtain a card that gets them through security quickly. Another is to show videos to distract cranky travelers. Nike offered advice on branding the new security agency, and also provided tips on how to enliven training for airport screeners. Marriot International and FedEx suggested ways to measure employee performance, and Intel lent an engineer to advise on equipment-related purchases.

Source material: Stephen Power (2002, Jan. 24) Disney, Nike give government advice on handling airport security lines. *The Wall Street Journal*, p. B1.

There is growing belief worldwide that businesses can and should "make a difference" in resolving intractable social problems. Former president of Czechoslovakia Vaclav Havel notes that growing problems in the world call for new responsibility for all agents of society. Some perceive businesses to be the only entities with the clout to resolve global social problems (Hawken, 1993). Edward Simon, President of Herman Miller, maintains that "business is the only institution that has a chance, as far as I can see, to fundamentally improve the injustice that exists in the world." Ways that businesses become better members of civil society include:

- Leaders who go beyond their own operations to promote global governance frameworks that institutionalize civil market behavior.
- Standardization and professionalization of disclosure and other external verification mechanisms (Zadek, 2001).

Businesses also shape global governance mechanisms via joint activities. For example, in 2003 a coalition of nine companies, including Gillette, Unilever, and DaimlerChrysler joined forces to encourage tougher anti-counterfeiting laws. This effort encouraged closer cooperation among governments, industries, and global enforcement agencies (de Jonquieres, 2003). Businesses also shape global governance mechanisms by joining forces with other organizations, such as the Global Compact described in Chapters 6 and 9.

Global Gangs

Using many of the same techniques as businesses and nongovernmental organizations, global gangs and criminals also influence balance between collective and individual interests.

Globalization of Gangs

Sometimes local gangs join forces globally. In this way the Chinese Triads, Japanese yakuza, the Sicilian and Russian Mafias, or drug cartels enlarge their worldwide presence. Chinese Triads, some with as many as 180,000 members worldwide, operate not only in Asia but smuggle weapons and people throughout the world, using local street gangs to penetrate new markets (Booth, 2000). Organized crime in Russia has established outposts in 29 countries outside the former USSR, and the Russian Mafia is responsible for most of the counterfeit US dollars held in Russian hands. Japanese yakuza have been accused of playing a major role in doubling of stock and land prices in Japan (How the mob, 1996). Other Asian gangs based in the Netherlands ship drugs to Australia where they are distributed by Lebanese and Romanian criminals (Robinson, 2000). Chinese Triads also commit high-tech crimes such as electronic counterfeiting and credit-card fraud (Booth, 2000).

The boxed examples above show that global gangs also derive opportunities from globalization. By moving their operations into financial and real estate sectors, they represent a competitive threat to legitimate commercial activities. In terms of management, global gangs are moving away from centralization to the same sort of global thinking and local action characteristic of many other types of global enterprises. According to Jeffrey Robinson (2000), the twenty-first century will belong to transnational criminals until the world revises its notion of policing to become global as well as national.

Other Global Actors

Still other entities shape governance on a global scale, often just by doing their jobs. For example, educational institutions shape attitudes about globalization and governance when they host foreign students. Religious institutions collect and disburse funds globally, and some develop statements on economic policy such as US Catholic bishops' 10-point "Catholic Framework for Economic Life." Hospitals as well as medical services of many kinds, for example plastic surgery and organ transplants, are also increasingly global, and they too require global governance mechanisms.

This examination of national and global governance issues shows that governmental actors face multiple and competing demands. National leaders seek the benefits of global trade at the same time as national sovereignty. At the global level, governmental leaders recognize that it is not possible to develop a single set of global trade rules without also incorporating rules governing human rights and environmental concerns. Responses to these interconnections is a complex challenge. Further, many actors vie to establish global rules of conduct including governments, businesses, not-for-profits, professional societies, and gangs. Decision-making now is distributed at the global level not just among superpowers but worldwide. This distribution almost guarantees disputes.

Global businesses also confront dual demands for stability and change. Their preferences for autonomy are difficult to realize in a global world where alliances are a norm. Yet the external alliances that allow for opportunity also require power sharing. Just as individual nations demand a greater voice in global decisions, consumers also demand a role in corporate governance. Managing these multiple and competing objectives requires exposure to risks and concerns such as human development and human rights that few organizations know how to address.

CHAPTER SUMMARY

A principal policy role for any government is to balance individual interests with common and collective interests of the governed.

Most governments are organized around sovereign and independent nation-states defined by geographic boundaries. But national economic prosperity depends on domestic activities and global ones.

Trade alliances and agreements are increasing in number and scope, expanding beyond regions to encompass diverse members, and expanding beyond cultural and political boundaries.

More global forms of governance can improve global trade and standards, create needed infrastructure and systems, and enhance global equity.

Armed conflict, global crime, and global terrorism are all on the increase, but global defense and security mechanisms are poorly equipped to manage them.

Businesses increasingly play roles once played solely by government actors. They coalesce to pressure governments, use professional groups to shape standards, and participate in activities to improve business practices.

REVIEW AND DISCUSSION QUESTIONS

1 In what ways have regional trade agreements failed to live up to their promise? What are the challenges of these to sovereign nations?

2 How are alliances like the EU similar to and different from alliances like the WTO? Relying on material provided here or elsewhere, describe the defining characteristics of each entity to make your points.

3 The traditional argument in support of government ownership of services like telecommunications, banking, or commercial air and train travel is that these industries are important to national defense. In view of almost worldwide privatization of these industries, how do you think nations expect to provide for their defense? Does privatization create risk for nations in a global world?

4 Visit the website for Transparency International (www.transparency.org). Examine countries that are most and least corrupt according to TI ratings; then consult with Table 8.2 on Economic Freedoms that appears in Chapter 8. What is the relationship you can see between corruption and economic freedoms? Among these nations, what is the relationship between corruption and economic growth?

Chapter 11
GLOBALIZATION OF TECHNOLOGIES

INFORMATION TECHNOLOGIES CONNECT THE WORLD

Information technologies such as telephony and the Internet provide instant connections for many to link to the world but, as this chapter demonstrates, older communication technologies remain important worldwide. Together new and old technologies foster many opportunities and create challenges for people and organizations of every size. The following vignettes illustrate how information technologies interconnect the world.

Internet: Adamee Itorcheak brought Internet service to remote northern Baffin Island—a Canadian region equal to the combined size of California and Alaska—via Nunanet Communications. The company became the first Internet service within 1,000 miles of the village of Iqaluit. Most Inuits who live on Baffin Island follow traditions that include dog sledding, seal hunting, and fishing. Their language is very visual and verbal, and is characterized by face-to-face communication and few tundra signposts. But a growing need for computers and growing desire to communicate with the outside world provided a business opportunity for Mr. Itorcheak. Fish plants use his services to communicate with wholesalers, and development officials connect to preserve native customs. Fishing and hunting guides use their connections to advertise, students enroll in distance-learning courses, and others visit chat rooms, play chess, or explore other hobbies and interests. Mr. Itorcheak was himself an Internet hobbyist until his wife suggested it might be cheaper to buy a server than rent services. Enter Nunanet Communications! Growing the nascent company made many demands on Mr. Itorcheak. For example, many of his first customers needed help to learn Internet protocol. The natural environment also creates the occasional challenge. For example, snowstorms can interrupt service, as did a hungry raven that devoured an antenna insulation.

Radio Technology: Radio technology may be a nineteenth-century discovery, but its recent introduction to Niger in Central Africa has led to a revolution in community building. Over 100 community stations in the Niger desert have developed with radio's cheap and simple technology. One example is Radio Afalla in Taureg. In this mostly Muslim and nomadic part of Niger, Radio Afalla's antenna stands out for miles of flat desert. The antenna captures radio signals using solar panels powered by a car battery and linked to a console of two tape players, two compact-disc players and one microphone. Many of the radio receivers the Tuaregs use are hand-crank models with second-hand transistors from the 1960s. This technological approach has been particularly appropriate in Niger where electricity and telephone lines are few. The station's goal is to focus on education, health, food, and childcare news in the local language. The DJs are locals and any music used is for background purposes behind "childbirth advice, vaccination updates, sanitation instruction, farming tips, candid talk on AIDS, and the occasional all-points-bulletin for lost camels" (Thurow, 2002: A1). The station also issues information on possible epidemics and offers precautions to prevent the spread of disease. At the station's official opening in 2002, the chief indicated that people were ready for more overseas news broadcast in the local language; ready to be part of a broader virtual community of listeners. Community also developed locally. For example, businesses such as vegetable vending operate near ▶

the station, and people within the broader community founded listener groups to discuss broadcast topics. Station funding comes from a growing coalition of aid groups such as Africare and Helen Keller International, UN agencies and the World Bank, and foreign governments including the US, France, and Switzerland. The success of these radio stations provides a valuable learning lesson for outside donors: listen to the people, build community, and work with appropriate technology.

Telephones: Vodacom, partially owned by Vodaphone, is a South African mobile-telephone operator that expanded to the Congo by serving homesick peacekeepers. But they discovered what many other telecommunications firms have learned from recent African experiences: opportunity. Vodacom has over 8 million customers in four African nations and its rival MTN counts another 6 million customers. Market share for Paris-based Alcatel is three times bigger in Africa than elsewhere, and many mobile-phone service companies find growth is greatest for them in sub-Saharan Africa. Nokia developed inexpensive handsets and networks to enter this market, Chinese companies like Huawei Technologies and ZTE Corporation have expanded to Africa, and other global companies like Ericsson and Motorola also invest in Africa. Mobiles allow Africans to leapfrog fixed-line telephony to gain access to the world; mobile phones already outnumber fixed-line ones by 2 to 1. This approach to telephone communication is being played out in many developing economies. For example, wireless technology grew 35 percent in Mexico in 2001 as compared to a 9 percent increase for fixed lines. Growth for mobile technology is drawing many businesses into developing economies. Competition among them has lowered consumer costs and moved developing nations one step closer to full capacity leading to Internet interconnections.

Source material: Africa: The next wide-open wireless frontier. (2004, Jan 28) *Business Week* [Electronic version]; Ain't no mountain high enough (2003, Nov. 1) *The Economist*, pp. 62–63; Solange De Santis (1998, Oct. 19) Across tundra and cultures, entrepreneur wires Arctic. *The Wall Street Journal*, pp. B1, B4; Roger Thurow (2002, May 10) In impoverished Niger, radio provides missing links in chain of development. *The Wall Street Journal*, pp. A1, A5; Will Weissert (2002, Mar. 4) Wireless is only way in rural Mexico. *The Seattle Times*, p. A7.

CHAPTER OVERVIEW

The chapter begins by defining technology, then considers how changes associated with both the Industrial and the Information Revolutions stimulate and have been stimulated by still other changes in many spheres of activity. The chapter reviews telecommunications connectivity to examine spillover effects on people, governments, and businesses.

TECHNOLOGICAL DEVELOPMENT

Many view technological shifts as *the* driving force for globalization (Naisbitt 1994; Ostry and Nelson, 1995; Friedman, 1999; Can there be a global standard for social policy?, 2000; The case for globalization, 2000; Mandel and Ferleger, 2000). The explosion of technological breakthroughs in telecommunications industries alone demonstrates that they rapidly move information, inventions, and innovations across national borders and boundaries of time and space. These rapid shifts affect almost every industry and reshape many core business technologies. Through interconnections with other global environments, they also reshape human lives.

Science is exploration for the sake of knowing. The resulting body of knowledge that science creates sometimes is not practical, but it becomes so with technology which is the application of science, usually in the interests of bettering human life. A cursory review of recent breakthroughs would show a tendency to focus most on "high" technology and on events in what is variously referred to as the Information Age or the Information/Knowledge Revolution. But "low" technologies and incremental changes in something so simple as a kitchen implement also have implications for people, businesses, and industries. As the example of Freeplay illustrates below, sometimes a combination of high and low technologies can produce a profound change.

Freeplay's Opportunity

In 1995 80 percent of the world's population had no in-home telephone, and over 50 percent had never used a telephone. Most were located in Africa where other technologies such as electricity and radio also are limited. At the same time, more advanced technologies elsewhere highlighted the plight of Africans caught by armed conflicts. In response to this dilemma, a South African firm called BayGen (renamed Freeplay Energy Group) introduced a wind-up radio to produce electricity sufficient to receive short wave, AM, and FM signals for about 40 minutes. Although far from high technology, the wind-up radio represents an important technological breakthrough to link isolated people. This device is a communication boon for developing economies and many war-torn sections of Africa, yet it operates much like a wind-up gramophone, is simple to use, inexpensive, and needs no batteries or plugs. Further, its discovery came from an older technology—the gramophone—rather than current or promised high-tech telecommunications technologies. One of the opening vignettes for this chapter illustrates how radios and transmissions shape community life in Africa. Freeplay also helps to shape children's lives through the Freeplay Foundation which donates radios to many of over 100,000 Rwandan children whose families were lost in conflict. The radios provide access to schooling, news, advice on avoiding diseases like AIDS, comfort and perhaps encouragement for children who otherwise have little of their own.

Freeplay's experience suggests that organizational attention can go not only to high technology solutions to business problems but also to incremental changes in existing or old technologies. In addition, although businesses often attend to new *product* technologies—especially the "bells and whistles" of information technologies—*process* technologies also have a significant impact on life and work. For example, total quality management brought about a revolution in workplaces no less significant than many product breakthroughs.

Technological competence in both product and process has been a critical success factor for businesses in most industries. Ability to create, develop, and apply new technologies (or revolutionize existing ones) is fundamental to success for companies of every size and type. And tomorrow's process and product technologies will inevitably propel others into industry leadership unless today's leaders remain technologically astute. According to Peter Drucker (1985) successful business innovation occurs when organizations examine internal opportunities and simultaneously monitor external shifts. Examples of oft-missed internal opportunities include failure to examine why unintended successes or failures occur, and ignoring gaps between what was supposed to happen and what occurred. External shifts include those described in other text chapters: changing cultural preferences, alterations in industry or market structure, and changes in awareness brought about by new knowledge. The example below illustrates that businesses sometimes can be very resistant to demand changes.

Did You Want that in Gray or Grey?

Like Henry Ford's auto that was delivered in any color so long as it was black, for their first decade personal computer manufacturers offered only gray—in cases, monitors, printers, you name it. Taiwan-based firm Acer expanded its PC market with colors to match walls, furniture, or personal preferences. Apple offers day-glo and even transparent models that expose the computer's innards. The long time lag between PC introduction and color choices shows that many in this industry failed to recognize an early opportunity for product differentiation.

The time it takes to develop a new technology varies as does consumer acceptance. For example, Internet technology seemed to develop almost overnight, and consumers embraced it readily. But it took 5–15 years for consumers to embrace some electronic technologies. For example, cable television was introduced in the 1960s, but had only about 60 percent penetration by 1996. VCRs introduced in the late 1970s had 90 percent penetration by 1996; PCs were introduced in the early 80s and had about 44 percent penetration by 1996. But cell telephones were introduced in 1985 and though they had 30 percent penetration by 1996, they experienced steep growth between 1992 and 1996 (New technologies take time, 1999). These examples show that business investments in technologies do not guarantee consumer interest in them or overnight success. Cultural habits, economic and political habits, the existing technological infrastructure, and industry readiness also shape product or service adoption for a global world. External factors like these converged to popularize the game of soccer.

Soccer Goes Global

Technological breakthroughs in satellite transmissions create worldwide opportunities for private broadcasters like BSkyB. This and other media companies pay billions for the rights to televise soccer games worldwide. Changes in immigration regulations have relaxed rules on the number of non-locals who can play in national teams, resulting in mini United Nations of team players selected from among the best in the world. Corporations are discovering the sponsorship value of soccer in reaching new audiences, and industries are altered as firms like Adidas and Disney produce merchandising tie-ins to link their products with soccer. With more viewers and more sponsors has come pressure on soccer teams and fans to tone down their language and behaviors. Players as well as managers increasingly view soccer as a business as well as a game. This example shows that technological change occurs in combination with governmental, business, and cultural changes.

Source material: Goodbye hoodlums, hello big money. (1996, Sept. 23) *Business Week,* pp. 66–68.

HISTORY AND WORK TECHNOLOGIES

Technological breakthroughs of almost every kind punctuate known history. Many led to revolutionary changes in work and personal life. Invention of the wheel represented a product breakthrough doubtless as profound for its time as assembly-line processes introduced by the Industrial Revolution. Beginning with cave dwellers' tools, technology has provided an endless stream of innovations, and every phase of history has been impacted in some way by technological advances leading to changes in how work is organized, completed, and evaluated, as well as new thinking about how the world of work is or can be organized. Table 11.1 provides examples of how technological changes led to changes for people.

Table 11.1 *Historical innovations and breakthroughs*

Approximate Years (from 2004)	Technology	Consequence
1,750,000	Primitive tools	Extended human capabilities
100,000	Making and using hunting gear	Extended access to food
5,500	The wheel	Improved speed of transport
3,500	Boats and sails	Extended geographic access
800	Clock, compass, and other measures	Improved navigation
500	Printing press	Ideas were recorded and shared
225	Engines	Mechanization becomes possible

Table 11.1 *Continued*

Approximate Years (from 2004)	Technology	Consequence
200	Railroads	Amount transported grows
175	Electricity	Day is extended
145	Image and sound reproduction	Groundwork for telecommunications
105	Telecommunications introduced	Expanded communication networks
100	Airplanes	Speed of travel increases
85	Automobiles and roads	Travel access is individualized
60	Nuclear power developed	Threats now worldwide
55	Computers	Improved data management
50	Transistors	Computers available to individuals
45	Satellites	Data transmission improves
40	Lasers	Speed of information transmission
35	Microtechnology	Chips, bioengineering, genetic engineering
34	Moon landing	The world expands

Source material: Spyros Makridakis (1989) Management in the 21st century. *Long Range Planning*, 22 (2): 37–53.

The Industrial Revolution

Production of goods prior to the Industrial Revolution depended on a crafts system, so-called because workers individually crafted a product or its parts. Craft products could be quite expensive and many were available only to a very few. In the absence of distribution systems, each geographic region had to employ multiple craftspeople and other specialists to produce paper, furniture, fabric, and so on. The numbers of jobs in these crafts were necessarily limited by geographic demand and its future depended on experts' ability to teach skills to others. These points are further explored with an example of craft production of watches and their production today.

The Crafts System of Watch Production

Two hundred and fifty years ago each of the many parts for watch making was individually crafted by a master, an assistant, and one to three apprentices. The time to produce a watch was about a month, and its estimated cost in 1994 US dollars was $10,000 (Makridakis, 1989). Each watch was unique and different from every other. By 1994 a watch could be manufactured in less than a minute for less than one US dollar. Each was exactly like every other.

The Industrial Revolution Alters Work

Steam power was introduced in the 1770s. This technology was used to power machines, and it was later enhanced by electrical power. Both stimulated an Industrial Revolution in Western nations that occurred from 1780 to 1930. Changes in work production were several.

First, work was relocated to factories. Towns grew around these factories, and eventually led to a massive shift of people from rural labor to industrial work in towns and cities. Second, industrialization closed gaps between aspirations and possibilities. Mass production lowered costs to levels that made many products more affordable for a wider range of buyers. This revolution ushered in an era of increasing demand for goods and services, and may have been the birth of a consumer society where acquisition had more to do with wants than with needs.

Third, control over how and when to work shifted from individuals to factory owners who began to regulate and standardize work. Worker innovations were discouraged in favor of efficiencies and predictable, fixed routines. The result was that specialized craft knowledge became less central to the production process. Managerial challenges included reshaping worker attitudes. For example, unlike craft labor, factory labor needed to begin and end at a specified time. This required new understandings about timeliness, and many owners built bell towers to call laborers to work. The following example shows how business needs began to shape other cultural and social values toward work.

Work as a Moral Good

At the dawn of the Industrial Revolution, industry required disciplined workers, but British workers were often transient, restless, and absent, especially at the beginning of the week. Further, when at work, people preferred to work intensely for periods of time and then to slack off, but this was contrary to assembly-work demands for steady routines. Work rules were imposed to instill discipline, including threats of dismissal, fines, and even beatings. Rewards such as payment based on results of work and subcontracting for group labor often were used to motivate adults. Finally, work was equated with moral values, and play with sloth and lack of Christian character. According to some, the drive to morally uplift the working class was linked more to the need for factory discipline than to any real concern for working-class souls.

Source material: Sidney Pollard (1963, Dec.) Factory discipline in the Industrial Revolution. *Economic History Review*, Second Series, 26 (7): 254–271.

As manufacturing work grew in popularity, many organizations grew in size to include many employees or even multiple factories. Owners found it difficult personally to coordinate and control all-important organizational functions. They began to hire others to help them make or enforce decisions. This new managerial class saw to it that workers arrived on time. They also established rewards and punishments, allocated resources, and otherwise accomplished the several managerial tasks now identified as traditional management ones: plan, organize, delegate, and control the work of others. This revolutionary change meant that in part managerial coordination of business activities replaced the "invisible hand" of market mechanisms (Chandler, 1977).

The Industrial Revolution Alters Human Life

The shift from craft to assembly work also transformed individual lives. Urban dwellers began to purchase goods like food that they'd previously produced, and their earnings afforded immediate gratification when purchasing luxuries like watches. But some changes took longer. For example, just as all family members had worked on farms, initially children also worked in factories. It was not unusual for children as young as 9 or 10 years to work six-day weeks, toiling in factories for 12–16 hours at a stretch. While this practice is held in low regard by the advanced economies today, it is less surprising in the context of its time.

Workers Lose Autonomy

Finally, it is important to recognize that standardization of work meant that the worker became a cog, and a replaceable cog at that, in the industrial process. Thus, while there were benefits associated with factory work, there were also costs. An individual cost of mechanization was loss of personal autonomy. Because factory workers were hired less for their minds than their ability to complete repetitive tasks efficiently, employees and employers alike sacrificed or ignored the organizational potential of individual innovation and of what now is thought of as knowledge work.

This loss in human development caused many to worry that machines would further diminish or replace human labor. Luddites were a group whose opposition was especially strong. For example, they attacked mechanical textile looms to preserve the craft nature of weavers' jobs. Those who oppose or question technological shifts are sometimes branded Luddites by those who believe technological change is only for the good.

Social Changes Produced by the Industrial Revolution

Daniel Rodgers (1978) believes the Industrial Revolution brought about five social changes between 1750 and 1830 that had their greatest effect on the Western world. These included:

1 The shift from agricultural to industrial economies.
2 Movement of people from rural to urban communities.

3 Unprecedented population growth.
4 An unprecedented high standard of living, and doubling of average life span in developed countries.
5 Continuous technological introduction and change that created a sense of constant change, and more change coming.

Viewed as constant and almost unstoppable, much as telecommunications breakthroughs are viewed today, the changes occasioned by the Industrial Revolution created opportunities and they posed threats such as those described above. So too the Information Revolution poses opportunities and threats.

INFORMATION TECHNOLOGIES AND GLOBAL INTERCONNECTIONS

Many technological breakthroughs connect the world. Digital electronics, miniaturization, telecommunications, computers, robotics, artificial intelligence, genetic engineering, low-flying satellites, and lasers are only a few among many information technologies that shape our lives. But other information-based industries such as medicine, education, and engineering have also witnessed breakthroughs that are also dependent on knowledge, computers, and networks. Examples from any one could be used to demonstrate that connectivity stimulated by technological change spills over into other global environments such as global culture, politics, and economics to create business opportunities and challenges. Development of and convergence among computers, the Internet and telephony illustrates how these three contribute to an interconnected world. They alter culture by providing access to alternative ideas, and are in turn altered by it with ideas that come from around the world. They alter economies through electronic fund transfers whose technologies are again reshaped by worldwide use and adaptation. They affect political views through worldwide mobilization of NGOs, and they alter work by making knowledge more important to many organizations than traditional factors such as seniority, age, or position.

COMPUTERS AND DIGITAL ELECTRONICS

According to Makridakis (1989), today's technological revolution began in the 1940s with mathematical demonstrations of computer concepts. The first commercial computer was available in 1952. Since then computerization has been at or near the heart of technological revolutions occurring almost worldwide. Digitalization or translation of signals into bits of 0s and 1s makes it possible to generate, process, store and transmit text, graphics or sound from one digital device to another. Computerization occurred in three phases (Bradley et al., 1993); each had different implications for businesses and for work.

The Data Processing Era for Computers

The Data Processing (DP) era from 1960 to 1980 was dominated by mainframe computers. These helped organizations improve information management efficiencies, but costs were very high, few were trained to use them, and fear caused many to resist them. For example, Arthur C. Clarke's book *2001: A Space Odyssey* depicted "HAL" as a thinking computer that shut down human life-support systems to protect itself. In honor of HAL's 2001 birthday, Artificial Intelligence (AI) leaders (those who explore the extent to which computers can simulate human thought processes) commented on the match between fiction and reality. Many conclude that advances in graphics and networking are far beyond those expected, but that, unlike the fictional HAL, computers are limited in their ability to take on complex thought processes.

As the following example illustrates, mainframes today scarcely resemble their DP era ancestors.

Mainframes, neither Gone nor Forgotten

The first commercial computer was unofficially known as the UNIVAC. It was a robust 16,000 pounds, measuring 8 feet high, 7 feet wide, and 14 feet long. Its 5,000 vacuum tubes could perform *1,000* calculations per second. Today's mainframes are far smaller machines with significantly more computing power. Used to manage tasks involving millions of calculations like those required for weather tracking or as models for nuclear explosions, they now can perform *trillions* of calculations per second. Disk storage also has improved. By as early as 1997, hard-disk storage for mainframes was the equivalent of paper stacked as high as a 15-storey building.

The Microcomputer Era

The first miniaturized transistor-driven computer led to micro-processors and later to personal computers. Personal computers became increasingly accessible because of what has been called "Moore's Law" after Intel's Gordon Moore who in 1965 predicted that the number of transistors on a computer chip would grow exponentially, doubling every two years. This has occurred due to technological breakthroughs. Costs also have fallen. But falling cost and growing speed are not the only factors that led to widespread computer adoption in homes and businesses: industry changes produced inexpensive and free software, introduction of hardware like monitors, printers, or scanners made computers more useful, and there was a growing worldwide sense that non-users would be left behind. Almost no one could have predicted the growing reach of micro-processors. Products such as automobiles, toys, and credit cards are manufactured with micro-processors that also are imbedded within them. The following example further illustrates the pervasive reach of micro-processors to the US middle class.

Micro-processor Before Noon

Before noon each day the average US person has contact with 70 micro-processors. These are imbedded in home products such as toasters, refrigerators, telephones, and pagers, and in every form of entertainment device including televisions, compact-disc player, radios, and VCRs. They are in the clock radio, the digital bathroom scale, the collar that silences the dog, robot toys; you name it, it probably depends on a micro-processor. In the garage are autos, garage doors, mowers, and other devices that also depend on micro-processors.

Source material: One digital day. (1998, June 8) *Fortune*, p. 100.

The Network Era

According to Bradley et al. (1993), the Network Era of computer use evolved: a) to meet combined demands for automating repetitive work and leveraging professional work; and b) to support smarter products and services. Local area networks (LANs) meant to link a firm's engineers soon expanded to include external networks of scientists, consumers, or government officials. This created broader knowledge networks that affected industry development in many ways. The example below illustrates how this occurred in the computer industry itself.

Industries Alter

1977 introduction of the personal computer divided the industry into two: mainframes and PCs. Subsequent technological development further divided hardware and software industries, and entire new industries emerged. For example, software had been an undifferentiated market but markets subsequently developed in categories such as communication software, personal finances, business spreadsheets, and gaming. Each of the latter now can be examined as a distinct subcategory in the software industry.

THE INTERNET LEADS TO THE WEB

Many believe that the Pentagon project that gave birth to the Internet was meant to sustain communication after a nuclear attack. But the real reason for Internet development is more mundane: it was to save on communication costs among research computers and scientists (Hafner and Lyon, 1996). Designed to allow any number of computer networks to link and transparently act as one, the result is a network that is loosely configured, transcends hardware and software boundaries, is largely ungoverned, and possibly ungovernable.

Post-1993 growth in Internet use occurred due to both technological and political change. In 1995 governmental permission was granted to use the Internet for commercial purposes. The technological breakthrough was development of hypertext markup language (HTML) to send, retrieve, and link graphic images and sound. Thus the world wide web (www) was born. Almost immediately the web became home to thousands then millions and billions of web pages. The web made the Internet attractive to businesses, spawning e-commerce activities for large and small firms worldwide. Business-to-business commerce grew particularly fast, developing rapid links between buyers and suppliers worldwide.

TELEPHONY CONNECTS

The telephone was invented in 1876, but the first regular transatlantic telephone service was introduced in 1956. Telephone technology moved slowly due to the mode of information transfer and governmental restrictions. For example, the copper wires along which telephone messages travel require costly landlines. Resource limits held telephone access to 1 percent or less in many economies, especially developing ones. This deterred business investments and development. Today, many of the same technological factors and cost conditions that fueled computer industry growth are revolutionizing telephony. Telephones now transmit graphics, video images, and text. Examples are free space optics and wireless technologies through which developing economies leapfrog infrastructure constraints such as limited landlines.

Governmental regulations on telecommunications also constrained telephone technologies. In many nations telephone networks were government owned and regulated, and this deterred business innovations. Recent privatization of telephony led to a boom in technological development, and to greater emphasis on worldwide telecommunications regulations. The following example illustrates how World Trade Organization agreements facilitate global telecommunications networking.

Telecommunications Deregulation

Sixty-nine nations agreed to liberalization of telecommunications services and expected this to reduce the average cost of an international call from $1.00 to 20 cents per minute even as it doubles or triples the revenues for global communications firms. In 1997, 40 governments agreed to begin cutting customs duties by the following July on information technology products to eliminate all duties by 2000. The latter agreement enhanced prior pacts on computers and together the two agreements cover about 90 percent of world information technology trade in computers, semiconductors, software, and similar products and telecommunications services.

Source material: *WTO Annual Report*. (1997) Geneva: WTO Publications

---

SIX FACTORS THAT CHARACTERIZE TECHNOLOGICAL CHANGE

Spyros Makridakis' (1989) review of technological development over time identified five factors reflective of technological development. These factors apply to connectivity of information technologies, and to them is added a sixth factor below:

1 The importance of technology has increased over time.
2 The rate of innovation has increased markedly during the last 200 years.
3 Innovations and breakthroughs often occur in clusters.
4 In every age, there have been considerable spin-offs from technology to all areas of personal and family lives.
5 Throughout history, the manual work of humans has been supplemented, substituted, or amplified by a variety of means. Telecommunications technologies have similarly affected knowledge work.
6 Interconnectivity has spillover effects in a global world.

The Importance of Technology has Increased Over Time

No business and few individuals are unaffected by changes due to information technologies. But the impact of those changes depends at least in part on where one lives and access to those technologies. In particular, information technologies have had greatest impact on societies that have well-developed infrastructures for electricity and telecommunications.

The Rate of Innovation has Increased

Most of the scientists who ever lived are living today, and their contributions to knowledge are shown in Figure 11.1. According to the *Encyclopedia of the Future* (Kurian and Molitor, 1996), these scientists are doubling the pool of scientific information every 12 years.

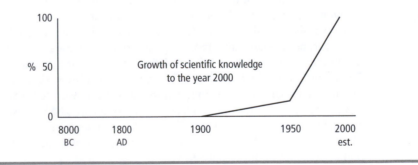

Figure 11.1 *Growth of scientific knowledge*

Source material: Bruce Merrifield (1994, Apr. 4) Wharton School. *Fortune*, p. 75.

Many scientists who contribute to the basic science of discovery lay the foundation for the Information Revolution and others devote their energies to applications leading to new technologies. The revolutionary changes introduced by new or improved products like computers have in turn led to technological breakthroughs in the processes by which we accomplish tasks or produce goods. As the example of Terabeam illustrates, technological breakthroughs often emerge due to shifts in other global environments.

Disaster Tries a New Technology

Terabeam Inc. produces "free space optics" through a device that transmits Internet and other data through the air along laser beams. This alternative to fiber-optic transmission attracted few customers until the 2001 terrorist destruction of the New York World Trade Center. Companies like Merrill Lynch turned to Terabeam because their landlines were destroyed, and many others found that tapping into air waves was the only way they could restore critical telecommunication links. Although free space technologies were introduced some 30 years ago, many companies had until 2001 considered them too new, too different, and unreliable. Change in these perceptions was motivated by a global political event and growing worldwide perception that terrorism affects everyone.

Source material: Dennis K. Berman (2001, Oct. 3) Disaster gives new life to wireless telecom firms. *The Wall Street Journal*, pp. B1, B4.

Global telecommunications interconnectivity has occurred very rapidly, producing changes in months, weeks or even days. Technological breakthroughs are accelerating at a rate directly proportional to falling technological barriers worldwide. Corporations are racing to take advantage of this trend and opportunities are available all over the world. For example, businesses now can hire skilled and educated workers from around the world. International Data Solutions, for example, scans case and client files for law firms and transmits them in digital form via satellite to the Philippines. Others use low-cost telephony to establish call centers around the world.

Economist Joseph Schumpeter argued that over time clustered technological innovations disrupt the status quo, replacing important industries in one time period with those in another. Valery (1999) observed that over time the types of industry cycles that Schumpeter described have peaked and waned in ever shorter cycles. For example, Schumpeter's first wave of innovations in water power, textiles, and iron covered 60 years. The cycle of steam, rail, and steel innovations was 55 years; electricity, chemicals, and the internal combustion engine was 50; petrochemicals, electronics, and aviation 40. More recently a fifth wave of digital networks, software, and new media has waxed and perhaps begun to wane in only 30 years.

Innovations Occur in Clusters

Innovations occur in clusters largely because a single but profound technological breakthrough often causes people to rethink traditional assumptions. Having seen one change, people imitate and then innovate, adding features to or finding new uses for technological advances. The homely example of the Guttenberg printing press below illustrates this point, showing that the process of innovation is nothing new.

> ### Innovation Dispersion Depends on Innovations in Other Industries
>
> Early advances in technology were dispersed only when people traveled. For example, when Johann Guttenberg introduced movable print type over 500 years ago, this technological shift had immediate impact only on the educated world because most people then were illiterate. Thus, the process technology for printing could not reach a full potential until educational technologies developed to teach reading. But another barrier was distribution technologies: there were no mail systems. Thus, books had to be carried one-by-one by travelers or on slow ships to spread this technology worldwide. It was nearly 400 more years after the invention of movable type before communication pioneers sent a telegraphic message to create the first telephone exchange in 1878 and lay the groundwork for what now is a global system for rapid communication. But the point is, rapid communication of information depends on people's ability to receive that information.

The same sort of clustered innovations that dispersed use of movable print type today occurs but much more rapidly as part of the information revolution. For example, as an opening vignette illustrates, telephony was adopted readily in developing economies following introduction of wireless approaches

Spin-offs from Technology Affect Life and Knowledge Work

You are probably a walking, talking example of how innovations alter life. Yes, you, with the Internet-accessed mobile telephone with games, photo imaging, text messaging, and other features. The communications networks you may take for granted have unfolded in your lifetime. Below we examine only a few among the many ways that telecommunications innovations like these have altered work and human life.

Unlike the land, labor, and capital factors so important to economic growth during the Industrial Revolution, the driving force behind the Information Revolution is intangible: information, and more specifically, knowledge. The amount of available information previously doubled every five years, but new forms of interconnectivity doubles information every two years. Given the ever increasing amount of information available in an average day, what may be most amazing is that we actually get anything done *except* consume new information. As the following example illustrates, information availability provides many worldwide with opportunities to adapt technologies to their own needs.

> ### A New Chip for Asia
>
> Until 2004 instructions inside computer chips were written in English. This forced reliance on English-language software protocols to write code, and it meant that Asian-language input and output for software contained layers of translation. A breakthrough came when Chinese computer scientist Chu Bong-foo found a way to put Asian characters in position to command binary codes. In practice, Chinese code writers now can

skip the translation process which will in turn speed the performance of digital products. Another possible result is that microchips will provide fewer benefits to companies from nations where Roman letters are used. This could mean more opportunities for Asian software companies. Culturecom Holdings Ltd. in Hong Kong introduced the first commercial uses of Chu's discovery with the introduction of a DVD player and a word-processing device.

Source material: Evan Ramstad (2004, Feb. 9) Chip that speaks languages of Asia levels playing field. *The Wall Street Journal*, p. B8.

Human Work Relies on Knowledge

The continuing shift from manual to knowledge work puts greater emphasis on intellect as a work input. This individual attribute can be continually renewed, but organizations cannot measure it as easily as manual labor. Many of the process technologies to support knowledge work are only now being discovered. For example, the accounting professional only recently began to think about how to account for intellect on a balance sheet.

Knowledge is a key resource for most organizations. Knowledge includes technical know-how of any type, organizational knowledge, and knowledge of self and others. Lane et al. define knowledge management as "the conscious and active management of locating or creating and assimilating, disseminating, and applying knowledge to strategic ends" (2004: 343). The growing importance of knowledge in global organizations suggests that today everyone needs to be a knowledge worker.

Knowledge helps organizations adapt to a global world and that is why most want to transfer knowledge quickly throughout the organization. The ability to learn continually can become a strategic advantage for some organizations (Senge, 1990), and it may be a critical success factor for most global firms. Authors Ikujiro Nonaka and Hirotaka Takeuchi (1995) view the knowledge creation process as a spiral that shares internal and external information at multiple levels. For example, internal networks share knowledge in meetings, social gatherings, and teamwork. These internal activities encourage people to transmit information to and from the external environment. Although knowledge generation is a critical concern for most companies, many US organizations find it difficult to leverage knowledge. Nonako and Takeuchi believe this is because of Western emphasis on the analytical nature of explicit knowledge. That is, conveying explicit information up or down organizational levels may reinforce facts, but it does not enhance understanding. The latter comes from implicit or tacit knowledge that is difficult to convey in a patterned way or in writing.

Knowledge and Power

Knowledge, like other sources of traditional power, has been viewed as a scarce resource, but knowledge-based systems treat it as a shared resource. Computer-based networks, for example, provide information access to many rather than a few managers. As more people acquire information, power derived from access to information erodes. Managers and workers become more equal; organizations become more democratic; and expectations grow for organizations to be community members. Further, according to Peter Drucker (1994a), the higher up the ladder one goes in knowledge work, the more likely it is for men and women to be doing the same work. Thus, knowledge becomes an equalizer in terms of work performed and may also be an equalizer in terms of pay and other work opportunities. The role of knowledge manager has taken on a formal dimension in advertising firm Saatchi and Saatchi as the following example shows.

What Does it Mean to be Director of Knowledge Management and Consumer Insights?

In 1997, Myra Stark's title as a Director of Knowledge was a new one in advertising and every other industry. She defined the role as directing and managing pursuit of all kinds of knowledge. Ms. Stark jets around the world to confirm consumer trends. For example, she observes that polenta has gained popularity in both the US and New Zealand, Internet cruising creates a state of mind where adults are no longer totally conscious of their surrounding, and boundaries of many types are blurring. Three examples: neutriceuticals combines food and health products; spirituality has reasserted itself in the US as a blend of Eastern and Western religious traditions; and localization of global products is evident when foie gras becomes "New York Hudson Valley foie gras" or calamari becomes "Montauk [NY] calamari." Although Ms. Stark's title was unusual at the time, the combined need for creativity and consumer information endemic to the advertising industry yielded a "department of the future" at ad agency TBWA International, and a "director of mind and mood" at Foote, Cone & Belding. Information or knowledge managers increasingly are part of the top management team in many organizations.

Source material: Yumiko Ono (1997, Feb. 28) Saatchi's 'Manager of Knowledge' keeps track of what's trendy. *The Wall Street Journal*, p. B5.

Spillover Effects of Telecommunications Connectivity

Telecommunication has enhanced global interconnectivity. Information is easily transmitted, leading to desired and unexpected and sometimes undesirable effects in many sectors. For example, Intel executives believe the Internet contributed to widescale media coverage of a flaw in the original Pentium chip. The story of this chip and the role Internet information played in discovering the flaw is an interesting one that illustrates the power of the Internet to shape information, business decisions, and development of computer-based industries.

Intel's Users Change (and so do their expectations)

Despite 24-hour testing that *Business Week* referred to as "the most exhaustive ever done on a computer chip," (Hof, 1994: 118) Intel discovered after release of the Pentium chip that it had a flaw: a floating decimal point affecting some high-precision division problems. The flaw was broadcast via the Internet, picked up by print news media, and soon became common knowledge among consumers. Accustomed to working with technical people and scientists rather than with consumers, and aware that the flaw was of limited scope, Intel originally offered to replace chips only for people affected by the flaw. Public outcry was immediate and harsh, and again the Internet played a significant role as the forum for consumer opposition. Eventually, Intel executives made a $500 million decision to replace all Pentium chips. Messages on the Internet immediately proclaimed small David's victory over the Intel Goliath. From this experience, Intel learned the important role the Internet could play in making world news out of what would have been a non-event in prior years, the difference between expectations of technical and consumer users, and the need to stand behind their "Intel Inside" product.

Source material: Robert D. Hof (1994, Dec. 19) The 'lurking time bomb' in Silicon Valley. *Business Week*, pp. 118–119.

Information Imbalances

The potential for equal access to information technologies is balanced by fears that those who do not have access will become the cyberspace equivalent of highway "road kill." There are concerns that disparities in access will lead to a division between those who have information and those who do not.

Despite fears about them, information technologies also provide new opportunities that include access to knowledge and business creation in developing and advanced economies alike. Israeli scientists and entrepreneurs, for example, are successful contributors to breakthroughs in advanced computer design, electric auto fuel, data networking, medical imaging, and electronic cash transfer. Companies like digital printer Indigo or voice imager VocalTech are only two of many companies founded on the strength of technological discovery and innovation. Israel is only one of national "hotspots" for technological breakthroughs. The following example shows where one might locate many computer hotspots.

Silicon Where?

Equivalents to California's Silicon Valley or Massachusetts' Highway 128 are springing up around the world in support of the computer industry, including the Silicon Forest in Seattle, the Silicon Glen in Scotland, Malaysia's high-tech Multimedia Super Corridor organized around Putrajaya, India's Silicon Valley near Bangalore, Cambridge, England's Silicon Fen, as well as similar tech centers in Singapore, Taiwan, Argentina, and Brazil. China fosters Silicon "Alleys" in the Zhongguancun near Beijing University where university graduates, students, and professors collaborate to develop high-tech companies.

The growing domain for scientific research and development experienced in the computer industry also applies to other industries including manufacturing, transportation, biotech, and environmental technologies. Many of the dominant national players in technology have had to cede ground to newer entrants, and others have responded by altering their focus. Intel, for example, no longer views the US as the most dynamic market for high tech and it derives more of its revenues from outside the US.

Equal access to information makes it possible for human rights groups to gather information that governments have long been able to suppress, and for television and similar entertainment modes to demonstrate possibilities and problems. Information sharing is yet another way to enhance equality, and this form of sharing generates global connectivity and creates many opportunities for individuals and businesses. The example below shows that Internet access provides business opportunities for Japanese women.

Japanese Women Mine Internet Business Possibilities

Despite government efforts to improve equality, cultural change in Japan has occurred slowly. For example, women are expected to marry and then drop out of the paid labor force. But as occurs elsewhere, some women in Japan want both a career and a family. This opportunity became more nearly possible with the Internet that allows women to set up "home work" centers providing services such as data entry, website design, and desktop publishing. Yumi Kasamatsu exemplifies this trend. She started out working alone on a used PC, but has since persuaded several big companies to consolidate their data-entry tasks through her and manages a nationwide network of home workers, most of whom are women. Along the way she has written six "how to" books on home work and become a popular seminar leader for women who want to set up their own Internet-intensive home businesses.

Source material: Robert A. Guth (2000, Feb. 29) Net lets Japanese women join work force at home. *The Wall Street Journal*, pp. B1, B20.

Instant on-line translators foster equality by reducing the English-language bias in the Internet. In Europe and in Asia, it is increasingly common for homepages to offer language alternatives. Interestingly, reasons to provide translations from English to non-English are business reasons: in many countries there are not enough English-readers to support English-only Internet services but translating devices remove this impediment to selling subscriptions or on-line memberships.

Cyberspace Governance

Internet use by pranksters, hackers, and electronic thieves has raised many issues around Internet use and access. The advantages of easy access to information creates opportunities for abuse and challenges such as loss of privacy. Additionally, inaccurate information can be harmful. Problems with "peepers" reading one's private mail, "hackers" obtaining banking and credit information, and Spam mail now show that Internet equal opportunity extends worldwide to pranksters, hackers, and thieves. The example of an attack on the US National Weather Service to follow shows how easily this can occur.

Attack on the US National Weather Service

Computer manager John Ward knew that hackers had penetrated the US National Weather Service's computers. Because these computers handle about 95 percent of computations that go into national weather forecasts that guide air travel, he also knew they had to be stopped. But despite months of effort, the hackers remained active. Ward discovered the hackers' port of entry was through an MIT computer, and so he installed an alarm system to alert the FBI whenever the hackers entered either the MIT system or the Weather Service computer. Often, hackers used the latter as a launching pad to jump into other computer networks and steal passwords. Working intensively with many, the case broke when MIT computer managers observed unusual activity on a computer telephone account and traced it through a local telephone call to Denmark. There, Danish police helped track down the hackers, seven young men between the ages of 17 and 23. Full details of the arrest were not released, but the Danish police were surprised because they believed Danish hacker attacks were coming from the US rather than the reverse. According to their own careful records, the hackers had put together a global network of computers and telephone lines to reach Israel, Brazil, and Japan as well as 32 different US systems.

Source material: John Falk (1994, Oct. 10) The latest flurries at weather bureau: Scattered hacking. *The Wall Street Journal*, pp. A1, A6.

Cyberspace governance is difficult to achieve because the Internet is not subject to the laws of any single country. It exists separate from the rules and regulations associated with geography and with traditional laws of most nations. Accordingly, governments have found it difficult to keep out unwanted cyber visitors or to limit use to legal, moral, or ethical ends. For example, although national regulations allowed Germany to block CompuServe on-line "newsgroups" judged to be pornographic, in fact German citizens could gain access to these and similar resources through Internet providers or by placing long-distance calls to servers in other nations. Table 11.1 demonstrates some of the challenges the Internet poses for national governments. In response to nations' efforts to curtail Internet use, the Internet Society works to develop standards of use. Called the Global Internet Project, organizational members including AT&T, MCI, IBM, Sun Microsystems, British Telecom, and BBN Corporation. This group informs members of pending worldwide legislation governing the Internet.

Table 11.2 *Internet use and national priorities*

Use	National Priorities
Saudi Arabian hackers debate topics from atheism to pornography via Internet servers in other countries	Saudi government fears they will lose control over political dialogue and public mores
Nongovernmental agencies use the Internet to rally support for their causes	Malaysian authorities examined financial and other records of local NGOs to explore the link between them and foreign subversives
BurmaNet lobbies businesses to discourage operations in Myanmar	Myanmar collects e-mail addresses of BurmaNet users
English-language dominance on the Internet	The French Association for the Defense of the French Language and the Future of the French language sued a Georgia Tech University (Georgia Tech Lorraine) to translate its Internet site into French
Information sharing	Grass-roots movements across countries use the Internet to share information, e.g., the Association for Progressive Communications created a homepage for the UN Fourth World Conference on Women
China's access to worldwide information	China's "Internet police" use filtering technology to block dissenting political views; Chinese company QQ offers software that filters banned words and phrases such as democracy, human rights, and Taiwan independence

Protecting Intellectual Property Rights

Many firms find that staying ahead technologically means protecting their ideas in a global market place. Reverse engineering, unlicensed borrowing, and outright stealing threaten companies' R&D investments in new products and services. Many firms vigorously defend their technologies at the global level by endorsing stronger intellectual property rights. Like corruption, intellectual property risk is widespread and occurs in part because of national differences in how property is defined. According to US government definitions, intellectual property refers to a broad collection of rights relating to human inventiveness and creativity. It comprises two main branches: first, industrial property, covering inventions, trademarks, and industrial designs; and, second, copyright of creative work such as books, music, or films.

Patents

A patent is a governmental grant of a property right to the inventor of a product or process that is new and has utility for an industrial application. A patent provides the inventor, or the inventor's successor in title, to exclusive rights that generally precludes others from making, using, or selling the invention. The Uruguay Round TRIPS agreement requires that a patent must be valid for a minimum of 20 years from the filing date of the application.

Trademark

A trademark is any word, symbol, design, or device used to identify a product. Service marks involve similar descriptors to identify a service. The purpose of a trademark or service mark is to identify goods put on the market, thereby distinguishing them from other goods and services, and to indicate their source or origin. To a large extent trademarks have become a guarantee of quality. The TRIPS agreement provides that initial registration of a trademark must be valid for a period of at least seven years with indefinite renewals.

The amount of counterfeit trade has increased four-fold in the last decade to total about 9 percent of total world trade (de Jonquieres, 2003). Previously limited to luxury goods such as jewelry, goods counterfeited today range from software, movies, music, and car components to pharmaceuticals. Brand-name goods are especially vulnerable, but everyday consumer products such as toothpaste are also subject to counterfeiting. This makes counterfeiting an issue for small firms as well as large ones; this point is illustrated by the following example of Ghana's Primtex Ltd.

Primtex Ltd. Fights Counterfeiting

Ghanaian fashion is defined by colorful textile designs, but many small Ghanaian firms are increasingly vulnerable to counterfeiting. For example, as soon as Primtex Ltd. issues a new design, it is transported to China, Pakistan, Nigeria, or India where locals will make cheap knock-offs that are then smuggled back into Ghana. This reverse engineering can occur in as little as a few weeks. An immediate result is reduced sales for Primtex. Primtex and three other primary Ghanaian textile companies lose an estimated $100 million per year to piracy and smuggling. The government also loses about $20 million in tariff revenues per year to smuggling. Another effect is price compression when consumers demand that local firms sell at the same low prices as imported knock-offs. Companies like Primtex can ill afford cost cutting and lost sales because their investments in designs and manufacturing are high. Accordingly, Primtex tries to protect its designs by closing its factory and posting signs to keep unwanted persons from the premises. The company also decided not to invest in e-commerce sales, fearing further incursions on their designs. Perhaps more importantly, as companies like Primtex lose sales and market share, they are further distanced from opportunities to sell to a more global community.

Source material: Michael M. Phillips (2002, July 12) Pilfered patterns. *The Wall Street Journal*, pp. B1, B4.

Copyright

Copyright usually refers to "literary and artistic works." US copyright law enumerates eight broad categories of subject matter that can be protected: a) literary works (which include computer software); b) musical works, including accompanying words; c) dramatic works, including accompanying music, pantomimes and choreographic works; d) pictorial, graphic and sculptural works; e) motion pictures and other audiovisual works; f) sound recordings; and g) architectural works. US law, consistent with the Berne Convention and the TRIPS agreement, protects a copyrighted work for the term of the author's life plus 50 years. In the EU, copyright extends 70 years beyond the author's death. Many nations do not provide protections for this form of intellectual property. This explains why street marketers in many places offer new movie and music releases so promptly; they have paid nothing for the property rights.

Common global policies on intellectual property have not emerged, in large part because many of the products they cover are evolving faster than rules can be written. Although GATT outlined an Agreement on Trade-Related Aspects of Intellectual Property Rights, most nations have yet to clarify how they will implement these rights.

Protecting Knowledge in Developing Economies

Many developing economies recognize that they too must protect their intellectual property. Companies in cosmetic and even toothpaste industries face growing allegations that they exploit indigenous people by using their knowledge of local plants without providing proper reimbursement for that knowledge. Following the 1992 Convention on Biological Diversity, Merck agreed to pay $1 million to Costa Rica's National Institute of Biodiversity to collect plants, insects, and microbes; they further agreed to pay royalties for discoveries made based on the Institute's help with research.

Pirating of software, books, and pharmaceutical goods reaches billions per year with huge losses to the computer software industry. The Business Software Alliance estimates that foregone revenue due to software piracy amounted to about $812 billion in 2003. Five common forms of software piracy include end-user piracy when an employee reproduces software copies without authorization; client-server overuse when too many employees on the same network use a central copy at the same time; Internet piracy that occurs when software is downloaded from the Internet; hard-disk loading when a business sells new computers with copies of illegal software; and software counterfeiting when someone illegally copies software for resale (Business Software Alliance, 2004: *http://www.bsa.org/usa/antipiracy/Types-of-Piracy.cfm*).

BUSINESS IMPLICATIONS OF TELECOMMUNICATION CHANGES

Many technological changes that affect businesses are industry-specific. For example, just-in-time management technologies primarily affect manufacturing firms. But every organization is affected by changes in telecommunication technologies that enhance the speed of information flow, provide opportunities to reduce information production, or transfer costs. These advantages are available to all organizations, and they stimulate illegal as well as legal business activities. In turn, they increase demand for risk management systems such as those described in Chapter 16.

Telecommunications technologies also provide access to more of the world for many businesses, and with this opportunity comes challenges. For example, access to new ideas and clients enhances creativity and innovation, but many companies in advanced economies find that they have new competitors from around the world. When worldwide competition increases, then all participants tend to increase efforts to develop new and better technologies.

The rapid speed of information transfer also alters many traditional assumptions about knowledge. For example, in the past technological breakthroughs were once the province of advanced economies, and knowledge was power in the hands of top managers. Today any person anywhere can provide and consume information. Within organizations, knowledge has become more central to organizational success and everyone is encouraged to leverage their knowledge to benefit the company. Because knowledge management is more central to organizational success, this former staff function is now located at the top of many organizational hierarchies who have Chief Knowledge or Information Officers. Additionally, in knowledge-intensive companies, there is greater reliance on and rewards for younger employees who can best leverage information breakthroughs. All of these changes alter sources of organizational power, they increase the speed of change, and they create additional demands for knowledge as an organizational input.

CHAPTER SUMMARY

Science is exploration for the sake of knowing, and technology is the application of science, usually in the interests of bettering human life. Technological competence in both product and process has been a critical success factor for businesses in most industries.

Technological breakthroughs of almost every kind punctuate known history, and many of these breakthroughs have brought about revolutionary changes in how work is accomplished. Technological revolutions also have had a profound impact on social and family life.

Telecommunications technologies demonstrate that connectivity spills over into other global environments such as global culture, politics, and economics to create business opportunities and challenges.

The Internet symbolizes the computer-based equivalent of boundarylessness: it is ungoverned, operates night and day around the world, is accessible to many, often free, and provides a knowledge-based window to the world. Easing of regulatory restrictions on the Internet in 1995 brought a flood of business uses to the Internet.

Unlike the land, manual labor, and capital factors so important to economic growth during the Industrial Revolution, the driving force behind the Information Revolution is an intangible: information, and more specifically, knowledge.

In the absence of global governance mechanisms, business leaders find it particularly difficult to protect intellectual property rights. Three types of mechanisms are meant to protect intellectual property: patents, copyright, and trademarks, but these are not uniformly applied worldwide.

REVIEW AND DISCUSSION QUESTIONS

1 The first chapter in this book weighed the positive and negative effects of globalization. Using information technology as the example, weigh the positives and negatives of this technology at four levels: global, national, business, and personal. Provide at least two examples of a positive and two examples of a negative for each level.

2 The content of the chapter focussed primarily on information technologies, but many other technologies are having a profound effect on people and organizations. Select a "breaththrough" technology outside the field of information technology (IT); possibilities include AZT medicine for AIDs, cloning, organ transplants, genetic engineering, and others. Choose one breakthrough technology and outline three ways it has, could, or will change work life in terms of organizing work; what we do when at work; how we accomplish tasks; how we interact with others. Map out first-, second-, and third-order effects of these technologies on the quality of human life.

Chapter 12
ORGANIZATIONAL GOVERNANCE AND STRUCTURE

EXIDE RESTRUCTURES

Exide Technologies describes itself as a global leader "providing stored electrical energy solutions" (Exide fast facts, 2003). With 2003 sales of about $2.4 billion, Exide is one of the world's largest producers and recyclers of the lead-acid batteries that power autos. They supply DaimlerChrysler, Fiat, Ford, Motorola and the navies of Norway, Spain, Sweden, and the US. Exide brands include Champion, Prestolite, Sonnak, Pacific Chloride, Exide, PCA, and Emisa.

In 1998 the company was accused of selling used and defective batteries as if they were new, leading to a guilty plea in US courts. The company itself filed suit against former executives to recover costs in resolving claims related to the fraud (three Exide managers later were convicted and sentenced to jail). The eventual cost to Exide exceeded $50 million, and the company sought protection from creditors by filing for bankruptcy. At the same time Exide purchased new entities and spun off existing ones, it faced growing competition for sales and buyers with price-reduction demands.

These and other challenges led to internal adjustments at Exide that included people, processes, and structures. A review of their restructuring efforts sets the stage for under-standing how and why companies restructure, and it demonstrates that structural arrangements also affect people and processes within the organization.

In 1995, CEO Arthur Hawkins was hired from ITT Corporation to rebuild Exide. His efforts mainly revolved around acquisitions from around the globe that put Exide into 89 countries. But each new company acquisition required a structural adjustment to coordinate among existing and new companies.

By 2000, Exide's structure was based on geographic divisions for markets it supplied with batteries. This meant there were country managers for each nation or region served, e.g., Britain, Germany, Austria, Italy, Spain, and Asia. Expected advantages of this approach were to streamline local decision-making, increase pricing flexibility, and access information to tailor products to specific countries or regions. There were also disadvantages of this geographic divisionalization. For example, managers recognized that it encouraged unnecessary plant construction in Asia. Further, a developing practice in Europe was that country managers—who were compensated based on their own sales—undercut one another's prices. For example, the manager of Country A reduced prices to sell more products in Country B. This induced Country B's manager to reduce prices still further, which could only lead to Exide losses. Profits fell and debts mounted.

Recognizing the dilemma, Exide's new CEO Robert Lutz took action to bring governance and structures in line. He fired or requested resignations from more than 50 executives, replaced the entire board, filed civil suits against former executives, and created a plan to revise the structure that took a year to develop and $8 million in costs.

Mr. Lutz's restructuring plan took time to "sell" the idea to existing country managers. He held five management retreats in eight months, then encouraged managers to work in teams to consider Exide's problems if it used the existing country manager model or alternatives. After much deliberation, Lutz decided to move toward divisionalization by product rather than geography. ▶

Initially, Exide created six business units organized around product lines, e.g., automobile batteries, industrial batteries. The global product divisional structure made it possible to eliminate manufacturing sites and coordinate production among those that remained. Further, the new structure eliminated incentives to undercut national prices. At the same time, there were far fewer product divisions than the geographic divisions they replaced. This meant that personnel were reshuffled in roles and even geographically. For example, Giovani Mele, who'd been Italy's managing director, was transferred to Frankfurt where he made less money and lived alone because his family would not move from Naples. Some former country managers quit outright, while others perceived that former career paths had closed and resigned within a few weeks.

Within six weeks of restructuring into the six product divisions, Exide purchased international battery maker GNB Technologies. The acquisition was meant to reestablish Exide in the North American industrial-battery market it abandoned a decade earlier. Although the structure required alteration to accommodate the new acquisition, CEO Lutz feared that GNB's president would leave if GNB were folded into existing product divisions. Accordingly, Mr. Lutz hybridized the new structure by adding GNB as a geographic division to existing product divisions. This led to internal clashes. For example, GNB's president thought he should be allowed to develop Exide in China, but the president of the automotive battery division thought China should be his territory because it represented the fastest growth territory for automotive batteries. This example illustrates that a change in structure often comes with its own problems.

Restructuring efforts that took Exide from geographic to product to a hybrid structure affected more people than top executives. Four distribution centers and 60 branch offices were closed, and 1,500 jobs were cut. At the same time, Exide introduced an EXCELL process (Exide's Customer-Focussed Lean Leadership system) to create a culture that encouraged employees to make process improvements. Other goals were to improve the costs of quality such as reducing scrap and waste and lower costs with fewer accidents and warranty redemptions. Further restructuring followed to organize Exide around three divisions: Global Network Power, Motive Power, and Transportation.

Source material: Exide fast facts. (2002, Nov. 1) http://www.exide.com; Exide files suit against former top execs. (2002, May 13) *American Metal Market*, p. 16; James E. Guyette (2003, Jan.) 'White-collar' crime nets former Exide chief 10 years in prison, $1 million in fines. *Aftermarket Business*, p. 9; Joann S. Lublin (2001, June 27) In choosing the right management model, firms seesaw between product and place. *The Wall Street Journal*, pp. A1, A8; A.P. Smith (2001, Nov. 2) Exide gives boost to consolidation efforts. *American Metal Market*, p. 2.

CHAPTER OVERVIEW

This chapter looks at governance and structural arrangements in global firms. Governance differences such as the relationship between top managers and their boards tend to differ on a global basis. This results in different structural arrangements among firms. The chapter examines traditional forms and hybrids as well as alliance forms of structure.

THE PURPOSE OF ORGANIZATIONAL STRUCTURE

Chapter 3 outlined five levels of strategy to show that the overall purpose of the firm shapes its portfolio, its competitive stance in each line of business, its operational features, and ideally the work each person accomplishes. This chapter focusses on an important dimension of operational strategy: governing and structuring the enterprise.

Organizational purpose is achieved in part via governance mechanisms and structural arrangements that outline relationships between people and their jobs. An organization's structure assigns decision-making authority, it allocates responsibilities, it identifies sources of power, and it shows how organizations link their activities with markets. For global firms, it demonstrates relationships between functions, geographic regions that may span the globe, and product or service divisions of the company. Structure is usually represented in organizational charts that often differ because structural arrangements differ. Visual representations of organizational structure include pyramids, circles, and networks to name a few.

Because an organization's structure underpins the relationships that facilitate organizational movement, one can think of an organization's structure as its skeleton. Just as human skeletons differ, so do the skeletons or structures of most organizations. That is, some are wide, some narrow, some small, and some large. Very large organizations typically have highly formalized and complex structures, whereas smaller firms usually rely on structures that are less formalized and less complex. Some structures function well, others do not. All articulate and manage formal relationships within an organization. In summary, although every organization has a structure, they differ from one organization to another depending on factors such as organizational purpose, preferences of top managers, company ownership, and even nation of origin.

Different terms are used to describe the same components of structure. For example, although this text uses the term organizational *structure*, others might refer to it as the organization's *design*. Job titles appearing on an organizational chart also vary from one to another. For example, the person who makes most strategic decisions in the US is the Chief Executive Officer (CEO); the analogous UK term is Managing Director. Global organizations increasingly borrow structural features and terms from one another.

REASONS TO STUDY STRUCTURE

Analysis of an organizational structure is instructive for several reasons. Perhaps most importantly, structural arrangements lay out sources and directions of organizational power. Among other things, structure shows who is in charge, where responsibilities lie, and the direction of communication flows.

Most big firms adopt at least some features of a hierachical structure. Harold Leavitt believes this occurs because hierachies "add structure and regularity to our lives. They give us routines, duties, and responsibilities" (2003: 101), which people need. Leavitt acknowledges that hierachies also can be problematic, but argues they provide a way for people to process—perhaps regularize—complexity. This being the case, a second reason to study structure is that a hierachy reflects priorities in perceived importance of functions, products/services, and global geographic markets to the firm. For example, when members of the top executive team are responsible for functions such as human resources, finance, or production, this suggests that coordination among functions is deemed most important to firm success. Certainly coordinating products/services and geographic markets is important, but coordination among these two is managed by first coordinating the functions. Thus, structural configuration first focusses attention on a particular organizational area, for example function, and then on others, such as products/services, nations, or regions. This first decision about structure guides resource flows and define control and other important processes.

Third, analyzing structure provides a way to examine the fit between what leaders say they want to do and what the organization is actually able to do. If resources are structured to flow in the strategic direction managers espouse, then the organization is better positioned to meet its objectives than when the structural configuration conflicts with strategic direction. For example, an organization that claims to be global would ordinarily be structured such that resources flow toward global rather than national, regional, or local units alone.

Structural analysis also facilitates career planning. People who begin their careers at or near the bottom of the organizational structure can examine structure to anticipate opportunities and barriers to promotion. For example, earning an MBA is desirable if everyone in top management has one. Structures also illustrate people's roles relative to those of others. Thus, structural examination can help one avoid dead-end assignments but seek those that enhance career progress. For career purposes, it is also important to realize that while an organizational structure illustrates formal power and responsibility, it often omits important informal relationships. The classic example is the secretary to the CEO whose role may not appear on the organizational chart but who can nevertheless wield considerable informal power.

SOURCES OF INFORMATION ON A COMPANY'S STRUCTURE

Formal structural configurations for any given organization typically are captured in an organizational chart that shows vertical and lateral relationships. For public companies, this chart often appears on a company's website, in corporate annual reports, or other published materials. Family-owned or privately held enterprises may provide little information on how they are structured.

As indicated earlier, organizational charts often resemble figures such as pyramids or circles. Globalization has increased structural options and brought about variation in the way organizational charts are drawn. Sometimes pyramids are depicted top to bottom, but others rest on their sides. Additionally, globalization has increased interconnections and brought about new organizational forms such as strategic alliances, joint ventures, and other collaborative relationships. These forms link structural features of one organization with structural features of another, and they increase structural diversity and complexity for firms.

Although it is more convenient to assess structure based on a formal organizational chart, analysts sometimes have to construct their own view of how a company is structured. Capsule commentaries in published materials can provide useful descriptions. For example, a company that refers to its "divisions" often is structuring work according to one of several forms of divisionalization described later in this chapter. Reports that appear in trade or academic articles also offer clues about an organization's structure. Additionally, one can examine officers' titles to interpret structure. For example, if an organization lists ten executive vice-presidents, then we can reasonably infer that these ten are at the same horizontal level in the organization. Above them would be jobs titles such as CEO or President, and below them would be people holding titles such as non-executive vice-president or director.

Varieties of Restructuring

Two types of restructuring activities occur in many companies. Financial restructuring occurs when a company consolidates its debts or otherwise reorganizes the way it manages finances. In the management field, restructuring refers to reorganization of jobs or organizational roles. The latter form of restructuring is the one of most interest to management analysts.

First, we look at those who make the most important decisions, then at structural arrangements among various divisions, products, and functions.

ORGANIZATIONAL GOVERNANCE

Although everyone in an organization has a place in its structure, most studies of structure concentrate attention on top levels where important decisions are made. In many organizations—especially those from Anglo-Saxon nations—organizational structures are hierarchical. That is, a limited number of people make the important decisions and many more at the bottom of the hierarchy support them. At top levels are senior managers and relevant policy review boards such as a Board of Directors. Decisions made at these levels often are subject to shareholder votes, and they are increasingly subject to public review and comment.

Students of globalization are interested in senior managers and policy review boards because the relationships among them and the decisions they make shape activities and outcomes. They also shape the enterprise strategy that defines organizational purpose and the corporate strategy that adds or deletes businesses from the corporate portfolio. The following review of jobs and relationships among Board and top managers illustrates the governance process.

Boards of Directors and Top Managers

The separate responsibilities of top managers and boards of directors are much the same worldwide, but the following sections show that governance relationships among them are managed in different ways.

The activities of top executives (such as a CEO or Managing Director) are usually monitored by a Board of Directors that numbers 10–15 people in the US but can be more or less elsewhere. Also depending on the nation, the Board of Directors usually answer to others such as shareholders or the government. Among typical Board responsibilities are:

- Review strategic decisions.
- Assess the company's current and future ability to meet shareholder and stakeholder expectations.
- Evaluate top-executive performance.
- Set executive pay and other forms of compensation.
- Hire or fire top managers.
- Select financial auditors; review the results.
- Oversee management, corporate strategy, and the company's financial reports to shareholders.

Although most boards play these roles, their composition varies worldwide. For example, China's national companies would normally include politicians among the Board members, but private Chinese companies would more likely be headed by founders. In Malaysia, a native Malay always heads the Board. In the wake of financial debacles in US and European firms such as Enron, Ahold, Parmalat, and Worldcom, many nations introduced new legislation mandating what and how boards were to monitor senior managers. For example, Singapore requires that auditors be changed no less frequently than every two years. These kinds of governances changes are occurring worldwide for reasons such as those described below.

Siemens' Managing Board

As Siemens is registered in Germany, it is subject to a German Corporation Act that requires a two-tier structure with a supervisory board and a managing (or executive) board. Additionally, *Mitbestimmung* or co-determination, entitles workers and union representatives half the seats on supervisory boards in large corporations. Responsibilities for Siemens' managing board are: to develop the company's strategic orientation, plan and finalize the annual budget, allocate resources, and monitor executive managers of each operating group. The managing board cooperates closely with the supervisory board and has ultimate authority over major management decisions. EU efforts to standardize corporate rules as well as labor concessions to prevent outsoucing undermine co-determination, and in the long run may lead to structural changes for Siemens and other global giants from Germany.

> ### Who Chooses Board Directors?
>
> People who serve on the Board of Directors for US public firms are nominated and then elected to serve. Often they are nominated by the CEO or current board members from among their circle of acquaintances. In the election process, every shareholder has a vote equivalent to the number of shares owned. However, aside from a paragraph or two (if that) individual shareholders typically have limited information to guide their election choices. Further, election outcomes usually are determined by majority stockholders—those who hold many shares rather than by individual votes from small shareholders.

Combined CEO and Chairman of the Board Roles

In the US, three out of four companies in the Standard & Poor's 500 combine the role of Chairman of the Board and CEO (The way we govern now, 2003). In practical terms, this means that the Board that reviews executive decisions and allocates CEO rewards is itself headed by the CEO. Moreover, in the US other Board members are often nominated by the CEO, usually from among other CEOs who have a commercial link with the company or a personal link with the CEO. This often creates what is called "interlocking directorates," meaning that CEOs very frequently are Board directors for one another. Other than the CEO, company managers such as division heads or directors are rarely members of US Boards of Directors.

Another concern is that current systems for assembling boards of directors tend to program out diversity. For example, studies conducted between 1998 and 2003 show there were no female members on the boards of directors for 10 percent of US firms, 53 percent of Australian firms, 58 percent of UK firms, 76 percent of Spanish firms, and 97 percent of Japanese firms (Flynn and Adams, 2004).

Several issues related to the combined CEO/Chairman of the Board model emerged from accounting and fraud scandals among large US firms in the early 2000s. Given that Board directors often are CEOs of other companies, many wonder if Board members have adequate time to review or oversee another company's results and activities. For example, US Boards meet 4–10 times a year for 2–4 hours; this may be too little time for work required. There is also an issue with cost/benefits of Board efforts. Many Board directors earn tens of thousands of dollars per year as Board members for what can be a small time commitment (The way we govern now, 2003).

A third issue deals with loyalty: if a director is nominated by the current CEO, to whom will that Board member be most loyal? For example, will Board members approve raises for the CEO simply because they owe that CEO their own position on the Board? In the case of interlocking directorates, that same CEO may be on the Board voting for one's own raise. Many believe that these arrangements, i.e., Chairman/CEO, interlocking directorates, create a power imbalance that favors the CEO. However, changes in US law such as the Sarbanes-Oxley Act may introduce controls. For example, the law mandates that only non-executive members of a Board can serve on audit or compensation committees.

Non-executive Chairman of the Board

Other Board/CEO models more nearly balance the power of the CEO with those of the Board. For example, in Britain and elsewhere in Europe someone who is not a company executive usually chairs the Board of Directors. One argument for this model is that the Chairman of the Board can take a more objective position on issues of executive compensation, strategic review, and so on. Further, unlike the US model, the British model usually includes several senior executives from the company, providing the Board with additional insider insight.

As indicated in the example of Siemens' Managing Board, German companies are legally required to structure chief executive/Board relationships around a two-tiered board that includes a management board that takes responsibility for operations and a supervisory board for strategic oversight that includes shareholder, worker, and union representatives. In those cases, the management board is not just a single CEO but rather a group of senior executives who work together to run the company. This contrasts sharply with the unitary CEO model usual to the US.

The Chief Managing Officer

Chief executives usually are at the top of an organization's operational hierarchy. Typical top-management titles are Chief Executive Officer (CEO), Managing Director, or Managing Board. These individuals or groups set organizational direction in consultation with the Board and are responsible for managing day-to-day responsibilities that yield profits and other social benefits. As shown in the Exide case, the top manager creates an operating structure to meet these objectives. Sometimes the CEO or Managing Director also is in charge of operations; other times the function is assigned to a Chief Operating Office (COO) who reports to the CEO or Managing Director. Some organizations create a team of two or more top managers who share the executive officer role. For example, until he stepped down in 2004 the founder of Dell Computer split the office of the CEO with a colleague. Michael Dell made most strategic decisions and his colleague made most operational ones, but both consulted with the other on all decisions. This shared approach to top management is unusual in US firms.

STRUCTURING FOR GLOBAL PRESENCE AND ACTIVITIES

Every global firm operates in many nations, many offer a wide array of products and services, and all rely on functions such as marketing, finance, operations, human resource management, and accounting. Integration among these functions as well as geographic and products/services integration is an important structural concern for the global firm. Students of globalization are interested in how well an organization's structure prepares it to operate in an increasingly global world. To assess this, one studies the vertical and horizontal linkages within the organization that affect global activities. This chapter shows that there is no single "best" structure; global firms use many different structural forms.

An analysis of structure might begin with questions such as: How does the organization manage its subsidiaries in various countries? Through what internal mechanisms are resources such as labor and supplies distributed? Where are decisions made? How does the organization integrate functions with products/services and nations? These questions can be approached through an examination of structural features. An important first decision is whether to centralize or decentralize decision-making worldwide.

Structure and Leadership Style

The traditional context for Western managers encouraged hierarchies that delegate authority downward from top to middle managers and then to employees. In a more diverse and global world, other models also appear. For example, in family-owned firms, final authority may reside in the patriarch or matriarch but management decisions often are reached via family consensus. In virtual firms, authority is necessarily distributed—often horizontally. The top-down authoritarian manager has by no means disappeared, but in fostering diverse organizations, globalization has also fostered diverse leadership styles as well as diverse structures.

Centralization and Decentralization

The decision to expand abroad raises questions about coordination and control of relationships between the parent company and its offspring. Some firms centralize control to make most important decisions at headquarters. Others decentralize, delegating important decisions to overseas managers or to those responsible for global products and services. Global firms like Makro and Eva Airlines decentralized decisions because top managers believe local managers are in a better position to make decisions. For example, Makro's Paul Van Vlisingen decentralized this retail giant to give local managers control over day-to-day decisions. Sweden's IKEA is also radically decentralized, depending mostly on in-person communication and other media to exchange information. At one point Ford Motor Company centralized many decisions to better achieve a worldwide integration strategy, but more recently Ford's move away from that strategy has led them to greater decentralization in decision authority. Philips has done both: decentralized and then centralized to improve coordination and control as it reduced the workforce. Bertelsmann did the opposite: they centralized and then decentralized. The reasons for the latter decisions appear in the box to follow.

Bertelsmann's Decentralization

Thomas Middelhoff, former CEO of Bertelsmann, tended to use a more Anglo-Saxon approach to managing a global firm. He centralized many decisions better to integrate among them. When Middelhoff was replaced by Gunter Thielen, the latter decentralized, believing that involving lower-level managers is an important way to generate steady company growth. Further, the company disbanded the management committees that Middelhoff had created, replacing them with a new executive board council to coordinate among divisions. Mr. Thielen also cut the 15-person office of the chairman.

Source material: Bertelsmann scraps ex-CEO's initiatives in pursuit of growth. (2002, Apr. 23) *The Wall Street Journal*, p. A5.

The choice of whether to centralize or decentralize depends in part on the strategy the firm pursues, and this is also reflected in the type of structure it creates. Below we examine several traditional approaches to structuring for global expansion. We begin with fairly simple structures that are easiest to describe, then look at complex structures that are more difficult to describe and to draw. However, our main focus is on how each type of structural arrangement is meant to aid the organization's adaptation to global shifts.

Ways to Structure For Global Expansion

An Export Office

Organizations new to international expansion often will organize their efforts around an export group responsible for activities abroad. Although the person responsible for exporting usually is at the second or third highest level of top managers, this role is often an "add on" rather than integral to the firm. Primary emphasis remains on the home country to which the organization is linked.

An advantage of an export office structure is that it organizes all international activities under a single role. This makes it easier for a single person, usually the export manager, to coordinate among various countries and regions. This export manager may report to the CEO as shown in Figure 12.1, but alternatively s/he can report to an intermediary, for example a vice president, who then reports to the CEO. A disadvantage of this structural approach is that it tends to separate international and organizational activities, and because of this anyone other than the export manager may be slow to identify opportunities (or threats) abroad. When exports increase to represent more of an organization's income, export activities need to be integrated more with those of the firm. For this reason, many firms abandon an export office structure when they go global.

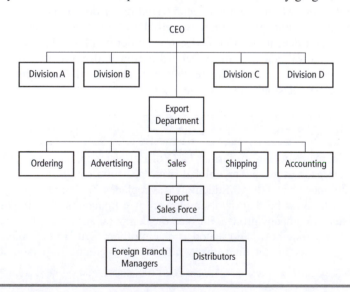

Figure 12.1 *Domestic divisional structure with an export office*

Functional Organizational Structure

One way an organization expands for global presence is with a functional structure where tasks are organized around principal *functions* such as marketing, accounting, operations, research and development (R&D), legal affairs, human resources or the like. Heads of these functions are senior managers with titles such as Vice President (VP) for Operations and VP for Legal Affairs, as shown in Figure 12.2. This example illustrates a clear set of priorities: first in priority are functions followed by product groups, followed by nations where products are produced or sold. Another company using the same functional approach could put secondary emphasis on nations followed by product groups. This example represents only one of many different ways that an organization can be structured along functional lines. A second point is that structural arrangements establish the relative order of importance of functions to geographic groups to products/services. In a functional structure, functions are deemed most important.

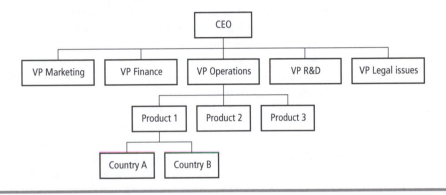

Figure 12.2 *Global functional structure*

In the functional structure shown in Figure 12.2, each functional manager is responsible for his/her function in all product lines and all over the world. Thus, the Marketing VP would manage products and then nations with respect to marketing concerns. Using this model, each functional manager takes on some responsibility for operations/activities outside the home nation. This differentiates this model from an export office approach that organizes all international activities around a single export officer.

Inditex—Functional Structure and Strategic Alliances

Inditex, parent to the Zara brand, is an apparel pioneer, and has used a functional structure to go global. At the top of the organization is majority owner Amacio Oretga who is chair of the Board. He works closely with a deputy chair/CEO who in turn supervises a managing director. Supporting their work are corporate departments organized by functions: tax, finance and management control, corporate communications, administrative systems, and human resources. The managing director has responsibility for additional functional support departments such as logistics and manufacturing.

Inditex also participates in strategic alliances. For example, they formed a strategic alliance with Italian Percassi group to reduce risk when developing the Zara brand in Italy.

Advantages of a functional structure on a global level are several: everyone knows her/his function; it makes good use of technical people and/or their specialized skills and knowledge; it limits resource duplication and permits the company to operate with a relatively lean managerial staff; and it allows for tight and centralized control over decisions. For example, hiring can be centralized with all applications, interviews, and hiring occurring in a single place. This model also allows the top executive to coordinate among functional areas.

The functional structural form also has disadvantages. For example, as a company grows or expands worldwide, it becomes more difficult for a single functional leader to manage everything. Thus, it may not be suited for a company that intends to grow. Functional specialization can lead to jealousies, particularly if resources are disproportionately allocated among functions. The functional structure also can create operational difficulties. For example, putting operations/production and marketing in different departments may make it difficult to manage product lines that require close coordination between marketing and production.

Further it may be difficult to coordinate among units that operate at great distances or when practices differ on a global scale. An example is that cost practices for accounting functions are difficult to coordinate globally because nations impose different requirements. Another disadvantage of this structural form is that new ideas may not be brought into the organization when functional specialists hire people trained to think like they do. Finally, if organizations do not reassign managers to other specialties or new locations they may lose opportunities to train senior managers for a more global world.

Divisional Structure

Organizations also can be divisionalized such that each role beneath that of top managers has authority for one or more divisions. Divisionalization can and does occur in several ways, principal ways to divisionalize are by product service lines, by geographic location, or took by customer such as industrial customers and consumers.

In 2003, toy manufacturer Mattel took a *product line* approach to divisionalization by structuring its activities around three product groups: a) the girls' division, b) the infant and preschool division, and c) the boys' entertainment, games and, puzzles division. It makes sense that Mattel—parent to the Barbie doll—concentrates on toys for girls in one division because a significant portion of Mattel products are for girls. What this example demonstrates is that Mattel continues to focus significant resources on the Barbie doll and girls' toys upon which the company was built. Figure 12.3 shows another way to structure around product divisions; it suggests that the three main products for a hypothetical cosmetics firm are fragrances, skin care, and hair care, and a fourth division contains everything else such as nail care and insect repellent.

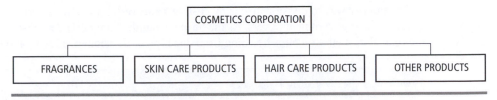

Figure 12.3 *Product division structure*

Another way to divisionalize is based on geographic areas served. Figure 12.4 represents divisionalization by *geographic area* because we see that it lists a Vice President for North America, another for Europe, a third for East Asia, and a fourth for Australasia. Reporting to each of these Vice Presidents are country managers. One example is shown under Australasia. In the boxes extending downward from Australasia, we see that functions such as marketing are managed within each country. We can assume that this would also be true for other geographic divisions in the same firm. An example of a company that uses a geographic divisional structure is Honda Motor Company. This company shifted to a geographic divisional structure in the early 1990s to correspond with different regions of the world they served: North America, Europe/Middle East/Africa, South America, Asia/Oceania and Japan. The purpose of this reorganization was to place decision-making responsibility for sales, manufacturing, and research in each region.

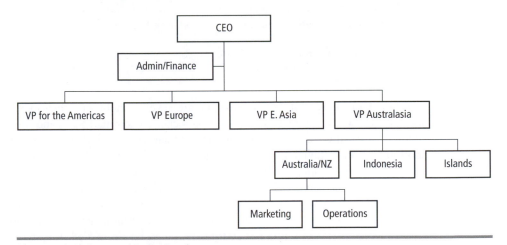

Figure 12.4 *Geographic divisional structure*

The Mattel example above showed that the girls' division remains high in company priorities. The visual of a geographic divisional structure shows that four geographic divisions are important enough to the firm to be part of the formal structure. This could mean that the firm operates only in those four regions. Other companies might geographically divisionalize with more nations or regions or fewer.

Yet another way to divisionalize is by *customers served*, for example commercial users, consumers, or government buyers. As the boxed example from P&G demonstrates, companies can alter their structures by going from one type of divisionalization to another.

P&G Alters Its Divisional Structure

In September 1998, P&G (Procter & Gamble) announced plans to revamp its corporate structure to boost sales and bring products to market faster. According to its annual report, the reorganization was expected to shift to product-based global business units of food and beverage, laundry and cleaning, paper, or beauty care with each of the four senior executives taking global responsibility for one product category. Prior structural arrangements followed a geographic divisionalization with senior executives responsible for North America, Asia, Latin America, and Europe, the Middle East, and Africa. According to a *Wall Street Journal* report:

> *Under the current structure, a P&G laundry product in Europe might compete for marketing funds against P&G diaper or tissue products in the region. Under the new organization, P&G will make decisions based on the company's global strategy for each product category rather than the spending levels of a particular region. In addition, P&G will create a global business services organization, bringing together business services such as finance, accounting and information technology that currently are dispersed throughout P&G's structure. By 2004, P&G had restructured again. Like many other global firms, they continually adapt their structure to meet organizational needs.*

Source material: Tara Parker-Pope (1998, Sept. 2) P&G, in effort to give sales a boost, plans to revamp corporate structure. *The Wall Street Journal*, p. B6.

General advantages of divisionalization are several, including: they locate functional specialties where they are needed (as we see occurs when marketing and operations concentrate on Australia and New Zealand) rather than organizing them in a central location; spotlighting those divisions most important to the firm provides a good way to remain focussed on what is important (four divisions in the visual); it becomes possible to measure performance by division; and the company can develop a unified approach to cover all divisions. Further, it may be easier to clarify goals and objectives within divisions, decision authority is moved downward such that decisions affecting a particular division are made closer to customers, and intraunit coordination may be simplified. Finally, a geographic divisional structure helps the company train executives worldwide, and this is important if the company believes that cross-national activities will remain important to its success.

However, as is true for any structural arrangement, the divisional form also has disadvantages, such as: often a large staff is needed for purposes of coordination; there may be costly forms of duplication, particularly if each division services its own functional needs, e.g., marketing; and divisions may become too independent, particularly if the division's competencies are distinctive or if it is difficult for the home office to communicate with the division because of geographic distance. This independence can prove costly if divisions compete with one another, if headquarters' managers over rely on poor information that division managers supply, or if division managers put local concerns ahead of needs the company may have to succeed globally. A particular disadvantage of geographic divisionalization occurs when managers perceive it to be more advantageous to work at headquarters rather than gain experience in other nations.

Family-owned Businesses

Most family-owned businesses operate solely in their nations of origin, but a growing number are global. About a third of listed companies in the *Fortune* 500 are family led. In Europe, 43 of Italy's top 100 firms are family owned; in France 26 of the top 100 are family owned; and in Germany 17 of the top 100 (Becht et al., 2003). The general information dearth for family-owned firms applies to governance and organizational structures.

Family-owned firms are typically managed by one or several members of the founding family, for example Ferrero. When the founding matriarch or patriarch is at the head of the organization the governance structure is fairly clear: papa or mama makes all the decisions; children and others follow their lead. This sometimes makes managing family-owned firms more complex than a firm with no family involvement because managers must manage family relationships as well as business relationships (Cadbury, 2000).

Governance characteristics of family-owned firms are several, depending on the stage of their development. The founder usually builds the firm as an owner and a manager in charge of everything. When the original owner dies or steps aside, he or she often leaves the company to children who operate the business as partners. When the reins are passed to the next generation, there may be many more children or grandchildren involved in management. Sometimes there are competing factions in the family. In the latter case, organizational structure may become less formal to allow fluid information exchange and decision sharing among family members. The latter structural arrangement tends to break down with future generations that involve marriages and involvement of ever more family members. Sometimes the company dissolves, other times it is retained but sold to a bigger company with professional management. In still other cases, the family-run firm continues and is managed or significantly influenced by family members.

Continued operation of a global family-owned firm usually requires that the firm adopt more formal structural mechanisms that include a Board of outside directors, a logical structure that separates strategic and operational responsibilities, and transparent recruiting and promotion policies that attract qualified employees (Cadbury, 2000). Without the latter, the family-owned firm might find it impossible to recruit desirable outside managers. The formal structures that family-owned firms adopt can be the same as those found in publicly owned firms, that is functional or divisional structures, or they may be hybrids of them. However, just as with all other firms, family-owned firms select or create any kind of structural configuration.

A Holding Company

A holding company is created when a company buys stock in other firms to gain voting control. Usually the holding company has majority voting control over a number of different entities. This occurs in the global advertising industry among firms like Omnicom and WPP that hold many different advertising companies located around the world.

Omnicom's Holding Company Structure
Global growth at advertising agency Omnicom has come through acquisitions of top advertising firms. To preserve the distinct character and creativity of each acquired firm, Omnicom is organized as a holding company. At the top of the organization are the Board and CEO and a layer of executive vice presidents who coordinate among businesses held: BBDO Worldwide, DDB Worldwide, DAS, TBWA Worldwide, and OMD Media Agency. The Worldwide companies all organize according to geographic divisions such as BBDO Taiwan and BBDO Asia Pacific.

What distinguishes the holding company structurally is that each company owned by the parent holding company functions as a distinct legal entity (Shim, 1989). Typically companies held within the holding-company portfolio are allowed management latitude that lets them structure their own activities. Within the same holding-company portfolio this could mean the portfolio contains one company structured functionally, another divisionalized by product, another divisionalized by geographic area, and a fourth that uses a matrix or some other hybrid form. Any study of the structure of a holding company therefore requires that one look at more than one of the companies held before reaching conclusions about structural configurations.

Advantages of a holding company are that it allows a company to use a small investment to control a large amount of assets. A holding company also protects the parent against some amount of financial risk because failure in one company does not cause the failure of others or of the holding company. In the case of a single failure, the holding company only loses its investment in the failed business. A final advantage is that no stockholder or management approval is required for purchasing sufficient stock to gain control over another firm.

A disadvantage of a holding company is that it is usually more expensive to administer each company because each operates according to its own charter and its own management prerogatives. This makes it almost impossible for holding companies to realize economies of scale or scope.

Divisional/Functional Hybrid Structures

Above we saw that there are advantages and disadvantages associated with both functional and divisional organizational structures. Some organizations attempt to maximize advantages and minimize disadvantages by creating hybrids. One type of hybrid combines the divisional and functional forms by putting roles associated with each on the same level (see example in Table 12.5).

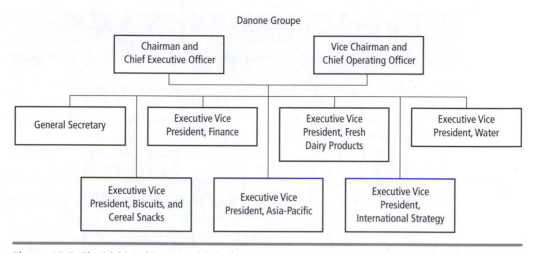

Figure 12.5 *The Divisional/Functional hybrid structure*

An advantage of the hybrid, for example combining divisional and functional features at the same structural level, is that it allows the organization to create a structure that best serves multiple needs. In the Danone example, placing products such as fresh dairy, water, and biscuits and cereal snacks on the same level as functions of finance and international strategy and the Asia-Pacific geographic region suggests that managers believe each to be equally important to success. A unique structure such as this may indicate that the organization does not feel bound by tradition or specialist training. It also could signal that the organization is willing to take risks to meet its objectives. Emerging structural hybrids are expected to address problems created with centralized and/or decentralized structures, but these alterations may create new challenges as well.

COMMON FEATURES OF "STAND ALONE" STRUCTURES

The many structures described above illustrate many differences, but they all have three common features. First, all are "stand alone" companies that preserve or protect organizational autonomy. That is, in consultation with their boards, top managers make autonomous decisions about the firm. Second, they all demonstrate fairly clear relationships meant to guide employee activities. Third, all are hierarchical in nature, meaning that decisions flow principally from the top to the bottom of the organization. Wherever practiced, this hierarchical form is often referred to as a bureaucracy. Its defining features are ones outlined by German theorist Max Weber who argued that this top-down hierarchical form is most efficient. The bureaucratic ideal is the pyramid-shaped hierarchy that remains popular today; it is sustained by clear divisions of labor, authority, and control, and supported by written rules and regulations.

Features of Bureaucracy and Scientific Management as "One Best Way"
1 Division of labor or specialization occurs—people are trained as experts in narrow areas.
2 Tasks are standardized to perform the same job in exactly the same way.
3 Hierarchy of authority is established.
4 Unity of command is established so no employee answers to more than one boss.
5 Span of control is limited to no more than 7 for any one supervisor.
6 Line and staff responsibilities are divided—line makes decisions, staff advises.
7 Decentralization locates authority at the lowest level possible without losing control over critical issues.
8 Structure is established according to purpose, function, geography, or by customer served to organize work in logical groupings.
9 Activities of the manager include planning, organizing, leading, coordinating, controlling.

John Fernandez (1991) identified five reasons it may be less possible to derive efficiencies from traditional hierarchical work arrangements today:

1 Rules rarely address unanticipated events; they are not flexible.
2 Rules can stifle creativity and innovations.
3 Needs for thinking may be limited by specialization.
4 Bureaucracies rarely encourage cooperation, teamwork or open communication.
5 Bureaucracies tend to create a sense of internal competition leading to win/lose positions even within organizations.

Although there may be limits for what bureaucracy can accomplish, most organizations are structured at least to some extent along hierarchical lines. This occurs in part because as organizations grow on a global scale, they have greater need for structural mechanisms that can help them remain efficient. This suggests that principles of bureaucracy have at least some currency today. At the same time, organizations face growing challenges to adopt new structural forms as well.

WHY ORGANIZATIONS RESTRUCTURE

Restructuring often results from global shifts and firms' efforts to adapt to them. For example, the late 1990s witnessed tremendous growth in merger and acquisitions activities as firms expanded into increasingly global industries. Mergers and acquisitions almost always lead to restructuring because existing organizations have to make room in the existing structure for the companies they have bought. Global competition that tends to drive down prices also leads to cost-containment efforts that often include restructuring to remove management layers.

Global competition also leads to top-management turnover. When this occurs, restructuring often follows with new managers who want to reshape the enterprise in their own image. These are only a few of the major reasons why restructuring occurs in global enterprises. Restructuring also affects processes and people. The interconnections among people, processes, and structures necessarily call on the former to adjust when the latter is changed. The example below describes changes that followed restructuring at FedEx.

More than a Simple Change

In 2000, FDX Corporation announced restructuring plans to combine the company's two primary brands: airfreight provider FedEx and ground-delivery provider RPS. The reorganization came on the heels of a public stock offering for competitor UPS that some feared would leave Federal Express in the dust. This reorganization meant top-management changes, but also affected some 4,000 sales people who'd previously sold FedEx and RPS services on separate teams. Affected processes included merging invoices for air and ground delivery into a single bill.

Source material: Rick Brooks (2000, Jan. 17) FDX plans restructuring of sales force. *The Wall Street Journal*, p. A3.

In summary, global shifts stimulate restructuring. The greater complexity faced by global enterprises calls on managers to consider structural alternatives to bureaucratic ones. It is this complexity that motivates many managers to adopt new structural forms or create hybrids of existing forms. These hybrids call for managers who are able to think "outside the box" of tradition—whatever that tradition may be. Leif Melin (1992) observes that firms can best expand beyond domestic bases by adopting a dynamic and complex view of organizations incorporating heterogeneity and diversity.

Within the last decade, suggested alternatives to existing structural arrangements have focussed on sustaining efficiency while also introducing flexibility. Additionally, there is much greater emphasis on using structure to integrate functions. Some emphasize shorter, flatter visualizations rather than a pyramid; others distribute decision-making; and others forge multiple rather than one-way relationships among people. Internal forms of restructuring include matrix structures, flat or horizontal structures, inverted pyramids, networks, spiderwebs, shamrocks, and virtuality. Sometimes integration comes from internal restructuring and other times it comes from external restructuring such as strategic alliances and joint ventures.

Intraorganizational Networks

Matrix Structure

Like hybrids, a matrix structure is intended to combine the advantages of different structures. Perhaps because they offer a way to manage the complexity usual to global enterprises, matrix structures were adopted by global giants such as Ford and Asea Brown Boveri. However, after several years of managing complex matrices, both Ford and ABB reduced the scale of their matrix designs. For example, ABB created a single layer of people between the top level and 1,300 operating units worldwide, retaining only 175 people in their Geneva headquarters. This suggests that a matrix form of structure such as in Figure 12.6, may be difficult to manage in the long-run.

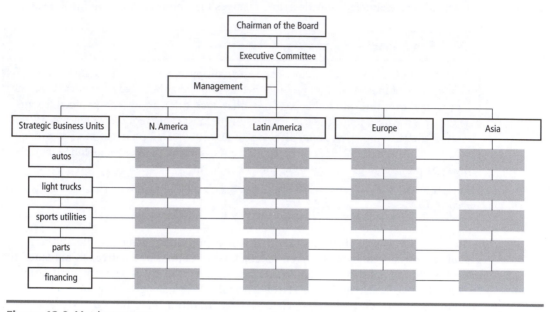

Figure 12.6 *Matrix structure*

In the matrix, people who "belong" in each strategic business unit also report to project teams that operate on either a relatively permanent or a temporary basis. For example, in the sample matrix structure in Figure 12.6 we see that work is organized by strategic business units (SBUs) on the vertical and by geographic divisions on the horizontal. What occurs is that members of the auto SBU team from various regions collaborate with one another on autos. In doing so, they generate cross-region synergies that could lead to development of a new automobile with attributes desirable in most or all nations served. At other times members of the auto team will meet with members of other product groups such as light trucks, SUV, financing to explore product-line synergies.

The auto illustration provides only one example. Bear in mind that a matrix could also be organized in other ways as well, for example with functional groups on the horizontal and geographic teams on the vertical. The point of the matrix is that the organization believes it can better achieve its objectives by combining functions, products, and divisions rather than having a single one dominate.

Integrative representation across groups is intended to reduce rivalry between groups; has the capacity to focus on requirements of external markets; and may promote creativity and flexibility less usual in a more bureaucratic structure. The teams created through matrix structure can be very innovative when ideas are traded freely between products, divisions, or geographic areas. However, there are also disadvantages with a matrix structure which include: the difficulty some people have when reporting to more than one boss (as would occur in the example in Figure 12.6 when the same person answers both to an SBU team and a geographic team); individual rewards are less likely because results emerge from a team; and many people prefer stability and control over their own destiny and therefore do not like to change groups frequently as can occur in a matrix. Finally, a matrix form of structure increases complexity for individuals located within the matrix and for top managers who oversee them.

Because they can be unique, hybrids usually force the organization to learn by doing. They often require experimentation as well as frequent visits and both telephone and e-mail messages among people involved in the hybrid. Ideally these informal forms of communication can improve flexibility without giving up useful controls.

Internal Networks

Ram Charan (1991) believes that as compared to traditional corporate structures, networks have the ability to muster the speed, focus, and flexibility needed to succeed in a dynamic world. Based on his studies of networks in ten large companies, for example Du Pont and CIGNA, Charan concluded that internal networks are relatively permanent structural arrangements intended to deliver on some aspect of corporate strategy. They are developed by senior managers to create a boundary-spanning structure composed of a select group of managers—usually no more than 100 or fewer than 25—whose skills and abilities are drawn from across the company's functions, units, geography, and existing hierarchy.

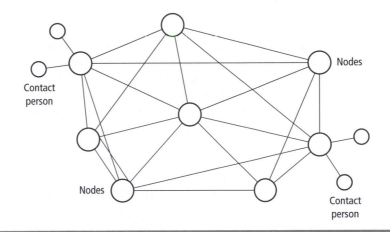

Figure 12.7 *Spiderweb network structure*

Source material: J.B. Quinn, Philip Anderson, and Sydney Finkelstein (1996) Leveraging intellect. *Academy of Management Executive*, 10 (3): 21.

A major purpose of an internal network is to transcend borders of functional or departmental interests, but other purposes include empowering managers to talk openly, build trust, and improve the quality of decisions by including more people in those decisions. Finally, and quite unlike the static nature of a traditional hierarchy, internal networks are dynamic because they permit information flows and decisions to travel in many directions at the same time.

Structural Contingencies for Knowledge Work

James Quinn et al. (1996) conclude that organizations based on professional intellect will continue to use hierarchical structures. However, professional knowledge in service industries like airlines, healthcare, and brokerage requires different structural forms. These forms will leverage intellect by removing hierarchical layers and pushing responsibility to the point of contact with customers. According to these authors, the spider's web form of the Internet allows information to wander freely, and it can be adapted to organizations. The free flow of information among subsidiaries and units in multiple locations in the same organization can be harnessed around single problems or challenges, but as Quinn et al. note, its success depends on individual identification with the problem at hand and a sense of interdependency. In a globalizing world, the network, shown in Figure 12.7, applies not only to organizations, but can be used to describe how dissimilar organizations coalesce around issues of common concern such as human rights or work conditions.

Source material: J.B. Quinn, Philip Anderson, and Sydney Finkelstein (1996) Leveraging intellect. *Academy of Management Executive*, 10 (3): 7–27.

An example of interlinkages appears in a structural arrangement that Philips developed some years ago (see Figure 12.8). The circles represent operating units and lines show relationships between them; some subsidiary relationships are facilitated through headquarters, for example South Africa and the UK, and others bypass headquarters, for example Japan and the US. These different linkages accommodate differences between Philips' operating units which range from single-function operations responsible only for research and development to large, fully integrated companies responsible for R&D, production, and marketing. Evidence of similar differentiated networks in large MNEs from all over the world, including Procter & Gamble, Unilever, Ericsson, NEC, and Matsushita led Ghoshal and Bartlett (1990) to argue that convergence toward patterns of linkages in many businesses may be indicative of broader and global societal changes.

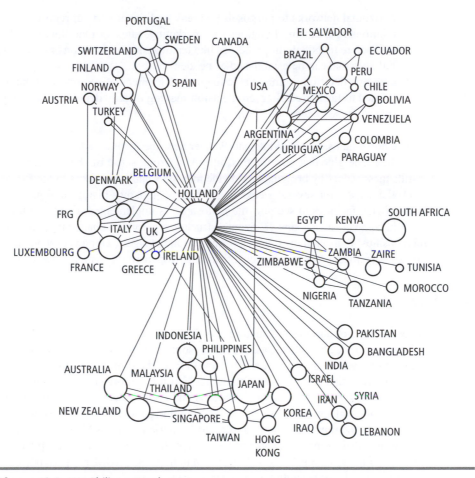

Figure 12.8 *N.V. Philips network structure*

Source material: S. Ghoshal and C. Bartlett (1990) The multinational corporation as an interorganizational network. *Academy of Management Review*, 15 (4): 605.

Horizontal Structure

Roderick White and Thomas Poynter (1990) believe a horizontal or "flat" structure makes it possible to respond to multiple and competing demands of worldwide integration in some lines and local responsiveness in others. Characteristics of the global horizontal structure include:

1 lateral decision processes bring together those most affected by decisions to collaborate on key issues that facilitate product flow, develop and adjust overlapping programs that deploy resources, and share information and knowledge;

2 horizontal networks to purposefully break traditional vertical reporting relationships, causing functions like marketing, sales, or manufacturing to operate as discrete units; lateral processes like teaming across functions provide flexible linkages that can be established as needed;

3 common decision premises able to cross differences of geography or nationality are needed to facilitate congruent decision-making usually depend on a strong and shared sense of corporate purpose.

The horizontal structure White and Poynter describe focusses attention where it is needed and when. The glue that ensures flexibility is a strong sense of shared values. Matsushita instills these values by bringing worldwide managers and supervisors to their training center in Osaka, Japan, for several weeks to study the company's history and philosophy. Then trainees visit factories to see how the philosophy is implemented. Dow also trains its managers in company philosophy. Horizontal structure represents a change in more than reporting relationships; it also requires process-oriented top managers, employees who share information and other resources, and personal flexibility responsive to changing demands.

Virtual Structure

A special case of horizontal structure is called the virtual corporation—organizations that exist more in electronic and occasional personal linkages than in geographic place. The concept of a virtual organization is borrowed from the term "virtual memory," describing configurations that cause a computer to act as if it has more storage capacity than it does (Byrne, 1993). As applied to organizations and their structures, it suggests an organization can be configured to appear to be something more than what objectively exists. Virtual organizations have been described in myriad ways as "lean" or "flat," as a conglomeration of companies brought together to serve a temporary purpose, or as a vertically integrated entity (Davidow and Malone, 1992). IBM's experience demonstrates one way a virtual organization can be structured.

Virtual Ambras
IBM's Ambras subsidiary adopted a virtual structure to market IBM personal computer clones. The firm drew on the core competencies of six independent companies to market a clone to almost any specification. Managers were in North Carolina, designers were in Singapore, but telemarketing, order taking, and final assembly were performed by other firms
Source material: S. Goldman (1994, July) Agile competitive behavior: Examples from industry. *Agility Forum Working Papers*, pp. 1–30.

The Ambras example shows the virtual organization need not exist in physical space, but it does require at least a core group of people who focus on strategic priorities.

Employees may be contract workers, often working from home via telecommuting technologies to complete work independent of constraints like place and time. By integrating computers and communications technologies, these contract workers become part of an entity that can be assembled and disassembled almost instantly. When people are not in the same place or work in different time zones throughout the world, it can be difficult to create processes like culture that reinforce a common sense of organizational purpose. This cultural challenge is exacerbated by a structural challenge that is in turn likely to alter processes and people willing to be part of the virtual corporation.

External Networks

The examples above describe activities that interconnect people internally. Other structural arrangements such as keiretsu and chaebol interconnect organizations externally.

Keiretsu and Chaebol

Keiretsu are a structural form unique to Japan partially adapted by South Korean chaebols. Keiretsu roots emerged in the late 1800s when the Japanese government developed industries such as shipbuilding that were then sold and managed as businesses. Efforts to build these industries and firms included government/business interconnections as well as business-to-business collaboration. These collaborative activities helped keiretsu develop into large informal networks of mutually supportive companies in a family of firms that usually include industrial firms, banks, trading houses, suppliers, and buyers. Close and ongoing relationships among keiretsu members develop trust and provide mechanisms for resource sharing. For example, 2003 losses due to bad debts at Mizuho—the world's largest bank—were covered with funds raised through keiretsu links. Similarly, a poorly performing company within a keiretsu might be supported with profits generated elsewhere in the same keiretsu group.

By the 1960s, the Japanese economy was dominated by large keiretsu like Mitsubishi, Fuyo, Toshiba, and Hitachi that forged clear links between business, government, and society. These were organized around different activities such as production, financing, distribution. Most encouraged internal loyalty and trust with practices such as lifetime employment and seniority-based promotions.

Chaebol are South Korean conglomerates developed along similar lines as keiretsu to concentrate resources. Most chaebol are family owned, decisions often are made outside public view, and activities may not be transparent. Recent government pressures on chaebol caused Daewoo to disband and encouraged other large chaebols to break with traditions. In 2003 government pressures on chaebol led to a full-scale investigation of six of the nation's biggest conglomerates including Samsung, LG Group, and Hyundai Group (South Korea moves, 2003). In response to these pressures, many chaebols restructured into holding companies. Once viewed as a key reason for national business success, keiretsu and chaebol face challenges in a more global world. For example, shareholders demand short-term income, and financial markets scrutinize credit ratings. Strong internal links among keiretsu partners may impede collaborative arrangements with firms outside Japan. For example, some believe that strong partners within the Mitsubishi keiretsu were an impediment to the failed external partnership with DaimlerChrysler (Bremner and Edmonson, 2004).

Interorganizational Networks

Sumantra Ghoshal and Christopher Bartlett (1990) believe that external and internal relationships for the same organization can be thought of as an interorganizational network capable of sustaining tight links in some parts of the world or among some products as well as looser links along other product or national lines.

The following example of IBM's 1996 restructuring illustrates how internal and external restructuring can occur simultaneously, often creating new questions and concerns as existing challenges are addressed.

IBM Alters Internal and External Structural Relationships

IBM products traditionally were sold through a special IBM sales force called "blue suits" because organizational culture at IBM traditionally reinforced blue suits as the norm. But many traditions changed at IBM to make it a more global company. First there was an external shift. Globalization of the computer industry produced thousands of independent distributors with a broader reach than a single firm. Like many other firms, IBM found it could sell more computers through distributors than through "blue suits" alone. Accordingly, IBM restructured the firm, creating a new position to oversee "direct" worldwide sales. This change represented an alteration in external relationships as boundaries between IBM sales agents and distributors became less clear. The internal adjustment was elimination of overlapping responsibilities and greater accountability for sales and service. By 2005 IBM undertook additional restructuring to accommodate its growing emphasis on business services.

Source material: Bart Ziegler (1996, Dec. 13) IBM revamps global units, sets one brand. *The Wall Street Journal*, A3.

Strategic Alliances

In the 1980s, strategic alliances began to grow in numbers. James and Weidenbaum describe strategic alliances as "cooperative, flexible arrangements, born out of the mutual need of firms to share the risks of an often uncertain marketplace by jointly pursuing a common objective" (1993: 61). Growth and expansion is costly not only because of fiscal concerns, but because expansion into new nations carries learning costs associated with culture, local conditions, politics, economics, and human resource management. Both economic and learning costs are reasons for firms to form strategic alliances. According to Farok Contractor and Peter Lorange (1988: 9), other reasons for structuring cooperative relationships include:

1 risk reduction
2 economies of scale and/or rationalization
3 technology exchange
4 co-opting or blocking competition
5 overcoming government mandates, trade or investment barriers
6 facilitating initial international expansion of inexperienced firms
7 vertical quasi-integration advantages of linking the complementary contributions of partners in a value chain.

According to Pekar and Allio (1994), a strategic alliance can include myriad non-equity as well as equity arrangements ranging from an independent entity in the form of an international joint venture to collaborative advertising, research and development partnerships, and cross-manufacturing, to name a few.

Arvind Parkhe (1991) believes competitive advantage depends not only on internal restructuring but also on structuring global strategic alliances (GSA) with other firms. According to Parkhe, diversity in reciprocal strengths and resources that lead to formation of an alliance can facilitate success, but diversity of societal, national, and organizational culture as well as diverse strategic directions and management practices in alliances could make them difficult to manage. He suggests these difficulties can be overcome with a commitment to organizational learning and a desire to create novel solutions to accommodate differences. Learning how to manage diversity from GSA experiences is important to firms in the long run, but the short-term costs of learning and the relative pain of working outside a known comfort zone may be a deterrent.

According to an early article on the topic, Perlmutter and Heenan (1986) observed that whether they were large or small, few firms could achieve industry leadership or be competitive globally without some set of global strategic partnerships (GSP) in their portfolios. Moreover, they observed that diverse backgrounds and cultures could lead to problems drawing attention to six areas:

1 Mission—each must be convinced the other has something they need and commit to a win/win sense of mission.
2 Strategy—must be clearly articulated to avoid intolerable overlaps between cooperation and competition.
3 Governance—observing that US firms historically harbor a belief in power over parity, they point out that the latter is the appropriate approach for collaborative arrangements.
4 Culture—the partners must be willing to shape a common set of values while also retaining national identities.
5 Organization—requires new organizational patterns capable of blending best practices of partners.
6 Management—unitary management methods must be adopted to reduce potential disputes.

At least initially, many were not enthusiastic about alliances. Porter (1990) viewed strategic alliances as risky and unstable arrangements inevitably dominated by the stronger partner. Further, early losses associated with strategic alliances often discouraged would-be allies. Television production is often used as an example. Once the bastion of television production, by 1994 the US had lost the capacity to manufacture televisions. Some believe the industry was undermined when RCA licensed color TV technology to a number of Japanese companies in the 1960s who copied the product, innovated, and successfully priced RCA and other manufacturers out of the market. Early experiments with cooperation in global markets favored partnerships between firms not otherwise competing. Backward or forward integration with suppliers and buyers to create just-in-time inventory systems are examples of alliances between non-competitors. The following example illustrates yet another form of alliance: cross-shareholding.

The GM-Fiat Cross-shareholding Alliance

Fiat's car division was the centerpiece of the Fiat dynasty—a model for powerful family firms in Europe. Led by Giovanni Agnelli, Fiat successfully expanded throughout Europe but by the late 1990s Fiat Auto car activities were generating losses. Family member Umberto proposed selling the auto division, but this was anathema to older brother Giovanni. Accordingly, Agnelli found a compromise to help Fiat "adapt to new global market conditions without selling the historical heart of the company." He agreed in 2000 to a cross-shareholding alliance that put 20 percent of Fiat's ownership into hands of General Motors' managers.

Source material: End of an era for European business. (2003, Jan. 25/26) *Financial Times*, p. 8.

Perhaps because of inexperience with them, organizations still face many challenges in structuring and managing alliances. Assessing internal needs and abilities to be part of an alliance, partner selection, relationship building, planning, and evaluating are challenges for formulating a joint venture.

Implementation is also problematic because partners with different national or organizational cultures produce managers with different views of what is normal, natural, or "right." Issues of control often are difficult to resolve, and cultural values can lead to different points of view on how people and processes should be managed. The success of alliances frequently depends on qualitative factors like trust and relationship building, but both are difficult to create when national or organizational cultures differ. Thus, forming an alliance by no means guarantees success. Further, success in strategic alliances appears to depend more on the "soft" side of management such as managing culture than on "hard" skills like financial acumen or technical expertise. Thus, the linear types of bottom-line decision-making that can more easily be made in a wholly owned subsidiary are complemented by cultural processes and less linearity in problem solving in cross-national strategic alliances. The following example demonstrates how cultures clashed in one strategic alliance.

Culture Clash at Triad

Siemens AG of Germany, Toshiba Corp. of Japan, and IBM of America joined forces as Triad to create a revolutionary computer memory chip, but culture clash among engineers and scientists impeded progress. Cultural groupings by nation created an "us versus them" atmosphere; imposing English as the common language was less comfortable for some than for others; and work habits differed. For example, Japanese were accustomed to working in open spaces and Germans were accustomed to windows, but Triad workers were assigned individual space without windows. This was more usual for US workers, but problematic for others. Communication styles also differed and were a barrier for information exchange. Thus, the structure selected affected work processes that in turn affected how people felt about the work.

The NUMMI GM/Toyota venture (New United Motor Manufacturing Inc.) was intended to blend the best of Japanese and US manufacturing practices in a car sold under both firm's names. The reality was that GM was unable to correct its weaknesses by venturing. The cars produced by NUMMI still sells six times as many cars under the Toyota name as with the GM name. Corning, on the other hand, successfully created and sustained alliances, defining itself as a network of organizations. Part of Corning's success with alliances may be that executives view alliances as long-term commitments. Corning seeks partners with compatible values and cultures, encourages 50/50 ownership, and clearly distinguishes the alliance from parent firms. In other words, alliances may be more successful when they are part of a longer-term vision.

IN A GLOBAL WORLD, WHAT STRUCTURE WORKS?

Examples above show that global businesses adopt many different organizational structures. Some rarely alter structure, others—like Exide—restructure with some frequency. A study of 778 major North American and European corporations revealed that half expected to alter their organizational structure within 3–5 years (Schellhardt, 1994), and a 1999 Conference Board survey noted that 85 percent of the global organizations they surveyed had restructured at least once in the 1990s (Getting a head, 1999).

One recommended structure for a global organization is to combine centralized decision-making within a worldwide product-division structure. But according to a 1993 McKinsey & Company study of the relationship between success and structural change, superior performance was not related to product or global divisions, centers of excellence, international business units, cross-border task forces, or globally integrated management information systems. These findings suggest that success depends on integrating structural form with people and processes. Table 12.1 shows that integration might also depend on how the company identifies itself as an entity. In practice, global managers increasingly mix structural forms by combining aspects of matrix with aspects of functional or divisional forms. These hybrids result in organizational charts that are necessarily "messier" than the charts shown above; they also are more challenging to manage.

Table 12.1 *Structure, strategy, and cultural behaviors appropriate to firms abroad*

	Domestic	**Multi-domestic**	**Multi-national**	**Global**
structure	centralized hierarchy	decentralized hierarchy	centralized hierarchy	networks and linkages
strategies for expanding beyond domestic markets	none	country specific; locally responsive	integrated worldwide	locally responsive and integrated worldwide
cultural perspective	parochial	culturally relative	HQ oriented	culturally synergistic
nature of cultural interactions	ignored	recognized but minimized	assimilated	source of organizational advantage
dynamics of cultural interaction	cultural dominance	cultural adaptation when necessary	cultural accommodation	cultural synergy, collaboration; learning

Source material: Nancy J. Adler and Susan Bartholomew (1992) Academic and professional communities of discourse: Generating knowledge on transnational human resource management. *Journal of International Business Studies*, 23 (3): 551–569.

CHAPTER SUMMARY

Organizational purpose is achieved in part via structural arrangements that outline the relationship between people and their jobs. Structural and other important organizational decisions are governed by a Board of Directors who ultimately answer to owners/shareholders and to an increasingly attentive public.

Global firms adopt structures that help them integrate functions, products/services, and nations worldwide, but they find that any structural form has advantages and disadvantages.

Restructuring often follows when: the company is involved in a merger or acquisition; when price competition necessitates removing organizational layers; and when there is top management turnover.

In general, more complex structural forms that integrate externally as well as internally tend to be more difficult to manage than simpler forms.

Although there is no single "best" global structure, there is evidence that global managers increasingly mix structural forms by combining aspects of matrix with aspects of functional or divisional forms. These hybrids result in charts that are somewhat "messier" than hierarchical charts. The challenge of mixed structures is that they are more complex to manage and they still are imperfect in balancing coordination and control.

REVIEW AND DISCUSSION QUESTIONS

1 Sony announced restructuring plans in 1999, and again in 2002 and 2003. Conduct research on Sony to analyze what structural plans they announced. What are the likely reasons for Sony to restructure so frequently?

2 In what ways might governance practices in family-owned firms help and hinder them when they go global?

3 Conduct research on keiretsu or chaebol to examine current relationships between these structural forms and their sponsoring governments.

4 Exide produces revenues, but it has not reported a profit since 1998. Conduct research on Exide better to understand the purpose behind its frequent restructuring efforts; also examine the effects on people and the results from the EXCELL improvement process it introduced.

Chapter 13
LEADERS, MANAGERS, CAREERS AND GLOBAL HUMAN RESOURCE SYSTEMS

LEADERS AND MANAGERS WORLDWIDE

In 1998, Motorola was counted among the largest semiconductor producers in the world. It was also well known for telecommunications products such as pagers, two-way private radios, and cellular phones. With annual sales of $27 billion (63 percent of them in foreign markets) and over 142,000 employees worldwide, Motorola's leaders implemented a global vision. For example, there were ambitious goals to hire more diverse employees worldwide. Worldwide training also had grown to include 14 locations worldwide whose activities consumed 4 percent of Motorola's annual payroll (as compared to the 1 percent of payroll most US firms allocate to training). For example, every employee worldwide was expected to complete at least 40 hours of classes per year. Employees could study English as a second language, creativity and innovation, and myriad other topics. Top managers often concentrated their training efforts on skills development such as envisioning the future. One example was a computer-based simulation full of external disasters like bankrupt customers and factory fires and internal shocks including a fired CEO. By 2003, competitors surrounded the company, Motorola had spun off its semiconductor unit, and revenues had fallen below 1998 levels. The somewhat plodding, engineering-driven culture that characterized Motorola left the company in the dust behind competitors in the fast-moving consumer electronics industry. CEO Christopher Galvin was replaced with Ed Zander who as president of Sun Microsystems had developed a reputation as an operational and marketing expert with a knack for developing new products. Market analysts argue that Zander's success depends on returning the company to profitability and the crucial ability to "see around corners" (Memo to, 2003).

Gerald Borenstein's selection for Bandag's Hong Kong office seemed a perfect fit for company needs. Borenstein had authored the company's marketing plan for China, he had lived in another country, and he had years of experience at Bandag—the leading US maker of retread tires. Borenstein himself had good reasons to accept an overseas assignment: the job offered a promotion, and future opportunities because Bandag derived a growing percentage of its revenues from global markets. In addition, the compensation package was very attractive, including a fully paid three-bedroom apartment in high-cost Hong Kong, a full-time housekeeper, private schools for the children, and travel allowances. Together, the compensation package far exceeded those usual at the Muscatine, Iowa home office for Bandag. Soon after Borenstein arrived in Hong Kong, Asian sales began to slow and domestic competitive pressures increased. Borenstein found it difficult to cut costs fast enough to satisfy headquarters, and those who had selected Borenstein for the Hong Kong job had retired or been reassigned. Within 18 months, Borenstein's Hong Kong job had evaporated, and the company was unable to find a new assignment for him. The family packed their belongings and returned to the US to relaunch Borenstein's career (Kaufman, 1999).

Stephanie Thompson followed her route to the world through New Zealand. Born in a rural town on the South Island, Stephanie was electrified by possibilities introduced in a dynamic university class. After completing an international studies degree, Stephanie explored those options teaching English in Ecuador. Her relieved family welcomed her return at the end of a year from her big OE (overseas experience). They were filled with ▶

pride as one success followed another: budding career, completion of a part-time MBA program, a series of promotions. But Stephanie felt there was something missing in her life, and after some years decided to return to Latin America. It took time for her family to accept the decision, and even more time to liquidate her belongings, but Stephanie returned to Ecuador with high hopes. Stephanie's personal network helped her secure a job she had first seen posted on the Internet—a job requiring Spanish-language skills and business acumen.

As a brand-new graduate of an Indian engineering university, Rajat Das had looked forward to beginning his career with a global company. He viewed it as a challenge to take his first post in the Middle East where he would be a third-country employee—neither a citizen of the Middle Eastern country where he would work nor of the employing German company. After his arrival at his Middle East post, he reveled in the opportunity to work on diverse project teams assembled of engineers educated almost everywhere in the world. Rajat had no difficulty settling into daily life, in part because he, like other expatriates, lived in a compound populated almost entirely with foreign nationals. To relieve the monotony of compound living and encourage social interactions, employing companies often organized social events that brought people together outside of work. Through these events and work projects, over time Rajat developed many friendships with other expatriates. Rajat was especially close to two co-workers—a German and a Canadian—whose age, education, and experiences were very similar to his own. One evening as the three chatted about future travel plans, the German declared his intention to purchase a "round the world" ticket for his upcoming vacation leave. Rajat was surprised to learn that the German was earning more vacation leave than he'd been granted, and even more surprised to learn that the Canadian engineer also had more annual leave. He cautiously raised the question of compensation, and his heart sank when he learned that both also were earning far more pay than he. To himself, Rajat said: "But we do the same job! How can our employer pay the German and Canadian engineers so much more than I? It is not fair."

Source material: Jonathan Kaufman (1999, Jan. 21) The castaways: An American expatriate finds Hong Kong post a fast boat to nowhere. *The Wall Street Journal*, pp. A1, A6; Glenn M. McEvoy and Barbara Parker (2000) The contemporary international assignment: A look at the options. In Mark Mendenhall and Gary Oddou (Eds), *Readings and Cases in International Human Resource Management (3rd edition)*, pp. 470–486. Cincinnati, OH: South-Western College Publishing; Memo to: Ed Zander; Subject: Motorola. (2003, Dec. 29) *Business Week*, p. 44.

CHAPTER OVERVIEW

Global business leaders almost uniformly agree that processes as well as structures are developed, implemented, and sustained by people. This has led to a growing emphasis on the "people" component of organizations, starting with top managers. This chapter examines leadership theories and research on global leaders to show how the two relate. But in a rapidly changing global world—where flexibility is a critical variable, resources are less than abundant, and learning and thinking at all levels have become important—lower-level employees also are critical to organizational outcomes. Accordingly, this chapter examines skills and abilities required not just from global leaders, but also from managers and other employees. It also looks at how individuals can build careers for a global world. Finally, it examines the process of human resource management to explore how organizations develop people through global human resource systems.

LEADERSHIP THEORIES

Ralph Stodgill (1974) observed there are almost as many definitions of leadership as there are people defining it. In general, studies of leadership can be organized around four types of studies that concentrate on leadership traits, leadership styles, contingencies that shape leadership requirements, and "new" or transformational leadership.

Trait Theories

Traits theories tend to examine personal characteristics of leaders. These traits include unyielding ones such as height, gender, or national origins, those based on values such as honesty or integrity that are not easily changed, or those such as emotional or cultural intelligence that can be developed.

Jack Welch on Leadership Traits

Jack Welch, former CEO of General Electric, believes there are four essential leadership traits.

1 Leaders should have lots of positive energy because they love action and enjoy change.
2 Leaders should be able to energize others because they love other people and can inspire them to reach lofty goals.
3 Leaders have to have "edge" or the courage to make tough decisions.
4 Leaders also have to execute, making sure that the job gets done.

Source material: Jack Welch (2004, Jan. 23) Four E's (A jolly good fellow). *The Wall Street Journal*, p. A14.

Leadership Style

Studies of leadership style or type focus on leadership behaviors. Early studies at Ohio University and Michigan State University suggest that most leaders emphasize either task accomplishment or consideration for others. Charles Farkas and Philippe De Backer (1996) interviewed leaders on six continents to discover five different styles among global leaders:

1 Strategic: the CEO is the top strategist responsible for vision and an outline for implementation.
2 Expertise: the CEO focusses organizational attention as champion of a specific, often proprietary form of expertise.
3 Box: the CEO develops rules, regulations, procedures, and values to control behavior and outcome within defined boundaries.
4 Change: the CEO acts as a radical change agent to transform bureaucracy.
5 Human assets: the CEO manages success through promoting programs, principles, and policies in support of the organization's human resources.

Among companies in their sample, Farkas and De Backer observed that the Human Assets approach to leadership was most frequently used; this suggests that consideration is important to global leadership style. Thirty percent of those interviewed, including global leaders at PepsiCo and Gillette, used this leadership style because they believe that success depends on people. Accordingly, they emphasize teamwork, empower workers, and develop others to become future leaders.

Leaders believe that global changes will require them to adopt different behaviors from those used in the past. For example, 1,500 senior executives in 20 countries (Korn, 1988) believed that they would be required to communicate more with others and make fewer decisions on their own. Other examples are shown in Table 13.1.

Table **13.1** *Changing behaviors for CEOs*

Behavior	1988 (%)	2000 (%)
Communicates frequently with employees	59	89
Communicates frequently with customers	41	78
Emphasizes ethics	74	85
Conveys strong sense of vision	75	98
Makes all major decisions	39	21

Source material: Lester B. Korn (1989, May 22) How the next CEO will be different. *Fortune*, pp. 157–59.

CEOs in small businesses identified their top five leadership skills as: financial management, communication (including informing, listening, oral and written forms), motivation of others, vision, and motivating self (Eggers and Leahy, 1994). Few believe that communicating more frequently will displace traditional management functions of planning, delegating, coordinating, organizing, and controlling. But the mix of styles may change to include more people skills.

Contingencies for Leadership

Contingency approaches to leadership generally conclude that situational factors such as environmental context call for different types of leaders. A study of MBA students in 15 nations illustrates this point, showing that while leader goals are often perceived to be the same, for example growth of the business, or personal reputation, importance goal rankings differ by country. For example, "honor, face, reputation" are the fourth most important goal for leaders in Germany, the Netherlands, and China, but they are sixth on the list of goals important to US, British, and New Zealand leaders (Hofstede et al., 2002).

These data suggest that leaders from different parts of the world will pursue different goals based on national culture. Therefore, to be successful, leaders' goals should match national ones. That is, success is contingent on the match between leader goals and national goals.

Toyota Workers in Five Nations

Among contingencies to which managers adapt are differences in work behaviors among those employed. Toyota manufactures its products in much the same way worldwide, but their managers find that work behaviors and motivations differ significantly among workers at US, French, British, Thai, and Japanese plants. For example, high unemployment in France motivates workers to retain jobs; British workers have trade unions that make them less concerned about job loss. These examples illustrate that although they employ a global workforce, a global firm cannot assume that workers will be the same around the world. Toyota works to globalize its workforce through training programs that develop employees who share skills and Toyota work values.

Source material: James Mackintosh and Peter Marsh (2003, Mar. 2) French work harder than British, says Toyota. *Financial Times* (Electronic version).

Theories of "New" Leadership

Finally, the "new leadership" approach views the leader as someone who manages meaning by developing and articulating a vision others will follow (Bryman, 1996). This new leader is sometimes referred to as a transformational or connective leader (Lipman-Blumen, 2000). Transformational leadership is believed to have four dimensions (Bass, 1985):

- The transformational leader stimulates followers by questioning assumptions and encouraging new approaches to thinking and working.
- The transformational leader focusses on developing followers, using empathy, showing consideration, or demonstrating support for employees.
- The transformational leader has charisma—people want to follow this leader because he/she demonstrates an ideal of leadership.
- The transformational leader has a vision that energizes and inspires followers.

LEADERSHIP THEORIES AND THE SIX COMPETENCIES OF GLOBAL LEADERS

The following box shows that researchers use all four theoretical perspectives to describe the global leader.

Leaderships Competencies of Global Leaders

Stephen Rhinesmith (2000) identified six global competencies important to the global leader:

1 managing competitiveness by looking at the "big picture"
2 managing complexity
3 managing alignment
4 managing change
5 managing teams
6 managing learning by being open and learning globally.

In their study of senior executives for *Fortune* 500 firms, Black et al. (1999) identified four skills important to global leaders:

1 inquisitiveness
2 an ability to embrace duality
3 character to develop trust and goodwill among people from different cultural backgrounds
4 "savvy" that allows a leader to see what needs to be done and marshal resources for accomplishment.

Rosen et al. (2000) surveyed over 1,000 CEOs to identify four "literacies" important to the global leader. These comprise:

1 personal literacy, including understanding oneself and one's own limitations and abilities
2 social literacy, to assemble strong teams and unleash collective strength
3 business literacy, including understanding the organization and its environment
4 cultural literacy, including knowing about and leveraging culture differences.

Based on interviews with 101 executives who their firms deemed to be extremely successful, McCall and Hollenbeck (2002) describe seven general competencies for the global leader:

1 open-minded and flexible in thinking and tactics pursued
2 cultural interest and sensitivity
3 ability to deal with complexity
4 resilience, resourcefulness, optimism, and energy
5 honesty and integrity
6 a stable personal life
7 technical or business skills.

The Global Mindset

As a group, these studies affirm assertions from Chapter 1: the global manager has a global mindset. This mindset frames the way a global manager thinks which in turn shapes behaviors. For example, managers with a global mindset are able to sustain a broad view of the organization and keep the details in mind. A global mindset helps this leader balance contradictions the organization faces, encourages reliance on processes to achieve success, helps the leader accomplishes work through diverse teams, and makes it possible for the leader readily to embrace change. These orientations and the gestalt mindset help the global leader engage in proactive and visionary behaviors (Harveston et al., 2000). A global mindset is a leadership trait, but it also reflects new leadership because with it managers interpret the meaning of events. These several studies on global leaders demonstrate five additional competencies for the global leader.

Know the Business and its Environment

Studies of global leaders demonstrate that technical skills as well as knowledge about the business and its environment are critical for achieving organizational objectives. This ability is what Rosen et al. (2000) called business literacy or an understanding of the organization and its environment. Black et al. (1999) similarly call for "savvy" that helps a leader to see what needs to be done in the "big picture" and also marshal internal resources for task accomplishment. Among Rhinesmith's (2000) six competencies are two that fit into this category: align the organization with its environment and manage competitiveness by looking at the "big picture."

This leader attribute is consistent with contingency theories that view leadership as a highly complex interaction between an individual and the task and social environment (Fiedler and House, 1994; Fiedler, 1996). In a global world, these environments differ because each firm faces a unique array of political, economic, cultural, and other global realities. Every leader should be knowledgeable about business and its environment, but the global leader must frame this knowledge such that it encompasses activities occurring not just locally or internationally, but throughout the world. Extensive knowledge of a business and industry helps the manager recognize when change is occurring or anticipate it.

Create and Convey a Clear Vision with Integrity

Global leaders of both large (Korn, 1989) and small firms (Eggers and Leahy, 1994) have a clear sense of organizational purpose and are able to convey their vision to others. This is important because the manager's job is to accomplish organizational objectives through the work of others. The ability to convey a clear vision portrays the global leader as a manager of meaning; the ability to convey this vision with integrity emphasizes leadership traits. For some, purpose is wealth creation; for others purpose is more broadly defined to include the "character" that generates trust, honesty, and integrity in others (Black et al., 1999; McCall and Hollenbeck, 2002). It is therefore essential that the global leader convey a vision sufficient to direct people in their daily work to accomplish the organization's strategies.

Thailand's Leadership Training Centre

During Thailand's economic boom, many Thais worried that leaders had lost their moral compass. The Leadership Training Centre developed to help leaders rediscover a sense of social responsibility in business. During a leadership retreat, leaders are encouraged to rethink their business philosophies and working styles, recognizing that the quality of a leader is to serve others. According to Chamlong Srimuang who runs the Centre, business leaders too often serve only themselves as commanders or receivers. Leaders have to be efficient, but they also have to be good people who think about the lives of their employees. Leaders who complete the program are also expected to return to their workplaces with reinforced commitment to virtues such as gratitude and devotion to the world.

Source material: A Buddhist boot camp for Thailand's elite. (2003, Jan. 8) *Financial Times*, p. 9.

Integrity can include a commitment to business ethics, or greater commitment to the company and its people than to personal self-interest. For example, Jim Collins' high-performance corporations (2001) were led by CEOs whose ambitions focussed on the company rather than on themselves. Integrity and a clear sense of purpose can also help the global leader manage ethical challenges that arise when cultural practices and values differ (Black et al., 1999). An example of personal character and integrity is reflected by Norbert Reinhart's actions; the example appears below.

"Your Shift is Over"

These were the words Canadian mining executive Norbert Reinhart uttered when he replaced employee Ed Leonard who'd been held for hostage by a Colombian rebel group. When hostage negotiations failed to progress, Reinhart packed, kissed his family goodbye, and left for Columbia where he spent three months as a replacement hostage for Leonard.

Source material: Ed Ungar (1999, Mar. 22) A matter of honor. *US New and World Report*, p. 36.

Principles of Ethical Leadership

Behavior is one way to demonstrate integrity. Managers may be better able to develop and express integrity by engaging in behaviors based on five ethical principles (Northouse, 2004):

- Ethical leaders respect others. This means valuing others, affirming them as individuals, and listening to and giving credence to their ideas.
- Ethical leaders also serve others, often putting their employees' welfare ahead of their own. Activities that demonstrate service to others include mentoring, team building, involving self or others in community-building activities, and empowering others (Kanungo and Mendonca, 1996).
- Ethical leaders are concerned about creating and sustaining a just and fair workplace. Fairness can be demonstrated with selection or promotional processes that provide equal opportunity and with compensation policies that reward (and punish) people equally.
- Ethical leaders are honest. When leaders report information—even negative information—in a timely manner, employees' recognize that the leader can be trusted to tell the truth. A leader who does what he or she commits to doing or explains why change is necessary also reflects honesty.
- Ethical leaders build community by recognizing that the common good is best served with input from employees as well as the top manager. Community building rarely occurs when the leader imposes his or her will on others.

Develop Self-awareness and Understanding

A first step to conveying vision is for the manager to *have* a vision; this comes from self-awareness. The "personal literacy" Rosen et al. (2000) identified as important emphasizes self-knowledge. As they describe it, self-understanding means knowing one's strengths and being aware of limitations. Rhinesmith notes that careful thought and consideration characteristic of reflection is a key personal characteristic of the successful global manager. According to Rhinesmith: "Reflection ... enables one to weave some sense of development and progress into the fabric of one's life and the life of the organization and the people with whom one works" (1993: 31).

For some, reflection might mean simply musing, but according to Mintzberg and Gosling (2002), in the global learning context reflection means probing, wondering, analyzing, synthesizing, and even struggling to understand events and one's role in them. Knowing oneself and understanding what is valuable and important provides a way to recognize one's own frameworks. Having recognized those frameworks, the global leader can reach beyond a single set of assumptions to identify competing assumptions operating globally and in the organization. This attribute reflects a leadership trait.

Values

McFarland et al.'s (1993) interviews with 100 top leaders of global organizations and academic institutions identified some of the core values around which leaders rally their work forces. Integrity and honesty, openness and trust, teamwork, caring, customer focus, respect for the individual and diversity, innovation, social responsibility, and life balance were a few values these top leaders mentioned repeatedly. The authors compared core values like these with values more traditionally found in organizations; some examples appear in Table 13.2.

Table **13.2** *Barriers and winning values for leaders*

Barriers	Winning Values
Hidden agendas, dishonesty, lack of openness	Open, honest, and fluid communication
Prejudiced and judgmental	Embraces diversity and differences
Sets and follows strict rules and rigid policies	Is flexible, fluid, and rapidly responds to change
Engages in win/lose activities	Engages in win/win activities that can produce bigger organizations pay-offs

Source material: Lynne Joy McFarland, Larry E. Senn, and John R. Childress (1993). *21st Century Leadership*, p. 155. New York: The Leadership Press.

Movement toward more values-based leadership is also reflected in Stephen Covey's emphasis on moral renewal, Peter Senge's application of concepts like Servant-Leadership (Spears, 1995), or Bolman and Deal's call for *Leading with Soul* (1995). A desirable result of personal-growth movements is to help people interact successfully with others who are different, to be more tolerant of uncertainty and irresolution, and to create organizations capable of playing multiple roles. Examining self and examining organizations are critical to defining self and strategy in a global world.

Manage Diversity

The studies reviewed above also assert that global leaders must be able to manage diversity. Managers relate to diverse groups in varied settings, including in teams (Rhinesmith, 2000; Rosen et al., 2000) and with individuals from different cultures (McCall and Hollenbeck, 2002; Rosen et al., 2000). An ability to manage diversity well creates the goodwill that is needed to help people from different backgrounds work together on the same tasks (Black et al., 1999). Diversity is a critical characteristic of a global world and managing it is further explored in Chapter 14. Managing diversity reflects leadership style, but it is also consistent with personal traits such as interest in others or ability to listen.

Continuously Learn

Finally, because global conditions change frequently, the global manager must be a continuous learner. Lifelong learning drives most successful global managers who recognize they can always learn more (Rhinesmith, 1993). Inquisitiveness is a factor that aids learning. Conditions that enhance learning are being open to others and understanding there are many ways to manage the same challenge.

Continuous learning can be achieved through formal education or less formally with daily habits of reading, listening, and interacting. For example, interacting with people from other cultures helps the manager learn more about cultural differences. Learning new computer programs helps the manager understand the challenges that employees face. Finally, global managers must continually learn about themselves. These skills and competencies for managing global interconnections are additions to rather than substitutes for technical skills business leaders need.

Leaders Who Fail

Studies above emphasize traits, skills, and competencies of successful global leaders. Several researchers have examined why leaders fail. For example, Sydney Finkelstein studied over 60 companies and interviewed nearly 200 leaders better to understand leaders who fail. He concludes that failed CEOs are similar to successful ones in being intelligent and ethical. However, he found that failed managers often pay too little attention to information that does not confirm their vision, tend to over-identify with the company such that there are few boundaries between personal and company interests, and fail to take actions needed. Ram Charan and Geoffrey Colvin believe that bad execution—including not getting things done, being indecisive, or failing to fulfill commitments—is a key failing for CEOs.

Source material: Ram Charan and Geoffrey Colvin (1999, June 21) Why CEOs fail. *Fortune*, pp. 69–78; Sydney Finkelstein (2003) *Why Smart Executives Fail*. New York: Putnam/Portfolio.

Gender and Global Leadership

Women in many nations encounter glass ceilings to promotions and "glass walls" that prevent lateral transfers into line positions. Overall, women have made greatest progress at lower-level managerial positions worldwide, but most have some difficulty obtaining mid-level business positions and much greater difficulty reaching top-level positions. Cultural practices such as discrimination may account for the barriers that women face in becoming managers, and cultural stereotypes about women play a role in shaping the educational, legal, and organizational opportunities available to prepare women for leadership.

The result is relatively few female CEOs in global firms. By 2003 only six *Fortune* 500 firms were headed by women; and another 393 *Fortune* 500 firms counted no women among their top five executives (Jones, 2003). A similar picture emerges worldwide. Often when women are in charge of companies, it is because they are members of the company's controlling family.

Some believe that women's management styles, interests, and business approaches differ from men throughout the world (Gibson, 1995; Helgesen, 1990; Rosener, 1990). Helen Fisher (1999) believes that women are able to see the big picture and willing to consider multiple points of view, and that these attributes equip them for leadership in a complex global world. Observations of few or no gender differences among managers (Powell and Graves, 2003) lead others to argue that while there are distinctions between leaders, few are due to gender alone (Due Billing and Alvesson, 2000). For example, when asked to describe their weaknesses, female business leaders for *Fortune* 500 firms felt they most needed to soften styles associated with male leaders, such as being forthright, tough, or a ferocious competitor (Sellers, 2002).

Women Business Leaders

Studies of women leaders in both Europe and the US show enough similarities to encourage development of global advancement strategies for women working in global firms. Most aspire to reach top leadership, and believe they will be best able to achieve top posts by exceeding performance expectations, having a recognized expertise, and taking on high-visibility assignments. Both studies also describe similar barriers to advancement, such as stereotyping and misconceptions about women's roles and abilities, lack of female role models, and lack of significant experience in general management or line positions. Another barrier to women is that senior managers do not assume accountability for women's advancement. Exclusion from informal networks was reported as much more of a barrier for US women leaders than for European ones.

Source material: Catalyst (2003) *Women in Leadership: A European Business Imperative: 2002* and *Women in US Corporate Leadership: 2003*. New York: Catalyst.

LEADING AND MANAGING

Zaleznik (1990) and Bennis (1993) proposed several ways to differentiate between leaders and managers. For example, leaders produce significant change, develop long-term visions, and embrace chaos and empowerment. Managers, on the other hand, produce orderly results, concentrate on the short run, and maintain control. Leaders grow by overcoming and mastering painful experiences and crises, but managers paths often are linear and focussed on vertical advancement through the organizational hierarchy. These differences suggest that to become leaders managers must play one role and prepare for a different one.

Middle Managers

Pressures from the top and organizational downsizing have increased the size, scope, and importance of middle managers' roles (Floyd and Wooldridge, 1994; Kraut et al., 1989). According to Harry Levinson (1988), like top managers middle managers need to be authoritative some of the time and participative other times. Other challenges include: a) closer involvement with subordinates to create commitments, b) understanding subordinates' personalities, and c) dealing with more significant personality differences and resulting conflicts. Because of increased interdependence worldwide and growing diversity, many managers are part of culturally diverse workplaces, and many more will manage organizations in a global context in the years ahead. Bartlett and Ghoshal (1995) believe a people-centered entrepreneurial managerial philosophy and style is essential to their success.

Managing Globally

Nancy Adler and Susan Bartholomew (1992) believe that global competence for managers will require skills that transcend those of managers in domestic or even international markets. These skills include a global perspective, local responsiveness, synergistic learning that makes it possible to work with and learn from people from many cultures, and an ability to collaborate with others on an equal basis.

Kenichi Ohmae (1990) believes global managers can be from any country, but they typically speak more than one language fluently and have lived and worked in more than one country. Often they have multiple passports, and frequently they are the children of parents from different nations. Global managers must have a broad nonparochial view of the company and its operations yet a deep understanding of their own business, country, or functional tasks (Bartlett and Ghoshal, 1992b; Reich, 1991a). Like leaders, global managers need cultural sensitivity. Thus these various studies suggest that global managers need to develop some of the same skills and abilities of global leaders. The following box shows why some fail.

Why Managers Derail

Center for Creative Leadership studies identified six reasons that "derail" a manager on the way to senior leadership:

1 difficulty in molding a staff that could include choosing people too much like oneself or being authoritarian;
2 difficulty in making strategic transitions from details to big picture thinking or from getting things done to accomplishing work through others;
3 lack of follow through;
4 poor treatment of others;
5 over-dependence on a single skill or on a single boss;
6 disagreements with higher-level managers about how the organization should be run that might include inability to adapt to a boss with a different style.

Source material: M. Lombardo and C. McCauley (1988) *The Dynamics of Management Derailment* (Technical Report 34). Greensboro, NC: Center for Creative Leadership.

Divergence and Convergence in Managerial Competencies

Project GLOBE is a multi-method, multi-phrase research program to test relationships between culture and leadership effectiveness. Over 160 social scientists and management scholars participate in these series of studies. By 2004, researchers had gathered information from over 17,000 middle-managers from more than 900 corporations in food processing, finance, and telecommunications industries in 62 cultures. These managers answered according to both cultural practices (as they are) and cultural values (as they should be). Results published in the first comprehensive report on GLOBE (House et al., 2004) reflect variations in management practices worldwide. However, when asked to indicate what "should be," respondents showed convergent views. For example, on gender egalitarianism—the degree to which a collective group minimizes gender inequality—managers indicated that gender inequalities should be far less than now practiced. Similarly on humane orientation—the degree to which a collective encourages and rewards individuals for being fair, altruistic, generous, caring, and kind to others—the mean score on practices was a full point lower than the mean score on what "should be" practiced. These results suggest that current practices among managers are divergent cross-culturally, but values may be converging. A premise to be tested in later phases of the GLOBE project is the extent to which effectiveness is a function of the interaction between leader attributes and organizational contingences (House et al., 2002).

Regional Convergence: Euro-managers

According to authors Roland Calori and Bruno Dufour (1995) European management style differs from US and Japanese styles in four characteristics:

1 a greater orientation toward people as individuals;
2 a higher level of internal negotiations between superordinates and subordinates;
3 greater skills at managing international diversity;
4 an enhanced ability to manage between extremes like short-run versus long-run goals.

Reporting on a study conducted by Assessment Circle Europe, Richard Hall (1994) found the most important qualities in Euro-managers—who he defined as anyone with managerial responsibilities in a multicultural organization—to be: language ability, communication and social skills, listening skills, a social personality, and the ability to work in a team. Additionally, this Euro-manager needs to develop initiative, be independent, and develop strong planning skills. Another study suggests that in Europe, the most admired senior managers are humane, professional, determined, close to employees, and communicate well (Brown, 1994).

Management in Asia

In a perceptual study of good leadership in Asian organizations, the top priority was honesty, followed by strategic vision, and recognizing good work in others (Selvarajah et al., 1995). But these attributes vary within Asia. For example, participative management is an important leadership attribute in Japan, but in Taiwan high priority is on a leader's ability to generate employee cooperation (Von Glinow et al., 1999).

Global Convergence in Management Practices

Chapter 4 showed how shareholder and stakeholder pressures combine to demand that global businesses from everywhere be both fiscally successful and socially responsive. That chapter also showed that managerial traditions previously found mainly within nations are now used worldwide. Examples are Asian firms more responsive to shareholders, US firms more responsive to stakeholders, and European firms that adopt new styles. For example, both Deutsche Telekom and Vivendi adopted US management models.

CAREER DEVELOPMENT

Interviews with executives and results of a career questionnaire completed by members of the International Association of Corporate and Professional Resources identified important knowledge, skills, and abilities for a successful 21st-century managerial career. Study authors Allred et al. (1996) grouped these success characteristics into five categories:

1 Knowledge-based technical specialty—as in the past, managers will begin their careers with a technical specialty, but will need strong computer literacy skills and must be able to interpret and use a broad array of data.
2 Future managers need not only multicultural and international experience; they must also have cross-functional expertise that allows them to be both managers and technical experts.
3 Future managers will be collaborative leaders, and will be part of both temporary and permanent groups over a career span.
4 Future managers will not only need to manage their careers and their time at work, they will need to rely on their own skills in balancing career and personal demands rather than on a boss who allocates time and tasks.
5 Flexibility will be the most important individual trait for successful managers, but integrity and trustworthiness are part of this equation as well.

Many find they must personally invest in acquiring skills and abilities important to success. Futurist William Van Dusen Wishard (1995) believes there is no blueprint for success, but suggests the following approach:

1 There is a need to discern what is permanent and immutable.
2 We must learn to make interconnections between people, events, and different categories of life because interdependence is an emerging condition of life.
3 We must learn to know ourselves.
4 We each need some understanding of how change and technology are affecting people and institutions.
5 We need to be open to dimensions of existence that are difficult to understand, value or control; within ourselves we need to value intuition.
6 There is a need to interact with people in a manner that will bridge racial and cultural differences.
7 There is a need to have a personal sense of creating something new for the future.

Authors Michael Arthur and Denise Rousseau (1996) believe boundarylessness will redefine careers such that they become a sequence of experiences that may or may not be related or progressive. This generates complexity for those who prefer linearity. As Table 13.3 suggests, with these new careers come new relationships between people and organizations.

Table 13.3 *Principles of new and old career paradigms*

Old Career Paradigms	New Career Paradigms
A formalized and static employment contract exchanges job security for employee compliance	Rewards are exchanged for performance, and contracts can be renegotiated as conditions change
People spend their careers in a single firm; the company trains for new needs	People work for many firms over a lifetime; the individual becomes responsible for career development and training
Employee allegiance is to the corporation and to permanent work groups	Employee transfers among projects generate project allegiances

Source material: Michael B. Arthur, Priscilla H. Claman, and Robert J. DeFillippi (1995) Intelligent enterprise, intelligent careers. *Academy of Management Executive*, 9 (4): 13.

Developing competencies appropriate to managing and leading requires balance that begins with a sense of personal priorities. For example, without a clear view of personal and professional priorities, individuals can easily lose the balance between personal life and work or become flexible at the cost of personal or profession integrity.

GLOBAL HUMAN RESOURCE SYSTEMS

Organizations also shape career development via human resource systems that recruit, select, compensate, train, and evaluate people's work. The integrative approach to human resource management found in global firms is increasingly called Strategic International Human Resource Management (SIHRM). These systems require strategically oriented HR managers able to integrate human resource activities on a global scale.

Scholars argue that SIHRM systems can help organizations facilitate strategic goal achievement (Schuler et al., 1993; Taylor et al., 1996), and that SIHRM facilitates global competitiveness, efficiency, local responsiveness, organizational flexibility, and organizational learning and knowledge transfer.

Managers play an important role in knowledge transfer, particularly when they travel and work in locations far from headquarters (Ondrack, 1985). However, many organizations have too few global leaders and many do not develop managers for global leadership. For example, about 85 percent of *Fortune* 500 firms lack global leaders (Gregerson et al., 1998).

Four Approaches to Cross-national Management

Heenan and Perlmutter (1979) outline four basic orientations to managing cross-nationally. Each orientation would lead to a different approach to managing people:

- An *ethnocentric* approach consolidates control at headquarters. Important decisions are made in the home country, and expatriates from the home country staff key posts abroad.
- A *polycentric* approach staffs abroad with host-country nationals who have some decision autonomy, but few of these managers are promoted to jobs at headquarters.
- A *regiocentric* approach employs a wider pool of managers within a geographic region like Asia or Latin America, employing host-country and/or third-country nationals. Although these managers have some degree of decision-making autonomy within their regions, they are seldom brought into jobs at headquarters.
- A *geocentric* approach to staffing identifies and selects the best person for the job regardless of nationality, and decision-making often is decentralized.

Selection

A successful domestic track record is reason enough for many US firms to select the managers they send abroad, but scholars observe that technical skills alone may not lead to managerial success abroad. Rosalie Tung (1987) shows that success in international assignments depends on three additional factors: personality traits such as relational abilities; environmental variables such as the place for the foreign assignment; and family situation.

Later work showed that expatriate success is also associated with adjustment (Black, 1988), and to job, organizational, and non-work variables (Black et al., 1991). Parker and McEvoy (1993) collapsed these many variables into three categories that shape expatriate success: a) individual variables; b) organizational variables; and c) contextual variables related to family or nation for the assignment.

Studies of non-US managers show they function differently and succeed in different ways than US expatriates (Andre, 1985; Zeira and Harari, 1977). Research on women managers abroad similarly shows that women succeed in international work but do not necessarily fit profiles based on US male experiences (Adler, 1987; Parker, 1991). Finally, a study that compared wholly owned subsidiary expatriate managers with international joint venture managers found the latter viewed adaptability as more important to their jobs than to subsidiary managers (Parker et al., 1996). These studies illustrate that factors contributing to success for the international assignment extend far beyond technical skills.

Staffing

In the 1990s, engineering company ABB was a model for the global firm; its leader Percy Barvenik was widely admired. He had this to say about how to develop a global manager:

Global managers are made, not born. ... You rotate people around the world..you encourage people to work in mixed-nationality teams. You force *them to create personal alliances across borders [because] mixing nationalities doesn't just happen. (Quoted in Taylor, 1991: 67–68)*

Managerial staffing abroad traditionally has been accomplished in three ways: sending an expatriate manager from the headquarters staff, hiring a host-country national, or hiring third-country nationals who share citizenship neither with the firm nor the host nation. Another staffing possibility is to hire from a local pool of "voluntary" expatriates—people who choose to live and work outside their nation of origin (Parker, 1991). For example, Stephanie Thompson's decision to move from New Zealand to Ecuador made her a voluntary expatriate.

Expatriate Staffing

Ethnocentrism is one reason a company might send an expatriate abroad. An expatriate in charge assures headquarters' control over decisions. But there are other reasons besides ethnocentrism that motivate expatriate staffing. An expatriate's knowledge of the company transfers knowledge from home to new cultures. Sometimes the job has technical requirements that only an expatriate can fill. In addition, expatriate postings develop employees for top-management slots. For example, Royal Dutch/Shell requires four global assignments before considering a manager for a senior position. Finally, the expatriate plays an important role: helping the organization interpret and integrate with the world. This was the role Bandag expected Gerald Borenstein to play in Hong Kong.

The benefits of knowledge transfer and management development may be offset by high compensation costs as much as triple those in the home office. In addition, nations may resent a company's propensity to expatriate top managers rather than hire locally.

Host-national Staffing

Among reasons to hire host nationals abroad is to fulfill a "social contract" to create jobs. In some nations, the social contract is formalized to require local hiring. In other cases, hiring host-country nationals for lower- to middle-level jobs may be a matter of expediency: there simply are not enough expatriates to fill all these jobs. Rosalie Tung (1982) notes there are also cultural reasons to hire host nationals: they are familiar with the host culture and speak the host language.

Third-country Staffing

The geocentric approach to staffing may lead to hiring a third-country national, like Rajat Das who worked for a German firm in the Middle East. Zeira and Harari (1977) studied third-country nationals to conclude that most are part of a competent and mobile group of managers with high adaptability and an open disposition to new cultures. This third-country national often carries dual citizenship or was born in one country and raised in another. Because they have lived within two cultures, many will have developed sensitivities to cross-cultural differences.

Voluntary Expatriate Staffing

Voluntary expatriates are professional or managerially prepared people who choose to live outside their nation of origin for a variety of possible reasons. They may be a trailing spouse to a national, feel the culture better fits their personal style, or find more job opportunities than in a home country. Often they speak more than one language and are adept in more than one culture. Thus voluntary expatriates provide yet another staffing option for managerial jobs abroad.

Staffing Issues

Rapid globalization creates reasons to combine staffing strategies. For example, few in Eastern European transitional economies were familiar with profit-oriented behaviors in 1989, leading firms to staff with third-country European nationals. But hiring locals helped them to develop as well.

Some "common sense" assumptions have not been supported by experience. For example, "hyphenated Americans," such as Chinese-Americans, often face barriers in countries of heritage because they are not perceived as being "real" Americans or "real" Chinese. In this case, an ability to bridge cultural borders can seem to work against managerial success. This suggests that global businesses can benefit from examining the validity of traditional staffing assumptions.

A company's business strategy also can drive staffing decisions. For example, Coca-Cola defines its business strategy as multilocal, and therefore prefers local managers who are responsive to and knowledgeable about local customs and needs. At the same time, Coca-Cola also expatriates parent-country nationals abroad to help them develop international knowledge.

The research on female expatriation is mixed. Some find that women succeed in them (Adler, 1987); others report that women confront more difficulties than men at every stage of the international transfer cycle (Mayrhofer and Scullion, 2002).

Managerial Attributes for Work Abroad

Generalist as well as specialist skills.

Technical skills may be less important that interpersonal skills, for example communicating well and getting along with others.

Individual competencies also can be important, such as adaptability, cultural empathy, ability to generate trust and respect, and willingness to learn.

Ascribed characteristics, such as health, nationality, gender, religion, and age may be important.

Repatriation

Most expatriates—especially those sent from headquarters—intend to return there. Often they confront repatriation difficulties such as readjustment to the home culture or limited organizational opportunities. In general, the longer the duration of the expatriate assignment, the harder it is to adjust upon return. Individuals accustomed to being general managers during their assignment abroad often find it difficult to return to specialist jobs or ones that have limited management scope. Organizational changes such as technological or structural ones may make it difficult for a returning expatriate to do his or her job well. Sometimes expatriates return to find that the job they left was restructured out of existence.

When Expatriate Support Is Missing

Some companies have an "out of sight, out of mind" orientation to managers abroad. In one company, a manager complained that headquarters routinely ignored his telephone calls. There was no organized social system of support for him or his family. Mentors were not assigned, and neither he nor his family received predeparture or in-country training. The resulting isolation put pressure on his marriage such that he sent his family home, and made preparations to return early from the expatriate assignment.

Source material: Mark Mendenhall and Gary Oddou (1988, Sept./Oct.) The overseas assignment: A practical look. *Business Horizons*, pp. 78–84.

Repatriation and opportunities for future advancement are also a concern for female expatriates (Culpan and Wright, 2002). Female managers in Western Europe often experience more difficulties at re-entry than males, suggesting that repatriation may be more stressful for them than the expatriate assignment itself (Linehan and Scullion, 2002).

Organizations and individuals relieve repatriation stress in several ways. Having a mentor at the home office during the overseas assignment can improve the expatriate's connection with organizational activities. On-going access to existing networks can also improve the repatriation experience. Organizations can further relieve stress by clarifying promotional paths for expatriates or by offering repatriation training to expatriates and family members.

Additional Ways to Develop Global Competencies

In addition to rotating managerial assignments worldwide, global companies develop managerial expertise in other ways. According to an Ernst and Young study, some of these methods include: forming an advisory council of senior executives in each country to guide the country managers on cultural issues; and facilitating a global communication network between managers to foster teaming and idea sharing (Donlon, 1996).

Temporary Assignments

Temporary assignments are yet another way to develop global expertise. For example, Rockwell International's Allen Bradley Company Division brings host nationals to the US for training. Similarly, Unilever found that hiring local managers provided a good perspective on India, but that to do their jobs well the Indian managers also needed exposure to Unilever's culture. In summary, managerial staffing decisions depend on the objectives deemed most important to organizational leaders at a given point of time. In global firms comprising many businesses and serving many markets, the selection approach may be a hybrid combination of ethnocentric to geocentric approaches.

Cross-cultural Training

Research shows a positive relationship between cultural training and performance outcomes (Black and Mendenhall, 1990; Deshpande and Viswesvaran, 1992). Yet many organizations provide little to no cross-cultural training. For example a survey of 228 global firms showed only 30 percent offered formal cultural training programs for an average three days of training (Solomon, 1994). Although many believe that training is more intensive for firms from other countries, Magoroh Maruyama (1992) shows that only some Japanese firms train extensively while others provide just two weeks' notice before sending their employees abroad. Matsushita, on the other hand, provides training of six months or more before the foreign assignment.

Organizations that provide cross-cultural training for existing employees choose from or combine four basic training options. Some, like Intel, combine these options, offering them to everyone in the workforce. Methods for training within sites are explored in Chapter 14.

Cognitive Training Methods

Cognitive training exposes employees to concrete knowledge about other people or places. Environmental briefings that describe climate, topography, infrastructure, population or housing in a nation are one form of cognitive training, Other forms provide information about cultural institutions, habits or national values, typically of the dominant culture. Cognitive awareness training may include lectures on national cultural habits, or it can be as simple as providing employees with a book. Many resources are available for cognitive-knowledge acquisition, ranging from tomes that list "dos and don'ts" for another culture, cultural briefings, such as Culturegrams, videos, CDs, and empirical research. Language acquisition also can be considered a form of cognitive training. Cognitive training is often the least expensive way for an organization to introduce a nation or culture.

Awareness Training Methods

Another training method encourages awareness of underlying cultural values and assumptions. This type of training often begins with self-assessments of management styles such as decision-style inventories that show most US decisions rely on facts whereas most Asian decisions are normative or concerned that decisions be fair. Awareness training of this type helps people understand that managerial styles differ because they are culturally based. Additional training may help people adapt their styles to cultural frameworks consistent with those managed. Awareness training takes longer and requires more organizational resources than cognitive training. In addition, it requires intellectual and emotional engagement from managers.

Behavioral Training Methods

The basic concept behind behavioral-training programs is "learning by doing," but there are many ways to provide this form of training. Cultural assimilators, for example, are written descriptions of a cultural encounter, usually of an expatriate interaction with a host national. The situation is usually relevant to tasks the trainee is meant to perform abroad, but the encounter presents a puzzling cultural situation that could be easily misinterpreted.

After reading the description, trainees choose from among three or four interpretations or explanations for the encounter. Each of the choices provides insight into basic concepts, attitudes, role perceptions, customs, and values in another culture, but one choice best reflects it. Cultural assimilators are developed for cultural pairs, so if French managers are expatriated to Colombia the assimilator would familiarize a French person with Colombian culture and customs.

Because they are labor intensive and specific to one culture, cultural assimilators can be quite expensive to develop. Globalization of knowledge also affects their longevity. For example, improved telecommunications expose many to cultural learning on a daily basis, and cultural convergence may alter business habits if not cultural values. Thus, currency can be a problem with cultural assimilators.

Cultural interactions invite people to engage with members of another culture in a purposeful way. For example, trainees may be required to attend a cultural activity in their own community to experience another culture. Reflection on this experience provides insight into not only cognitive knowledge gained, but also self-awareness of how the individual felt in a new "culture." This approach to awareness training places the learning burden on the individual.

Experiential exercises such as BaFa BaFa or Ecotonos are simulations that can immerse people in new cultures for a few hours. From participating in them, people gain experiential knowledge of how culture operates and the behaviors that cultures foster. This kind of training helps people learn about the relationship between values and behaviors. It also helps them observe their own behaviors when they enter a new culture. However, these types of training usually require sufficient organizational commitment to purchase the simulation, teach people how to administer it, and assemble a group to participate in it.

Immersion Training Methods

Short, exploratory visits to another nation, in-country immersion programs, and long-term sojourns in other nations all are field experiences used for cultural training. For example, some South Korean firms establish "culture houses" where employees live and speak like natives of the country where they will work. These types of programs are the most expensive among cultural training ones.

Compensation

Compensation has three measurable components. The first component is direct pay or the amount an employee receives for work. Managers typically are paid a salary and expected to work as many hours as necessary. Laborers more frequently earn an hourly rate, often receiving additional pay for overtime work. In the US, pay typically is about 70 percent of annual compensation, but in other countries the reverse is the case.

NEC's Compensation and Flextime Work Systems
Individual compensation may be a "people" issue, but systems for managing compensation call for integrated processes. NEC first introduced a flexible work system in 1993. It proved so successful that NEC rolled out a flexible work system and compensation plan that lets 7,000 managers choose their own hours and work priorities. With this system, NEC pays regular salaries but allows for only one hour of overtime pay.
Source material: NEC introduces flextime for 7,000. (2002, Oct. 24) *The Japan Times* (Electronic version).

A second component of compensation is incentives such as profit sharing, for example stock ownership or gain-sharing or bonuses. In some sectors and many nations, bonus pay represents a significant portion of annual pay. In Singapore, Indonesia, and Thailand salaried workers typically receive a 13th month of pay as an annual bonus, and a vacation bonus is typical in Western Europe. In Mexico, workers are paid for 365 days a year but expect a month's pay premium at Christmas, an 80 percent monthly bonus in addition to paid vacation time, and a year-end bonus based on punctuality. Some US managers earn many millions in annual bonuses.

Shred-It's Incentive Plan
Shred-It, a Toronto-based mobile document shredding and recycling service, operates in ten nations. Its early experiences in North America led to an incentive plan for sales people that provided performance awards such as electronics and experiential activities such as space camp or flying lessons. But Shred-It found that Brazilian sales people did not value the same incentives. Accordingly, Shred-It adopted a regional

> incentive plan for each continent, providing different awards based on different cultural preferences. The up-side is that Shred-It has adapted its incentives to regional needs; the down-side is that Shred-It now runs different incentive programs on every continent rather than a single, integrated program.
>
> Source material: Libby Estell (2001, Aug.) i see London, i see France. *Incentive*, 175 (8): 58–64.

Compensation, bonuses, and other incentives vary widely from country to country. For example, Japanese CEOs earn about 10-20 times more than the average worker in their firms. In comparison by the end of the 1990s the average CEO salary for *Fortune's* top 100 was $37.5 million or 1,000 times the level for ordinary workers. The growing number of lawsuits against top managers illustrates public frustration with high pay and incentives and the lavish lifestyle they support.

> ## CEO Charged under Sarbanes-Oxley
>
> Former HealthSouth CEO Richard Scrushy was the first CEO charged under the 2002 US Sarbanes-Oxley law to target corporate wrongdoing. In November 2003, Mr. Scrushy was charged with 85 counts of fraud that prosecutors say funded a lavish lifestyle that included a Cessna airplane, Chagall and Miro paintings, late-model Lamborghinis and a Rolls-Royce Corniche, two yachts, four homes, and jewels such as a 21.8 carat diamond.
>
> Source material: Jay Reeves (2003, Nov. 5) HealthSouth founder indicted. *The Seattle Times*, pp. E1, E6.

Benefits

Finally, the third component of compensation is benefits or indirect pay in the form of health insurance, educational rebates, vacations, holidays, and the like. Managers' benefits can include perquisites or "perks" like mobile-phone service, chauffeurs, or housing allowances. As is true for salaries and incentives, benefits vary widely on a global basis. In Western Europe, for example, the average worker earns six weeks of vacation per year plus many holidays. In the US, the average worker earns only one to two weeks of vacation and enjoys the fewest holidays of any advanced nation. Many US firms counter the effects of so little vacation time with other benefits such as sabbaticals or periodic paid leave. Sabbaticals such as those described in Table 13.4 improve employee retention; they are offered most when employees have abundant job options.

National differences in compensation raise issues of fairness affecting organizations that want to be "fair" and also benefit from labor wage differences. Perceptions of unequal treatment can undermine employee morale (as for Rajat Das) or bring about frequent revisions in global compensation systems. Both entail organizational costs.

Table 13.4 *Sabbaticals from businesses*

Company	Benefit
Adobe Systems (software)	3-week paid sabbatical every 5 years
IVillage (women's Internet site)	Month-long sabbaticals after 2.5 years
Intel (computer chips)	8 paid weeks every 7 years
Morningstar (mutual fund tracker)	6-week paid leave every 4 years

Source material: Sabbatical snapshot (2000, May 5) *The Wall Street Journal*, p. W4.

Expatriate Compensation

An expatriate's direct pay is usually equivalent to that of the home office, amounting to about $175,000 for upper-middle managers by the late 1990s. However, a cost of living adjustment may be necessary for cities and nations with a high cost of living. Sometimes expatriates receive a "signing" bonus similar to those used for professional athletes.

In addition to the usual benefits, the expatriate may receive extra vacation time for travel to and from the home nation, plus airfare for family travel. Some firms pay for emergency leave for family illness or death. Additional expatriate benefits can include relocation fees, housing subsidies, or possible "hardship" pay in developing or dangerous locales. In the latter cases, organizations often purchase special insurance policies to cover costs should the manager be kidnapped or harmed. If there are accompanying children, companies often provide an educational subsidy. Finally, the company may pay for sales costs or manage rentals of the expatriate's home-country residence.

As might be evident, compensation and benefits for an expatriate can result in significant outlays for the expatriating company. Although the expatriate may be able to save a good deal while working abroad, he or she sometimes faces a double income-tax burden, and lost income if an accompanying spouse or partner cannot obtain a work permit.

A Change in Structure Leads to a Compensation Change

A change in 3M's structure from country managers to regional ones led to a needed change for expatriate compensation. Managers who'd once expected to spend their entire career in one nation were being transferred to other nations where living costs differed. 3M introduced a more integrative approach by comparing net salaries (with some adjustments) in both new and old countries. The transferred executive then receives whichever pay is highest. Because local-housing costs are part of salary adjustment, the company neither pays a bonus nor subsidizes higher housing costs.

Source material: J. Flynn (1995, July 3) Continental divide over executive pay. *Business Week*, pp. 40–41.

Motivation and Compensation

Motivation is willingness to work hard to achieve a desired goal. Organizations try to channel employee energy in productive ways by matching rewards to the goals people want and will work hard to achieve. Tangible rewards such as money offered as US performance incentives are based on assumptions of economic rationality. However, researchers show that these assumptions do not apply to all settings. For example, an early study of Russian workers showed that consumer goods were better motivators than cash (Welsh et al., 1993). Similarly, incentive pay failed to improve employee morale in Poland's 400-employee Ahlstrom Fakop plant, but morale and sales both increased when the firm offered to maintain staffing at current levels if the plant met sales targets. These examples show that assumptions of economic rationality are not necessarily applicable worldwide.

Motivation at Home Depot Canada

Leaders at Home Depot Canada believe that the company's success is the sum of actions for all the people employed there. This means creating a culture of performance that has an emotional appeal so that people feel good about working for the company. Employees are partners, as demonstrated by Home Depot's commitment to providing healthcare benefits to part-time employees and bonus programs that include everyone. Home Depot Canada leaders also believe that if the company is socially responsible, people will also feel good about it. This is why Home Depot employees donate over six million person hours to community service per year.

Source material: Mike Troy (2002, Jun. 10) Motivating your workforce: A Home Depot case study. *Retailing Today*, 11: 29.

The goals people will work hard to achieve vary cross-culturally. Among family-owned businesses, it may be more important to please one's family than to achieve high economic returns. In Latin America countries where family and community affiliation are important, helping a friend win a job may be more important than what he or she contributes to the organization. According to Robert Moran and John Riesenberger (1994), the problems of motivating excellence among global employees occur because borders are blurring and employees are challenged to know where home is or to decide where they will place their loyalties. They argue this problem will be overcome when employees are motivated by empowerment, believing it is the CEO's job to see that all employees are empowered.

However, desire for empowerment may be easier to tap in cultures that encourage autonomy and less relevant where individual needs are subordinate to group or collective needs. National and individual motivational differences suggest managers balance among a wide variety of needs and desires when managing employees. Work/family balance, loyalty exchange, values, beliefs, and priorities are all among the challenges managers face globally. According, SIHRM leaders must examine workforce assumptions to consider worldwide applicability. For example, if part of the pay-off from work is intellectual stimulation from others, then a main work incentive may be provided when the organization creates that environment. To foster ongoing development of intellectual capital, organizations may need to create a workplace where people want to be.

In summary, motivation of a heterogeneous global workforce with differing needs and values requires a manager adept at understanding cultural differences in motivation. Recognizing these and other variations in work orientation is more demanding than assuming workforces are homogeneous. Recognizing variations and developing diverse skills is another of the many challenges the global HR manager faces.

Building Strategic and Global Human Resource Systems

Global SIHRM integration may be difficult to achieve with some parts of the HR function yielding more readily to integration than others. Earlier we saw that integration of compensation programs is fraught with challenges. However, cross-cultural training may be more easily integrated on a global scale. Staffing integration also requires trade-offs between host-nation expectations and company needs to develop global managers. One way to manage SIHRM integration is to develop common ethics and principles worldwide (Donlon, 1996) to help managers achieve a common vision.

CHAPTER SUMMARY

Studies of global leaders trace their roots in four distinct theories of leadership: trait theory, leadership style theory, contingency theory, and "new" leader theory. Global leaders tend to have six competencies: they operate from a global mindset, have strong knowledge of the business and its environment, create and convey a clear vision with integrity, develop self-awareness and understanding, manage diversity, and continuously learn.

Leaders and managers differ along several dimensions. Leaders produce significant change, develop long-term visions, and embrace chaos and empowerment. Managers, on the other hand, are expected to produce orderly results, concentrate on the short run, and maintain order and control. Differences between leaders and managers suggest that would-be leaders will have to develop leadership skills when practicing managerial ones.

Career development increasingly is an individual responsibility. Individuals can best reach their career goals if a) they can articulate their own goals, and b) they have a plan for attaining it. Organizations shape careers via Human Resource systems that recruit, select, compensate, train, and evaluate people. The integrative approach to human resource management found in global firms is increasingly called Strategic International Human Resource Management (SIHRM).

Most companies base their human resource practices on cultural values and domestic realities within nations. When the company expands globally, these practices and the assumptions upon which they are based bear reexamination.

In view of worldwide differences in HR practices, global SIHRM integration may be difficult to achieve. However, some aspects of the HR function, for example training may be more readily integrated than others such as compensation.

REVIEW AND DISCUSSION QUESTIONS

1 Which of the four theories of leadership is most satisfying to you? Support your opinion with examples from people you consider good leaders.

2 Defend one of the following assertions with research evidence: leadership success has nothing to do with gender; men inherently are more successful leaders than women; women inherently are more successful leaders than men.

3 Many organizational leaders have been taught to think that incentive pay motivates employees to achieve company goals. What are the cultural explanations you can offer when incentive plans fail to achieve desired results? What does this say about the universality of incentive pay systems?

Chapter 14
MANAGING DIVERSITY AND TEAMS

TRANSCENDING INTERNAL BOUNDARIES AT SAFEWALL

At its inception, Safewall Incorporated transcended traditional internal business boundaries even as its initial products—software firewalls to protect sensitive data—were expected to etch boundaries in cyberspace and earn the company a place on the *Fortune* 500. This seeming contradiction delighted Safewall's founders, who, like many in the software industry, enjoyed a mix and match approach to business by combining tradition (*Fortune* 500 aspirations) with innovations like overcoming internal boundaries.

Key readings for founding executives included traditional management classics and also newer ideas expressed by Peter Senge's *The Learning Organization* and Geoffrey Moore's *Crossing the Chasm*. Discussions of these and related ideas led to bold decisions for establishing Safewall Incorporated. For example, contrary to most business managers who at the time saw diversity principally as a problem to be solved, Safewall's executives recognized diversity as a business advantage. Diverse employees brought new knowledge and contacts to the organization, and they helped others see old challenges in new ways or new challenges with a twist on tradition. In other words, diversity was viewed as a source of organizational learning that could transform an organization. Whereas some organizational leaders fear change, Safewall leaders viewed transformation as a positive outcome. If there was to be a status quo at Safewall, it was to be built around the idea of constant change. Leaders wanted to create an innovative, robust, and diverse corporate culture—one where people would be assertive and willing to take risks. So they built the organization around people willing to take risks, starting with the hiring process.

All would-be hires for the new company needed good technical qualifications. What followed for qualified candidates was an initial $1\frac{1}{2}$-hour interview with the Vice President of Human Resources and two or three others. The interview rarely covered technical background, but focussed instead on exploring the candidate's character. Highly sought qualities included intelligence—defined as insight and problem-solving abilities—interpersonal skills, and ability to leverage business knowledge. This meant bringing experience to Safewall that could help the company achieve its mission. A satisfactory initial interview led to a second more extensive interview with six or more people that yielded further insight into the candidate's character.

Interview questions covered ground unfamiliar to many applicants, ranged widely, and often focussed on applicants' likes, dislikes, interests or enthusiasms. Questions the employee might be asked were: Who do you admire most? When do you know it is time to go home from work? The answers themselves were immaterial. Instead, the interviewers were trying to learn answers to their own questions, such as: Does this individual bring an approach that is unique? Is there an enthusiasm that could help us grow? Is there a will to work closely with others? Is there a commitment to challenging authority? Following the second interview, those present voted on one of three options: postpone a decision (pending additional interviews), no hire or hire. The latter received immediate Safewall job offers.

Once hired, new Safewall employees were part of a one-week orientation session, the purpose of which was to teach Safewall norms. Key norms were: question authority, participate fully, be part of the team. Organizational stories recounting past successes and ▶

failures reinforced norms. For example, trainers described Juan, a customer-service representative who traced half of reported problems to the same source. Because he didn't want to cause trouble for his boss or team, Juan spent about six months of his own time secretly working toward a successful correction. Rather than gaining kudos, Juan was admonished in view of potential costs, had the problem been corrected too late. The story targets a challenge typical for many Safewall employees: verbal and even philosophical commitment to challenging authority is quite different from *actually* challenging authority.

Many employees—even enthusiastic ones who adopted Safewall values—found it difficult to operationalize company values. For example, most had come from technology-intensive businesses where they worked on their own. This made it hard for them to engage fully in team projects, and some found it irritating to interact with team members rather than work on direct project tasks. Others felt team members could be too dominating, stubborn, or competitive.

One of the earliest steps toward creating a high-innovation culture was to organize people into product-development teams that were cross-functional by design. Leaders believed that since it takes Sales, Marketing, Engineering, Test, Quality Assurance, and Operations to get a product from conception to customer, all of these diverse functions should be represented on the Product Development Team (PDT). Each PDT incorporated individual diversity of age, race, and national origin as well. But since people served on multiple teams simultaneously and were assigned special individual projects, team membership sometimes occurred more by chance than design. Inherent to the teams was natural conflict between individuals that led to overt or covert tussles for control. For example, on a cross-functional product development team, the product engineer might lobby for technical advantages while the marketing manager would stress value to the end customer. This created ongoing group tension, and it made decision-making difficult.

Employees served on many PDT groups because they were reassigned as soon as the work of one finished. In the interests of reducing hierarchy and sharing authority, each PDT member was responsible for product integrity. This created a peer-authority system that meant individuals had to work well with one another. Although this usually occurred, the system was not without its problems. For example, resolutions were hard to achieve because no one, including the Project Manager, had final authority. Sometimes team members could not bring themselves to challenge the group. For example when Mike, a Chinese programmer, found a fatal flaw in his PDT's product, he took it to a senior executive rather than the team. When asked, Mike explained he had not spoken to the team because he perceived them to be "loud Americans" who did not listen to his input, and he feared that the older, more experienced Project Manager would lose face if Mike brought the problem to her.

Another challenge with the PDT system was the peer-review process. Some employees felt that favorable reviews depended less on one's work than on one's ability to "schmooze" with others. According to company rumor, some female employees felt they were given little chance to contribute fully in team meetings or that teams favored dominant males. Finally, rapid employee growth and high team turnover were making it less feasible for executives to monitor or develop employees. Some believed that the current system had outlived its usefulness, and this led to calls for greater control over projects, ▶

specific job descriptions, and a much more rigorous approach to evaluation and human resource development. The Vice President of Human Resources was asked to review these concerns, and bring forward an "idea to reality" plan for how the company could continue to grow and remain true to its commitment to individual action, learning, innovation, and diversity.

CHAPTER OVERVIEW

Hiring from a global pool increases human diversity in global businesses. In addition, global businesses pursue diverse processes and create diverse structures to manage them. All require integrative diversity management initiatives. This chapter focusses on integrative initiatives for managing organizational diversity worldwide. Strategic orientations to diversity, creating an inclusive culture, and teamwork development are three ways organizations integrate diversity worldwide.

MANAGING DIVERSITY

For many organizational leaders, the first challenge of diversity is defining it. Organizations typically begin with a focus on visible dimensions of human resource diversity such as gender, race, nationality, age, and physical abilities. Often an emphasis on visible forms of diversity leads to recognition that organizations house many *less* visible forms of diversity such as religion, marital status, sexual orientation, values, or economic class. Organizational leaders also manage structural diversity and often they balance diverse processes worldwide.

Cultural Diversity

Hiring from a global labor pool results in cultural diversity in global organizations. Growing diversity within nations increases cultural diversity in domestic workplaces as well. For example, at its top levels New York-based Coty includes US CFOs and HR directors, an Indian operations manager, a French division president, a Danish group president, and a German CEO. Unilever's top 200 leaders represent 40 nationalities.

Visible and less visible forms of human diversity are important to organizations first because they are important to employees. If an employee believes he or she is less valuable to the organization due to gender, nationality, or some other factor, this perception creates potential for poor employee morale, lowered performance, or turnover. Any one of these results increases organizational costs. Second, diversity is important to organizations because a diverse workforce reflects the global world in which companies operate. Ideally diversity in the workforce makes global organizations more alert and responsive to their world. Managing a diverse workforce depends on integrative mechanisms that facilitate efficient and effective work. This includes appropriate human resource practices for recruiting, hiring, developing, and evaluating people. As occurred at Safewall, changes in these practices may come slowly.

In recent years, discussion of what makes cultural diversity "work" in organizations has shifted from (a) figuring out ways to attract and hire a diverse set of people to (b) trying to understand what makes people from diverse backgrounds operate effectively within organizations (Ely and Thomas, 2001). Researchers such as Davidson and Ferdman (2002) believe that the diversity/effectiveness link is strongest in organizations where everyone feels included by the organization. Organizations can best develop inclusive networks when they a) reexamine their norms or traditional ways of doing things, b) seek and value similarities as well as differences as sources of competitive advantage, and c) train people for skills that enhance a sense of inclusion. An example to be explored later in this chapter is training for multicultural teamwork.

Structural Diversity and Diverse Processes

In addition to diverse people, global organizations often accommodate diverse structural forms and diverse processes. Structural diversity results from activities that involve decision-sharing such as strategic alliances and cross-sectoral partnerships. Depending on the types of businesses held in the corporate portfolio, companies may need to structure for diversity in products/services or nations served.

Processes also are diverse. For example, firm acquisition brings compensation systems, information management systems, and even organizational cultures that differ from those of the acquiring firm. Although some global firms pursue integration tactics to create homogeneous processes for all subsidiaries, full integration and consistency is quite difficult. For example, Levi Strauss uses the same human resource management principles everywhere. At the same time, due to national differences, Levi does not compensate everyone the same worldwide. The result is diverse compensation systems dependent on national economic practices. In other cases, technological factors may constrain integration of worldwide processes. For example, a weak telecommunications infrastructure in many African nations limits Internet use as a company-wide communication medium.

Leveraging Diversity

Defining diversity or believing that it is important to be diverse are preliminary steps to leveraging diversity as a business advantage. Lisa Hoecklin (1995) believes that global leaders must recognize that cultural diversity can simultaneously cause problems and provide benefits to organizations. Efforts to balance benefits against costs have yielded different approaches to managing diversity.

Incorporating Cultural Diversity

According to David Thomas and Robin Ely (1996), business leaders tend to adopt one of three different views to incorporate cultural diversity in their organizations.

1 The discrimination and fairness paradigm has been most used in US organizations. This approach assumes that prejudice has kept members of certain groups out of organizations and can be remedied by focussing on equal opportunity, fair treatment, and compliance with Equal Employment Opportunity laws. Remedies consistent with this paradigm favor assimilation such that newcomers become more like existing employees.

2 The access and legitimacy paradigm emerged from the competitive business climate of the 1980s and 1990s, relying more on acceptance and valuing of difference than the discrimination and fairness paradigm. This paradigm was motivated by awareness that diversity outside the organization required greater diversity within. Among the limitations of this paradigm is that it accepts diversity without really understanding how diversity can or does change the way work is accomplished. Although boundaries to acceptance can be transcended with this paradigm, boundaries to understanding remain.

3 Learning is a third and emerging paradigm. This perspective not only values diversity, it also argues that differences in perspectives can help organizations learn. Like the fairness paradigm it promotes equal opportunity and like the access paradigm it acknowledges cultural differences, but it transcends both to make learning the glue through which an organization integrates because of its differences, not in spite of them.

Integrating Diverse People, Processes, and Structures

Dass and Parker (1999) believe that organizational responses to diversity depend on external and internal pressures for diversity and top-management commitment to leveraging diversity. Some organizations undertake diversity initiatives because of high leader commitment to it. For example, Levi Strauss opened integrated factories in the 1940s, predating the US Civil Rights movement by two decades. The company also launched other diversity initiatives well before others. For example, it became a leader in promoting AIDS awareness in 1982 and in the early 1990s became the first *Fortune* 500 company to offer full medical benefits to unmarried partners.

In the late 1990s leaders at Ford Motor Company recognized that their future success depended on fully utilizing the company's depth of human diversity. In 1998, Toyota established a Corporate Diversity Department to guide the company in making diversity an integral part of every aspect of their business. Specifically, this Department provides strategic guidance, support for specific initiatives, and helps develop and promote education and awareness throughout the organization. Thus we see that diversity initiatives emerged at Levi, Ford, and Toyota because top managers viewed diversity as a strategic initiative.

Other organizations develop diversity initiatives in response to external or internal pressures for it. External pressures for diversity can come from different sources such as stakeholders, nongovernmental or governmental actions, or media. Internal pressures for diversity often come from shareholders, employees, or unions. Whatever their source, organizational leaders become attentive when pressures for diversity—be they external or internal—increase.

Dass and Parker (1999) further argue that organizational efforts to incorporate diversity differ because organizations pursue different diversity strategies. As shown in Table 14.1, organizations that simply react to diversity pressures (boxes 1, 2, and 3) pursue different activities than organizations that take a proactive stance (boxes 10–12). Different

Table 14.1 *Strategic responses for managing diversity and their implementation*

	Episodic	Freestanding	Systemic
Reactive	**1** Deny an assignment to an employee because a client might object to the employee's nationality, race, gender, age, etc.	**2** Choose to risk fines or other costs, rather than engage in equal employment opportunity practices	**3** Choose geographic locations for the business which avoid diversity/where the local workforce does not contain protected classes
Defensive	**4** In response to a governmental employment audit, provide a workshop for protected groups on "how to succeed by adapting to fit into the organization"	**5** Regular sexual harassment training which focusses on how to avoid a legal liability	**6** Performance appraisal standards for managers include specific targets/quotas for hiring of protected groups
Accommodative	**7** To increase diversity awareness for managers, bring in a speaker to tell them how to value the diversity of their employees	**8** Sponsor an annual event that celebrates a protected group, e.g., Special Olympics	**9** To ensure equal pay, program the HR computerized management system to annually review and adjust pay differentials between non-protected and protected groups
Proactive	**10** Pilot an employee network conference that engages employees and their managers in reciprocal learning activities	**11** Regularly include vendors, suppliers, and customers in the organization's diversity training offerings to increase their involvement in and contribution to diversity efforts	**12** Different business units continually share information about their diversity successes and failures, then adapt and integrate them into their businesses

Implementation (Episodic, Freestanding, Systemic). Strategic responses for managing diversity. Pressures for Diversity: Low→High. Executive priorities for managing diversity: Marginal ← → Strategic.

strategies such as reactive (resistance), defensive (discrimination and fairness), accommodative (access and legitimacy), and proactive (learning) (Dass and Parker, 1999; Ely and Thomas, 2001; Thomas and Ely, 1996) represent different levels of structural and process level integration, for example performance appraisal and promotion processes, or agenda-setting processes.

Organizational leaders who embark on diversity initiatives should be aware there can be a time lag between diversity initiatives and results. For example, US affirmative-action laws dating to the 1960s produced few changes at the top. For example, among *Fortune* 500 firms, only six had female CEOs by 2004. The following example similarly shows few African-Americans lead major US corporations. This pattern reoccurs worldwide; there is very little diversity among top managers or corporate boards worldwide.

African-American Business Leaders

Franklin Raines, CEO of Fannie Mae, became the first African-American to run a *Fortune* 500 company.

Richard Nanula was named CEO of Starwood Lodging in 1998.

Robert Johnson founded Black Entertainment TV and owns BET Holdings which he took private in 1998 so he could expand without worrying about earnings impact or shareholder concerns.

Chester Davenport became the chairman of Envirotest, the largest owner-operator of vehicle-emission testing centers in the US. Davenport also created remote sensing technology (RST) to simplify auto exhaust testing.

R. Donahue Peebles was the founder and became chief executive of Peebles Atlantic Development Corporation, the largest 100 percent black-owned hotel and real-estate development company in the US.

Source material: Competitive practices for a diverse workforce. (1998) *Business Week*, special advertising section, S1–S18.

Diversity and Performance

In the last two decades, interest in diversity has grown almost exponentially, yielding insight into a wide variety of diversity issues. However, research results on the diversity/performance link are decidedly mixed. For example, research on the efficacy of diverse top-management teams variously demonstrates that diversity is positive (Amason, 1996; Bantel and Jackson, 1989; Murray, 1989); negative (Dess and Origer, 1987); contingent on other variables (Hambrick, 1987) and; curvilinear (Wiersema and Bantel, 1992). Research on work teams shows a similar range of findings and this same pattern also appears in research relating to strategic forms of diversity (for example product diversification and internationalization of markets). This creates challenging questions for researchers and practitioners, and may demonstrate that the diversity/performance link is part of a complex process whose outcome is defined by more than diversity alone.

Successful Diversity Initiatives

Business leaders such as those for Safewall believe diversity is important to their future. Bigger companies like DuPont, Avon, and Honda also believe that managing diversity well provides a global competitive advantage to them. For example, Group Danone brings together researchers, engineers, and technicians from over 20 nations to develop new products. Doing so leads to unique products that help Danone respond to rapid changes in consumer tastes and preferences worldwide.

According to Ann Morrison (1992), author of *The New Leaders: Guidelines for Leadership Diversity in Business*, successful diversity initiatives at the organizational level include:

1 Top managers intervene to establish the need for diversity.
2 Non-managers are recruited for managerial jobs to improve diversity.
3 Internal advocacy groups are established to provide diversity champions.
4 Company profiles/statistics are developed to provide a baseline for diversity.
5 Appraisal is tied to diversity progress.
6 Promotion criteria and processes change.
7 Succession planning is modified to incorporate diversity goals.
8 Diversity training occurs.
9 Informal networks and support groups are developed.
10 Work/family policies are developed.

Ways to Enhance the Value of Diversity

Being diverse in terms of organizational demographics or markets served is a necessary but not sufficient condition for making diversity a sustainable advantage. This advantage comes from an organization's ability to integrate diversity. General recommendations include:

1 Develop a diversity policy for all organizational levels that outlines what is meant by diversity.
2 Practice checking the assumptions behind decisions, and ask others to do the same.
3 Create a high-trust work environment that discourages disparaging jokes or comments, facilitates opportunities among workers, and incorporates people from all levels in projects and processes.
4 Get to know people as individuals to discover their points of view.
5 Expect to be a teacher as well as a learner about diversity.
6 Recognize that resistance and anger are likely responses to changing a homogeneous culture.
7 Reward small successes and progress.
8 Hire talented trainers or encourage people to enroll in training offered.
9 Encourage formation of interest groups and diversity learning inside and outside of work.
10 Embed the planned change in all processes and structures.

Creating a Culture that Values Diversity

A powerful integrative mechanism is organizational culture. According to the Conference Board (Winterle), "unless an organization develops a culture that understands, respects, and values differences, diversity is likely to result in decreased organizational effectiveness" (1992: 19). Motorola's key beliefs include constant respect for people and uncompromising integrity. Global retailer Makro emphasizes core values of integrity and trust. Guinness' five-point Star System reinforces quality, safety, people, productivity, and information as priorities. These firms put people at the center of the organization's culture. Table 14.2 lists many other ways leaders shape advantages from diversity.

Table 14.2 *Corporate diversity initiatives*

Communications	Education and Training	Employee Involvement
CEO speeches	Diversity briefings for managers	Task forces on diversity
Written diversity policy; Diversity brochures	Awareness training for everyone	Interest groups for members of diverse populations
Second-language publications	Diversity-skills training	Company time provided for diversity planning
Reports to the public or to shareholders	Multicultural team training	Networking groups
Press releases	Sexual harassment training	
Career Development	**Performance and Accountability**	
Mentoring	Define behaviors that enhance inclusion	
Succession planning for diversity	Monitor and report on diversity progress	
Individual development plans	Link rewards to achieving diversity objectives	
Assign people to diverse jobs over a career	Develop diversity measures that are both qualitative and quantitative	
Networking directories		

Changing organizational culture by hiring people with differences is only one step toward managing heterogeneity. It is also important that people within the organization be encouraged to view these changes as positive and useful to organizational performance.

Transcending implicit boundaries that include narrow definitions of "who we are" makes this difficult, particularly if efforts to incorporate diversity occur only at the surface level. A change in culture to value diversity more must be embedded in processes and structures such that people have an incentive to change their behavior and their thinking. Incorporating diversity in an organization is more than hiring; it includes recruiting, training, and reaching outside the organization to cultivate community relations and establish a reputation for being an organization that hires and promotes from diverse pools. Changes in culture that accommodate greater diversity also require changes in patterned thinking among managers and other employees.

From the person leading organizations to the shop floor, managing diversity begins first with knowledge and understanding of why culture is important. It is critical for people to understand their own national cultures and assess the strengths and weaknesses that culture offers in a globalizing world. Within the organization, it is important to make features of culture explicit, to ask as is done in process reengineering: why do we do what we do in the way we do it?

Adaptive organizations identify opportunities associated with globalization of culture that include a growing consumer society, experiments that lead to organizational innovations, and combine traditional and non-traditional management techniques in new ways to manage structures, processes, and people for a global market.

Toyota's New Perspectives

Toyota President Hiroshi Okuda created the Virtual Venture Co. division with a team of young employees who work far from HQ. Their job is to find ways to attract young buyers to Toyota automobiles, and their solution was the Toyota Scion. The company believes that if it can't attract today's youth, they will not be able to attract them when they are older. The Virtual Venture Co. initially assembled eight young employees from different parts of the company, but hired 25 new employees whose average age was 34. Employees in this division get more autonomy than colleagues in the parent company, and they design entirely new models for the youth market. The group also proposed a $107.5 million theme park featuring classic, current, and futuristic autos intended for a shopping mall in a trendy Tokyo Bay location.

Source material: Lisa Shuchman (1998, July 21) Toyota creates traditional team to lure disaffected young buyers. *The Wall Street Journal*, p. A11.

Developing Individual Cultural Sensitivity

Managers who want to leverage diversity at work must themselves be aware of and responsive to cultural differences. According to Milton Bennett (1993), many deny that cross-cultural differences matter. Denial would not be a helpful way to manage diversity. Another approach that impedes multicultural management is to visualize diversity from a defensive framework that reflects "us versus them" thinking. The third stage of "minimization" recognizes and accepts superficial cultural differences, such as food preferences, but people in the minimization stage retain a strong belief that at some level people are all the same. A fourth stage of cultural sensitivity is acceptance of differences. Once a person accepts that differences occur, then adaptation can follow. Finally, the sixth stage of cultural sensitivity is to integrate differences to understand and internalize them. This model of cultural sensitivity was developed with the expatriate or long-term sojourner in mind, but it is equally applicable to the global manager in organizations where diversity is the norm.

TEAMWORK

Organizations create cultures and provide spaces where people work, interact, and sometimes play. In organizations that employ more than a handful of employees, groups begin to emerge. Some of these groups are naturally occurring social groups of people who spend time together outside work. Other groups are formally assembled to accomplish work-related tasks that include idea development, product assembly, and organizational learning.

Teams Assemble in Different Ways

Work teams are defined as officially formed groups assembled to accomplish an organizational task. Team members can self-select or be appointed by supervisors or managers. Teams can be composed of people from the same work unit or come from among different work units. Some organize to manage an ongoing function, for example top-management teams, but others organize to manage a single project, for example review an existing reward system or develop a new product or work process. In a global world, many members of groups are from different cultural backgrounds.

Teams Work on Different Types of Tasks

Teams can be assembled to work on different tasks as well. For example, some teams face ambiguous tasks whereas others confront a clearly defined task. Team production of an automobile is a clearly defined task. When the design phase is complete, various parts of the task are assigned to individuals or groups who assemble the car. A product-development team may be assigned to an ambiguous task such as new product creation. The general intent is clear, but the team cannot know in advance what attributes will appeal to customers, what the product should look like, or how it should operate. Resolving these ambiguities is part of the project-development team's task. Individual responsibilities are less easily assigned in advance to teams with ambiguous tasks.

Teams have long been a part of the organizational landscape in Japan and elsewhere in Asia where collectivism is a dominant cultural norm. In the US where individualism is a stronger norm, teams became popular as a management tool only in response to growing Japanese competition in the mid-1970s. Today teams are a distinctive feature of most organizations, particularly global ones.

Teams Function for Different Time Periods

Some teams work together over long time periods; others are of short duration. For example, so-called "hot" groups or teams are relatively short-lived and disband once their task is complete (Lipman-Blumen and Leavitt, 1999). A crisis-reaction group such as the one Johnson and Johnson assembled following Tylenol poisonings is one example of a hot group. Other characteristics of hot teams are a shared sense of being part of a vital mission and task dominance that can drive out other considerations including interpersonal ones. The flame of hot teams can lead to burnout or personal flare-ups in a short time period. This suggests that the characteristics of hot teams can lead to dysfunction when introduced to a team whose work is accomplished over a long time period.

Teams Malfunction

Sometimes teams do not function well, but this can occur for many reasons such as the flame-out factor for hot teams. Some teams become dysfunctional due to personal conflict among team members. For example, a group with too many leaders can explode. Conversely, if no one is willing to lead, the group can stagnate. These examples suggest that managers should answer the following questions before assembling a team:

1 Are team members capable of completing the task; that is, does each have the skills needed for the team's task?
2 Are team members able to work well together?
3 Will the leader be chosen by the group or by the manager? The latter choice can circumvent some team leadership problems.
4 What training is needed to prepare team members for any group process problems they might confront?
5 How can group members be rewarded for their work when it is likely that some will work harder than others?

Some teams fail because they are not well structured for success. For example, sometimes a team is assigned to a project without sufficient resources, such as time or information, to accomplish its task. In a worst-case scenario, a manager might assemble a team of people who do not work well together for the very purpose of delaying or destroying a distasteful idea. This can lead to morale problems among team members when they realize their work is not valued.

Creating a Sense of Team

The Boeing Corporation found that a sense of engineering primacy was an impediment to them in their attempt to streamline aircraft design and manufacture. In the past, Boeing engineers created aircraft designs without consulting manufacturing. Thus, they rarely knew if their designs could be built. Newly forced to collaborate ▶

with manufacturing in the design phase, many engineers initially objected or were unwilling to listen to manufacturing people's suggestions. At least initially while they were learning, manufacturing personnel found it difficult to contribute fully to the collaborative process. Observing these initial reactions, organizational leaders recognized that crossing functions required more than an order: it meant training in teamwork; it meant recognizing assumptions and perceptions of who was most and least important to the organization and why; and it meant changing the way people viewed themselves relative to others. Crossing functional boundaries between design and manufacturing took time and effort at the Boeing Company, but the company persisted to remain in the global market for airplane design and production.

Building Effective Teams

When they do function well, teams contribute to organizational success. Well-balanced teams that combine insights, abilities, and skills of several or many people provide a means for maximizing the advantages of diverse thinking. Additionally, teams tend to perform well when there is top-management support for them, when appropriate skills are represented on the team, when leaders have high-level personal skills that satisfy task and the social needs of group members, and when managers help team members respect and trust others. Writing in *The Wisdom of Teams*, Jon Katzenbach and Douglas Smith (1993) believe highly successful teams share the following characteristics:

1 They are small, preferably less than 10 members.
2 They mix people who have complementary skills in terms of technical expertise and ability to solve problems or manage interpersonal conflict.
3 They share common commitment to a realistic and do-able goal.
4 They set specific performance goals.

Phases of Team Development

One team challenge is to function as a group rather than as a bunch of autonomous individuals. According to management scholars, virtually every successful project or team group transitions through five project stages:

1 The forming stage is characterized by hopeful uncertainty as individuals get to know one another and struggle to define the project and the role of each in it. People are usually well disposed to work together, but some will be anxious to get on with the task and others will want to develop trust. Both sets of needs must be met at this stage, and so it is imperative to take the time to talk out individual interests and concerns; to be honest about constraints faced; to describe past experiences with groups to help the group pool prior learning. Most groups are

composed of people who have the technical skills and abilities to succeed nicely in the assigned task, but projects fail when social needs go unmet.

2 In the storming stage, individuals work out differences in approach, opinion, interests, and personality. Many individuals are uncomfortable with conflict, and will try to smooth it out before it is resolved. Cross-cultural differences in resolving conflict need to be described and decisions made to ensure that all are able to contribute fully to the group.

3 In the norming stage, members of the group become a group, establishing explicit and implicit expectations of each other. In this stage, it is imperative for individuals to share their expectations of each other and create a performance appraisal system for group use. The latter is difficult to do but provides a mechanism for dealing with problems that may arise later. Rotating meeting leadership or other roles provides insight into the work others do.

4 In the performing stage, the group completes its tasks and achieves set objectives. It assesses its performance against standards established in the norming stage.

5 In adjourning, some people will feel elated at task accomplishments; others will feel sad because the group's work is done. The group should find ways to accommodate both.

Most reviews of these five stages of group development imply that group-development processes are linear and sequential. However, Appelbaum et al. (1998) believe that teams can get stuck in a particular process phase, for example storming, or they can loop back to an earlier stage. For example, a group with a common set of norms may need to revise norms as tasks evolve. Further, changes in team membership or even absence and illness among group members may result in new rounds of conflict or "storming" as members realign themselves and their roles.

Leading and Managing Teams

Much occurs in a team that transcends the obvious and explicit purpose of task accomplishment. For example, interpersonal relations are an important part of the group process. Managing these dynamics requires a team leader with more than technical skills; also important are personal skills such as patience and persistence and work-related skills such as an ability to interpret cross-cultural cues. In addition, managing teams requires some awareness of how differing teams can be managed. Hackman (2002) notes that different types of teams require different levels of authority. For example, the team that executes a task will be manager-led, but a team that executes, monitors, and manages the work process needs to be self-managing. Teams that execute, self-manage, and design context are self-designing teams, and teams that do all of the above and also set the team's overall direction are self-governing teams. These examples illustrate that managers need to consider many factors from team type and purpose to desired outcome when assembling teams.

Global Teams

Global teams are defined as groups from different nationals who cross cultures and time zones for an extended period of time to work on a common project (Marquardt and Horvath, 2001). These authors note that global teams face challenges of coordination and control, geographic distance, and cultural differences that impede communication and make it difficult to maintain a sense of team. A study of teams in global organizations showed that team performance also is affected by autonomy, recognition, and appropriate rewards for team performance (Borelli et al., 1995).

Global teams also can be assembled in a single place. For example, Danone created its Vitapole location in France to bring together researchers, scientists, and engineers on a periodic basis. The Vitapole location houses over 1,000 people representing 20 nationalities. These scientists also use the company website to communicate with one another when they are dispersed.

Table 14.3 lists some of the personal, work-related, and social/intellectual skills important to a global team leader.

Table 14.3 *Characteristics of successful global team leaders*

Personal	Work-related	Intellectual/social
Patient/persistent	Capable of systems thinking	Curious intellectually and socially
Emotionally stable	Can make decisions in ambiguous situations	Able to form personal relationships and build rapport
Able to live with failure	Capable of pushing cultural limits	Knowledgeable about historical and current social developments
Open-minded	Able to model behavior valued in a specific cultural context	Sensitive to the values of each person
Humble	Able to read cross-cultural business cues	Motivated to work cross-culturally
Strong imagination	Able to adapt management style	
	Technically competent	

Source material: Mary O'Hara-Devereaux and Robert Johansen (1994) *Globalwork*, p. 106. San Francisco, CA: Jossey-Bass. This material is used by permission of John Wiley & Sons, Inc.

MANAGING MULTICULTURAL TEAMS

Natural challenges arise in teams, even when members of the team are from the same background and national culture. This occurs because individuals differ. They bring different personalities, different intellectual and interpersonal skills, and different work experiences to the team. In addition to individual differences, multicultural teams also confront differences in behaviors, expectations, and values due to cultural background. For example, people from collectivist cultures value group cohesion and are likely to have considerable experience working on teams. People from highly individualist cultures are less likely to bring this experience to the group. Instead, they may have more experience working alone—so much so that some believe group work is a big waste of their time.

Cultural Diversity in Teams

There were few examples to guide Khanh Vu in managing 35 engineers from 11 nations in an engineering department of Sun Microsystem. All the engineers shared technical expertise, but few were fluent with US culture and fewer still with the free-wheeling culture of California's Silicon Valley where Sun is headquartered. Accordingly, Vu and his group had to invent the future. For example, many of the engineers were from Asian cultures where conflict and criticism would not be tolerated in meetings. These people wondered how criticism of work could be anything other than criticism of a person's character. Vu himself wondered how people could shout at one another in a meeting, yet walk out the door as friends. As a group, the engineers realized that certain topics were culturally sensitive and could not be discussed in casual conversation, including sex, religion, politics, money, and relationships.

Source material: Marilyn Lewis (1993, Feb. 3) Multicultural companies invent the future as they go. *The Seattle Times*, p. E9.

Cultural differences of many types affect team dynamics. Table 14.4 illustrates value-based differences likely to lead to behavioral differences for team members.

Table 14.4 *Cultural contrasts affecting teamwork*

Use time to build relationships that facilitate work	*Ways to use time*	Use time to accomplish tasks
Problem solving is circular	*Ways to reason*	Linear and logical problem-solving
The group is most important	*Self vs. group*	The individual is most important
One's accomplishments are to enhance the group	*Modesty vs. boasting*	One's accomplishments enhance a career
Find ways to maintain harmony	*Responding to others*	Tell it like it is; be direct
Time is elastic	*Use of time*	Time is money

Table 14.4 illustrates contrasting and learned cultural styles that may affect group dynamics. These can create conflict among group members, and further shape how conflict is perceived, handled, or resolved (Appelbaum et al., 1998). For example, behavioral differences can generate mistrust that communication differences encourage. In the Safewall case, the Chinese programmer distrusted American colleagues because he believed they were "loud." When conflict occurs in multicultural groups, Appelbaum et al. (1998) suggest that managers define conflict issues from the point of view of all cultures represented, uncover cultural interpretations of specific issues, and help group members see how cultural knowledge can lead to synergy rather than group dysfunction.

One Team Leads to Another

Levi Strauss leaders decided to institute a shared success program for employees worldwide. They began with a global task force of line managers and people representing important company functions such as human resources, finance, tax, and communications. This team had to begin at ground zero to articulate plan purpose and decide on issues such as eligibility, payout criteria, and so on. The design process took five months, and was followed by an implementation phase that included educating worldwide employees about the plan. This phase began with global communications teams who took charge of information distribution. The latter group had to be aware of differences including legal and cultural ones that impede or enhance communications. Finally, on-site groups located around the world developed additional teams to implement within nations and regions. Multicultural membership in each of these teams helped facilitate development and implementation of the plan worldwide.

Culture affects work groups most when the task is ambiguous, when interactions occur over a long period of time, and when outcomes of the group task are important (Thomas, 2002). A strong organizational culture that encourages teamwork can help to overcome these challenges. Compensation systems that reward people for their performance in a group also aid performance as does intercultural teamwork training. The following example from Intel shows that training can take many forms.

Intel's Intercultural Training

Intercultural Awareness: managers and employees are introduced to information about how workers from different cultures perceive the business structure, processes, and procedures.

Multicultural Integration: a series of workshops provide skill building and career development for foreign-born professionals.

Culture Specific Training: when groups are to work with others from a specific culture, they receive training better to understand their own cultures and to learn about cultural nuances of the other group.

▶

> *Training for International Assignments*: usually a training consultant who has lived and worked in the assigned country is brought in to orient the newly assigned person to the language, culture, and practices of the host country.
>
> *Intact Team Training*: consultants are brought in to act as liaisons, translators or intervention providers to encourage positive ways for people from different cultures to work together.

Informational forms of training enhance cognitive knowledge and improve awareness of behavioral differences, but more intensive (and expensive) cultural learning may be needed to move analysis beyond the surface level of culture. Whether offered to enhance cross-cultural or diversity understanding, more intensive forms of cultural learning such as sensitivity training often are resisted, perhaps because they ask people to reach a new level of awareness about themselves or to examine negatives of their own cultural values and behaviors.

TEAMWORK IN VIRTUAL ORGANIZATIONS

Growing demand for coordination and integration motivates organizations to assemble virtual teams of people who are geographically and organizationally linked via telecommunication technologies (Bell and Kozlowski, 2002; Townsend et al., 1998). Among benefits of virtual teams is that people working all over the world can contribute to the same project. Their virtuality reduces travel costs, may improve cycle time for projects, can reduce organizational duplication, and can provide greater flexibility for people whether they work at home or elsewhere (Bell and Kozlowski, 2002; Kayworth and Leidner, 2000). The virtual team also confronts challenges.

According to authors Michael Kossler and Sonya Prestridge (1996), these challenges include communication, conflict resolution, decision-making, and members' abilities to feel the sense of team unity valuable to success. These authors distinguish between virtual teams—defined as temporary and geographically dispersed teams—and globally dispersed teams (GDT)—defined as relatively permanent. This distinction suggests that a virtual team suffers from the same problems any temporary team faces, that is, lack of commitment to the team or divided interests. The GDT might be more akin to permanent teams whose members commit to each other because the team will operate over the long term.

Establishing Virtual Teams

Kossler and Prestridge (1996) suggest that a virtual team might benefit from following guidelines such as:

1 Hold an initial face-to-face start-up meeting.
2 Establish interdependency among team members.

3 Establish a schedule of periodic face-to-face meeetings.
4 Agree on what, when, and how information will be shared and how team members are to respond to information that is shared.
5 Establish clear norms and protocols for surfacing assumptions and conflicts.
6 Clarify need for members to nurture each other and credit relationships.
7 Recognize and honor diversity of cultures.

CONTRIBUTORS TO TEAM SUCCESS

In summary, teams can be local or they can be virtual. They can be big, small, project oriented, or managerial. Although teams share characteristics—such as transitioning through the five developmental stages—the particulars for each team will vary. Managers who want to encourage team success will:

- Select team members with care to provide needed skills and abilities.
- Provide training to encourage team success.
- Assess team progress at critical intervals.
- Encourage development of team members.
- Assure that teams have the resources needed to accomplish their assigned tasks.

In global organizations, member selection is likely to include diversity, and this may require training for intercultural awareness.

Contributors to Virtual Team Success

Research on virtual teams is somewhat limited. However a university study provides some direction (Kayworth and Leidner, 2000). Twelve virtual teams were assembled, composed of 5–7 members from three universities located in Mexico, the US, and Europe. Half the groups observed that cultural differences affected their ability to coordinate the project and communicate with one another. Those teams that used multiple communication modes such as e-mail, web-based communication tools, and a team website, tended to be more satisfied with their ability to communicate and outcomes than did groups that used e-mail as their single communication mode. This suggests that many forms of communication may help to compensate for the loss of face time.

Interestingly, only four of the twelve groups judged their leader effective. Common characteristics among leaders judged to be effective were: ability to articulate project goals and assign responsibilities for specific schedules and deadlines, a high priority for regular communication, high flexibility and empathy for team members, and cultural awareness. This suggests that virtual team leaders enhance team success when they combine task skills such as goal setting with personal skills such as empathy for others.

For team members, successful team participation begins with recognition that team members were assembled *because* of their differences, and that all bring technical competence to the task. In order to make the most of the team process, members need to encourage expression of differences rather than ignore or suppress them. Thus, it is important for team members to solicit input from each other, and to withhold judgment when team members have different preferences for speaking or listening. Finally, it may be valuable for team members to avoid conflict around leadership by recognizing that all team members can develop the capacity to lead and to follow. This can be practiced by sharing or rotating leadership tasks.

It is clear that global organizations—indeed, most organizations—increasingly accomplishing their tasks through teams. Accordingly, over an entire career, most people will be on many teams; on some they will lead, on others they will follow. This being the case, it is important to understand and develop skills to lead and to follow.

CHAPTER SUMMARY

Hiring from a global labor pool results in cultural diversity in global organizations with worldwide facilities. Growing diversity within nations also increases cultural diversity in domestic workplaces. Diversity of three types is important to organizations: human diversity, structural diversity, and diversity among organizational processes.

Organizational responses to diversity, that is diversity strategies, depend on external and internal pressures for diversity and top-management commitment to leveraging diversity. These various responses are characterized by different behaviors in terms of organizing people, processes, and structures.

Organizations assemble teams or groups to accomplish work-related tasks that include idea development, product assembly, and organizational learning. Increasingly, teams are virtual.

Different types of teams require different forms of leadership. In general teams require a leader with more than technical skills. Also important are personal skills such as patience and persistence and work-related skills such as an ability to interpret cross-cultural business cues.

Culture affects work groups most when the task is ambiguous, when interactions occur over a long period of time, and when outcomes of the group task are important.

REVIEW AND DISCUSSION QUESTIONS

1 In what ways is inequality inefficient at the global, national, and firm levels? When there are inequalities in the firm, are there some that people will accept and others that might be counterproductive? What would these be, and what is the basis for acceptable versus unacceptable forms of inequalities?

2 Have you ever been on a dysfunctional team? Analyze the organization that assembled the team to consider how organizational culture may have contributed to team dysfunction. Also analyze team members (yourself included) to explore the team's dysfunction. Use the five stages of a group to analyze the team's progress; did the group move smoothly through each stage or get stuck at one?

Chapter 15
CORPORATE SOCIAL RESPONSIBILITY AND ETHICS

VALUE ADDED AND VALUE EXPECTED

The public increasingly calls for corporate social responsibility (CSR) and ethical behaviors. Some practice one without the other, creating public suspicion of all companies. For example, philanthropic giving and responsiveness to community needs at Enron led to public belief that the company was a great corporate citizen. Later it was revealed that leaders engaged in illegal and unethical activities. For example, top managers encouraged employee investments even when they were selling their own shares of the firm. Similarly, Parmalat SpA leaders showed good corporate citizenship, but as the evidence below suggests, they also behaved in illegal and unethical ways. These examples demonstrate that companies must be *both* socially responsible and ethical.

The Parmalat case which follows shows why CSR and ethical behaviors are increasingly important to a global public. The first Tanzi in what became the Parmalat empire supplied cured meat near Parma. In 1961 the company passed to his 22-year-old son Calisto Tanzi who dutifully abandoned his university studies to take the helm. The firm he called Parmalat was named after his home city and the "latte" the company distributed via a Swedish invention called Ultra Heat Treatment (UHT) that extends milk's shelf life. Tanzi expanded a growing product line offered in many countries. By 2003 the company owned dozens of food lines such as boxed milk, tomato paste, and cookies produced and sold in over 30 nations. It employed 36,000 people worldwide and was Italy's eighth largest company.

The public bought 49 percent of the company's equity shares in 1990 and thereafter the company added debt largely underwritten by global firms such as J.P. Morgan, Morgan Stanley, and Merrill Lynch. Parmalat the public company was part of a complex holding company structure based in Italy.

Calisto Tanzi proved to be a beneficent employer and philanthropist, giving $2 million to restore the 16th-century Correggio frescoes at Parma Cathedral. Unbeknownst to the global public, Calisto Tanzi often siphoned money from the public Parmalat into the family-owned Parma AC and travel company Parmatour. According to reports, he told financial officers to record false credits in Parmalat accounts. But attorneys attest that Calisto did not think he was doing anything out of the ordinary when he shifted hundreds of millions of dollars from Parmalat's accounts to those of the soccer team. In his defense, lawyer Michele Ributti claimed, "It's an Italian way of thinking" (Menn, 2004: A3).

In 1999 the Borsa Italiano stock exchange had introduced a new code of ethics requiring a minimum number of independent directors on every board, but exceptions were made for large companies like Parmalat that could explain their decisions to the public. Parmalat provided its rationale, the public accepted it, and Parmalat's board operated as an exception to the new code of ethics. According to news reports, Calisto Tanzi never stopped thinking of Parmalat as a family-owned firm. Parmalat's chief executive was Stefano Tanzi, and its board of directors included other Tanzi family members. Son Stefano Tanzi was chairman of Parma Calcio the soccer team, and daughter Francesca Tanzi headed Parmatour. Exemption from ethics standards and the holding company structure shielded the company in part from public scrutiny.

In many nations, managers are agents for rather than company owners. This agency model is often criticized because the agent's interests are most likely to be self-oriented. ▶

For example, in the interests of his/her annual compensation, an agent may be motivated to improve short-term performance even at the expense of long-term growth. After all, the agent may not even be there in the long term. Family ownership is often lauded as a contrast because family members have long-term interests in the firm's performance and may make necessary sacrifices to ensure long-term success and firm survival. The thinking goes that the family has a vested interest in being responsible because the family's future depends on the company's future.

But there is a downside to family ownership evident in Parmalat's failure. Family and business interests can become entwined such that managers do not differentiate between their own and public interests. For Parlamat the result was family disgrace, company failure, and job losses around the world when managers went beyond the boundaries of ethics and the law. For example, Calisto Tanzi was arrested and marched off to aging San Vittore prison. Weeks later three other family members and several Parmalat employees also were jailed to prevent possible destruction of evidence against Parmalat. Latin American milk suppliers filed suit against the company, fearing they would never be paid for milk delivered, and around the world Parmalat employees wondered if their jobs would disappeared.

Although the senior Mr. Tanzi admitted he knew the books were fraudulent, he initially denied responsibility. The fall of Parmalat led to criticism of an Italian approach to global business that encourages family networks of companies whose members play leadership roles in Italian politics, culture, and civil society organizations.

The moral of this story is that the type of company, its size, the way it is structured and even its country of origin shape a company, its activities, and its approach to CSR and ethics. It also suggests that survival and success in a global world increasingly relies on doing well financially and also doing good work in the eyes of the public. That is, companies are expected to be socially responsible and ethical according to external standards. In a global world, these two processes become not so much value-added as value-expected activities.

Source material: Alessandra Galloni (2004, Feb. 18) Children of Parmalat founder are arrested as probe widens. *The Wall Street Journal*, p. B2; Joseph Menn (2004, Jan.14) 'The family way' backfires for food conglomerate. *The Seattle Times*, p. A3.

CHAPTER OVERVIEW

This chapter examines two important processes that facilitate business interactions with stakeholders and with mediating organizations: corporate social responsibility (CSR) development and ethics processes. Both are increasingly integrative, helping global firms to organize internally and adapt to external shifts.

Processes are systematic or continuous activities to accomplish organizational purposes. Unlike programs that can be easily added or deleted, processes tend to be long term and embedded within the organization. Usually they are integrated with people, structure, and other organizational processes. In most firms, for example, strategic management is part of a continuous process that shapes structure and outlines what jobs need to be accomplished. Processes like internal supply-chain management help organizations coordinate production. This chapter examines two processes that link the organization to its external environments: corporate social responsibility and ethics. Worldwide integration of these two helps organizations adapt to and anticipate external environmental shifts and work with mediating organizations.

CORPORATE CITIZENSHIP AND SOCIAL RESPONSIBILITY INITIATIVES

In the 1990s, social expectations encouraged businesses to integrate self-interest with community interest. Those communities are increasingly international and even global (Waddock and Boyle, 1995). Corporate social responsibility (CSR) is the process by which businesses negotiate their role in society. For a business, this would mean developing a CSR process with internal standards. These standards vary, activities vary, and companies engage in CSR activities for many reasons.

Reasons for CSR Initiatives

CSR initiatives are important to a global public. For example, a study of 25,000 consumers in 23 nations showed that two-thirds of those surveyed want companies to go beyond fiscal responsibility to also take on social roles (Millennium Poll, 2000). This research also showed the public forms their opinions about a company based in part on CSR activities. In a 2002 study of British adults, half said that a company should give equal attention to society, the environment, and financial performance (The public's view, 2002).

Due to globalization of information, the public is better informed about business activities. Cultural shifts encourage them to use this information to evaluate corporate social responsibility. Echo Research's (2003) study found that monthly media volume on CSR issues has almost quadrupled since 2000. This pattern is found in Europe, the US, China, Australia, and South Africa. Social responsibility is increasingly viewed as a positive. For example, a social responsibility measure is included in *Fortune*'s annual list of "Global Most Admired" companies.

A second reason for CSR initiatives is they help organizations hire and retain the people they want. The Echo study (2003) also found that business decision-makers believe CSR initiatives help them attract, retain, and motivate employees. A US study showed employee morale is higher in organizations that are involved in their communities (Lewin and Sabater, 1996). Freight firm TNT measured satisfaction among their employees, finding that 94 percent of employees approve TNT's responsible attitude toward the community.

Third, CSR initiatives relate to business performance (Lewin and Sabater, 1996). Firms that pursued a triple bottom line of economic, environmental, and social sustainability outperformed the Global Index (Green is good, 1999). Businesses leaders with CSR processes in place believe that rather than being a substitute for profitability, social responsibility is a means of achieving profitability. For example, the Millennium Poll of over a thousand chief executives in 33 nations in Europe, Asia, and the Americas indicates that most CEOS think responsible behavior toward employees, shareholders, and communities is a core concern for firm profitability (DiPiazza, 2002).

Cargill: Doing Well by Doing Good

Cargill is a food and agricultural business. Their stated purpose is "to be the global leader in nourishing people." They further define nourishment to include "feeding people better" and "providing whatever is necessary for life, health and growth." This "requires taking care with each individual we touch. Yet it also embraces the idea of using our know-how to spur environmentally sustainable economic development for society at large." Cargill notes that measures of successful performance include both "enriched communities and profitable growth."

An example of how Cargill integrates this purpose worldwide is found at their Saraburi, Thailand facility which operates using the same safety and health standards in all Cargill plants. But the Saraburi plant has the best safety record in the industry and in Cargill. Fewer accidents mean safer employees, less stress and cost to the communities in which they live, and a better use of economic and human resources.

Source material: Cargill Identity Guidelines (2002): *http://www.cargillbrandidentity.com/strategy/vision.htm* (accessed Nov. 14, 2003); (1999) Washington, DC: US Chamber of Commerce Center for Corporate Citizenship.

CSR initiatives vary almost as much as firms. Some of these CSR variations appear on the continuum in Figure 15.1. Firms that adopt minimum to no CSR initiatives occupy the three positions on the left of the continuum. For example on the far left is the firm that puts profit motives ahead of all social objectives. This firm is willing to forgo morality to achieve profits; it subscribes to no CSR initiatives. This firm is unlikely to survive in the long run, often because it engages in illegal behaviors to achieve its goals. At the second point on the continuum is the firm that fights CSR initiatives, perhaps by rejecting stakeholder dialogue or lobbying against legal changes. This company usually conforms to laws because active opposition to social initiatives puts it above the public's radar screen.

In the third position is a firm that complies with rather than fights CSR laws. This company reflects the level of social responsibility recommended by Milton Friedman who maintains there is one and only one social responsibility of business—to use its resources and engage in activities designed to increase its profits so long as it stays within the law. According to Zadek (2002), in future the public will reject this as a CSR minimum.

Firms that exceed CSR minimums cluster on the right side of the continuum. These firms engage in a wide range of CSR activities. What the continuum shows is that leaders who were inspired by CSR only a few years ago now are integrating CSR with other organizational practices. Moreover, movement to the right of the continuum is accompanied by more integration of CSR initiatives with an organization's people, other processes, and structures. Below are examples of how this occurs.

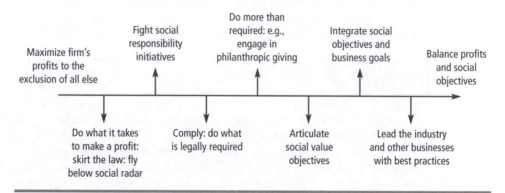

Figure 15.1 *A corporate social responsibility continuum*

Philanthropic Giving

Philanthropic giving is one way companies demonstrate good citizenship. According to the AAFRC Trust for Philanthropy (Charity holds, 2003), in 2002 US companies gave $12.19 billion to charities. An integrative form of charitable giving is called strategic philanthropy wherein a corporation gives to a cause aligned with its own strategies. For example, Avon Products Inc. "the company for women" donates funds to breast cancer research.

The Gates Foundation and the Global Alliance for Vaccines and Immunization (GAVI)

The Bill and Melinda Gates Foundation are separate from Microsoft, but Bill Gates founded both. Observing that UNICEF had insufficient resources, the Gates donated over a billion dollars to immunize children through GAVI. GAVI uses corporate style methods to allocate money and supplies. For example, recipients of GAVI funds must provide clear outlines for fund use, are subject to auditing, and must report results. But many of the nations where vaccine is needed do not keep good records, and this makes it hard for them to conform to the application process. According to Gates, the process assures that the money will go to children's needs, but some criticized the process. For example, some believe that Western accountability standards are too high/too soon for developing economies. Others believe that adoption of objective systems could divert time and interest from meeting children's direct needs. Nevertheless, by 2002 GAVI had provided vaccine for 7 million children, saving an estimated 700,000 young lives in developing economies.

Source material: Rachel Zimmerman (2001, Dec. 3) Gates brings his business sensibilities to efforts to vaccinate the world's poor. *The Wall Street Journal*, pp. A1, A8.

Some companies donate gifts such as volunteer time or goods. For example, pharmaceutical giant Johnson and Johnson donates medical supplies to Operation Smile—a charitable organization that repairs cleft lips and palates for children worldwide.

Employee Volunteerism

Many companies encourage employee volunteerism. But Husky Injection Molding System has taken it to a whole new level. Through a Green Shares program, Husky gives stock to employee volunteers. Husky especially encourages environmental causes that are of greatest concern to CEO and founder Robert Schad. Each of Husky's 3,000 employees worldwide can earn as many as 30 shares per year. The company developed a special tally for employees to total their share earnings. For example, bicycling to work can earn one tenth of a share per day. This program encourages employees, and contributes to the environmental quality of communities in which Husky operates.

Source material: Larry M. Greenberg (2000, Jan. 24) Canada's Husky Injection awards stock to employees who perform good deeds. *The Wall Street Journal*, p. B13A.

On the face of it, it might seem that corporate giving is a good thing. But findings from the Reputation Institute (Alsop, 2002b) indicate that philanthropy will not enhance corporate reputation if a company a) fails to live up to its philanthropic image or b) if consumers perceive philanthropy to be manipulative. For example, some members of the public take a cynical view of Philip Morris's charitable giving because of the company's endorsement of tobacco products (Alsop, 2000b).

Reputational Capital

A 2004 Harris Interactive and Reputation Institute report indicates that three-quarters of US respondents rate the image of big corporations as either "not good" or "terrible." The study suggests that once lost it is difficult for organizations to rebuild their reputation. Companies that ranked high on the 2004 reputational measure were Honda, which was rated high for corporate sincerity, being a good place to work, trust, admiration, and respect. Global nonprofit organizations also were rated for reputation in 2004. At the top of the list were Doctors Without Borders and Habitat for Humanity; at the bottom were Greenpeace and People for the Ethical Treatment of Animals whose respective reputational ratings were 44 percent and 35 percent.

Source material: Ronald Alsop (2004, Feb. 19) Corporate scandals hit home. *The Wall Street Journal*, pp. B1, B2 and online Journal.

Alsop (2004) suggests it is sometimes difficult to balance image and action. For example, both Procter & Gamble and Honda Motor Company donated supplies in the aftermath of New York terrorist attacks in 2001. Both companies decided not to publicize their involvement, but those who thought they'd done nothing subsequently criticized them.

Articulate Social Value Objectives

Some business leaders are simply committed to developing an integrative global approach to managing corporate social responsibility. They do this is various ways. Some, like McDonald's, incorporate values in their vision statements, making it part of an articulated belief system:

> We believe that being a good corporate citizen means treating people with fairness and integrity, sharing our success with the communities in which we do business, and being a leader on issues that affect customers. (McDonald's Corporation, 1992)

Philips' General Business Principles serve the same purpose: they articulate a single set of principles to guide employees throughout the world. These and similar "values" statements provide a specific outline of the company's expectations of themselves and their employees, and they illustrate that the company is willing to go public with its values.

Philips' General Business Principles

The purpose of the Philips' General Business Principles is to establish guiding principles of Philips' ethics in business conduct. These principles describe the organization's commitment to employees and the commitment expected from employees and it outlines specific expectations in terms of maintaining the integrity of financial records, gift giving and accepting, outside interests, bribery, and community activities.

Source material: Royal Philips Electronics annual report to shareholders. (2000).

Starbucks Coffee Company found that an aspiration to improve the quality of life in coffee-producing countries involved more than a statement of commitment. The Starbucks experience described below shows that considerable managerial resources are needed to create what became a short document titled "Starbucks Commitment ... To Do Our Part."

"Starbucks Commitment ... To Do Our Part"

Starbucks' senior vice president Dave Olsen described the six-month process that yielded a four-page document of company beliefs and plans to improve the lives of people in coffee-producing countries. He said the document involved more than a product; it caused top managers to "explore our own values and beliefs" and examine past actions as well as involve themselves in "a lot of soul searching to come to an understanding of how we can live up to our sense of responsibility to make a difference in the world." Olsen described this process at an Economic Justice Forum held at Seattle University. Following his presentation, a member of the audience promptly asked: "Why haven't you done more?"

Integrate Social Objectives and Business Goals

Engage with Stakeholders

Broadly defined, stakeholders are individuals and groups who are affected by or can affect company decisions. Primary stakeholders are internal to the company such as owners, employees, labor unions, customers, and suppliers (Clarkson, 1995). Secondary stakeholders are usually external to the firm; they could be nongovernmental organizations, social activists, community groups, and governmental organizations (Waddock et al., 2002). Other external stakeholders can be those who live in communities near global company sites or where the company's products are sold. Many of these stakeholders take an active interest in CSR activities.

Top leaders worldwide report that responsible treatment of stakeholders is an important element of CSR initiatives (Corporate social responsibility gaining, 2002). Pressure from stakeholder groups to improve or change conduct ranked second most important among company challenges in 2000 (Most respected, 2000). Further, a study of stakeholder relationships showed they have a direct impact on financial performance (Berman et al., 1999). This suggests that positive connections with key stakeholders can improve firm profitability.

The introductory case for Chapter 3 showed how Shell stakeholders were at first ignored. Later Shell engaged in dialogue with stakeholders that eventually brought the latter into Shell's decision-making processes. The example also illustrates that negative stakeholder action can profoundly affect firm performance. This is one reason to engage with stakeholders. Another reason for stakeholder engagement is the innovation that results with diverse perspectives on the same challenges. The Clarkson Principles of Stakeholder Management (The Clarkson Centre, 1999: 4) outline company activities that enhance stakeholder interactions:

Principle 1: Managers should acknowledge and actively monitor the concerns of all legitimate stakeholders, and should take their interests appropriately into account in decision-making and operations.

Principle 2: Managers should listen to and openly communicate with stakeholders about their respective concerns and contributions, and about the risks that they assume because of their involvement with the corporation.

Principle 3: Managers should adopt processes and modes of behavior that are sensitive to the concerns and capabilities of each stakeholder constituency.

Principle 4: Managers should recognize the interdependence of efforts and rewards among stakeholders, and should attempt to achieve a fair distribution of the benefits and burdens of corporate activity among them, taking into account their respective risks and vulnerabilities.

Principle 5: Managers should work cooperatively with other entities, both public and private, to insure that risks and harm arising from corporate activities are minimized and, where they cannot be avoided, appropriately compensated.

Principle 6: Managers should avoid altogether activities that might jeopardize inalienable human rights (for example the right to life) or give rise to risks which, if clearly understood, would be patently unacceptable to relevant stakeholders.

Principle 7: Managers should acknowledge the potential conflicts between (a) their own role as corporate stakeholders, and (b) their legal and moral responsibilities for the interests of stakeholders, and should address such conflicts through open communication, appropriate reporting and incentive systems, and, where necessary, third-party review.

Cause-related Marketing

Other companies initiate "cause-related" marketing initiatives. In one variation, the company donates a portion of sales on selected products to the charitable organization. Welch Foods Inc. and Johnson & Johnson donate in this way to the World Wildlife Fund. Worldwide initiatives like these have increased revenues for causes from $75 million in 1988 to $535 million by 1997 (Kadlec and Van Voorst, 1997).

Cause-related marketing usually is an integral part of the company's marketing efforts, and many of these campaigns enhance the public's view of the organization. For example, a study of US households revealed that 83 percent of people have a more positive image of a product or company when the company supports a cause they care about. Sixty-six percent viewed cause-related marketing as a good way to help solve social problems, and 61 percent thought it should be a standard company activity (Companies and causes, 2000). In the same study, two-thirds of consumers say that if price and quality are equal, they are likely to switch to a brand or retailer backing a good cause. In a British study, cause-related marketing was shown to have a significant increase on brand affinity, with 48 percent of consumers actually changing buying behavior to companies involved in cause-related marketing (Brand benefits, 2003).

Cause-based Partnerships

Cause-based partnerships (CBP) are alliances between businesses and not-for-profit organizations that simultaneously respond to the values of civil society and address organizational needs. CBPs organize to alleviate a social problem, for example poverty, environmental degradation, social injustices or satisfy a social need, such as Special Olympics. The number of these relationships has grown (Berger et al., 1999; Crane, 2000). Major businesses and nonprofits such as General Motors, McDonald's, the World Wide Fund for Nature, and Greenpeace engage in CBPs and their numbers are expected to grow (Elkington and Fennell, 2000). The recent focus of most CBPs is economic development, environmental concerns, and public issues like health and education (Waddell and Brown, 1997). Environmental CBPs are particularly active (see Bendell, 2000b; Lober, 1997; Murphy and Bendell, 1997).

Austin (2000) notes that some CSR activities are transactional in nature or conducted at arm's length. For example, affinity charge cards produce revenue for a social need, but they require little company/CSO interaction. CBPs involve continual interactions between partners' managers and are usually more integrative than transactional. An example is Starbucks/Conservation International efforts to promote fair-trade coffee. Another is the CARE/Glaxo/Bangladeshi government partnership to eradicate parasites in Bangladeshi communities. The Marco Polo partnership between MCI/Worldcom, National Geographic, the Kennedy Center ArtLinks, and US teachers worked to reduce the digital divide for low-income children. All these require ongoing interaction between managers from different sectors who do not necessarily "speak the same language" in term of vision, values, or operational activities.

CBPs can involve many partners or two, combine organizations of different sizes and scope, are initiated by outside influences, organizational leaders, grassroots efforts among employees, or they can be forced. Whether they come about by chance or design, these kinds of partnerships create managerial linkages that connect businesses to social goals. This increases the complexity of managing CBPs.

Lead the Industry with CSR "Best Practices"

Many business leaders believe morality and profits are served when social objectives are integrated with other business activities. Companies like The Body Shop and Esprit base their global reputations on this approach. The Body Shop, for example, strives to provide effective cosmetic products and be a CSR leader. According to founder Anita Roddick:

> We take care in the manufacture of our products to minimize damage to the environment. Our Fair Trade policy establishes trading partnerships with indigenous people in the developing world. And we actively campaign for human rights and a ban on animal testing in the cosmetics industry. We wish to leave the world a better place, and in better shape, than we found it. (1996 The Body Shop catalogue)

Most CSR leaders concentrate on a limited number of social issues. For example, C&A, a Dutch retail chain, established a code of conduct to help abolish child labor, and IKEA will not sell carpets without certification that they did not require child labor. The following example concentrates on human rights as one instance of CSR leadership activities. A similar review of another social issue such as environmental protection, child labor, job creation, educational and digital inequities, disaster relief, worldwide safety standards, healthcare, and so on would highlight many of the same points.

Human Rights Initiatives

Levi Strauss is one of the best-known CSR leaders on human rights. In 1991, Levi Strauss became one of the first multinational companies to develop a comprehensive code of conduct to ensure that workers making their product anywhere in the world work in safe conditions and are treated with dignity and respect (Levi Strauss, 2002). Evidence of human rights violations caused Levi Strauss to introduce new terms of association with business partners in 1993, thereby becoming one of the first multinationals to adopt guidelines covering worker treatment. These guidelines covered suppliers and subcontractors who might otherwise use child labor or force employees to work unacceptable hours. Levi hires private inspectors to monitor human rights in their manufacturing plants around the world.

Businesses that lead on CSR activities often draw criticism. For example, stockholders may prefer they devote themselves to profits alone and social-action groups may use them to spotlight unmet needs. The following example shows how CSR leaders can be held to a higher standard than other firms.

Phillips-Van Heusen Corporation

Globalization of the textile industry touched off fierce competition for low-wage labor. Companies like Phillips-Van Heusen (PVH), manufacturer of brand name products Izod and Gant, have been caught between simultaneous demands for low costs and the desire to improve working conditions and pay. PVH chief executive Bruce Klatsky recognized that the firm had to import from lower-wage countries, but at the same time he took unusual steps to improve labor conditions. For example, in Guatemalan plants, PVH contributed more than $1.5 million to improve nutrition and schools in the villages where workers live; offers subsidized lunches and free on-site healthcare for employees; provides school supplies for workers' children; equips sewing workers with ergonomic chairs; and pays higher wages than could be earned for similar jobs in Guatemala.

Yet PVH Guatemala became the target of human rights activists who claimed PVH's shirt-making operation was paying wages below the poverty line, hired contractors that used underage workers, and intimidates union organizers. Human rights advocates acknowledge that PVH has worked hard to improve working conditions in Guatemalan plants, but claim that more progress can and should be made.

CSR activities like those above often are integrative mechanisms for adapting people, processes, and global structures. In addition, these activities help an organization live with, respond to, and anticipate needs of a global community.

ETHICS

Encouraging the same ethical behaviors worldwide also calls for internal organizational integration. In turn, ethical behaviors help organizations adapt to external expectations of them. Ethics are grounded in a moral philosophy that helps people discern between right and wrong. In the business world, ethics is the study of morally appropriate behaviors and decisions, examining what "should be done." This section looks at how ethical values emerge in organizations, followed by an examination of how these "home grown" values play out in international and then global markets.

Ethics in Domestic Organizations

National Culture Influences Organizational Ethics and Responsibility

Researchers note that national culture plays a key role in shaping organizational values and ethical behaviors (Becker and Fritsche, 1987; Hofstede, 1980; Buller et al., 1997; Vitell et al., 1993). As noted in Chapter 7, most businesses develop within nations by adopting dominant cultural values, beliefs, and behaviors such as obeying national laws and regulations and conforming to national norms.

Both laws and norms reflect national cultural values and together they outline "right" and "wrong" business behaviors. Except for laws, most of these absolutes are not written. Nevertheless, most people within a nation can distinguish between right and wrong behavior, and they carry this knowledge into the workplace. In this way, a nation's ethics significantly influences organizations and their ethics. Organizations often rely on implicit national values rather than formal ethical codes in a domestic setting. Exceptions can occur when the organization expands beyond its immediate environment to operate throughout a nation. An example is Sears. When it expanded in the US, Sears confronted regional cultural differences that it dealt with by creating some 29,000 pages of policies and procedures in 100 years.

Top Managers Also Influence Organizational Ethics

An organization's culture reflects the culture surrounding it (Laurent, 1999), and also top-managers' cultural orientations (Trompenaars and Hampden-Turner, 1998). Together these two exert a powerful influence on organizational behaviors (Adler, 1997).

Top-managers' values are particularly evident at an organization's founding or with a new chief officer. Some managers shape organizational culture with written statements such as the organization's vision, purpose, mission, or values. According to Beyer and Nino (1999), top managers create ethics-positive cultures by articulating organizational purpose in terms of social as well as business goals. Additionally, they carefully design reward systems that do not (however inadvertently) reward unethical behavior. They stay in touch with what is occurring in their own organizations and finally, they exemplify desired values in their own behaviors and decisions.

The Effects of Ethics-negative Managerial Behaviors

Ethics-negative behaviors can counteract ethics statements. Examples below illustrate that managers must do more than sign off on an ethics plan; they must live them as well.

> ### Walk the Talk
>
> In one workplace, a top manager smoked cigarettes in his office despite his own written smoking ban. The smoke-laden air traveled through the heating ducts, but little was done when nonsmokers objected. The result was ongoing tension between smokers and nonsmokers about "right" behavior. In another case, a hotel manager habitually parked his car beneath a sign reading "parking is not allowed." Among the implicit messages he conveyed is: it is acceptable to break the rules—if you are powerful enough to get away with it.

When managers behave unethically, employees can be demoralized or even leave their jobs. Others might follow-the-leader and engage in unethical behaviors themselves. Events associated with Enron and Arthur Andersen show that such tactics may yield short-term benefits, but they are unsustainable and can lead to an organization's demise.

> ### Enron's Culture Encouraged Unethical Behaviors
>
> High demands for performance and profitability led Enron employees first to cut ethical corners and finally to break laws as well. According to one Enron controller, the logic was as follows: "If your boss was [fudging] and you have never worked anywhere else, you just assume that everybody fudges earnings. Once you get there and you realized how it was, do you stand up and lose your job? It was scary. It was easy to get into 'Well, everybody else is doing it, so maybe it isn't so bad.'"
>
> Source material: John Byrne (2002, Feb. 25) The environment was ripe for abuse. *Business Week*, pp. 188–120.

In summary, the values and behaviors of top managers intersect with those of a nation to permeate an organization. Both external cultural values and internal organizational ones help employees make decisions about what is right and wrong. When—as occurred at Enron—top managers violate national cultural norms, the results can be disastrous. Organizations whose ethical standards are not congruent with their home culture may move their headquarters offshore in a search for lower ethical standards.

Ethics initiatives within a domestic culture are likely to be ad hoc because it is assumed that everyone knows what is expected. However, formal ethics initiatives might emerge in response to a specific problem. For example, in the 1970s many US companies created ombuds offices to field a growing number of discrimination complaints. Often these initiatives are stand-alone ones that are not integrated with other organizational activities.

ETHICS IN AN INTERNATIONAL CONTEXT

The main focus of international business is on interactions *between* nations. Thus, internationalization enlarges the scope of organizational initiatives, including ethics. Practically speaking, crossing national borders requires that organizational leaders manage more differences, it incorporates more diverse values into decision-making processes, and it exposes the organization to many more stakeholders whose values may be based on a different moral philosophy. These and other differences challenge organizations to establish and maintain strong and ethical corporate cultures that can reach across national boundaries and distances (Beyer and Nino, 1999).

Ethical Values Internationally

Sometimes a company simply assumes that their values can cross national borders. The following example from Nike illustrates what can happen when a company makes this assumption.

Nike—Founded on a Handshake
NIKE Inc. was "founded on a handshake" with implicit belief that "business with all of our partners [would be] based on trust, teamwork, honesty and mutual respect. We expect all of our business partners to operate on the same principles." But Nike discovered that their overseas subcontractors were not treating workers with the same level of respect expected in the US. This suggests that Nike's assumptions were unfounded.

As is true within nations, top business leaders instill ethics abroad (Donaldson, 1985) by providing ethical guidelines and themselves acting ethically. However, it may be difficult for a single manager to effectively convey ethical values internationally. For example, top managers in the home office are usually only occasional visitors to international sites. Thus they rely more on others to reinforce organizational values abroad such as general managers who more frequently deal with day-to-day ethical concerns such as equity and fairness at work (Smith, 1990). Richard De George (1993) believes organizations confront three types of ethical conflicts when operating outside national borders: pressures on individuals to violate their personal norms, pressures that arise when cultural norms differ, and pressures that arise when the company confronts a conflict between home and host-country interests.

Adaptive Ethics

Many large firms have followed one of two adaptive ethical paths when they go international: ethical absolutism or ethical relativism.

Ethical Absolutism—They Adapt to Us

One adaptive approach reflects what Heenan and Perlmutter (1979) called ethnocentrism—putting home-company interests first. In an ethnocentric firm, employees of the host culture are expected to adapt to the cultural norms and values of the employer. Ethnocentric practices may unfold somewhat invisibly when host and home culture are very similar or, as in the case of Nike, they rest on assumptions that are unfounded.

Ethical problems with ethnocentrism become noticeable when home and host cultures differ, particularly when a company tries to dominate and control in the host culture. The latter occurred in Central America's so-called "Banana Republics." Powerful North American business interests almost entirely dominated these cultures in the 1950s, often operating there as virtual fiefdoms with little regard to local custom or needs.

Although the ethnocentric approach to managing ethics can unfold in different ways, its common core is ethical absolutism that judges home-culture values as "right" and host culture values as "wrong" or at least secondary in importance. This absolutism requires little adaptation from the firm. However, host-country nationals usually resent ethical absolutes that conflict with their own values. In addition, an ethnocentric approach does not help managers develop a worldview that recognizes value differences.

Ethical Relativism—the Company Adapts

Some firms pursued a second adaptive approach that reflects cultural relativism. The cliché "when in Rome, do as the Romans do" best characterizes this approach. The international firm that adopts a relativist approach engages in host-country practices in that nation. Unless forbidden by law, this could mean paying bribes if that is the standard business practice. For example, Arvind Industries compromised their own ethical standards by bribing Taiwanese officials because company leaders believed it important to communicate and engage with businesses in nations where bribery is more a norm (Birchard, 2000); Arvind reported the bribes in their financial statements.

This approach to ethics recognizes that cultural values differ and it adapts accordingly. In practice the relativist firm will develop different ethical practices for different nations. With relativism, corporate conduct is tailored to the specific and unique situation often found in each country (Baker, 1993). In the absence of universals, the culturally relative firm must clearly outline expectations in written documents such as compliance guidelines that identify correct and incorrect behaviors. Thus, the rules are more formalized than the implicit rules of organizational or national culture. Because laws vary by country, compliance statements also can vary. Sethi (1999) notes that most multinational corporations respond to public pressures for ethical behavior by means of compliance to local laws and standards.

A compliance approach to managing international ethics initiatives usually has more resources devoted to it than are required when rules of ethics are implicit for the organization or embodied in national cultural norms. For example, preparation and dissemination increases the cost of having formal ethical guidelines. Implementation costs increase when there are different codes for each country. Costs also increase to monitor behaviors. For example, compliance efforts need to be formally assigned to someone in the organization. Often this role is allocated to the legal department because it is they who are most likely to know the law, but sometimes the role goes to a Human Resources Department. Titles for this position include Compliance Director or Director of Business Conduct. Training facilitates compliance and also entails costs.

Problems with a Culturally Relative Ethic

Managerial transfers that often occur in international business invite and even encourage managers to develop culturally relative values that change depending on place. This is problematic because most people do not find it easy to substitute one set of values for another. Thus, as Laurent (1999, 1986) notes, cultural relativism complicates organizational development. For individual managers whose ethical values are more absolute, it might mean operating from a "true" sense of ethics in one country and a "false" set in another.

A second challenge to managing ethics with cultural relativism is that the burden to write new rules increases with each country entered. The end result may be a dense set of compliance statements. If the latter are written in the highly specialized legal language of each country, they may be inaccessible to managers. In other words, despite the existence of compliance documents, managers may not understand them or feel they are too much trouble to consult. Additionally, compliance with different national guidelines may complicate financial and other forms of organizational reporting and impede coordination among functions or divisions.

Finally, while adaptation via compliance fulfills public duties to obey the law, adaptation may not help managers understand or learn about the culture and its underlying values. In other words, legal compliance may offer too little managerial insight into the basis of a culture. Cultural ignorance could prevent managers from tracking activities in the nation that have implications for the firm such as a shift in public sentiment that leads to changed norms or new laws.

Legal Guidelines Lag Cultural Change

New laws for a nation usually arise in response to an external shock or to change in public sentiment or cultural belief. This inevitably means that legal guidelines will lag cultural shifts. Thus the business whose managers do not learn the "whys" of culture may be blindsided by growing stakeholder sentiment for change. This is especially likely in nations different from the home culture where it may be difficult to identify important stakeholder groups or trends they represent.

In summary, both forms of ethical adaptations create business advantages and disadvantages. As a tactic, adaptation may best serve an organization when home and host cultures are similar, when the company operates in relatively few international markets, when business expectations are well described by law, and when national cultural values are presumed to be stable. In the following section, we see that when these conditions change, companies approach ethics via an integrated approach.

ETHICS IN A GLOBAL CONTEXT

A global ethic suggests it is possible to develop "a basic consensus on binding values, irrevocable criteria and personal basic attitudes" (Kung, 1998) on a worldwide scale. While the main purpose of this section is to look at how organizations operate ethically on a global scale, it is important to look first at the context that created demand for a global ethic.

The Growing Need for Global Ethics Initiatives

Whereas international companies sometimes find it possible to operate in an "out of sight, out of mind" context, worldwide interconnections make business activities more visible to the public. This centrality includes growing concern for how businesses contribute to global problems and also in what businesses can and should do to address problems, including ones they did not create. Thus one result of growing global interconnections is a growing sense that responsibility for righting social wrongs belongs to businesses as well as to governments and civil society organizations.

The public increasingly demands that businesses be socially responsible and ethical. They put most emphasis on ethical issues that are most evident to them, such as labor and human rights and environmentalism, and may be less aware of complex ethical issues such as financial reporting (Boatright, 2000). Many global organizations concentrate their ethical initiatives on issues pertinent to their own industry or stakeholders. For example, cosmetics firms are particularly responsive to animal testing, and the timber industry is most responsive to sustainable development in the natural environment.

Business Ethics Activities in a Global World

Internal integration provides an important mechanism through which global businesses respond to global shifts and demands. Thus we might expect the global business to create an ethics approach that is also integrative in nature.

When businesses expand their activities throughout the world, their managers often "search for principles for action that transcend national borders and cultural values, and modes of operation that will achieve the broad purposes of the corporation on a long-term and sustainable basis" (Clarkson Centre, 1999: 1). This search is meant to help them create synergies from integration. According to Laurent (1999), the most successful multinational companies are those able to integrate among different cultural frameworks. Although companies realize that they cannot easily adopt one or more sets of business principles for overseas markets and others for their domestic market, in practice many find it difficult to create a single, integrated ethic.

Universal ethical principles are not thick on the ground because, as Chapter 7 demonstrates, people share few values worldwide. As the following example shows, even within nations people have different values especially when social norms are in flux. US West faced protests for charitable giving to Boy Scouts of America because the latter does not permit gay troop leaders. But when the company withdrew their financial support from BSA, then religious groups protested perceived support of gay rights (Jennings and Entine, 1998).

Global businesses reach beyond regulatory or even cultural limits of nations to face ethical challenges that are worldwide in scope. In the absence of global governance mechanisms to regulate and discipline companies that violate ethical standards, businesses face a disorganized and fragmented ethics framework. Some managers of these businesses believe that it is important for them to help clarify how business can or should contribute to creating an environment for ethical business, but their motivations may differ to include some or all of the following:

- Voluntary guidelines may be viewed as less problematic than those created by governments.
- Guidelines may stimulate all firms to operate according to the same principles and thus create a 'level playing field' for all organizations.
- Ethical conduct is needed in an increasingly interdependent world.
- Norms of ethics reduce operating uncertainties.
- It is simply the "right" thing to do.

According to Business for Social Responsibility (2002), the business case for ethics is that ethical behaviors enhance corporate reputation and brand image; improve risk and crisis management; create a cohesive corporate culture; and avoids fines, sanctions, and litigation. One business person turned social activist notes that businesses can either develop appropriate company policies or be forced to do so by public opinion (Chandler, 1999). Many prefer to do the former to participate actively in shaping policies that affect them.

While some undoubtedly view ethics initiatives as public-relations tools, others worldwide are acting to move social responsibility initiatives away from manipulation and influence of the public and toward serious dialogue and debate (Steinmann and Lohr, 1992). Below we see that ethics initiatives that emerge from this dialogue can be internally or externally focussed.

Internal Focus of Ethics

In their study of *Fortune* 500 firms, Weaver et al. (1999) found that practices that reinforce ethics depend on top managers' commitment to ethics. In other words, when external pressure is the reason for ethics programs, adopted practices often are not integrative. Examples include memos, reminders, and policy documents. Conversely, when the reason for ethics initiatives is top management commitment, ethics practices are more likely to be integrative such as linking annual rewards to managerial behaviors that reinforce ethical ideals.

Company Codes of Ethics

Many companies develop explicit codes of ethics. A few examples from the apparel industry include Hennes & Mauritz, Inditex, Gap, and Levi Strauss. These codes typically explain the "why" of a global ethic. The following paragraphs review ethics codes to show an increased use of them and expanding scope.

Many large multinationals introduced formal codes of ethics beginning in the early 1990s (Center for Business Ethics, 1992; Webley, 1992). A 1999 Conference Board study found 78 percent were setting up ethics standards, an increase of 41 percent from 1991 and 21 percent from 1987. Joanne Ciulla (1991) observed that most companies develop internal ethics codes by looking at codes collected by centers like the Ethics Resource Center in Washington, DC or London's Institute of Business Ethics. Most are modeled along similar lines to include: 1) contracts (such as conflict of interest, bribery, security of proprietary information, and receiving gifts) and 2) legally or generally accepted standards (such as sexual harassment, workplace safety, or political activities).

According to Business for Social Responsibility (2002), codes of ethics have expanded beyond these two major issues to additionally focus on the natural environment, child labor, human rights, and other concerns (Business for Social Responsibility, 2002). The result is that many more ethics codes include statements about:

- fundamental honesty and adherence to the law
- product safety and quality, workplace health and safety precautions
- conflicts of interest
- employment practices
- fair practices in selling and marketing products or services
- financial reporting
- supplier relationships
- pricing, billing, and contracting
- trading in securities and/or use of insider information
- payments to obtain business
- acquiring and using information about others
- security and political activities
- environmental protection
- intellectual property or use of proprietary information (Business Roundtable, 1988).

More recently, ethics codes incorporate treatments of Internet and e-commerce activities. In their written "Standards of Business Conduct," Sun Microsystems specifically describes what constitutes "reasonable personal use of Sun's information resources" (Sun Microsystems, Inc., Standards, 2001: 8). Other companies might outline the ethics of information acquisition or activities such as data mining.

Benefits of Company Codes of Ethics

Ethical codes may not ensure success, but even when flawed they may prevent failures. Their existence makes it less likely that leaders or managers will unwittingly guide the firm into an ethical morass, or that individuals will rely on conflicting personal ethics when acting on behalf of the firm. This is particularly important at a global level because cultural differences in beliefs and values do lead to cross-cultural differences in behaviors. Among the most important variables for ethics codes are: top-management commitment; rewards and sanctions have to be in place; and it has to be a process more than a written product. Whatever form it takes (and there are many), leaders of ethics programs need to connect their written commitments to ethical behaviors. This is part of the integrative process.

Problems with Company Codes of Ethics

Enron had articulated a global vision of ethics, had a global code of ethics, and was often applauded for its socially responsible behavior. This suggests that under some circumstances a code of ethics may function more as a public-relations tool than as a behavioral guide. Codes of ethics such as Enron's have little practical value when top managers flout them.

Other criticisms of corporate codes of ethics are that they lack specific content, they ignore the rights of key stakeholders in their dealings with the organization, or code compliance is not well integrated into organizational procedures. Additionally, many codes fail when they provide no framework for communicating with external communities about their success or failure in achieving the code's objectives (Sethi, 1999). These challenges show why it is important to do more than simply write up a code—codes must be part of an integrated system for decision-making. Implementation includes at least four important activities:

- Communicate with employees so they understand what behaviors are expected and why. Communication should also include notice of sanctions for ethical violations.
- Monitor actual behavior which might include periodic inspections or progress reports.
- Link ethics to rewards and integrate ethics codes into everyday activities of employees.
- Audit results for feed-through to next-step processes.

Other Internal Approaches to Integration of a Global Ethic

Codes of ethics have received most attention as a global business process, but other mechanisms integrate ethics worldwide. For example, Desai and Rittenburg (1997) suggest an ethics committee headed by an advisor who can create ethical awareness throughout the organization. This individual also manages and monitors knowledge transfer on ethics to subsidiaries and affiliates abroad. The company can also monitor and respond to measures of ethics. For example, it might choose to do business only in nations where the Transparency Index is high and the Corruption Index low.

Another approach more typical for large firms than small ones is to push ethics through supply chains by asking or even demanding that suppliers understand and comply with established ethical standards. For the most part, these types of networks are vertically configured external networks managed via internal mechanisms. The following example from Hennes & Mauritz illustrates why companies develop supply-chain codes and the issues they cover.

Hennes & Mauritz

H&M does not have any factories of its own. Instead we buy all our garments and other goods from over 900 suppliers, primarily in Europe and Asia. Since we do not have direct control over this production we have drawn up guidelines for our suppliers, which together form our Code of Conduct. The Code includes requirements concerning:

- the working environment;
- a ban on child labor;
- fire safety;
- working hours;
- wages;
- freedom of association.

Source material: H&M Code of conduct. (2003, Dec. 28) http://www.hm.com/us/hm/social/coc.jsp

---

Integrative Global Ethics Activities

Activities typical for an integrative corporate ethics program include training, methods for auditing and evaluating ethical behaviors, disciplinary processes used when ethical expectations are not met, ethics telephone lines, and formal ethics departments and officers (Weaver et al., 1999). An important mechanism for integrating ethical behaviors and ideals throughout the organization is to link them to rewards for all employees, but especially leaders and managers. Examples of these activities appear in Table 15.1.

Table 15.1 *Develop, monitor, enforce*

Develop	Monitor	Enforce
Statement of corporate principles	Ethics audit	Link rewards to ethical behaviors and ideals
Ethics code or conduct code	Assess compliance worldwide	Punish failures
Adopt existing code	Produce a separate ethics report at periodic intervals	Provide non-punitive communication channel for whistleblowers
Train employees	Provide "hotlines"	Hold top officer to ethical standards

Table 15.1 *Continued*

Create clear lines of ethics responsibility	Create ombuds office for complaints/concerns
An office for ethics and ethics officer	Adhere to professional and other standards
	External audits

Source material: Arlene Broadhurst (2000) Corporations and the ethics of social responsibility: An emerging regime of expansion and compliance. *Business Ethics: A European Review*, 9 (2): 86–98. Reprinted with permission of Blackwell Publishing Ltd.

When ethics ideals are integrated with other organizational processes, then the global firm is better prepared to convey its ethical stance globally. Typically it has mechanisms for training employees worldwide. It also has mechanisms for responding to deviations from ethical standards. However, inasmuch as values are nation-based, in the short-term companies will find it difficult to fully integrate corporate ethics into behaviors of all employees worldwide. Thus, companies must continually invest in ethics initiatives.

External Sources of Ethics

Companies can use external certification programs that hold employees to ethical standards and encourage employees to conform to professional standards. Rather than develop their own codes, companies can also adopt principles and practices suggested by industry groups or coordinating organizations.

The Ethical Trading Initiative

In the UK the Department of International Development and Department for Trade and Industry were instrumental to the Ethical Trading Initiative. This alliance of companies, NGOs and trade unions operates from the UK to work worldwide, ensuring that goods produced for UK markets come from global suppliers who are working to improve labor conditions. Included in the nine-point Base Code are statements covering forced labor and rights to collective bargaining. These and other Code statements are discussed with supply-chain members. Although both auditing and monitoring follow, the main purpose of the Code and supplier discussion is to develop and maintain long-term and positive relationships with suppliers and their employees.

Source material: Jane Collier (2000) Editorial: Globalization and ethical global business. *Business Ethics: A European Review*, 9 (2): 71–75.

The search for a global ethic is not new. Meeting in 1893, the Council of the Parliament of the World's Religions assembled people from every possible religion to prepare a declaration for a global ethic. The resulting declaration concentrates on three main principles: the full realization of the intrinsic dignity of the human person, the inalienable freedom and equality in principle of all humans, and the necessary solidarity and interdependence of all humans with each other, both as individuals and as communities (Kung, 1998). The council continues to meet (see http://www.cpwr.org). An example of a recent global approach to business ethics is the Global Compact described in Chapters 6 and 9.

The Caux Round Table Principles for Business

The Caux Round Table Principles (1995) also outline global ethical business practices. Developed through collaborative activities among leaders of businesses and other organizations, these principles were translated into many languages for worldwide introduction. The CRT Principles call for responsiveness to stakeholders as well as shareholders; efforts to create justice and world community; and business behaviors that conform to the spirit as well as the letter of the law. A noteworthy feature of the CRT Principles is that they reflect efforts to create a hybrid founded on two basic ethical ideas: the shared existence and common good of *kyosei* representing Japanese cooperation and the more Western notion of individualism reflected in an emphasis on human dignity.

Challenges to Global Ethics Codes

There are several challenges to a global code of ethics that can be applied to all companies. First, since global rules are likely to emerge from a negotiation process, they are unlikely to reflect values and habits of all cultures. To the extent that these rules are developed by firms from the Westernized countries, they may better reflect Western values than those of the world. Second, global ethics may be viewed as an end rather than a beginning point for global ethics. When conditions change, organizations may use codes to fight change. Finally, a global code of ethics may also serve to depress innovation, since some will hesitate to act in the absence of clear guidelines. However, ethics, like every other process associated with globalization, is dynamic rather than static.

CHAPTER SUMMARY

There are three principal reasons for a business to undertake corporate social responsibility (CSR) initiatives: the public expects responsibility and increasingly monitors company behaviors, CSR helps organizations attract and retain people, and CSR is a correlate of financial performance.

A CSR continuum ranges from companies that do not obey the law to those that are leaders for CSR initiatives. The range of CSR initiatives include philanthropic giving and volunteerism, well-articulated social-value objectives, integration of social objectives and business goals, and leading the industry and others in CSR best practices. Each level of CSR activity on the continuum requires more integrative CSR mechanisms in the firm.

Ethics are grounded in a moral philosophy that helps people discern between right and wrong. In the business world, ethics is the study of morally appropriate behaviors and decisions, examining what "should be done." The challenge of global business ethics is to develop a hierarchy of what is good or "right" in a world where there are few widely accepted absolutes.

Global firms increasingly integrate a single ethic throughout their worldwide operations. This adaptive process makes it possible for the global firm to operate ethically wherever their activities are located.

REVIEW AND DISCUSSION QUESTIONS

1 The review of company human rights activities illustrates some of the challenges for CSR leadership. Conduct research on a similar social issue such as environmental protection, child labor, educational inequities, disaster relief, worldwide safety standards, or health care, to report on what businesses do and the public's response to CSR leadership.

2 To what extent should business organizations be held accountable for social injustices?

3 Companies like Mattel, H&M, Pearson, Sara Lee, and Levi Strauss all have strong codes of ethics. Conduct research on one of these firms to identify elements of their ethical codes. Assess them according to the Business for Social Responsibility list of expanded scope for codes of ethics.

Chapter 16
DECISION-MAKING, INNOVATION AND CREATIVITY, RISK, AND CONFLICT MANAGEMENT

SAMSUNG'S NEW APPROACH

In 1995, Samsung Electronics faced financial disaster when business strategies did not lead to intended pay-offs. These strategies included manufacturing components for better-known global brands and selling copycat products of microwaves or televisions such as Sanyo to consumers. Few outside Samsung even knew it as a global company—its strategies kept it hidden from public view. Worse, even fewer cared. By July of 1998, Samsung Electronics was losing millions of dollars per month, causing CEO Yun Jong Yong to organize a retreat with nine other senior managers. The group decided to cut costs drastically, and each pledged to resign if objectives were not met. The company met the objectives but Yun departed from South Korea's tradition of lifetime employment by firing some senior managers and replacing them with younger, English-speaking ones.

By 2004, Samsung Electronics had significantly changed. Their global market share in big-screen televisions, cell telephones, flash memory, LCD displays, MP3 players, dram chips, DVD players, and microwave ovens was in the top three, boosted by Samsung's decision to abandon a tradition that emphasized a low-risk follower strategy.

Based in South Korea, Samsung Electronics is part of the Samsung chaebol. SE alone employs more than 88,000 people who staff offices in more than 47 nations. It competes in many industries, but often collaborates with competitors. For example, Samsung competes with Sony in the electronics industry but sells them semiconductors and displays and collaborates on big-screen televisions. It is also in partnership with Dell, Hewlett-Packard, and IBM. And now that it has begun to establish global brands, Samsung Electronics also wants to become Korea's first great global company.

Implementation of its turnaround strategy called for many changes. SE streamlined processes to improve the speed of product introduction. For example, in 1995 it took 14 months between product idea and its introduction; that was reduced to less than five months. Decision-making was decentralized, moving from top executives in Korean to global-brand managers. Contrary to the past, managerial risk and innovation were encouraged. For example, in 2002 Chin Dae Je, the head of the digital media division sent a laptop to Michael Dell. And the risk proved worth the reward: Samsung began to produce a similar model sold under the Dell label.

Changes in people included many new hires who would have been unwelcome in South Korean firms in the not-so-distant past. For example, SE recruited 47-year-old Korean-American Eric Kim to take over marketing and create a global brand. Kim consolidated worldwide advertising, hiring a Madison Avenue firm to enhance the company's brand image. Chin Dae Je also was hired following education and employment in the US. Chin noted that he had initial difficulty with Samsung's hierarchical culture, finding he was the only person asking questions at strategy meetings. He noted: "People blushed and turned red. They were upset. I didn't care. I just kept asking questions" (quoted in Holstein, 2002: 92). Other Korean-Americans and Koreans with experience abroad were hired, creating a culture in which questions were asked and answers found.

At the same time, Samsung released 30,000 of its workers, keeping twice as many designers as it once did. The latter differ from the traditional Korean worker not only in looks that include dyed hair and casual work clothes but also in work behaviors that ▶

emphasize creativity and innovation. These product developers, management innovations, and vertical links between Samsung Electronics and Samsung affiliates are three reasons that CEO Ki Tae Lee believes Samsung telecommunications products have been successful in recent years (Lee, 2003).

Structures also altered at Samsung. Managers go through relatively few layers of bureaucracy for plan approval. They communicate with one another and also with employees in other Samsung subsidiaries. For example, Chin encouraged development of a combined cell phone and handheld computer by assembling teams of engineers and designers from throughout the company. Samsung has developed partnerships with telecommunications companies and retailers outside the company, blurring the boundaries of its structure. Doing so has helped Samsung attract new customers. For example, Samsung convinced Sprint they could manufacture better equipment than European competitors. The company has shed non-core units and emerged as a leader in melding wireless technologies with gadgets ranging from personal digital assistants to refrigerators.

These examples illustrate that Samsung Electronics departed in significant ways from traditional South Korean business practices to introduce simultaneous changes in people, processes, and structures. With these changes, Samsung became a brand powerhouse that now threatens to unseat Sony as the best-known brand in consumer electronics.

Source material: Cliff Edwards, Moon Ihlwan, and Pete Engardio (2003, June 16) The Samsung way. *Business Week* , pp. 56–64; William J. Holstein (2002, Apr. 1) Samsung's golden touch. *Fortune*, pp. 89–94; Sang Lee (2003) Samsung CEO Ki Tae Lee on expanding the global market. *Academy of Management Executive*, 17 (2): 27–29; Jay Solomon (2002, June 13) Seoul survivors: Back from brink, Korea Inc. wants a little respect. *The Wall Street Journal*, pp. A1, A8.

CHAPTER OVERVIEW

Processes of many types become important business tools. This chapter examines five essential processes for managing a global firm: decision-making, innovation, creativity, risk, and conflict management.

THE DECISION-MAKING PROCESS

Decision-making means choosing from among alternatives. This may seem like a simple enough process, but global managers face growing complexity when weighing available alternatives. Sometimes the alternatives are not even clear. For example, choosing an expansion strategy is more complex when everywhere and anywhere are among the options. Additionally, information in the form of raw data is globally abundant, but transforming it into useful knowledge may prove difficult. Time is also a constraint on global decision-making. Finally, managers know that global competitors are often weighing the same decision alternatives, but they may be using different criteria and access different information. Complexity, information access, time, and diverse competitors all increase the challenge of global decision-making.

Rational Decision-making

The traditional Western approach to decision-making is scientific and analytical. This tradition is part of a scientific revolution that emerged in the 1700s and persists today. Central to this tradition are three important assumptions (adapted from Harman, 1993):

1 The *objectivist assumption* is that the universe can be explored and understood by using quantitative methods of scientific observation. In other words, the scientific process can help us objectively understand how the business world works.
2 The *positivist assumption* is that what is real is that which is physically observable. In business, we might be encouraged to pay most attention to what can be measured and ignore those things that are less easily measured.
3 The *reductionist assumption* is that complex phenomena can be scientifically explained by reducing phenomena to basic levels. For example, business activities are responses to stimuli. (See Harman, 1993 for a short description of rational and intuitive decision-making; see Capra, 1984 for a comprehensive history of the scientific revolution.)

In the business world, these three rational assumptions foster a decision-making process that is reductive, linear, and begins with problem identification. Steps in the process are shown in Table 16.1.

Table 16.1 *Linear steps in the rational decision-making process*

Decision-making Step	Assumptions
Problem identification	Assumes that a distinctive problem can be isolated for resolution
Identify decision criteria	Assumes all criteria are identifiable
Allocate weights to criteria	Assumes agreement on importance of each criteria
Develop alternatives	Assumes that a comprehensive list of alternatives can be developed
Analyze alternatives on weighted criteria	Assumes the consequences for each alternative can be known
Select an alternative	Assumes maximum profit, minimized cost
Implement the alternative	Assumes everyone will pursue the same alternative
Evaluation	Assumes the outcome can be objectively measured against the original problem

This step-by-step process assumes the following conditions are met:

- The problem is clear and unambiguous.
- A single (or at least limited), well-defined goal is to be achieved.
- All alternatives and consequences are known.
- Preferences are clear.
- Preferences are constant and stable.
- There are no time or cost constraints.
- Final choice will maximize economic pay-offs.

Many conditions of rational decision-making are violated in the global sphere: problems are ambiguous; many alternatives are not known; preferences are unclear or dynamic; and there are time constraints. Further, diverse participants in the global business world make decisions using criteria other than economic rationality. When decisions are influenced by factors such as political processes, rational decision-making may not even be a good way to reach a decision. For example, business and government activities are closely linked in a Japanese keiretsu leading to decision distribution among multiple powerful groups. Identified alternatives would be limited to those that can be negotiated, and the existence of self-interested groups might de-emphasize rules over interests. Organizations such as governments and civil society organizations that mediate between businesses and global shifts also make decisions more political.

Bounded Rationality

Herbert Simon (1955) defined "bounded rationality" as behavior rational within a simplified problem framework. Simon argues that few decisions are truly rational because in most organizations decision-making is distributed, access to information is limited, and decision-makers tend to pursue acceptable rather than perfect alternatives. Choosing an acceptable alternative is known as "satisficing," which may be necessary when market information is not perfect.

Table 16.2 compares attributes of three views of decision-making: rational, organizational process, and political process. As indicated, each approach makes different assumptions about who makes decisions, the search for available alternatives, alternative selection, and methods of implementing decisions made.

Table 16.2 *Approaches to decision-making*

	Rational	**Organizational process**	**Political process**
Decision-maker	Unitary; made at the peak of a steep hierarchy	Distributed among process participant	Distributed among members of the dominant coalition
Search for alternatives	Exhaustive search for the single best alternative	Search for acceptable alternatives (bounded rationality)	"Might" (power) makes "right;" dominant people prevail
Basis for alternative selected	Quantifiable: maximize benefits; minimize costs	Satisfice important actors in the environment	Satisfy important participants
Methods for implementation	Rules; top-down hierarchy; formal planning and performance reviews	Provide inducements sufficient to motivate desired contributions	Appeal to self- or group-interest; de-emphasize rules

Intuitive Decision-making

Another approach to decision-making is based on intuition which is defined in simple terms as the process of knowing that does not rely consciously on rational or linear thought processes. Shapiro and Spence define intuition "as a nonconscious, holistic processing mode in which judgments are made with no awareness of the rules or knowledge used for inference and can feel right despite one's inability to articulate the reasons" (1997: 64). Words like "hunches," "feelings," or "instincts" might be used to describe the intuitive process. Some think of it as a sixth sense, an innate personality trait, or even a paranormal capacity (Shirley and Langan-Fox, 1996). In the business world, most think of intuition as accumulated experience (Burke and Miller, 1999). In other words, experience teaches people how to make decisions even if they cannot explain the process in rational terms. This suggests that intuition is more than guesses. Instead, it is a process that relies on mental models and values that are neither easily measured nor described.

According to Daniel Isenberg (1984), intuition plays an important business role because it can help managers to:

1 sense when a problem exists;
2 perform well-learned behaviors and patterns rapidly;
3 synthesize isolated data into an integrated picture;
4 rein in over-reliance on rationality.

Researchers find that managers often display quite high levels of intuition (Blattberg and Hoch, 1990). A nine-nation study of over 1300 business managers (Parikh et al., 1994) found 54 percent used intuition (at least in part) in decision-making.

Willis Harman (1993) believes renewed interest in organizational intuition is very positive for organizations and society. He believes that over reliance on rationality has led to organizational decisions that are unwise, and that intuition can improve decisions because it uses more of human knowledge, it provides a way for businesses to reassess the role of business in the world, and it may have global implications for changing the assumptions that shaped the past. He points to global problems such as terrorism and extinction of species as interrelated consequences of having put our faith in science to the exclusion of values.

Developing Complementary Decision-making Approaches

One's preferred approach to decision-making is probably cultural. That is, each of us approaches decisions using a learned framework. For people whose dominant culture is rational and linear, the "right" approach to decision-making is likely to be linear. For people whose dominant culture is more relational, the "right" approach to decision-making is likely to be the one that analyzes relationships. In a global world where decision-making preferences differ, managers need to develop both linear and intuitive skills. Table 16.3 describes thinking in terms of two metaphors: chains are step-by-step linear decisions and circles are relational forms of decision-making. The attributes in the table might show where your preferences lie.

Table 16.3 *Features of chain and circle decision-making*

Chain	Circle
Analytical	Relational
Emphasizes beginnings and endings	Emphasizes cycles
Describes attributes and properties	Describes interactions
Sees causality as linear	Sees causality as nonlinear, even random
Identifies values, principles, motives, and laws that determine behaviors	Identifies contexts that determine behaviors

Source material: Jonathan King, Jonathan T. Down, and David A. Bella (2002) Learning to think in circles. *Journal of Management Inquiry*, 11 (2): 161–170.

Paul Nutt (2002) argues that the type of decision-making approach used depends on the challenge faced. He notes that rational analysis may be best suited to tasks that are objective and can produce tangible results. On the other hand, when objectives sought and the means of producing results are ambiguous, a better approach to decision-making might be inspiration derived from working with stakeholders to learn from them. Similarly, Shapiro and Spence (1997) argue that less structured problems that senior managers confront, such as new product planning or strategy formation, are likely to require intuitive as well as analytical decision-making skills.

In summary, although most approach decision-making in singular ways, a global world calls for decision-makers who can bring both linear and intuitive thinking to the decision-making process. As John Patton (2003) describes it, this means relying on a combination of intuition, logic, and emotions to make decisions. Making decisions based on multiple modes of knowing may facilitate the rapid decision-making often required in a global world. For most this is going to mean recognizing one's own preferences, and finding ways to expand on them.

Approaches to Expanding Decision-making Style

One approach is to practice making decisions in groups comprising people who practice different decision-making styles. Another is to look at the same challenge using intuitive and linear decision-making lenses simultaneously. People low on intuition might improve it with activities such as meditation, reflection, journal keeping, or exercises that stimulate recognition of interconnections. People low on linear forms of rationality may develop it with activities such as fishbone techniques, mind mapping, or scenario planning.

Bolman and Deal (1991) believe that expanded management thinking might include:

1 A holistic framework that encourages inquiry into a range of issues rather than focussing on single issues one at a time.
2 Awareness of a set of options that range from dependence on skills to dependence on abilities like bargaining.
3 Creativity and a willingness to risk.
4 An ability to ask the right questions more than to find the right answers.
5 An ability to remain flexible to external events.

Decision-making according to linear, rational models dominant in the US are expanding to accommodate more process-oriented modes of thinking. People who manage global enterprises increasingly rely on intuition as well as economic rationality and an understanding of political processes to reach decisions.

INNOVATION

Inventions usually involve a new discovery. Individuals and small companies often invent new products. For example, 20th-century inventions by small US firms include air conditioners, the FM radio, microprocessors, fast-frozen food, soft contact lenses, and the zipper (US Small Business Administration, 1994). Innovations often disrupt the status quo in big companies, and this makes it difficult for them to accommodate innovation easily (Christensen, 1997). Organizational leaders at companies like 3M and Rubbermaid believe that innovation is an important source of their strategic advantage. Other companies undertake operational innovation, meaning that they create a new business process (Hammer, 2004). Here innovation is defined as constant development and refinement of both products and processes. Others believe that innovation is the basis for a nation's strategic advantage as well, and would therefore argue that it is important for national governments to stimulate national innovation.

Organizations innovate for many reasons: to maintain market share in an industry, be part of a changing industry, or create new organizational opportunities. Often organizations become alert to the need to innovate because of changes in buyer habits. Club Med has responded to growing interest in adventure traveling by establishing outposts in ever more exotic locations.

Cultural Change Leads to Business Innovations

When a growing number of women begin to work outside the home, there is typically a decrease in the number of times people shop for groceries. Additionally, more meals will be purchased rather than prepared at home. Retailers alert to this cultural change innovate by offering ready-made meals or making it easier to consolidate shopping. Entrepreneurial businesses might emerge to deliver groceries or fully cooked meals. Manufacturers develop new products, for example a combined oven and refrigerator, or make changes to existing ones, such as bigger or smarter refrigerators that keep track of groceries consumed. The opportunities are limited only by the imagination that stimulated innovations.

Research and Development

Organizational innovation often results from research and development investments of different types. Larger firms like Rubbermaid, 3M, Sony, and Toyota rely on in-house or internal research teams to generate new products. Additionally, firms may joint venture with competitors or collaborate with noncompetitors to develop new products. Research and development also can come from external sources. Most process-oriented breakthroughs come from external sources and many product ideas come from government funding for basic research that later is adapted to consumer use. For example, scopolamine was developed to suppress astronaut air sickness but later became available for queasy travelers. In many nations, a significant amount of research and development is government sponsored. For example, some governments fund research labs or offer tax breaks in research-intensive industries. Rising costs and diminishing supplies of natural resources like oil stimulate government research subsidies for wind, sun, and other energy sources. External innovation is sometimes purchased. For example, a good deal of Microsoft's growth has come from buying small companies that developed innovative products. In general, most innovation comes from smaller firms.

Almost 96 percent of national R&D traditionally has been conducted by wealthy industrialized nations such as Japan, the US, Germany, France, and others in Western Europe. The World Economic Forum produces a Creativity Index that rates national involvement in innovations. Among the top ten innovators in 2000 were the US, Finland, Israel, Taiwan, and Hungary. Other countries such as Singapore are not themselves high in innovation, but rapidly import new technologies. In general, the most innovative nations also tend to be those that create an infrastructure that encourages business start-ups. Many newly Asian economies nations have become more innovative with investments that upgrade the technological base. This includes approaches such as increased expenditures on R&D, improved education, FDI incentives, and making the home country more attractive to home-country engineers and scientists.

With regard to stimulating change, former GE Chairman Jack Welch asked: "Are you regenerating? Are you dealing with new things? When you find yourself in a new environment, do you come up with a fundamentally different approach? That's the test. When you flunk, you leave [the industry]!" (Peters, 1994). This pretty well sums up the attitude it takes to stimulate technological breakthroughs. The need for continuous breakthroughs occurs because new products and processes can be copied by others, and because the pace of invention is rapid. In turn, this calls for organizational efforts to engage all members of the organization—from top to bottom—in the innovation process.

Although rigid, bureaucratic mechanisms can depress organizational innovations, this does not need to be the case. For example, 3M is a highly structured organization and also one that is well known for product innovations. One way 3M encourages innovation is by stimulating risks. When risks fail people are not punished, sending the message that failures are a natural and expected part of risk taking.

Creating an Innovation Culture

Gary Hamel (2000) believes there are ten "rules" for designing organizations that inspire innovation. These are:

- Set unreasonable expectations—aspire high.
- Stretch the business definition to make innovation possible.
- Create a cause, not a business.
- Listen to new voices.
- Design an open market for ideas.
- Offer an open market for capital to fund idea development.
- Open the internal market for talent; let people move within the organization.
- Lower the risks for experimentation; don't punish failure.
- Divide and divide into new units.
- Pay innovators really well.

Internally, innovative ideas often are brought to production by "idea" champions—people who believe in ideas enough to invest time and energy developing them. In *Winning Through Innovation*, authors Michael Tushman and Charles O'Reilly III (1997) argue that successful innovation is difficult to sustain because of both structural and cultural inertia within organizations. That is, over time organizations develop structures, processes, and systems to manage work, but changing them is costly because employees resist change. This cultural inertia of how things are or should be done often proves more intractable than structural change, but Tushman and O'Reilly believe inertial resistance can be overcome if organizational leaders emphasize constant learning. Although their focus is on innovation, the thesis for these authors is one seen throughout this text: changes in one part of an organization necessarily affect other parts of an organization. Thus a change in the innovation process requires a change in people and in structures.

CREATIVITY

Innovation is often stimulated by creative thinking on the part of people who are willing to think "outside the box" or sponsor ideas others might consider far-fetched or just plain wrong. John Kao (1996) argues that the only way for businesses to generate new ideas is to hire creative people and then give them an environment where they are free to develop their ideas and also directed toward focussing on tasks and working with others. According to the Center for Creative Leadership, organizational stimulants to individual creativity include providing six features listed below:

1 Freedom in deciding what work to do or how to do it.
2 Challenge to work hard on important projects.
3 Resources needed to do the work.
4 Encouragement from a supervisor who is a good work model, who sets appropriate goals, who supports and has confidence in the work group.
5 Work group supports diverse skills, such as people who communicate well are open to new ideas, constructively challenge one another's work, are committed to their work, and trust and help each other.
6 Organizational encouragement in a culture that supports creativity and communicates a shared vision of the organization.

Factors that depress creativity include: 1) organizational impediments such as internal political problems, harsh criticism of new ideas, destructive forms of internal competition, avoidance of risk, and overemphasis on the status quo; and 2) workload pressure such as unrealistic expectations, too many distractions, or extreme time pressures (KEYS, 1995).

Creativity and a Computer?

Most people think of creativity as an individual attribute. But Jacob Goldenberg and David Mazursky believe people can get a little help from their friend the computer. These two researchers developed five templates for analytical thinking that help people rethink existing relationships and produce more creative product innovations. The templates invite people to rethink attribute dependency (what attributes can be changed), component control (the way the product is linked to its environment), replacement (replace a product part), displacement (remove a component of a product), or division (separate a product into two parts). A divisional innovation is separation of shampoo from conditioner. An attribute replacement innovation for disposable diapers is a pleasant scent that signals need for a change.

Source material: Jacob Goldenberg and David Mazursky (2002) *Creativity in Product Innovation*. Cambridge: Cambridge University; David Rosenberg (2002, May 13) The brainstormer. *The Wall Street Journal*, p. R14.

Although creativity may come naturally to some people, individual intelligence as well as past experience also play a role. Creative people like John Kao often attribute creativity to environmental rather than genetic factors.

Creativity as a Natural Occurrence

John Kao, author of *Jamming*: *The Art and Discipline of Business Creativity* (1996), has abundant natural creative gifts. In addition to having been an executive producer in the film business, he played piano for Frank Zappa, has a passion for multimedia, and owns his own creative consulting firm. His intelligence is reflected by academic accomplishments that include a PhD in psychiatry and an MBA. However, he attributes his own skills to his Chinese-American background and to a father who combined Chinese and Western-style medicine. Mr. Kao's example suggests that creativity may be stimulated by diversity, and that people provide strong models for others to develop their own creative potential.

Source material: John Kao (1993, Mar./Apr.) The worldwide web of Chinese business. *Harvard Business Review*, pp. 24–38.

According to James Higgins, author of *Escape From the Maze* (1997), personal creativity is stimulated in nine steps:

1 Accept innate creativity by consciously trying to use imagination and intuition.
2 Unlearn how not to be creative by breaking habits of predictable thinking developed in the past.
3 Expand personal problem-solving styles; for example, people who are intuitive should practice being rational and vice versa.

4 Use creativity techniques such as brainstorming.

5 Practice thinking more in pictures and visual images than just in words.

6 Learn when to think because both vigorous exercise and sleepiness tend to turn off internal mental censors that program out creativity.

7 Think in new ways by looking for solutions in unfamiliar places and using multiple techniques.

8 Keep a creativity record, perhaps a notebook to preserve ideas.

9 Face complexity by realizing that few problems have simple answers.

Tapping into Your Own Creativity

Creativity is learned, but it's a lifelong process. For example, if you feel you are not creative, here are some things you can do to stimulate creativity. Most involve breaking out of existing "rules" that govern your life.

■ Imagine yourself as someone you are not: an actor, a singer, your nonexistent twin.

■ Begin a conversation with someone you don't know or would ordinarily avoid.

■ Practice guessing who is telephoning (don't peek at caller ID).

■ Do an activity with your nondominant hand.

■ Develop and refer often to a statement you create that asserts you are creative.

Source material: Creativity Central. (2001) *Fanning the Creative Spirit: Two Toy Inventors Simplify Creativity*. Duluth, MN: Creativity Central.

MANAGING RISK

The possibility of risk is embedded in most situations, especially new or unaccustomed ones. Mihaly Simai defines international risks as "important, potentially disturbing and destabilizing factors or acts originating with, or generated by, various actors on different structural levels, and having spillover consequences for other members of the international community" (1994: 258). This definition notes that risk comes from different sources, and it has spillover effects. The following examinations of political risk, currency-exchange risk, and corruption risk show how risk has expanded in a global world. The material also demonstrates how global organizations are managing long-standing and relatively new forms of risk.

Political Risk

Much of the business literature defines international political risk narrowly as risks to company resources because of political decisions. Growing awareness that political systems are interdependent with other systems led to recognition that political risk includes social as well as political decisions, events, or conditions that could cause investors to lose money or opportunities (Howell and Chaddick, 1994). Political risk is assessed by private organizations such as Political Risk Services, Business Environment Risk Intelligence, or the Economist Intelligence Unit. These groups measure activities such as societal conflict or currency exchange controls to build indices of country risk.

Llewellyn Howell and Brad Chaddick (1994) compared data produced by published and private sources to find that existing measures of risk generally are poor predictors of specific outcomes. Based on their research, they concluded that individual factors of regional hostility and authoritarian government were better predictors of potential problems than indices combining all risk events.

Assessing Political Risk

Organizations calculate risks by creating internal systems for risk analysis, via projections based on published risk analyses, or on purchased reports. For example, Citibank established a Market Risk Policy Committee to oversee market risk (Citicorp Annual Report, 1995: 34). Although it is customary to build sophisticated, multivariate models of risk, Howell and Chaddick's (1994) research suggests that a simple approach might be as effective. This advice is counter to the "bigger-is-better" assumption for model building.

Business–government alliances represent another way to reduce organizational risk. In partnerships with governments, businesses induce government commitment to their interests. The trade-off is that organizations then relinquish some amount of decision control. Organizations also manage political risk by taking a longer-run view of the risk. For example, following economic turmoil in Brazil, Avon chose to cut prices to remain in the market. Many firms made similar decisions during Asia's 1997 currency crisis. An example follows in the box below.

McDonald's Stays the Course

In response to an economic crisis in Latin America, McDonald's representative Jim Cantalupo had this to say:

> *We've been through similar situations before in Latin America ... and we've learned that you have to stay the course. In Brazil we've survived seven economic reform plans, five currencies, five presidents, two constitutions and 14 finance ministers. Today in Brazil, McDonald's is the unchallenged market leader. In the past three years, our same-store sales have doubled—in an economy that very recently was described in the same dire terms used to characterize conditions in some Asian markets today.*

Source material: Can the US weather Asia's storm? (1998, Jan. 5) *The Wall Street Journal*, p. A22.

Currency-exchange Risk

According to Kim and Kim (1993), three types of currency-exchange fluctuations create potential risk:

1 Translation or "paper" exposures occur when the company consolidates financial statements from all nations. For example, Coca-Cola lost $13 million on currency translation in 1988, gained $20 million in 1989, and lost $500,000 in 1990.

2 Transaction exposure involves real losses or gains arising from transaction settlements involving exchange rates. The parent company for Swatch watches experienced a currency loss of 140 million francs ($123 million) in 1995.

3 Exposure to changes in the economic situation of nations represents an economic exposure over the lifetime of the enterprise.

Managing Currency Risk

Many forms of economic exposure can legitimately be considered political risk factors, and paper losses or gains may be difficult to manage. But the real concern for global firms is transaction exposure to actual currency exchange and losses. The vacillating value of the US dollar in world markets together with a propensity to use dollar-denominated transactions increases this exposure. For firms like Nestlé, Unilever, and Coca-Cola whose revenues and profits come primarily from outside their home countries, currency transactions can represent volatile losses and gains. Small firms are particularly vulnerable to currency risk. Firms manage currency risk in a number of ways:

- Over four-fifths of company treasurers manage currency risk with hedging strategies that use financial instruments to guarantee exchange rates.
- Bartering also provides a means for reducing exchange rate risk.
- Sony's overseas sales are 97 percent in foreign currencies and it promotes currency-swap agreements among their units to minimize risk.
- Motorola uses a currency-netting system to collect and disburse cash payments among Motorola companies and their suppliers (Holland, 1994).
- Wedco Technology, which custom grinds plastics and other materials for US and European companies, hedges against currency risk by billing in dollars; it also forces customers to supply their own raw materials so Wedco avoids currency risks for imports.
- Currency-exchange risk also can be hedged with short terms for payment, or buying forward contracts from banks that lock in exchange rates.

Hedging Currency-exchange Exposure

One way to reduce currency exposure is to locate production facilities in local markets, but even then interdependencies among units of the same worldwide firm may lead to currency exchange exposure. For example, although products for Siemens' medical technology division contain about 70 percent of local products in the US, Siemens faces a risk for the remaining 30 percent.

Source material: Terence Roth (1995, Mar. 9) In Europe, strengthening of currencies is causing headaches for many exporters. *The Wall Street Journal*, p. A14.

Corruption Risk

Chapter 10's consideration of corruption notes that it can include a broad range of activities including bribery, counterfeiting, smuggling, tax evasion, business irregularities like insider trading or kickbacks, price-fixing, fraud, and extortion. The economic costs of corruption are several. Corruption misuses productive factors, may result in reduced shareholder returns, can hurt a company's reputation, and can reduce employee morale. Thus, a company that competes in markets where corruption occurs faces corruption risk.

Corruption is widespread, even among nations that have worked particularly hard to eradicate business and political corruption. Moreover, corrupt practices vary worldwide and the reasons for corruption also vary. Whereas corruption in Asia and Eastern Europe tends to enrich individuals, particularly politicians, corruption in Western Europe and the US more likely serves business interests. For example, a manager pays off a government official to secure a business contract. A study of the relationship between low wages and corruption showed that corruption is lower where public employees are paid relatively well (Van Rijckeghem and Weder, 1997). Corruption is less when business behavior is clearly defined in written form or according to commonly shared values, and where there are legal or industry sanctions against corruption accompanied by strict enforcement policies.

The Foreign Corrupt Practices Act

The US Foreign Corrupt Practices Act (FCPA) was introduced in 1977 with considerable effect on US business practices. Features of the FCPA include:

- No employee of a US firm can corrupt foreign officials, politicians, or political candidates with bribes.
- Firms must keep detailed records of their actions, and they must provide reasonable assurance to show that all transactions were within the law.
- Facilitating payments are allowed when paid to lower-level employees or clerks to speed up duties they would have performed. An example would be a "grease" payment to a customs official to clear a delivery sooner rather than later.
- Fines of up to $1 million and/or 5 years in jail for offenses.

CONFLICT AND MANAGERIAL RISK

Managerial risk takes many forms including three the global manager faces: psychological risk from stress, personal risk from travel and work abroad, and personal risk arising from conflict and violence at work. Neither stress nor conflict are inherently negative. In fact, both are believed necessary to induce desired action or create desirable results. However, taken beyond optimal levels, stress and conflict produce dysfunctional consequences such as substance abuse, noncompliance, or escalating violence at work.

Stress

Stress is a normal and natural part of life and work. Some amount of workplace stress motivates and energizes work productivity, and many believe that a moderate amount of stress produces highest levels of personal productivity. The stress curve in Figure 16.1 shows these relationships. It also shows that too much stress can lead to brownout or lower productivity and more can lead to burnout when the person can no longer work effectively.

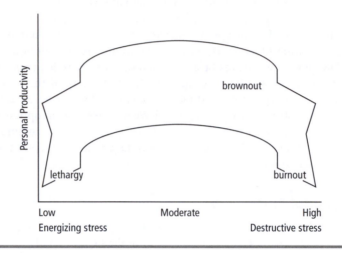

Figure 16.1 *A stress curve*

Work-related stress is escalating worldwide, exacerbated by the potential for working every hour of the week, a growing sense that hard work is the only way to sustain jobs, growing pressure to do more with less, and almost constant demands to learn new skills. Some managers face stress due to business travel which—due to globalization—can be more frequent and be completed in shorter time periods (Miller, 1996). A faster pace provides constant exposure to new cultures and new experiences, producing stressors that create anxieties and can disrupt work places. Additional travel stressors come from global shifts that include Middle East hostility, terrorist attacks, disease outbreaks, and executive kidnappings.

For US managers, business travel increased 20 percent between 1990 and 1995 to allow more travel in less time. For example, as many as 25 percent of business travelers return within 24 hours (Miller, 1996). This pace can lead to overwork, family estrangement, drug and alcohol abuse, and dysfunctional workplace conflict.

Whereas stress symptoms such as substance abuse traditionally were viewed as personal problems, organizations increasingly take on some responsibilities for stress reduction. Evolving Systems, Inc. is a software developer with a mission to provide an excellent work environment for employees that fosters growth and job satisfaction. They aim to reduce workplace stress for engineers by hiring an "office mom" to make sure employees eat regularly, host holiday and birthday parties, water the plants, and make sure sick workers get care. Others firms such as Deloitte Touche provide an office concierge to handle personal needs such as laundry, car repairs, theater tickets, and the like. The following examples show how companies reduce stress for business travelers:

Stress Reduction for Travelers
Hewlett Packard provides an 800 number for traveling executives to use for family contacts; executives can use the number even to read to their children by telephone.
American Family Insurance provides an on-site convenience store for travelers to pick up last-minute travel items like hosiery, shaving cream, and snacks.
Price Waterhouse flies its consultants home from wherever they are in the US because they felt executives were spending too many weekends away from home.
An informal policy at EDS provides a day or two off for employees who have been on the road for four or more days so they can reacquaint themselves with their families and catch up on personal errands and tasks.
Source material: Laundry and dog-walking. (1996, Nov. 1) *The Wall Street Journal*, p. B9.

About 28 percent of 243 locations worldwide are ranked high for poor personal security or sociopolitical tensions (Lublin, 2003), and terrorism increases the risk of travel. Additionally, kidnappings are on the rise for executives. From 20,000-30,000 people are kidnapped per year (Auerbach, 1998); almost 2,000 executives were kidnapped and held for ransom in 1999 (Flynn, 2002). In some cases, family members or colleagues of executives are kidnapped, held for ransom, hurt, or killed. Businesses respond to these risks with security measures ranging from evasive driving school, to bodyguards, preventive training (for example follow different routes to work), attack dogs, walled housing compounds, and kidnap and ransom insurance.

Managing Conflict at Work

Conflict involves disputes that are difficult to resolve because of differences of opinion or practice. Accountemps surveyed executives to find they spend 9 percent of management time in conflict resolution; this percentage increased to 13 percent in 1991 and to 18 percent by 1996. On the eve of Britain's introduction of new Dispute Resolution Regulations, a study of organizations who together employed 4 million people showed the average employer devoted 450 days of management time to conflicts and disputes. Total time devoted to managing conflict in each firm is the equivalent to that of two full-time managers (Conflict at work costs employers 450 days management time every year, 2004). In a global world with greater diversity, differences of opinion and conflict may be inevitable and they are escalating. This suggests that every manager must develop skills for managing conflict. Leonard Greenhalgh (1986) suggests a framework for conflict diagnosis that can help managers recognize and address dimensions of conflict. For example, as shown in Table 16.4, conflict is more difficult to resolve when those involved view the conflict as a matter of principle. In the global workplace, conflicts over religious practices have proved particularly challenging because they involve important principles. Sanyo Electric Company banned headscarves at its Jakarta subsidiary, and then those affected marched to the Indonesia House of Representatives in protest. Headscarves are also a focal issue in French schools. Cultural clashes like these throughout the world focus attention on profound differences in principles that are played out in workplace conflict.

Table 16.4 *Conflict diagnosis model*

Conflict Dimension	Difficult to Resolve	Easier to Resolve
Issue at question	A matter of principle	A divisible issue with no principle at stake
Size of the stakes	Large stakes	Small stakes
Interdependence of parties	Not interdependent	Very interdependent
Likelihood of future interactions	Low	High
Leadership and followers	Weak leader; factionalized followers	Strong leader with cohesive followers
Third-party involvement	No neutral third party	Trusted and powerful third party
Events to this point	One party feels more harmed than another	Balanced; a sense of equal harm to this point

Source material: Leonard Greenhalgh (1986) Managing conflict. *Sloan Management Review*, 27 (4): 45–51.

Managing Violence at Work

Violent solutions to workplace challenges also are growing. The ILO's report *Violence on the Job* (1998) observes that outbursts of violence occur at workplaces around the globe. Factors that increase the likelihood of workplace violence include: a) changes in an individual's social-support system, b) shrinking labor-market opportunities, and c) changing societal values (Allen and Lucero, 1996). According to Bemsimon (1994), violence appears to occur more frequently when stressors such as heavy workloads, understaffing, lay-offs, restructurings, and other workplace change occurs.

Bemsimon notes that indicators of a stressful workplace include persistent and widespread complaints about working conditions, labor/management conflict, frequent grievances and injury claims, and high absenteeism. Allen and Lucero (1996) believe workplace violence is preceded by exhibitions of anger, resentment or frustration, and will be targeted at the person perceived to be most responsible for the aversive treatment; this person often is a manager. In summary, managers increasingly manage not only stress but violence at work that may be targeted at them.

Allen and Lucero (1996) believe managers can take the following steps to reduce workplace violence:

1 Practice fair treatment of all employees; provide clear expectations and performance feedback.
2 Provide supervisory training for those closest to employees.
3 Develop employee assistance efforts to help employees deal with difficult transitions.
4 Develop termination practices that are fair; extend assistance to the employee in finding other work.
5 Provide a security system limiting workplace access, especially for those who have been recently fired or made redundant.

This review of organizational responses to risk, stress, and conflict illustrates that many organizations face increased risks. Many of these risks are new ones with which managers have little experience, and all reflect increased variety of actions and beliefs associated with greater workplace diversity.

CHAPTER SUMMARY

Decision-making means choosing from among alternatives. Decision-making according to linear, rational models dominant in the Western world are expanding to accommodate more process-oriented modes of thinking such as intuition.

Innovation is constant development and refinement of both products and processes, and it can be an important source of company advantage.

Workplaces that stimulate individual creativity often are those where people are encouraged to innovate but have guidelines and objectives in place. They require organizational structures that allow flexibility but also provide direction, and processes that facilitate rather than impede the innovations that often emerge from creativity.

The possibility of risk is embedded in most situations. Evidence of growing political risk and foreign currency exchange risk, corruption risk, and personal risk show how the concept of risk has expanded in a global world. Managers increasingly face three kinds of personal risk: psychological risk from stress, personal risk from travel, and conflict and violence at work.

REVIEW AND DISCUSSION QUESTIONS

1 Assess your own decision-making style, selecting characteristics from rational and intuitive decision styles that best reflect your habits.

2 James Higgins, author of *Escape From the Maze* (1997), believes that personal creativity is stimulated in nine steps outlined earlier in the chapter. Assess yourself on these nine steps to estimate the extent to which you are creative.

3 Use Greenhalgh's Conflict Diagnosis Model to analyze conflict in Palestine. Which elements are in place? What are your predictions for near-term resolutions?

Chapter 17
A LOOK AHEAD

DUE DILIGENCE AT NEW ZEALAND STEVEDORING COMPANY LIMITED[1]

An unanswered telephone ringing in the distance broke Lindy Hebert's concentration. She glanced out at the splendid view of Auckland's waterfront, wondering yet again why no one was answering the phone. At the headquarters, work came first. Lindy herself had worked as hard as possible in the last four weeks—even spending evenings and weekends at work. Her due diligence report on New Zealand Stevedoring Company Limited (NZSC) would be the go/no go for a possible purchase.

Lindy and colleague Brad Shorten were in Auckland for Portland, Oregon company Dockmovers Associates—the largest independent terminal operator and stevedore company in the US. Privately held, Dockmovers recently established an international subsidiary to develop worldwide business opportunities. Limited growth opportunities and increased competition from abroad almost mandated worldwide expansion. Shipping had become a global industry, and Dockmovers wanted to be part of the action.

Dockmovers' leaders were looking at a New Zealand firm because national norms and practices were expected to be similar to those of the US Pacific Northwest; this could help with transition after an acquisition. For example, like in the Pacific Northwest, New Zealanders have a high regard for the natural environment and people were known to be hard workers. After four weeks of reviewing the books, observing employees, and listening to unanswered telephones Lindy wondered if there were more national differences than Dockmovers anticipated.

Like many New Zealand firms, NZSC was an indirect result of what was popularly known as "Rogernomics" because Labour Party economic adviser Roger Douglas had helped initiate changes such as deregulation of foreign exchange, fewer import restrictions, and export incentives. A later move toward industry privatization included stevedoring. Lindy and Brad wondered why changes brought about by privatization were still having an impact years later.

Organized around the national government's Waterfront Industry Commission (WIC), New Zealand stevedoring (movement of goods from ship to shore and vice versa) had been controlled by local harbour boards. Under the auspices of the WIC, these boards owned dock terminals, sheds, cranes, and other equipment but the WIC was the ultimate owner and employer. To hire stevedores, companies had to accept labor costs and people the WIC sent to them.

New Zealand's commitment to a uniformly high standard of living, generous benefits, and substantial retirement packages led to high labor costs in every industry. Additionally, and unlike elsewhere, New Zealand regulations made it impossible to fire stevedores. This forced up the price of shipping costs for meat, dairy, and wool exporters who began to agitate for change. A waterfront reorganization in 1989 disbanded the WIC and replaced it with port companies that operated more like for-profit businesses. Port companies traded shares for port assets such as terminals and sheds, and paid dividends on their profits to local government councils. The port companies eliminated many employee redundancies, reducing the number of stevedores from 1,600 in 1989 to 540 by 1997. Workers also were more productive, handling double the number of containers per day. At the time of the Dockmovers review, these improvements were less evident than the confusion and concern that often reigns during transition from an old system to a new one.

▶

Because the new rules of privatization and deregulation were complex, NZSC organized the 12 New Zealand locations as separate and autonomous legal entities. Management was decentralized and except for a computer link, few systems were integrated. The CEO was far from a "people" person, but his leadership style was not unusual for New Zealand where the work ethic was expected to motivate people. Unfortunately, the due diligence review had showcased all the flaws of the current system. First, decentralization made it impossible to compare units easily. Second, since there were no integrated systems in place all 12 sets of books had to be evaluated manually. Third, the head office had been lax on the rules and some companies hadn't yet gotten around to rolling end-of-year net income into retained earnings. Fourth, there appeared to be overspending.

The gleaming wood and pleasing sea-blue and salmon color scheme in the NZSC office was one example. The office was far nicer than anything Dockmovers' employees enjoyed. Then there were work issues. NZCS employees were unused to working more than eight hours a day; their families complained at the longer hours required for what they'd been told was an audit. Many believed the audit created unrealistic deadlines. Further, the CEO's autocratic style had driven away many good employees, and those who remained were hesitant to make decisions. The "tall poppy" syndrome tended to discourage individual initiative. What this meant is that someone who did more than others was subject to peer pressure to stop. Finally, there seemed to be an issue of "attitude" among existing staff. It was an attitude Lindy found difficult to pinpoint but something she had noticed at her first day at NZSC.

That first work day followed 18 air hours to New Zealand, but Brad and Lindy had planned their trip to arrive early in the morning to begin work at 7:00 a.m. on Monday morning. From their command post in the many-windowed conference room, they observed workers trickling in—seemingly on their own schedules. One day Lindy and Brad arrived at the office and no one was there to admit them. As planned, Brad spent a good deal of his time with the CEO, attorneys, and external accountants. Accustomed to 55-hour work weeks that extended to 60 and 70 hours during accounting end-periods, Lindy reviewed on-site documents. At first she'd asked employees to find papers for her, but after growing impatient for more information, soon she'd begun to sort through file-room cabinets on her own. Employees were disturbed by this behavior, but the CEO had shouted down the corridor, "Never mind, Lindy has access to personnel files—and everything else." After that, employees helped most by getting out of the way.

When asked to recall the "audit," one NZSC employee's most vivid mental image was of Lindy "haring" down the hallway as Brad called out from the conference room "Are you done yet?" Frequent telephone, fax, and e-mail communications to the parent company in Portland expressed Brad and Lindy's emerging concerns: reliable data were difficult to obtain; managers were causing delays by working 8:30–6:30 days; there was no master plan; past decisions had committed the company to above-market leases and equipment prices; and there was a fixed workforce with seven weeks of paid holidays a year. Lindy wondered if it could ever be worth it for Dockmovers to acquire NZSC. But where else in the wide world could the company begin its all-important global expansion plan?

CHAPTER OVERVIEW

The introductory case illustrates that businesses and business people operate in an expanding world, making interconnections that encompass issues of culture, politics, economics, businesses and industries, the natural environment, and technology. Each enables globalization and each generates challenges. This concluding look at prior chapters shows that businesses are increasingly interconnected not only with one another but with a world that is global.

ORGANIZATIONS OPERATE IN WORLDWIDE SYSTEMS

The Dockmovers Case illustrates that even small firms go global. It also shows that growing interconnections of business, politics, time, and space sometimes confront national and cultural differences in how, when, and who participates in business. These types of challenges will increase in the foreseeable future as diverse nations like China and India become stronger economic players. China's economy alone is expected to be bigger than that of the US or the EU by 2020. Companies from all over the world and of every size and shape contribute to economic growth, but they begin with differing perspectives on relationships between business and society. For example, some operate strictly as wealth generators while others build companies to provide jobs, develop a nation, or improve social conditions. Many civil society organizations (CSOs) are also global ones whose interests increasingly overlap with business concerns. Corporate social responsibility, global codes of ethics, labor rights and protection, and preservations of the natural environment on a global scale are a few among many concerns that global CSOs believe must be part of the global landscape for business.

The interconnections that shape globalization add several layers of complexity to the management task. Accordingly, organizational efforts to go global are likely to be confronted by at least some of Dockmovers' challenges. Although some challenges can be anticipated, such as political differences, others come as a surprise. For example, in the Dockmovers case shared use of the English language did not mean New Zealanders and US workers could communicate perfectly.

Prior chapters identified challenges like these, noting that global managers can best prepare for global participation by recognizing their roles in a worldwide system characterized by global shifts occurring in six environments. The core argument is that organizations are interconnected to their world, operating in a system that is increasingly global rather than merely local or regional. The idea that organizations operate within systems is hardly a new one, but what is new to most managers is that the system is worldwide in scope. In this worldwide system, many global shifts that affect organizations occur "out of sight," and their effects are often difficult to anticipate. Characteristics of globalization such as growing interconnections, a rapid and discontinuous pace of change, and the increased number and diversity among global organizations all create complexity for organizational managers. This book demonstrates that interconnections affect business, governmental, and social actors, forcing them too to develop relationships that can help or hurt. In particular, we observed that many shifts in global environments like culture, politics, or economics are mediated by governmental and/or civil society organizations.

Managers respond to some amount of growing global complexity by recognizing, analyzing, and even anticipating global shifts. This analysis better prepares organizations for global shifts and some are adept enough to shape outcomes of those shifts. At the same time, there is chaos in this system of worldwide interconnections that makes it difficult to anticipate everything that can affect an organization.

ORGANIZATIONAL MANAGERS ADAPT STRUCTURES, PROCESSES, AND PEOPLE

Organizations differ worldwide because each makes different use of internal resources like people, processes, and structures. Earlier chapters demonstrated that organizations experience global shifts in different ways due to configurational differences. They necessarily respond to global shifts in distinctive ways as well. However, the core task is the same for global organizations: on a worldwide scale to integrate internal mechanisms of structure, people, and processes better to respond to real or anticipated global shifts.

An organization's structure provides the framework for organizational action (see Chapter 12). It shows relationships between people and their jobs, determines the direction in which resources like power, information, and money will flow, and helps the global organization establish priorities among *functions* such as marketing, finance, or production, *geographic regions* served, and *products or services*. Global giants increasingly develop structures that accommodate global expansion. These structures often follow mergers, acquisitions, or divestitures, and they frequently accommodate diverse organizational types, for example wholly owned subsidiaries *and* joint ventures. The latter structural form connects global organizations to one another. Dual needs for centralization and decentralization often challenge structural integration for large global firms like St. Gobain, McDonald's, Coca-Cola, Henkels, Sanro, Samsung, Siemens, and Cemex that generate billions in revenues, manage hundreds of thousands of employees, and operate in more than 100 nations. Even a large team of top managers would find it hard to direct all of these activities simultaneously, and that is why many delegate. Smaller global competitors also distribute worldwide or source from global pools. Although the scope of their activities is necessarily smaller, their managers must also decide if they will make decisions in a centralized location or delegate more broadly.

Because structures, people, and processes co-exist in the same organization, a change in one is bound to affect the others. For example, acquisitions often disrupt systematic or continuous process activities that accomplish organizational purposes; they disrupt existing structures, and often they lead to changes in personnel and in job assignments. The success and retention of a process-oriented change depends very much on its integration with structure and with an organization's people. In the early days of computerization, many organizations learned this lesson the hard way when fearful employees left them or disgruntled ones "accidentally" spilled coffee into mainframes. Many stimulants—internal and external—can bring about changes in organizational processes. Growing worldwide risk forces many companies to develop comprehensive safety processes; technological changes require information processing changes; and global supply chains call for integrative management systems. These and many other global processes stimulate internal integration of PPS (Chapter 16).

Perhaps more than processes and structures, people—from top managers to individual employees—make or break organizations. The Strategic International Human Resource Systems (Chapter 13) to select, develop, train, compensate, and otherwise manage human resources efficiently are difficult to integrate. For example, cultural differences are an impediment to integrating people worldwide around a common purpose. Differences in how people think, the time they are willing to devote to organizations, the skills and abilities they have or can acquire, or the compensation they expect vary widely. The diversity they bring to organizations and to team efforts are the subject of Chapter 14.

Leaders of global organizations (see Chapter 13) achieve integration using a global mindset that simultaneously views both the big picture and the details. A global mindset becomes possible for managers who can think outside their own culture to recognize the conflicting priorities and demands the firm faces. Global leaders tend to be people with intimate knowledge of their organization and its environment. They are able to create and convey a clear organizational vision with integrity, they develop self-awareness and understanding, they are continuous learners, and they are able to manage diversity well.

ORGANIZATIONS INTERCONNECT WITH ONE ANOTHER

Examples above illustrate that global adaptations of structures, processes, and people increasingly interconnect businesses to other organizations. For example, suppliers can mediate the relationship between an organization and developing technologies, while buyer groups can mediate the relationship between an organization and cultural shifts. Increasingly, global shifts are also mediated by organizations outside the business sector; governmental, non-governmental, and intergovernmental organizations are three examples. These and other mediating organizations often stand between the focal organization and global shifts, and they affect global businesses in two principal ways: they shape the meaning of global shifts, and they shape the options available to businesses. The activities of mediating organizations interconnect them with business activities worldwide. One result is growing worldwide demand for businesses that are responsible and responsive global citizens.

THE CHANGING LANDSCAPE FOR BUSINESS

In addition to generating profits, global businesses—especially global giants—face growing pressure to participate in social problem-solving. Some of these problems are directly related to business activities, for example labor standards and environmental protection, while others are less direct, for example worldwide equity. For global giants, these types of activities are not only value-added but are value-expected by a global populace. In turn, global giants introduce and transmit higher standards to their suppliers. Through educational campaigns, buyers are also encouraged to recognize their global problem-solving roles. Simultaneously, global governance mechanisms such as ISO standards and codes of ethics and responsibility emerge and interconnect businesses with the world (see Chapter 15). Many of these results come about through business, government, and nongovernmental partnerships that further interconnect them to each other.

In the last half decade, the world has witnessed considerable turmoil and uneven progress in worldwide development. But there is a growing awareness that all members of society have a role to play in attaining "globalization for good." This awareness is reflected by political activities such as the UN's Global Compact, new WTO initiatives that link labor, the environment, and trade, and G8 focus on economic development in Africa. For the natural environment, responses to globalization are reflected in vaccine availability for all children and worldwide responses to natural disasters or to global diseases. Worldwide response to the SARS virus (described in Chapter 6) shows how scientists for the first time collaborated rapidly to identify and isolate a disesase. Economic systems to manage global FDI, trade, capital, and labor are fraught with challenges, but worldwide systems are developing to monitor exchange, drive out fraud, and provide access to capital for the world's poor through new institutions and activities such as microenterprise lending. Telecommunications technologies facilitate many of these activities, but they too face challenges such as information excess and inaccuracy.

These examples demonstrate that globalization is a process whereby worldwide interconnections in virtually every sphere of activity are growing. Some of these interconnections lead to integration/unity worldwide; others do not. For example, there is a growing sense that the world needs a common security system. However, addressing this or any other global challenge means reaching consensus worldwide, and that is easier said than done. Consensus is difficult to reach for several reasons explored in this text: available information differs, individuals have different values, and many begin with different ends in mind. Examples of enterprise strategy listed in Chapter 3 show that business organizations are chartered for different reasons. Reviews of different economic theories in Chapter 8 show that many take different positions about the value of business/government relationships. Finally a 2004 meeting of Nobel Prize winners in economics illustrates how information access and utilization lead to differences in opinion. When asked which would be the largest economy in 75 years, these respondents listed: China, the European Union, or the US. Joseph Stiglitz responded "It's too difficult to make a projection 75 years from now" (Nobel laureates, 2004). General predictions were that the world economy would continue to grow, developing economies would continue to grow, and some indicated that social, political, and economic policy integration would lead to higher standards of living. For example, Lawrence Klein admired this integration in Norway which produces "fairness among many segments of the population." (Good news, 2004: A7).

THE GLOBAL CITIZEN

Organizations clearly play important roles in the globalization process. But organizations exist to serve society. Most organizations developed to serve the needs of domestic or regional societies now operate in and increasingly serve a global world. This world shelters the rich and poor, the educated and undereducated, the healthy and the ill. As shown throughout the text, an interconnected world does not mean common response to any single issue, but there is a growing sense that a peaceful world cannot be achieved without equity. Achieving that equity becomes the job not only of organizations but also of citizens worldwide.

A return to chapter materials identifies some common themes on how equity may be achieved. First, there is growing worldwide interest in and embrace of market economics as a medium for economic development (see Chapter 8). Disappointing results from many free-market experiments demonstrate their limits and show that government intervention in markets sometimes helps and sometimes hurts. Thus economic development initiatives come with efforts also to improve governance, and they are undertaken by considering many global influences rather than single ones. The World Values Survey (see Chapter 7) demonstrates a powerful relationship between economic development and cultural values. Results from the WVS show that shifts from an agrarian to an industrial society—such as is occurring today in many nations— bring with them a reorientation from traditional to more secular-rational views that question authority, discourage male dominance, and encourage personal freedoms. This suggests that many more people worldwide will question authority, including that of wealthy and powerful global businesses. Finally, there is growing evidence that the world's challenges must be addressed by all nations rather than just a few. The consensus-based approach of the World Trade Organization and halting progress toward agreements on telecommunications, agriculture, and services shows that worldwide agreement on any global issue will take years rather than months. Progress may be slow and discontinuous, and for some that will be discouraging. Citizen protests that drew prominent media attention beginning with the 1999 WTO meeting show that civil society organizations increasingly demand a voice in establishing trade regimes. In particular, they are voices for protecting the natural environment, for civil rights, and for labor improvements worldwide.

The slow global pace of equity proves frustrating to many in the advanced economies and disastrous for many in developing ones. Accordingly, global progress toward equity requires more than organizational efforts. It requires individual efforts that begin with knowledge and result in action. As noted in Chapter 1, people operate from mental frameworks to identify priorities and shape action. Usually these frameworks are built around domestic concerns and domestic values. But just as business managers must reframe their thinking for a global world, so too individuals must expand their mental frames better to see the whole world rather than just their part in it.

This book explores global interconnections of many types, with each chapter examining different perspectives on interconnections. Ideally, having provided a beginning point for readers, this text will motivate them as citizens, voters, and employees to utilize a global mindset when working to balance self-interest and societal interests in work, political, and personal life.

NOTE

1 Development of this case study was supported by a Faculty Development Grant from the University of Washington Center for International Business Education and Research.

References

Abramovitz, Janet N., and Mattoon, Ashley T. (1999) Paper cuts: Recovering the paper landscape. http://www.worthwatch.org/Pubs/paper/149.html

Adair, Anthony (1999) Codes of conduct are good for NGOs too. *IPA Review*, 51 (1): 26–27.

Adler, Nancy J. (1987) Pacific Basin managers: A Gaijin, not a woman. *Human Resource Management*, 26: 169–191.

Adler, Nancy J. (1997) *International Dimensions of Organizational Behavior* (3rd edn). Cincinnati, OH: South-Western Publishing.

Adler, Nancy J., and Bartholomew, Susan (1992) Academic and professional communities of discourse: Generating knowledge on transnational human resource management. *Journal of International Business Studies*, 23 (3): 551–569.

ADR Reference Guide (2002/03) at: http://www.adr.com/jpmorgan/corpactions/ADR ReferenceGuide.pdf

AIDS epidemic 2003. (2003) UNAIDS/WHO report. http://www.unaids.org

Albert, Michel, Haviland, Paul, and Rohatyn, Felix G. (1993) *Capitalism vs. Capitalism: How America's Obsession with Individual Achievement & Short-term Profit has Led it to the Brink of Collapse*. New York: Four Walls Eight Windows.

Allen, R.E., and Lucero, Margaret A. (1996) Beyond resentment: Exploring organizationally targeted insider murder. *Journal of Management Inquiry*, 5 (2): 86–103.

Allred, Brent B., Snow, Charles C., and Miles, Raymond E. (1996) Characteristics of managerial careers in the 21st century. *Academy of Management Executive*, 10 (4): 17–27.

Alsop, Ronald (2002a, Jan. 16) Companies' reputations depend on service they give customers. *The Wall Street Journal*, p. B1.

Alsop, Ronald (2002b, Jan. 16) For a company, charitable works are best carried out discreetly. *The Wall Street Journal*, p. B1.

Alsop, Ronald (2004) *The 18 Immutable Laws of Corporate Reputation*. New York: Free Press Wall Street Journal Book.

Altadis SA Annual Report. (2000) Paris: Altadis SA Corporate Communications Department.

Amason, Allen C. (1996) Distinguishing the effects of functional and dysfunctional conflict on strategic decision making: Resolving a paradox for top management team. *Academy of Management Journal*, 39: 123–149.

Andre, R. (1985) The effects of multinational business training: A replication of INSEAD research in an institute in the United States. *Management International Review*, 25: 4–15.

Anholt, Simon (2000, Nov./Dec.) The nation as brand. *Across the Board*, pp. 22–27.

Annan, Kofi (2000, May) *We the peoples: Millennium Report of the Secretary-General of the UN*. New York: United Nations.

Appelbaum, Steven H., Shapiro, Barbara, and Elbaz, David (1998) The management of multicultural team conflict. *Team Performance Management*, 4 (5): 211–225.

Applebaum, Richard P., and Henderson, Jeffrey (1995) The hinge of history: Turbulence and transformation in the world economy. *Competition and Change*. Germany: Harwood Academic Publishers, pp. 1–12.

Arab Human Development Report 2003. (2003) New York: United Nations Development Program.

Arthur, Michael B., Claman, Priscilla H., and DeFillippi, Robert J. (1995) Intelligent enterprise, intelligent careers. *Academy of Management Executive*, 9 (4): 7–22.

Arthur, Michael B., and Rousseau, Denise M. (1996) *The Boundaryless Career*. New York: Oxford University Press.

Asahi Beer Company homepage. (2002, July 3) http://www.asahibeer.co.jp

Ascarelli, Silvia (1999, Aug. 12) Latest test of unity in Europe may take Orange from Dutch. *The Wall Street Journal*, pp. A1, A6.

Ashkenas, Ron, Ulrich, Dave, Jick, Todd, and Kerr, Steve (1995) *The Boundaryless Organization*. San Francisco, CA: Jossey-Bass.

Asia's competing capitalisms. (1995, June 24) *The Economist*, pp. 16–17.

Asia's labor pains. (1995, Aug. 26) *The Economist*, pp. 51–52.

Asian business survey. (2001, Apr. 7) *The Economist*, p. 5.

Auerbach, Ann Hagedorn (1998) *Ransom: The Untold Story of International Kidnapping*. New York: Henry Holt.

Austin, James (2000) *The Collaborative Challenge*. San Francisco: Jossey-Bass.

Back office to the world. (2001, May 5) *The Economist*, pp. 59–62.

Baglole, Joel (2001, Mar. 13) Iceland transforms itself into a hotbed of new industries. *The Wall Street Journal*, p. 21.

Baker, M.B. (1993) Private codes of corporate conduct: Should the fox guard the henhouse? *University of Miami Inter-American Law Review*, 24: 400–433.

Bangert, David C., and Pirzada, Kahkashan (1992) Culture and negotiation. *International Executive*, 34 (1): 43–64.

Bannock, Graham, Baxter, R.E., and Davis, Evan (1998) *Dictionary of Economics*. New York: Wiley.

Bannon, Lisa (1994, Nov. 17) Natuzzi's huge selection of leather furniture pays off. *The Wall Street Journal*, p. B4.

Bannerjee, Subhabrata Bobby, and Linstead, Stephen (2001) Globalization, multiculturalism and other fictions: Colonialism for the new millennium? *Organization*, 8 (4): 683–722.

Bantel, K.A., and Jackson, Susan E. (1989) Top management and innovations in banking: Does the composition of the top team make a difference? *Strategic Management Journal*, 10: 107–124.

Barber, Benjamin (1992, Mar.) Jihad vs. McWorld. *Atlantic Monthly*, 269 (3): 53–61.

Barber, Benjamin (1996, Mar.) *Jihad vs. McWorld*. New York: Ballantine Books.

Barnett, Richard, and Cavanagh, John (1994) *Global Dreams: Imperial Corporations and the New World Order*. New York: Simon and Schuster.

Barney, Jay (1991) Firm resources and sustained competitive advantage. *Journal of Management*, 17 (1): 99–120.

Bartlett, Christopher A., and Ghoshal, Sumantra (1989) *Managing Across Borders: The Transnational Solution*. Boston, MA: Harvard Business School Press.

Bartlett, Christopher A., and Ghoshal, Sumantra (1992a) *Transnational Management*. Boston, MA: Irwin.

Bartlett, Christopher A., and Ghoshal, Sumantra (1992b, Sept./Oct.) What is a global manager? *Harvard Business Review*, pp. 124–132.

Bartlett, Christopher A., and Ghoshal, Sumantra (1995, May/June) Changing the role of top management: Beyond systems to people. *Harvard Business Review*, pp. 132–142.

Bartlett, Christopher A., and Ghoshal, Sumantra (2000, Mar./Apr.) Going global: Lessons from late movers. *Harvard Business Review*, pp. 132–142.

Bass, Bernard M. (1985) *Leadership and Performance Beyond Expectation*. New York: Free Press.

Beamish, Paul, Killing, J. Peter, Lecraw, Donald J., and Crookell, Peter (1991) *International Management*. Burr Ridge, IL: Irwin.

Becht, Marco, Betts, Paul, and Morck, Randall.(2003, Feb. 3) The complex evolution of family affairs. *Financial Times*, p. 6.

Becker, Helmut, and Fritzsche, David (1987) A comparison of the ethical behavior of American, French, and German managers. *Columbia Journal of World Business*, 22 (4): 87–95.

Begley, Thomas M., and Boyd, David P. (2003) *MIT Sloan Management Review*, 44 (2): 25–33.

Bell, Bradford S., and Kozlowski, Steve W.J. (2002) A typology of virtual teams. *Group and Organization Management*, 27 (1): 14–49.

Bell, Jim, McNaughton, Rod, and Young, Stephen (2001) "Born-again global" firms: An extension to the "born global" phenomenon. *Journal of International Management*, 7: 173–189.

Bemsimon, H.F. (1994) Crisis and disaster management: Violence in the workplace. *Training and Development*, 28: 27–32.

Bendell, Jem (Ed.) (2000a) *Terms for Endearment*. Sheffield, UK: Greenleaf.

Bendell, Jem (2000b) Working with stakeholder pressure for sustainable development. In Jem Bendell (Ed.), *Terms for Endearment*, pp.14–30. Sheffield, UK: Greenleaf.

Bennett, John W., and Dahlberg, Kenneth A. (1993) Institutions, social organizations, and cultural values. *The Earth as Transformed by Human Action*. New York: Cambridge University Press.

Bennett, Milton (1993) Towards ethnorelativism: A development model of intercultural sensitivity. In Michael R. Paige (Ed.), *Education for the Intercultural Experience*, pp. 21–71. Boston: Intercultural Press.

Bennis, Warren (1993) Managing the dream: Leadership in the 21st century. In W. Rosenbach and R. Taylor (Eds), *Contemporary Issues in Leadership*, pp. 247–260. Boulder, CO: Westview.

Berger, I., Cunningham, P., and Drumwright, M. (1999) Social alliances: Company/ nonprofit collaboration. *Social Marketing Quarterly*, 5 (3): 49–53.

Berger, Peter L. (1997) Four faces of global culture. *The National Interest*, 49: 23–30.

Berle, Adolph, and Means, Gardiner (1932) *The Modern Corporation and Private Property*. New York: Macmillan.

Berman, Shawn L., Wicks, Andrew C., Kotha, Suresh, and Jones, Thomas M. (1999) Does stakeholder orientation matter? The relationship between stakeholder management models and firm financial performance. *Academy of Management Journal*, 42 (5): 488–506.

Beyer, Janice M., and Nino, David (1999) Ethics and cultures in international business. *Journal of Management Inquiry*, 8 (3): 287–298.

Bhagwati, Jagdish (2002, June 22) The poor's best hope. *The Economist*, pp. 24–26.

Birchard, Bill (2002, June) Global profits, ethical peril. *Chief Executive*, pp. 48–54.

Black hole. (1999, Aug. 28) *The Economist*, p. 59.

Black, J. Stewart (1988) Work role transitions: A study of American expatriate managers in Japan. *Journal of International Business Studies*, 19: 277–294.

Black, Stewart J. and Mendenhall, Mark (1990) Cross-cultural training effectiveness: A review and a theoretical framework for future research. *Academy of Management Review*, 15 (1): 113–136.

Black, J. Stewart, Morrison, Alan, and Gregersen, Hal B. (1999) *Global Explorers: The Next Generation of Leaders*. New York: Routledge.

Black, J.S., Mendenhall, Mark, and Oddou, Gary (1991) Toward a comprehensive model of international adjustment: An integration of multiple theoretical perspectives. *Academy of Management Review*, 16: 291–317.

Blackhurst, Chris (2002, May) Family fortunes. *Management Today*, pp. 54–60.

Blanchflower, David G., and Slaughter, Matthew (1998) The causes and consequences of changing earnings inequality: W(h)ither the debate? *Global Trade and Wages*. New York: Council on Foreign Relations.

Blattberg, Robert C., and Hoch, Stephen J. (1990, Aug.) Data models and managerial intuition: 50% model + 50% manager. *Management Science*, pp. 887–899.

Boatwright, John R. (2000) Globalization and the ethics of business. *Business Ethics Quarterly*, 10 (1): 1–6.

Bolman, Lee, and Deal, Terry E. (1991) *Reframing Organizations*. San Francisco, CA: Jossey-Bass.

Bolman, Lee, and Deal, Terry E. (1995). *Leading with Soul*. San Francisco, CA: Jossey-Bass.

Booth, Jason (2001, Oct.16) Terror attacks to harm Asian economies. *The Wall Street Journal*, p. A23.

Booth, Martin (2000) *The Dragon Syndicates*. New York: Carroll and Graf.

Borrelli, G., Cable, J., and Higgs, M.J. (1995) What makes teams work better? *Team Performance Management*, 1 (3): 28–35.

Borrus, M., and Zysman, J. (1998) Wintelism and the changing terms of global competition: Prototype of the future. BRIEF Working Paper 96B, Berkeley, CA.

Bosch, Gerhard, Dawkins, Peter, and Michon, Francois (1993) *Times are Changing: Working Time in 14 Industrialized Countries*. Geneva: International Institute for Labour Studies, ILO.

Boston, William (2002, June 18) Tainted food roils Germany's organic farmers. *The Wall Street Journal*, p. A13.

Boyacigiller, Nakiya A., and Adler, Nancy J. (1991) The parochial dinosaur: Organizational science in a global context. *Academy of Management Review*, 16 (2): 262–290.

Brabet, Julienne, and Klemm, Mary (1994) Sharing the visions: Company mission statements in Britain and France. *Long Range Planning*, 27 (1): 84–94.

Bradbury, Hilary, and Clair, Judith A. (1999) Promoting sustainable organizations with Sweden's Natural Step. *Academy of Management Executive*, 13 (4): 63–74.

Brademas, John, and Heimann, Fritz (1998, Sept./Oct.) Tackling international corruption. *Foreign Affairs*, pp. 17–22.

Bradley, S.P., Hausman, J.A., and Nolan, R.L. (1993) *Globalization, Technology, and Competition*. Boston: Harvard Business School Press.

Brand benefits—cause-related marketing. (2003) Brand Benefits 2003. http://www.bitc.org.uk/resources/research/research_publications/brand_benefits.html

Brandenburger, Adam, and Nalebuff, Barry (1996) *Co-opetition*. New York: Doubleday.

Brecher, Jeremy, and Costello, Tim (1994) *Global Village or Global Pillage?* Boston, MA: South End Press.

Bremner, Brian, and Edmonson, Gail (2004, May 10) Japan: A tale of two mergers. *Business Week*, p. 42.

Broadhurst, Arlene (2000) Corporations and the ethics of Social responsibility: An emerging regime of expansion and compliance. *Business Ethics: A European Review*, 9 (2): 86–98.

Brown, Andrew (1994) Top of the bosses. *International Management*, 49 (3): 26–29.

Brown, Juanita (1992) Corporation as community: A new image for a new era. In John Renesch (Ed.), *New Traditions in Business*, pp. 123–139. San Francisco, CA: Berrett-Koehler.

Brown, L. David, Khagram, Sanjeev, Moore, Mark H., and Frumkin, Peter (2002) Globalization, NGOs, and multisectoral relations. *Journal of Marxism and Reality*, 3 (6): 271–298.

Brown, Lester, Lenssen, Nicholas, and Kane, Hal (1995) *Vital Signs*. Washington, D.C.: Worldwatch Institute.

Bryman, Alan (1996) Leadership in organizations. In Stewart R. Clegg, Cynthia Hardy, and Walter R. Nord (Eds), *Handbook of Organization Studies*, pp. 276–292. London: Sage.

Buck, Susan J. (1998) *The Global Commons: An Introduction*. Washington, D.C.: Island Press.

Bulkeley, William M. (2004, Jan. 19) IBM documents give rare look at sensitive plans on "offshoring." *The Wall Street Journal*, pp. B1, B8.

Buller, Paul F., Kohls, John J., and Anderson, Kenneth S. (1997) A model for addressing cross-cultural ethical conflicts. *Business & Society*, 36 (2): 169–193.

Bureau of Labor Statistics (data from 2000 for textile, apparel and leather products manufacturing). (2003, Nov.19) http://ftp.bls.gov/pub/special.requests/ForeignLabor/ind2231.txt

Burke, Lisa A., and Miller, Monica K. (1999) Taking the mystery out of intuitive decision making. *Academy of Management Executive*, 13 (4): 91–98.

Business for Social Responsibility. (2002, Mar. 11) Corporate ethics: A prime business asset. http://www.bsr.org

Byrne, John (1993, Feb. 8) The virtual corporation. *Business Week*, pp. 98–103.

Cadbury, Sir Adrian (2000) *Family Firms and Their Governance*. Great Britain: Egon Zehnder International.

Calori, Roland, and Dufour, Bruno (1995) Management European style. *Academy of Management Executive*, 9 (3): 61–77.

Campbell, Alexandra, and Verbeke, Alain (1994, Apr.) The globalization of service multinationals. *Long Range Planning*, 27 (2): 95–102.

Can there be a global standard for social policy? The "Social Policy Principles" as a test case. (2000, May 2). Overseas Development Institute Briefing Paper: www.odi.org.uk/briefing/2_00.html

Capra, Fritzof (1984) *The Turning Point*. New York: Bantam Books.

Carrington, Tim (1994, June 22) Gender economics. *The Wall Street Journal*, pp. A1, A6.

Carstairs, Robert T., and Welch, Lawrence S. (1982/1983). Licensing and internationalization of smaller companies: Some Australian evidence. *Management International Review*, 22 (3): 33–44.

The case for globalisation. (2000, Sept. 23) *The Economist*, pp. 19–20.

Castells, Manuel (1996) *The Rise of the Network Society*. Oxford: Blackwell.

Castells, Manuel (1998) *The Information Age: Economy, Society and Culture*. Malden, MA and Oxford: Blackwell.

Castells, Manuel, and Portes, Alejandro (1989) World underneath: The origins, dynamics, and effects of the informal economy. In Alejandro Portes, Manuel Castells, and Lauren Benton (Eds), *The Informal Economy: Studies in Advanced and Less Developed Countries*, pp. 11–37. Baltimore, MD: Johns Hopkins University Press.

Catalyst fact sheet. (1999) Women of color in corporate management: A statistical picture. New York: Catalyst.

Caux Round Table Principles for Business. (1995) Reprint from Business Ethics. Minneapolis: Business Ethics.

Cavusgil, S. Tamer, and Knight, Gary A. (1997) Explaining an emerging phenomenon for international marketing: Global orientation and the born-global firm. Working paper: Michigan State University CIBER.

Center for Business Ethics. (1992) Instilling ethical values in large corporations. *Journal of Business Ethics*, pp. 863–867.

Cetron, Marvin J., and Davies, Owen (2001, Jan./Feb.) Trends now changing the world. *The Futurist*, pp. 40–43.

Chakraborty, S.K. (1995) *Ethics in Management: Vedantic Perspectives*. Delhi: Oxford University Press.

Champy, James (1995) *Reengineering Management: The Mandate for New Leadership*. New York: HarperBusiness.

Chandler, Alfred (1977) *The Visible Hand: The Managerial Revolution in American Business*. Cambridge, MA: Belknap Press of Harvard University Press.

Chandler, Sir Geoffrey. (1999, Feb. 1). The new corporate challenge. *Time*, p. 68.

Charan, Ram (1991) How networks reshape organizations—for results. Reprinted in *Fast Forward*. (1996) Cambridge, MA: Harvard Business School Press, pp. 15–38.

Charity holds it own in tough times. (2003) AAFRC. http://aafrc.org/press_releases/trustreleases/charityholds.html.

Che non ci sera. (1995, Apr.) *The Economist*, pp. 75–76.

Christensen, Clayton (1997) *The Innovator's Dilemma: Why New Technologies Cause Great Firms to Fail*. Cambridge, MA: Harvard Business School Press.

Cisco aims to train 100,000 workers in India by 2006. (2001, Jan. 16) *The Wall Street Journal*, p. A19.

Citicorp Annual Report. (1995) New York: Citicorp.

Ciulla, Joanne B. (1991, Fall) Why is business talking about ethics? Reflections on foreign conversations. *California Management Review*, pp. 67–86.

Clair, Judith, Milliman, John, and Mitroff, Ian (1995) Clash or cooperation? Understanding environmental organizations and their relationship to business. In Denis Collins and Mark Starik (Eds), *Research in Corporate Social Performance and Policy*, Supplement 1, pp. 163–193. Greenwich, CT: JAI.

Clark, William C. (2000) Environmental globalization. In Joseph S. Nye, Jr., and John D. Donahue (Eds), *Governance in a Global World*, pp. 86–108. Washington, D.C.: Brookings Institution Press.

Clarkson Centre for Business Ethics. (1999) *Principles of Stakeholder Management*. Toronto: The Clarkson Centre.

Clarkson, M.B.E. (1995) A stakeholder framework for analyzing and evaluating corporate social performance. *Academy of Management Review*, 20 (1): 92–117.

Cleveland, Harlan (1990) *The Global Commons*. Lanham, MD: University Press of America.

Click, Reid W., and Harrison, Paul (2000) Does multinationality matter? Evidence of value destruction in U.S. multinational corporations. Washington, D.C.: US Federal Reserve Board paper.

Clough, Michael (1996) *Shaping American Foreign Relations: The Critical Role of the Southeast*. Muscatine, Iowa: Stanley Foundation New American Dialogue.

Clougherty, Joseph A. (2001) Globalization and the autonomy of domestic competition policy: An empirical test on the world airline industry. *Journal of International Business Studies*, 32 (3): 459–478.

Colborn, Theo, Dumanoski, Dianne, and Myers, John Peterson (1996) *Our Stolen Future*. New York: Dutton.

Collier, Paul, Elliot, Lani, Hegre, Havard, Hoeffler, Anke, Reynal-Querol, Marta, and Sanbanis, Nicholas (2003) *Breaking the Conflict Trap: Civil War and Development Policy*. Washington, D.C.: The World Bank.

Collins, Jim (2001) *Good to Great*. New York: HarperCollins.

Commission on Global Governance (1995) *Our Global Neighborhood*. New York: Oxford University Press.

Companies and causes. (2000, Dec. 18) *Business Week*, online edition.

Conflict at work costs employers 450 days management time every year—Hopes high that new Dispute Resolution Regulations will cut costs. (2004, Sept. 30) Press release from the Chartered Institute of Personnel and Development, accessed Dec. 5, 2005: http://www.cipd.co.uk/press/PressRelease/Conflict_300904_PR.htm

Contractor, Farok J., and Lorange, Peter (1988) Why should firms cooperate? The strategy and economics basis for cooperative ventures. In F.J. Contractor and Peter Lorange (Eds.), *Cooperative Strategies in International Business*, pp. 3–30. Lexington, MA: Lexington Books.

Corporate social responsibility gaining higher awareness among CEOs, says PwC survey report. (2002) PriceWaterhouseCoopers. http://www.pcwglobal.com/extweb/ncinthenews.nsf

Cosmeceuticals. (2000, Dec. 9) *The Economist*, p. 115.

Coviello, Nicole E. and McAuley, Andrew (1999) Internationalisation and the smaller firm: A review of contemporary empirical research 1. *Management International Review*, 39 (3): 223–256.

Coviello, Nicole E., and Munro, Hugh J. (1995) Growing the entrepreneurial firm: Networking for international market development. *European Journal of Marketing*, 29 (7): 49–61.

Cowan, Scott (1996, July) Presidential speech. American Assembly of Collegiate Schools of Business. St Louis, MO.

Crane, Andrew (2000) Culture clash and mediation. In Jem Bendell (Ed.), *Terms for Endearment*, pp.163–177. Sheffield, UK: Greenleaf.

Crawford, Lesley (2001, March 30) Allzarage. *ROB Magazine*. http://www.robmagazine.com

Culpan, Oya, and Wright, Gillian H. (2002) Women abroad: Getting the best results from women managers. *International Journal of Human Resource Management*, 13 (5): 794–802.

Dalby, David, Barrett, David, and Mann, Michael (1999) *The Linguasphere Register of the World's Languages and Speech Communities*. Hebron, Wales, UK: Published for Observatoire Linguistique by Linguasphere Press/Gwasg y Byd laith.

Daly, Herman (1996) *Beyond Growth: The Economics of Sustainable Development*. Boston: Beacon Press.

Daniels, John D., and Radebaugh, Lee H. (1992) *International Business* (6th edn). Reading, MA: Addison-Wesley.

Dass, P. and Parker, Barbara (1999) Strategies for managing human resource diversity: From resistance to learning. *Academy of Management Executive*, 13 (2): 68–80.

D'Aveni, Richard A. (1995) *Hypercompetitive rivalries*. New York: The Free Press.

Davidson, Martin N., and Ferdman, Bernardo M. (2002) Inclusive and effective networks: Linking diversity theory and practice. Academy of Management Conference, Denver, Aug. 8–12.

Davidow, William, and Malone, Michael (1992) *The Virtual Corporation: Structuring and Revitalizing the Corporation for the 21st century*. Burlingame, NY: Harper.

De George, Richard (1993) *Competing with Integrity in International Business*. New York: Oxford University Press.

de Geus, Arie (1997) *The Living Company*. Boston, MA: Harvard Business School Press.

de Jonquieres, Guy (2003, Jan. 27) Multinationals move to stem tide of fakes. *Financial Times*, p. 2.

De Soto, Hernando (2000) *The Mystery of Capitalism: Why Capitalism Triumphs in the West and Fails Everywhere Else*. New York: Basic Books.

De Villiers, Marq (2000) *Water: The Fate of Our Most Precious Resource*. New York: Houghton Mifflin.

Delaney, Kevin J. (2003) Outsourcing jobs—and workers—to India. *The Wall Street Journal*, pp. B1, B2.

Demick, David H., and O'Reilly, Aidan J. (2000) Supporting SME internationalisation: A collaborative project for accelerated export development. *Irish Marketing Review*, 13 (1): 34–45.

Desai, Ashay B., and Rittenburg, Terri (1997) Global ethics: An integrative framework for MNEs. *Journal of Business Ethics*, 16 (8): 791–800.

Deshpande, S. P., and Viswesvaran, C. (1992) Is cross-cultural training of expatriate managers effective? A meta-analysis. *International Journal of Intercultural Relations*, 16: 295–310.

Dess, Greg, and Origer, Nancy (1987) Environment, structure, and consensus in strategy formulation: A conceptual integration. *Academy of Management Review*, 12: 313–330.

Dicken, Peter (1992) *Global Shift* (2nd edn). London: Guilford Press.

Dicken, Peter (1998) *Global Shift* (3rd edn). New York and London: Guilford.

Dimson, Elroy, Marsh, Paul, and Staunton, Mike (2003) *Global Investment Returns Yearbook*. ABN Amro.

DiPiazza, Jr., Samuel (2002) Survey highlights. http://www.pwcglobal.com/extweb/ncsurvres.nsf

Dollar, David, and Kraay, Aart (2002, Jan./Feb.) Spreading the wealth. *Foreign Affairs*, pp. 120–133.

Doh, Jonathan P., Rodriguez, Peter, Uhlenbruck, Klaus, Collins, Jamie, and Eden, Lorraine (2003) Coping with corruption in foreign markets. *Academy of Management Executive*, 17 (3): 114–127.

Donaldson, Thomas (1985) Multinationals' decision making: Reconciling ethical norms. *Journal of Business Ethics*, 4: 357–366.

Donlon, J. (1996, Sept.) Managing across borders. *Chief Executive*, p. 58.

Dow Jones Sustainability Indexes 2004 press release. (2004, Sept. 2) Accessed Nov. 11, 2004: http://www.sustainability-indexes.com/djsi_pdf/news/PressReleases/DJSI_PressRelease_040902_Review.pdf

Dowling, Michael J., Roering, William D., Carlin, Barbara A., and Wisnieski, Joette (1996) Multifaceted relationships under coopetition. *Journal of Management Inquiry*, 5 (2): 155–167.

Drucker, Peter F. (1985) *Innovation and Entrepreneurship: Practice and Principles*. New York: HarperBusiness.

Drucker, Peter F. (1987) Social innovation: Management's new dimension. *Long Range Planning*, 20 (6): 29–34.

Drucker, Peter F. (1994a, Oct. 17) The continuing feminist experiment. *The Wall Street Journal*, p. A14.

Drucker, Peter F. (1994b, Dec. 20) The new superpower: The overseas Chinese. *The Wall Street Journal*, p. A14.

Drucker, Peter F. (1999) *Management Challenges for the 21st Century*. New York: HarperBusiness.

Due Billing, Yvonne, and Alvesson, Mats (2000) Questioning the notion of feminine leadership: A critical perspective on gender labeling of leadership. *Gender, Work, and Organizations*, 7 (3): 144–157.

Dufour, Bruno (1994) Dealing in diversity: *Management education in Europe*. Selections, pp. 7–15.

Dunne, Nancy (2003, Mar. 21) Workplace happiness is all in the family. *Financial Times*, p. 1.

Dunning, John (1988) *Explaining International Production*. London: Unwin Hyman.

Dunning, John (1993) *The Globalization of Business*. London: Routledge.

A dynamic new world economy. (1994) *Business Week*, 21st Century Capitalism, pp. 22–23.

Easterbrook, Gregg (1995) *A Moment on the Earth*. New York: Viking.

Echo Research. (2003) CSR & the financial community: Friend or foe? http://www.echoresearch.com

Eggers, John H., and Leahy, Kim T. (1994) Entrepreneurial leadership in the US. *Issues and Observations* (Center for Creative Leadership publication), 14 (1): 1–5.

Elkington, John, and Fennell, Shelly (2000) Partners for sustainability. In Jem Bendell (Ed.), *Terms for Endearment*, pp.150–162. Sheffield, UK: Greenleaf.

Ellis, Vernon (2001) Can global business be a force for good? *Business Strategy Review*, 12 (2): 15–20.

Ely, Robin J., and Thomas, David A. (2001) Cultural diversity at work: The effects of diversity perspectives on work group processes and outcomes. *Administrative Science Quarterly*, 46: 229–273.

Emerging issues in development economics. (1997, Oct./Dec.) *World Bank Policy and Research Bulletin*, pp. 1–4.

Emerging nations win major exporting roles. (1997, Feb. 24) *The Wall Street Journal*, p. Al.

Emery, Fred, and Trist, Eric (1965) The causal texture of organizational environments. *Human Relations*, 18: 21–32.

Engendering development through gender equity. (2000, July–Sept.) *World Bank Policy and Research Bulletin*, 11 (3): 1–5.

Entrepreneurial fresh air. (2001, Jan. 13) *The Economist*, p. 60.

The Environmental Literacy Council. (2003, April 14). www.enviroliteracy.org/subcategory.php/202.html

The environment is good business in France. (1992, Mar.) *Civil Engineering*, pp. 66.

Erlich, Paul R. (1969) *The Population Bomb*. Binghamton, NY: Vail-Ballou.

Erlich, Paul R., and Erlich, Anne (2004) *One with Nineveh*. Washington, DC: Shearwater Books.

Evans, Philip, and Wurster, Thomas S. (2000) *Blown to Bits*. Cambridge, MA: Harvard Business School Press.

Evans, Paul, Doz, Yves, and Laurent, Andre (Eds) (1990) *Human Resource Management in International Firms: Change, Globalization, Innovation*. New York: St. Martin's Press.

An evil unbearable to the human heart. (1993) *World of Work—US*. 4: 4–5.

Exchange places. (2001, May 5) A survey of global equity markets, *The Economist*, survey insert.

Experts work to eradicate use of child labour. (1997, Oct. 29) *New Zealand Herald*, p. A8.

Falk, Richard (1993) The making of global citizenship. In Jeremy Brecher, John Brown Childs, and Jill Cutler (Eds), *Global Visions*, pp. 39–50. Boston, MA: South End Press.

Falk, Richard (1998) *Law in an Emerging Global Village*. Ardsley, NY: Transaction Publishers.

Families and Work Institute. (2003) *2002 National Study of the Changing Workforce*. Boston: Families and Work Institute.

Family Inc. (2003, Nov. 10) *Business Week*, pp. 100–114.

Farkas, Charles M., and De Backer, Philippe. (1996) *Maximum Leadership*. New York: Henry Holt.

Farnham, Alan (1994, June 27) Global—or just globaloney? *Fortune*, pp. 97–100.

Farrell, Christopher (1994, Nov. 18) The triple revolution. *Business Week*, Special issue, pp. 16–25.

Feigenbaum, Harvey B. (2001, Nov.) *Globalization and cultural diplomacy*. Washington, D.C.: Center for Arts and Culture, Issue paper.

Fernandez, John (1991) *Managing a Diverse Work Force*. Lexington, MA: Lexington Books, pp. 23–25.

Fiedler, Fred E. (1996) Research on leadership selection and training: One view of the future. *Administrative Science Quarterly*, 42 (2): 241–250.

Fiedler, Fred E., and House, Robert J. (1994) Leadership theory and research: A report of progress. In Cary L. Cooper and Ivan T. Robertson (Eds), *Key Reviews in Managerial Psychology*, pp. 97–116. Chichester, UK: Wiley.

Finnegan, William. (2002, Apr. 8) Leasing the rain. *New Yorker*, pp. 43–53.

A firm focus on family affairs. (2003, Dec. 23) *Financial Times*, p. 7.

Fischel, Daniel (1995) *Payback: The Conspiracy to Destroy Michael Millken and his Financial Revolution*. New York: HarperBusiness.

Fisher, Ann B. (1993, May 31) Japanese working women strike back. *Fortune*, p. 22.

Fisher, Helen (1999) *The First Sex: The Natural Talents of Women and How They are Changing the World*. New York: Random House.

Floyd, Steven W., and Wooldridge, Bill (1994) Dinosaurs or dynamos? Recognizing middle management's strategic role. *Academy of Management Executive*, 8 (4): 47–58.

Flynn, Dennis, and Giraldez, Arturo (2002) Cycles Of silver: Global economic unity through the mid-18th century. *Journal of World History*, 13 (2): 391–427.

Flynn, Julia (2002, May 11) Global kidnappings climb to a new peak. *The Wall Street Journal*, p. A21.

Flynn, Patricia M., and Adams, Susan M. (2004, Sept./Oct.) Women on board. *BizEd*, pp. 34–39.

Foreign friends. (2000, Jan 8.) *The Economist*, pp. 71–74.

Foreign investment in US plunges nearly 80%. (2003, June 20) *The Wall Street Journal*, p. A6.

Foust, Dean (1995, Feb. 20) What the IMF needs is a good alarm system. *Business Week*, p. 55.

Fowler, Geoffrey A. (2002, Mar. 6) "Green" sales pitch isn't helping to move products off the shelf. *The Wall Street Journal*, pp. B1, B4.

France left behind, politicians keep quiet. (2001, Nov. 12) *Le Figaro*.

Frank, Robert (2001, May 22) Checks in the mail. *The Wall Street Journal*, pp. A1, A16.

Frank, Robert H., and Cook, Philip J. (1995) *The Winner-take-all Society*. Cambridge, MA: The Free Press.

Freedman, Laurence (Ed.) (2003) *Superterrorism: Policy Responses*. London: Blackwell.

French, Hilary (2003) *Vanishing Borders: Protecting the Environment in the Age of Globalization*. New York: Norton Paperbacks.

French, Howard W. (2003, July 25) Japan's neglected resource: Female workers. *New York Times*, p. A3.

Friedheim, Cyrus (1998) *The Trillion Dollar Enterprise*. Old Tappan, NJ: Addison-Wesley Longman.

Friedman, Thomas L. (1999) *The Lexus and the Olive Tree*. New York: Farrar Straus and Giroux.

Fritsch, Peter (2002, Apr. 22) A cement titan in Mexico thrives by selling to the poor. *The Wall Street Journal*, pp. A1, A8.

Fujita, Masataka (1995) Small and medium-sized transnational corporations: Trends and patterns of foreign direct investment. *Small Business Economics*, 7 (3): 183–204.

Fukao, M. (1993) International integration of financial markets and the costs of capital. *Journal of International Securities Markets*, 7:

Fukao, M. (1995) *Financial Integration, Corporate Governance and the Performance of Multinational Corporations*. Washington, D.C.: Brookings Institution.

The future of fertility in intermediate-fertility countries. (2002) United Nations Population Division.

A game of international leapfrog. (1994, Oct. 1) *The Economist*, pp. 6–9.

Garrett, Laurie (1994) *The Coming Plague: Newly Emerging Diseases in a World Out of Balance*. New York: Farrar Straus and Giroux.

Garten, Jeffrey E. (1998, Feb. 9) Globalism doesn't have to be cruel. *Business Week*, p. 26.

Garten, Jeffrey E. (2003, Jan. 4) A new year; a new agenda. *The Economist*, pp. 53–56.

GATT and FTAs: No longer foes. (1992, Oct.) *International Business*, pp. 6–14.

Gereffi, Gary, Garcia-Johnson, Ronie, and Sasser, Erika (2001, July/Aug.) The NGO-industrial complex. *Foreign Policy*, 125: 56–66.

German shoppers get coupons. (2001, Apr. 5) *The Wall Street Journal*, p. A1.

Getting a head. (1999, July 3) *The Economist*, p. 54.

Ghemawat, Pankaj, and Ghadar, Fariborz (2000, July/Aug.) The dubious logic of global megamergers. *Harvard Business Review*, pp. 65–72.

Ghoshal, Sumantra, and Bartlett, Christopher (1990) The multinational corporation as an interorganizational network. *Academy of Management Review*, 15 (4): 603–625.

Ghoshal, Sumantra, and Bartlett, Christopher (1995, Jan./Dec.) Changing the role of top management: Beyond structure to processes. *Harvard Business Review*, pp. 86–96.

Gibson, Cristina B. (1995, 2nd quarter) An investigation of gender differences in leadership across four countries. *Journal of International Business Studies*, pp. 255–279.

Gidoomal, Ram, and Porter, D. (1997) *The UK Maharajahs: Inside the South Asian Success Story*. London, England: Nicholas Brealey Publishing.

Glasius, Marlies, and Kaldor, Mary (2002) In Marlies Glasius, Mary Kaldor, and Helmut Anheier (Eds), pp. 1–33. *Global Civil Society*. Oxford: Oxford University Press.

Global Alliance for Vaccines and Immunizations. (2003, Apr. 14) http://www.vaccinealliance.org

Global Employment Trends. (2003) Geneva: International Labour Organization.

The Global Investor and Corporate Governance. (2001) New York: The Conference Board.

Globalization, Growth and Poverty. (2001, Dec.) World Bank policy research report.

Goffman, E. (1974) *Frame Analysis: An Essay on the Organization of Experience*. Boston: Northeastern University Press.

Goldman, Abigail (2004, Nov. 28) Mattel struggles to balance profit with morality. *The Seattle Times*, pp. A1, A24.

Gomez-Buendia, Hernando (1995) The politics of global employment: A perspective from Latin America. In Mihaly Simai (Ed), *Global Employment: An International Investigation into the Future of Work*, pp. 65–93. London and New Jersey: Zed Books.

Gomes-Casseres, Benjamin (1994, July/Aug.) Group versus group: How alliance networks compete. Reprinted in Garten, Jeffrey E. (Ed). *World View*, pp. 127–141. Boston: Harvard Business Review Book.

Good news for the globe. (2004, Sept. 3) *The Wall Street Journal*, pp. A7, A9.

Goodall, Jane (1995, Dec.) A message from Jane Goodall. *National Geographic*, p. 102.

Govindarajan, Vijay, and Gupta, Anil K. (2000) Analysis of the emerging global arena. *European Management Journal*, 18 (3): 274–284.

Graham, John W., and Havlich, Wendy C. (1999) *Corporate Environmental Policies*. Lanham, MD: Scarecrow Press.

Green, Carolyn, and Ruhleder, Karen (1996) Globalization, borderless worlds, and the Tower of Babel. *Journal of Organizational Change*, 8 (4): 55–68.

Green is good. (1999, Sept. 11) *The Economist*, p. 7.

Greenemeier, L. (2002, Feb. 11) Offshore outsourcing grows to global proportions, *Information Week*, 875: 56–58.

Greenhalgh, Leonard (1986) Managing conflict. *Sloan Management Review*, 27 (4): 45–51.

Greening Industry: New Roles for Communities, Markets, and Governments. (1999) New York: Oxford University Press.

Gregersen, Hal B., Morrison, Allen J., and Black, J Stewart. (1998) Developing leaders for the global frontier. *Sloan Management Review*, 40 (1): 21–32.

Grupo Industrial Bimbo SA Website. Accessed 2004 Nov. 30 at http://www.grupobimbo.com

Gupta, Anil K., and Govindarajan, Vijay (2002) Cultivating a global mindset. *Academy of Management Executive*, 16 (1):116–126.

Haass, Richard N., and Litan, Robert E. (1998, May/June) Globalization and its discontents: Navigating the dangers of a tangled world. *Foreign Affairs*, 77 (3): 2–6.

Hackman, J. Richard (2002) *Leading Teams: Setting the Stage for Great Performances*. Boston: Harvard Business School Press.

Hafner, Katie, and Lyon, Matthew (1996) *Where Wizards Stay up Late*. New York: Simon & Schuster.

Halal, William (1996) *The New Management*. Thousand Oaks, CA: Sage.

Haley, George T., and Haley, Usha C.V. (1997) Making strategic business decisions in South and Southeast Asia. *Conference Proceedings of the First International Conference on Operations and Quantitative Management*. Jaipur, India, Volume II, pp. 597–604.

Haley, George T., and Haley, Usha C.V. (1998) Boxing with shadows: Competing effectively with the overseas Chinese and overseas Indian business networks in the Asian area. *Journal of Organizational Change*, 22 (4): 301–319.

Haley, George T., and Tan, C.T. (1996) The black hole of Southeast Asia: Strategic decision making in an informational void. *Management Decisions*, 34 (9): 43–55.

Hall, Richard (1994) *EuroManagers and Martians*. Brussels: Europublications.

Hambrick, Donald C. (1987) The top management team: Key to strategic success. *California Management Review*, 30 (1): 88–109.

Hamel, Gary (1996, July/Aug.) Nine routes to industry revolution. *Harvard Business Review*, pp. 72–72.

Hamel, Gary (2000) *Leading the Revolution*. Cambridge, MA: Harvard Business School Press.

Hamel, Gary, and Prahalad, C.K. (1985, July/Aug.) Do you really have a global strategy? *Harvard Business Review*, pp. 139–148.

Hamel, Gary, and Prahalad, C.K. (1994) *Competing for the Future*. Boston, MA: Harvard Business School Press.

Hammer, Michael (2004) Deep change. *Harvard Business Review*, 82 (4): 84–94.

Hampden-Turner, Charles, and Trompenaars, Alfons (1998) *Riding the Waves of Culture*. New York: McGraw-Hill.

Handy, Charles (1994) *The Age of Paradox*. Cambridge, MA: Harvard Business School Press.

Hardin, Garrett (1968) The tragedy of the commons. *Science*, 162: 1243–1248.

Harman, Willis (1993) Intuition in decision-making. In Brenda Sutton (Ed.), *The Legitimate Corporation: Essential Readings in Business Ethics and Corporate Governanc*e, pp. 224–235. Cambridge, MA: Blackwell Business.

Harris, Phillip R., and Moran, Robert T. (1996) *Managing Cultural Differences* (4th edn). Houston, TX: Gulf Publishing.

Harrison, Lawrence E., and Huntington, Samuel P. (2000) *Culture Matters*. New York: Basic Books.

Harveston, Paula D., Kedia, Ben L., and Davis, Peter S. (2000) Internationalization of born global and gradual globalizing firms: The impact of the manager. *Advances in Competitiveness Research*, 8 (1): 92–99.

Harzing, Anne-Wil, and Hofstede, Geert (1996) Planned change in organizations: The influence of national culture. In Peter A. Bamberger, Miriam Erez, and Samuel B. Bacharach (Eds), *Research in the Sociology of Organizations*, 14: 297–340. Greenwich, CT: JAI Press.

Hawken, Paul (1993) *The Ecology of Commerce*. New York: HarperBusiness.

Heenan, David A., and Perlmutter, Howard V. (1979) *Multinational Organization Development*. Reading, MA: Addison-Wesley.

Heinrich, Joseph, Boyd Robert, Bowles, Samuel, Gintis, Herbert, Fehr, Ernest, and Camerer, Colin (Eds) (2004) *Foundations of Human Sociality: Ethnography and Experiments in 15 Small-scale Societies*. London: Oxford University Press.

Held, David, McGrew, Anthony, Goldblatt, David, and Perraton, Jonathon (1999) *Global Transformations*. Stanford, CA: Stanford University Press.

Helgesen, Sally (1990) *The Female Advantage: Women's Ways of Leadership*. New York: Doubleday/Currency.

Helliker, Kevin (2002, June 7) In natural foods, a big name's no big help. *The Wall Street Journal*, pp. B1, B4.

Henderson, Hazel (1996) *Building a Win-Win World: Life Beyond Global Economic Warfare*. San Francisco, CA: Berrett-Koehler.

Henderson, Hazel (1999) *Beyond Globalization: Shaping a Sustainable Global Economy*. West Hartford, CT: Kumarian Press.

Higgins, James M. (1997) *Escape from the Maze*. Winter Park, FL: New Management Publishing.

Hillman, Amy J. (1998, Sept. 16) Diversified boards enjoy enviable benefits of higher shareholder gains. *Seattle Times*, p. B5.

Hilsenrath, Jon E. (2003, Apr. 9) How your trash helps fuel boom in China's economy. *The Wall Street Journal*, pp. A1, A2.

Hilsenrath, Jon E., and Buckman, Rebecca (2003, Oct. 20) Factory employment is falling world-wide. *The Wall Street Journal*, pp. A2, A8.

Hoecklin, Lisa (1995) *Managing Cultural Differences: Strategies for Competitive Advantage*. Reading, MA, and Wokingham: Addison-Wesley.

Hofstede, Geert (1980) *Culture's Consequences*. Beverly Hills, CA: Sage.

Hofstede, Geert (1983) The cultural relativity of organization practices and theories. *Journal of International Business Studies*, 14 (2): 75–90.

Hofstede, Geert (1994) The business of international business is culture. *International Business Review*, 3 (1): 1–14.

Hofstede, Geert (2001) *Culture's Consequences* (2nd edn). Thousand Oaks, CA: Sage.

Hofstede, Geert, Van Deusen, Cheryl A., Mueller, Carolyn B., Charles, Thomas A., and the Business Goals Network (2002) What goals do business leaders pursue? A study in fifteen countries. *Journal of International Business Studies*, 33 (4): 785–803.

Holland, Christopher P. (1994, Fall) The evolution of a global cash management system. *Sloan Management Review*, p. 38.

Holmlund, Maria, and Kock, Soren (1998) Relationships and the internationalisation of Finnish small and medium sized companies. *International Small Business Journal*, 16 (4): 46–63.

Holstein, William J. (1992, Apr. 13) Little companies; big exports. *Business Week*, pp. 70–72.

Holstein, William J. (2002, Apr. 1) Samsung's golden touch. *Fortune*, pp. 89–94.

Hookway, James (2004, May 26) Vote-guarding in Philippines. *The Wall Street Journal*, p. A16.

How the mob burned the banks. (1995, Aug. 21) *Business Week*, pp. 42–47.

Hoover's online. (2003) Accessed January 22, 2003 at http://www.hoovers.com

Hordes, Mark W., Clancy, J. Anthony, and Baddaley, Julie (1995) A primer for global start-ups. *Academy of Management Executive*, 9 (2): 7–11.

Hours of work. (2002, July 8) International Labour Organization. Key Indicators of the Labour Market 6: http://www.ilo.org/public/english/employment/strat/kilm/kilm06.htm

House, Robert, Javidan, Mansour, Hanges, Paul, and Dorfman, Peter (2002) Understanding cultures and implicit leadership theories across the globe: An introduction to Project GLOBE. *Journal of World Business*, 37: 3–10.

House, Robert J., Hanges, Paul J., Javidan, Mansour, Dorfman, Peter W., and Gupta, Vipin (2004) *Culture, Leadership, and Organizations*. Thousand Oaks, CA: Sage.

Hout, Thomas, Porter, Michael E., and Rudden, Eileen. (1982, Sept./Oct.). How global companies win out. *Harvard Business Review*, pp. 98–108.

How mergers go wrong. (2000, July 22) *The Economist*, pp. 19–20.

How Shell's move to revamp culture ended in scandal. (2004, Nov. 2) *The Wall Street Journal*, pp. A1, A14.

How to live long and prosper. (1997, May 10) *The Economist*, p. 59.

Howell, Llewellyn D., and Chaddick, Brad (1994, Fall) Models of political risk for foreign investment and trade. *Columbia Journal of World Business*, 29 (3): 70–91.

Hu, Yao-Su (1992, Winter) Global or stateless corporations are national firms with international operations. *California Management Review*, pp. 107–126.

Human Development Report 1994. (1994) New York: Oxford University Press.

Human Development Report 1995. (1995) New York and Geneva: United Nations.

Human Development Report 2000. (2000) New York and Oxford: Oxford University Press.

Human rights. (1995, June 3) *The Economist*, pp. 58–59.

Hunt, Shelby D., and Morgan, Robert M. (1995) The comparative advantage theory of competition. *Journal of Marketing*, 59 (2): 1–22.

Huntington, Samuel (1993, Summer) The clash of civilizations. *Foreign Affairs*, pp. 22–49.

Husband, Charles (1996) The right to be understood: Conceiving the multi-ethnic public sphere. *Innovation*, 9 (2): 205–211.

Ibbotson, Roger G., and Brinson, Gary P. (1993). *Global Investing*. New York: McGraw-Hill.

ICGN (International Corporate Governance Network). (2002, June 28). http://www.icgn.org

Inglehart, Ronald, and Baker, Wayne E. (2000) Modernization, cultural change, and the persistence of traditional values. *American Sociological Review*, 65 (1): 19–33.

Inheriting the bamboo network. (1995, Dec. 23) *The Economist*, pp. 79–80.

Interbrand and Kochon, Nick (1997) *The World's Greatest Brands*. Washington, NY: New York University Press.

International Food Policy Research Institute. (2003, Apr. 25) http://www.cgiar.org/ifpri

Is the world's population explosion over? (1998, Feb. 2) Population Reference Bureau. http://www.prb.org/prb/info/popexplo.htm

Isenberg, Daniel J. (1984, Nov./Dec.) How senior managers think. *Harvard Business Review*, 62 (6): 81–90.

It's time to redefine the World Bank and the IMF. (1994, July 25) *The Wall Street Journal*, p. Al.

James, Harvey S., and Weidenbaum, Murray (1993) *When Businesses Cross International Borders*. Westport, CT: Praeger Publishers.

Jennings, Marianne M., and Entine, Jon (1998) Business with a soul: A reexamination of what counts in business ethics. *Hamline Journal of Public Law and Policy*, 20, pp. 1–88.

Johanson. Jan. and Mattsson, L.-G. (1988) Internationalisation in industrial systems: A network approach. In N. Hood and J.E. Vahlne (Eds), *Strategies in Global Competition*, pp. 287–314. London: Croom Helm.

Johanson, Jan, and Mattsson, L.-G. (1992) Network positions and strategic action – An analytical framework. In B. Axelsson and G. Easton (Eds), *Industrial Networks: A New View of Reality*, pp. 205–217. London: Routledge.

Johanson, Jan, and Vahlne, Jan-Erik (1977) The internationalization process of the firm— International Food Policy Research Institute. (2003, Apr. 25). http://www.cgiar.org/ifpri

Johanson Jan and Wiedersheim-Paul, Finn (1975, Oct.) The internationalisation of the firm: Four Swedish cases. *Journal of Management Studies*, pp. 305–322.

Johnston, William B. (1997) Global work force 2000: The new world labor market. In Heide Vernon-Wertzel and Lawrence H. Wortzel (Eds), *Strategic Management in a Global Economy*, pp. 368–381. New York: John Wiley.

Jolly, V., Alahuhta, Ml., and Jeannet, J. (1992) Challenging the incumbents: How high technology start-ups compete globally. *Journal of Strategic Change*, 1: 71–82.

Jones, Daniel, and Womack, James (1996) *Lean Thinking*. New York, NY: Simon & Schuster.

Jones, Del (2003, Jan. 27) Few women hold top executive jobs, even when CEOs are female. USA Today/on-line edition.

Jones, Marion V. (2001) First steps in internationalization—Concepts and evidence from a sample of small high-technology firms. *Journal of International Management*, 7 (3): 191–210.

Kadlec, Daniel, and Van Voorst, Bruce (1997, May 5) The new world of giving. *Time*, pp. 62–65.

Kahn, Jeremy (2002, Apr. 29) Deloitte restates its case. *Fortune*, pp. 65–72.

Kahn, Joel S. (1995) *Culture, Multiculture, and Postculture*. Beverly Hills, CA: Sage.

Kanter, Rosabeth Moss (1995, Sept./Oct.) Thriving locally in the global economy. *Harvard Business Review*, pp. 151–160.

Kanter, Rosabeth Moss, and Dretler, Thomas D. (1998) *Academy of Management Executive*, 12 (4): 60–68.

Kanungo, R.N., and Mendonca, M. (1996) *Ethical Dimensions of Leadership*. Thousand Oaks, CA: Sage.

Kao, John (1996) *Jamming: The Art and Discipline of Business Creativity*. New York: HarperBusiness.

Kapur, Devesh, and Ramamurti, Ravi (2001) India's emerging competitive advantage in service. *Academy of Management Executive*, 15 (2): 20–32.

Katzenbach, Jon R., and Smith, Douglas K. (1993) *The Wisdom of Teams*. Cambridge, MA: Harvard Business School.

Kayworth, Timothy, and Leidner, Dorothy (2000) The global virtual manager: A prescription for success. *European Management Journal*, 18 (2): 183–194.

Keay, John (1991) *The Honourable Company: A History of the English East India Company*. London: HarperCollins.

Keen, Peter G.W., and Knapp, Ellen M. (1996) *Every Manager's Guide to Business Processes*. Boston, MA: Harvard Business School Press.

Keohane, Robert O., and Nye, Joseph S. Jr. (2000) Introduction. In Joseph S. Nye, Jr. and John D. Donahue (Eds), *Governance in a Global World*, pp. 1–41. Washington, D.C.: Brookings Institution Press.

Kester, W. Carl (1996) American and Japanese corporate governance: Convergence to best practice? In Suzanne Berger and Ronald Dore (Eds), *National Diversity and Global Capitalism*, pp. 107–137. Ithaca and London: Cornell University Press.

KEYS: New survey measures creativity in the workplace. (1995) *Issues and Observations*, 15 (3): 2, 9. KEYS: Assessing the Climate for Creativity by the Center for Creative Leadership from the work of Teresa Amabile and Stan Gryskiewicz, published by the Center for Creative Leadership, Greensboro, NC.

Kim, Suk H., and Kim, Seung H. (1993) *Global Corporate Finance*. Miami: Kolb Publishing.

Klein, Alec (1999, Mar. 16) Say "freeze!": Kodak brings film to land of penguins and ice flows. *The Wall Street Journal*, p. B1.

Klein, Naomi (2000) *No Logo*. New York: St. Martin's Press.

Kluckhohn, C., and Strodtbeck, Fred L.(1961) *Variations in Values Orientations*. Westport, CT: Greenwood Press.

Knight, Gary A., and Cavusgil, S. Tamer (1996) The born global firm: A challenge to traditional internationalization theory. *Advances in International Marketing*, 8: 11–26.

Knight, Gary A., and Cavusgil, S. Tamer (2004) Innovation, organizational capabilities, and the born-global firm. *Journal of International Business Studies*, 35: 124–141.

Knoke, William (1996) *Bold New World*. New York: Kodansha Intl.

Kobrin, Stephen J. (1991) An empirical analysis of the determinants of global integration. *Strategic Management Journal*, 12 (Special Issue): 17–31.

Kobrin, Stephen J. (1994) Is there a relationship between a geocentric mind-set and multinational strategy? *Journal of International Business Studies*, 25 (3): 493–511.

Korn, Lester B. (1989, May 22) How the next CEO will be different. *Fortune*, pp. 157–59.

Korten, David C. (1995) *When Corporations Rule the World*. San Francisco, CA: Berrett-Koehler.

Kossler, Michael E., and Prestridge, Sonya (1996) Geographically dispersed teams. *Issues and Observations*, 16 (2/3): 9–11 (a publication of the Center for Creative Leadership, Greensboro, North Carolina, USA http://www.ic.ncs.com/cds).

Kotkin, Joel (1993) *Tribes*. New York: Random House.

Kraar, Louis (1994, Aug. 8) Your next PC could be made in Taiwan. *Fortune*, pp. 90–96.

Kraut, Allen I., Pedigo, Patricia R., McKenna, D. Douglas, and Dunnette, Marvin D. (1989) The role of the manager: What's really important in different management jobs? *Academy of Management Executive*, 3 (4): 286–293.

Krugman, Paul (1994) Competitiveness: A dangerous obsession. *Foreign Affairs*, 73 (2): 28–44.

Krugman, Paul (1996) *Pop Internationalism*. Cambridge, MA: MIT Press.

Krugman, Paul (1998) *The Accidental Theorist and Other Dispatches from the Dismal Science*. New York and London: W.W. Norton.

Kung, Hans (1998) *A Global Ethic for Global Politics and Economics*. Oxford: Oxford University Press.

Kurian, George Thomas, and Molitor, Graham (Eds) (1996) *Encyclopedia of the Future*. New York: Macmillan Library Reference.

Kwan, C.H. (1996) A yen bloc in Asia. *Journal of the Asia Pacific Economy*, 1 (1): 1–21.

La Porta, Rafael, and Lopez-de-Silanes, Florencio (1999) Corporate ownership around the world. *Journal of Finance*, 54 (2): 471–518.

Lachica, Eduardo (1998, July 8) Japan to lose 1.4% of its 1997 GDP due to Asia's turmoil, study says. *The Wall Street Journal*, p. A12.

Landes, David S. (1998) *The Wealth and Poverty of Nations*. New York: Norton.

Lane, C. (1989) *Management and Labour in Europe: The Industrial Enterprise in Germany, Britain and France*. Aldershot: Edward Elgar.

Lane, Henry W., Greenberg, Danna, and Berdrow, Iris (2004). Barriers and bonds to knowledge transfer in global alliances and mergers. In Henry Lane, Martha Maznevki, Mark Mendenhall, and Jeanne McNett (Eds), *The Blackwell Handbook of Global Management: A Guide to Managing Complexity*, pp. 342–361. Malden, MA and Oxford, UK: Blackwell.

Laurent, Andre (1986) The cross-cultural puzzle of international human resource management. *Human Resource Management*, 25 (1): 91–102.

Laurent, Andre (1999) Re-inventing management at the crossroads of culture. Paper presented at the Summer Institute of Intercultural Communication. Forest Grove, OR.

Leavitt, Harold J. (2003) Why hierarchies thrive. *Harvard Business Review*, 81 (3): 96–102.

Lee, Chris (1994) Open-book management. *Training*, 31 (7): 21–27.

Lenartowicz, Tomasz, and Roth, Kendall (2001) Does subculture within a country matter? A cross-cultural study of motivational domains and business performance in Brazil. *Journal of International Business Studies*, 32 (2): 305–325.

Levi Strauss homepage. (2002, Mar. 27) http://www.levistrauss.com

Levinson, Harry (1988) You won't recognize me: Predictions about changes in top-management characteristics. *Academy of Management Executive*, 2 (2): 119–125.

Levitt, Theodore (1983, May/June) The globalization of markets. *Harvard Business Review*, pp. 92–102.

Lewin, David, and Sabater, J.M. (1996) Corporate philanthropy and business performance. In Dwight F. Burlingame, and Dennis R. Young (Eds), *Corporate Philanthropy at the Crossroads*, pp. 105–126. Bloomington and Indianapolis, IN: Indiana University Press.

The life cycle of money. (1999, May 17) *Seattle Times*, p. A6.

Light on the shadows. (1997, May 3) *The Economist*, pp. 63–64.

Linehan, Margaret, and Scullion, Hugh (2002) Repatriation of European female corporate executives: An empirical study. *International Journal of Human Resource Management*, 13 (2): 254–268.

Lipman-Blumen, Jean (2000) *Connective Leadership: Managing in a Changing World*. New York: Oxford University Press.

Lipman-Blumen, Jean, and Leavitt, Harold J. (1999) *Hot Groups*. New York: Oxford University Press.

Lipsey, Robert E., Blomstrom, Magnus, and Ramstetter, Eric D. (2000) Internationalized production in world output. Working paper. Washington, D.C.: National Bureau of Economic Research.

Lober, D.J. (1997, Feb.) Explaining the formation of business-environmental collaborations: Collaborative windows and the paper task force. *Policy Sciences*, 30: 1–24.

Lodge, George C. (1995) *Managing Globalization in the Age of Interdependence*. San Francisco, CA: Jossey-Bass.

Lomborg, Bjorn (2001) *The Skeptical Environmentalist: Measuring the Real State of the World*. London: Cambridge University Press.

Lublin, Joanne S. (2000, June 27) In choosing the right management model, firms seesaw between product and place. *The Wall Street Journal*, pp. A1, A4.

Lublin, Joanne S. (2003, Sept. 29). No place like home. *The Wall Street Journal*, p. R7.

Luttwak, Edward (1999) *Turbo-capitalism: Winners and Losers in the Global Economy*. New York: HarperCollins.

McCall, Morgan W., Jr., and Hollenbeck, George P. (2002) *Developing Global Executives*. Boston, MA: Harvard Business School Press.

McDougall, Patricia Phillips, Shane, S., and Oviatt, Benjamin (1994) Explaining the formation of international new ventures: the limits of theories from international business research. *Journal of Business Venturing*, 9, pp. 469–487.

McFarland, Lynne Joy, Senn, Larry E., and Childress, John R. (1993) *21st Century Leadership*, p. 155. New York: The Leadership Press.

McRae, Hamish (1994) *The World in 2020*. Boston, MA: Harvard Business School Press.

Madsen, Tage Koed, and Servais, Per (1997) The internationalization of born globals: An evolutionary process? *International Business Review*, 6 (6): 561–583.

Magnusson, Paul (1994, Oct. 3) The IMF should look forward, not back. *Business Week*, p. 108.

Makhija, Mona V., Kim, Kwangsoo, and Williamson, Sandra D. (1997, 4th quarter) Measuring globalization of industries using a national industry approach: Empirical evidence across five countries and over time. *Journal of International Business Studies*, pp. 679–710.

Makridakis, Spyros (1989) Management in the 21st Century. *Long Range Planning*, 22 (2): 37–53.

Malaysia plans Islamic global bond. (2002, June 12) *The Wall Street Journal*, p. A14.

Management barometer. (2003) Quarterly survey in US and Western European findings reported from 14 different countries. PriceWaterhouseCoopers/BS/Global Research Inc.

Mandel, Jay R., and Ferleger, Louis (2000, July) Preface. *The Annals of the American Academy of Political and Social Science*, 570. Thousand Oaks, CA: Sage.

Mankiw, Gregory (1995, September) The growth of nations. New York: The Brookings Institution, Brookings Papers on Economic Activity.

Mapes, Timothy, and Madani, Puspa (2001, Apr. 16) Indonesia's financial woes find another victim: Its forests. *The Wall Street Journal*, pp. A10, A12.

Marquardt, Michael J., and Horvath, Lisa (2001) *Global Teams*. Palo Alto, CA: Consulting Psychologists Press; Davies-Black Publishing.

Marstrander, Rolf (1994) Industrial ecology: A practical framework for environmental management. *Environmental Management Handbook* (Chapter 12). London: Pitman Publishing.

Martin, Joanne, Feldman, Martha S., Hatch, Mary Jo, and Sitkin, Sim B. (1983) The uniqueness paradox in organizational stories. *Administrative Science Quarterly*, 28: 438–454.

Mayrhofer, Wolfgang, and Scullion, Hugh (2002) Female expatriates in international business: Empirical evidence from the German clothing industry. *International Journal of Human Resource Management*, 13 (5): 815–837.

Mayruth, Andrew (2002, Mar. 24) Somalia is sacrificing its trees for profit. *Seattle Times*, p. A4.

Maruyama, Magoroh (1992) Lessons from Japanese management failures in foreign countries. *Human Systems Management*, 11 (1): 41–48.

Mauro, Paulo (1995) Corruption and growth. *Quarterly Journal of Economics*, 110 (3): 681–712.

McDonald's Corporation Annual Report. (1992) Oak Brook, IL: McDonald's Investor Relations.

Melin, Leif (1992). Internationalization as a strategy process. *Strategic Management Journal*, 13: 99–118.

Merrill Lynch advertisement. (1995, June 12) *Fortune*, p. 49.

Microbial threats to health: emergence, detection, and response. (2003, Mar. 18) Washington, DC: Institute of Medicine. http://www.ion.edu

Millenium Poll (2000) http://www.pwcglobal.com

Miller, Lisa (1996, May 31) Pace of business travel abroad is beyond breakneck. *The Wall Street Journal*, p. B1.

Miller, John J. (2002, Mar. 8) How do you say "extinct"? *The Wall Street Journal*, p. W13.

Millman, Gregory (1995) *The Vandals' Crown: How Rebel Currency Traders Overthrew the World's Central Banks*. Cambridge, MA: Free Press.

Millstein, Ira (2000, Summer) Corporate governance: The role of market forces. *OECD Observer*, 221/222, p. 27.

Mintzberg, Henry, and Gosling, Jonathan (2002) Educating managers beyond borders. *Academy of Management Learning and Education*, 1 (1): 64–76.

The missing link. (1994, Oct. 1) *The Economist*, The global economy survey, pp. 10–14.

Mitchener, Brandon (2001, Nov. 13) EU needs joint border police and security policy, Prodi says. *The Wall Street Journal*, p. A18.

Moore, James (1996) *The Death of Competition*. New York: HarperBusiness.

Moran, Robert T., and Riesenberger, John R. (1994) *The Global Challenge*. London: McGraw-Hill.

Morris, Michael H., Davis, Duane L., and Allen, Jeffrey W. (1994) Fostering corporate entrepreneurship: Cross-cultural comparisons of the importance of individualism versus collectivism. *Journal of International Business Studies*, 25: 65–89.

Morrison, Ann M. (1992) *The New Leaders: Guidelines for Leadership Diversity in Business*. San Francisco, CA: Jossey-Bass.

Morrow, David J. (1993, Nov. 7) Women exposing sex harassment in Japan. *Seattle Times*, p. D9.

Moses, Elissa (2000) *The $100 Billion Allowance: Accessing the Global Teen Market*. New York: John Wiley & Sons.

Most respected companies. (2000) PriceWaterHouseCoopers survey. http://www.pwcglobal.com

Murphy, David F. and Bendell, Jem (1997) *In the Company of Partners: Business, Environmental Groups and Sustainable Development Post-Rio*. Bristol, UK: The Policy Press.

Murray, Alan I. (1989) Top management group heterogeneity and firm performance. *Strategic Management Journal*, 10: 125–142.

Museveni, Yoweri (2001, Nov. 11) Globalisation. UN General Assembly address, accessed through allAfrica.com

Naisbitt, John (1994) *Global Paradox*. New York: Easton Press.

The new geography of the IT industry. (2003, July 19) *The Economist*, pp. 47–49.

New technologies take time. (1999, Apr. 19) *Business Week*, p. 8.

No school, no future. (1999, Mar. 27) *The Economist*, pp. 45–46.

No title. (2001, Mar. 31) *The Economist*, pp. 20–22.

Nobel laureates offer views on the economy. (2004, Sept. 3) *The Wall Street Journal* Online, wsj.com

Nonaka, Ikujiro, and Takeuchi, Hirotaka (1995) *The Knowledge-creating Company*. New York: Oxford University Press.

Nordhaus, William D., and Tobin, James (1972) *Economic Research: Retrospect and Prospect: Vol 5. Economic Growth*. Cambridge : National Bureau of Economic Research.

Northouse, Peter G. (2004) *Leadership: Theory and Practice* (3rd edn). Thousand Oaks, CA: Sage.

Nutt, Paul (2002) Making strategic choices. *Journal of Management Studies*, 39: 67–96.

O'Driscoll, Gerald P., and Holmes, Kim R. (2002) *The 2002 Index of Economic Freedom*. Washington, D.C.: Heritage Foundation; New York, NY: *The Wall Street Journal*.

Ohmae, Kenichi (1990) *The Borderless World: Power and Strategy in the Interlinked Economy*. London: Collins.

Ohmae, Kenichi (1995) *The End of the Nation State*. Cambridge, MA and New York: Free Press.

Olson, Mancur (2000) *Power and Prosperity: Outgrowing Communist and Capitalist Dictatorships*. New York: Basic Books.

Ondrack, Daniel (1985, Fall) International transfers of managers in North American and European MNCs. *Journal of International Business Studies*, pp. 1–19.

O'Neill, Helen (1997) Globalisation, competitiveness and human security: Challenges for development policy and institutional change. In Kay Cristobal (Ed.), *Globalisation, Competitiveness and Human Security*, pp. 20–21. London: Frank Cass.

O'Rourke, Kevin, and Williamson, Jeffrey (2000) *Globalization and History: The Evolution of a Nineteenth-century Atlantic Economy*. Boston, MA: MIT Press.

Osland, Joyce S., De Franco, Silvio, and Osland, Asbjorn (1999) Organizational implications of Latin American culture: Lessons for the expatriate manager. *Journal of Management Inquiry*, 8 (2): 219–234.

Ostry, Sylvia, and Nelson, Richard R. (1995) *Techno-nationalism and Techno-globalism: Conflict and Cooperation*. Washington DC: Brookings Institution Press.

The outlook. (1998, Jan. 26*) The Wall Street Journal*, p. A1.

Oviatt, Benjamin, and McDougal, Patricia Phillips (1995) Global start-ups: Entrepreneurs on a worldwide stage. *Academy of Management Executive*, 9 (2): 30–43.

Parikh, Jagdish, Neubauer, Franz, and Lank, Alden G. (1994) *Intuition: The New Frontier of Management*. London: Blackwell.

Parker, Barbara (1991) Employment globalization: Can "voluntary" expatriates meet US hiring needs abroad? *Journal of Global Business*, 2 (2): 39–46.

Parker, Barbara, and McEvoy, Glenn (1993). Initial examination of a model of intercultural adjustment. *International Journal of Intercultural Relations*, 17: 355–379.

Parker, Barbara, Zeira, Yoram, and Hatem, Tarek (1996) International joint venture managers: Factors affecting personal success and organizational performance. *Journal of International Management*, 2 (1):1–29.

Parkhe, Arvind (1991) Interfirm diversity, organizational learning, and longevity in global strategic alliances. *Journal of International Business Studies*, 22 (4): 579–601.

Passage back to India. (1995, July 17) *Business Week*, pp. 44–46.

Patton, John (2003) Intuition in decisions. *Management Decision*, 41 (10): 989–996.

Pekar, Peter Jr., and Allio, Robert (1994, Aug.) Making alliances work: Guidelines for success. Long Range Planning, pp. 54–65.

Perlmutter, Howard V., and Heenan, David A. (1986, Mar./Apr.) Cooperate to compete globally. *Harvard Business Review*, pp. 136–152.

Perrin, Jane, and Nishikawa, Clare (2003) Global mega brand franchises: Extending brands within a global marketplace. *Consumer Insights Magazine*. Accessed online October 14, 2003 at http://acnielsen.com/pubs/ci/2003/ql/features/mega.htm

Peters, Tom (1994, Aug.) How life really works. *Quality Digest*.

Peters, Tom, and Waterman, Robert Jr. (1982) *In Search of Excellence*. New York: Harper & Row.

Pfeffer, Jeffrey (1994) *Competitive Advantage Through People*. Boston, MA: Harvard Business School Press.

Phatak, Arvind V. (1992) *International Dimensions of Management* (3rd edn). Boston, MA: PWS-Kent.

Phillips, Don (1994, Aug. 22) Culture may play role in flight safety. *Seattle Times*, pp. E1, E3.

Pieterse, Jan N. (1995) Globalization as hybridization. In Mike Featherstone, Scott Lash, and Roland Robertson (Eds), *Global Modernities*, pp. 45–68. London: Sage.

Pilot analysis of global agrosystems. (2001) International Food Policy Research Institute. http://www.ifpri.org/pubs/books/page/agroeco_exesum.pdf

Pomfret, John (2001, June 10) Baby-boy boom engulfs China. *Seattle Times*, p. A22.

Population Reference Bureau. (1998) http://www.prb.org

Porter, Michael E. (1980) *Competitive Strategy*. New York: Free Press.

Porter, Michael E. (Ed.) (1986) *Competition in Global Industries*. Boston, MA: Harvard Business School Press.

Porter, Michael E. (1990) *The Competitive Advantage of Nations*. New York and Boston: Free Press.

Porter, Michael E., and van der Linde, Claas (1995) Green and competitive: Ending the stalemate. *Harvard Business Review*, 73 (5): 120–134.

Powell, Gary, and Graves, Laura M. (2003) *Women and Men in Management* (3rd edn). Thousand Oaks, CA: Sage.

Power, Stephen (2002, Jan. 24) Disney, Nike give government advice on handling airport security lines. *The Wall Street Journal*, p. B1.

Prahalad, C.K., and Doz, Yves L. (1987) *The Multinational Mission: Balancing Local Demands and Global Vision*. New York: The Free Press.

Prahalad, C.K., and Lieberthal, Kenneth (1998) The end of corporate imperialism. *Harvard Business Review*, 76 (4): 68–79.

Prahalad, C.K., and Ramaswamy, Venkatram (2002) The co-creation connection. *Strategy and Business*, 27: 50–61.

Preamble to the Earth Charter. (2003, May 2) http://www.earthcharter.org/earthcharter/charter.htm

Prestowitz, Jr., C.V., Tonelson, A., and Jerome, R.W. (1991, Mar./Apr.) The last gasp of GATTism. *Harvard Business Review*, pp. 130–138.

Privatisation. (2000, July 22) *The Economist*, p. 99.

The public's view of corporate responsibility. (2002) Key findings 2002 for BITC website. http://www.bitc.org.uk/docs/MORI_article.doc

Raghavan, Anita, and Steinmetz, Greg (2000, Mar. 31) Europe's family firms become a dying breed among succession woes. *The Wall Street Journal*, pp. A1, A10.

Recent privatization trends in OECD countries. (2002, June) *Financial Market Trends*, 82: 43–58.

Reich, Robert (1991a, Fall) The stateless manager. *Best of Business Quarterly*, 84–91.

Reich, Robert (1991b) *The Work of Nations: Preparing Ourselves for 21st Century Capitalism*. New York: Alfred A. Knopf.

Reid, Stan D. (1983) Firm internationalization, transaction costs, and strategic choice. *International Marketing Review*, 1 (2): 44–56.

Reid, Stan D. (1984) Market expansion and firm internationalization. In Erdener Kaynak (Ed.), *International marketing management*, pp. 197–206. New York: Praeger.

Renesch, John (Ed.) (1992) *New Traditions in Business*. San Francisco, CA: Berrett-Koehler.

Revenue from illicit drugs: $400 billion. (1997, June 24) *World Drug Report*. Geneva: United Nations.

Reverse linkages—Everybody wins. (1995, May) Development Brief. (Additional information appears in World Bank (1995). *Global Economic Prospects and the Developing Economies 1995*. Washington, D.C.: World Bank.)

Reynolds, Paul D., Camp, S. Michael, Bygrave, William D., Autio, Erkko, and Hay, Michael (2001) *Global Entrepreneurship Monitor 2001 Summary Report*. London Business School and Babson College. http://www.gemconsortium.org

Rhinesmith, Stephen H. (1993) *A Manager's Guide to Globalization*. Alexandria, VA and Homewood, IL; American Society for Training and Development and Business One Irwin.

Rhinesmith, Stephen H. (2000) *A Manager's Guide to Globalization*. New York: McGraw-Hill.

Ricardo, David (1817) *On the Principles of Political Economy and Taxation*. London: J. Murray.

Robertson, Roland (1995) Glocalization: Time-space and homogeneity-heterogeneity. In Mike Featherstone, Scott Lash, and Roland Robertson (Eds), *Global Modernities*, pp. 25–44. London: Sage.

Robinson, Jeffrey (2000) *The Merger*. Woodstock, NY: Overlook Press.

Robinson, Richard (1981 Spring/Summer) Background concepts and philosophy of international business from World War II to the present, *Journal of International Business Studies*, 13–21.

Rodgers, Daniel (1978) *The Work Ethic in Industrial American 1850–1920*. Chicago: University of Chicago Press.

Rodrik, Dani (1997) *Has Globalization Gone Too Far?* New York: Institute for International Economics.

Rondinelli, Dennis S., and Berry, Michael A. (2000) Environmental citizenship in multinational corporations: Social responsibility and sustainable development. *European Management Journal*, 18 (1): 70–84.

Root, Franklin (1987) *Entry Strategies for International Markets*. Lexington, MA: Lexington Books.

Rosen, Robert, Digh, Patricia, Singer, Marshall, and Phillips, Carl (2000) *Global Literacies: Lessons on Business Leadership and National Cultures*. New York: Simon & Schuster.

Rosener, Judith (1990, Nov./Dec.) Ways women lead. *Harvard Business Review*, pp. 119–125.

Royal, Weld F. (1994, Dec.) *Passport to Peril? Sales & Marketing Management*, pp. 74–78.

Rugman, Alan M. (2001) *The End of Globalization*. New York: AMACOM/McGraw-Hill.

Sai, Yasutaka (1995) *The Eight Core Values of the Japanese Businessman: Toward an Understanding of Japanese Management*. Binghamton, NY: Haworth Press.

Said, Edward (1998) *The Myth of the "Clash of Civilizations."* (Video). Boston: Media Education Foundation.

Salamon, Lester M. (1994, July/Aug.) The rise of the nonprofit sector. *Foreign Affairs*, pp. 109–122.

Salamon, Lester M., and Anheier, Helmut K. (1994) *The Emerging Sector*. Baltimore, MD: The Johns Hopkins University Institute for Policy Studies.

Salamon, Lester M., and Anheier, Helmut K. (1998) *The Emerging Sector Revisited*. Baltimore, MD: The Johns Hopkins University Center for Civil Society Studies.

Salamon, Lester, Sokolowski, S. Wojciech, and List, Regina (2004) In Lester Salamon, S. Wojciech Sokolowski and associates (Eds), pp.1–14. *Global Civil Society, Volume II*. Bloomfield, CT: Kumarian Press.

Sampson, Anthony (1995) *Company Man*. New York: Times Business.

SARS deals blow to Asian economies. (2003, Apr. 21) *The Wall Street Journal*, p. A10.

Scandals reduce U.S. sparkle as icon of marketplace ideas. (2002, June 28) *The Wall Street Journal*, pp. A10, A11.

Schellhardt, Timothy D. (1994, Oct. 28) Major firms in North America, Europe plan marketing changes, survey shows. *The Wall Street Journal*, p. A5B.

Schein, Edgar H. (1992) *Organizational Culture and Leadership*. San Francisco: Jossey-Bass.

Schiffrin, Anya (1996, Nov. 1) Dutch firms debate whether employees or shareholders should get priority. *The Wall Street Journal*, p. A7A.

Scholte, Jan Aart (1996) Toward a critical theory of globalization. In Eleonore Hoffman and Gillian Young (Eds), *Globalization: Theory and Practice*, pp. 43–57. London: Pinter.

Schonberger, Richard (1996) *World Class Manufacturing: The Lessons of Simplicity Applied*. New York: Free Press.

Schuler, Randall S., Dowling, Peter J., and De Cieri, Helen (1993) An integrative framework of strategic international human resource management. *Journal of Management*, 19 (2): 419–450.

Schwartz, Shalom H. (1992) Universals in the content and structure of values: Theoretical advances and empirical tests in 20 countries. *Advances in Experimental Social Psychology*, 1–62.

Sellers, Patricia (2002, Oct. 14) True grit. *Fortune*, pp. 101–112.

Selvarajah, Christopher T., Duignan, Patrick, Suppiah, Chandrseagran, Lane, Terry, and Nuttman, Chris (1995) *Management International Review*, 35 (1): 29–44.

Sen, Amartya (1999) *Development as Freedom*. New York: Random House.

Senge, Peter (1990) *The Fifth Discipline: The Art and Practice of the Learning Organization*. New York, NY: Doubleday.

Sera, Koh (1992) Corporate globalization: A new trend. *Academy of Management Executive*, 6 (1): 89–96.

Sethi, S. Prakash (1999) Codes of conduct for global business: Prospects and challenges of implementation. In Clarkson Centre for Business Ethics, Principles of stakeholder management, pp. 9–20. Toronto: Clarkson Centre for Business Ethics.

Shapiro, Spence, and Spence, Mark (1997) Managerial intuition: A conceptual and operational framework. *Business Horizons*, 40 (1): 63–69.

Sharma, D. (1992) International business research: issues and trends. *Scandinavian International Business Review*, 1 (3): 3–8.

Sharp, Margaret (1992) Tides of change: The world economy and Europe in the 1990s. *International Affairs*, 68 (1): 17–35.

Shim, Jae K. (1989) *The Encyclopedic Dictionary of Accounting and Finance*. New York: MJF Books, p. 220

Shirley, D.A., and Langan-Fox, I. (1996) Intuition: A review of the literature. *Psychological Reports*, 79: 563–584.

Shiva, Vanda (2002) *Water Wars: Privatization, Pollution and Profit*. Cambridge, MA: South End Press.

Simai, Mihaly (1994) *The Future of Global Governance*. Washington, D.C.: United States Institute of Peace.

Simon, Herbert (1955) A behavioral model of rational choice. *Quarterly Journal of Economics*, 69: 99–118.

Simon, Julian (1981) *The Ultimate Resource*. Oxford: Martin Robinson.

Simon, Julian (1998) *The Ultimate Resource 2*. Princeton, NJ: Princeton University Press.

Simpson, Glenn R. (2001, Nov. 13) "Hawala" played a global role in criminal acts. *The Wall Street Journal*, p. A15.

Simon, Herman (1996) *Hidden Champions: Lessons from 500 of the World's Best Unknown Companies*. Boston, MA: Harvard Business School Press.

Sins of the secular missionaries. (2002, Jan.29) *The Economist*, pp. 25–57.

Slywotzky, Adrian J. (1996) *Value Migration*. Boston: Harvard Business School Press.

Small and medium-sized enterprises: Local strength, global reach. (2000, June) *OECD Policy Brief*. http://www.1.oecd.org/publications/pol_brief/2000/2000_02.pdf

Smith, Adam (1776) *An Inquiry into the Nature and Causes of the Wealth of Nations*. Dublin, Whitestone.

Smith, J. (1990, Autumn) Do the right thing: Ethical principles and managerial decision making. *SAM Advanced Management Journal*, pp. 4–7.

Software piracy: What you should know. (1995) http://www.bentley.com/anti.piracy.html, pp. 1–2.

Solomon, Charlene (1994, July) Global operations demand that HR rethink diversity. *Personnel Journal*, 73 (7): 40–49.

Solomon, Steven (1995) *The Confidence Game*. New York: Simon & Schuster; also see Deane, Marjorie, and Pringle, Robert(1995) *The Central Banks*. New York: Viking; or Millman, Gregory (1995) *The Vandals' Crown*. Cambridge, MA: Free Press.

South Korea moves ahead with chaebol inquiry. (2003, Mar. 5) *The Wall Street Journal*, p. A13.

Spears, Larry (Ed.) (1995) *Reflections on Leadership*. New York: John Wiley.

Specter, Michael (1994, Aug. 14) A Russian outpost now happily embraces Asia. *New York Times*, p. A1.

Stead, W. Edward, and Stead, Jean Garner (1996) *Management for a Small Planet* (2nd edn). Thousand Oaks, CA: Sage.

Steadman, Mark E., Zimmerer, Thomas W., and Green, Ronald F. (1995) Pressures from stakeholders hit Japanese companies. *Long Range Planning*, 28 (6): 29–37.

Steenkamp, Jan-Benedict EM, Batra, Rajeev, and Alden, Dana L. (2003) How perceived brand globalness creates brand value. *Journal of International Business Studies*, 34 (1): 53–65.

Steingard, David S., and Fitzgibbons, Dale E. (1995) Challenging the juggernaut of globalization: A manifesto for academic praxis. *Journal of Organizational Change Management*, 8 (4): 30–54.

Steinmann, Horst, and Lohr, Albert (1992, Apr.) A survey of business ethics in Germany. *Business Ethics: A European Review*, pp. 139–141.

Stodgill, Ralph M. (1974) *Handbook of Leadership: A Survey of the Literature*. New York: Free Press.

Sun Microsystems, Inc. (2001, Jan. 1) Standards of business conduct: Our reputation – a shared responsibility. Palo Alto, CA: Sun Microsystems, Business Conduct Office.

A survey of global equity markets. (2001, May 5) *The Economist*, survey insert.

Swerdlow, Joel L. (1999, Aug.) Global culture. *National Geographic*, pp. 2–5.

The tap runs dry. (1997, May 31) *The Economist*, pp. 21–23.

Taylor, Sully, Beechler, Schon, and Napier, Nancy (1996) Toward an integrative model of strategic international human resource management. *Academy of Management Review*, 21 (4): 959–985.

Taylor, William (1991) The logic of global business. reprinted in *Fast Forward*. (1996) Cambridge, MA: Harvard Business School Press, pp. 61–88.

Terpstra, Vern, and David, Kenneth (1991) *The Cultural Environment of International Business* (3rd edn). Cincinnati, OH: South-Western Publishing.

Thomas, David A., and Ely, Robin J. (1996, Sept./Oct.) Making differences matter: A new paradigm for managing diversity. *Harvard Business Review*, pp. 79–90.

Thomas, David C. (2002) *Essentials of International Management*. Thousand Oaks, CA: Sage.

Through the wringer. (2001, Apr. 14) *The Economist*, pp. 64–66.

Tomlinson, John (1991) *Cultural Imperialism*. Baltimore: John Hopkins University Press.

Top 10 facts about women business owners. (2003) Center for Women's Business Research. On line, accessed 2003, Oct. 15: http://www.nfwbo.org/key.html

Tornow, Walter W. (1994) Center for Creative Leadership Conference report. *Issues and Observations*, 14 (2), p. 7.

Townsend, A.M., DeMarie, S., and Hendrickson, A. (1998) Virtual teams: Technology and the workplace of the future. *Academy of Management Executive*, 12 (3): 17–29.

Trompenaars, Alfons (1994) *Riding the Waves of Culture*. Burr Ridge, IL: Irwin.

Trompenaars, Alfons and Hampden-Turner, Charles (1998) *Riding the Waves of Culture*. New York: McGraw-Hill.

Tully, Sean (2000, May 15) Water, water everywhere. *Fortune*, pp. 342–354.

Tung, Rosalie (1982) Selection and training procedures of US, European and Japanese multinationals. *California Management Review*, 25 (1): 57–71.

Tung, R.L. (1987, May) Expatriate assignments: Enhancing success and minimizing failure. *Academy of Management Executive*, 1 (2): 117–126.

Turner, Adrian (2001) *Just Capital*. London: Macmillan.

Tushman, Michael L., and O'Reilly, Charles A., III. (1997) *Winning Through Innovation*. Boston: Harvard University Press.

Twenty lessons in twenty years of global growth. (2003, Nov. 18) Accessed Nov 2004. http://www.dominos.com/C1256B420054FF48/vwContentByKey/W25TLJLG823DOMBEN

UNCTAD (2003, July 7) World market for corporate HQs emerging. http://www.unctad.org/Templates/Webflyer.asp?docID=3768&intItemID=1528&lang=1

Underground economy. (2001, Feb. 3) *The Economist*, p. 108.

The United Nations Population Fund. (1999, October) http://www.unfpa.org

United Nations Conference on Trade and Development. (1993) *Environmental Management in Transnational Corporations: Report on the Benchmark Corporate Environmental Survey*. New York: United Nations.

Up the ladder. (2000, Nov. 6) *Business Week*, pp. 78–84.

Urbanization. (2000) Millennium in maps: Population. *National Geographic*.

US Small Business Administration. (1994) Office of Advocacy. Washington, D.C.: US Government Printing Office.

Valery, Nicholas (1999, Feb. 20) Innovation in industry survey. *The Economist*.

van Bergeijk, Peter A.G., and Mensink, Nico W. (1997) Measuring globalization. *Journal of World Trade*, 31 (3): 159–168.

Van Dusen Wishard, William (1995) *We have crossed over the border of history*. Potomac, MD: Porter McGinn Associates.

Van Rijckeghem, Caroline, and Weder, Beatrice (1997, May) Corruption and the rate of temptation: Do low wages in the civil services cause corruption? Washington, D.C.: IMF Working Paper.

Vernon, Raymond (1966, June) International trade and international investment in the product cycle. Quarterly *Journal of Economics*, pp. 190–207.

Veseth, Michael (1998) *Selling Globalization: The Myth of the Global Economy*. Boulder, CO and London: Lynne Rienner Publishers.

Violence on the job: A global problem. (1998) Geneva: ILO.

Viotzthum, Carlta (1995, July 21) "Corporate governance" is bringing change to the boardrooms of Europe. *The Wall Street Journal*, p. A5A.

Vitell, Scott J., Nwachukwu, Savio L., and Barnes, James H. (1993) The effects of culture on ethical decision-making: An application of Hofstede's typology. *Journal of Business Ethics*, 12: 753–760.

Vogel, Steven (1997) *Freer Markets, More Rules*. Ithaca, NY: Cornell University Press.

von Weizsacker, Ernst, Lovins, Amory, and Lovins, Hunter (1998) *Factor Four: Doubling Wealth, Halving Resource Use*. Snowmass, CO: Rocky Mountain Institute.

Von Glinow, Mary Ann, Huo, Y. Paul, and Lowe, Kevin (1999) Leadership across the Pacific Ocean: A trinational comparison. *International Business Review*, 8: 1–15.

Waddell, Steve (1999, Aug.) Business-government-nonprofit collaborations as agents for social innovation and learning. Paper presented at the Academy of Management Meeting, Chicago.

Waddell, Steve (2001, July/Aug.) The role of civil society in business strategy. *The Corporate Ethics Monitor*, pp. 57–59.

Waddell, Steve (2001/2002) Societal learning: Creating big-systems change. *The Systems Thinker*, 12 (10): 1–5.

Waddell, Steve and Brown, L. David (1997) Fostering intersectoral partnering: A guide to promoting cooperation among government, business, and civil society actors. *IDR Reports*, 13 (3): 1–27.

Waddock, Sandra, and Boyle, Mary-Ellen (1995) The dynamics of change in corporate community relations. *California Management Review*, 37 (4): 125–141.

Waddock, Sandra, and Smith, Neil (2000) Relationships: The real challenge of corporate global citizenship. *Business and Society Review*, 105 (1): 47–62.

Waddock, Sandra, Bodwell, Charles, and Graves, Samuel B. (2002) Responsibility: The new business imperative. *Academy of Management Executive*, 16 (2): 132–148.

Walters, Mark Jerome (2003) *Six Modern Plagues and How We Are Causing Them*. Washington, D.C.: Island Press.

Ward, Diane Raines (2002) *Water Wars: Drought, Flood, Folly, and the Politics of Thirst*. New York: Riverhead Books.

Watkins, Kevin (2002, Mar.) Making globalization work for the poor. *Finance & Development*, pp. 24–27.

Watson, Adam (1995) The prospects for a more integrated international society. In Kanti P. Bajpai and Harish C. Shukul (Eds), *Interpreting World Politics*, pp. 130–138. New Delhi: Sage.

The way we govern now. (2003, Jan. 11) *The Economist*, pp. 59–61.

We the Peoples: Executive Summary of the Millennium Report. (2000) New York: United Nations.

Weaver, G.R., Trevino, Linda K., and Cochran, Philip L. (1999) Integrated and decoupled corporate social performance: Management commitments, external pressures, and corporate ethics practices. *Academy of Management Journal*, 42 (5): 539–553.

Webley, Simon (1992) *Company Values and Codes: Current Best Practices in the United Kingdom*. London: Institute of Business Ethics.

Welsh, Dianne, Luthans, Fred, and Sommer, S.M. (1993) Managing Russian factory workers: The impact of US based behavioral and participative techniques. *Academy of Management Journal*, 36 (1): 58–79.

What concerns do cross-border M&As raise for host countries? (2000) *World Investment Report*. New York and Geneva: United Nations.

White, Roderick, and Poynter, Thomas (1990) Organizing for world-wide advantage. In C.A. Bartlett, Yves Doz and Gunnar Hedlund (Eds), *Managing the Global Firm*, pp. 95–113. London: Routledge.

Who wants to be a giant? (1995, June 24) *The Economist*, Multinational Survey, p. 4.

Why can't a country be like a firm? (1995, Apr. 22) *The Economist*, p. 79.

Wiersema, M.F., and Bantel, K.A. (1992) Top management team demography and corporate strategic change. *Academy of Management Journal*, 35: 91–121.

Williamson, John G. (1996, Mar.) Globalization and inequality: Then and now. Working Paper 5491. Cambridge, MA: National Bureau of Economic Research.

Wilson, Edward O. (2002, Feb.). The bottleneck. *Scientific American*, pp. 82–92.

Winterle, Mary J. (1992) *Workforce Diversity: Corporate Challenges, Corporate Responses*. New York: Conference Board.

Women and men in the informal economy: A statistical picture. (2002) Geneva: International Labour Office.

Women entrepreneurs are a growing international trend. (1997, Feb. 28) Washington, D.C.: Center for Women's Business Research.

Women in leadership: A European business imperative. (2002) New York: Catalyst.

Wood, A. (1994) *North–South Trade, Employment and Inequality: Changing Fortunes in a Skill-driven World*. Oxford: Oxford University Press.

World Bank figures for 2000. (2002, Jan. 25) New York: World Bank.

World Development Report. (1997) New York: World Bank.

World Development Report. (2001) New York: World Bank.

World Development Report, 2000/2001. (2001) Attacking poverty. World Bank: Oxford University Press.

World Disasters Report 2003. (2003) New York: Red Cross.

World Disasters Report 2004. (2004) New York: Red Cross.

World Employment Report 2001. (2001) Geneva: International Labour Organization. http://www.wallstreetview.com/GDPRankings.html

World exports of commercial services by region and economy, 1980–2001. (2002) Washington, DC: US Department of Commerce.

World Investment Report 1993. (1993) New York: UN, UNCTAD.

World Investment Report 1995. (1995) New York: UN, UNCTAD.

World Investment Report 2000. (2000) Cross-border mergers and acquisitions and Development. Geneva: UN, UNCTAD.

World Investment Report 2001. (2001) New York and Geneva: UN, UNCTAD.

World moves forward on plans for free-market energy. (2001, Dec. 6) *The Wall Street Journal*, p. A8.

World Resources Institute (1996/1997) *A Guide to the Global Environment: The Urban Environment*. Oxford and New York: Oxford University Press.

Worldwatch Institute (2001) *Vital Signs*. Washington, DC: Worldwatch Institute.

World Water Development Report: Water for People, Water for Life. (2003). New York: The United Nations.

http://www.unctad.org/Templates/webflyer.asp?docid=3768&intlItemID=1634&lang=1

Wright, Richard W., and Ricks, David A. (1994) Trends in international business research: Twenty-five years later. *Journal of International Business Studies*, 25 (4): 687–701.

WTO Annual Report. (1996) Geneva: World Trade Organization

WTO Annual Report. (2002) Geneva: World Trade Organization.

WTO News (2002, May 2) Trade to pick up slightly in 2002 after sharp drop in 2001. http://www.wto.org/english/news_e/pres02_e/pr288_e.htm

Yip, George S. (1995) *Total Global Strategy*. Englewood Cliffs, NJ: Prentice Hall.

Yip, George S., Johansson, Johny K., and Roos, Johan (1997) Effects of nationality on global strategy. *Management International Review*, 37 (4): 365–385.

Zachary, G. Pascal (1994, July 28) Exporting rights. *The Wall Street Journal*, pp. A1, A5.

Zadek, Simon (2001) *The Civil Corporation*. London: New Economics Foundation.

Zadek, Simon (2002) *The Civil Corporation: The New Economy of Corporate Citizenship*. London: Earthscan Publications.

Zafarullah, Mohammed, Ali, Mujahid, and Young, Stephen (1998) The internationalisation of the small firm in developing countries: Exploratory research from Pakistan. *Journal of Global Marketing*, 2 (3): 21–40.

Zaleznik, Abraham (1990) *The Managerial Mystique: Restoring Leadership in Business*. New York: Harper & Row.

Zeira, Yoram, and Harari, E. (1977) Genuine multinational staffing policy: Expectations and realities. *Academy of Management Journal*, 20 (2): 327–333.

Zero Population Growth (2003, Apr. 13) http://www.zpg.com

Zwingle, Erla (1998, Oct.) Women and population. *National Geographic*, pp. 40–47.

Zwingle, Erla (2002, Nov.) Cities. *National Geographic*, pp. 40–47.

Index